LIFE UPON THESE SHORES

LIFE UPON THESE SHORES

LOOKING AT AFRICAN AMERICAN HISTORY

1513–2008

Henry Louis Gates, Jr.

Alfred A. Knopf   New York   2011

THIS IS A BORZOI BOOK
PUBLISHED BY ALFRED A. KNOPF

Library of Congress Cataloging-in-Publication Data
Gates, Henry Louis.
Life upon these shores : looking at African American history, 1513–2008 / Henry Louis Gates, Jr.
Includes bibliographical references and index.
ISBN 978-0-307-59342-9 (hardback)
1. African Americans—History. 2. African Americans—History—Pictorial works. 3. United States—
Civilization—African American influences. I. Title.
E185.G27 2011
973'.0496073—dc22
2011014277

Front-of-jacket image: © Exactostock/SuperStock
Spine-of-jacket images (top to bottom): Digital Vision/Getty Images;
(next two) Ken Chernus/Getty Images; Exactostock/SuperStock
Jacket design by Chip Kidd

Manufactured in the United States of America
First Edition

In memory of Henry Louis Gates, Sr. (1913–2010)

and in honor of

Donald and Susan Newhouse

and

Daniel and Joanna Rose

The deep immortal wish,
the timeless will:

> Cinquez its deathless primaveral image,
> life that transfigures many lives.

Voyage through death
                to life upon these shores.

—Robert Hayden,
"Middle Passage"

CONTENTS

ACKNOWLEDGMENTS

I would like to thank the following for their work on *Life Upon These Shores*:

Donald Yacovone, for helping me to conceive almost every aspect of this massive undertaking—suggesting entries to be included, providing the research for most of those entries, and supervising fact-checking. He and his team researched and wrote every caption for every image that appears in this volume. This book could not have happened without his attention and expertise. Donald's credentials as a historian of African America are impeccable, and the Du Bois Institute is fortunate to have him as research manager.

Abby Wolf, for putting on her research hat to provide comprehensive endnotes for this book.

Robert Heinrich, a graduate of Brandeis University and currently an adjunct faculty member there, for his invaluable assistance in researching the majority of entries for the twentieth century.

P. J. Dickson, a graduate student in American history at Brandeis University, for contributing extensive research for much of the late nineteenth century.

Anne Arsenault, a lawyer with Rahdert, Steele, Reynolds & Driscoll, P.A., in St. Petersburg, Florida, for her counsel on the sections dealing with legal cases and constitutional law.

Shirley Sun, a graduate student at Harvard University, for managing the vast image database for this project and contributing significant research to the entry for Ellison's *Invisible Man*.

Julie Wolf, a writer and editor in Boston, for her care and precision in editing a draft of the manuscript.

Everyone involved made this a better project. Their commitment to it was a blessing.

As always, Amy Gosdanian, Vera Grant, and Joanne Kendall at the Du Bois Institute have provided invaluable support throughout this project. Maggie Gates and Liza Gates continue to sustain me, wherever I go.

I wish also to acknowledge the unflagging support of my agents, Tina Bennett, Bennett Ashley, and Paul Lucas, at Janklow & Nesbit, and especially of my friends and colleagues Larry Bobo, Caroline Elkins, Evelyn Brooks Higginbotham, Mariel Iglesias Ustet, and Marcy Morgan.

Richard Philpott and his team at ZOOID have been terrific partners throughout.

Erroll McDonald, vice president and executive editor at Random House, made this project possible, and I am indebted to him for his faith and friendship.

INTRODUCTION

Before the pen of Jefferson etched the majestic words of the Declaration of Independence across the pages of history, we were here. For more than two centuries our forebears labored without wages; they made cotton king . . .—and yet out of a bottomless vitality, they continued to thrive and develop. If the inexpressible cruelties of slavery could not stop us, the opposition we now face will surely fail . . . because the goal of America is freedom. Abused and scorned though we may be, our destiny is tied up with America's destiny.

—Martin Luther King, Jr.
"Letter from Birmingham Jail," April 16, 1963

In *Life Upon These Shores,* I set out to picture African American history, to find a new way of looking at its full sweep. I imagined a book with an abundance of images of the great and small events and of the significant individuals who shaped the heritage of the African American people and the history of our nation. *Life Upon These Shores: Looking at African American History* draws upon a treasury of illustrations at once to visualize and to write the history of black people in America, which begins as early as 1513, when the free black conquistador Juan Garrido accompanied Ponce de León on his first expedition to Florida. So the book ranges from the exploration of the New World and the long ordeal of slavery through Emancipation and the Civil War; from the era of Reconstruction through Jim Crow and World War I; from the Great Migration of 1910 to 1930—including the Harlem Renaissance and the Jazz Age—through the Great Depression and World War II; from the civil rights movement and its aftermath, and the Black Power insurgence, on to the age of hip-hop and the rise of the Joshua Generation, leading to the election of the first African American president of the United States. *Life Upon These Shores* illustrates the richness of this history through ancient maps, manuscripts and documents, portraits, postcards, posters, sheet music, car-toons, drawings and photographs, and even film stills.

We have combed through more than four hundred years of public records and private collections for the names, stories, and images of not only well-known African Americans but also others who have been consigned to oblivion even as they too were instrumental in shaping African American history day to day. To be sure, here are the transcendent personalities: among many, Phillis Wheatley, Sojourner Truth, Henry Highland Garnet, Harriet Tubman, Anna Julia Cooper, Ida B. Wells, Booker T. Washington, Frederick Douglass, Madam C. J. Walker, Jack Johnson and Joe Louis, W. E. B. Du Bois, Alain Locke, Langston Hughes, Josephine Baker, George Schulyer, Zora Neale Hurston, Richard Wright, Ralph Ellison, Althea Gibson and Arthur Ashe, Charles Hamilton Houston, Thurgood Marshall, Constance Baker Motley, Elijah Muhammad and Muhammad Ali, Adam Clayton Powell, Martin Luther King, Jr., Malcolm X, John Lewis, James Meredith, Charlayne Hunter-Gault, James Baldwin, Eldridge Cleaver, Huey P. Newton, Stokely Carmichael, H. Rap Brown, James Brown, Amiri Baraka, Shirley Chisholm, Jesse Jackson, Michael Jackson and Prince, Colin Powell, Condoleezza Rice, and Barack Obama. Their vaunted contributions to politics, sports, literature, the arts, religion, and education have indelibly colored the canvas of American culture and society. But this book also aims in part to restore to the historical record the names and achievements of significant men and women long forgotten: among them Onesimus, the slave who taught Cotton Mather to inoculate the Massachusetts colony against smallpox; the pre–Civil War, wildly popular black ventriloquist and magician Richard Potter; Stagecoach Mary, a post–Civil War driver for Wells Fargo; and the famous cowboy Deadwood Dick.

As I have studied the remarkable visual depictions collected in *Life Upon These Shores,* I have been struck by the sheer diversity of African American expression throughout our nation's history—how there has never been only one way to be black, religiously, politically, socially, artistically, professionally, sexually, or stylistically. I have tried to showcase the multiplicity of cultural institutions, political strategies, and religious and social perspectives defining black culture and society from slavery to freedom, from the plantation to the White House. Although, for example, debates between such central figures as Booker T. Washington and W. E. B. Du Bois, or Malcolm X and Martin Luther King, Jr., are familiar in the academy, they remain largely unknown to the general public, as do controversies involving their lesser-known peers; the latter too have a place at the table. These and all the other images and stories in this book help us to understand the complexity of the African American people, the rich and honest diversity of opinion that has always characterized the black experience in America.

Life Upon These Shores seeks not only to elucidate the pressing issues faced by each generation of African Americans but also to evoke the limitless variety of African American life: for instance, the experience of slavery in the North as opposed to slavery on a Southern plantation or in the West; the experience of being a freedperson as opposed to a slave; the experience of being a sharecropper in the South in the early twentieth century as opposed to a dockworker in Oakland or an autoworker in Detroit; the experience of being a black woman as opposed to a black man. Here are images of African Americans from different African ethnic groups dragged into slavery, forced to imagine new identities upon these shores; images of free blacks alongside their enslaved brethren in the South, forming their own religious, social, and cultural institutions in the North; images documenting the myriad ways in which some resisted slavery and segregation even as others sought accommodation, all the while forging family ties and communal bonds "behind the veil," as W. E. B. Du Bois put it.

The illustrations also offer a glimpse at how global affairs influenced African American history. So it was that the Haitian Revolution (1791–1804) sparked demands for the abolition of slavery and for equal rights up through the Civil War, while inspiring slave rebellions in America. A century and a half or so later, African movements for independence from colonialism informed the American civil rights movement, which in turn was to have a profound influence on the release of Nelson Mandela from prison and the dismantling of apartheid in South Africa.

A collective visual history of persons of African descent in America since their arrival in the sixteenth and seventeenth centuries, *Life Upon These Shores*—by examining defining issues, controversies and debates, and the achievements of people who shaped the history day to day for more than four hundred years—reveals, in all its human glory, the generally unacknowledged multifaceted nature of the black experience in these United States.

This is a general history for a general audience and relies on an enormous body of scholarly literature. The book stands on the shoulders of true giants. To retain its appeal, I have limited intrusive scholarly apparatus and identified sources only for direct quotes or for information not readily accessible. For those seeking verification of facts or additional information, one should consult the extended bibliography, which lists all of the major works used in this study.

HENRY LOUIS GATES, JR.
Oak Bluffs, Massachusetts
August 31, 2010

PART ONE

ORIGINS

1513–1760

AFRICAN SLAVES,
AFRICAN CONQUISTADORS

Juan Garrido attends to the horse of Hernando Cortés, conqueror of Mexico, as Aztecs give the
Spaniard a neckband. Illustration from Diego Duran, *Historia de las Indias,* 1579.

The history of the African American people in what is now the United States began in late August 1619, when the first cargo of "20 and odd" Africans aboard an English ship called the *White Lion* landed in Jamestown, Virginia. These twenty Africans had been born in Angola. And how they ended up in Jamestown tells us quite a bit about the origins and nature of the slave trade to North America, and its multinational and multicultural roots, inscribed in this curious institution from its very beginnings.

These twenty Angolans were captured either in military campaigns in 1618 and 1619, led by the Portuguese governor of Angola, Luís Mendes de Vasconcellos, in the highlands between the Kwanza and Lukala rivers, or in a civil war in the kingdom of Kongo between King Álvaro II and the rebel

Duke of Mbamba, Pedro da Silva, both Angolans, who would have sold their captives to the Portuguese. (The historians John Thornton and Linda Heywood conclude that 90 percent of the 12.5 million Africans shipped to the New World between 1501 and 1866 as slaves were captured by African elites and sold into slavery to Europeans.)[1] Sovereigns such as Queen Nzinga Mbande, the monarch of Ndongo and Matamba, Dom Garcia II of Kongo, and King Kpengla of Dahomey profited enormously from the slave trade.

The twenty black people who ended up in Jamestown sailed from Angola, along with three hundred other captives, on a Portuguese ship named the *São João Bautista,* heading for Veracruz, Mexico. The slave trade began and ended much earlier in Mexico than it did in the United States, and Mexico received

more slaves than the United States did. Two privateers, the *White Lion* (carrying letters of marque, documents allowing them to seize the goods of other nations, from William of Orange, the Dutch prince) and a companion ship, the *Treasurer* (carrying letters of marque from the Duke of Savoy), captured about fifty of the slaves onboard the *São João.*

The two warships did not have the capacity to carry many slaves, so they divided the fifty between them. Virginia authorities refused to allow the slaves aboard the *Treasurer* to land because the Duke of Savoy, an independent entity, had made a treaty of peace with Spain and was not, therefore, eligible to raid Spanish ships. (Spain and Portugal were under one flag between 1580 and 1640.) The *Treasurer* took its human cargo to Bermuda, returning to Jamestown a year later. After being plundered, the

São João Bautista continued to Veracruz, on the Gulf Coast of Mexico, stopping briefly in Jamaica, where it sold forty-seven of its captives who were children in exchange for supplies. Even as early as 1619, the capture and sale of only twenty Angolans involved, in one way or another, no less than eight regional entities: Angola, Portugal, Spain, Holland, England, Mexico, Jamaica, and the British colony of Virginia, plus the Duke of Savoy!

Americans tend to forget that the slave trade to the New World was already a full century old by the time it began in the United States in 1619, a year before the *Mayflower* landed at Plymouth Rock. In fact, only a very small percentage of all the slaves shipped to the New World even came to the United States. In a sense, these twenty Angolans are the progenitors of the 40 million African American people in the United States today—not genetically but metaphorically, institutionally. They constituted the first group

Esteban accompanying Hernando Cortés in Mexico, ca. 1550.

of the total of 450,000 people who would be shipped from Africa to the United States over the entire course of the slave trade. It is difficult to comprehend the enormity of the slave trade: incredibly,

Slaves working a Latin American gold mine. The Drake manuscript, *Histoire Naturelle des Indes* (*Natural History of the Indies*), ca. 1590.

no fewer than 12.5 million Africans were shipped to the New World between 1501 and 1866. Fifteen percent died in the dreaded Middle Passage, meaning that more than 11 million Africans survived this ordeal and disembarked in the New World. And fewer than a half million of these became slaves in the United States.

It is no accident that the first African Americans should have arrived from Angola. The effect of the slave trade on Angola was devastating: 5,494,000 Africans were shipped to the New World from there alone, and 5,694,000—45 percent, incredibly, of all the Africans enslaved through the history of the slave trade—were shipped from the area called West Central Africa, the region from Cape Lopez in the nation of Gabon today south to Namibia, of which Angola is a major part. In other words, if we did a DNA analysis on all of the descendants of all of the slaves in North and South America and the Caribbean, 45 percent of us could trace either our maternal or our paternal roots back to this region.

Where in the New World did the rest of these millions of Africans end up? Almost half went to Brazil alone; Cuba received 779,100, far more than the United States did. Jamaica received just

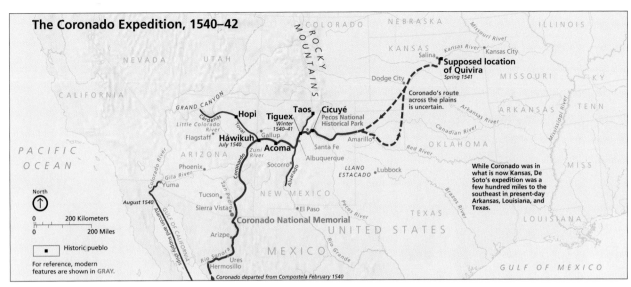

The Coronado Expedition, 1540–42

While Coronado was in what is now Kansas, De Soto's expedition was a few hundred miles to the southeast in present-day Arkansas, Louisiana, and Texas.

Coronado departed from Compostela February 1540

Spanish exploration in the Southwest, 1540–42.

over one million, while Haiti received 773,700. Our neighbor, Mexico, not generally associated with the slave trade or thought of as a site of black culture, received about 550,000, one hundred thousand more Africans through the trade than the United States did. Even Peru, which today we think of as the home of Inca civilization and as having little to do with black people or slavery, received a total of approximately 150,000 African slaves, about a third of the number who came to our country. Slavery, as we can see, was a shared enterprise among the major powers of Europe, in hot pursuit of its enormous profits, and its victims were scattered widely throughout the New World.[2]

The African slaves experienced their enslavement primarily in the Dutch, Portuguese, Spanish, and French languages, since they were deposited mainly in European colonies in the Caribbean islands and throughout much of the continent of South America. In other words, the transatlantic slave trade was an extended multicultural, multinational, multilinguistic series of exchanges and encounters, and the interactions that it induced among Europeans, Africans, and Native Americans created new peoples and cultures in the Western Hemisphere, including every sort of possible genetic admixture. While it is quite surprising to us today,

given the large size of the current African American population, overall only a relatively small percentage of these Africans were settled in English-speaking countries such as the United States and the English-speaking Caribbean, such as Jamaica.

The African presence in the New World was more than a hundred years old by the time these twenty Angolan slaves found themselves in Jamestown; indeed, black men had played a key role in the quests of the Spanish conquistadors from their very beginnings, commencing in the first decade of the sixteenth century, and not just as slaves: some of these men were free and were conquistadors themselves. And these black conquistadors were motivated by lust for wealth and power, just as their white peers were.[3]

For example, Vasco Núñez de Balboa's expedition, which "discovered" the Pacific Ocean in 1513, included thirty Africans, among them a man named Nuflo de Olano. Hernando Cortés's expedition to Mexico in 1519 included several black men, slave and free, among them Juan Garrido, who would claim to be the first person to "plant and harvest the first wheat crop in the New World," as we will see. And when Cortés brutally conquered the Aztec Empire in 1521, black men also took part in the slaughter.[4] When Álvar Núñez Cabeza

de Vaca traveled overland from Florida through Texas into Mexico in 1528, black men traveled with him. Francisco Pizarro's expedition to Peru in 1531 and his conquest of the Inca Empire in 1532 included black men, who would "carry his body to the cathedral after his assassination" in 1541, as the historian Evelyn Brooks Higginbotham puts it. When Pedro de Alvarado arrived in Quito in 1534, two hundred black men arrived

Queen Nzinga (1583?–1663). Nzinga became queen of the Mbundu in 1626; she proved a formidable leader and skilled diplomat when dealing with the Portuguese.

King of Congo, West Africa, receiving Portuguese emissaries, ca. 1491.

with him. And black men accompanied Hernando de Alarcón and Francisco Vásquez de Coronado when they explored Arizona, New Mexico, and the Colorado River between 1540 and 1542.[5] From the very beginnings of Spanish efforts to colonize the New World, then, blacks played a fundamental part. As early as 1570, more than 23,000 people of African descent lived in Spanish colonial Mexico, which then stretched north into modern-day Arizona and New Mexico and west to the Pacific Ocean. While most of these black people were slaves, many would earn or purchase their freedom. By 1810, New Spain contained 624,000 free blacks, about 10 percent of its total population.

Several of these black people made quite a name for themselves. I have mentioned Juan Garrido. Garrido was born in West Africa in about 1480 and arrived in Lisbon as a teenager, and as a free man. He soon became one of the first black conquistadors, and perhaps the most famous. In 1503, he sailed from Seville to Santo Domingo, before joining the Spanish conquistador Juan Ponce de León as part of the Spanish colonization of Puerto Rico and Cuba, and de León's expeditions to Florida in 1513 and 1521. He also participated in Hernando Cortés's army's destruction of the Aztec Empire.

Garrido spent seven years in Santo Domingo before settling in San Juan, Puerto Rico, where he fought with de León. His exploits with de León brought him to present-day Florida, where he became the first African to reach lands embraced by the modern-day United States. He met Cortés in Cuba and in 1519 accompanied him in the campaign against the Aztecs. By one account, he took responsibility for burying his dead Spanish comrades and erected a chapel to them in Tenochtitlán, the Aztec capital. He participated in other Spanish explorations and in 1524 settled in Mexico City, where the Spanish declared him a resident, provided him with a plot of land in the city's center, and made him first doorman of the town council, then caretaker of the city's aqueduct. By 1528 he had left the city for Zacatula province, where he began a gold-mining operation with slave labor. Wealth eluded him, so he rejoined Cortés in the 1530s for an expedition into lower California and spent his last years back in Mexico City, where he died in the late 1540s.

Astonishingly, Garrido left us a brief but revealing account of his life in a petition to Charles V, the king of Spain, in 1538:

I became a Christian in Lisbon, of my own will, spent seven years in Castile, and landed in Santo

Domingo . . . where I was for some time. From there I ventured to San Juan de Puerto Rico . . . where I spent considerable time . . . afterwards landing in New Spain; I was present at the taking of Mexico City and in other conquests . . . ; I was the first to plant and harvest wheat in this land, from which has come all that there now is; and brought to New Spain many vegetable seeds.[6]

While Garrido and other blacks were settling in Mexico City, the capital of New Spain, other Africans—most likely black slaves—ventured into lands that would become the United States. For example, some black people accompanied Lucas Vázquez de Ayllón in 1526 on an expedition from Hispaniola to San Miguel de Gualdape, somewhere along the southern Georgia coast. Although some of the Africans may have been skilled artisans, most likely the majority accompanied the six hundred Spanish settlers as slaves or servants meant to do the backbreaking work of establishing a settlement. Disease, starvation, and Ayllón's own death doomed the enterprise. Dissidents mutinied against the colony's weakened leadership, but, surprisingly, the Africans attacked the mutineers, burning their refuge. Local Indians then attacked the Spanish, driving out the

surviving settlers, while the Africans settled among the Guale Indians, establishing the first settlement of Maroons (runaway slaves) in North America.

Sometimes black slaves could gain fame for their adventures in the New World, just as Garrido had done as a free man. In the spring of 1536, a band of Spanish explorers under Diego de Alcaraz left Mexico City, traveling deep into the northern lands. They had gone far past the frontier settlement of Culiacán, near the Gulf of California, in search of Indians to enslave, when they encountered a ragged, blond-haired European and a black African, both men wearing feather headdresses and carrying symbols associated with Indian medicine men. Alcaraz and his men had discovered the long-lost Spanish explorer Álvar Núñez Cabeza de Vaca and Esteban (or Estévan, Spanish for "Stephen"), the most famous African slave explorer.

The property of Captain Andrés Dorantes de Carranza, Esteban had participated in the exploration of Florida in April 1528 as part of the expedition of Pánfilo de Narváez. Narváez divided his force, leaving three hundred men behind when their transport vessels returned to New Spain. Wandering across the territory and attacked by indigenous people, they eventually constructed rafts and sailed across the Gulf of Mexico to present-day Galves-

ton, Texas, where a storm sank three of the five makeshift vessels. Esteban, his master, and thirteen others survived the storms and deprivation during the winter of 1528 and pressed inland.

Karankawa Indians enslaved the party for five years; twelve of the men died during their ordeal. In 1534, Esteban and the four other survivors (including Cabeza de Vaca) escaped their captors and encountered friendlier tribes that mistook them for healers or medicine men. Esteban became especially skilled at speaking the indigenous languages and became a kind of cultural broker as the small band wandered west through Texas and northern Mexico in search of New Spain. By the time Alcaraz encountered Cabeza de Vaca and Esteban in 1536, the two had wandered more than fifteen thousand miles. They regaled their Spanish colleagues with tales of golden cities—the famed Seven Cities of Cibola—and Esteban bragged that he was the "Son of the Sun," as various Indians had dubbed him. Three years later Esteban set out on another expedition. Dressed in animal pelts, bells, feathers, and turquoise, he gathered about him hundreds of admiring native followers. He was executed in May 1539 by the Zuni of Hawikuh in New Mexico, who rightly viewed him as a harbinger of more unwanted and dangerous visitors.

ORIGINS OF NORTH AMERICAN SLAVERY

Long before Columbus's famed voyages to the New World, Europeans had been engaged with Africa in the slave trade. But the Spanish and Portuguese, in the rush to exploit the resources of the Western Hemisphere and increase their power and wealth, intended to use Native Americans, not Africans, as the source of free or cheap labor. The prospect of Amerindian slavery was so attractive that as early as 1495 Columbus transported five hundred Native Americans back to Seville. The venture proved a success, and he planned to establish a regular trade to the Iberian Peninsula, Italy, and the Atlantic islands like Madeira, which had taken the lead in the European development of slavery. The Spanish uprooted tens of thousands of Amerindians in the fifteenth and sixteenth centuries, sending them to Panama, Peru, and the Caribbean to work the cane fields and the mines. They labored under the *encomienda* system, a mix of feudalism and slavery that helped further decimate the indigenous populations who possessed no resistance to many European diseases. While the Spanish did not intend to destroy Indian populations—they wanted their labor—the impact of the European presence proved catastrophic. Within seventy-five years of their first contact with the Spanish, the population of Mexico had diminished, incredibly, by 90 percent, with similar results in Peru and Chile. On Hispaniola, where Columbus first landed, by the 1540s the native population had been nearly wiped out, reduced to only five hundred.

The *encomienda* system, especially the horrid gold- and silver-mining practices as depicted by the De Bry brothers (influential Flemish engravers), was unconscionable. The callous disregard

One of the first depictions of slavery in the Western Hemisphere. From Girolamo Benzoni's *Americae Pars Quinta Nobilis & Admiratione* (Frankfurt, 1595).

for human life displayed by the Spanish colonizers became known, and Bishop Bartolomé de Las Casas and others exposed the enslavement of the Indians as crimes against humanity. King Charles V of Spain was forced to act: in 1542 he banned Indian slavery in Spanish America and promoted basic rights for Indians such as the right to own property. The law did little to reform colonial Spanish attitudes, but it did put an end to Indian enslavement and offered a measure of protection to indigenous peoples, even to women of mixed heritage like Isabel de Olvera, who in 1600 petitioned a Spanish official for protection while she accompanied the expedition of Juan Guerra de Resa to New Spain. "I therefore request your grace," she wrote, "to accept this affidavit, which shows that I am free and not bound by marriage or slavery."[7] But the

1542 ban on Indian slavery came too late to benefit the millions who already had perished of disease and maltreatment. Equally important, Las Casas and others proposed to solve the New World labor problem and eliminate the abuse of Amerindians by replacing Indian slaves with African ones. Indeed, when the native populations of Hispaniola declined, the Spanish acquired blacks from "Guinea" (one of Europe's several names for the West African coastal civilizations) and began to import them in great numbers.

When the Spanish explorer Pedro Menéndez de Avilés established St. Augustine, Florida, in 1565, he discovered a mulatto named Luis, a free African who probably washed up on shore after a 1554 shipwreck, living with the Calusa Indians. Luis, because of his skill with native languages, proved

St. Augustine, Florida, hand-colored engraving, 1589.

vital to Spanish interests and helped negotiate the release by a rival captain of several shipwrecked captives, including Spaniards, mestiza women (females of Amerindian and European ancestry), and one "unnamed black woman." To reward such useful service, Menéndez de Avilés made Luis an official military interpreter, and he and other individuals of African descent who lived among the indigenous population played critical roles in the release of many other captives. But Luis and his Spanish allies could do little to prevent slaves from fleeing their masters to live with native tribes. Such losses were especially painful to slave owners in a region desperate for workers. Menéndez de Avilés had gained permission to import as many as five hundred black slaves, but he probably did not acquire more than fifty at the time of settlement. The cost of slavery proved daunting, even to the wealthy, who were the only members of the society in a position to own such "property." With each male slave worth about two hundred pesos (a small fortune), the loss of a slave could be financially devastating. Still, black slaves were so desirable that some Spanish soldiers who sought to recoup back pay from the Crown preferred to be paid in slave licenses rather than in currency.[8]

FROM RED TO BLACK SLAVERY

In 1610 a Maroon settlement, San Lorenzo de los Negros (founded near modern Veracruz in the 1570s), gained freedom and municipal status from the Spanish Crown after a war led by a black former slave named Nyanga (or Gaspar Yanga). In other words, nine years before the Angolans came to Jamestown as slaves, a free and self-governing black municipality existed in the New World.

But most Africans brought to the New World faced a different fate than that of Yanga's determined Maroons. Even the freedom of Yanga's settlement rested on an agreement to return any fugitive slaves to Spanish authorities. The decimation of Amerindians, the outlawing of their enslavement, and the growth of the English colonies along the North American coast became turning points in the development of African slavery in the Western Hemisphere. While

Spain, and to a lesser degree Portugal, dominated the slave trade in the sixteenth century, the English broke into it through piracy and privateering.

As we have seen, the first slaves introduced into the English colonies, at Jamestown, were the "20 and odd Negroes" mentioned in a famous letter dated January 1620.[9] They originated in Angola and had been shipped under the Portuguese flag to Mexico. Just outside Veracruz, a major slave-trading port on the Gulf of Mexico, English privateers, under Dutch and Italian letters of marque, intercepted two vessels and transferred about fifty of the slaves to their own ships, leaving the remainder to proceed with the other cargo to grateful Spanish merchants, who sold them as plantation workers, personal servants, or even craftsmen.

The introduction of slaves into the English colonies thus resulted from the

Virginia tobacco production, uniting the colony's cash crop with African slavery. A seventeenth-century depiction.

struggle of the English and Dutch with Portugal for control of an increasingly lucrative trade in people legally "stolen" from Africa. In fact, a successful and profitable trade in African slaves could not have existed without some African

The first African slaves landing at Jamestown, Virginia, in 1619. Howard Pyle's (1853–1911) depiction originally appeared in *Harper's Monthly Magazine* in January 1901.

King Garcia II (Nkanga a Lukeni) of Kongo ruled 1641–61. The king is receiving a Dutch embassy in 1642 to negotiate a slave trade agreement.

António Manuel (Nsaku Ne Vunda), Kongo's ambassador to the Vatican, died shortly after arriving in Rome in 1608.

Queen Nzinga meeting with the Portuguese governor of Luanda. According to Giovanni Antonio Cavazzi, who witnessed the scene, when Queen Nzinga entered the room, the governor occupied the only seat. So she summoned a female assistant, who became her seat.

Miguel de Castro was one of several Kongo ambassadors to the Portuguese colony in Brazil and the Netherlands. De Castro communicated with his Dutch counterparts in Latin and was part of a Kongo elite fluent in Portuguese.

leaders' willingness to sell enemies captured in war to whomever offered the highest price. One of the most important monarchs was the legendary Queen Nzinga of Angola.

In 1637, the Dutch began buying slaves directly from Africa. A 1642 engraving shows Dutch emissaries paying homage to an African leader, most likely King Garcia II Nkanga a Lukeni of the Kongo, in an attempt to break into the Portuguese-dominated slave trade.

Contrary to popular assumptions, African elites during this period often had direct contact with Europeans in Europe, even exchanging ambassadors. Several of these ambassadors had their portraits painted, including Miguel de Castro, Kongo's ambassador to the Netherlands (1646) and António Manuel, Kongo's ambassador to the Vatican (1608). Emissaries from European nations visited the monarchs of African kingdoms as early as the sixteenth century, as paintings of the Dutch ambassador and Portuguese officials paying tribute to the king of Kongo in the late sixteenth century attest.

While the English moved toward a slave-based labor system only gradually and fitfully, white colonists rapidly introduced African slaves into most of the English colonies. In Virginia black slaves, white indentured servants, and Native Americans were the colony's primary sources of labor. Virginian slavery developed slowly during the seventeenth century as the Crown tried to restrict the planting of tobacco there, because it competed with tobacco cultivation in the British West Indies. The Virginia colonists resisted, and ultimately tobacco came to underpin the colony's economic life. After prolonged (and dubiously legal) attempts to extend the contracts of white indentured servants, white planters found that, over the long term, slave labor produced tobacco far more profitably than free labor ever could. The race for African slaves was on.

The kings of Kongo and Angola, ca. 1680.

FIRST AFRICANS AND THE GROWTH OF NORTHERN SLAVERY

Not all of the first Africans to settle in the United States were slaves. In the summer of 1627, a vessel from the Dutch West India Company seized a Portuguese shipment of Angolans off Cuba and delivered an undetermined number of slaves to New Amsterdam; other slaves captured from Spanish vessels also found their way into Dutch hands in the future New York. While these were the first slaves in the city, the first African to arrive on modern Manhattan Island was a free black man, Jan Rodrigues, who landed there in 1613—six years before the Angolans disembarked in Jamestown. He lived there for many years, marrying a Native American. Rodrigues worked to protect Dutch settlement claims to the region and insisted that they compensate him.

Rodrigues was an "Atlantic Creole" (as defined by the historians Ira Berlin and John Thornton).[10] The Atlantic Creoles played an important role in the colonization of North America. In 1634, when English Catholics established a colony at St. Mary's City, Maryland, another Atlantic Creole was among the several Africans who accompanied the white settlers. Mathias de Sousa, a Catholic of Portuguese and African descent, was among the original Maryland settlers; likely the Jesuits who employed him subsidized his transportation costs. De Sousa was a freeman who enjoyed all the rights and responsibilities held by his fellow white colonists. He signed contracts with whites, became the head of a trading expedition, participated in court proceedings, voted on colony matters, and eventually, because of unpaid debts, became an indentured servant. He was, in other words, an equal member of early Maryland society. But such

A slave auction in New Amsterdam, depicted by Howard Pyle, 1895.

racial freedom, whether in Maryland or in New Amsterdam, would not endure.

In New Amsterdam, as elsewhere, the Dutch demand for labor far outstripped any available supply, and the colonists rapidly turned to the African slave trade. The Dutch West India Company delivered the first cargo of Angolans to New Amsterdam in 1627, then promised to deliver twelve Africans for every white Dutch settler in the region. Only three years later, fifty Angolan Africans, cap-

tured off Brazil from a Portuguese slave trader, arrived in modern Staten Island and New Jersey, with more to come. Rather than laboring as personal servants, these enslaved Africans cleared land, cut timber, helped erect military defenses, built houses, and planted crops. The governor of the colony, Peter Stuyvesant, made it clear that he wanted more slaves—"stout and strong fellows, fit for immediate employment . . . , also, if required, in war against the wild barbarians, either to pursue them when retreating, or else to carry some of the soldiers' baggage."[11]

The status of the first black slaves brought to New Amsterdam remained ambiguous; many served terms identical to those of white indentured servants. This had also been the case in Virginia, but by 1662 Virginians had moved toward associating blacks with permanent, inheritable slavery. Connecticut and Massachusetts (in 1641) recognized the legality of slavery and restricted the institution to those of African descent. In New Amsterdam, however, small black neighborhoods developed as early as 1639, some free, some slave. By mid-century, the Dutch West India Company offered freedom to various classes of Africans, both male and female, reveal-

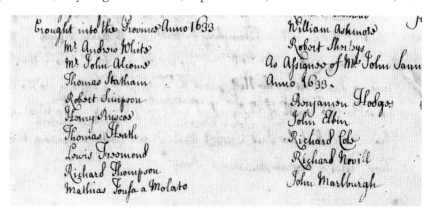

Mathias de Sousa is listed as a mulatto in this Maryland Land Office record, 1639.

ing the complex and halting movement to permanent racial enslavement. A similar pattern developed in Rhode Island, which would soon come to dominate the American slave trade.

Prior to 1700, many Africans served as slaves for a specific term of years, although the trend was to extend the period of service far beyond whatever limitations colonial legislatures had imposed. As John Thornton and Linda Heywood show, even in this indeterminate period, the status of Africans was already subject to debate rooted in the various meanings of the word "negro," which often was used as a simple ethnic marker but was also used to denote the status of a slave. It was only with what Thornton and Heywood call the "Plantation Generation" that enslavement of

Newport, Rhode Island, 1730. By the mid-eighteenth century Rhode Island had become the center of the American slave trade.

Africans came to be seen as perpetual and heritable.[12] Thus, by 1650 Indians and some whites may have been slaves, but only Africans served life terms. By 1700 Rhode Island mandated by law that only Indians and Africans could be enslaved for life.

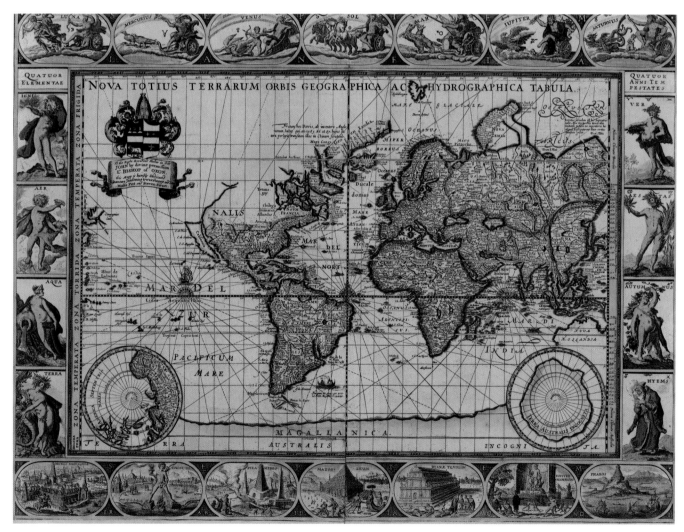

The Atlantic world, in 1680, at the onset of the slave trade.

ROYAL AFRICAN COMPANY

To solve vexing labor shortages in its Caribbean colonies, the English Crown in 1663 granted a slave-trading monopoly to the Company of Royal Adventurers to Africa. But in the early 1670s the firm failed, and most of the vessels returned to privateering. Then the Royal African Company was founded in 1672 to organize and expand the English slave trade and thereby provide the colonies with a reliable source of labor. Among its investors were the Duke of York (later James II), members of the royal family, and various peers.

Another investor was the famed philosopher John Locke, who served as secretary of the Committee on Plantations. His *Two Treatises on Government* (1689) would form the backbone of American revolutionary ideology in the next century. In the second treatise Locke exclaimed that all men should be protected from the "Arbitrary Will of another Man," but in the same pages he also defended the permanent enslavement of captives taken in war. He approved the charter for the Carolina colonies that granted free white men total domination over their black slaves. Locke's *Two Treatises* expressed the traditional European understanding of the relationship of war to enslavement, but it also conveniently enhanced his investment in the Royal African Company. In 1690, the first rice was planted in the Carolinas, and within forty years the region would produce rice prodigiously, as shown in a late-eighteenth-century advertisement. For the cultivation of this staple crop, the Carolinas were dependent on the labor of African slaves.

Seeking to increase its share of the African slave trade, the company enlisted the services of Ayuba ibn Suleiman Diallo, better known as Job ben

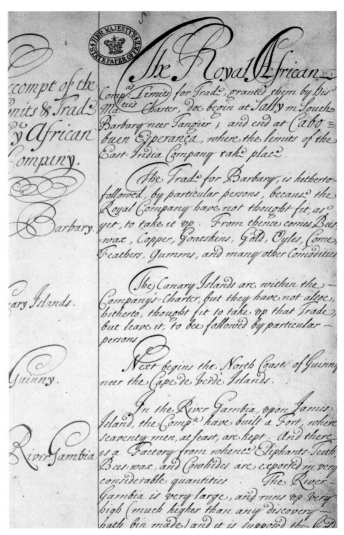

As part of the Crown's chartering of the Royal African Company, it carefully defined the geographic scope of the monopoly's operations.

Solomon (Jallo). Born in Senegal in 1702 to a prosperous and influential Muslim family, Diallo trained in Koranic and Arabic studies. In 1730, Mandingo kidnappers seized him and sold him to an English trader, who then transported him to Annapolis, Maryland. Put to work on a tobacco farm, he ran away but was quickly captured and imprisoned. One day, most improbably, Diallo sat down in his prison cell and wrote a letter in Arabic to his father, back in Senegal; a

lawyer named Thomas Bluett, who just happened to be traveling through Annapolis, obtained the letter and sent it to James Oglethorpe, director of the Royal African Company. Oglethorpe had it translated by a distinguished professor of Arabic at Oxford. Realizing that Diallo was the son of a prominent family, Bluett raised funds to purchase the African's freedom and brought him to London, where he became the toast of the town. Bluett had Diallo's portrait

Ayuba ibn Suleiman Diallo (1702–73).

painted and even published a memoir in 1734 about this African Muslim. In London, Diallo came to the attention of the Royal African Company, which saw in him an ingenious way of penetrating the dominance of the French in the slave trade in Senegal. Issued a French passport and loaded with supplies, Diallo returned to his homeland, ironically, to do the work of the Royal African Company. He remained on its payroll until the firm's demise.

Between 1673 and 1725 the Royal African Company sold about 75,000 slaves to British North American buyers, earning its investors about a 12 percent return. Although the company lost its monopoly in 1698, it remained far and away the largest English slave-trading venture, dwarfing all the independent shippers. It became successful largely because of the many forts and ports it established on the West African coast; these facilities were critical in protecting English traders and their vessels from their European and African competitors and from Africans opposed to the slave trade. But the company often erected these forts at the request of African kings to protect their economic interests in the trade. Additionally, the company received support from a royal tax on each slave purchased by independent traders. After the company lost its monopoly, an exclusive contract to provide slaves to the South

TO BE SOLD on board the Ship *Bance-Island*, on tuesday the 6th of *May* next, at *Ashley-Ferry*; a choice cargo of about 250 fine healthy NEGROES, just arrived from the Windward & Rice Coast. —The utmost care has already been taken, and shall be continued, to keep them free from the least danger of being infected with the SMALL-POX, no boat having been on board, and all other communication with people from *Charles-Town* prevented.

Austin, Laurens, & Appleby.

N. B. Full one Half of the above Negroes have had the SMALL-POX in their own Country.

In the coastal regions of the Carolinas, rice planters depended upon Africans with experience in rice cultivation, as this newspaper advertisement indicates. The firm of George Austin, Henry Laurens, and George Appleby imported thousands of slaves into Charleston during the second half of the eighteenth century.

Sea Company gave it renewed support. In 1731 the company abandoned the slave trade for the traffic in ivory and gold, then dissolved in 1752.

Slave coffle, depicted in 1866.

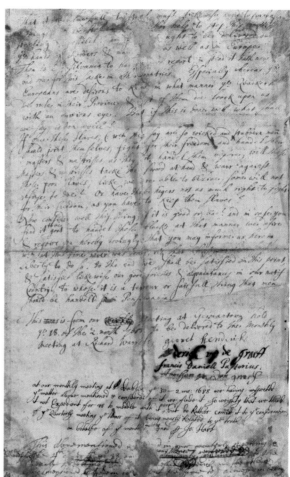

Quaker petition against slavery, Germantown, Pennsylvania, April 1688.

While slaves produced great wealth in England's North American colonies, the institution did not go entirely unchallenged. Slavery had existed in nearly all human communities, including African ones, from the very beginning of civilization. Indeed, many African kings welcomed the presence of European slave traders as a convenient way to dispose of competing tribes, enemies, and criminals, and to earn considerable wealth. Meanwhile, few Europeans found cause to question the institution. As late as the 1730s, a slave trader named Jean Bar-

bot considered himself a compassionate man because he refused to allow the fear-stricken, captured Africans on his slave ships to starve themselves to death; he instead smashed their teeth so they could be force-fed. Another slave trader, Thomas Phillips, cultivated a similarly "altruistic" self-image by not cutting off the arms and legs of slaves who attempted suicide, a punishment employed by other traders in an effort to set an example for slaves contemplating the same desperate act. In a brutal world in which chained prison convicts were sent to the colonies on vessels vir-

tually indistinguishable from slave ships, such "mercy" might appear as Christian benevolence to its practitioners.

But not to the Quakers of Germantown, outside Philadelphia. Many Quakers were descended from German Mennonites, who had fled their homes in Krefeld, in western Germany, to escape religious persecution. In the Germantown Protest, a petition penned in 1688, they explicitly connected the religious persecution that they themselves endured to the bondage of Africans. According to the petition, a person could have no liberty of conscience without lib-

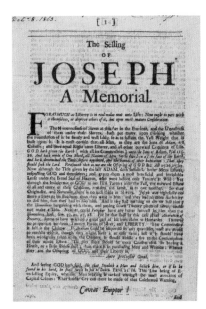

Samuel Sewall, *The Selling of Joseph,* 1700.

Samuel Sewall (1652–1730). Oil on canvas by Nathaniel Emmons, 1728.

this is not done at that manner we will be done at, therefore we contradict & are against this traffick of men body. And we who profess that it is unlawfull to steal, must lickewise avoid to purchase such things as are stollen, but rather help to stop this robbing and stealing if possibel. and such men ought to be delivered out of the hands of the Robbers, & made free as well as in Europe.

While awkwardly crafted, the petition's meaning and passion are clear. Indeed, the fellow Quakers to whom it was addressed considered it so clear and so threatening to the social order that they took no action on it and buried it in their files, where it was not rediscovered until the nineteenth century.

The same fate awaited *The Selling of Joseph,* written in 1700, the first pamphlet in North America to argue against slavery. Its author, the Massachusetts judge Samuel Sewall, best known for his role in the Salem witch trials, denounced slavery and the slave trade as "man stealing." Just as in the Quakers' 1688 petition, Sewall (who was not a Quaker) declared in his 1700 tract, "The Sin of Slaveholding," that "liberty is in real value next unto Life: None ought to part with it themselves, or deprive others of it, but upon most mature Consideration." He went on to recognize

erty of the body. It was not enough, they argued, to show mercy and kindness to slaves. Africans had been criminally seized from their homes and shipped to the New World without their consent. Rejecting John Locke's justification for enslaving captives in war, the petition asserted that purchasing African slaves was the equivalent of purchasing stolen goods:

Pray, what thing in the world can be done worse towards us, then if men should robb or steal us away, & sell us for slaves to strange Countries, separating housband from their wife and children. Being now

Africans as the children of God, just as Europeans were, and deserving of respect. His essay, part of an emerging international "conversation" on religion, slavery, and social ethics, also responded to local circumstances. A slave and his wife who claimed to be unjustly held in bondage had petitioned him as a judge, forcing him to think about the institution of slavery in ways that most people had not. Additionally, the number of slaves in the colony had grown considerably. Sewall determined that blacks were a kind of "extravasat Blood," inherently outside the mainstream of European life and culture. They did not belong, he held, among whites. The publication quickly dropped from sight and was not reprinted until 1863.

FEAR AND RESISTANCE

After 1700, as the population of black slaves in the northernmost colonies grew, so too did apprehension and guilt among whites. Colonial legislatures adopted laws restricting black conduct.

Most African slaves retained African religious beliefs, although many of those from Kongo and Angola had been converted to Roman Catholicism before being shipped to the New World. The Church of England was the first and the most aggressive denomination to evangelize African Americans. In 1703, under the auspices of the church's Society for the Propagation of the Gospel, Elias Neau, a French-born Huguenot who had arrived in New York via the West Indies in the 1690s, opened a school for the religious instruction of slaves. Neau

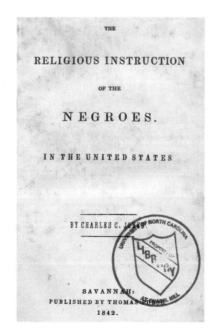

Trained in New England and at Princeton University, Charles Colcock Jones, a Georgia Presbyterian minister and plantation owner, wrote one of the earliest accounts of Elias Neau's education efforts among black New Yorkers.

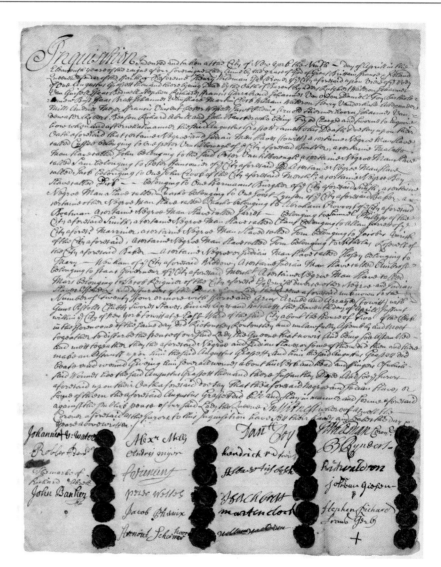

Coroner's inquest into the murder of Augustus Grasset by the slave Toby and thirty-seven accomplices during the 1712 New York slave revolt. The accused Africans had recently arrived from the Gold Coast and never accepted their status as slaves. Indeed, several committed suicide rather than submit to capture by New York authorities.

had spent much of his career as a slave trader, but his own imprisonment in France had instilled in him a degree of empathy for those in bondage. He did not question the legality or morality of slavery, but he did assert that even slaves had a right to religious instruction and to an opportunity to convert to Christianity.

His religious instruction, mostly offered in his own home, proved enormously popular with the city's slaves, who listened hungrily as he emphasized the sufferings of Christ and spoke of Christian hope. Restive under the tightening controls, they eagerly took advantage of any opportunity to gain education. Before long more than one

The trial proceedings of those, black and white, accused in the 1741 New York conspiracy.

This 1731 New York law barred all Africans, free or slave, and Indians over the age of fourteen, from being on the streets one hour after sunset.

hundred slaves were attending his classes. Even black merchantmen from Bermuda and the West Indies stopped into his school during their brief stays in port. Very likely they all drew unintended lessons about liberation in this world and the next from the simplified theology offered in Neau's classes.

But whites in the general population became increasingly hostile to efforts to educate blacks and disapproved of evangelical efforts to convert black souls to Christianity. White ministers resented Neau's efforts and the support he received from London. New Yorkers generally feared that educating slaves would only encourage them to resist. To quell such anxiety, Neau supported new laws to guarantee that the baptism of a slave would have no impact on his bondage. In 1704 and 1706, first New Jersey and then New York passed such legislation, increasing Neau's confidence that he could continue his evangelizing undisturbed.

Nevertheless, white hostility to his efforts continued, even though New York governor Robert Hunter endorsed the school. But in 1708 an Indian and a black female slave murdered a master and his family, including five children. It inflamed public opinion, especially as more individuals beyond the two killers appeared to have been involved. Hanging the male slave and burning the female did not extinguish the white rage.

In 1711 Governor Hunter widely circulated a proclamation urging all masters to send their slaves to Neau's school, believing that religious instruction would help preserve the social order. In 1712, 1731, and 1741, white anxiety and black resistance to white domination led to rebellion, insurrection, and tragedy. In the spring of 1712, a conspiracy of slaves in New York set fire to the house of a white owner, and as the occupants fled the flames, the slaves waited outside to butcher them. Authorities swiftly rounded up about twenty-one conspirators (many of whom white people merely suspected had been involved) and quickly executed eighteen of them. Some they broke on the wheel, others they hanged with chains, and several they burned to death. Bodies and severed heads ornamented public thoroughfares for weeks as a warning to other slaves in the city. The governor intervened to halt the orgy of revenge and pardoned several of the accused, including two Spanish blacks who had been illegally enslaved by privateers. He also advised masters to keep the peace by employing

This map of New York City, made in 1813, is the recollection of the seventy-six-year-old New Yorker David Grim. It shows some eleven hundred houses, sixty landmarks, and the place where city officials executed—by burning—those Africans accused in the 1741 conspiracy.

white indentured servants rather than importing more slaves. Instead, slave imports increased dramatically, doubling the region's slave population in the following decades. In December 1712, the state legislature adopted a series of harsh measures to rivet the chains of slavery even tighter on African Americans, quashing any attempts by masters to free their property.

In the following years, plots, both real and imagined, punctuated New York and New Jersey society. Whites treated

threats, or rumors of threats, to burn their cities with special attention, leading lawmakers to ban the congregating of blacks after sunset. The words of one inebriated slave in 1731 were sufficient to start a fury of judicial killings, whippings, and mutilations. Attempted rape, or even the charge that a slave had attacked a white woman, immediately led to a public burning. New York slaves may have sought to return the favor. Two thousand of them now lived in a city with a total population of ten thousand.

In 1741, Fort George, the home of New York's governor, burned to the ground. Fires then broke out in other parts of the city, in New Jersey, and on Long Island. Whites claimed that they had overheard slaves taking credit for the fires and plotting a general insurrection and the destruction of the city. Authorities believed that secret black societies and gangs were planning a revolt, inspired by a conspiracy of priests and their Catholic minions—white, black, brown, free and slave. Additionally, they asserted, the evangelizing of slaves by Neau and by the itinerant Great Awakening minister George Whitefield had encouraged slaves to rise up against their masters. (Whitefield symbolizes the complexity of Christian attitudes toward slavery: at the same time that he was committed to bringing Christianity to slaves and spoke passionately of the "un-Christian" cruelties inflicted on them, he also urged the legalization of slavery in 1751.) Many of the fires remained unexplained; some blacks gave forced confessions.

The government seized dozens of slaves and four whites, tried them, and found them guilty. For the next several months, execution by hanging or burning became an almost daily occurrence. Slaves were offered huge rewards for informing on alleged plotters, leading to tainted but compelling testimonies and seemingly endless retribution. Several plotters confessed, and a black doctor said he had threatened to help poison whites; the plot seemed as real as any that had recently taken place in the Caribbean. A slave named Will explained that he was enraged at his master for refusing to allow him to see his wife and thus was ready to kill.

Confession did not necessarily mean a pardon; Will was burned at the stake anyway.

But slave prisoners told their white captors whatever they wanted to hear, allowing authorities to exaggerate and twist idle talk and righteous anger into an imminent bloody conspiracy. Thus, many innocent African Americans went to brutal deaths. Within a year, however, many New Yorkers began to doubt the tales of revolt and papist conspiracy, anxious about the kind of society they all had a hand in creating.

INOCULATION

I had from a Servant of my own, an Account of [inoculation] being practised in Africa. Enquiring of my Negro-man Onesimus, who is a pretty Intelligent Fellow, Whether he ever had ye Small-Pox; he answered, both, Yes, and, No; and then told me, that he had undergone an Operation, which had given him something of ye Small-pox, & would forever præserve him from it. He described ye Operation to me, and shew'd me in his Arm ye Scar."[13] In this July 12, 1716, letter, the great Puritan Cotton Mather revealed how in 1713 an African brought a life-saving medical technique to the greater European world.

Back in 1706, several parishioners in Mather's congregation had bought their minister a "good servant" for about £50, "a very likely Slave," as Mather recorded in his diary, "a young Man, who is a Negro of a promising Aspect and Temper."[14] Mather had a variety of servants, male and female, but he owned Onesimus, whom he named after the slave owned by St. Paul. We know precious little about Onesimus, but it is a near

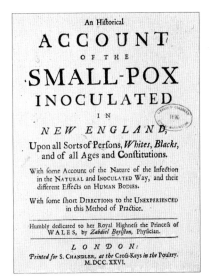

An Historical

ACCOUNT

OF THE

SMALL-POX

INOCULATED

IN

NEW ENGLAND,

Upon all Sorts of Perfons, *Whites*, *Blacks*, and of all Ages and Conftitutions.

With fome Account of the Nature of the Infection in the NATURAL and INOCULATED Way, and their different Effects on HUMAN BODIES.

With fome fhort DIRECTIONS to the UNEXPERIENCED in this Method of Practice.

Humbly dedicated to her Royal Highnefs the Princefs of WALES, by *Zabdiel Boylfton*, Phyfician.

LONDON:

Printed for S. CHANDLER, at the Crofs-Keys in the Poultry. M.DCC.XXVI.

In 1726, Zabdiel Boylston (1679–1766), member of a dynasty of Boston physicians, published an account of the controversy over inoculation.

certainty that he was born in Africa. He chafed under his slave status and, through his recalcitrance and resistance, eventually compelled Mather to allow him to buy his freedom. The relationship, however, proved fruitful in ways no one could have predicted.

For years, Boston had been periodically afflicted with smallpox epidemics. In 1702 all three of Mather's children fell ill with the disease, striking fear in the minister that God would take them in retribution for whatever sins he had committed. In one month that year, eighty Bostonians died from the pox. When an outbreak terrorized Boston again in 1721, Mather led a very controversial—albeit thoroughly justifiable—campaign to employ the new preventive measure that he had learned from his slave. The idea of inoculation, however, was radical and completely counterintuitive. After learning about the practice from Onesimus, Mather interviewed other Africans in the Boston area to confirm the story. All affirmed its widespread use in Africa and even showed him the scars on their arms to prove it. The Africans also informed him that slave traders on the African coast regularly inoculated their cargoes before shipping them to the New World colonies.

Mather detailed the practice to the Royal Society in London, where pox

Cotton Mather (1663–1728).

ery, especially Benjamin Coleman, who also had interviewed Boston's African community about the practice. The only physician to support the move was Zabdiel Boylston, who with Mather penned a pamphlet to urge immediate and widespread adoption of the practice. Coleman also published his findings about inoculation, and all three men emphasized the experience of Africans to demonstrate its effectiveness. Understanding that the public would resist the idea that Africans could teach white people anything about medicine, they asserted that anyone who accepted Indian remedies for poisonous snakebites had no cause to object to African remedies.

But white Bostonians angrily resisted inoculation, in part because Africans suggested it, and went so far as to throw

a bomb into Mather's home. Prominent among Mather's opponents was the editor of *The New England Courant,* James Franklin (the older brother of Benjamin, who worked as an apprentice in the newspaper's office during the controversy). Nevertheless, Boylston found enough people willing to be inoculated to prove its efficacy. Those who refused it died in much higher percentages. Mather, Coleman, and Boylston won their point—and showed how much African people could contribute to European medicine and science. But subsequent accounts of the history of inoculation focused on the heroism of Mather and Boylston rather than on the wisdom of Onesimus and his fellow African Americans.

outbreaks were even more devastating than in the colonies. The Boston public thought the idea of injecting a disease into people to prevent the disease outrageous—and they resisted. A few ministers supported Mather's discov-

FORT MOSE:
A DIFFERENT TRAJECTORY

During the first half of the eighteenth century, African Americans along the southeastern coast exploited the struggle between England and Spain, finding openings to resist slavery and gain freedom. Slavery had become increasingly racialized and more integral to New World economies, but since the mid-sixteenth century people of African descent had assumed important military roles throughout the Caribbean for a Spanish Crown chronically short of manpower. In 1683, for instance, blacks in Spanish-controlled St. Augustine had been organized into a military company for defense against the English and local Indians.

In the early eighteenth century, Spanish raids on English settlements in the Carolinas—and later Georgia—and retaliatory English attacks on Indian

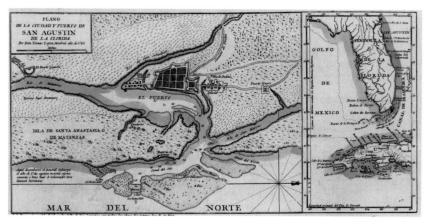

Map of St. Augustine, hand-colored. Fort Mose lies to the east of the city.

and black settlements were destabilizing the region. The conflicts also intensified the desire of English-held slaves to rebel and escape south—and the Spanish encouraged such flights by offering freedom to all runaways. The flow of fugitives from the Carolinas, especially

after rebellions in 1720 and 1724, significantly increased the number of blacks in St. Augustine and of those eager to take up arms in support of Spanish rule. The city's black militia unit came under the command of Captain Francisco Menéndez (a Mandinga, or Atlantic Creole),

St. Christopher medal, handmade
silver, excavated at Fort Mose.

who would serve Spain for more than forty years. The black troops under his command performed so well that they earned praise from the king, who, in 1733, reissued his offer of freedom to any slaves that escaped from the English colonies.

In 1738, the runaways and other blacks then living in St. Augustine moved about two miles north of the Castillo de San Marcos to a village and fort that would become known as Gracia Real de Santa Teresa de Mose, or Fort Mose. The settlement, much like a South American Maroon society, came under the command of Captain Menéndez and another black officer, Antonio de la Puente, but operated with the full backing and support of colonial authorities. Indeed, the Spanish wanted the blacks at Fort Mose to become even more numerous and powerful as a check on English military power and as a perimeter defense for St. Augustine. The Spanish oversaw construction of the fort and surrounding homes (which the black residents actually owned); the blacks received

Spanish weapons and benefited from the ministrations of a priest, assigned to the settlement, who baptized willing converts. This St. Christopher medal, recovered during recent archaeological excavations, could have been obtained in Florida, in other parts of the Spanish Empire, or even in the Kongo, where many Catholic converts lived. As the patron saint of travelers, St. Christopher remains a remarkable symbol of the black diaspora.

Fort Mose's hundred or so first inhabitants were quickly augmented by more runaways, such as a group of twenty-three men, women, and children who had escaped from Port Royal, off the South Carolina coast, in a stolen skiff. Such escapes increased so dramatically that the English resorted to public executions of captured runaways in an attempt to stanch the flow to Florida.

On September 9, 1739, at a branch of the Stono River near Charleston, South Carolina, about twenty slaves under the leadership of a slave named Jemmy broke into a store to seize arms and ammunition. They executed the white owners and deposited the victims' heads on the store's front steps. The rebels then proceeded toward St. Augustine, gaining additional insurgents (perhaps as many as fifty) and leaving destruction in their wake. They successfully fought off the English for more than a week before their defeat and deaths, although some of the rebels might have reached Fort Mose.

The next year another slave rebellion took place in the same region, leading to the execution of at least fifty rebels. All had the same goal: to reach Spanish Florida and freedom. The English struck back, laying siege to St. Augustine and forcing the evacuation of Fort Mose, which they then razed. But in 1741 Menéndez and his militia retook the outpost and helped drive out English forces. The Spanish government took particular note of the heroism of the black troops:

Fort Mose, artist's rendering.

The constancy, valor and glory of the officers here are beyond all praise: the patriotism, courage, and steadiness of the troops, militia, free blacks, and convicts have been great. . . . Even among the slaves a particular steadiness has been noticed, and a desire not to await the enemy within . . . [Fort Castillo] but to go out to meet him.[15]

Fort Mose blacks gratefully went on serving the Spanish Crown. The Spanish offer of emancipation continued to draw fugitive slaves to St. Augustine, where they could own property and live in relative freedom. In 1752 a new Spanish governor sought to reestablish Fort Mose with former residents and new escapees from the English colonies. Again commanded by Captain Menéndez, Fort Mose's defenses were buttressed by six cannons and a detachment of Spanish cavalry. Many of the fort's former residents understandably preferred to remain in St. Augustine, so the governor added to the fifty or so residents new settlers from the Canary Islands. Despite the stronger force and new defensive works, the fort declined, and when Spain turned over the region to England in the 1763 Treaty of Paris, the residents—black, brown, red, and white—permanently abandoned the settlement. It was not rediscovered until the twentieth century.

23

PART TWO

FORGING FREEDOM

1760–1804

Briton Hammon, Jupiter Hammon, and Phillis Wheatley inaugurated the African American literary tradition. Their work, crafted between 1760 and the late 1780s, emerged during the formation of free black communities, as black challenges to the institution of slavery had begun to multiply (especially in the North), and as free blacks like Jean Baptiste Point du Sable began exploring the West and forging business alliances with powerful white leaders. Du Sable and Wheatley in particular displayed impressive abilities to cultivate contacts in the white world, becoming clever business, social, and intellectual entrepreneurs.

Du Sable, who associated with the white St. Louis businessman and judge Jacques Clamorgan, arrived in New Orleans from Haiti in 1764. Within a year he completed a six-hundred-mile journey up the Mississippi River with

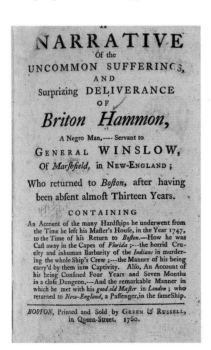

Briton Hammon's *Narrative*, 1760, published a year after his escape.

Clamorgan and claimed hundreds of acres of land in Peoria, Illinois. Several years later he established a trading post and farm at present-day Chicago, thus becoming the city's founder. Despite the growing importance of slavery in American life, du Sable, Wheatley, and the Hammons created unprecedented opportunities for themselves and, more important, cleared vital pathways for other African Americans.

Briton Hammon and Jupiter Hammon (unrelated despite sharing a surname) published the first writings by African Americans. *A Narrative of the Uncommon Sufferings, and Surprizing Deliverance of Briton Hammon,* appearing in 1760, was the first slave narrative published in North America. Briton Hammon, a slave in coastal Marshfield, Massachusetts, had received permission from his owner in 1747 to undertake a long voyage. Shipwrecked off the Florida coast, he spent the next dozen years in an odyssey of capture and imprisonment in Florida and Cuba, and in military service. After his escape from Spanish authorities, he joined the British Royal Navy, which discharged him in 1759 for wounds he received in battle. In an ironic twist typical of such publications, on his return voyage to Boston he sailed on the same vessel as his master, who happened to have visited London and had long ago concluded that his property had died. Hammon's astonishing account of his life, capitalizing on the Indian captivity narrative tradition (perfected by Mary Rowlandson in the previous century), claimed a space for blacks in the developing print community of the greater Atlantic world, and created a model for the hundreds of slave narratives that would follow in the next century.

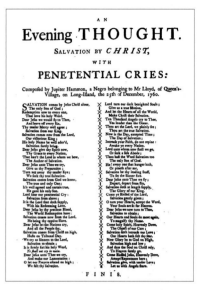

Jupiter Hammon (1711–1806?), "An Evening Thought," 1760.

Jupiter Hammon's "An Evening Thought" was the first published poem by an African American. A slave born on the Henry Lloyd plantation on Long Island, Jupiter Hammon received his

Phillis Wheatley (1753?–84). This colorized image comes from the frontispiece of her book, *Poems on Various Subjects, Religious and Moral,* 1773.

Jean Baptiste Point du Sable (1745?–1818), artist's rendering, 1884. Du Sable was the founder of Chicago.

education from a Harvard graduate named Nehemiah Bull and from Daniel Denton, a British missionary. Except for a brief stay in Hartford, Connecticut, during the Revolution, Hammon spent his entire life on the Lloyd plantation working as a skilled craftsman and as a preacher. Converting to Wesleyan Methodism during the First Great Awakening, Hammon published his devotional poem "An Evening Thought" on Christ-mas Day 1760. The work revealed the influence of English hymns, but more important, it displayed black religiosity at a time when most whites questioned the capacity of blacks to comprehend Christian dogma. Moreover, it contained a subversive equalitarian subtext in assuring fellow African Americans that they could, with all others, share in Christian salvation: "Let us with Angels share."

Phillis Wheatley's *Poems on Various Subjects, Religious and Moral* (1773), and her later work, similarly drew public attention to the capacity of blacks to acquire the essential tools of European cultural expression. While her work is careful, measured, and somewhat rigid for modern tastes, it conformed beautifully to eighteenth-century standards. It conformed so well, in fact, that her book included a statement from a committee of "eighteen most respectable characters" of Boston, including the governor of the colony and John Hancock, to authenticate it as genuine, to assuage the doubts of those who believed that Africans lacked the requisite degree of reason ever to write anything as complex as a poem.

Wheatley, born in Senegal or Gambia and sold as a slave in Boston in 1761, quickly mastered English and wrote her first poem four years later. But her October 1770 elegy to the English evangelical George Whitefield brought her attention throughout the Atlantic world, ultimately earning her the friendship and patronage of the Countess of Huntington, a woman who that same year helped publish the slave narrative of James Albert Ukawsaw Gronniosaw in Bath, England. Selina Hastings, the countess, was at the center of the antislavery Methodist circle and was eager to use the writings of former slaves themselves as prima facie evidence against slavery. As du Sable had skillfully used his contacts with prominent whites to advance his career,

The site of du Sable's first settlement at the location of modern-day Chicago, artist's rendering, 1884.

Wheatley employed the influence of her owners John and Susanna Wheatley to contact the countess in London. The countess republished her elegy and then supported publication of her book, the first book of poems published in English by a black person. (Juan Latino, who was both a professor and a slave in Spain, published the very first book of poems by a black person, in Latin, in 1573.)

Wheatley, who had become an important part of the developing black Atlantic world, probably knew Gronniosaw, since they shared a patron. Another former slave, Ignatius Sancho (whose collected letters would be published posthumously in 1782), certainly wrote about the unjustness of Wheatley's enslavement. (Despite the letter of attestation, no one would publish Wheatley's book in Boston, so her master sent her to London, where it was published on September 5, 1773.) Wheatley most certainly knew the Boston blacks who repeatedly petitioned the legislature for freedom during the Revolutionary era. Her work, such as her 1768 poem "America" (not published in her lifetime), possessed a more distinct antislavery character than even that found in Jupiter Hammon's better-known 1787 "Address to the Negroes in the State of New York," which claimed that God would "set us free . . . in his own time, and way." "Thy Power, O Liberty, makes strong the weak," Wheatley wrote, "And (wond'rous instinct) Ethiopians speak."[1]

Her poems and published letters, as well as those of Jupiter Hammon (who addressed a poem directly to Wheatley in 1778), existed within a larger colonial debate over the boundaries of liberty and freedom that ultimately led to national independence and growing antislavery sentiment. In fact, the very year that Wheatley published her book, Harvard graduates Theodore Parsons and Eliphalet Pearson debated the institution of slavery at commencement, and published it as *A Forensic Dispute on the Legality of Enslaving Africans.* The famed revolutionary and physician Benjamin Rush found Wheatley's work so compelling that he cited it as evidence of human equality, and her book of poetry may have convinced one Virginia master to give up his slaves. Wheatley and the other early African American writers inserted an African American voice into the ideology of the American Revolution and claimed a moral authority that clearly challenged whites of her era:

> How, presumptuous shall we
>   hope to find
> Divine acceptance with th'
>   Almighty mind—
> While yet (O deed ungenerous!)
>   they disgrace
> And hold in bondage Afric's
>   blameless race![2]

CRISPUS ATTUCKS AND THE FREEDOM STRUGGLE

Crispus Attucks, a brave sailor, probably of black, Indian, and white ancestry, was the first colonist to be killed in the series of volatile events that led to the American Revolution. Most likely a runaway slave from Framingham, Massachusetts, Attucks served on a Nantucket whaler at the time of his fateful role on the evening of March 5, 1770, protesting the presence of royal troops in Boston.

Little is known about Attucks, and no contemporary image of him survives. But according to some eyewit-

The Boston Massacre, lithograph by J. H. Bufford, 1856. This reimagining places Crispus Attucks at the focus of the incident.

29

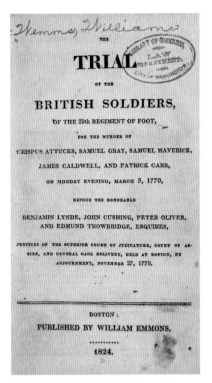

THE

TRIAL

OF THE

BRITISH SOLDIERS,

OF THE 29th REGIMENT OF FOOT,

FOR THE MURDER OF

CRISPUS ATTUCKS, SAMUEL GRAY, SAMUEL MAVERICK,

JAMES CALDWELL, AND PATRICK CARR,

ON MONDAY EVENING, MARCH 5, 1770,

BEFORE THE HONORABLE

BENJAMIN LYNDE, JOHN CUSHING, PETER OLIVER,

AND EDMUND TROWBRIDGE, ESQUIRES,

JUSTICES OF THE SUPERIOR COURT OF JUDICATURE, COURT OF AS-
SIZE, AND GENERAL GAOL DELIVERY, HELD AT BOSTON, BY
ADJOURNMENT, NOVEMBER 27, 1770.

BOSTON:

PUBLISHED BY WILLIAM EMMONS.

1824.

Trial transcript of the British soldiers accused of murdering Crispus Attucks and four other colonials in the Boston Massacre. John Adams successfully defended the soldiers.

nesses to the event, he was a strong and fearsome-looking person, perhaps in his late forties. Hearing a commotion during dinner, he abandoned his meal to lead a body of sailors (several of whom were black) and other "rabble" (as John Adams referred to them in his defense of the soldiers during their trial), to confront the unwanted Redcoats. Accounts differ as to what took place, but the rioters did throw debris at the soldiers, and Attucks may have grabbed a soldier's bayonet, or merely waved a barrel stave. Regardless, by the end of the incident he and four other rioters lay dead, only steps from the Old State House. Adams gained acquittals for most of the soldiers involved in the tragic incident; two others found guilty of manslaughter were branded on their thumbs and released. Curiously, Attucks seems to have been forgotten for the next eighty years. Then, in 1850, the explosive Fugitive Slave Act was adopted, and the abolitionist movement turned Attucks into an iconic patri-

otic figure—illustrative of the black role in the nation's founding and of blacks' singular devotion to American freedom. Paul Revere, in his contemporary rendering of the Boston Massacre, either left Attucks out or rendered him white like others who participated in the riot. But in the black abolitionist William C. Nell's important book *Colored Patriots of the American Revolution* (1855) and in the accompanying 1856 lithograph, Attucks is moved front and center to emphasize his role in the massacre and in helping to establish American independence. During the Civil War, recruiters employed images of Attucks and the Boston Massacre to rally enlistments for the commonwealth's three African American regiments. Ever since, he has remained in the nation's patriotic lexicon.

The Boston Massacre, one of many critical incidents during the contentious 1770s, took place amid rancorous debates on both sides of the Atlantic over the meaning of liberty and freedom. Another was the June 22, 1772, *Somersett* case in Britain. Chief Justice Lord Baron Mansfield, in his celebrated legal opinion, freed a slave named James Somersett, asserting that no British law existed to hold Somersett as a slave or to sell him abroad. But Mansfield's ruling did not end the institution in Britain, and as late as 1827 British courts held that a female slave named Grace Jones remained a slave under West Indian law, although she had lived as a free woman in Britain for a year. Still, many maintained that the court's decision represented a deadly blow to slavery. Although historians disagree on its full impact, reformers throughout the Atlantic world believed that it was a pivotal milestone in overturning the institution.

The court's controversial decision in the *Somersett* case and the passionate debates concerning the extent of imperial authority over the American colonies inspired African Americans. Royal taxation, the quartering of soldiers in private homes, restrictions on trade and domestic industries, and nullification

Granville Sharp the Abolitionist Rescuing a Slave from the Hands of His Master, oil on canvas by James Hayllar, 1864. Sharp (1735–1813), one of Britain's leading abolitionists, regularly brought cases of slaves and kidnapped Africans before the bar of justice. He achieved his greatest success in the *Somersett* case.

of laws adopted by colonial legislatures incited countless colonial tirades against royal tyranny and alleged attempts by the Crown to enslave American colonists. These intense and well-crafted rants sounded sweet to the ears of real slaves. Many African Americans used the colonists' rhetoric of opposition to call for their own liberation. In an April 20, 1773, petition to the Massachusetts legislature, which probably also circulated as a leaflet, four slaves asked lawmakers to extend the freedom they claimed for themselves to those truly in chains:

> The efforts made by the legislative of this province in their last Sessions to free themselves from slavery, gave us, who are in that deplorable state, a high degree of satisfaction. We expect great things from men who have made such a noble stand against the designs of their fellow-men to enslave them. We cannot but wish and hope Sir, that you will have the same grand object, we mean civil and religious liberty, in view in your next session. The divine spirit of freedom, seems to fire every human breast on this continent.[3]

COLORED PATRIOTS

African Americans are among the most overlooked participants in the American Revolution. Historians estimate that at least five thousand black men fought for the Continental army; thousands more, in some way or another, supported both sides in the war, all drawn by the possibility of freedom. Peter Salem, Salem Poor, Barzillai Lew, Prince Estabrook, and a few others fought in the Battles of Lexington and Concord and at Bunker Hill. Peter Salem is customarily credited with killing Major John Pitcairn at Bunker Hill, and in the early 1960s a musket purported to be Salem's held an honored place at the Bunker Hill Museum. Historians also routinely point to the petition submitted to the Massachusetts legislature by fourteen white officers praising the heroism of Salem Poor.

John Trumbull's emblematic painting of the death of Joseph Warren at Bunker Hill includes one African American, a "faithful negro" (as the artist called him), who is usually assumed to be the slave of the white officer he stands behind. As in so many eighteenth-century American and British paintings, the black figure is marginalized, to affirm the importance of the white subject as the focus of

The Death of General Warren at the Battle of Bunker Hill, oil on canvas by John Trumbull, 1786.

the painting. Trumbull's painting, and historians' episodic mentions of individual blacks in the Revolution, take on a sometimes patronizing character in a carefully filtered story of national self-creation. The face of history is changed, however, when we realize that at least 103 African American men fought side by side with white men at Bunker Hill.

The estimate that five thousand black soldiers fought in the Continental army would certainly be considerably higher if one included all officers' servants, stevedores, teamsters, and spies (male and female). Perhaps the most celebrated black patriot spy was James Armistead Lafayette, depicted in this 1783 portrait (page 32) as General Lafayette's groom. Armistead masqueraded as a runaway slave and scouted British encampments in Richmond and then at the war's final

American soldiers at Yorktown, 1781, including an African American from a Rhode Island regiment, watercolor. The stylized image is from the diary of Jean Baptiste Antoine de Verger, an officer in Count Rochambeau's army.

James Armistead (1760–1830), engraving with General Lafayette's letter verifying his invaluable services during the Revolutionary War.

battle at Yorktown, providing vital information that the Americans employed to secure victory. In 1784, Lafayette, the famed French volunteer, penned a glowing testimony of Armistead's wartime bravery. When Lafayette revisited the United States in 1824, the Richmond, Virginia, artist John Blennerhasset Martin created a broadside featuring Lafayette's text and a likeness of Armistead, who then took on the Frenchman's surname to honor him.

But serving the American cause proved difficult. At the very beginning of the war, black soldiers fought in integrated units along with whites and some Native Americans, even in units from Virginia. Ten months after Lexington and Concord, however, some of the states began excluding blacks, especially slaves, from their militias, for fear of inciting slave rebellions. In early July 1775 the Continental army officially excluded all blacks from its ranks. In January 1776, the Congress decided that those free blacks who had already served in the army could continue, but it would not permit General Washington to recruit additional ones. Soon

General Lafayette at Yorktown Attended by James Armistead, oil on canvas by Jean-Baptiste Le Paon, ca. 1783.

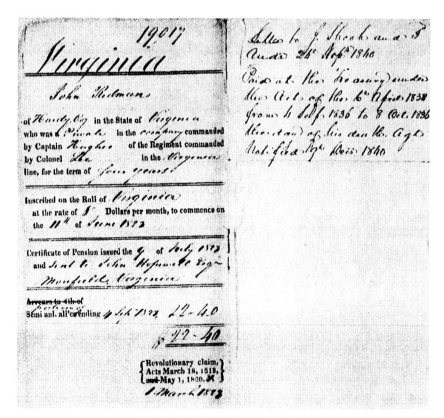

John Redman's pension application.

afterward, Massachusetts and the other New England states adopted legislation to exclude all blacks and Indians from their militia ranks.

As the war ground on and the states found it increasingly difficult to fill their recruitment quotas, however, black men began reentering the service—except in the Deep South. My fourth great-grandfather, John Redman, for example, a free Negro, mustered into the army on Christmas Day 1778 and served until the spring of 1784, participating in a battle near Savannah, Geor-gia. Redman received a pension for his service. Congress turned a color-blind eye to the black troops and by 1779 was even ready to recruit thousands of slaves. It even suggested that South Carolina and Georgia raise a force of three thousand blacks to repel the king's troops.

Although several southern states re-coiled at the thought of arming their slaves, many others, especially in the North, included some blacks in the ranks of most of their regiments. One Rhode Island unit contained between 150 and 200. Black patriots fought at the Battles of Monmouth, Red Bank, and Trenton, suffered with white troops at Valley Forge, and celebrated the final victory at Yorktown. About five hundred, mostly from Haiti, served with the French after that country agreed to support the Patriot cause. Many more served on the high seas, providing the manpower that made the margin of difference between victory and defeat. From the beginning of the Republic, African Americans have served their country nobly.

THE KING'S FREEDOM

Incentive for the Continental Congress to reconsider its ban on black recruits for the army came from an unlikely source. On November 7, 1775, aboard the HMS *William* off the Norfolk, Virginia, coast, John Murray, fourth Earl of Dunmore, issued a proc-lamation offering freedom to all inden-tured servants and slaves if they would be "willing to bear Arms, . . . joining HIS MAJESTY'S TROOPS as soon as may be, for the more speedily reducing this Colony to a proper Sense of their Duty, to HIS MAJESTY'S Crown and Dignity."[4] Shock waves rippled through the colo-nies as slave owners contemplated the full meaning of Dunmore's act. Not surprisingly, slaves from New York to the Carolinas began disappearing. Even some of George Washington's property took flight and made for a British war-ship. Washington remained unmoved and refused to reconsider the ban on recruiting black soldiers. The idea of slaves running away to His Majesty's troops, however, compelled many Amer-icans to reconsider their exclusionary laws and regulations. It also forced them

Lord Dunmore's proclamation, November 7, 1775.

to allocate men to slave supervision who otherwise would have been avail-able for combat duty. American colo-nists offered a pardon to those blacks who quickly returned to the Patriot side and promised swift executions for those who did not, although Virgin-ians proved reluctant to kill very many blacks who sought freedom among the British.

Dunmore's Ethiopian Regiment, in total about three hundred men who wore uniforms emblazoned with "Lib-erty to Slaves," proved more important for its symbolic value than for its effec-tiveness as a fighting force. Its only sig-nificant engagement, at Great Bridge on December 9, was a galling defeat. Nev-ertheless, slaves continued to flee by any means available, and Dunmore effec-tively used them as sailors and pilots aboard his vessels and as foraging units to resupply all his men. But by July 1776 many of the troops had died of disease, and the remainder fled aboard the few ships remaining to Dunmore, bound for St. Augustine, Florida, and Bermuda.

Dunmore's "Ethiopians" were not alone among blacks in supporting the Loyalist cause. A slave in Monmouth County, New Jersey, who gained fame as "Colonel Tye" fled his cruel master in November 1775 and eagerly joined Dun-more's regiment. After its demise, he returned to New Jersey and joined his

The Death of Major Pierson, oil on canvas by John Singleton Copley, 1782–84.

British allies at the Battle of Monmouth, even capturing a rebel militia captain. He then formed his own guerrilla unit, the Black Brigade, becoming a kind of black Swamp Fox for the king, spreading terror throughout the region where he had been held as a slave. In late 1779 his unit joined the Queen's Rangers and attacked Patriots around New York City. The next year his brigade returned to New Jersey, where it continued to wreak havoc among the Patriots.

The willingness of blacks to fight for Great Britain, as depicted in John Singleton Copley's *The Death of Major Pierson,* if nothing else reflected their desire for freedom. That desire also helps explain why so many African Americans, from New York to South Carolina, chose to flee with the evacuating British rather

than trust their fate to their former masters. Estimates vary wildly on the number; in Virginia alone, Thomas Jefferson believed that about thirty thousand slaves attempted to reach British lines, although clearly most did not make it. Jefferson himself lost thirty of his own slaves to British offers of freedom. Some historians estimate that tens of thousands of slaves sought to escape their bondage during the war—the largest act of slave resistance in American history. We know for certain that about fourteen thousand blacks fled from various occupied American cities when Britain withdrew at the end of the war. Many resettled in Nova Scotia. Rose Fortune was the daughter of a free black named Fortune and his unidentified wife, who had departed with the English at the

close of the Revolution. Rose lived in Annapolis Royal, an important port and military installation, where she labored as a baggage carrier and died in 1867.

Rose Fortune, watercolor, ca. 1830. She was the daughter of Fortune, a free black refugee who settled in Nova Scotia at the close of the Revolutionary War. Fortune lived in Annapolis Royal. She gained local celebrity through her numerous jobs, especially carrying the baggage of travelers on the local ferry. She died in 1867, possibly ninety years old.

DECLARING INDEPENDENCE

We hold these truths to be self-evident, that all men are created equal, that they are endowed by their Creator with certain unalienable Rights, that among these are Life, Liberty and the pursuit of Happiness. That to secure these rights, Governments are instituted among Men, deriving their just powers from the consent of the governed.

These words of Thomas Jefferson that begin the second paragraph of the Declaration of Independence offered powerful justification for the colonies' separation from Great Britain. In time they would underpin the abolitionists' indictment of the institution of slavery and racial prejudice; later still, for black people fighting for civil rights, these words would embody the very meaning of freedom in the United States. But did Jefferson have African Americans in mind when he wrote those words? Abraham Lincoln thought so, but the evidence is ambiguous at best.

In 1774, in his *Summary View of the Rights of British America,* Jefferson declared, "The abolition of domestic slavery is the great object of desire in those colonies, where it was unhappily introduced in their infant state." More suggestively, he condemned the Crown (as he would two years later in his draft of the Declaration) for forcing slavery upon the colonies, which "deeply wounded" the "rights of human nature." No abolitionist tract, this document summarized the unjust policies the Crown had inflicted upon the colonists. As a relatively young man in his early thirties, Jefferson, in the *Summary View* and especially in his draft of the Declaration, sought to cinch the case for independence by pinning the most diabolical violation of human rights directly on the king. In a statement that his colleagues in the Continental Congress excised from the final Declaration, Jefferson asserted that the king has waged cruel war against human nature itself, violating its most sacred rights of life & liberty in the persons of a distant people who never offended him, captivating & carrying them into slavery in another hemisphere, or to incur miserable death in their transportation thither. This piractical warfare, the opprobrium of infidel powers, is the warfare of the CHRISTIAN king of Great Britain. . . . He is now exciting those very people to rise in arms among us, and to purchase that liberty he has deprived them, & murdering the people upon whom he also obtruded them; thus paying off former crimes committed against the liberties of one people, with crimes which he urges them to commit against the lives of another.[5]

Even in his most blistering prose, Jefferson expressed more outrage at the "sins" of the king, and especially at British willingness to turn slaves against their colonial masters, than at the "sin" of slavery. The signers of the Declaration too had expressed little unease about slavery and rather more about their own safety and the protection of their precious property; so blaming the king for creating the basis for the colonies' burgeoning wealth would have made little sense. In fact, the great English wit and writer Samuel Johnson, in a 1771 pamphlet, famously pointed out

Thomas Jefferson (1743–1826). Photomechanical reproduction based on the 1805 Rembrandt Peale portrait held by the New-York Historical Society.

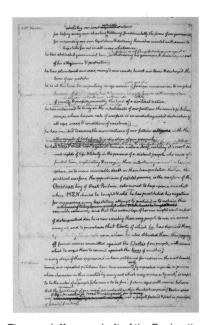

Thomas Jefferson, draft of the Declaration of Independence, 1776. The draft included his censure of the king for forcing slavery upon the American people and encouraging the slaves to rise up against the colonists.

the glaring inconsistency of the Americans. "How is it," he asked, "that we hear the loudest yelps for liberty from the drivers of Negroes?"[6] Jefferson may well have regretted that his colleagues dropped his words of righteous indignation from the Declaration, but not because they expressed his heartfelt rejection of the institution of slavery.

The degree to which Jefferson felt the contradiction between his words and his deeds as a slave owner will always remain uncertain. During the later controversy over the statehood of Missouri, he expressed deep apprehension over the fate of the nation because of slavery. But he never developed a detailed principled stand against it; he refused to divest himself of his human property; and he unabashedly deni- grated the character of African peoples to whomever would listen. Thus, when Jefferson penned the draft of the Declaration of Independence, the only images of Africans that likely came to mind were those bound in chains or those marching with Lord Dunmore with the words "Liberty for Slaves" emblazoned on their royal uniforms.

UNLEASHING FREEDOM

The American Revolution's rhetoric kindled sentiments favoring the abolition of slavery. African Americans submitted legislative petitions demanding equal rights, initiated court challenges to racial discrimination, and performed valiant military service; in all these ways they demanded a fuller definition of "liberty" than American colonists sought. No genuine Patriot could fail to recognize the contradiction between the quest for independence from a monarchy and the evil of holding other human beings in bondage. The hypocrisy was palpable. Accordingly—slowly, gradually— anti-slavery sentiment spread, and several states adopted gradual emancipation laws. In 1777, Vermont abolished slavery altogether. The Quakers, as a denomination, moved fitfully toward excluding slave owners from fellowship, and individual members like Anthony Benezet forcefully denounced slavery. Benezet's fellow Philadelphian Dr. Benjamin Rush published calls for equality and for an end to the institution. But these new voices based their appeals largely upon high moral or ideological principles, ones that simply could not penetrate the dense barriers of economic self-interest and ingrained racial prejudice. Thomas Jefferson certainly understood the inconsistency between his belief in the equality of all "men" and his ownership of slaves. But discomfort with the

Paul Cuffee (1759–1817).

contradiction lost most (but not all) of its force in light of his fear of traumatic economic loss and his unbending belief in the innate intellectual inferiority of people of African descent. As he once wrote, slave owners had the wolf by the ears and could not safely hang on or let go.

Along King's Road from Philadelphia to the Lehigh Valley, the Rising Sun Tavern had refreshed travelers and provided a forum for political debates since 1746. In 1775, a group of Pennsylvanians led by Benjamin Rush founded the Society for the Relief of Free Negroes Unlawfully Held in Bondage, a Quaker-dominated group that later became the Pennsylvania Abolition Society. The new society agreed to take up the case of Dinah Nevill, an African American who claimed freeborn status. Although Nevill and the society lost their legal case against her presumed Virginia master, the group did manage to arrange for the purchase and manumission of her and her two children. The Nevill case marked the beginning of organized resistance to slavery in America.

Two years later, speaking for "A Great Number of Blacks detained in a State of slavery in the bowels of a free & Christian Country," an anonymous group of African Americans petitioned the Massachusetts legislature for their freedom. Their appeal drew upon the era's liberal Christian ideals and the language of the Declaration of Independence. They asserted their "Natural and Unaliable Right to that freedom which the Grat Parent of the Unavers hath Bestowed equalley on all menkind."[7] They instructed the lawmakers that all

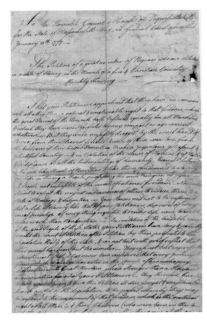

Petition to the Massachusetts legislature requesting freedom for all people of African descent held in bondage, January 13, 1777.

Act for the Gradual Abolition of Slavery, March 1, 1780.

Elizabeth Freeman (1742?–1829). Miniature portrait, watercolor on ivory by Susan Anne Livingston Ridley Sedgwick, 1811.

the arguments that they had employed against Britain in favor of their own rights applied a thousand times more to "your petitioners." Then, in February 1780, Paul Cuffee (who would later become a wealthy black merchant and sea captain and would actively advocate the emigration of blacks back to Africa), joined with six other free blacks to insist that since they could not vote, the state must exempt them from payment of taxes. The next year Cuffee requested that the selectmen in his hometown of Dartmouth, Massachusetts, offer voting privileges to all the town's African Americans.

Also in 1780, the state of Pennsylvania enacted a gradual emancipation law, which Connecticut and Rhode Island similarly adopted in 1784. The next year the state of New York freed all slaves who had served in the army during the Revolution, but it did not actually end slavery itself until 1827. African Americans and white antislavery allies like Benezet pressed for a more definitive end to slavery, while slave owners tried to extend the time blacks would have to remain

in bondage. One recently emancipated slave who signed his name "Cato" published a protest against such measures in the September 21, 1780, issue of the Philadelphia *Freeman's Journal*. "I am a poor negro," he wrote, who with his wife and children had been freed by the state, and now he feared that it would "send us all back to our masters." This would be the cruelest act, Cato lamented, preferring that the state "hang us all" rather than send them back to slavery. He also drew upon the Revolutionary experience, reminding Philadelphians that they all had resisted the slavery that the king of Great Britain had imposed on America. "Now surely . . . ," he cried, it cannot be possible "that the assembly will take from us the liberty they have given."[8]

Massachusetts also delivered to slavery a series of blows. In 1781 slaves there instigated several court cases to secure their freedom. Levi Lincoln and Caleb Strong, prominent state attorneys, handled such a case on behalf of a slave named Quock Walker. The state constitution's proclamation, they argued, that "all men are born free and equal,

and have certain natural, essential, and unalienable rights" effectively abolished slavery. After lengthy trials, the court eventually agreed. But the commonwealth's chief justice, William Cushing, who presided over the court that rendered the final ruling in the Walker cases, refused to emancipate his own slave; he did so only after the state attorney general threatened to sue him.

More famous is the 1781 case of Elizabeth Freeman, better known as Mumbet. A slave for decades in the home of John Ashley in Sheffield, Mumbet was assaulted by her owner. She then secured one of the state's most prominent lawyers, Theodore Sedgwick, to bring a freedom suit for her and another slave, known as Borm. Based on the commonwealth's constitutional guarantee of equality for all, Sedgwick convinced a jury to grant both slaves their freedom. Mumbet spent the rest of her life as a paid and much-loved servant in the home of the Sedgwick family, eventually earning enough money to purchase her own home.

FREEDOM, TECHNOLOGY,
AND KING COTTON

The Founding Fathers of the American government left succeeding generations a divided legacy on the issue of slavery. On July 13, 1787, the nation's first government under the Articles of Confederation adopted a plan for the settlement of the Northwest Territories, a region that includes the present states of Ohio, Indiana, Illinois, Michigan, and Wisconsin. Based on a 1784 report by Thomas Jefferson, this Northwest Ordinance detailed how the lands would be settled and politically organized. The Confederation Congress paid special attention to guaranteeing the free exercise of religion, and the sixth and final provision declared:

> There shall be neither slavery
> nor involuntary servitude in the
> said territory, otherwise than in
> punishment of crimes whereof
> the party shall have been duly
> convicted: Provided always,
> that any person escaping into
> the same, from whom labor or
> service is lawfully claimed in
> any one of the original states,
> such fugitive may be lawfully
> reclaimed.

But the new federal constitution hammered out in Philadelphia during the spring and summer of 1787 failed to build on the ordinance's antislavery precedent. James Madison's brilliant theoretical handiwork, and the convention delegates' deft political compromises, overcame all the competing interests but one. Madison's notes on the Constitutional Convention's proceedings, if nothing else, revealed the delegates' reluctance to confront slavery. He tried his best to shield his own slaves from the harsher aspects of the institution, and

The Northwest Ordinance, 1787.

The U.S. Constitution, 1787.

James Madison (1751–1836), fourth president of the United States.

the document if it had included provisions attacking slavery. More important, the document's infamous provisions to count three-fifths of the number of slaves in the South to determine representation in Congress, to allow the slave trade to continue for another twenty years, and to offer slave owners the right to recapture their runaways, all directly perpetuated slavery as an economic institution. In addition, the document's incorporation of strong property rights and its pledge to have the Congress ensure "domestic tranquility" fortified slavery rather than weakening it.

Nevertheless, the Constitution—certainly with the additional Bill of Rights—contained potential antislavery elements; and many Founding Fathers hoped that slavery would wither and die with an end to the slave trade. But one man's innocent excursion to Savannah, Georgia, in 1792 dealt an unpredictable and final blow to the prospect of a painless end to slavery. After graduating from

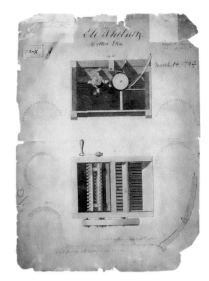

Eli Whitney's cotton gin, patent application, March 14, 1794.

they considered him a kindly master, but he never found a way to end his own dependence on involuntary servitude, much less the nation's. Several Founding Fathers believed that the Constitution would gradually reduce national dependence upon slavery, but many others rejected that notion. South Carolina, for instance, would never have ratified

Yale College, the Massachusetts-born inventor Eli Whitney traveled south to take up a tutoring position not far from the plantation of Catharine Littlefield Greene, widow of the Revolutionary War general Nathanael Greene. There he decided that he enjoyed the widow Greene's company and tinkering with agricultural equipment more than tutoring. With advice from Greene and area businessmen, Whitney worked on a model machine that would gin, or remove the seeds from, short-staple cotton. His creation worked with stunning efficiency: one production model could extract as many seeds as could one thousand slaves. Thus did the cotton gin make large-scale cotton production possible. On March 14, 1794, Whitney received a patent from the U.S. government. His idea spread uncontrollably, and many firms quickly pirated Whitney's creation. By 1805 American cotton production had leaped from two million pounds a year to sixty million, forever altering American economic history, the history of slavery, and American race relations.

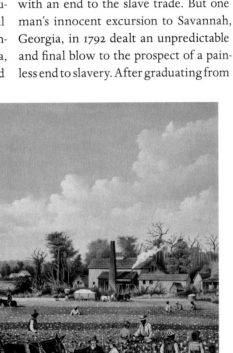

Slaves picking cotton, Currier and Ives lithograph, from an image by William Aiken Walker, 1884.

ESTABLISHING FREEDOM

Prince Hall (1735?–1807). Hall was the founder of black Freemasonry and the leader of eighteenth-century black Boston. This is one of many imagined images; no actual portrait of him exists.

Freemason degree of Richard P. G. Wright, June 23, 1799. Wright and his son, Theodore Sedgwick Wright, were influential abolitionists and Freemasons.

At the end of the eighteenth century, the emergence of free black communities in the North offered practical illustrations of how African Americans could succeed in freedom. By establishing churches, businesses, schools, and fraternal lodges, black Americans contradicted the stereotypes of racial inferiority that whites had developed to justify their enslavement. Nevertheless, as blacks developed enduring institutions and assumed more visible roles throughout American society, white racial intolerance only hardened.

A leather dresser named Prince Hall, freed by his Boston owners in 1770, wasted no time in assuming community leadership. In March 1775, along with fourteen other men, Hall became a Freemason, inducted by British soldiers stationed in Boston to keep watch on the restive Patriot movement. Hall tried to build a black lodge in the city but found the local white Freemasons hostile and unwelcoming. But in 1787 he received a charter from the Grand Lodge in London officially to establish Lodge No. 459. Today Lodge No. 459 is the oldest black institution in North America. It spawned others across the North (and after the Civil War throughout the South), becoming a moving force in the black antislavery movement and producing many of the nation's black community leaders. Hall, among his many activities, petitioned the Massachusetts legislature to end the institution of slavery, to support black education, and to support black emigration. Moreover, he fearlessly condemned the brutality that whites regularly inflicted on Boston's black citizens and called out for social and political equality. White political and social leaders recognized Hall as the spokesman for his community and trusted his opinions. His business success and his prominence as a Freemason made his name one of the most recognizable of all African Americans in the North. At his death in 1807, newspapers around the country registered the loss.

Richard Allen (1760–1831), founder of the African Methodist Episcopal Church;
William White (1748–1836), bishop of the Episcopal Church of America and
founder of a school for African Americans and Indians; and Absalom Jones
(1746–1818), first black Methodist Episcopal minister. Engraving, 1922.

Richard Allen's Bethel African
Methodist Episcopal Church,
Philadelphia. Engraving, 1829.

New York African Free School, engraving
from a drawing by Patrick H. Reason, 1830.

Absalom Jones, the son of Delaware slaves, gained his freedom in 1784 and quickly emerged as a leader among Philadelphia's black Methodist Episcopalians. In 1787, he and Richard Allen were members of St. George's Methodist Church in Philadelphia, an interracial congregation. Allen was a preacher there. One day while Jones was in prayer, white members rudely interrupted him and tried to move him to a less conspicuous place in the building. He, Allen, and other black church members walked out. They organized the Free African Society and in 1794, with the help of Benjamin Rush and others, founded the St. Thomas African Episcopal Church of Philadelphia, the first independent black church in North America. Allen, however, remained a Methodist and in 1791 broke ground for the Mother Bethel African Methodist Episcopal Church. Finally organized in 1816, it quickly developed into an important black denomination, establishing congregations throughout the North and operating a prodigious publication program and later a denominational newspaper, *The Christian Recorder,* which reported on black arts, culture, and politics.

In 1794 Jones had voted to remain with the Methodist Episcopal denomination rather than join Allen's more independent-minded group. Jones was ordained in 1804, becoming the country's first black priest, and his church, St. Thomas's, was the first and most important black Episcopal church in North America. Both churches anchored the prosperous Philadelphia black community; Jones's church soon gained more than five hundred members.

Every significant northern city and town offered at least some educational opportunities for African Americans. Where whites closed public education to black students, black parents organized privately supported schools, either themselves or in conjunction with sympathetic whites. In 1789, New York's Episcopal denomination, with the New York Manumission Society, opened the African Free School, one of the earliest and best-known schools for black students. In 1800 it began receiving tax subsidies and soon grew to be the largest school in the city, with as many as 160 students. Over the next decades the school—which hired black teachers—trained more than 2,300 students. Several would become national leaders, including Henry Highland Garnet, James McCune Smith, Theodore S. Wright, and Alexander Crummell.

CREATING A BLACK ATLANTIC

As we have seen, during the era of the American Revolution, African Americans published appeals in popular newspapers and pamphlets to assert their right to full citizenship. As a people associated in white minds with slavery and intellectual inferiority, they also employed print to repudiate racial stereotypes. In the late eighteenth century, several black women and men in the United States and Britain published important accounts of their enslavement and eventual freedom as well as other texts that demonstrated their innate abilities and remarkable talents. These publications constituted the beginnings of a black Atlantic literary tradition, a formal conversational exchange, and it provided prima facie testimony about the horror and evil of slavery and about the intellectual equality of blacks and whites. James Albert Ukawsaw Gron-

niosaw, Phillis Wheatley, Ignatius Sancho, John Marrant, Ottobah Cugoano, Olaudah Equiano, and Benjamin Banneker may or may not have known one another personally, but they certainly knew of one another through their writings. Moreover, echoes and references in their texts tell us that they read each other. Black authors, thus, wrote not in isolation but from within a reinforcing transatlantic community.

Slave owners like Thomas Jefferson privately dismissed Wheatley and Banneker as unworthy of recognition or as frauds. But this growing display of black intellectual talent in the arts and sciences, which proponents of the Enlightenment like Jefferson claimed to respect, slowly, cumulatively, put defenders of slavery on the defensive by assaulting ingrained prejudices about the nature and quality of the African American mind.

Ignatius Sancho, probably born in 1729 aboard a slave vessel, grew up in Britain and came under the tutelage of the Duke of Montagu, a wealthy philanthropist interested in the natural "capacities" of black people. He gave Sancho full access to his considerable library and encouraged him to read and write. By 1774 Sancho had established a grocery store and accumulated enough wealth and property to vote in parliamentary elections—an extraordinary achievement in an age when less than 10 percent of all British people could exercise that privilege. He gained some renown as an author and playwright but especially for his unusually numerous and influential letters to and from well-known correspondents, including the novelist Laurence Sterne and Jabez Fisher, a Philadelphia Quaker. Fisher provided him with books about the slave

Ignatius Sancho (1729–80), portrait by Thomas Gainsborough, oil on canvas, 1768.

trade, very likely ones by Anthony Benezet. After Sancho's death in 1780, one of his correspondents, Frances Crewe, collected and published two volumes of his letters in 1782. The work established the former slave as a well-educated, sentient man who had possessed a level of eloquence that relatively few of his contemporaries either in Britain or the United States could demonstrate.

Olaudah Equiano, one of the best-known British antislavery activists, published his *Interesting Narrative of the Life of Olaudah Equiano, or Gustavus Vassa, the African* in 1789. It quickly became a best seller, seeing nine British editions and at least one American edition during the author's lifetime, and was translated into Dutch, German, and Russian. Equiano lectured extensively throughout the British Isles, publicizing his story and selling his book, which evidently earned him handsome returns. Although his African origins are in some dispute, his *Narrative* is the only substantial description of the Middle Passage from the slave's viewpoint. His book influenced generations of African Americans, relat-

Benjamin Banneker (1731–1806). Banneker produced several editions of his *Almanac* between 1792 and 1797.

Olaudah Equiano (1745?–97),
frontispiece of his *Narrative*, 1789.

ing an exciting story of danger, adventure, war (on two continents), and world travel, and it became a model for others who sought to tell their slave narratives.

Equally important, it was a powerful and eloquent indictment of slavery—by a former slave—at a time when whites in Europe and the United States had just begun to question the institution.

Just a few years later, in 1792, Benjamin Banneker published the first of his many *Almanac*s. Freeborn in Maryland, Banneker had demonstrated great facility in math from a very early age and at twenty, without any assistance or training, built a clock that kept time for more than forty years. About 1789, he became fascinated by astronomy, read all the books on the subject he could acquire, and began making mathematical projections of lunar and solar eclipses. In 1791 his talents came to the attention of Major Andrew Ellicott, whom President George Washington had appointed

to survey lands for the new capital. For a brief time Ellicott hired Banneker to maintain the project's astronomical field clock and other instruments, make astronomical recordings, and determine latitude. The next year Banneker wrote his first *Almanac* and sent a copy to Thomas Jefferson with a letter urging him to put an end to slavery. Jefferson conducted a polite and respectful correspondence with Banneker, which itself was published in Philadelphia as a separate pamphlet. Privately, however, Jefferson doubted that Banneker was capable of such scientific work. Others harbored no such doubts, and Banneker's work gained him international attention and African Americans a rightful claim to achievement in math and science.

TOUSSAINT!

American slave owners often justified slavery by claiming that as docile and intellectually inferior beings, Africans were well suited for enslavement. But their private fears of slave rebellion, and the knowledge that black people were just as complexly human as white people, belied such public justifications. The revolution of the slaves in Haiti (1791–1804) made real every slave owner's worst nightmare.

Haiti, or Saint-Domingue, as it was known in the eighteenth century, produced about half of all the sugar and coffee consumed in Europe and substantial amounts of cotton, indigo, and other produce. Occupying the western half of the island of Hispaniola, Saint-Domingue was the wealthiest colony in the Caribbean, earning the sobriquets "Pearl of the Antilles" and "Eden of the Western World." About

8,000 plantations, occupied by about 40,000 whites and about 500,000 slaves, generated an astonishing amount of wealth for France. The colony also possessed about 30,000 free people of color, many of whom were well-to-do mulattoes and some of whom owned slaves themselves, but who nevertheless suffered discrimination. Some of these free men of color gained invaluable military knowledge from the French army and served in a special black unit that the French brought to America in 1781 to help the colonists defeat Great Britain; in just a few years, veterans of this unit would become leaders of the revolution on Saint-Domingue.

Unrest began in 1790, fueled by American independence and the advent of the French Revolution, with its proclamation of the rights of man. Then, in 1791, an organized slave revolt broke out

Toussaint L'Ouverture (1743–1803),
hand-colored lithograph portrait by
Nicolas Eustache Maurin. One of a series
sold in Paris and Boston in 1832.

Toussaint L'Ouverture, engraving executed in Paris, 1802.

Jean-Jacques Dessalines (1758–1806). Dessalines assumed leadership of Haitian forces after the capture of Toussaint L'Ouverture. He crowned himself emperor and, fearing a return of French forces, ordered the liquidation of all remaining whites on the island. His rule inspired great dissension and a coup on August 17, 1806. The plotters murdered him and dragged his body through the streets before dismembering it. Wooden bust, nineteenth century.

that would continue for twelve years, involving France, Great Britain, Spain, and the United States in a complex series of shifting racial and political alliances and competition for European colonial domination. Toussaint L'Ouverture emerged as the primary rebel leader (receiving secret American assistance); he defeated the French and then allied with them to defeat the English invasion of 1793—the same year that France ended slavery, thereby establishing equality in Haiti. He became governor of the colony in 1796 and led the resistance to Napoleon's attempt to reestablish slavery; but he was deceitfully captured in 1802 and eventually died a slow death from cold and starvation in a French prison. In 1803, General Dessalines, Toussaint's successor, led a brutal war of extermination against the French, ending in the declaration of Haitian independence on January 1, 1804. Dessalines would serve as Haiti's

first emperor. He would be assassinated two years later.

For people of African descent around the world, the Haitian Revolution stood as a monument to black equality and independence. As Frederick Douglass explained in 1893, the Haitian revolutionaries "struck for the freedom of every black man in the world."[9] In the wake of the revolt, slave rebellions, actual and threatened, occurred in North and South America, many citing the Haitian experience as their motivation. In Cuba, Jamaica, Louisiana, and even in Charleston, South Carolina, blacks seeking freedom named Haiti as their inspiration.

In August 1800, the Virginia slave Gabriel planned a revolt in Richmond that would include the ransoming of the state's governor, James Monroe. Rumors of French involvement swept through the city. By October twenty-six slaves, including Gabriel, had been executed and eight others transported to New Orleans. In 1822 in Charleston, South Carolina, the slaves in the Denmark Vesey conspiracy had Haiti in mind when they planned to burn the city and escape. In fact, many of the slaves in the Charleston region (the same thing happened in Cuba) had come with their owners from Haiti, and at least two were among the Vesey plotters. In all, as many as twelve thousand former French slaves—who saw Toussaint L'Ouverture as a liberator—had been transported to the United States in the wake of the Haitian rebellion.

White Americans might have interpreted the Haitian Revolution as a warning about the inherent dangers of slave ownership, but they took a different lesson. Thomas Jefferson admonished that Haiti proved what could happen if the United States followed the French into emancipation. South Carolina, with its majority black population, had sent thousands of dollars to help put down the insurrection in Saint-Domingue.

Henri Christophe (1767–1820). Freeborn, probably from Granada, Christophe served in the French army during the American Revolution. He then moved to Haiti, where he rose to prominence and became a general under L'Ouverture. After independence, he was elected to the effectively powerless position of president. He set up a rival government in 1807 and in 1811 established a royal government with himself as king. A form of slavery returned to the northern part of the island, increasing its wealth but impoverishing the island's southern regions. Resentment over his feudal policies threatened another coup, and rather than face execution, King Henri I shot himself with a silver bullet. Oil on canvas by Richard Evans, 1818.

Afterward Saint-Domingue declined as an economic powerhouse. American and Cuban slave imports increased as whites saw it as an opportunity. By 1840 Cuba would supplant Haiti as the world's leading producer of sugar. (Slavery would remain legal in Cuba until 1886.) Nevertheless, the Haitian Revolution became a turning point in Western history. It was the first successful slave rebellion in the New World. It produced the first black republic in the history of the world. It would dominate the thinking about emancipation in every country in the New World from 1804 until slavery finally ended in the Western Hemisphere in Brazil in 1888.

PART THREE

"IT SHALL EVER BE OUR DUTY TO VINDICATE OUR BRETHREN"

1800–1834

TRACING THE TRADE

Scene on the Coast of Africa, by Charles E. Wagstaff, engraving, 1844, after *Slave Trade,*
by François-Auguste Biard, oil on canvas, 1840.

Between 1701 and 1825 Americans purchased about 299,000 African slaves—a substantial number, certainly, but not even close to the total number of slaves brought to the Western Hemisphere. During the same period about 8.4 million enslaved Africans made the fateful voyage to the Americas, the vast majority shipped by Portugal, Spain, and Great Britain to Brazil, Jamaica, Cuba, and other parts of the Caribbean. Over the course of the transatlantic slave trade from 1501 to 1866, more than 12.5 million Africans experienced the Middle Passage, the largest coerced movement of a people in history. Without this trade, the Netherlands, France, Great Britain, Portugal, and Spain could neither have grown the crops nor exploited the New World resources that their populations demanded. The amount of wealth that Europe obtained from the trade was exceeded only by the depth of the tragedy it caused.

But responsibility for the trade's origins, if not for its total economic impact or the extended suffering it caused the slaves and their descendants, lies equally at the doorsteps of European traders and African elites. The slaves that white men bought along the West African coast were people whom local African leaders wished to sell—members of enemy clans or competing ethnic groups. Such sales not only enriched the coffers of African kings, their families, and their supporters, they weakened their enemies considerably. Given the seemingly insatiable European hunger for slave labor, African leaders saw the slave trade as a vital self-interest.

As cotton, coffee, sugar, rice, and tobacco production increased in the New World, the demand for labor rose correspondingly; such demand never could have been filled from available labor pools in Europe. By the mid-eighteenth century, all regions of West Africa had seen dramatic increases in the sale of slaves; the vast majority came from West Central Africa, which provided more slaves than all other areas of Africa combined. Luanda (in modern Angola) alone supplied about 1.3 million people to the traffic.

White traders participated eagerly, gaining enormous wealth and inflicting savage brutality. Below decks during the infamous Middle Passage, traders divided their human cargo by gender. To maximize carrying capacity, they kept them unclothed, chained, and packed, although rarely as densely packed as depicted in the British broadsides of slaving vessels that became iconic images in the campaign against the trade. The pencil-and-watercolor image below is one of the few eyewit-

"The Trade of Particular Towns" and "The Import and Export of Negroes,"
page from *Report of the Lords of the Committee of Council*, 1789.
The tables show the trade in slaves from Bristol and the general level
of the trade in slaves to Britain's Caribbean possessions.

View of the Deck of the Slave Ship Alabanoz, by Lieutenant Francis Meynell, pencil and watercolor, 1846.
This eyewitness rendering depicts conditions endured by slaves during the Middle Passage.

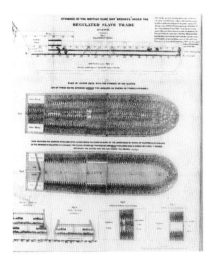

Stowage plans aboard the largest vessels engaged in the slave trade, 1788. British abolitionists effectively employed this iconic image to rally opposition to the slave trade.

Abolition of the Slave Trade, by George Cruikshank, engraved colored print, 1792. In 1792, William Wilberforce accused John Kimber, captain of the slave ship *Recovery,* of punishing a fifteen-year-old African girl for refusing to dance naked on the deck of his vessel, and causing her death. Cruikshank, an influential British cartoonist, published this image in solidarity. Kimber was then tried before the High Court of Admiralty, but the jury concluded that the young girl died of disease rather than the punishment inflicted upon her, and acquitted Kimber.

ness depictions of the cruel and cramped conditions found below decks. About 26 percent of those shipped west in such conditions were children, like Phillis Wheatley. All spent about two months in transit from the African coast to the American auction block. The filthy conditions, and the lack of clean water and food, guaranteed that about 15 percent died before reaching their destinations. Conditions could be so brutal that ships' crews perished in about equal percentages. Any hint of resistance on the part of slaves—and resistance was common—was met with swift brutality. The slave punishment drawn by the English satirist George Cruikshank in 1792 in fact took place, and the abolitionist William Wilberforce denounced the man responsible for it, Captain John Kimber, in Parliament.

Most of the slaves brought into North America came directly from Africa, although some came from the Caribbean, and most who came before the trade was abolished in 1807 arrived in British-owned vessels. When Americans entered the trade, they did so at a disadvantage, since Britain controlled most access points along the West

African coast. Additionally, British vessels could hold up to 273 slaves per trip, while Americans used smaller vessels, holding only about 124 slaves. To pay for their slaves, Americans exchanged vast amounts of New England–made rum, most of it manufactured in Rhode Island, the epicenter of the American slave trade. During the 1770s, Rhode Island exported about 536,000 gallons per year, about 52 percent of total production. The Brown, De Wolf, and Vernon families were the most active slave importers in the state, earning great wealth and bringing their cargoes to all regions of the East Coast, especially to South Carolina. In one seventy-five-year period before January 1, 1808, the date on which the importation of slaves to the United States was legally banned, 934 vessels left the state for the West African coast.

But natural increase, rather than

Runaway slave advertisement. This advertisement is typical of those that appeared in most American newspapers during the eighteenth century.

importations, accounted for the vast majority of the slaves who lived in the United States. By 1780 Virginia, for instance, had almost halted slave imports. The significance of the trade for the economic and political development of the nation, however, remained enormous.

END OF THE SLAVE TRADE IN BRITAIN AND THE UNITED STATES, 1807 AND 1808

Innocent men, women, and children, stripped bare, are packed like lumber in suffocating ships' holds. Beautiful young girls corralled in barracoons refuse to eat, wither, and quickly die. Other men and women, seeing the coast vanish from their sight, leap to their deaths from a ship's deck. Chained men in the depths of another darkened vessel resist their confinement, and though bound to one another, rise up and reach the main deck. Fear-stricken sailors wait the rush and shoot dead as many of the men as they can; the surviving rebels are heaved overboard. One hundred, out of 190 entrapped passengers, are deliberately thrown into the sea.

Why is Africa a scene of blood and desolation? Why are her children wrestled from her, to administer to the luxuries and greatness of those whom they never offended? And why are these dismal cries in vain? Alas! I reply again, can the cries and groans, with which the air now trembles, be heard across this extensive continent? Can the southern winds convey them to the ear of Britain?[1]

Thomas Clarkson's 1788 *Essay on the Slavery and Commerce of the Human Species* detailed these actual conditions of the slave trade to his fellow Englishmen. Through such accounts, he and his close friend in Parliament, William Wilberforce, sought to humanize the victims of the trade. In their many pamphlets and speeches, rather than providing mere numbers in the debit and credit columns of a ledger, they described the effects of enslavement upon the men, women, and children whom British merchants

"Am I Not a Man and a Brother," by Josiah Wedgwood, medallion, 1787. Wedgwood (1730–95), British potter, created this medallion in support of efforts to end the slave trade; it became the central icon of the antislavery movement. Americans later created a companion image of a female slave with the phrase "Am I Not a Woman and a Sister?" The image is often criticized for portraying Africans as submissive, but abolitionists employed it to emphasize the godliness and religiosity of the slaves.

"We Are All Brethren," medal, 1807. This medal was struck to commemorate abolition of the British slave trade. The banner expresses the antislavery movement's Christian equalitarianism, but its depiction of nearly naked Africans only reinforced a sense of "otherness" and cultural inferiority.

and Caribbean planters removed from the African continent. Clarkson, who had a gift for recognizing a poignant and telling incident, made their suffering real. With Wilberforce and a host of other abolitionists, he campaigned against the power of the Liverpool merchants and Jamaican planters and lobbied Parliament to end the brutal trade in human flesh. Abolitionists organized boycotts of slave-made produce, especially sugar, and Josiah Wedgwood, a wealthy manufacturer, mass-produced an iconic image of a kneeling slave to display the Christian virtue of a people he hoped would be freed from servitude. Carl Bernhard Wadström, a Swedish abolitionist who lived in Britain, made the astonishing engraving of a planter

and his slave reproduced on page 54; he sought to convince the public—and West Indian planters—that black and white could live in peace and that whites could perform a noble deed by bringing education to Africans. The same year as Clarkson's 1788 essay, one hundred anti-slave-trade petitions poured into Parliament. Despite pleas of "national interest" and long-standing "privilege," a number of parliamentarians did not wish to have their humanitarianism brought into question or give their liberal political enemies a potent political lever.

Still, as Wilberforce pleaded in the House of Commons for the humanity of Africans, many could be heard snickering. Parliamentary opponents of

Abolition of the Slave Trade, by Henry Moses, 1807; engraving by Joseph Collyer, 1808. The official British recognition of the end of the slave trade focuses on Member of Parliament William Wilberforce and celebrates the legislation as an expression of English liberty.

"Am I Not a Woman and a Sister?" engraving, 1830s. This antislavery emblem, based on the original Wedgwood medallion, employed widespread cultural belief in the unique religiosity of women and their presumed moral superiority.

Thomas Clarkson, by Carl Frederik von Breda, oil on canvas, 1788. Clarkson (1760–1846) devoted his life to ending the slave trade and British slavery in the Caribbean. One of the original 1787 members of the Committee for Abolition of the African Slave Trade, he traveled tens of thousands of miles to personally investigate the true conditions of the trade and worked closely with William Wilberforce to advance the abolition cause in Parliament.

the slave trade met countless crushing defeats and delays. In 1792 the Commons voted to "gradually" end the trade, only to find that war with France diverted attention from the cause. By early 1807 British interests in the Caribbean reigned unchallenged, but profits declined. Abolitionists, the Commons, and the ministry then cooperated to push an abolition bill through the balky House of Lords, which, at the king's urging, drafted its own abolition bill, and on March 25, 1807, it declared the trade illegal after May 1 of that year: "hereby utterly abolished, prohibited, and declared to be unlawful."

Ending the external slave trade in the United States proved far easier since article 1, section 9 of the Constitution drafted in Philadelphia mandated gradual abolition. But the lack of a nationwide campaign against the trade, as had occurred in Britain, worked to hinder the advance of abolitionism. On March 2, 1807, the Congress passed enabling legislation to end American participation in the trade after January 1, 1808. Among its various provisions were rigorous penalties, including a $20,000 fine and forfeiture of the vessel used to transport "any negro, mulatto, or person of color . . . for the purpose of selling them in any port or place within the jurisdiction of the United States." While its original advocates intended it as an antislavery measure, the ban adopted in

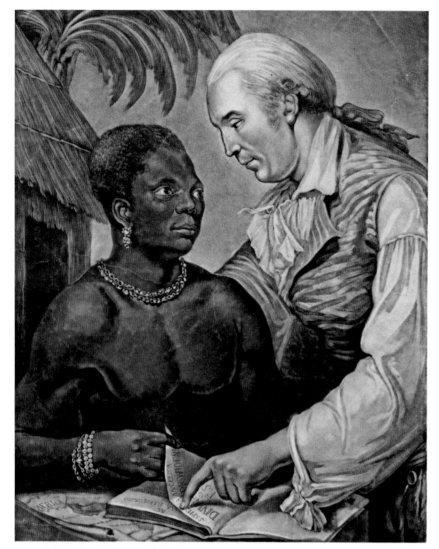

The Benevolent Effects of Abolishing the Slave Trade, by Carl Bernhard Wadström, engraving, June 1792. The Swedish-born Wadström (1746–99) moved to Britain in 1788 and became a prominent abolitionist. An exponent of Swedenborgian theology, he came to believe in the religious superiority of Africans. This extraordinary engraving, depicting the inherent fraternal bonds between master and slave, assured viewers of the positive outcome of ending the slave trade and, ultimately, slavery.

William Wilberforce, by John Rising, oil on canvas, 1790. Wilberforce (1759–1833), perhaps the best-known British abolitionist, was the son of a prosperous merchant and one of the youngest members of Parliament. Having experienced a religious conversion in 1785, he became a social reformer and then an abolitionist after reading the evidence against the slave trade amassed by Thomas Clarkson. He was Parliament's leading voice against the slave trade, and after its abolition in 1807 he continued the fight against British slavery. He died on July 26, 1833, three days after Parliament passed emancipation.

1807, if anything, buttressed the institution of slavery. By limiting the supply, the measure increased the value of slaves within the United States; by failing to provide the president with any enforcement mechanism for an additional twelve years, Congress blunted the impact of its own legislation. States like Virginia then became slave exporters in a vigorous internal trade—untouched by federal legislation—and demand for slave labor grew enough to support profitable smuggling operations. The 1807 measure held no dangers for the interests of slave owners in the United States; ironically, they had every reason to welcome it.

SERVING FREEDOM IN THE WAR OF 1812

The Battle of New Orleans by William Momberger, engraving, 1861. While the total number of African Americans who served in the War of 1812 is not known, at least six hundred fought alongside General Andrew Jackson in the victory over invading British troops in New Orleans.

In September 1814, near the close of the War of 1812, British forces were threatening New Orleans. General Andrew Jackson issued a call to black Louisianans to help defend "our country." As "sons of freedom," Jackson pleaded, "you are now called upon to defend our most inestimable blessings." Black citizens responded by the hundreds. First came 350 black militiamen, with an experienced black soldier named Vincent Populus helping to command the unit. Another force of 250 African Americans, under the command of Joseph Savory—a black officer—joined

Jackson's force. On the eve of battle on December 18, the general thanked them—in French—for rallying to assist their "fellow citizens" in their time of crisis.

From December 1814 through January 8, 1815, both units helped fend off the English invasion and proved critical to the American victory, earning Jackson's enthusiastic praise. The popular *Niles Weekly Register* of February 25, 1815, carried the general's tribute: "The two corps of colored volunteers have not disappointed the hopes that were formed of their courage and perseverance in the

performance of their duty." He singled out Joseph Savory for commendation. Although word of the peace treaty concluded between the United States and Great Britain arrived too late to avoid the bloodshed, the battle proved the most successful of the war. In the next decades, prior to the Civil War, African Americans would point to Jackson's statements, especially his references to blacks as citizens, as proof of black claims to equal rights.

African Americans, with their long history of service in the maritime trades, also served in the navy during the war.

Courageous Act of Cyrus Tiffany in the Battle of Lake Erie, Sept. 13, 1813, by Martyl Schweig, mural painted for the WPA in Washington, D.C.'s, Recorder of Deeds Office, 1942. African Americans, with experience in the maritime trades, proved indispensable to Perry's victory on Lake Erie.

At least 10 percent of Commander Oliver H. Perry's men in the Great Lakes were black, and their heroism, especially on Lake Erie, proved decisive. While a large number of Perry's own crew were black, few names of specific black sailors are known. But on September 10, 1813, Perry won a decisive battle against British naval forces at Put-in-Bay, on Lake Erie. His own vessel, the USS *Lawrence,* absorbed a crushing broadside, killing about 80 percent of his crew. According to popular legend, Cyrus Tiffany, an elderly black sailor, helped save Perry's life as his vessel began to sink. More likely, as a longtime friend to the commander, Tiffany stuck close by Perry's side and assisted him in transferring command to the *Lawrence's* sister ship, the USS *Niagara.* Perry never hesitated to praise his black sailors, saying they acted without regard to the danger they faced.

YARROW MAMOUT BY CHARLES WILLSON PEALE AND THE RISE OF A PEOPLE

By the beginning of the nineteenth century and especially by 1820, some free African Americans began to enjoy tangible success. Important black communities had developed in New York, Philadelphia, Baltimore, and Boston. In 1820 the black population of Brooklyn reached about 12 percent; it was about 9 percent in New York City; nearly 12 percent in Philadelphia; more than 23 percent in Baltimore, of which more than 16 percent were free; and about 4 percent in Boston. Almost 4,000 African Americans dwelled in the Washington, D.C., area, nearly 1,700 of them free. New York and Baltimore had the largest free black populations, with more than 10,000 residing in each city. By 1820 blacks in all these cities had orga-

nized profitable businesses, churches, self-help or aid societies, schools, and fraternal lodges—undeniable symbols of success. With caterers, barbers and hairdressers, waiters, ministers, craftsmen, and hotel stewards as its members, a black middle class began to emerge even in the face of mounting racial prejudice.

Yarrow Mamout, probably born in the Senegal-Gambia region, had been enslaved as an adult and arrived in Maryland sometime before the American Revolution. (He chose to place his surname, Yarrow, first in keeping with Muslim naming conventions.) In 1783, his owner moved with him to Georgetown, in the District of Columbia. In the summer of 1796, after his owner's

Yarrow Mamout, by Charles Willson Peale, oil on canvas, 1819.

Pierre Toussaint and his wife, Mary Rose Juliett Toussaint (sometimes identified as Juliet Noel), symbolized the growing success of northern free blacks. Watercolor miniatures by Anthony Meucci, ca. 1825.

James Forten (1766–1842), after a watercolor by an unknown artist.

death, Yarrow gained his freedom and made enough money through his bricklaying and basket-making skills to support a small family and to invest in a local bank—one that included George Washington among its stockholders. By 1800 Yarrow had earned enough money to purchase his own Georgetown home. He gained renown among local whites as a successful and distinctive free man—and a vigorous one, who took a daily swim into his eighties. He proudly professed his Muslim faith.

In 1819, Charles Willson Peale, of the famous artistic Peale family, came to Washington to paint President Monroe's portrait and heard about Yarrow, who was rumored to be 134 years old. Yarrow, probably only ten years older than Peale, sat for his portrait on January 30 and 31; the completed likeness hung in Peale's Philadelphia museum until 1854. Yarrow lived out his final years in his own home, sustained by the income of his investments, which were now large enough for him to loan money to others.

The Pierre and Mary Rose Juliett Toussaint family of New York traced a similar trajectory. Brought to the United States from Saint-Domingue as a slave in 1787, Pierre Toussaint became a highly skilled hairdresser. His owner, Jean-Jacques Bérard, died unexpectedly, leaving his widow, Marie Elizabeth Bérard, virtually penniless. Toussaint supported himself and his owner through his growing hairdressing business. After her second marriage, Bérard formally emancipated Toussaint at a ceremony held in the city's French consulate on July 2, 1807. Toussaint then built an extremely profitable business, attending to the city's wealthy white women. He became so successful that he bought his own home in the city and purchased the freedom of a sister and another fugitive from Saint-Domingue, Mary Rose Juliett, whom he married in August 1811. He became a popular city philanthropist, supporting Catholic churches, St. Patrick's Orphan Asylum, and numerous destitute black children. His wife also served New York's Haitian community and helped sustain the city's African Hall for Mutual Relief.

A number of African Americans of the period attained significant wealth, especially James Forten. Born free in Philadelphia in 1766, he stood in the crowd outside Philadelphia Hall to hear the first reading of the Declaration of Independence. After service in the Revolution, Forten became a master sailmaker and eventually bought the business of Robert Bridges, his white employer. He was close friends with Paul Cuffee and initially supported Cuffee's plans for the emigration of free blacks to Liberia. He proved as accomplished a businessman as a sailmaker and acquired great wealth, investing his profits in real estate, banks, and a canal, and later in railroad stock. His marriage to Charlotte Vandine produced eight children, including Margaretta Forten, Harriet Forten Purvis, Sarah Forten Purvis, and Robert Bridges Forten, the cream of Philadelphia's black elite and active abolitionists. James Forten became one of the central figures in the antislavery movement—his financial support in the early 1830s made possible the publication of William Lloyd Garrison's *Liberator*.

COLONIZATION AND LIBERIA

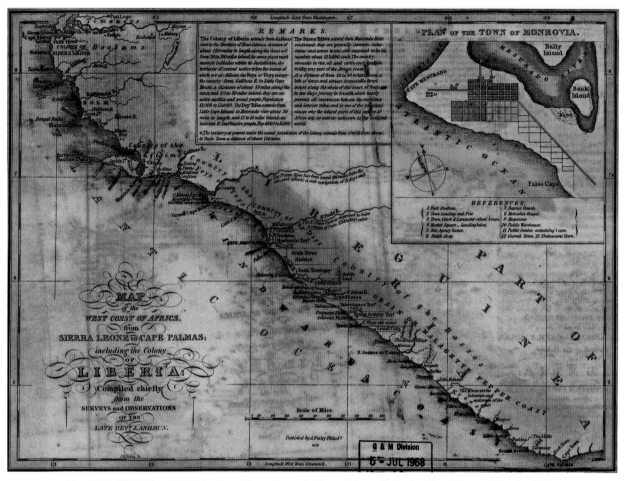

Map of the West Coast of Africa from Sierra Leone to Cape Palmas, including the Colony of Liberia, 1830.

On December 28, 1816, Speaker Henry Clay, Representative John Randolph of Virginia, Elias B. Caldwell, secretary of the U.S. Supreme Court, and other political leaders met in the chambers of the U.S. House of Representatives to found the American Colonization Society (ACS), which would establish the colony of Liberia and transport thousands of African Americans to West Africa.

Moved by Gabriel's 1800 rebellion and the rising tide of racial animosity, these political leaders hoped gradually to end the institution of slavery and thus the problem of race by remov-

ing all the slaves and former slaves back to Africa. During the Society's first years, some free northern blacks like Paul Cuffee, Richard Allen, and James Forten supported the society and similar efforts to offer blacks an escape from American racial oppression. Proponents of the ACS like Henry Clay, Daniel Webster, James Madison, James Monroe, Francis Scott Key, Andrew Jackson, and Abraham Lincoln all believed that blacks and whites could not coexist in freedom and, thus, sought to remove as many free blacks from the United States as possible. In 1818, Maryland established its own colo-

nization movement, and Pennsylvania, Connecticut, and New Jersey quickly followed with resolutions in support. Before long, ACS auxiliaries sprang up throughout the North and even in many southern states, although scant interest existed in the Deep South.

In 1819, the U.S. Congress appropriated funds and authorized President Monroe to secure land in West Africa to return Africans who had been captured during the navy's effort to enforce the federal ban on participation in the international slave trade. The ACS then cooperated with the government to find suitable land near

Life membership certificate for the American Colonization Society.

Daniel Coker, engraving by John Sartain, 1891. Coker (1780?–1835?), the AME Church founder and educator, represented some African Americans of the 1820s who, disillusioned with the nation's growing racism, cooperated with white colonizationists in hopes of finding freedom and equality in the British colony of Sierra Leone.

Sierra Leone, a British colony that had been formed as a home for freed British slaves. In January 1820 more than eighty blacks—primarily from New York and Philadelphia—under the leadership of the Baltimore AME minister Daniel Coker, arrived in Sierra Leone to begin the search for a new home. Coker, born a slave, worked with Richard Allen to build the AME Church and is credited with publishing in 1810 the first antislavery tract written by an African American. Many of these initial settlers soon died, the agents from the ACS and the federal government died, and a year later no new American colony had been established.

In 1821, thirty-three additional blacks from Virginia and Maryland arrived in West Africa and settled at Cape Mesurado. Coker led the remnants of his group to a permanent location on the Liberian coast and was joined by his wife, Maria, and his family. In 1827, Maryland resettled some African Americans at Cape Palmas, followed by separate groups from Pennsylvania and Virginia. In 1838, the various settlements combined into one colony, and in 1847, Liberia declared independence. The ex-Virginian Joseph Jenkins Roberts served as the colony's first governor and the country's first president. Depicted here is Jane Waring Roberts, who emigrated from Virginia and married Joseph in 1836. She remained in Liberia and dedicated her life to a variety of Christian charities and to the promotion of women's education. As a tribute to his wife's concerns, President Roberts established a foundation that still supports Liberian education today.

Opposition to the ACS became a core principle of the black abolitionist movement, because it and its allied societies opposed equal rights and citizenship for African Americans. The ACS finally dissolved in 1964.

Jane Waring Roberts, daguerreotype, probably copied by Rufus Anson before 1860, from an earlier image created by Augustus Washington. Roberts (1819–1914) emigrated to Liberia from Virginia in 1824 and in 1836 became the second wife of Liberia's first president, Joseph Jenkins Roberts. She spoke French fluently, accompanied her husband on official diplomatic missions, and in 1887 initiated a project to build a hospital in Monrovia. As part of her fundraising, she dined with President and Mrs. Grover Cleveland in the White House.

Formation of the American Colonization Society and establishment of the Liberian colony reflected the growing national debate over the problem of slavery and the North's mounting racial strife. Just before statehood, Ohio adopted a constitution in 1802 that based legislative representation strictly on "the number of white male inhabitants." In 1810, the federal government barred blacks from carrying U.S. mail, and in 1820 it limited the election of District of Columbia officials to whites only. In 1818, the state of Connecticut, in its new constitution, disenfranchised all its black voters, followed by Rhode Island in 1822. In 1817, New York adopted a law that would free all remaining slaves on July 4, 1827, but its constitution of 1821 included property requirements that effectively disenfranchised the majority of adult black males, while eliminating all such requirements for whites.

The 1820s also saw disturbing race riots in Philadelphia, Boston, and Hartford, Connecticut. In 1829, whites rioted in Cincinnati, after which about half of the city's black population was expelled. In 1824, a white mob in Providence, Rhode Island, enraged by the idea of racial mixing, rampaged through the black section called Hard Scrabble, destroying a number of black-owned homes. This broadside lampooned the black community and satirized the destruction of their homes and property: "Poor Cato's hut prop't up, and Cezer's ley sprawling / And ours goody gui ! nothing left but de cellar!"[2] Such incidents increased in frequency and number during the 1830s and 1840s.

In 1824, in response to the increasingly hostile conditions, about six thousand blacks from Philadelphia, New York City, and Baltimore sold their

"Hard Scrabble," 1824. This racist broadside defended a race riot against the black settlement in Providence, Rhode Island. Other such broadsides in the 1820s lampooned the small but growing antislavery movement and the northern black community.

homes and moved to Haiti, seeking a future away from American racism. The Reverend Richard Allen led the organizing effort in Philadelphia; the Haitian president had convinced him of the wonderful opportunities available there, conveniently ignoring the new black republic's extreme poverty and declining population. Allen's own brother traveled to Haiti and encouraged him to send emigrants. But those who went turned out to be urban dwellers, not the agricultural workers that the Haitians wanted and needed. Within two years, one-third of the surviving emigrants returned to the United States disenchanted.

Most explosive and worrisome was

James Tallmadge, by Alexander Hay Ritchie, engraving, 1826. Tallmadge (1778–1853), a lawyer and New York congressman from Dutchess County, in 1819 initiated the crucial debates over slavery in Missouri.

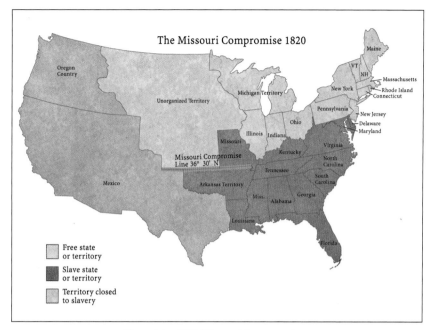

Map of the 1820 Missouri Compromise.

the national debate over Missouri's quest for statehood. The question of whether to allow slavery into the territories acquired in Thomas Jefferson's Louisiana Purchase exposed the paradoxical foundations of the new American republic. In 1819, the Missouri Territory applied for statehood, and a bill to enable Missourians to draft a constitution and form a government came before the U.S. House of Representatives. New York congressman James Tallmadge attached a rider to the bill that banned slavery in the new state and in the remaining portion of the Louisiana Purchase. The congressional debates that followed shook former president Jefferson. In a letter from Monticello, dated April 22, 1820, to Massachusetts congressman John Holmes (who supported admission of Missouri as a slave state), he explained that the debates struck him as "a fire bell in the night, awakened and filled me with terror. I considered it at once as the knell of the Union." Finally, in 1820, Henry Clay and others orchestrated a compromise that allowed Missouri to have slaves but banned slavery in the remaining portion of the Louisiana Purchase and admitted Maine as a free state. The Great Compromise may have "hushed" the controversy for the moment, Jefferson thought,

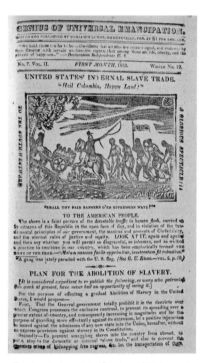

Benjamin Lundy's *Genius of Universal Emancipation,* title page, 1823.

but it would rise again. As it is, he went on to say, "we have the wolf by the ear, and we can neither hold him, nor safely let him go. [J]ustice is in one scale, and self-preservation in the other." The failure of the new generation of political leaders to settle the controversy amicably grieved him deeply. It was "suicide," he lamented, and "treason against the

Benjamin Lundy, engraving by unidentified artist after portrait by A. Dickinson. Lundy (1789–1839), a tireless editor, was one of the earliest white abolitionists to believe in racial equality. He had a great influence upon the Boston radical William Lloyd Garrison.

hopes of the world." The "unwise and unworthy passions of their sons," he feared, would destroy the great nation he and the other Founding Fathers had made.

Jefferson and his old ally John Adams both died on July 4, 1826, by which time new voices were questioning the divided political legacy of the Revolu-

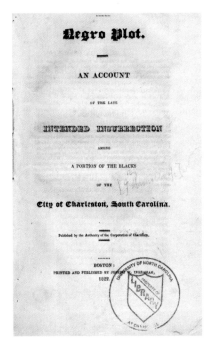

Negro Plot, title page, 1822. This work was the first account of the Denmark Vesey conspiracy.

tionary generation. In the North, black abolitionists organized a movement to resist the American Colonization Society's schemes and to raise awareness about the injustice of slavery. Individual Quakers were among the first to join their campaign. Nineteen-year-old Benjamin Lundy, born to New Jersey Quakers in 1789, saw a coffle of slaves trudging to their fate and was transformed. In 1821, in the wake of the Missouri Compromise debates, Lundy founded *Genius of Universal Emancipation.* The most radical antislavery newspaper prior to the founding of *The Liberator* in 1831, Lundy's *Genius* helped organize and connect scattered antislavery forces, giving voice to a wide variety of antislavery tactics. It was also the first antislavery paper to publish the views of African Americans. The country's failure to abandon slavery, Lundy warned, courted the possibility of a slave insurrection as terrible as the one in Haiti. To the South, his remarks proved shockingly prescient in 1822, when South Carolina authorities uncovered a plot by the former slave Denmark Vesey. A highly literate, multilingual businessman, Vesey had bought his own freedom in 1799 and became a leader of Charleston's large black community. With a number of other blacks, Vesey planned to seize weapons, burn the city, assassinate the governor and the mayor, and kill as many whites as they could find before escaping to Haiti. Several blacks betrayed the conspiracy, and after the summary trials the authorities hanged thirty-five conspirators and transported forty more out of the state. Vesey faced the gallows on July 2, 1822.

FREEDOM'S JOURNAL AND WALKER'S APPEAL

On March 16, 1827, just prior to the end of slavery in the state of New York, *Freedom's Journal,* the nation's first African American newspaper, published its first words: "We wish to plead our own cause. Too long others have spoken for us. Too long has the publick been deceived by misrepresentations, in things which concern us dearly. . . . The civil rights of a people being of the greatest value, it shall ever be our duty to vindicate our brethren." The paper reflected the growth and development of northern black communities and testified to black capability in an era dominated by relentless and demeaning racial prejudice. "Our vices and our degradation are ever arrayed against us," the paper announced in its front-page editorial statement, "but our virtues are passed by unnoticed." *Freedom's Journal* pledged to familiarize the country with the accomplishments of black citizens and to offer them advice on how to further advance socially and economically. The paper helped knit together blacks from across the North, bringing them information about other black communities and businesses, and issues related to abolitionism and African colonization; it also promoted education and the temperance reform cause.

The careers of the paper's two editors reflected central trends of the black North. Samuel E. Cornish, born in Delaware in 1795, became a minister and served Presbyterian congregations in Maryland and New York. He campaigned against the American Colonization Society and promoted education, moral reform, temperance, and self-help as ways to improve black

Freedom's Journal, front page, 1827.

John B. Russwurm (1799–1851),
engraving, 1891.

Samuel E. Cornish (1795–1858),
engraving by Francis Kearney, 1825.

life. He founded various black organizations, helped establish the black convention movement of the 1830s, and worked with leading white abolitionists to launch the New York Anti-Slavery Society. When *Freedom's Journal* folded in 1829, he immediately followed it up with another paper, *Rights of All*. In 1837, he founded *The Colored American,* one of the most successful and aggressive of the early black newspapers.

The other editor of *Freedom's Journal* was John Russwurm. Born in 1799 to a Jamaican slave and a British merchant, Russwurm would become a widely experienced and cosmopolitan leader. He attended school in Quebec and taught briefly in Boston, then graduated from Bowdoin College in 1826, the second African American to receive a

formal college education. He moved to New York the next year and joined forces with Cornish. But their alliance must have been difficult, as Russwurm chose to support the colonization movement while Cornish labored in service of its destruction. When *Freedom's Journal* ceased publication, Russwurm accepted an appointment with the Maryland Colonization Society and moved to Monrovia, Liberia, where he became superintendent of education. He eventually resumed his career as a journalist and edited the *Liberian Herald.* Blacks at home burned him in effigy for supporting the hated Colonization Society, and radical white abolitionists repudiated him as a traitor. But Russwurm's assertion that blacks needed and deserved their own nation as a prerequisite to ending American slavery prefigured the later ideas of Martin R. Delany and other black nationalists. He remained in Africa for the rest of his life and helped negotiate the merging of Liberia with the Maryland-in-Liberia settlement, which took place in 1855, four years after his death.

Of all the early publications by African Americans, none proved more important than David Walker's *Appeal,* serialized in 1829 and published in pamphlet form in 1830. Walker, born free in North Carolina, may have been living in Charleston in the days leading up to the Denmark Vesey incident. He had been active in the city's AME Church, but he either had left the city by 1822 or simply avoided accusations of complicity with Vesey. By 1825 he had moved to Boston, where he opened a used-clothing store, joined the Prince Hall Freemasons, served as an agent for *Freedom's Journal,* and helped establish the General Colored Association, an antislavery political organization. In the fall of 1829 Walker published his *Appeal to the Colored Citizens of the World,* the most aggressive repudiation of slavery and racial prejudice to have appeared anywhere. "Blacks or Coloured People," Walker wrote, "are treated more cruel

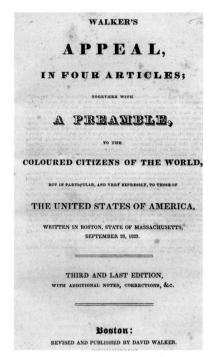

David Walker's *Appeal,* title page, 1830.

by the white Christians of America, than devils themselves ever treated a set of men, women and children on this earth." He rejected the racist assertions of Thomas Jefferson point by point and urged his brethren to organize and battle American oppression:

> Now, I ask you, had you not
> rather be killed than to be a slave
> to a tyrant, who takes the life of
> your mother, wife, and dear little
> children? Look upon your mother,
> wife and children, and answer
> God Almighty; and believe this,
> that it is no more harm for you to
> kill a man, who is trying to kill
> you, than it is for you to take a
> drink of water when thirsty.[3]

Walker had hoped to distribute his pamphlet throughout the country, especially in the South, by having black ministers give it out to their congregations and by employing the network of black mariners that plied the nation's coastal routes. But he died before he could proceed with any plans, thus depriving the growing black abolitionist movement of its most passionate spokesman.

THE LIBERATOR AND
WILLIAM LLOYD GARRISON

The peaceable minister Samuel Joseph May warned the fiery William Lloyd Garrison to control his language. You are, he said, "too severe" and endangering the antislavery cause. As the two men walked the streets of Boston, May advised his close friend to cool off—"You are all on fire." Garrison stopped, placed his hand on his colleague's shoulder, and replied, "Brother May, I have need to be all on fire, for I have mountains of ice about me to melt."[4] True to his word, when Garrison published the first issue of *The Liberator* on January 1, 1831, he erupted with volcanic force:

> I do not wish to think, or speak, or write with moderation. No! no! Tell a man whose house is on fire to give a moderate alarm; tell him to moderately rescue his wife from the hands of the ravisher; tell the mother to gradually extricate her babe from the fire into which it has fallen;—but urge me not to use moderation in a cause like the present. I am in earnest—I will not equivocate— I will not excuse—I will not retreat a single inch—and I will be heard.

Born in coastal Newburyport, Massachusetts, in 1805, Garrison spent his life as a zealous journalist, first with a local Federalist paper, then moving on to Benjamin Lundy's *Genius of Universal Emancipation* in 1828. Through his work with Lundy and contact with the black community in Baltimore, where Lundy published his paper, Garrison embraced the idea of immediate emancipation—the concept that slavery was a sin and so must be immediately

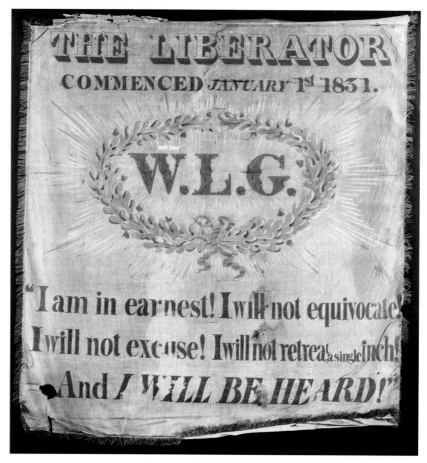

"The Liberator Commenced," cotton banner, ca. 1841. To commemorate the founding of *The Liberator,* the banner quotes William Lloyd Garrison's opening editorial.

abandoned. Although prior to 1831 others had made the same assertion, no one had made it with such stunning force. Boston's churches refused to allow Garrison to speak from their pulpits, and most public halls closed their doors to him, fearing that his words threatened the foundations of the republic.

The nation had been debating the issue of slavery for decades, but suddenly the tone changed dramatically. To northerners (often prejudiced against black people) and to southerners (dependent upon slavery for their livelihood, and living in fear of an American repetition of the Haitian Revolution), Garrison's words rained down like flaming meteorites from the night sky. He exposed the hypocrisy of American republicanism and censured its Christians who refused to condemn the greatest sin ever committed by mankind. He took aim at the American Colonization Society, and his 1832 book, *Thoughts on African Colonization,* exposed it as an impractical and racist scheme to deport African Americans against their will. The last third of his book reprinted remarks from many African American meetings and speeches protesting the colonization scheme as a violation of their rights as U.S. citizens.

William Lloyd Garrison (1805–79). A fiery Boston abolitionist, Garrison advocated the immediate end of slavery, racial equality, disunionism, pacifism, temperance, and women's rights. Boston blacks remained loyal to Garrison, even when they rejected his extreme views against voting and on disunionism.

Over the next decade, Garrison broadened his antislavery ideology to attack racial prejudice, to support equal rights for women, and to repudiate war and all forms of violence; he then called for the separation of the South from the Union. In time, many other eloquent white reformers, such as Wendell Phillips, Charles Sumner, Gerrit Smith, and Theodore Parker, would join Garrison, but his radical reform program remained central to the antislavery movement.

While he gave countless speeches, published many pamphlets, and attracted thousands of followers across the North, Garrison's most potent weapon remained *The Liberator*. Begun in January 1831 with a small circulation and a limited supply of talented contributors, it depended upon African American communities across the North for its survival. Especially during its first difficult years, blacks served as its distribution agents; wrote letters, essays, and announcements for publication; and contributed money for its support. In fact, without the support of black communities and especially the financial contributions of black leaders like James Forten and Robert Purvis, the paper would have quickly collapsed. Instead, it enjoyed the longest publication run of any antebellum antislavery newspaper, attracted a very loyal following in the black community, and more than any other single publication helped spread antislavery sentiment. It continued to publish until the close of 1865 and the end of slavery.

NAT TURNER

I entered my master's chamber, it being dark, I could not give a death blow, the hatchet glanced from his head, he sprang from the bed and called his wife, it was his last word, Will laid him dead, with a blow of his axe, and Mrs. Travis shared the same fate, as she lay in bed. The murder of this family, five in number, was the work of a moment, not one of them awoke; there was a little infant sleeping in a cradle, that was forgotten, until we had left the house and gone some distance, when Henry and Will returned and killed it."[5] In these words, recorded by his captors, Nat Turner recounted the start of nineteenth-century America's bloodiest slave insurrection.

Turner, born around 1800 on the Southampton County, Virginia, slave plantation of Benjamin Turner, was the son of a slave named Nancy, who may have been brought from Haiti with her owner to escape the Haitian Revolution. From early childhood, both whites and blacks recognized Nat's special gifts. He quickly learned to read, and his owner presented him with a Bible, a gift the young boy cherished. He gained access to books owned by local whites, reinforcing his unique position as a slave. Both his mother and his grandmother cultivated a strong sense of self-worth in him, frequently telling him that he was destined to fulfill some great purpose. Whites also recognized his ability and charisma.

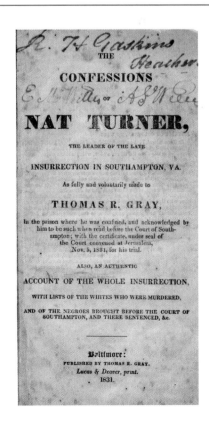

Thomas R. Gray, *The Confessions of Nat Turner* (Baltimore: Thomas R. Gray, 1831). Gray's interview with Turner (1800?–31), included in this pamphlet, contains the only recorded words of the leader of the country's bloodiest slave insurrection.

Horrid Massacre in Virginia, woodcut, 1831. This popular depiction tells the story of the Turner revolt, from the initial attack to the military intervention. It displays the innocence of the victims and the perfidy of the insurrectionists.

August 22, 1831, Nat Turner and about seventy armed slaves and free blacks took history into their hands. They would put an end to slavery in Southampton County, Virginia, the rebels decided, or they would die in the attempt. By the end of the next day, they had attacked about fifteen homes and killed between fifty-five and sixty whites. After white militia began attacking Turner's men, other slaves who had planned to join the rebellion suddenly turned against it, concluding that it would fail. Most of the rebels were quickly captured, but Turner eluded authorities for more than a month. On Sunday, October 30, Benjamin Phipps, a local white, stumbled onto Turner's hideout and seized him. A special Virginia court tried him on November 5 and sentenced him to hang six days later. Afterward enraged whites took his body, skinned it, and rendered his remains into grease. Twenty-one of his fellow rebels also went to the gallows, and another sixteen were sold away from the region.

The Turner Rebellion, the most famous of the slave revolts—and threatened revolts—in the South, stretching

Even his owner believed that Nat would not be well suited for slavery: he sold him and his mother to a nearby plantation belonging to Benjamin Turner's son, Samuel. When Samuel died in 1822, Nat's wife—perhaps a woman named Cherry—was sold off to settle the estate. The loss embittered him. He began a series of fasts and prayers and reported having prophetic visions: black and white spirits in battle, the sun going dark, thunder rocking the heavens, and blood flowing in streams. He held a series of religious revival meetings that attracted many slaves and at least one white man, who asked Turner to baptize him. In 1828 his visions became even more intense. His new owner then died, and Turner and sixteen other slaves found themselves under the supervision of yet another master. Then in February 1831 an eclipse of the sun foretold to Turner that the time had come to take up the yoke of Christ and put slavery down.

He conspired with four men he had known for years and planned to act on July 4. But Turner became ill and the plot was delayed; he also may have been awaiting word from conspirators in nearby North Carolina. Exactly what Turner planned beyond rising up in Southampton is unclear—and it may have been unclear to him as well. Nevertheless, beginning at two a.m. on

Nat Turner with other conspirators, colorized steel engraving, after Felix O. C. Darley, 1863.

back to the early eighteenth century, sent shock waves throughout the country. Coming after the searing debates over Missouri, the Denmark Vesey conspiracy, and the emergence of radical abolitionism in the North, Nat Turner's bloody insurrection transformed southern thinking on the institution of slavery. The Virginia legislature debated ending it; the state's governor John Floyd declared that only manumission would head off further rebellions. Even Thomas Jefferson Randolph resurrected his grandfather's plan for colonization, hoping to hinder future Nat Turners. Had the state adopted a policy of manumission, no matter how gradual, the nation might have avoided civil war. Instead, the South's view of slavery hardened, and state legislatures adopted stronger and more restrictive laws for both slaves and free blacks. Southerners after 1831 began describing slavery not as a danger to the republic or a regrettable inheritance from the Founding Fathers, but as a positive good, a beneficial institution to both slaves and whites.

THE FOUNDING OF THE AMERICAN ANTI-SLAVERY SOCIETY AND MARIA STEWART

The formation of the American Anti-Slavery Society in 1833 was one of the most important events in the development of the abolitionist movement. The new organization built on the earlier experiences of the Pennsylvania Abolition Society; the American Convention of Abolition Societies, which first met more than forty years earlier; and other groups in Boston, New York, and Philadelphia. Led by Boston's William Lloyd Garrison and New York's Arthur and Lewis Tappan, northern abolitionists met in Philadelphia in December 1833 to unite the movement's disparate elements around the idea of immediate emancipation. White liberal Christians and orthodox Protestants met in the Quaker city with black abolitionists James McCrummell, Robert Purvis, James Forten, and James G. Barbadoes. Together they signed the society's "Declaration of Sentiments," in a dramatic ceremony that mimicked the signing of the Declaration of Independence.

The public responded with outrage at the interracial meeting and called for

"Declaration of the Anti-Slavery Convention," Philadelphia, December 4, 1833.

the execution of the society's leaders, fearing that its program of immediatism would destroy the republic. Nevertheless, the American Anti-Slavery Society spawned auxiliaries across the North,

held countless conventions, published newspapers and pamphlets, and sent out hundreds of agents, black and white, to spread the antislavery message. The most important antislavery organization, it remained active until adoption of the Fifteenth Amendment to the Constitution in 1870 appeared to assure full civil rights for blacks.

But African Americans had already been organizing against the American Colonization Society. In September 1830 black leaders from the greater Philadelphia region, Maryland, Delaware, New York, Connecticut, Rhode Island, and Virginia, under the direction of the Reverend Richard Allen, met to form the American Society of Free Persons of Color. The following year many of the same delegates reconvened in Philadelphia for the first annual convention "of the people of colour" in June 1831. These black national conventions would meet periodically until 1864. The convention movement became one of the most important venues for debate on all the major issues facing African Americans before the Civil War. Such

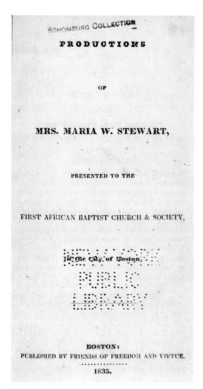

While living in New York, Maria W. Stewart (1803–79) published a collection of her first speeches.

Jarena Lee (1783–?). Born free in Cape May, New Jersey, she experienced a religious conversion in 1804, at the beginning of the Second Great Awakening, and spent her life preaching. Although she married the Reverend Joseph Lee in 1811, he did not support her desire to become a minister. The AME Church's leader Richard Allen believed Lee had been called by God to preach, but the denomination refused to approve her, and few churches would open their doors to her.

Robert Purvis (1810–98). Son of mixed-race Charleston, South Carolina, parents, Purvis moved to Philadelphia in 1819 and rose to become the city's most important black leader and one of the North's most influential black abolitionists. His prominence and his demands for justice made him a target for racists, and in 1838 and 1842 his city residence was besieged by rioters, compelling him to buy a gun, despite his professed Garrisonian principles of nonresistance. Although he moved to the countryside, Purvis remained active in the abolitionist movement. He served as vice president of the American Anti-Slavery Society from 1841 to 1865. This daguerrotype was taken in the 1840s.

face-to-face meetings increased solidarity and offered opportunities to convene with white allies, such as William Lloyd Garrison, Benjamin Lundy, and Arthur Tappan.

A month after Garrison formed the New England Anti-Slavery Society in January 1832, black women in Salem, Massachusetts, established the first women's antislavery society. Meeting on George Washington's birthday, the Female Anti-Slavery Society of Salem pledged to work "for our mutual improvement, and to promote the welfare of our color."[6] Led by Mary A. and Dorothy C. Battys, E. A. Drew, Charlotte Bell, Hannah B. Fowler, and Eleanor C. Harvey, the new society allied itself with *The Liberator,* praising its opposition to the colonization scheme. The women also pledged their resources to help the poor,

refute racial prejudice, and disseminate antislavery publications.

Perhaps no woman made a greater impact during the formative years of the antislavery movement than Maria W. Stewart. Born Maria Miller in Hartford in 1803, she moved to Boston at age five and obtained an education through Sabbath schools and her own efforts. She married James Stewart in 1826, and the two worked closely with the radical abolitionist David Walker. Her husband's death in 1829 and Walker's in 1830 moved Stewart to become fully committed to the antislavery cause. Her 1831 address, "Religion and the Pure Principles of Morality," is the first political manifesto published by an African American woman. Stewart also became the first woman to address audiences of mixed races and both genders, and she

tirelessly defended her right as a woman and an African American to speak out. An enemy of the colonization movement, she preferred death to deportation and urged her brethren to commit to the antislavery fight. Unhappy with the level of activism in Boston, she left the city in 1833 and never returned. She eventually moved to Washington, D.C., where she aided former slaves and Civil War veterans.

Stewart's eloquence is thought to have inspired other black women to write their autobiographies, such as Jarena Lee, whose *The Life and Religious Experiences of Jarena Lee* was published in 1836. Lee was called to preach in 1817 at the AME Church in Pennsylvania; she was initially approved by Bishop Richard Allen but was, as she put it, "measurably debarred" because of her gender.[7]

BRITISH EMANCIPATION

That such a system should so long have been suffered to exist in any part of the British Empire will appear, to our posterity, almost incredible [and that it] continued for two centuries, and by a people who may, nevertheless, I trust, be affirmed to be the most moral and humane of nations, is one of those anomalies which, if it does not stagger the belief, will, at least, excite the astonishment of future ages."[8] William Wilberforce's 1823 appeal sheds light on why Great Britain willingly abolished slavery in its Caribbean colonies at a time when it reaped enormous profits off the uncompensated labor of its African slaves. Wilberforce, as the illustration on the following page shows, was most closely associated with the end of British slavery, but Thomas Clarkson, Thomas F. Buxton, and Granville Sharp were equally important, and African Americans honored their work by naming schools, colleges, and antislavery societies after them. Several of the black settlements in Canada West also took the names of these men in recognition of their enormous contributions to the growth of black freedom. Thousands of others in Great Britain joined organizations such as the London Anti-Slavery Society or labored tirelessly as individuals to overcome the power of the Caribbean planters to halt a practice that contradicted the image that Britain wished to project to the world.

The English abolitionists who had ended the slave trade in 1807 viewed their success as a prelude to the eventual end of slavery itself. They assumed that if planters could not import additional slaves, they would be compelled out of their own self-interest to better treat the ones they owned. Under improved conditions, the early abolitionists hoped, the humanity of the slaves would be recognized and the institution would become odious to all, and unnecessary. Such did not happen.

The campaign to end slavery, however, underwent a seismic shift in perspective with the publication of Elizabeth Heyrick's *Immediate, Not Gradual Abolition* in 1824. Thereafter, in England and in the United States, gradualist schemes to place slavery on the road to extinction struck many as no longer sufficient. All were implicated in the sin of slavery, Heyrick asserted, and no

To the Friends of Negro Emancipation, engraving by David Lucas after a painting by Alexander Rippingille, 1834. Newly freed slaves celebrate the end of slavery by burying the tools of suppression. The text below the image reads: "A glorious and happy era on the first of August, bursts upon the Western World; England strikes the manacle from the slave, and bids the bond go free."

"The year of release is at hand," engraving by T. S. Engleheart, originally published in Mary Ann Rawson, *The Bow in the Cloud; or, The Negro's Memorial: A collection of original contributions, in prose and verse, illustrative of the evils of slavery, and commemorative of its abolition in the British colonies* (London: Jackson and Walford, 1834). The engraving's title comes from Deuteronomy 15:9 (King James version).

"Koo, Koo, or Actor Boy," a Jamaican John-Canoe celebration, 1836. John-Canoe is an anglicized version of Jonkonnu, Junkanoo, Jonkanoo, or Jankunu, a Caribbean dance celebration of West African origin, perhaps from an Igbo secret society; it occurs the day after Christmas and on New Year's Day. In Jamaica before emancipation, white planters permitted the slaves to perform these secular celebrations, as did the slave masters in coastal North Carolina.

one could remain neutral on the great moral question of the age: one either supported slavery or actively opposed it. "The slave has a right to his liberty," she exclaimed, "a right which it is a crime to withhold—let the consequences to the planters be what they may."[9] Between 1823 and 1833, the popular clamor for an end to slavery reached unprecedented levels. In 1833 alone, Parliament received more than five thousand antislavery petitions containing about 1.5 million signatures. One petition stretched for more than half a mile, carefully sewn and pasted together by a team that included Priscilla Buxton, the daughter of the great abolitionist; it contained the signatures of 350,000 women.

On July 26, 1833, bowing to intense public pressure, Parliament adopted legislation that would free the nearly eight hundred thousand British Caribbean slaves on August 1, 1834. Wilberforce was lying on his deathbed when he heard the news, and thanked God "that I should have lived to witness" this day.[10] But Parliament subjected the slaves to a long period of uncompensated apprenticeship (ultimately reduced to four years) and compensated the slave owners with 20 million pounds (perhaps equivalent to several trillion dollars today) for the loss of their property. While compensated emancipation set an unfortunate precedent—compensating the slave owners rather than the slaves—African Americans and their allies on both sides of the Atlantic proclaimed August 1 an international day of celebration. If nothing else, it proved that a nation could end slavery without violent revolution.

PART FOUR

RACE AND RESISTANCE

1834–1850

OBERLIN COLLEGE

Female graduates of Oberlin College, daguerrotype, 1855. Ann Hazle, an African American from New Bern, North Carolina, attended Oberlin from 1853 to 1855. She died in Ohio in 1862.

No college or university in the United States can match Oberlin College's legacy on race. Founded in 1833 by John Shipherd and Philo Stewart as part of a communitarian settlement, Oberlin admitted more black students before 1865 than all other American colleges and universities combined.

Begun as the country's first coeducational institution, Oberlin received a substantial antislavery boost when fifty-one students led by Theodore Dwight Weld withdrew from Cincinnati's Lane Seminary to assert their right to discuss abolitionism. At its formative stage, the new college needed the infusion of students and several new faculty members, but unexpectedly the Lane rebels, as they were called, insisted that Oberlin accept black students as the price of their own enrollment. Arthur and Lewis Tappan sweetened the students' demands by offering a $10,000 endowment (equal to well over $2 million today) if the college agreed. The town and a slight majority of the students opposed the move. Some female students threatened to wade through Lake Erie and go home if the school admitted blacks. The trustees and faculty nevertheless narrowly agreed to accept the Lane rebels' terms and the Tappan brothers' offer. In 1835 the college officially accepted the change, and James Bradley, who arrived with the original Lane students, enrolled in the school's preparatory department and became the first African American at Oberlin.

When the financial panic of 1837 struck the Tappan brothers, they withdrew their financial support. Much to Oberlin's credit, it unwaveringly maintained its policy to accept all qualified students regardless of race or gender. Nearly one-third of the school's black students came from the Cincinnati region, many after graduating from Gilmore High School, a private black preparatory school founded in 1844. By the close of the Civil War, Oberlin had accepted forty-five African American men and women in its regular bachelor's program and graduated thirty-two, fifteen of whom were women. The daguerreotype shows female graduates proudly posing with Ann Hazle, originally from New Bern, North Caro-

Oberlin College campus, engraving, 1840s. This image originally appeared in Henry Howe's *Historical Collections of Ohio*, 1847.

John Mercer Langston (1829–97), daguerrotype, 1849.

Among the college's other regular graduates were abolitionists George B. Vashon, who in 1844 earned the distinction of becoming the first black graduate of the college; William Howard Day, who earned his diploma in 1847; and John Mercer Langston, who graduated in 1849. Abolitionist, politician, legislator, and educator, Langston went on to earn a theological degree in 1853 under the great Oberlin evangelical Charles Grandison Finney. The college's most illustrious early black graduate, Langston later founded the law school at Howard University and became its first dean. As with many of the black students who attended Oberlin, other members of the Langston family also enrolled. Langston's two older brothers, Gideon and Charles, attended the school's preparatory department.

Most black students, male or female, never entered the formal bachelor's program but, like the Langston brothers, attended the school's preparatory program. In all, 141 black women enrolled in it before 1865. In 1842, Sarah Watson had been the first, but in 1850 Lucy Stanton of Cleveland was the first to complete the program. The famed fugitive slave Anthony Burns also enrolled

George B. Vashon (1824–78), born free in Carlisle, Pennsylvania, grew up in Pittsburgh, where he joined that city's active black abolitionist community. He graduated from Oberlin in 1844, the first African American to do so, and returned to Pittsburgh, where he joined forces with the great black nationalist Martin R. Delany and helped edit the newspaper *The Mystery*. He later studied law, but the Pennsylvania bar refused to admit him because of his race.

lina, who began her studies in 1853 and graduated with her class in 1855. She went on to a teaching career and died in Ohio in February 1862. The image testifies to the depth of change that had occurred on campus with the presence of black students. The educator and AME Church leader Fanny Jackson Coppin, who earned her B.A. degree in 1865, actually taught white students at Oberlin's preparatory department, an astonishing arrangement in a state that had one of the North's most odious racial codes.

in the preparatory department, as did Frederick Douglass's daughter Rosetta, and the son of the black editor John Russwurm. Mary and Emily Edmonson, two sisters who were captured in the ill-fated escape of the *Pearl* and were then

Anthony Burns, 1855. Burns (1834–62), born a slave in Virginia, was permitted to earn wages, the majority of which he turned over to his owner. He escaped in 1854, and his arrest in Boston caused a national furor over the legitimacy of the 1850 Fugitive Slave Act. He was returned to slavery and sold to an owner in North Carolina. The black abolitionist Leonard Grimes arranged for Burns's purchase, after which he attended Oberlin College and received training for the ministry.

purchased and freed by abolitionists, also entered the preparatory department. The antislavery author Harriet Beecher Stowe paid for their education.

Oberlin's commitment to racial equality weakened during the 1880s, as the nation moved more forcefully and violently toward Jim Crow culture. In 1882, the school began compelling black students to eat at separate tables, and several white female students refused to share their dinners with African Americans. The college also began segregating its dormitories, and when Mary Church Terrell—who had graduated from the college in 1884—sent her daughters there in 1913, they faced restrictive housing rules. She protested, and the school relaxed but did not fully end its discriminatory policies. Not until 1948 did the college hire a black faculty member. Although blacks never exceeded 5 percent of total student population, Oberlin College nevertheless was exceptional in terms of racial justice in American higher education.

MAGICIAN AND VENTRILOQUIST

When we consider nineteenth-century black performers, most of us think of minstrel shows. But African Americans excelled in the full range of the performing arts, even well before the Civil War. Dramatic readers like Louise De Mortie, gifted singers like Elizabeth Greenfield (the Black Swan), and actors like Ira Aldridge, one of the most nuanced Shakespeareans of any time or any race, attracted large audiences both in the United States and in Europe. Additionally, blacks joined circuses and traveling troupes, performing in popular meeting places like taverns and hotels, following in a tradition that stretched back at least to the Middle Ages. Black performers knew no boundaries, apparently: Richard Potter (1783?–1835), the son of a Massachusetts slave named Dinah Swan, became a well-known and quite successful magician and ventriloquist.

As a ten-year-old cabin boy, Potter had traveled to Britain, where he saw a performance by John Rannie, a Scottish magician and ventriloquist. He became an apprentice to Rannie, and at age eighteen joined a traveling circus with him. In 1807, Rannie booked performances in Boston. He continued to work until 1811, when he retired and gave all his equipment and props to Potter. While

Richard Potter gravesite.

Rannie and Potter worked together, they incorporated magic acts into their performances of plays. One production, *The Provoked Husband,* ironically led to the marriage of Potter and the female lead, Sally Harris. Potter's solo career flourished, and by 1813 he had earned enough money to purchase land in New Hampshire. Between 1818 and 1831 he performed in Boston, New York, and Raleigh, North Carolina. While the Nat Turner Rebellion likely put a stop to his travels below the Mason-Dixon Line, his career was astonishing as it occurred during an era of hardening racial lines and declining economic opportunities for African Americans in the North.

JULIA CHINN

The 1836 election of Martin Van Buren as U.S. president reverberated throughout American politics and offered unexpected insight into the realities of slavery. Van Buren's running mate, Richard Mentor Johnson (1780–1850), lived in Scott County, Kentucky. He had begun his political career in the U.S. House of Representatives in 1806 and entered the Senate in 1819, during the Missouri debates. A hero of the War of 1812 and a devoted admirer of Andrew Jackson, he lost his reelection bid in 1828 but soon returned to the House of Representatives. Johnson won working-class Democratic support in the North to become Jackson's running mate in the 1832 election, but doubts about his suitability left him off the ticket. In 1836 he emerged as the strongest candidate to become Van Buren's running mate. Ironically, most of his support to fill the bottom half of the ticket came from the North, rather than the South, where his colleagues considered him a disturbing political liability because of his "domestic relations."

Early in his career, Johnson had been a close ally of Thomas Jefferson, sharing far more than republican principles with the third president. While Jefferson never discussed any relationship with his slave Sally Hemings, Johnson displayed no such reluctance to acknowledge intimacy with his own "property." On the contrary, he paraded his unofficial marriage to Julia Chinn, a slave he had inherited from his father, before the public in ways that outraged his fellow slave owners and became a national scandal. Johnson never married and may have taken up with Chinn to spite his family, who had objected to a woman he wished to marry, or he may simply have loved his mulatto slave, popular opinion be damned. Liaisons with female slaves

were roundly condemned by abolitionists and former slaves like Harriet Jacobs. The South Carolina slave owner James Henry Hammond maintained the public fiction of marriage to his white wife while turning his plantation into a personal bordello. North Florida's Zephaniah Kingsley believed in slavery—but not racism—and apparently provided for several black slave "wives," refusing to disrupt the domestic lives of his slave families.

Johnson and Julia Chinn apparently became devoted to each other, and she bore him two daughters, Imogene and Adaline, whom Johnson treated as family and educated as if they had been white. When out of town, he entrusted operation of his estate to his "wife," who managed it admirably. He brushed off criticism and even brought his family to a Fourth of July celebration. As he escorted his family onto the speaker's platform, however, the white women in the audience fled in disgust.

When Chinn died during a cholera epidemic in 1833, Johnson began a similar relationship with one of her sisters. He made sure that his light-skinned daughters married white men in Washington, D.C., who could provide for them, and he included them in his will. Johnson also took an interest in Marcellus Chinn, Julia's brother, bringing him with him to New York during the 1836 campaign. Marcellus, however, fled to the abolitionist Lewis Tappan. When Johnson made another trip north, this time to Detroit, he brought Daniel Chinn, the father of Marcellus and Julia, with him as a body servant. Daniel fled to Canada and freedom.

As much as Johnson wished to maintain his family, the pressures overwhelmed him, and the political costs

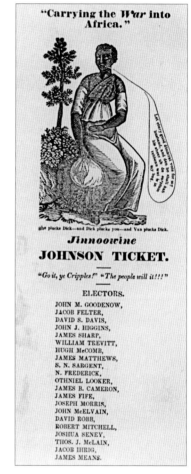

"Jinnoowine [Genuine] Johnson Ticket," broadside, 1836. This racist handbill was produced by Democrats, the party of the candidates on this ticket. Clearly, elements of the Democratic Party did not approve of Martin Van Buren's running mate, Richard M. Johnson. In this image, Julia Chinn declares: "Let ebery good dimicrat vote for my husband, and din he shall had his sheer ub de surplum rebbenu [surplus revenue] wat is in my bag." Underneath her image the handbill states: "She plucks Dick [Johnson]—and Dick plucks you—and Van [Buren] plucks Dick."

proved high. His conduct became an acute embarrassment to his fellow Democrats. As the accompanying illustration shows, they criticized their own candidate, using rude language to depict Julia Chinn's appeal to Johnson. Whig and later Republican rivals repeatedly cited the relationship as representative of the immorality of slaveholders. During their famed Illinois contest for the U.S. Senate in 1858, Stephen Douglas repeatedly accused Abraham Lincoln of favoring miscegenation. In response, Lincoln pointed out that racial mixing took place most often where slavery existed, not in the free North, and he pointed to Douglas's "good friend" Richard M. Johnson as evidence. That always raised a chorus of laughter.

Johnson's relationship also proved personally damaging to his surviving daughter and her family. Johnson's brothers challenged his will in court, successfully asserting that since their brother had never been married, he left no legally recognized children to inherit his estate.

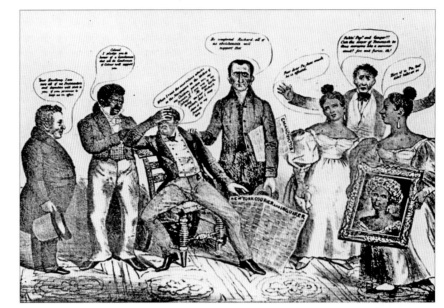

"An Affecting Scene in Kentucky," 1836. This racist attack on vice presidential candidate Richard M. Johnson ridicules his "domestic life." A distraught Johnson drops a copy of the *New York Courier and Enquirer,* lamenting: "When I read the scurrilous attacks in the Newspapers on the Mother of my Children, pardon me, my friends if I give way to feelings!!! My dear Girls, bring me your Mother's picture, that I may show it to my friends here."

AN UNCOMPROMISING TALENT

James McCune Smith (1813–65), one of the most accomplished and influential of northern black leaders, was the first African American to receive a medical degree. The son of a slave in New York City, Smith gained his freedom when the state's emancipation law took effect on July 4, 1827. He graduated from the city's African Free School system. (Founded in 1787, it had grown to six schools in the early 1830s. Many future antislavery leaders attended the schools, including Alexander Crummell and Henry Highland Garnet.) Smith attended African Free School No. 2, taught by Charles Andrews, an English instructor, who operated the school from 1809 to 1832. New York City blacks initially supported the system with enthusiasm, but in 1830, when Andrews

voiced his support for the American Colonization Society, they repudiated it. Growing resistance eventually forced Andrews's retirement and compelled the schools to begin hiring African American instructors.

Smith, although a talented student, was apprenticed to a blacksmith after graduation. Unsatisfied, he applied to the medical schools at Columbia College and Geneva, New York, but was rejected because of his race. With the assistance of Peter Williams, Jr., of St. Philips Church, the nation's first black Episcopal minister, Smith entered the University of Glasgow in Scotland. He completed his bachelor's degree in 1835 and a master's degree in 1836; after finishing clinical work in Paris, he received his medical degree in 1837.

Smith returned to New York City

James McCune Smith (1813–65), engraving by Patrick H. Reason.

and established a practice in Manhattan as a surgeon and a general practitioner for both blacks and whites. He became the staff physician for the New York Colored Orphan Asylum and opened a pharmacy on West Broadway, the first such business owned by an African American.

Smith gained most renown, however, as a radical abolitionist, an essayist, and an intellectual. Immediately upon returning to the United States, he joined the American Anti-Slavery Society. Before the end of the 1840s, he broke with William Lloyd Garrison and his followers, favoring political abolitionism over Garrison's moral suasion and nonresistance tactics. He helped lead the campaign for black suffrage in New York, which placed minimum property-owning requirements on black male voters. He quickly moved into the orbit of the radical white abolitionist Gerrit Smith, who attempted to establish a black settlement in the vast lands he owned in the Adirondack Mountains. James McCune Smith also became a member of the Liberty Party, which his friend Gerrit Smith helped lead.

Both men also became involved in the Radical Abolition Party, successor to the Liberty Party, which in 1857 nominated McCune Smith as its candidate for secretary of the state. Smith wrote many letters and essays for the New York *Weekly Anglo-African* (the preeminent black newspaper of the 1860s), the *Anglo-African Magazine,* and for *Frederick Douglass' Paper.* His extensive newspaper letters under the moniker "Communipaw" (the Native American name of the town where he lived near Jersey City) sparked extensive debates among African Americans across the North and helped shape the aims of black abolitionism. His introduction to Frederick Douglass's second autobiography, *My Bondage, My Freedom* in 1855, testifies to his place among northern blacks. He wrote passionately against colonization and all emigration schemes as inherently destructive to black claims to full and equal American citizenship.

Gerrit Smith (1797–1874), photograph by Mathew Brady, ca. 1860. Smith, a wealthy New York philanthropist, congressman, and associate of John Brown, bought land in New York's Adirondack Mountains to create an African American community. Because of his generosity, Smith earned the enormous respect of blacks across the North. James McCune Smith was one of his most frequent correspondents.

OPPOSING BLACK FREEDOM

The growing antislavery movement and increased immigration proved a volatile mixture in the years before the Civil War. From Boston to Philadelphia and the Midwest, opponents of abolition combined with recent immigrants—who competed with African Americans for employment—to oppose the antislavery movement and the black communities. Beginning in 1829, Cincinnati officials moved to restrict the freedom of African Americans, and the next year a riot drove out more than one thousand city blacks, many of whom made their way to the Wilberforce settlement in Canada. In the 1830s rioters ended efforts to establish a black manual labor school in New

Haven, Connecticut. In Canterbury, in eastern Connecticut, protesters broke up a school for black girls run by Prudence Crandall, a white woman; authorities then put her on trial for educating black students who were not residents of the state. In rural New Hampshire, rioters used about one hundred oxen to drag the Noyes Academy for black children off its foundation. When antislavery lecturers attempted to speak in public, rocks and the contents of outhouses rained down on them. Even William Lloyd Garrison was seized by a mob and dragged through the streets of Boston with a rope around his neck. A mob caught the abolitionist Amos Dresser carrying abolitionist literature on the

streets of Nashville and publicly flogged him. In November 1837, a seething Alton, Illinois, mob pillaged the offices of the antislavery publisher Elijah P. Lovejoy, destroying his press and killing him. During the 1830s and 1840s few northern cities or towns with any significant black communities escaped violence.

In Philadelphia, white and black abolitionists worked with the Pennsylvania Anti-Slavery Society to raise funds to erect Pennsylvania Hall, a facility where abolitionists could meet safely in a city increasingly torn over race and Irish immigration. Black leaders Frederick A. Hinton and James McCrummell served on the hall's business committee, and other blacks invested in the build-

Pennsylvania Hall, color lithograph, 1838.

ing's construction. Opening on May 14, 1838, beautiful Pennsylvania Hall hosted a meeting of the Female Anti-Slavery Society. The light-skinned Robert Purvis escorted his darker-colored wife Harriet Forten Purvis to the gathering. Mistaking Purvis for a white man, whites began rumors that Pennsylvania Hall existed primarily to foster amalgamation. Two light-skinned women walking with their darker male cousin were also mistaken for white. The idea that a "negro" would escort two white women on city streets inflamed Philadelphians, elites and working class alike.

When angry whites began milling around the facility, hall managers approached the city's mayor asking for protection. On May 17 Mayor John Swift convinced the abolitionists to temporarily halt their meetings and give him the keys to the building. Mayor Swift then addressed the protesters, perhaps as many as fifteen thousand, assuring them that no further antislavery assemblies would take place and that they should "keep the peace." He bade them a friendly good evening and left. The crowd cheered for the mayor.

Then when he was sufficiently out of sight, they attacked the building. They broke down the doors and ran through the hall, turning on the gas jets. Three days after Pennsylvania Hall opened for business, it lay in ruins. Over the following two nights rioters attacked the Shelter for Colored Orphans and the First African Presbyterian Church on Lombard Street. Several black homes also

came under attack. While the white elite appeared to be behind the destruction of Pennsylvania Hall, the mob that attacked the other buildings and black-owned property was largely composed of the white working class.

The year before, a constitutional convention had met in Harrisburg. The delegates, fearing that blacks had become so successful and numerous

The destruction of Pennsylvania Hall on May 17, 1838, wood engraving by John Archibald Woodside, Jr., 1838.

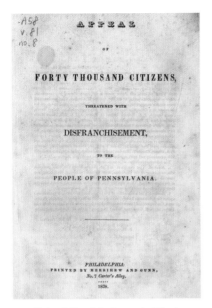

Robert Purvis's *Appeal of Forty Thousand Citizens,* 1838.

The murder of Elijah P. Lovejoy.

that they would soon begin electing members of their race to office, drafted a new state constitution that introduced the word "white" into the definition of voter qualifications. Frederick A. Hinton and Charles W. Gardner penned an appeal to the convention to retain black voting rights. In January 1838 the convention moved to Philadelphia and received Hinton and Gardner's petition but rejected it. The new constitution then went before the state's voters. Robert Purvis headed a committee of black Philadelphians that penned *Appeal of Forty Thousand Citizens* to demonstrate that blacks merited retaining the right to vote. Presenting evidence of black citizenship stretching back to the Revolution, the value of accumulated black property, and the amount of taxes blacks paid, the pamphlet rightly took pride in black achievement and assured white voters that "our country has no reason to be ashamed of us." Whatever whites had heard about African Americans, the pamphlet explained that "THEY ARE FOR THE GREATER PART, INDUSTRIOUS, PEACEABLE, AND USEFUL PEOPLE."[1] Despite their tireless campaign, on October 9, 1838, the voters approved the new constitution, ending the right to vote that African Americans had exercised since the beginning of the republic.

Life in Philadelphia, by Edward Clay, engraving by Charles Hunt, ca. 1840s. Clay and many other whites produced countless popular caricatures of African Americans. Clay especially enjoyed ridiculing what he understood as black aspirations to middle-class gentility and respectability.

THE AMISTAD AND THE CREOLE

"Death of Capt. Ferrer," by John Warner Barber, lithograph, 1839. This iconic image, engraved by the Connecticut artist Barber, accurately depicts a scene from the *Amistad* mutiny. The black cook, who had earlier taunted the captives, is seen dead at the feet of Captain Ferrer.

African resistance to slavery disrupted white stereotypes of inherent black docility and contentment, and when that defiance occurred on the high seas, it had important international ramifications. In early July 1839, a group of fifty-three African captives found themselves aboard the Cuban schooner *Amistad,* in the midst of a long and miserable journey. Months earlier, Portuguese slave traders had kidnapped them from the Sierra Leone region of Africa and brought them to Cuba, in flagrant violation of the 1817 treaty between England and Spain prohibiting the slave trade. Spaniards disguised the Africans' origins by giving them Spanish names and fabricating paperwork that claimed they had come from Cuba. José Ruiz and Pedro Montes purchased the Africans and shipped them along the Cuban coast, intended for another Caribbean destination.

On July 2, the captives staged a mutiny. Sengbe Pieh (popularly known as Joseph Cinqué) managed to free himself from his chains and helped many of his companions escape their irons. They located a cache of knives aboard the ship. As thunder rumbled and rain poured down, they attacked and killed the ship captain, Ramón Ferrer, as well as a black cook who, likely, had been taunting the captives; he can be seen lying on the left-hand portion of the lithograph by John Warner Barber. The mutineers kept Ruiz and Montes alive and commanded them to steer the ship back to Africa. The Spaniards agreed, but although they sailed east during the day, they pointed the ship north and west at night, putting them on a course for the United States. On August 25, the ship and its tired and starving passengers landed on Long Island. Four days later an American naval vessel took control of the *Amistad* and towed it to Connecticut. The Africans were taken to a New Haven jail, where they aroused intense public interest, to await their fate.

As the captives sat in jail, debate ensued over how the case should proceed. Ruiz and Montes held that the slaves should face murder charges. The Spanish government believed that since the slaves (allegedly) came from Cuba, the U.S. government should return them as property. Abolitionists, led by the wealthy New Yorker Lewis Tappan, formed the *Amistad* Committee to expose the fraudulent enslavement and to secure the freedom of the Africans. New York City blacks raised money to support the captives in a number of ways, including the production of the play *The Black Schooner, or, The Private Slaver* Amistad. The case slowly wound its way through the federal court system to the U.S. Supreme Court in 1841, where former president John Quincy Adams argued for the defense. Led by Justice Joseph Story, the court ruled in an eight-to-one decision that the African captives were not criminals or slaves but kidnapped Africans who deserved to go free. The one legitimately Cuban slave aboard the ship—who had belonged to Captain Ferrer—left for Canada via the Underground Railroad. The *Amistad* Committee and the Union Missionary Society (formed by black ministers and later merged with the American Missionary Association) raised enough money to transport thirty-six surviving Africans back to Sierra Leone.

"Joseph Cinquez," by James or Isaac Sheffield, lithograph, 1839. This is one of many popular images of the recognized leader of the mutiny. Most differ vastly from one another.

Washington forced the white overseer to sail the ship to Nassau, Bahamas—a British colony. One white man died during the fighting. When the ship arrived in Nassau, the British government imprisoned the nineteen rebels on mutiny charges but freed the remaining slaves, as slavery had officially ended in the British Empire in 1833.

Back in the United States, the antislavery congressman Joshua R. Giddings of Ohio introduced a resolution calling for the freedom of the imprisoned slaves, since Virginia law did not apply to areas outside the United States. The House censured him, and he resigned—only to win overwhelming reelection. The British government then freed the accused slaves after they served a few weeks in jail. Secretary of State Daniel Webster initially argued that the British should return the slaves to their masters, but he did not further pursue the matter. He feared that pressing the issue could jeopardize the important Webster-Ashburton treaty, which would end a contentious border dispute between the United States and Great Britain. As a result, Madison Washington and his compatriots gained their freedom.

As the *Amistad* slaves prepared to return to Africa, another slave rebellion with diplomatic consequences erupted. One hundred thirty-five slaves were sailing aboard the ship *Creole* as it traveled from Richmond to New Orleans. On November 7, 1841, the slave cook Madison Washington organized an uprising. With the help of eighteen other slaves,

John Quincy Adams (1767–1848), lithograph, 1846. Adams was the sixth president of the United States and a Massachusetts congressman. By the mid-1830s he was an abolitionist, aggressively defending the antislavery movement's right to petition the federal government. He served as the *Amistad* defendants' attorney before the U.S. Supreme Court.

FINDING FREEDOM IN MASSACHUSETTS

In 1783, the Massachusetts judiciary declared slavery illegal based on the state's 1780 constitutional provision that "all men are born free and equal, and have . . . the right of enjoying and defending their lives and liberty." The U.S. Constitution, however, implicitly supported slave owners' rights to hold human property and even directed that slaves escaping to other states "shall be

George Latimer (1818–80?), lithograph, 1840s. Latimer was the son of a white stonemason and a slave named Margaret Olmsted, the property of his father's brother. He was a house servant until age sixteen, when he became a drayman, earning twenty-five cents a day. He was hired out to a variety of jobs and, ironically, received some of his worst treatment from black masters. But his last owner, James B. Gray, a white storekeeper who specialized in selling alcohol to Norfolk's black population, repeatedly beat him. Latimer ran away first in 1840 and a second time in 1842, with his wife. The Reverend Nathaniel Colver, a Baptist minister and lecturer for the American Anti-Slavery Society, helped Latimer, purchased the runaway slave from Gray, and gave him his freedom.

"$50 Reward," 1842. Gray's advertisement for the return of Latimer.

"Great Massachusetts Petition," 1842. The Latimer Committee sent this petition form to every Massachusetts town to gain signatures for passage of personal liberty laws to prevent the seizure of alleged fugitive slaves.

delivered up on Claim of the Party to whom such Service or Labour may be due" (article 4, section 2). The Fugitive Slave Act of 1793 reinforced this provision, explicitly legalizing the recapture of slaves and authorizing state or federal magistrates to issue certificates of removal to return slaves from one state to another.

The Fugitive Slave Act met with resistance in northern states, mostly from African Americans, Quakers, and some abolitionists, but it was not until the 1840s that opposition gained more widespread strength. In 1842, the U.S. Supreme Court in *Prigg v. Pennsylvania* upheld the constitutionality of the 1793 law but declared that state authorities could not be forced to act in fugitive slave cases. One year later, in the city of Boston, the capture of the escaped slave George Latimer exposed the ugly realities of fugitive slave rendition.

On October 4, 1842, George Latimer and his wife, Rebecca, fled Norfolk, Virginia, heading north. Latimer's owner, James B. Gray, published an ad in the *Norfolk Beacon* on October 15, 1842:

RANAWAY on Monday night last my Negro Man George, commonly called George Latimer. He is about 5 feet 3 or 4 inches high, about 22 years of age, his complexion a bright yellow, is of a compact, well made frame, and is rather silent and slow spoken.— I suspect that he went North Tuesday, and will give Fifty Dollars reward and pay all necessary expenses, if taken out of the State. Twenty Five Dollars reward will be given for his apprehension within the State.

Latimer was quickly spotted in Boston by William R. Carpenter, a former employee of Gray, and at Gray's request, he was arrested on charges of larceny and jailed in preparation for his return to Virginia. Rebecca Latimer went into hiding.

George Latimer's incarceration prompted public outrage and galvanized the abolitionist community into action. On the night Latimer was incarcerated, a crowd of some three hundred mostly free black males gathered outside the courthouse to prevent Latimer's return to Gray and to ensure that proper legal procedures were followed. Counsel for Latimer, Samuel E. Sewall and Amos B.

Merrill, filed a writ of habeas corpus, but Chief Justice Lemuel Shaw denied it and ordered that Latimer be held in custody until Gray could procure evidence for trial. Latimer remained in jail for several weeks. Protesters signed petitions and held public meetings at Faneuil Hall to discuss ways to prevent his return to slavery. William Lloyd Garrison publicly criticized the seizure of the fugitive in *The Liberator,* and William Francis Channing and Dr. Henry Ingersoll Bowditch began publishing *The Latimer Journal and North Star* to apprise citizens of the case and to rally support for Latimer's release. Ultimately, the outcry proved effective. The day before the hearing that would determine Latimer's fate, Gray agreed to release his slave for a sum of $400. On November 18 Latimer was formally manumitted and released from custody.

Public mobilization did not end there. Fifty thousand people of Massachusetts signed a petition asking Congress to amend the Constitution to prevent similar outrages. Another 65,000 petitioned the Massachusetts legislature, demanding reform of fugitive slave rendition practices in the state. They submitted that the legislature should (1) forbid all persons who hold office under the government of Massachusetts from aiding in or abetting the arrest or detention of any person who may be claimed as a fugitive from slavery; (2) forbid the use of the jails or other public property of the state for the detention of any such person before described; (3) and propose an amendment to the U.S. Constitution to forever separate the people of Massachusetts from all connection with slavery. The legislature agreed to most of the citizens' demands and passed an 1843 statute, popularly known as the Latimer Law, for "the protection of personal liberty." The statute prohibited all state officers and jail facilities from being used to assist in fugitive slave recapture. Several other northern states followed suit, enacting or strengthening personal liberty laws to protect against the loathsome practice. Vermont and Ohio passed laws in 1843, Connecticut in 1844, Pennsylvania in 1847, and Rhode Island in 1848. Although the *Prigg* decision had authorized fugitive slave rendition on a national level, northerners were intent upon making the practice too costly or time-consuming for slave owners to pursue. Southerners did not take this affront lying down. On January 3, 1850, Senator James Mason of Virginia announced his intention to introduce a bill that would strengthen the Fugitive Slave Law of 1793 and force northern states to comply. The resulting Fugitive Slave Law of 1850 would ultimately divide the nation, pushing it toward civil war.

FREDERICK DOUGLASS

The *Narrative of the Life of Frederick Douglass, An American Slave* launched its author into international celebrity. Since its publication in 1845, the book has been a touchstone of American literature and an archetype of redemptive autobiography. The first of his three autobiographies, the *Narrative* traced Douglass's early life in slavery to his freedom in the North. When the famed antislavery newspaper *The Liberator* announced the book's imminent publication on May 9, 1845, it made sure to state that it "was written entirely by Mr. Douglass." That a slave could write startled many; that one could write so powerfully simply astonished. Indeed, when whites protested that no slave could write such a book, Douglass agreed—an enslaved mind could never accomplish it. What more powerful antislavery statement existed? For years the North had heard testimony from whites about the evils of slavery, but it took the words of one who had lived the evils to authenticate the antislavery message. While many former slaves would speak from countless antislavery platforms, none

The North Star. Douglass's first newspaper was published weekly from 1847 to 1849 and intermittently in 1851.

spoke—or wrote—with the brilliance of Frederick Douglass.

"I was born in Tuckahoe, near Hillsborough, and about twelve miles from Easton, in Talbot county, Maryland. I have no accurate knowledge of my age. . . . By far the larger part of the slaves know as little of their ages as horses know of theirs, and it is the wish of most masters . . . to keep

Frederick Douglass (1818–95), daguerrotype, 1855.

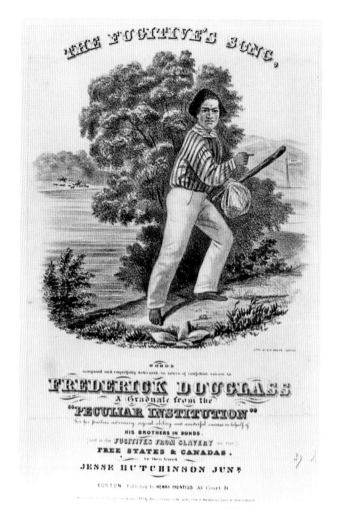

"The Fugitive's Song," sheet music cover, 1845. The song, marking Douglass's escape from slavery, was composed as a token of esteem by Jesse Hutchinson, Jr. It was performed by the Hutchinson Family Singers, a popular antislavery chorus.

their slaves thus ignorant."[2] Douglass (1818–95), who barely knew his mother and suspected that his owner was also his father, grew up in the cabin of his maternal grandparents. At about eight years of age, he was sent to the home of Hugh and Sophia Auld in Baltimore, where he lived for seven years in relative freedom. He taught himself to read, and at about thirteen he bought a copy of *The Columbian Orator,* a popular textbook with unmistakable antislavery influences. At about fifteen his owner shipped him to another plantation, to break the young Douglass of his growing self-possession—an undesirable trait that masters interpreted as unruliness. Douglass resented the efforts to "break" him and in a pivotal moment successfully challenged slavedriver Edward Covey's harsh discipline. As a result, Douglass was returned to Baltimore in 1836, where his labor was sold to a local shipyard, and he learned the caulking trade. Two years later, dressed as a sailor and carrying the free papers of another man, he escaped to New York City and freedom.

In August 1841 Douglass came to the attention of Boston's abolitionist community when William Lloyd Garrison heard him speak on Nantucket Island. "I shall never forget his first speech," Garrison wrote in the narrative's introduction, "the powerful impression it created upon a crowded auditory, completely taken by surprise—the applause which

followed from the beginning to the end of his felicitous remarks."[3] When Douglass completed his speech, Garrison rose and proclaimed that Patrick Henry never made a more eloquent address in defense of liberty.

Douglass's star rose meteorically, and he became the face—and voice—of the antislavery movement. He toured widely and quickly outgrew the limited role that his white colleagues imagined for him. By the time he published his *Narrative* in 1845, Douglass was impatient with the paternalism of his new associates, especially those who told him that he spoke too intelligently and that when addressing the public, he should put some of the old plantation talk in his speeches to keep his stories believable. He would have none of it and left for

England. The 1855 daguerreotype captures a man bursting with confidence, power, and success.

Having attracted enough backing, he launched his own independent newspaper, *The North Star.* Most black newspapers had perished or struggled with limited circulations. Published in his new home of Rochester, New York, *The North Star* (the first of Douglass's three antebellum newspapers) carried his uncompromising views on abolition, civil rights, women's rights, temperance, and many other reform movements. Its banner proclaimed "Right is of no Sex—Truth is of no Color." More important, the paper provided Douglass—and black abolitionism—with a monumental and independent voice.

CROSSCURRENTS OF 1848:
FRENCH ABOLITION AND THE *PEARL*

Abolition of Slavery in the French Colonies, by François-Auguste Biard, oil on canvas, 1849.

At midcentury the debate over the expansion of slavery reached a new level of intensity in the United States. In France, however, the tide turned in the opposite direction. France had ended slavery in 1794, in the afterglow of the French Revolution, but Napoleon reintroduced it in 1802, during the Haitian Revolution, shortly before he had Toussaint captured and brought to France. The European revolutions of 1848 led to the overthrow of the French king Louis-Philippe and had enormous consequences throughout Europe, but for blacks in the French Empire, one consequence in particular stood out: abolitionists came to positions of influence in the new government. They immediately sought an end to slavery. They worked with their British counterparts and ended Britain's insistence on searching French vessels for slaves on the high seas—which had been an enormous barrier to the growth of French antislavery sentiment. The French could now demand an immediate end to slavery without hearing the objection that abolition was a British plot to attack French wealth in the Caribbean. Antislavery petitions poured into the Chamber of Deputies, most important by French women, who rarely if ever signed legislative petitions. Even by the beginning of 1848—prior to the European revolutions—antislavery forces claimed to have thirty thousand petition signatures.

The Second Republic's provisional government convened a committee, led by abolitionist Victor Schoelcher, to write an emancipation act. After forty-three meetings, the committee on April 27, 1848, finally announced to the world that "slavery will be completely abolished in all the colonies and the French possessions, two months after the promulgation of the present decree in each of them." All members of the Second Republic's provisional government signed the decree, which freed all the slaves in Guadeloupe, Martinique, Réunion, Guiana, Senegal, and Madagascar. Slaves in Martinique, informed by British traders that the home government would end the institution of slavery, sped up the process by threatening a slave insurrection, which prompted the provisional governor of the island (and the governor of Martinique) to declare immediate emancipation. Fifteen years after the British Empire freed its slaves, France had followed suit.

In the United States, however, slavery grew. Not two weeks before the passage of the French emancipation law, and just as the federal government was

Daniel Drayton (1802?–57). Captain of the *Pearl,* Drayton authored *Personal Memoir of Daniel Drayton, for four years and four months a prisoner (for charity's sake) in Washington jail: including a narrative of the voyage and capture of the schooner Pearl.* (Boston: B. Marsh; New York: American and Foreign Anti-Slavery Society, 1855).

Mary (1832–53) and Emily (1835–95) Edmonson were born in Montgomery County, Maryland, as slaves. Their father was a free landowner, but they remained in bondage and hired out their work as servants to elite white families in Washington, D.C. The sisters and four of their brothers were among the seventy-seven would-be escapees on the *Pearl.* After their recapture, the sisters were sent to New Orleans to be sold, but fearing that their health might be damaged, their owners reshipped them to Alexandria, Virginia, where they did sewing and were locked up at night to prevent their escape. The famed Congregational minister and abolitionist Henry Ward Beecher arranged for the sisters' purchase on November 4, 1848. They became popular attractions on the antislavery circuit, and through Beecher and his sister, Harriet Beecher Stowe, they attended the Young Ladies Preparatory School at Oberlin College. In this 1850 daguerrotype, they are standing on either side of Gerrit Smith and behind Frederick Douglass.

celebrating the ascension of the new French Republic, an attempted slave escape in Washington, D.C., took the country by storm. On April 13 a white man named Daniel Drayton sailed the schooner *Pearl* to a local wharf. Edward Sayers, the ship's owner; Drayton (who was paid $100 for his services); the ship's cook, Chester English; two slaves, Paul Jennings and Samuel Edmonson; a free black couple, Daniel and Mary Bell; and William Chaplin, a daring abolitionist, worked together to assist several local slaves to escape. The well-organized black community in the District spread the word about the escape attempt, and on April 15, much to the astonishment of Sayers and Drayton, seventy-seven slaves marched through the night rain and boarded the *Pearl* in hopes of finding freedom. Among those fleeing were several members of the Edmonson family, including the young sisters Mary and Emily Edmonson.

The organizers planned to follow an improbable route, sailing down the Potomac River, up Chesapeake Bay, and to the Delaware River and Philadelphia. But bad weather kept them from proceeding very far, and the *Pearl* anchored near Point Lookout, off the southern tip

of the Maryland peninsula. Meanwhile, in Washington, a posse formed to find the escapees. They made no headway—until they received a tip from an unexpected source. Judson Diggs, an African American, had hauled materials to the wharf for one of the slaves, but the slave could not afford to pay him. Diggs, who also had been spurned by one of the Edmonson sisters, grew angry and retaliated by telling the slave catchers about the escape plan. The posse commandeered the steamship *Salem* and tracked down the *Pearl.* After taking control of the vessel, the posse brought the slaves back to Washington. The captives arrived to a waiting mob; one man in the crowd cut Drayton's ear with a knife. Police arrested Drayton and Sayers, although they believed English's excuse that he did not know the slaves had escaped.

Congressman Joshua Giddings visited the jailed conspirators to provide

legal advice, sparking outrage from the mob outside. Only a large number of police officers prevented the angry whites from lynching Giddings. During the trial, the congressman, reformer, and abolitionist Horace Mann provided legal defense, but Sayers and Drayton received life sentences. In 1852 President Millard Fillmore pardoned the two men. But most of the slaves met a different fate: those who had sought escape were consigned to the Bruin and Hill slave traders, which proceeded to break up the families and sell them to the Deep South. The Edmonson sisters, however, were bought and freed by the Reverend Henry Ward Beecher. With the financial help of his sister Harriet Beecher Stowe, the two attended Oberlin College and afterward appeared often on the antislavery lecture circuit. Although it failed, the *Pearl* incident was the largest peacetime slave escape attempt in American history.

RUSH FOR GOLD

The "whole country... is filled with gold." Northern newspapers from 1848 until the mid-1850s proclaimed that enormous wealth could be easily plucked from the ground in California. Even Frederick Douglass's *North Star* carried stories of the golden opportunity waiting in the West. In early 1850 Garrison's *Liberator* carried a report of San Francisco blacks who earned $100 to $300 a month—more than a year's income, for many—in the gold fields. In reality, few people black or white found wealth in the West, and most who did succeed accomplished that unlikely feat by selling supplies or services to miners rather than by being one, such as Levi Strauss, whose blue jeans we still wear. But enough true stories filtered back east to entice those seeking opportunity or an easy road to wealth. One black, known only as "Hector," a naval deserter, quickly earned $4,000 in gold, and another, remembered only as "Dick," earned the fabulous sum of $100,000 in gold, only to lose it on a San Francisco gaming table.

Blacks from across North America, nearly every major black community, many southern slaves, and many from the Caribbean found their way to the gold fields. Some others, like Samuel D. Burris of Delaware, fled to California to escape enslavement for his successful Underground Railroad activities. Rather than gold, Burris found security for his family and, later, the opportunity to build schools, fight for civil rights, and develop San Francisco's growing black community.

But for every story about success or fabulous wealth, blacks in the East could also read detailed accounts of the rampant discrimination awaiting them in the western territories: they could not

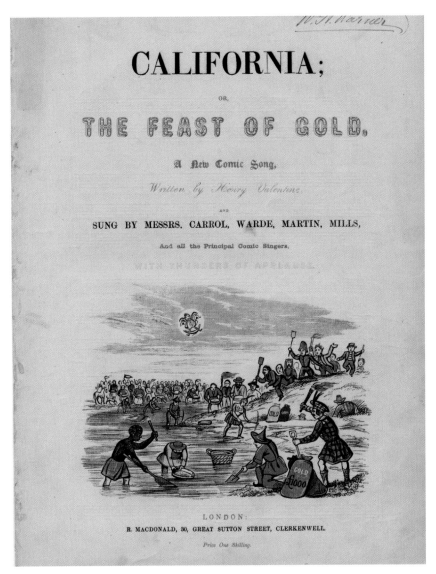

"California; or, The Feast of Gold," sheet music cover. Music like this captured the hysteria over the possibility of quick wealth.

vote or hold office there, provide testimony in court cases, or secure an education for their children. In fact, according to the 1850 census, only about seven hundred blacks resided in the territory (soon to become a state), and slightly less than half were slaves, brought by their owners to work the gold mines. Two years later the black population climbed to about two thousand. Half of them lived

in the mining districts, and most of the remainder lived in San Francisco or Sacramento; only forty-five lived in Los Angeles County.

For those who worked the mines and waterways in search of gold, the labor proved onerous, dirty, and at times dangerous. Whites, jealous of or threatened by a black individual's success, could expel blacks from an area in which they

White and black miners at Spanish Flat, California, 1852.

Black gold miner in Auburn Ravine, California, 1852.

had worked for many months, or simply kill them. Thus, black prospectors and miners formed mutual aid societies or companies to protect their interests. Because the region attracted so many people from around the world, black miners sometimes formed cooperative agreements with white immigrants—Germans and Scots, for instance—who opposed slavery or who simply did not share American racial prejudices. European immigrants also benefited from business projects such as dam construction, and they occasionally formed joint ventures with blacks to exploit a claim. Blacks also enjoyed a great deal of cooperation with the Mexicans and Chinese who were brought in specifically for their labor. The various nonwhite groups generally had good relations, but when conflict arose, none of them could obtain legal recourse, as the court system—where it existed—accepted testimony only from whites.

HARRIET TUBMAN, AMERICAN ICON

In 1849, Harriet Tubman, fearing that the recent death of her master would mean her sale into the Deep South—the fate of three of her sisters—ran away from her Maryland owners. Born Araminta Ross on Maryland's eastern shore about 1822, Tubman had eight siblings and grew up in a mixed community of free and enslaved African Americans. Even as a child, she resisted her enslavement and once hid from her mistress for five days, fearing a beating for stealing a lump of sugar. As a teenager, she was ordered to participate in the punishment of a fellow slave who had left his owner's property without permission. When she refused to help tie down the man to prepare him for a beating, the overseer smashed her skull with a two-pound weight. For the rest of her life, she would be plagued with narcoleptic seizures. The incident, and the sale of her niece and the niece's daughter, convinced her and her brothers to escape. Her husband, a free black named John Tubman whom she had married in about 1844, refused to participate, and her brothers soon abandoned the attempt. Harriet, however, left her husband and walked across Maryland and Delaware, trekking to Philadelphia and Cape May, New Jersey, where she found labor as a cook, domestic, and laundress.

Harriet Tubman (1822?–1913). This photograph was taken by H. B. Lindsley, probably around the time of the Civil War.

Swing Low: A Memorial to Harriet Tubman, by Alison Saar, 2007.

Railroad quickly took on mythic status that only grew with the passage of time. For generations she has symbolized the African American quest for freedom and resistance to slavery. She has been the subject of countless depictions, most notably by the black artists Aaron Douglas and Jacob Lawrence.

Less known but equally astonishing was Tubman's work during the Civil War. In 1862, she traveled to Union-occupied South Carolina and tended to wounded soldiers and freedpeople; she also cooked and sold food to local residents. She roamed the region, acting as a spy. She gathered information on Confederate supplies and troop disposition, which she shared with the Union command. She became well acquainted with Colonel James Montgomery of the Second South Carolina Volunteers, an African American infantry regiment, and provided him with invaluable military intelligence. One of her missions up the Combahee River resulted in the seizure of Confederate supplies and the liberation of 756 slaves. At war's end she traveled to Virginia, where she nursed black patients at the James River contraband hospital, and then she became the matron of the black hospital at Fortress Monroe, which had housed contraband since the beginning of the war.

In 1869 she married Nelson Davis, a former Union soldier who was twenty years younger than she. For twenty-five years Tubman attempted to receive a pension from the federal government in recognition of her wartime service. Colonel Thomas Wentworth Higginson, the former commander of the First South Carolina Volunteers, and General Rufus Saxton, the former head of the Department of the South, both lobbied on Tubman's behalf, but to no avail. In 1888, however, two years after her husband's death, Tubman (who retained her name) received a widow's pension.

Determined to have as much of her family with her as possible, within a year Tubman returned to Maryland to begin rescuing family members. The new Fugitive Slave Law made such exploits all the more dangerous, and by 1855 she had moved to the black community in St. Catharines, Ontario, Canada. She then returned to Maryland to retrieve her elderly parents, an extraordinary feat since they had to travel by wagon. With the help of New York's William Seward (later Lincoln's secretary of state), she settled them on property in Auburn, New York, where Tubman herself would later reside.

While exact numbers will never be known, Tubman made fourteen trips back to Maryland and liberated at least seventy slaves and gave assistance to others who may have indirectly freed another fifty. Fearless and determined, she carried a gun during her trips south and preferred to travel in winter when the days were shortest. She became intimately familiar with the best routes and took full advantage of the underground resistance movement, in which African Americans and white abolitionists (mostly Quakers) provided safe houses and helped move slaves north to vigilance committees in Philadelphia, New York, Boston, and elsewhere.

Tubman's labors in the Underground

THE *ROBERTS* CASE AND THE BIRTH OF JIM CROW

Abiel Smith School, Boston's segregated school on the north side of Beacon Hill, founded in 1835.

More than a century before the Supreme Court's landmark 1954 *Brown v. Board of Education* decision struck down racial segregation of public schools, Boston abolitionists sought to establish equal education rights for black schoolchildren. By the 1790s Massachusetts had largely abolished slavery, but segregated schools remained one of the last strongholds of institutionalized racial prejudice.

In 1848, in an effort to put an end to the offensive practice, one of Boston's most vocal black civil rights activists, Benjamin Roberts, tried to enroll his five-year-old daughter, Sarah, in a public school near their home. The whites-only school rejected Sarah, and her father filed suit. He hired Robert Morris, the

first black lawyer admitted to the bar in Massachusetts, to sue the school board and the city of Boston for its requirement that black and white children must attend separate schools. *Roberts v. City of Boston,* the first case challenging school segregation in the North, reached the Supreme Judicial Court of Massachusetts in 1850. Morris, along with his co-counsel, the young lawyer, abolitionist, and future U.S. senator Charles Sumner, argued that the constitution of Massachusetts guaranteed that "all men, without distinction of color or race, are equal before the law." They asserted, "The separation of children in the public schools of Boston, on account of color or race, is in the nature of caste, and is a violation of equality."[4]

Chief Justice Lemuel Shaw, however, was unmoved by Sumner and Morris's arguments. In his opinion delivered in March 1850, Shaw maintained that "prejudice, if it exists, is not created by law, and probably cannot be changed by law."[5] The school committee decided that separate schools would best serve the needs of both groups of children. As such, the city could rightfully require separate facilities.

Despite the disappointing outcome, activists persisted in their efforts to strike down the city's racist policy. Led by Roberts and other abolitionists, particularly the black leader William Cooper Nell, they moved their dispute out of the courtroom and into the streets, launching demonstrations and school

Robert Morris (1823–82). Morris was likely the second African American to practice law in the United States. The Salem-born Morris moved to Boston at the age of thirteen and trained under the antislavery attorney Ellis Gray Loring. He passed the state bar in 1847, then used his skills (as the NAACP would in the next century) to attack the legal structure of racism. Although he initiated the *Roberts* case, he deferred to Charles Sumner as the lead attorney.

"Jim Crow," one of the most popular racist characterizations of African Americans in the nineteenth century.

Charles Sumner (1811–74). A founder of Massachusetts's Free Soil Party in 1848, Sumner won election to the U.S. Senate as a Democrat in 1851 and later joined the Republican Party, becoming one of its leading radicals. He is perhaps best remembered for the beating he received in the Senate chamber from South Carolina congressman Preston Brooks on May 22, 1856.

boycotts and sending petitions to legislators. Nell's Equal School Association had been rallying against Boston's segregated schools since the 1840s, and following the failure of the *Roberts* case the organization appealed to the legislative branch to end public school segregation. An 1851 bill failed, but after several years the protestation and petitioning paid off. In March 1855 the Massachusetts legislature enacted a bill prohibiting segregation in schools, and it was signed into law the following month.

While integrationists ultimately triumphed in Massachusetts, segregationists prevailed on the national level. *Roberts v. City of Boston* provided a persuasive precedent for the "separate but equal" doctrine pronounced by the U.S. Supreme Court in *Plessy v. Ferguson* (1896). Shaw's reasoning, which *Plessy* enshrined into constitutional law, would be used to uphold racial segregation for more than fifty years. While "Jim Crow" is customarily associated with the South's institutionalization of segregation, it was actually born in Boston.

PART FIVE

EMERGENCE

1850–1860

THE NEW FUGITIVE SLAVE LAW

By the 1840s slavery had weakened the bonds of union throughout the United States. The annexation of Texas, the 1848 Mexican Cession, and the settlement of lands previously acquired increased the likelihood that the "peculiar institution" would spread westward. The growing number of abolitionists and the rising power of the South within the federal government caused countless political clashes and intense sectional rivalry. In an attempt to defuse a growing political crisis, the Congress stitched together a series of compromises: ending the slave trade in Washington, D.C., and admitting California as a free state.

Most controversial of all, it legislated a particularly pugnacious strengthening of the 1793 Fugitive Slave Law. The 1793 law explicitly authorized the recapture of runaway slaves and authorized state or federal magistrates to issue certificates of removal to return slaves from one state to another. It had long been contentious: slaveholders argued that the law simply reinforced their constitutional right to reclaim their human property, while northern opponents viewed it as loathsome and offensive. High-profile cases, such as George Latimer's in Boston in 1842, led many northern states to enact personal liberty laws to prevent state officials and facilities from aiding slave renditions. Although

the Supreme Court in *Prigg v. Pennsylvania* (1842) upheld the constitutionality of the 1793 law, enforcement was left to federal authorities and often became too

"The Fugitive Slave Law," broadside, published in Hartford, Connecticut, by S. M. Africanus, 1850.

costly and time-consuming for slaveholders to pursue.

On January 3, 1850, Senator James Mason of Virginia announced his intention to introduce a bill that would strengthen the 1793 law to compel

the North's cooperation. Senators on both sides opposed the bill, claiming it did not go far enough to protect their respective interests. A month later, Senator Henry Clay of Kentucky adopted the idea as part of his compromise bill. Clay, along with the great unionist senator Daniel Webster of Massachusetts, persuaded many to accept a new fugitive slave law for the larger sake of preserving the Union. Debate raged in Congress for the better part of the year, but President Millard Fillmore signed the new law on September 18, 1850.

The new Fugitive Slave Law authorized the appointment of fugitive slave commissioners who would issue warrants for the arrest of runaway slaves. The commissioner was charged with determining whether an accused fugitive matched the claimant's description of his escaped slave. The alleged fugitive could not testify on his own behalf, and no jury was allowed to hear the case. The commissioner received his pay from the slaveholder claimant—five dollars if the alleged fugitive was released, but ten dollars if the prisoner was returned to the claimant—a provision that provoked intense derision among the law's northern opponents. The law further provided that anyone interfering with rendition proceedings or attempting to rescue, aid, or harbor a fugitive could be fined as much as $1,000, jailed for up to

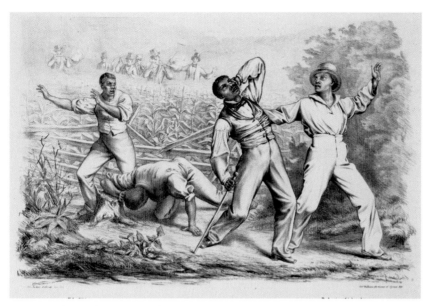

Effects of the Fugitive-Slave-Law, published by Hoff and Bloede, 1850.

"Caution!!" broadside, April 24, 1851. Abolitionists posted this sheet around the city of Boston.

six months, and possibly charged with treason.

Passage of the new law set thousands of blacks fleeing to Canada, fearing arrest and enslavement. Black and white abolitionists who rallied against the law formed new Underground Railroad "stations" and rescue leagues. In Boston black churches became vital links in underground activities and centers of resistance to the law. Despite the law's threat to punish violators, resistance continued and occasionally turned violent. Vigilance committees, vowing to thwart slave catchers by any means necessary, organized throughout the North and rescued several slaves facing recapture. Still, hundreds of fugitive slaves were returned to their owners, even as late as June 1863; the law would not be repealed until 1864. Although it was intended as part of the compromise package designed to decrease tensions between North and South, it ultimately increased the likelihood of civil war.

Church of the Fugitive Slaves in Boston, engraving, 1856. This depiction of Leonard A. Grimes's Twelfth Baptist Church comes from Charles Emery Stevens's *Anthony Burns, a History.*

RESISTING THE FUGITIVE SLAVE LAW

The Christiana Tragedy, wood engraving, 1872. This depiction comes from William Still's *The Underground Railroad* (Philadelphia: Porter, 1872).

Under the strict provisions of the Fugitive Slave Law, the alleged fugitive was not permitted to testify on his own behalf, no jury was allowed to hear the case, and anyone interfering with rendition proceedings or attempting to rescue, aid, or harbor a fugitive could be fined as much as $1,000 or jailed for up to six months. In the first full year of the law's enforcement, four major events called attention to its injustices and revealed how much it forced the North to bend to the will of the South.

Boston abolitionists achieved an early victory in the fight against slave rendition. Shadrach Minkins, born into slavery in the early 1800s, had been sold to John Debree, a purser in the U.S. Navy. In May 1850, Minkins fled to Boston, where he worked at the Cornhill Coffee House as a waiter under the assumed name Frederick Jenkins. With the passage

of the Fugitive Slave Law four months later, Minkins's refuge in Boston was no longer safe. In February 1851, Norfolk constable John Caphart arrived in Boston to reclaim Debree's escaped property. On February 15, federal authorities issued a warrant for Minkins's arrest. News of his seizure spread quickly, and the Boston Vigilance Committee sprang into action—attorneys Robert Morris (one of the nation's first black lawyers), Richard Henry Dana, Jr., and Ellis Gray Loring came to his aid. While the lawyers planned his defense, a large crowd, mostly African American, stormed the courtroom and grabbed the prisoner. They hurried him out of the building, through the courthouse square, and off to Cambridge. Next they shuttled him through the Underground Railroad system to Montreal, beyond the reach of federal authorities. Eight men were

indicted for aiding in Minkins's escape, but the federal government proved unable to secure even one conviction against the rescuers.

Following this embarrassing defeat, the federal government determined to flex its muscle and enforce the law stringently. On April 3, Thomas Sims was arrested in Boston on charges of theft and placed in the custody of the U.S. marshal. Sims, who maintained that he was a free man, had arrived in Boston in February 1851. James Potter, a Georgia slave owner, sent his agents to Boston to bring Sims back to his plantation. Large crowds gathered at Courthouse Square, and the Boston Vigilance Committee met to devise a rescue plan. This time, however, the government reacted swiftly, with increased police presence. It placed chains around the courthouse to keep the protesters at bay, an image

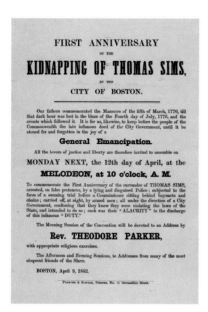

"First Anniversary of the Kidnapping of Thomas Sims," broadside, April 9, 1852.

that abolitionists used to maximum effect. The mayor of Boston called out the militia to secure the courthouse, and the federal troops were placed on alert at the nearby Charlestown Navy Yard. The heavy guard made a courtroom rescue like that of Minkins impossible. The vigilance committee hatched a plan to have Sims jump from his third-floor cell into a pile of mattresses placed below.

Lewis Hayden (1811–89). Hayden escaped Kentucky slavery in 1844 with his wife and a son and rose to become a leader of the Boston black abolitionist community. He became a confidant of Governor John A. Andrew and, after the Civil War, a Massachusetts state senator. No one in Boston, white or black, could match his energy on behalf of fugitive slaves.

But the night of the planned escape, iron bars were placed in Sims's cell window, thwarting the rescue. On April 11, Commissioner George Ticknor Curtis ordered Thomas Sims to be returned to his owner. Early the next morning a force of three hundred armed guards marched the accused fugitive to the wharf; Sims then boarded the *Acorn*, bound for Savannah.

In rural Christiana, Pennsylvania, blacks took up arms to thwart an attempt to recapture fugitive slaves. On September 11, 1851, Maryland plantation owner Edward Gorsuch, his son, and a nephew arrived in Christiana in search of four escaped slaves, Noah Buley, Nelson Ford, George Hammond, and Joshua Hammond. A team of U.S. marshals led Gorsuch and his men to the home of William Parker, where they believed two of the runaways had taken refuge. As the party neared the home, onlookers sounded horns to alert others of the slave catchers' presence. A crowd of about a hundred responded to the alert and arrived armed with guns and clubs to fight Gorsuch and his men. The crowd attacked the would-be capturers. Shots rang out, and Gorsuch fell dead; his son was severely wounded; three others died before the incident ended. Parker and the Gorsuch slaves fled to Canada. President Millard Fillmore sent a group of marines to investigate the shootings, and thirty-eight people were arrested. Ultimately, however, the government secured no convictions, and charges were dropped for lack of evidence. Southerners fumed that the rioters had evaded punishment, and the Fillmore administration became deeply embarrassed by yet another failure to enforce the law.

Two weeks later, in Syracuse, New York, additional, organized opposition broke out. Fugitive slave William McHenry (popularly known as Jerry) was arrested on October 1 and taken into custody for a hearing in front of Commissioner Joseph F. Sabine. Jerry, a robust and handsome slave born in Bun-

Jermain Wesley Loguen (1813–72). Engraving from *The Rev. J. W. Loguen, as a Slave and as a Freeman: A Narrative of Real Life* (Syracuse: J. G. K. Truair, 1859). Loguen was an AME Zion clergyman and abolitionist leader. He escaped slavery in Tennessee in 1835 and traveled to Canada, where he received an education, then attended the famed Oneida Institute. Afterward he opened several black schools and received his ordination in 1842. He founded six churches in western New York and worked with Frederick Douglass and other abolitionists on the Underground Railroad. As a minister in Syracuse, he became one of the leading figures in the Jerry Rescue.

Samuel Joseph May (1797–1871). This Boston-born minister was a radical abolitionist, temperance and peace advocate, education reformer, and early supporter of women's rights. He moved to Syracuse in 1845 to take up the city's only Unitarian pulpit. He agonized over the legitimacy of using violence to free fugitive slaves, but overcame his reservations to become one of the leaders of the Jerry Rescue.

Samuel Ringgold Ward (1817?–66). This leading black abolitionist ministered to a white Congregational church in Cortland, New York, where he edited an antislavery newspaper and joined the abolitionist Liberty Party. On October 1, 1851, he helped other conspirators, white and black, to rescue the fugitive slave Jerry McHenry in Syracuse. The photo comes from Ward's *Autobiography of a Fugitive Negro* (London: John Snow, 1855).

Boston Courthouse, where abolitionists rescued Shadrach Minkins.

combe County, North Carolina, had been sold in Missouri and in 1843 escaped from his new master, John McReynolds of Marian County. His arrest coincided with the annual Liberty Party convention, an abolitionist political group formed in 1840. When news of his arrest spread, a crowd of two thousand or more gathered outside the courthouse. The protesters attempted to rescue Jerry, but he was recaptured and incarcerated at the commissioner's office. That afternoon the local vigilance committee and Liberty Party members met to discuss plans for Jerry's liberation. Activists such as the wealthy abolitionist and congressman Gerrit Smith, Unitarian

minister Samuel Joseph May, and two local black ministers and abolitionists—Samuel Ringgold Ward and Jermain Wesley Loguen—agreed to take action. That night, as the crowd outside the jail swelled to three thousand, a group charged the door with a battering ram, broke into the jail, and carried Jerry out of the building.

After a few days in hiding, Jerry crossed the border to Canada, where he lived until his death two years later. Once again the Fillmore administration sought to punish those who had aided in the rescue effort. The grand jury indicted twenty-six individuals, but only one, a black man named Enoch Reed,

was convicted, but not under the Fugitive Slave Law. Instead, he was charged with resisting a federal officer discharging his official duties. The government secured no other convictions, but Syracuse abolitionists swore out an arrest warrant for McReynolds's agent and charged the marshal who had arrested Jerry with violating the state's 1840 personal liberty law. While newspapers throughout the South railed against the Jerry Rescuers and condemned their conduct as treason, antislavery forces celebrated what they saw as a great defense of liberty, and each year until the Civil War, the city celebrated "Jerry Rescue Day."

MARTIN R. DELANY AND
HARRIET BEECHER STOWE

Two landmark books that altered the course of African American and American history appeared in 1852. Martin R. Delany (1812–85) was born to a slave father and a free black mother in Virginia. His mother fled to Pennsylvania to evade punishment for teaching her children to read, and his father joined them the following year after purchasing his own freedom. The young Delany excelled in school and later began an internship with a white doctor in Pittsburgh, then gained acceptance to Harvard Medical School in 1850. While he would eventually practice medicine, his time at Harvard did not last long—protests from white students forced him and two black classmates out of the school.

Even before Harvard, Delany had

"Little Eva reading to Uncle Tom." This image, from *Uncle Tom's Cabin,* represents one rendering of the scene. Scores of different versions of this scene exist. Publication of *Uncle Tom's Cabin* began in the abolitionist weekly *The National Era,* 1851–52.

"Eliza's Flight," sheet music cover, 1852. This song by E. J. Loder was just one of innumerable songs and plays that appeared after publication of Stowe's novel.

been writing about racial issues. Beginning in 1843, he published the newspaper *The Mystery,* and four years later he joined Frederick Douglass in Rochester, New York, to coedit *The North Star,* staying until 1849. Toward the end of his time in Rochester, Delany began to emphasize black self-sufficiency in his writings. Equally important, when the 1850 Fugitive Slave Law brought the reach of slavery into the North, Delany reconsidered his previous opposition to emigration plans.

He solidified his reputation as one of the most radical American abolitionists with his 1852 work, *The Condition, Elevation, Emigration and Destiny of the Colored People of the United States.* It served as an inspiring foundation for the early black nationalist movement, but abolitionists—black and white—bristled at its call for blacks to leave the United States. To African Americans who insisted on their right to full American citizenship, Delany's call for emigration sounded uncomfortably

Harriet Beecher Stowe (1811–96). The daughter and wife of ministers, she authored or edited about twenty books.

similar to the American Colonization Society's unwanted schemes and undercut the foundation of black abolitionism.

Delany, however, asserted that racial discrimination ran so deep in American society that free blacks could never achieve equality. Undeterred by the criticism of his peers, he organized emigration conferences in the following years. He advanced a variety of emigration plans, first to Canada and then, in 1854, to the West Indies, Central America, and South America. Just before the Civil War, Delany even considered the possibility of resettling in Africa and, with fellow explorer Robert Campbell, explored Liberia and the Niger Valley. The emigration movement peaked at the beginning of the Civil War. Delany returned to the United States, worked as a recruiter for black troops, and eventually received a major's commission, making him the highest-ranking African American in the war.

With its incisive critique of American racism, Delany's *Condition, Elevation, Emigration and Destiny of the Colored People* would remain a powerful text for succeeding generations of African Americans.

But an antislavery novel by a New England white woman, published at the same time, struck a far more resounding moral chord. That the story of Lincoln greeting Harriet Beecher Stowe with the words "So you're the little woman who wrote the book that made this great war!" is sometimes represented as apocryphal hardly diminishes its point (certainly, James McPherson's reporting of it makes a strong case for its accuracy): Stowe's novel *Uncle Tom's Cabin* (1852) radically altered the national conversation about slavery.

The daughter of an influential clergyman and a member of an astonishing family that included nineteenth-century America's most influential minister, Henry Ward Beecher, she lived in Connecticut before moving with her family to Cincinnati. In 1836, she married Calvin Stowe, with whom she would eventually move to Brunswick, Maine, where he was a professor of American religion at Bowdoin College. It was during her years in Ohio that Harriet Beecher Stowe developed a political consciousness and became an outspoken critic of slavery. Like Delany, she felt outrage over the 1850 Fugitive Slave Law; in Cincinnati she came under the influence of evangelical abolitionists and received a firsthand education in the workings of the Underground Railroad. Also like Delany, she turned her disgust with slavery into words of protest.

Perhaps encouraged by the solitude of the Maine woods, she reflected on the debate raging over the Fugitive Slave Law and what she had seen in Ohio. She always said that the hand of God had moved her pen, but divinely or otherwise, she became inspired. Little point existed in cataloging the many crimes of slavery, as she memorably wrote— the thing itself was a crime against God. *Uncle Tom's Cabin* made its first appearance in *The National Era*, an antislavery newspaper, serialized between June 1851 and April 1852 under the title "The Man That Was a Thing." It appeared in book form in March and has remained in print ever since. During the 1850s and afterward, several versions of the book ran simultaneously as plays in New York and reached an unprecedented level of popularity. *Uncle Tom's Cabin* sold more than 300,000 copies in 1852. A host of Southern versions sought to refute Stowe's so-called exaggerations and distortions and reveal the "true" paternalism of slavery. Stowe's complex narrative actually displayed many sides of slavery, while centering on its inherent evil. Kindly slaveholders, who even treated their property as family members, in the end could offer no lasting protection to human chattel.

Primary among its black characters are Eliza Harris and Uncle Tom, both owned by Arthur Shelby, a relatively kind slave owner. When Harris finds out that Shelby plans to sell his slaves to pay off his debt, she escapes with her child, traveling to Ohio, memorably crossing a frozen Ohio River with the child in her arms; she eventually meets up with her husband at a Quaker settlement. The family successfully makes the journey to Canada and to freedom. Uncle Tom, on the other hand, stays behind and meets a much different fate. Augustine St. Clare purchases him and, at the behest of his daughter, eventually agrees to free him. But Augustine dies before finalizing Tom's emancipation. His new owner is Simon Legree, a brutal

Martin R. Delany (1812–85). Delany is best remembered for his *Condition, Elevation, Emigration and Destiny of the Colored People of the United States*. He also served in the Union army and received the rank of major, the highest rank achieved by an African American during the Civil War.

man—originally from the North—who unleashes a reign of terror on Tom that eventually kills him.

Although *Uncle Tom* mania seized the North, black abolitionists ultimately found the book objectionable, since Stowe's only answer for the problem of slavery was colonization, a denial of the African American right to full citizenship. While modern eyes see little but submission in the Uncle Tom character, Stowe and the nineteenth-century North admired his Christlike endurance of suffering and ultimately of death, displaying what Stowe viewed as the noble and Christian character of African Americans.

INSTITUTE FOR COLORED YOUTH

Based on a bequest from the Quaker philanthropist Richard Humphreys, the Institute for Colored Youth (ICY) became the most important black school in Philadelphia. Opening as a high school in 1837, the ICY erected a spacious building in 1852, in the heart of the city's African American community. Charles L. Reason, a black abolitionist leader and the nation's first black college professor, served as principal until 1855, instituting a challenging classical curriculum, founding a library, and establishing a public lecture program. For the faculty, he drew on the city's back elite, including Grace A. Mapps and her cousin Sarah Mapps Douglass. He proved an able leader and increased school enrollment from 6 students to 118 by the time he left.

Also in 1855, the school hired Robert Campbell as an instructor of geography, natural sciences, algebra, and Latin. Born in Kingston, Jamaica, Campbell lectured as well for the city's Banneker Institute, a private black literary and debating society for the young black sons of elite families. To develop his knowledge of science, Campbell attempted to enroll in a lecture series at the Franklin Institute, but was barred because of his race. The incident made him an instant abolitionist, and thereafter he assisted in Underground Railroad activities. Sickened by the depth of

The Institute for Colored Youth. This photograph comes from Fanny Jackson Coppin's *Reminiscences of School Life, and Hints on Teaching* (Philadelphia: L. J. Coppin, 1913).

American racial prejudice, he became an advocate of black emigration to Africa and the Caribbean.

Ebenezer D. C. Bassett, who later became the nation's first black diplomat, took over from Reason as principal. He diminished the curriculum's emphasis upon science and moved it toward civics and reform. He invited many prominent black leaders, like Frederick Douglass and Henry Highland Garnet, to offer public lectures. The school also developed a teacher-training program and produced many black faculty members for the city's segregated schools.

During the Civil War the ICY became a hub of recruitment for the black regiments. In 1869, Fanny Jackson Coppin (1837–1913), a graduate of Oberlin College, became the director of the school's teacher preparatory department and within a year doubled its enrollment. The school's managers recognized her abilities and talents as a public speaker and made her principal the following year. She abolished corporal punishment and built a solid and enduring relationship among parents, students, and faculty. Her administration and the academic achievement of her students became so well known that visitors flocked to the school to see her work firsthand.

Coppin built on the high caliber of the teachers at the ICY and hired the best black faculty the nation produced. She added Richard T. Greener, the first black graduate of Harvard College, to the English department; Edward Bouchet, Yale's first black graduate, to head the science program; and Philadelphia's Octavius V. Catto, who had graduated from the ICY in 1858 and become a prominent educator and political leader, to assume

Fanny Jackson Coppin (1837–1913).

direction of the school's "Boys' Department." Coppin was so successful that she remained at the helm for twenty-one years, becoming a prominent educational leader and public intellectual.

She expanded the school and added the kind of industrial education that would later be advanced by Booker T. Washington, without diminishing the emphasis on teacher training. As she remarked in her 1913 *Reminiscences:*

The Academic Department of the Institute had been so splendidly successful in proving that the Negro youth was equally capable as others in mastering a higher education, that no argument was necessary to establish its need, but the broad ground of education by which the masses must become self-supporting was, to me, a matter of painful anxiety. Frederick Douglass once said, it was easier to get a colored boy into a lawyer's office than into a blacksmith shop; and on account of the inflexibility of the Trades Unions, this condition of affairs still continues, making it necessary for us to have our own "blacksmith shop."[1]

Although many of the city's black elite resented the emphasis on vocational training, the program proved an enormous success. Students who desired to learn the printing, shoemaking, and dressmaking businesses, or carpentry and metalwork, had no other options but the ICY. By the 1890s the school added typing and stenography to the list of course offerings. In just two months after the opening of the voca-

Charles L. Reason (1818–93). New York City–born and educated at the African Free School, Reason became a leading black abolitionist. Rejected for the Episcopal ministry because of his race, he became an educator and professor at the interracial New York Central College in McGrawville. In 1852, he left Central College for teaching at the ICY. Engraving by J. C. Buttre (1821–93), from Julia Griffiths, *Autographs for Freedom* (1854).

tional department, 325 students signed up for the program's waiting list. Before the end of the century, three-fourths of all the black teachers in the Philadelphia–New Jersey area had graduated from the ICY.

THE BLACK SWAN

On March 31, 1853, more than two thousand people jammed New York City's Metropolitan Hall to hear the voice of Elizabeth T. Greenfield. The Leontyne Price of her era, Greenfield had astonishing vocal range and depth, perhaps reaching more than three octaves, a talent she displayed across the United States and in Europe.

Her rise to stardom began in slavery in Natchez, Mississippi. Born about 1817, she was the property of a wealthy Quaker widow, Elizabeth Holliday Greenfield, who moved to Philadelphia in the 1820s. She lived in freedom, and when her mistress died in 1845, she received only a token inheritance, as Greenfield relatives contested the will. The young songstress probably sang at church events and at private parties before a more formal debut in Baltimore about 1849. In October 1851, a Buffalo

Elizabeth T. Greenfield (1817?–76), by John William Orr, engraving, 1873.

attorney and his wife heard Greenfield sing, became her patrons, and promoted her to other city elites.

She soon gained local renown and received very favorable comparisons to the great Swedish singer, Jenny Lind (the "Swedish Nightingale"), and Catherine Hayes (the "Irish Swan"). Initially dubbed the "African Nightingale," Greenfield quickly became known as the "Black Swan." Less than a year later she began a national tour, gaining additional fame virtually by the day. Her concert at the Metropolitan in New York catapulted her into international celebrity but also brought out racists, who belittled her with the sobriquet "African Crow" and protested the interracial audiences that flocked to her performances.

She then traveled to London, where she met Lord Shaftesbury and other wealthy Britons. Impressed with her talent, the Duchess of Sutherland became her patron. Additional training during her English sojourn led to a performance for Queen Victoria on May 10, 1854. She won the queen's admiration—and a financial gift—which raised her spirits and eased the uncertainties of her life. She returned to the United States in July 1854 and toured major American cities, which she continued in the midst of the Civil War. Finally she settled in Philadelphia, where she founded the Black Swan Opera Troupe. She took on many students in her later years, including Carrie Thomas, who would become the leading soprano of the Hampton Institute Singers. Testifying to the persistence of her fame, Harry H. Pace in the early 1920s named his legendary recording company after her: Black Swan Record Company.

CLOTEL; OR, THE PRESIDENT'S DAUGHTER AND COLORED PATRIOTS OF THE AMERICAN REVOLUTION

At a time when northern whites considered African Americans to be incapable of sustained thought, the large number of publications by black abolitionists, and especially former slaves, became powerful antislavery acts. The many black-authored newspapers, pamphlets, petitions, essays, historical studies, personal narratives, fiction, and poetry, dating back to the eighteenth century, created a black presence in the arena of public debate and refuted stereotypes about the limits of black intelligence. People of African descent had a long history of publication, especially in Europe, where the first novel by an African American appeared in 1853.

William Wells Brown, born a slave in 1815 in Lexington, Kentucky, lived in St. Louis with his owners and hired out his labor to a wide variety of employers, including Elijah P. Lovejoy, the Illinois editor who was murdered in 1837 defending his antislavery newspaper. Brown also worked on a number of steamboats that plied the Mississippi

William Wells Brown (1815–84).

River delivering slaves to New Orleans. His first escape attempt ended with his mother shipped south to the Louisiana slave markets; then Brown successfully fled on January 1, 1834. He made his way to Cleveland, where he helped other runaways get to Canada. In the 1840s, he moved to Boston and gained renown as an eloquent antislavery lecturer. Publication of his *Narrative* in 1847 made him an international star. Fearing recapture, he traveled to Europe in 1849, meeting many European leaders and intellectuals including Victor Hugo and Alexis de Tocqueville. Friends collected a fund to secure his freedom, whereupon Brown returned to the United States in 1854, the year after publication of his novel *Clotel; or, The President's Daughter*.

The novel focuses on the tragic ordeal of Clotel, a beautiful sixteen-year-old quadroon and daughter of President Thomas Jefferson. Playing off rumors that had circulated for about fifty years that Jefferson had sired children with his slave Sally Hemings, Brown used the conventions of the sentimental novel and irony to expose the hypocrisy of American democracy. Brown, who wrote with authority on the subject of slavery, traced the struggles of Clotel and her daughter Mary against rapacious masters and the inhuman system of bondage. Clotel, who has been sold south, escapes and attempts to rescue her daughter. She is caught, however, and sent to the slave pens in the nation's

"The Death of Clotel," illustration from the 1853 edition of *Clotel; or, The President's Daughter* (London: Partridge and Oakey).

capital. Determined to be free, she escapes again, but slave catchers corner her on a bridge over the Potomac River. Rather than submit to reenslavement, she leaps to her death. Her daughter continues the freedom struggle and after a series of plot twists ends her days free in Europe with her lover—an associate of Nat Turner—but never able to return to the United States lest she be reenslaved. Brown revisited the novel three times, publishing variations of the book under different titles in 1860, 1864, and 1867. The final version included new chapters on the Civil War and a daring rescue of ninety-three soldiers from the notorious Andersonville Confederate prison.

Two years after the first edition of *Clotel,* William Cooper Nell published *The Colored Patriots of the American Revolution.* As a schoolboy, Nell, born in Boston in 1816, had felt the bitter sting of racial prejudice when city fathers denied him the Franklin Medal, a citywide academic award, because he was black. He later interned in a Boston law office but never practiced. Instead, in 1831 he began a career-long association with William Lloyd Garrison, *The Liberator,* and the fight for civil rights. He briefly assisted Frederick Douglass in Rochester, publishing *The North Star,* but soon returned to Boston and *The Liberator.* He ran the newspaper office and led movements

to end desegregation in many Boston facilities, including public schools, performance halls, and the railway. In 1850, he ran for the state legislature on the Free Soil ticket. He also researched the history of black military service and in 1851 published a booklet, *Services of Colored Americans in the Wars of 1776 and 1812.*

Four years later he completed the influential *Colored Patriots,* the first assessment of the African American military role in the nation's struggle for independence and in the War of 1812. The text creatively used oral history and careful scholarship to trace the black

military contribution. With important prefatory remarks by Harriet Beecher Stowe and abolitionist Wendell Phillips, the book stood as a monument to black courage and patriotism, even though, as Phillips remarked, blacks had been "denied a country."[2] The book proved more wide-ranging than its title implied, showing connections to Nell's own times and offering important biographical information on other black leaders and events such as the 1822 Denmark Vesey plot in Charleston.

Perhaps among the book's greatest achievements was its influence on the Boston merchant and Republican political activist George Livermore, leading him to craft his own careful exploration of the Founding Fathers' attitudes toward black military recruitment during the Revolution. Livermore's 1862 *Historical Research Respecting the Opinions of the Founders of the Republic on Negroes as Slaves, as Citizens, and as Soldiers* helped change President Lincoln's views on the ability of African Americans to be soldiers— a change that he famously included in the Emancipation Proclamation.

William Cooper Nell (1816–74). Ubiquitous in the antislavery community, Nell became a pioneer in collecting black oral history and memorabilia.

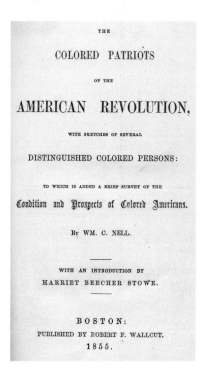

THE

COLORED PATRIOTS

OF THE

AMERICAN REVOLUTION,

WITH SKETCHES OF SEVERAL

DISTINGUISHED COLORED PERSONS:

TO WHICH IS ADDED A BRIEF SURVEY OF THE

Condition and Prospects of Colored Americans.

By WM. C. NELL.

WITH AN INTRODUCTION BY
HARRIET BEECHER STOWE.

BOSTON:
PUBLISHED BY ROBERT F. WALLCUT.
1855.

Nell's influential *Colored Patriots of the American Revolution* (Boston: Robert F. Wallcut, 1855), title page.

ANTHONY BURNS

In March 1854, Anthony Burns boarded a ship in Richmond, bound for Boston. Upon arrival, like most newcomers, he sought a job and a place to stay. He found employment with Mr. Coffin Pitts, a Boston clothing dealer, and wrote a letter to inform his brother back home. Unfortunately, Burns's missive about his recent hire found its way into the hands of Charles Suttle, a slaveholder in Alexandria, Virginia—and Burns's former master. When Suttle learned of Burns's whereabouts, he traveled to Massachusetts to reclaim his property. Burns was little more than chattel to Suttle; having wrongfully escaped from his possession, he was legally bound to return with Suttle to the plantation. Although Massachusetts was a free state that had enacted personal liberty laws to protect escaped slaves, the 1850 Fugitive Slave Law obliged federal courts to return runaway slaves to their owners. On May 24, Burns was arrested and jailed, in preparation for his return to involuntary servitude.

A furor erupted in Boston over the Burns case. In 1851, the city had successfully defied the law in the case of Shadrach Minkins, although it failed to prevent Thomas Sims's return to slavery in Georgia. A guard of three hundred had escorted the unfortunate Sims to the vessel that then carried him back south. Now abolitionists, black and white, were determined that Burns would not meet a similar fate. On May 25, handbills

appeared throughout the city reading, "The Man Is Not Bought" and "Kidnapping again!! A man was stolen last night by the Fugitive Slave Bill Commissioner! He will have his mock trial

The title page of an 1854 pamphlet describing the case of Anthony Burns (1834–62). Jeffrey Ruggles's *The Unboxing of Henry Brown* (2003) asserts that this image is actually of the fugitive slave Henry Box Brown. Other images of Brown, however, do not support that assertion.

on Saturday, May 27, at 9 o'clock in the Kidnapper's 'Court,' before the Hon. Slave Bill Commissioner, at the Court House in Court Square. Shall Boston steal another man?"[3]

Outrage quickly spread. On Friday evening the Boston Vigilance Committee sponsored a meeting at Faneuil Hall to discuss Burns's fate. Receiving word that a small group of blacks led by Lewis Hayden had gathered outside the courthouse to rescue Burns, the Faneuil Hall group rushed to join them. Perhaps as many as two thousand black and white abolitionists, led by Martin Stowell and the Unitarian minister Thomas Wentworth Higginson, stormed the courthouse, beating down the door with a battering ram. Amid gunshots and drawn knives, one deputy marshal trying to resist the mob was fatally stabbed. The rioting lasted several hours, finally quashed by federal deputies. Pro-slavery president Franklin Pierce seized the opportunity to display the federal government's commitment to enforce the Fugitive Slave Law: he sent several thousand soldiers, marines, and voluntary militia to guard the courthouse for the duration of the Burns trial.

The trial commenced the following day, presided over by federal slave commissioner Edward G. Loring. Burns's zealous young attorney, Richard Henry Dana, Jr., managed to delay the proceedings until Monday. His arguments detailed the unconstitutionality of the Fugitive Slave Law, and witness accounts about Burns's whereabouts conflicted, but the outcome was hardly in doubt. Loring delivered his ruling on the morning of June 2, 1854. Later that

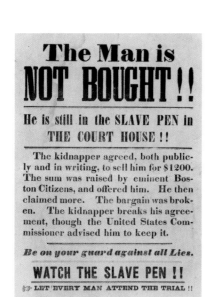

"The Man Is Not Bought!!" Antislavery broadside posted during the Burns trial, 1854.

"Marshal's Posse with Burns Moving Down State Street," illustration from Charles Emery Stevens, *Anthony Burns, A History* (Boston: John P. Jewett and Co., 1856).

day Burns, shackled and escorted by armed guards, walked to Boston's wharf to begin his journey back to Virginia. Fifty thousand people, guarded by thousands of troops, gathered along the route between the courthouse and the wharf.

Burns returned to Virginia, where he was placed in the Lumpkin slave jail in Richmond. No longer of use to his master Charles Suttle, Burns was held in solitary confinement for several months,

then was sold to David McDaniel, a North Carolina slave trader, for $905. News of Burns's sale spread to Boston. The city's black abolitionist minister Leonard Grimes and members of his Twelfth Baptist Church, along with the Reverend G. S. Stockwell of Amherst, arranged to purchase his freedom for $1,300; the checks Grimes used to purchase Burns's freedom were dated on George Washington's birthday.

His freedom secured, Burns went on to attend Oberlin College and became the pastor of a Baptist church in St. Catharines, Ontario. He died of tuberculosis in 1862 at the age of twenty-nine.

Anthony Burns was the last fugitive returned to slavery from New England. His infamous trial invigorated the abolitionist movement in the North and intensified popular opposition to the growing power of the South.

JOHN MERCER LANGSTON AND THE BAR OF JUSTICE

In the spring of 1855, white voters in Brownhelm, near Oberlin, Ohio, elected John Mercer Langston as township clerk, making him the nation's first elected black official. Langston, who ran on the Free Soil ticket, was born in 1829 and had graduated from Oberlin College at age twenty; he remained in the region for about fifteen years thereafter. Voters repeatedly elected him to the town council and the local board of edu-

cation, happy to select a man of superior managerial skills and sound grasp of the law.

Langston had not come by his legal training easily. At the time of his college graduation, only three or four African Americans in the entire county had received legal training, and none in the Midwest. So Langston's career decision represented a direct challenge to the legal establishment; it rebuffed the State

John Mercer Langston (1829–97), by William J. Simmons, engraving, 1887.

"The Admission to the Ohio Bar, 1854," illustration from John Mercer Langston's
From the Virginia Plantation to the National Capitol, 1894.

of Ohio, which barred most blacks from voting and serving on juries. Only in 1849 did blacks win the right to testify in court cases involving whites.

No law school in the country would admit Langston, and for several years he searched in vain for a white lawyer who would take him on as an apprentice. He eventually found an antislavery lawyer who agreed to train him, but the man quickly abrogated the agreement. Langston decided to return to Oberlin for a theological degree.

Then, in 1853, Langston became the apprentice of Philemon Bliss, an Ohio lawyer, publisher, and abolitionist. He dedicated himself completely to his studies, rigorously reviewing the law regarding real and personal property, contract law, and courtroom procedure. He attended county court sessions to see the law applied, then returned to

Bliss for further grilling. While deep in his studies, he drafted a petition to the state legislature insisting that all African Americans in the state be given the right to vote. At that point state law only permitted the lightest-skinned blacks to vote. The legislators refused to permit Langston even to address them, then rejected his written request that the state adopt a constitutional amendment granting blacks the vote.

Outraged and profoundly disappointed, Langston nevertheless benefited from his work on the case. On September 13, 1854, he appeared before a five-member review panel at the district court, convened to give Langston his bar examination. Most of the panel members hated the idea of a black bar member, but his answers to their interrogations left them stunned. None had imagined they would ever hear such

legal acuity coming from the mouth of an African American. They approved his admission, albeit reluctantly.

Fittingly, but also ironically, his first case was in defense of a white farmer—and a neighbor—whose very home was at stake. Langston approached the case as if his own future depended on its outcome—which it might have. The trial, which took place in a barn, lasted over eight hours. The lawyers for both sides presented their summations. The many spectators were riveted by Langston's presence. At last, without even leaving their seats, the jury decided in favor of Langston's client. Had he lost, Langston might have had to return to farming. That would have denied the antislavery movement one of its finest minds and Howard University the 1869 founder of its legal department.

BEREA COLLEGE AND
WILBERFORCE UNIVERSITY

Julia Maria Fairchild Ladies' Hall, the first brick structure at Berea College, dedicated 1873.

During the mid-1850s African Americans could attend two new colleges that were completely open to their education.

In 1855, the abolitionist John G. Fee founded Berea College, near Lexington, Kentucky, the first integrated, coeducational school in the South. Although little more than a one-room school when it opened, the existence of the private college nevertheless incited the wrath of white supremacists throughout its early years. Indeed, Kentucky's increasingly violent proslavery contingent forced Fee and other Berea workers out of the state in 1859. But during the war Fee returned to teach and preach to black Union soldiers at Camp Nelson, the state's largest black recruitment center. For about eighteen months he helped provide

facilities for the freedmen and their families; he also raised funds for barracks, a hospital, a school, and a church. Before the close of 1866, Berea College had attracted 187 students, 96 black and 91 white. It offered mostly preparatory classes, to ready students for advanced study at the college level, and began enrolling full-time college students in 1869. It awarded its first undergraduate degrees in 1873. The town of Berea developed around the school and Fee's church, and a number of freedpeople migrated there after emancipation.

But this remarkable experiment—an integrated student body and faculty in an increasingly integrated town—could not last in the post-Reconstruction South. In 1904 Democratic state representative Charles Day introduced a bill

"to prohibit white and colored persons from attending the same school." The state superintendent of schools, horrified by the implications of Booker T. Washington's dinner at the White House with President Roosevelt that year, championed the new segregation law. Over objections from the Berea College administration, the bill passed, and the private school faced the choice of segregation or paying a fine it could not afford. Unwilling to close, administrators instituted segregation until 1950, when the state legislature amended the law to permit integration at the collegiate level.

The year after Berea's founding, the Methodist Episcopal Church—with the help of the African Methodist Episcopal Church—founded a new college

111

Wilberforce University, lithograph by Middleton, Wallace & Co., ca. 1850s.

"Bishop Daniel A. Payne," frontispiece, from Payne's *Recollections of Seventy Years* (Nashville: Publishing House of the AME Sunday School Union, 1888). Payne (1811–93) studied at the Lutheran Theological Seminary in Gettysburg, but left the Lutherans for the AME Church because they proved reluctant to give a black minister a parish.

about two hundred miles to the north, in Tawawa Springs (later Xenia), Ohio. It planned to educate African Americans, and in the spirit of this mission, it named the school after William Wilberforce, the eighteenth-century British abolitionist. During the Civil War Wilberforce University faced major financial problems, as its enrollments collapsed. It closed in 1862. But the following year, the AME Church bought Wilberforce for $10,000, reopened the school, and installed the AME bishop Daniel A. Payne as president.

A native of Charleston, South Carolina, Payne was long dedicated to black education. In 1828, at the age of seventeen, he had opened a school in South Carolina for African Americans. When the state forced him to close it, he moved north and studied theology at the Evangelical Lutheran Seminary in Gettysburg, Pennsylvania. He could not complete his studies because of his failing eyesight; still, he became the first African American ordained by the Franckean Lutheran Synod. All the while he continued to focus on black education, opening a school for African Americans in Philadelphia in 1840. The following year he left the Lutheran Church to join the AME. Payne had led the charge to purchase Wilberforce.

During his thirteen years as university president, Payne shepherded its rapid expansion. In 1866 he established a theology department that eventually grew into its own school, the Payne Theological Seminary. He created science and classics departments in order to bolster its academic standing. Even after he left the presidency, he continued to play an important role as dean of the theological school. In 1887, Wilberforce began receiving funds from the state of Ohio, making it a hybrid public-private school. At the end of the nineteenth century it counted W. E. B. Du Bois and Hallie Quinn Brown, the writer and civil rights advocate, among its notable faculty members.

DRED SCOTT

On March 6, 1857, the U.S. Supreme Court handed down one of its most controversial opinions. *Dred Scott v. Sanford,* commonly known as "the *Dred Scott* decision," infamously ruled that African Americans had no rights under the Constitution. Often referred to as one of the worst, yet most important, decisions ever issued by the Supreme Court, *Dred Scott* sparked intense debate over the future of slavery in the United States and helped spur the country toward civil war.

Dred Scott, a slave living in St. Louis, had brought his case to a Missouri state court in 1846, claiming that he, his wife, and his two daughters were legally entitled to freedom. Because he and his family had lived on free soil in Illinois and Minnesota for several years, they had become free, he argued, and remained so despite returning to Missouri, a slave state.

After eleven years of victories and reversals in the court system, Scott's appeal finally reached the Supreme Court. Chief Justice Roger B. Taney wrote for the majority in a 7–2 decision; the ruling went well beyond the issue of Scott's right to freedom. Encouraged by President-elect James Buchanan, the Court, with a stroke of the pen, attempted to quash the debate once and for all between North and South over the issue of slavery.

Taney presented several major conclusions. First, he held that African Americans and their descendants were not protected by the Constitution and thus could not be citizens. Second, as noncitizens, blacks had no privileges granted by the Constitution and were not entitled to sue in court. Taney could have stopped there, dismissing Scott's case on his lack of standing alone. How-

NOW READY:
THE
Dred Scott Decision.

OPINION OF CHIEF-JUSTICE
ROGER B. TANEY,
WITH AN INTRODUCTION,
BY DR. J. H. VAN EVRIE.
ALSO,
AN APPENDIX,
BY SAM. A. CARTWRIGHT, M.D., of New Orleans,
ENTITLED,
"Natural History of the Prognathous
Race of Mankind."
ORIGINALLY WRITTEN FOR THE NEW YORK DAY-BOOK.

THE GREAT WANT OF A BRIEF PAMPHLET, containing the famous decision of Chief-Justice Taney, in the celebrated Dred Scott Case, has induced the Publishers of the DAY-BOOK to present this edition to the public. It contains a Historical Introduction by Dr. Van Evrie, author of "Negroes and Negro Slavery," and an Appendix by Dr. Cartwright, of New Orleans, in which the physical differences between the negro and the white races are forcibly presented. As a whole, this pamphlet gives the *historical, legal,* and *physical* aspects of the "Slavery" Question in a concise compass, and should be circulated by thousands before the next presidential election. All who desire to answer the arguments of the abolitionists should read it. In order to place it before the masses, and induce Democratic Clubs, Democratic Town Committees, and all interested in the cause, to or-

"Now Ready," 1860. J. H. Van Evrie's advertisement for his edition of Chief Justice Roger B. Taney's decision.

ever, he went on to rule that Congress had no authority to regulate slavery in the territories, thereby invalidating the 1820 Missouri Compromise. Finally, he stated that slaves were private property and thus should be treated as any other property and could not be seized without due process.

Taney, a slave owner himself, claimed to be following the Constitution's "true intent and meaning when it was adopted." Because the framers considered blacks "a subordinate and inferior class of beings," he reasoned, they had "no rights or privileges but such as those who held the power and the Government might choose to grant them."[4] Since the framers had not expressly granted blacks any rights to citizenship, the Court could not recognize any.

Taney's sweeping opinion not only rejected Dred Scott's legal battle for

freedom but relegated all blacks to a permanent status of inferiority. Dashing the hopes of antislavery reformers, the decision also carried frightening implications for all African Americans. Many concluded that it spelled the end of their quest for equal rights. Interest in colonization and emigration movements was renewed, and even Frederick Douglass considered moving to Haiti. Hopes for adoption of even the most gradual emancipation schemes withered, as free blacks, in Taney's determination, possessed no rights that white men were bound to respect. With regulation of slavery snatched from the province of the U.S. Congress, antislavery groups rightly feared that slavery could return to the free states. Abraham Lincoln, who opposed the antislavery movement, asserted that the nation was only one court case away from the destruction of all the North's antislavery laws and constitutions.

The Court's decision incited all sides of the question to action. J. H. Van Evrie, well known for his support of slavery and for his intensely racist depictions of blacks, published Taney's decision in cheap pamphlet form. The Republican Party—founded three years earlier as a political haven for Free Soilers, former members of the Whig Party, and moderate abolitionists—soon transformed Dred Scott's defeat into a catalyst for social change. The party's fight to gain control of the White House, Congress, and the courts led to the election of Abraham Lincoln in 1860 and ultimately to the Civil War. Although never officially overruled, the *Dred Scott* decision was effectively overturned following the Civil War by the Thirteenth, Fourteenth, and Fifteenth amendments to the Constitution.

FRANK LESLIE'S ILLUSTRATED NEWSPAPER

Entered according to Act of Congress, in the year 1857, by FRANK LESLIE, in the Clerk's Office of the District Court for the Southern District of New York. (Copyrighted June 22, 1857.)

No. 82.—VOL. IV.]   NEW YORK, SATURDAY, JUNE 27, 1857.   [PRICE 6 CENTS.

TO TOURISTS AND TRAVELLERS.

WE shall be happy to receive personal narratives, of land or sea, including adventures and incidents, from every person who pleases to correspond with our paper.

We take this opportunity of returning our thanks to our numerous artistic correspondents throughout the country, for the many sketches we are constantly receiving from them of the news of the day. We trust they will spare no pains to furnish us with drawings of events as they may occur. We would also remind them that it is necessary to send all sketches, if possible, by the earliest conveyance.

VISIT TO DRED SCOTT—HIS FAMILY—INCIDENTS OF HIS LIFE—DECISION OF THE SUPREME COURT.

WHILE standing in the Fair grounds at St. Louis, and engaged in conversation with a prominent citizen of that enterprising city, he suddenly asked us if we would not like to be introduced to Dred Scott. Upon expressing a desire to be thus honored, the gentleman called to an old negro who was standing near by, and our wish was gratified. Dred made a rude obeisance to our recognition, and seemed to enjoy the notice we expended upon him. We found him on examination to be a pure-blooded African, perhaps fifty years of age, with a shrewd, intelligent, good-natured face, of rather light frame, being not more than five feet six inches high. After some general remarks we expressed a wish to get his portrait (we had made

ELIZA AND LIZZIE, CHILDREN OF DRED SCOTT.

efforts before, through correspondents, and failed), and asked him if he would not go to Fitzgibbon's gallery and

have it taken. The gentleman present explained to Dred that it was proper he should have his likeness in the "great illustrated paper of the country," overruled his many objections, which seemed to grow out of a superstitious feeling, and he promised to be at the gallery the next day. This appointment Dred did not keep. Determined not to be foiled, we sought an interview with Mr. Crane, Dred's lawyer, who promptly gave us a letter of introduction, explaining to Dred that it was to his advantage to have his picture taken to be engraved for our paper, and also directions where we could find his domicile. We found the place with difficulty, the streets in Dred's neighborhood being more clearly defined in the plan of the city than on the mother earth; we finally reached a wooden house, however, protected by a balcony that answered the description. Approaching the door, we saw a smart, tidy-looking negress, perhaps thirty years of age, who, with two female assistants, was busy ironing. To our question, "Is this where Dred Scott lives?" we received, rather hesitatingly, the answer, "Yes." Upon our asking if he was home, she said,

"What white man arter dad nigger for?—why don't white man 'tend to his own business, and let dat nigger 'lone? Some of dese days dey'll steal dat nigger—dat are a fact."

DRED SCOTT. PHOTOGRAPHED BY FITZGIBBON, OF ST. LOUIS.   HIS WIFE, HARRIET. PHOTOGRAPHED BY FITZGIBBON, OF ST. LOUIS.

Frank Leslie's Illustrated Newspaper, front page, June 27, 1857. The popular paper showed images of Dred Scott (1800?–58), his wife, Harriet (1818?–76), and their two daughters, Eliza and Lizzie.

OUR NIG

My mistress was wholly imbued with southern principles. I do not pretend to divulge every transaction in my own life, which the unprejudiced would declare unfavorable in comparison with treatment of legal bondman; I have purposely omitted what would most provoke shame in our good anti-slavery friends at home."[5] With these words, Harriet Wilson, born in 1825, set the context for her 1859 novel, *Our Nig: or, Sketches from the Life of a Free Black,* the first novel published by an African American woman. Based on her own life, *Our Nig* records the horrifying experiences of Frado, a free black servant in the rural North. Frado is the daughter of a white woman and a free black man. After her father dies, her mother abandons the six-year-old to become an indentured servant in the Bellmont family. Mrs. Bellmont and her daughter Mary inflict brutality on Frado (our "Nig," in an ironic turn). In one instance, the daughter falsely accuses "Nig" of pushing her into a stream, whereupon the mother "commenced beating her inhumanly; then propping her mouth open with a piece of wood, [and] shut her up in a dark room, without any supper."[6] Near the close of the book Frado is temporarily rescued by a woman who teaches her the craft of sewing bonnets. Then Frado marries a fugitive slave lecturer, but he is a fraud—he has never been in the South—and merely panders to abolitionists for money. In the end, he abandons her as well, and she is forced to give up her son to the poor farm.

She survives only because of the inexplicable kindness of a friend, who provides her with "a valuable recipe, from which she might manufacture a useful article for her maintenance."[7] In real life,

Our Nig, title page, 1859.

Wilson invented a hair tonic that she sold throughout New England. After the publication of *Our Nig* and the death of her son, Wilson became a prominent Spiritualist in Boston. She died at the turn of the century.

In her preface, Wilson advised her readers, whom she assumed would be largely African American, that the

events in Frado's life were not nearly as bad as the actual treatment she endured. Living as she had in the hotbed of New England antislavery activism, Wilson had every expectation of receiving fairness and respect from a group that loudly professed to have the best interests of African Americans at heart. But she endured maltreatment from "professed abolitionists," as she lamented, "who didn't want slaves at the South, nor niggers in their own houses, North. Faugh! To lodge one; to eat with one; to admit one through the front door; to sit next to one; awful!"[8] She wrote the novel, as she admitted in her preface, to help support herself and her son, who died only five months after its publication. Very likely, however, she earned little, as the popular press ignored *Our Nig,* and even the antislavery press, African American newspapers included, never acknowledged its appearance.

The book's condemnation of northern prejudice certainly did not threaten black abolitionists, many of whom freely criticized their white brethren who manifested the slightest degree of racism. But in the course of *Our Nig,* Wilson criticized all the prime constituencies for her book, even professed Christians, which guaranteed its quick disappearance (until authenticated and republished in 1983). A commercial failure in its own time, *Our Nig* testifies today, as no other work of its era does, to the depths of racial prejudice in the North.

PART SIX

WAR AND ITS MEANING

1859–1865

"Harper's [*sic*] Ferry Insurrection—Interior of the Engine-House, just before the gate is broken down by the storming party." Wood engraving from *Frank Leslie's Illustrated Newspaper,* November 5, 1859.

Burglary is common, but State-breaking is a new species of crime. . . . John Brown, with twenty-one other men, a few days ago threw himself against the State of Virginia." On November 19, 1859, the *Weekly Anglo-African* advised its readers that John Brown and his men, including five African Americans, had broken into the state of Virginia. But unlike common criminals, they did not want to steal anyone's possessions. Rather, they sought to "obtain and restore stolen chattels to their proper owners—to restore the slave to himself." The October 16, 1859, raid on the federal arsenal at Harpers Ferry became the single most important event, next to Lincoln's election, that drove the nation to civil war. It convinced southerners that northern-

ers would stop at nothing to attack their "peculiar institution," and it gave the North a heroic figure whose death, Ralph Waldo Emerson exclaimed, would "make the gallows as glorious as the cross."[1]

Brown, who had declared war on slavery and had led an antislavery insurrection in Kansas, had been secretly planning an attack on the South. In 1857 he was seeking support among black and white abolitionists. The philanthropists and antislavery leaders Theodore Parker, Gerrit Smith, Thomas Wentworth Higginson, Samuel Gridley Howe, Franklin Benjamin Sanborn, and George Luther Stearns supplied him with money, guns, and pikes, although they obtained no specific details about the plan. Other abolitionists hesitated. The Quaker poet

John Greenleaf Whittier, after examining one of the pikes meant for the slaves, remarked that it looked too much like a murder weapon. Many blacks sympathized with Brown's intent, and had he been better prepared, black militia units from Ohio and Canada West might have joined him. But even Frederick Douglass (who did not learn any details until just before the raid) refused to participate, fearing (like many others) that Brown could not possibly succeed or that the backlash against the participants' families would be devastating. Finally, black abolitionists like James McCune Smith and George DeBaptiste preferred even more violent plans than Brown's and simply did not trust the plans of professed white friends.

The collection of misfits, roman-

"Effect of John Brown's Invasion at the South," *Harper's Weekly,* November 19, 1859. This issue dramatically asserts that John Brown's attempt to "rescue" slaves in the South would only incite slaves *against* the abolitionists. The cook in the upper-right corner declares: "What's dem fool niggers fraid on? I'd like ter see one o' dem folks oxdertake to carry me off, I would!"

Bird's-eye view of Harpers Ferry, from Edward Beyer, *Album of Virginia: or, Illustration of the Old Dominion* (Richmond: Enquirer Book, 1857).

John A. Copeland (1834–59). Freeborn in North Carolina, Copeland moved to Oberlin, Ohio, and briefly attended the college's preparatory department. He dedicated himself to the Underground Railroad and abolitionism. He was related by marriage to Lewis S. Leary, also of Oberlin, who recruited him into John Brown's force. Copeland was captured during the raid, tried with Brown, convicted of treason and insurrection, and executed.

Shields Green (1836–59). A slave from Charleston, South Carolina, Green fled to Canada and was recruited into Brown's conspiracy by Frederick Douglass. But when Green and Douglass learned more details of Brown's intended raid, Douglass backed out, fearing it would end in disaster. Green, however, refused to abandon the project. He turned to Douglass and said, "I believe I'll go with the old man." He was captured alongside Brown in the engine house and later hanged.

Lewis Sheridan Leary (1835–59). Freeborn in Fayetteville, North Carolina, Leary moved to Oberlin in 1856. In September 1858 he participated in the Oberlin-Wellington fugitive slave rescue. He met John Brown in March 1859 and joined his band. During the Harpers Ferry raid, Leary held the rifle factory with Copeland and John Kagi, a twenty-five-year-old white man from Ohio. Shot by the town's defenders, he suffered for eight hours before dying.

Osborne P. Anderson (1830–72). Freeborn in Chester County, Pennsylvania, Anderson fled to the black community at Chatham, Ontario, after passage of the Fugitive Slave Law in 1850, where he assisted Mary Ann Shadd Cary, the editor of the *Provincial Freeman.* He met John Brown at the 1858 Chatham antislavery convention and helped lay plans for the government they would form after the liberation of the South's slaves. During the Harpers Ferry attack, he distributed pikes to slaves and joined with Leary and John Kagi to guard the arsenal they had seized. Somehow Anderson—he was the only participant to do so—and wrote about his experience in *A Voice from Harper's Ferry,* 1861.

Dangerfield Newby (1820?–59). Newby was born a slave in Culpeper County, Virginia, but in 1858 his white slave-owning father uprooted his slave wife and twenty of his former slaves and moved to Bridgeport, Ohio. As a blacksmith, Newby possessed sufficient means to buy his wife and children from their new owner, Dr. Lewis A. Jennings. His attempts, however, failed, and he joined Brown in a desperate effort to free his family. Newby was one of the first killed in the raid. His wife and several family members survived the Civil War to see freedom.

tics, sons of John Brown, and five blacks—Osborne P. Anderson, Dangerfield Newby, Shields Green, Lewis S. Leary, and John A. Copeland—who undertook the raid on Harpers Ferry likely assumed that once word circulated about the insurrection, thousands of slaves would appear, ready to seize their freedom. Instead, whites reacted with horror and spread alarm all the way to the nation's capital. In short order, a detachment of federal troops, led by Robert E. Lee, cornered the men in the arsenal's firehouse, and after negotiations proved fruitless, they rushed the building and seized the wounded Brown and his surviving conspirators.

Dangerfield Newby, born a slave, had joined the raid in hopes of freeing his slave wife and family; he and Lewis Leary, a free black activist who lived in Oberlin, Ohio, were both killed

early in the raid, their bodies used for target practice. Osborne Anderson, a Pennsylvania-born free black, had fled to Canada after passage of the Fugitive Slave Law and worked on the staff of the *Provincial Freeman,* an antislavery newspaper edited by Mary Ann Shadd Cary. During the raid Anderson succeeded in arming about thirty slaves on the nearby plantation of a descendant of George Washington; they managed to destroy some property but had no real impact on the raid. He escaped capture, returned to Canada, and later wrote an account of his participation in the attack.

Shields Green and John Copeland were captured along with Brown and placed on trial for treason. They shared a jail cell with their fellow white conspirator Albert Hazlett and watched workmen construct their gallows. Little is known about Green, other than

that he was an escaped South Carolina slave who had earned the nickname of "Emperor." Copeland, a nephew of Lewis Leary, was born in Raleigh, North Carolina, a free man, and lived in Oberlin, Ohio, where he became a devoted abolitionist and worker on the Underground Railroad. His last letters, written from his cell, survive. A man of conviction and courage, Copeland wrote his parents on November 26 that he had no regrets, "for remember the *cause* in which I was engaged; *remember it was a holy cause,* one in which men in every way better than I am, have suffered & died. Remember that if I must die, I die in trying to liberate a few of my poor & oppressed people from a condition of servitude against which God in his words has hurled his most bitter denunciations."[2] He was executed on December 16, 1859, in Charlestown, Virginia.

"THIS IS A WHITE MAN'S WAR!"

"Bombardment of Fort Sumter, Charleston Harbor: April 12 and 13, 1861,"
Currier and Ives, hand-colored lithograph, ca. 1861.

The "fire-eating" secessionist and Virginia slave owner Edmund Ruffin fired the first cannon at Fort Sumter on April 12, 1861, igniting the Civil War. While the Upper South hesitated to fully embrace secession, the Confederate seizure of Fort Sumter compelled unity around the idea of Southern nationhood.

At first the attack exerted a similar tendency in the North, based on the outrage that traitors had fired on the flag and taken the fort. The heroic stand of the fort's commander, Major Robert Anderson, inspired even the political opponents of Lincoln and the Republican Party. Northern blacks reacted with equal patriotic fervor, although with far less cause than their white brethren. Thousands of blacks pledged their honor to defend the nation against Southern treason. Groups in Boston, New York City, Philadelphia, and elsewhere imme-diately began raising militia companies for federal service.

Within a month, just in the city of Philadelphia, six companies formed and equipped themselves. A correspondent for Horace Greeley's *New-York Tribune* reported that Philadelphia blacks already were drilling and that five thousand more could be raised if the government asked for them. One of the companies even attired themselves in the exotic red, blue, and white of the Zouaves, Algerians who had fought with the French army in Europe; the Union army had more than seventy Zouave regiments, most of them white. Ironically, the white Zouave regiments would earn a reputation for the most vicious racism of any Union regiment. The New York *Weekly Anglo-African,* the most important black paper of the era, on April 27 proclaimed that the time had finally come: "We want Nat Turner—not speeches; Denmark Vesey—not resolutions; John Brown—not meetings."

On April 13, the day Fort Sumter surrendered, the paper called on blacks to take up weapons and, like the Italian secret revolutionary societies the Carbonari, assassinate any slave catcher they might meet on the street: "Let the infamous wretches understand that the issues between freedom and slavery are the broad issues of life and death." On April 27, with the smell of black powder still in the air, the *Anglo-African* also quoted the wisdom of Frederick Douglass—"One man in the right is a majority"—and urged blacks to form guerrilla bands and descend on the South to destroy slavery. Five hundred of these men, the paper explained, could do more damage than five thousand regular soldiers. The time was urgent—it "only wants men determined to do or die."

"Bombardment of Fort Sumter by the Batteries of the Confederate States," wood engraving, 1861.

Nick Biddle (1796–1876), from a carte de visite, 1861.

But the Lincoln administration and state governors across the North repeated countless times that the Union army wanted "no niggers": "this is a white man's war." White soldiers recoiled at the prospect of uniformed black men. Send blacks as diggers or laborers but never as soldiers, Yankee soldiers wrote back home—real men used weapons of war, blacks used shovels. Perhaps the words of Ohio congressman Chilton A. White best embodied the North's attitude in 1861 toward black soldiers: "This is a government of white men, made by white men for white men, to be administered, protected, defended and maintained by white men."[3]

Arrogantly shoved aside, Northern blacks debated how to respond to the war. Most believed that they owed no allegiance to a nation that spurned their patriotism. Even the African Methodist Episcopal Church concluded that blacks had no business fighting for a government that oppressed them. Most blacks, however, believed with Frederick Douglass that ultimately the North would be forced to wage war, not just for the Union, but against slavery. Until that time, as the *Weekly Anglo-African* counseled, they should support the slaves and wait for opinions to change.

But others could not ignore the slaves' call and volunteered for service in any way they could. A few, like H. Ford Douglas, Joseph T. Wilson, and the mixed-blood Connecticut soldier Meunomennie L. Maimi, served in white units, while others, like the journalist William H. Johnson, became officers' attendants or teamsters—anything to get into the fight and help slaves escape. Nick Biddle, from Pottsville, Pennsylvania, who might have escaped from slavery in Delaware during the 1830s, accompanied the five-hundred-man "Washington Artillerists" unit through secessionist Baltimore in 1861 on their way to defend Washington, D.C. As Biddle's photograph shows, he wore the uniform of a Union soldier but was not officially enrolled.

On April 18—the day before mobs assaulted the Sixth Massachusetts Regiment, leaving four soldiers and twelve rioters dead—enraged secessionists assaulted the Pennsylvania unit as it passed through Baltimore to board a train for Washington. Even the police, detailed to escort the men to the train station, turned on the Pennsylvanians. Many received terrible wounds; one man had several teeth knocked out. The brave Biddle suffered a stone to the head, leaving him dazed and bloodied. After the story circulated that President Lincoln visited the unit (and saw each wounded man) that had come all the way from Pennsylvania to defend him, Unionists used the incident, and the irresistible irony, to proclaim Biddle the first man wounded by hostile forces in the Civil War.

CONTRABAND

The very stomach of this rebellion is the negro in the form of a slave. Arrest that hoe in the hands of the negro, and you smite the rebellion in the very seat of its life." As Frederick Douglass explained in his *Monthly* in July 1861, the best way to attack the South was at its strongest and most vulnerable point: the institution of slavery. But at the beginning of 1861, most of the North did not fully appreciate the South's determination to gain independence. Moreover, slavery remained legal in the border states—states only precariously remaining in the Union; the Fugitive Slave Law remained in effect; and the Supreme Court's 1857 *Dred Scott* decision, proclaiming that blacks had no rights that white men were bound to respect, still reigned.

Shortly after the start of the war, three slaves who had been compelled to work for the Confederates escaped to Union-held Fort Monroe, a fortified complex near Hampton, on the tip of the Virginia Peninsula. The Lincoln administration had immediately made sure to increase its hold on the strategic fort. On May 23, the three escaped slaves arrived at Fort Monroe, and the next day they

Patriotic cover depicting Fort Monroe as a popular destination for runaway slaves at the start of the Civil War. Such covers—or envelopes—became popular collectibles and often carried demeaning images of African Americans.

met its commander, General Benjamin F. Butler. A controversial and mercurial Massachusetts lawyer and politician, Butler learned that two of the escaped slaves had wives and families in nearby Hampton. What should he do with the three? Indeed, what could he do?

The next day, Confederate Major John B. Cary, who had known Butler before the war, approached the fort under a flag of truce and on behalf of the slaves' owner (a Colonel Mallory) asked for the return of the man's property under the Fugitive Slave Law. Butler reminded Cary that as Virginia claimed to have left the Union, his "client" Mallory could not ask for redress under the Constitution he had repudiated. Butler then declared the men "contraband" of war and put them to work for the Union. But as a reporter for *The Atlantic Monthly* would explain in November

1861, if one slave on the Potomac heard something about emancipation "in a few days it will be known by his brethren on the Gulf. Such is the mysterious spiritual telegraph which runs through the slave population." Soon fugitives began collecting at Fort Monroe, and by July about a thousand former slaves had found refuge under Butler's protection. As the number of fugitives would only increase, Butler sought clarification of official policy from the War Department. Should he consider these people free or slaves? What impact did the war have on their legal status? If they remained property, who owned them?

The Lincoln administration had no ready answers to Butler's queries and wished to avoid any direct challenges to slavery, fearing that such action would alienate the border states. In fact, Lincoln specifically reversed General John

Benjamin F. Butler, glass, wet collodion image. Butler (1818–93) was a Lowell, Massachusetts, politician who won appointment as a major general in the Union army. He is best remembered for his creative use of the word *contraband* and for his wartime rule over Union-occupied New Orleans. He later won election as governor of his home state.

Former slaves, or "contraband," at "Foller's house" in Cumberland, Virginia. Stereoscope view by James F. Gibson, May 14, 1862.

C. Frémont's emancipation order in Missouri because it went beyond military necessity and, according to Lincoln, violated the constitutional rights of property owners. Butler's earlier decision to proclaim slaves that came into his lines "contraband," however, gave the Congress the lead it needed to move more strongly against slavery. While the Congress recognized that it could not arbitrarily seize slaves, it could certainly seize the "property" of those who had committed treason. Thus, on August 6, 1861, it passed the first of two Confiscation acts, declaring:

> Any property of whatsoever kind or description, with intent to use or employ the same, or suffer the same to be used or employed, in aiding, abetting, or promoting such insurrection or resistance to the laws . . . all such property is hereby declared to be lawful subject of prize and capture wherever found; and it shall be the duty of the President of the United States to cause the same to be seized, confiscated, and condemned.

THE PORT ROYAL EXPERIMENT

The question of what to do with freed slaves loomed large from the earliest days of the Civil War. Indeed, many of the issues central to Reconstruction would first arise in the heat of the war.

As the Union military moved South, Confederate planters often faced a choice between fight or flight. On November 7, 1861, planters living on the Sea Islands, off the coast of South Carolina, chose to flee and left without their property—including their slaves. The U.S. Navy moved into Port Royal Harbor, seized the land, and took on the task of determining what to do with the ten thousand "contraband" slaves. For the federal government, Port Royal provided what the historian Willie Lee Rose called a "rehearsal for Reconstruction."

Various Northerners rushed to the bucolic region to implement their own program. Secretary of State Salmon P.

An African American church on the Smith Plantation on Port Royal Island, South Carolina. Sketch by Alfred R. Waud.

Chase asked his friend Edward L. Pierce, a Boston lawyer, to travel to Port Royal and direct federal efforts there. Pierce formed a group of missionaries and teachers called Gideon's Band, and in March 1862 fifty-three Northerners arrived to help the freed slaves make the transition to freedom. Although paternalistic, they sincerely sought to demonstrate that free blacks could become good citizens and make meaningful contributions to society. Charlotte Forten,

Charlotte Forten (1837–1914). Philadelphia-born, Forten was a prominent member of the city's black elite. She taught at a previously all-white school in Salem, Massachusetts, then joined the band of teachers and Gideonites who traveled to the Sea Islands in 1862 to help "prepare" the former slaves for their transition to freedom. A diarist, abolitionist, and educator, she married the ministerial student Francis J. Grimké In 1878.

a Philadelphia black teacher and diarist, was among the many reformers, black and white, who tried their hand assisting the former slaves.

But like her white colleagues, Forten possessed no understanding of local traditions and saw the former slaves as exotics, lacking the rudiments of civilization. To that end, she and others focused on establishing schools, inculcating Northern values, and implementing a free-labor economy. The North kept a close eye on the "Port Royal Experiment," but the former slaves expressed their own ideas of freedom—ideas that ran counter to the goals of the Gideonites and federal representatives. They resisted growing cotton, which only reminded them of their years in slavery working to enrich their masters' coffers. Much to the chagrin of government officials, many blacks outright destroyed cotton gins. Instead, they grew corn and potatoes for their own subsistence. African Americans believed that land, not cash, held the key to real independence, and they wished to have the stake in society that they and generations of their ancestors had long since earned.

These conflicts would come to a head when the federal government seized the abandoned lands in the region and, in

"Port Royal, South Carolina. Slave Quarters," glass, wet collodion image by Timothy H. O'Sullivan, April 1862.

March 1863, sold them. African Americans purchased only 2,000 of the 21,000 acres initially for sale; most went to government officials and speculators. Boston abolitionist Edward Philbrick formed a joint-stock company and purchased eleven plantations, leased two more, and amassed 7,000 acres of land. Philbrick transformed his land into a free-labor cotton plantation, maintaining that succeeding in the marketplace

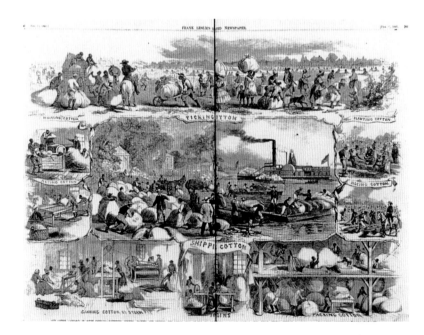

"Picking Cotton, Shipping Cotton," illustration from *Frank Leslie's Illustrated Newspaper,* February 15, 1862. While the former slaves were interested in freedom, and the abolitionists were interested in imparting middle-class values to the Sea Islands blacks, the federal government was interested in cotton production. "Our cotton campaign in South Carolina—Gathering, Ginning, Packing, and Shipping the Cotton Crops of the Sea Island, Port Royal, by the Federal Army, under General Sherman," reads the caption.

General William T. Sherman (1820–91). A racist who refused to permit black soldiers in his army, Sherman nevertheless issued Field Order No. 15, designating the entire region of the Sea Islands—from Charleston south to Florida's St. Johns River and thirty miles west along the coast—as a region for exclusive black settlement.

would provide the best path of advancement for African Americans. While Philbrick did make money on the land, he grew tired of blacks' insistence on subsistence agriculture and moved back to Massachusetts.

This tension between the desires of blacks and those of whites pervaded the Port Royal Experiment. The beginning of the end came, ironically, when the former slaves received what they wanted. On January 16, 1865, General William Tecumseh Sherman issued Field Order No. 15, granting to the local blacks about 400,000 acres of land on the Sea Islands and along the South Carolina coast. But soon President Andrew Johnson allowed former slaveholders to take back any of their land that had gone unsold. And the following year, the military forced blacks off the land if they did not sign a lease agreement with the original white owners. A largely compliant Congress worried over the constitutionality of the land seizures and permitted the dispossession of the former slaves. As a result, the majority of blacks lost their claim to "Sherman Land" and any hope for a secure future. The promise of the Port Royal Experiment could not withstand the social and political tensions that would undermine attempts to achieve equality for African Americans during Reconstruction.

"AN ACT FOR THE RELEASE OF CERTAIN PERSONS HELD TO SERVICE, OR LABOR IN THE DISTRICT OF COLUMBIA"

I have never doubted the constitutional authority of congress to abolish slavery in this District; and I have ever desired to see the national capital freed from the institution in some satisfactory way." Thus, on April 16, 1862, President Abraham Lincoln signed the new federal law ending slavery in the nation's capital.

In a letter to the Congress concerning the bill, Lincoln accurately described his lifelong belief that Congress possessed such authority. But in a March 24 letter to the great New York publisher Horace Greeley, he confessed to being "a little uneasy about the abolishment of slavery in this District."[4] For Lincoln, timing was critical, and as in all things related to slavery, he wished to move deliberately—he had one eye on Northern public opinion and the other clearly fixed on the border states. He preferred that one of the border states, particularly Delaware, rather than the Congress, move first against slavery; a vigorous federal move, he feared, would alienate loyal slave owners and drive Kentucky, or even Maryland, into the arms of the Confederacy. Additionally, he wanted the bill to include a measure for compensation—to the slave

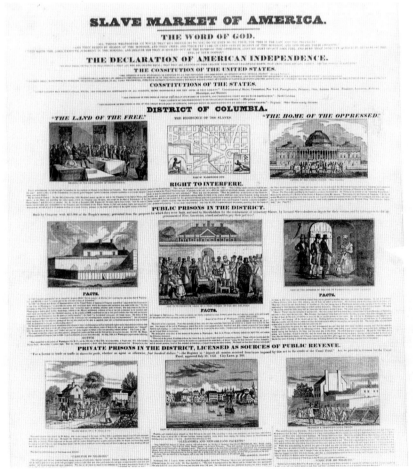

"Slave Market of America," broadside, 1836, published in
New York by the American Anti-Slavery Society.

owners, not the slaves—to preserve the constitutional protection of property. He also supported the inclusion of a provision to offer voluntary colonization to those freed by the new law, which he believed might attract additional white support for the move and be less threatening to loyal slave owners. Perhaps harboring thoughts that the South still might be enticed back into the Union, he held that the government ought to act "persuasively, and not menacingly," toward the South.

But such constitutional scruples and patience toward the South won Lincoln no friends among abolitionists, black leaders, or even those pushing for a vigorous prosecution of the war. That Lincoln could gain so much congressional support for the modest bill abolishing slavery in the District reflected the low expectations of many congressional Republicans regarding the president as much as the merits of the bill.

Since the beginning of the nineteenth century various bills to outlaw slavery in the District had come before both houses of Congress. Even Lincoln had introduced one in 1849, during his only term in the House of Representatives. In December 1861, Massachusetts senator Henry Wilson introduced a bill outlawing District slavery, immediately sparking intense debate. As the Senate galleries filled with local black residents, Senator Garrett Davis from Kentucky proposed an amendment to Wilson's bill mandating the forced expulsion and colonization of all slaves emancipated by Wilson's bill. It took the tie-breaking vote of Vice President Hannibal Hamlin to defeat the offensive amendment. Not until the following April did the Senate find enough support to pass the bill, which the House of Representatives immediately took up. One day shy of the first anniversary of the Confederate attack on Fort Sumter, the House passed the measure.

ROBERT SMALLS AND THE *PLANTER*

In the predawn hours of May 13, 1862, a crew of African American deckhands quietly set about unmooring the *Planter* from its berth in the Charleston harbor. Their journey that day would be fairly short, just beyond the outer harbor, but for its crew it would mean the difference between life and death. At the helm was Robert Smalls, like the rest of his crew a slave. After weeks of careful planning, and relying on the intimate knowledge of local waterways and Confederate defenses that he had accumulated over a year while sailing aboard the *Planter,* Smalls and his compatriots embarked on a daring break for freedom.

Before the outbreak of the Civil War, the *Planter* ferried cotton in and out of Charleston harbor. Almost 150 feet long and about 30 feet wide, the *Planter* could carry 1,400 bales of cotton. Designed to ply shallow water, and equipped with dual steam-powered engines, the ship was swift, agile, and well suited to navigating the inland waterways of the Car-

Robert Smalls, captain of the gunboat *Planter,* illustration from *Harper's Weekly,* July 14, 1862.

olina coast. At the outbreak of hostilities, the *Planter*'s owner leased the vessel and its slave crew to the Confederate navy to transport troops and munitions. For more than a year Smalls helped pilot the vessel through the coastal inlets, under the direction of Captain C. J. Relyea and two other Confederate officers.

When the Union navy began its blockade of Charleston harbor, Smalls and his fellow crew members planned their escape. One night when the three white officers of the *Planter,* in violation of standing orders, all left the ship to sleep onshore, Smalls executed his plan. Carrying four large guns, including one that he claimed had been seized from Fort Sumter, the *Planter* set out at three a.m. He raised the Confederate and South Carolina state flags and ordered the crew to stoke the boilers. As they steamed past the first crucial checkpoint, a Confederate sentry, Smalls stood in the pilot house in Captain Relyea's coat and trademark straw hat. In the faint light, the sentry could detect nothing amiss. Smalls and the *Planter* then stopped to take on several women and children, including Smalls's own wife and children. The vessel then approached the Confederate outpost at Castle Pinckney, gave the correct signal from the ship's whistle, and received clearance to proceed. Similarly, the ship passed Fort Ripley without incident.

Now only Fort Johnston (from which the first shots had been fired on Fort Sumter in 1861) lay between the *Planter* and open waters. Smalls and his crew played the roles they knew so well, operating the ship as they had for many months. By the time Confederate forces realized the ship was steaming toward the Union blockade, the *Planter* was beyond the reach of the fort's guns. Smalls then ordered the Confederate colors struck and raised a white flag. The USS *Onward,* a clipper built in 1852, received the ship and helped celebrate the victory and Smalls's new-found freedom. Dispatched to Port Royal, in the Sea Islands, Smalls officially turned the *Planter* over to Admiral Samuel F. Du Pont, commander of naval forces in the Department of the South.

Smalls and the rest of his crew were compensated for the seizure of the *Planter,* following standard military practice. In addition to providing the *Planter,* its armaments, and cargo of weapons, Smalls himself turned out to be an invaluable asset to Union forces. His knowledge of Carolina waterways, Confederate naval defense strategies, and even the location of mines he had helped lay in Charleston harbor, proved invaluable. Equally important, his exploits found their way into many Northern newspapers, which abolitionists used to refute racial stereotypes, especially the obnoxious notion that slaves were content in bondage. Smalls served the navy honorably during the war, transporting troops throughout the region. Afterward Congress enacted special legislation that made him an official member of the U.S. Navy, qualifying him for a pension. Smalls went on to become a prominent figure in South Carolina politics during Reconstruction, eventually serving in the U.S. House of Representatives.

PRESIDENT LINCOLN AND COLONIZATION

On August 14, 1862, President Lincoln met with Edward M. Thomas, the Reverend John F. Cook, Cornelius C. Clark, John T. Costin, and Benjamin McCoy, ministers, Freemasons, abolitionists, and leading organizers of the Washington, D.C., black community. At the president's request, the five men came to hear his colonization plans. Throughout his life Lincoln had supported efforts to colonize blacks outside the United States, especially to Liberia, as the best answer to America's racial problem. The president's political hero, Henry Clay, had been an active supporter of the movement and a founder of the American Colonization Society. Next to temperance, colonization was the single most popular "reform" movement of the nineteenth century, and all Northern states had branches of the colonization society. Support for colonization was so strong in Maryland, for example, that it established its own separate settlement in Liberia—which later merged with the Colonization Society's main colony, around Monrovia. In the summer of 1862, while Lincoln probably had other political motives for advancing colonization, like making more acceptable his planned Emancipation Proclamation, his support for some version of colonization was a core political principle.

Whatever his motives, Lincoln's statements to the delegation, widely reported in the popular and black press, outraged most Northern blacks. As *The Christian Recorder* reported on August 23, he told the group that he had no intention of discussing the merits of his plans. They should instead listen and then return to their community and convince their brethren of the merits of his case. He prefaced his remarks with a basic assumption:

Abraham Lincoln (1809–65), by J. H. Bufford & Sons, lithograph, after a Mathew Brady photograph, 1865.

You and we are different races. We have between us a broader difference than exists between almost any other two races. Whether it is right or wrong, I need not discuss; but this physical difference is a great disadvantage to us both, as I think your race suffer very greatly, many of them, by living among us, while ours suffer from your presence. In a word, we suffer from each other.

Since black and white could never live together in freedom, he said, blacks should leave the country. But more pointedly, he placed entire blame for the Civil War on blacks: "But for your race among us there could not be war. . . . I repeat, without the institution of slavery and the colored race as a basis, this war could not have an existence. It is better for us both, therefore, to be separated." Thus, not only did Lincoln attack black hopes for full American citizenship, he blamed them for causing the war.

The sense of shock and disappointment was palpable among blacks. Many Washington blacks denounced their leaders for attending the meeting and for failing to denounce the president's statements. The famed poet Frances Ellen Watkins Harper spoke for most blacks when she expressed her astonishment that in the midst of a bloody civil war, the president was still "dabbling with colonization." In *The Christian Recorder,* Harper advised her many readers that Lincoln's fixation with colonization "just now suggests to my mind the idea of a man almost dying of a loathsome cancer, and busying himself about having his hair trimmed according to the latest fashion."[5] Forget colonization, she cried out. Send black men to the battlefield. But at the president's urging, the Congress had appropriated funds for colonization. He even appointed the Reverend James Mitchell, who had been a colonization agent in Indiana, as commissioner of emigration in the Interior Department to plan for the settlement of freed slaves in the Isthmus of Panama and on Cow Island, off the southern coast of Haiti. Both projects proved dismal failures and were soon abandoned.

Frances Ellen Watkins Harper (1825–1911). Born free in Baltimore, Harper was the most widely read black poet prior to the Harlem Renaissance. She took up the antislavery cause after passage of the Fugitive Slave Law, later moved to Philadelphia, and became active in the Underground Railroad. Her 1858 poem "Bury Me in a Free Land" came to symbolize the black quest for freedom and equality. This engraving originally appeared in William Still, *The Underground Railroad,* 1871.

FIRST IN THE FIELD

Until January 1863 the U.S. government refused to recruit African Americans for the army. Although it publicly rejected countless black requests to volunteer for service, the Lincoln administration responded inconsistently to individual efforts by a few Union officers determined to enlist black soldiers.

In August 1862, General James H. Lane, who was also a U.S. senator, organized the First Kansas Colored Infantry. A fiery abolitionist with repugnant racial views, Lane had been battling proslavery forces since the days of John Brown. He made no secret of his raids across the Kansas border into Missouri to liberate slaves and continued the practice after the start of the war, seizing hundreds, if not thousands of them. Refusing to allow any source of Union manpower to go untapped, he placed the liberated "property" in his regiment, which at the time operated under state, rather than federal, authority.

On August 4, 1862, he opened a recruitment office in Leavenworth, Kansas. The secretary of war told him the unit would

"Corps d'Afrique, 1864," by Fritz Kredel, from F. P. Todd, *Soldiers of the American Army,* 1941.

"A Detachment of the First South Carolina," from Frank Leslie's *Famous Leaders and Battle Scenes of the Civil War* (New York: Mrs. Frank Leslie, 1896). Thomas Wentworth Higginson's First South Carolina Volunteers repel an attack.

not be accepted into federal service, but Lane pushed ahead nevertheless, recruiting free and enslaved blacks, Indians, and those of mixed blood into the unit. He even appointed William D. Matthews, a free black of Leavenworth, as a first lieutenant—something that the U.S. Army would not permit until near the end of the war. By September, Lane was drilling as many as six hundred "colored" recruits, with more coming in every day.

On October 26, 1862, 224 members of the First Kansas Colored Infantry left Fort Lincoln in search of Confederate raiders across the border in Missouri. Two days later the regiment encountered a larger force of rebel cavalry, killed several, and later fought off an even stronger enemy counterattack at Island Mound, Missouri—the first official engagement between black Union soldiers and Confederate troops. Among the Union heroes of the day was John Six-Killer, a mixed Indian and black soldier who killed four Confederate soldiers before falling. Rebel troops killed a white Union officer from the unit and left an unmistakable message for his comrades: one bullet in the heart and another in the groin. Kansas newspapers hailed the valor of the black soldiers, and one report, reprinted in the *New-York Tribune* on November 11, 1862,

exclaimed: "It is useless to talk any more of negro courage. The men fight like tigers, and each and every one of them."

But the president, the army, and Northern public opinion would not yet accept the idea that African Americans could become soldiers. Evidence of black military ability—in the face of prohibitions against it—was needed. After Union forces seized New Orleans early in 1862, black officers from the Native Guards, a black Confederate unit formed in defense of the region, offered their services to General Benjamin F. Butler. Previously at Virginia's Fort Monroe, Butler now commanded the occupation forces and held responsibility for defending New Orleans and surrounding areas from concerted rebel efforts to retake them. Short-handed, Butler pondered the black unit's offer of service. Most of the men were light-skinned members of the city's black elite. With the enemy bearing down on him, he decided to enroll them. On September 27, 1862, he organized the First Regiment Louisiana Native Guard, followed later by the Second and Third Guards.

After January 1863, the army added more units and referred to them as the Corps d'Afrique. Butler permitted the Guards to keep their black officers, a deci-

sion later reversed by the War Department. The men received training and at first performed mostly garrison duty. But at the Battle of Port Hudson on May 27, 1863, and again at Milliken's Bend on June 7, 1863, the black soldiers of the Louisiana units performed with extraordinary heroism, convincing ever more Union commanders that black soldiers could perform at least as well as white troops.

Perhaps the greatest boost to the drive to recruit black soldiers began in the spring of 1862, when General David Hunter took over the Department of the South—a command encompassing the South Carolina, Georgia, and north Florida coasts. He immediately declared martial law and issued an emancipation order, which the Lincoln administration just as quickly voided. He also began raising a regiment of black soldiers. Although the War Department rejected his request for official permission to muster the unit, he persisted. At one point the House of Representatives investigated Hunter's efforts and demanded to know if he, in fact, had organized a unit of former slaves in violation of federal law. On June 23, Hunter replied to the House inquiry stating that "no regiment of 'fugitive slaves' has been or is being organized in this department.

"Colored Men Attention!"
Recruitment advertisement for
the Second Kansas Colored
Volunteers, from the Leavenworth
Daily Conservative, July 17, 1863.

There is, however, a fine regiment of persons whose late masters are 'fugitive rebels.'"[6] When Hunter's reply was read to the Congress, howls of laughter shot up from Republican supporters, while conservatives growled in disgust. His letter went on to praise the men under his command, and he advised the Congress that by the end of next fall he could have as many as fifty thousand men ready to fight the rebellion.

The War Department ended Hunter's efforts, but his successor, General Rufus Saxton, with the surprising cooperation of the War Department, reversed course and mustered the First South Carolina Volunteers on November 7, 1862. Thomas Wentworth Higginson, a Unitarian minister and former supporter of John Brown, took command of the regiment and within six days led it into action. Commanded by white officers, but with black noncommissioned officers, and composed entirely of former slaves from the region, the unit performed with exceptional efficiency and daring against the soldiers' former owners. Higginson, who later went on to a distinguished literary career, wrote many letters back home to the popular press, well aware that what his men did and what he said about them would determine the future of black recruitment and therefore the course of the war. On February 11, 1863, in the *Boston Daily Evening Traveller,* for instance, Higginson assured Northern readers that his black troops had indeed faced enemy cavalry, infantry, and cannon. In "every instance," he proudly explained, they came off "not only with unblemished honor, but with undisputed triumph."

EMANCIPATION PROCLAMATION

In his famous public reply to the New York journalist Horace Greeley in August 1862, President Abraham Lincoln declared, "If I could save the Union without freeing any slave I would do it, and if I could save it by freeing all the slaves I would do it; and if I could save it by freeing some and leaving others alone I would also do that. What I do about slavery, and the colored race, I do because I believe it helps to save the Union."[7] The president received endless opinions on what to do about slavery and the Confederacy. Antislavery forces in and out of government pressed him

Slaves listening to a reading of the
Emancipation Proclamation, by J. W.
Watts, steel engraving, 1864. The image
originally appeared in a pamphlet with the
proclamation, printed by Lucius Stebbins.

The First Reading of the Emancipation Proclamation Before the Cabinet, by Alexander Hay Ritchie, engraving, 1866, from a painting by F. B. Carpenter, 1864.

to use the opportunity the war provided to end its primary cause. Lincoln demurred. While General Robert E. Lee started his drive north in September 1862, a delegation of Chicago ministers presented Lincoln with several antislavery memorials.

The president listened to their appeals but only joked that everyone appeared to know the Lord's will except him; he wrote on September 13, 1862, "And if I can learn what it is I will do it!"[8] Still, in all the discussions during August and early September, Lincoln never hinted that he had already decided to issue a preliminary Emancipation Proclamation (he had decided by mid-July) and was just awaiting the right moment. When General George B. McClellan's Army of the Potomac intercepted Lee's advancing army at Antietam (also known as the Battle of Sharpsburg, Maryland) on September 17, 1862, Lincoln decided that the bloody engagement (the most deadly single day in all American history) was the right moment to reveal his strategy for defeating the South and restoring the Union.

As Lincoln's critics charged, the proclamation pertained only to slaves that Lincoln had no control over, and ignored the slaves of owners who lived in loyal states or who had pledged their loyalty to the Union. As Lincoln had hinted in his reply to Greeley, he chose a strategy that would keep the border states loyal and restore the Union by freeing some slaves and leaving others alone. As he stated in the September 22 proclamation, "all persons held as slaves within any state, or designated part of a state, the people whereof shall then be in rebellion against the United States, shall be then, thenceforward, and forever free." The September document said nothing about employing slaves or any other African Americans as soldiers against the South; it sought only to deprive those states in rebellion of a vital resource. Rather than aiming to change opinion in the South, the proclamation sought to attack the root of the rebellion—break its back, as the cartoon depicts—and turn European public opinion against the Confederacy. Without this move, European recognition of the South as an independent

nation was likely, which would render a Union victory more remote.

Abolitionists and Northern blacks, who never trusted Lincoln, lacked confidence that the president would keep his word and issue the final Emancipation Proclamation. When word arrived on January 1, 1863, jubilation swept through scores of gatherings across the North that had been waiting impatiently for the news. In Boston, black and white abolitionists filled Tremont Temple, and when Lincoln's stiff legal words floated above the throng, a roar of cheers exploded and hats flew into the air. Frederick Douglass thanked God for moving the president at long last, even to the point of accepting blacks into the army. "We have had a period of darkness," he declared, "but are now having the dawn of light."[9] Much sacrifice lay ahead, he warned, but Northern opinion had clearly changed. Just a few years earlier, Douglass remarked, abolitionists would have been chased out of Tremont Temple with knives and pistols; but now most of Boston celebrated the beginning of the end of slavery.

Word of the proclamation slowly

"Breaking that Backbone," by Benjamin H. Day, Jr., and published by Currier and Ives, ca. 1862. The print shows Generals Henry W. Halleck and George B. McClellan wielding the sledgehammers of skill and strategy to break the back of "the Great Southern Gyascutis." Waiting their turn are Secretary of War Stanton, with the army draft, and President Lincoln, with the Emancipation Proclamation. Lincoln wields an ax rather than a hammer.

spread southward. A majority of Southern slaves never heard of it or were convinced by their owners that it was yet another Yankee trick to capture and sell them off to Cuba. The jubilation of slaves in the border states and in northern Virginia proved short-lived when their owners reminded them that they would remain slaves so long as their owners drew breath from the air. As the months passed, the episodic effectiveness of the proclamation convinced most abolitionists that Lincoln's promise of freedom meant little, and the president's words, as the *Weekly Anglo-African* explained, were "no more humanitarian than a hundred pounder rifled cannon."[10] But as time would show, aimed in the right direction, that cannon could prove lethal.

CARNIVAL OF FURY

From July 13 to July 17, 1863, racial and class hatred erupted in New York City in the nineteenth century's largest and deadliest urban riot. On March 3, in response to the sagging war effort and staggering casualty lists, the U.S. Congress had adopted a new conscription law. New York Irish found the new law offensive as it required men as old as forty-five to enroll in the draft and took single men before those with families, placing a burden on immigrants, who often arrived unmarried. And the measure's provision allowing anyone to hire a substitute for a $300 fee clearly favored the wealthy over the poor immigrant. "A rich man's war and a poor man's fight" became the rallying cry against the law. The ability of the wealthy to avoid military service provoked vitriolic outrage and incited class antagonism. Amid the sweltering July heat, the city's opposition press

"The Riots in New York: Conflict Between the Military and the Rioters in First Avenue," from *Illustrated London News,* 1863.

stoked anger against the Conscription Act, and even the state's governor, Horatio Seymour, voiced his objections. After draft officials drew the first names

for induction, union artisans went out in the streets to protest. But soon unskilled workers, and even boys and women, poured into the streets, attack-

"The Riots in New York: Destruction of the Colored Orphan Asylum," from *Illustrated London News,* 1863.

ing draft officials and policemen. The mob quickly turned against pro-Lincoln newspaper offices and the homes of well-known abolitionists.

But the largely Irish white working class took out their anger, frustration, and fears on city blacks, whom they perceived as competitors for available employment. Moreover, they believed that a war fought for the emancipation of the slaves would lead to the mass migration of Southern blacks to the North, further reducing economic opportunities for recent immigrants. The hatred was palpable. Rioters burned the city's respectable black orphanage and then attacked any black within reach and destroyed as many black homes and businesses as possible. As the accompanying image accurately shows, in at least one case whites hanged a black resident from a tree, built a fire under him, and then stripped the flesh off his legs. For five days the mob rampaged through the black community, killing or beating as many African Americans as they could find.

Most of the black residents fled for their lives, preferring the swamps of New Jersey to the death that awaited them in New York. William P. Powell, who for years had run the Colored Seaman's Home, leaped with his family, including his disabled daughter, from their rooftop to a neighboring one. "King mob," as he lamented in *The Liberator* on July 24, destroyed his home and business, obliterating at least $3,000 worth of property and a lifetime of work. Not only was Powell a devoted Unionist, but he even had a son who served as a surgeon in the army. Why had the mob attacked so loyal a citizen? "What more could I do?" he cried out. "What further evidence was wanting to prove my allegiance in the exigencies of our unfortunate country?"

In one of the saddest tragedies related to the riot, relatives of the men in the 54th Massachusetts Volunteer Infantry—who would attack Fort Wagner the day after the riot—were either killed, beaten, or driven from the city. As Sergeant George E. Stephens recovered on Morris Island, South Carolina, after the battle, he responded to the mayhem in the August 22 issue of the *Weekly Anglo-African:* "while your mob-fiends upheld the assassin knife, and brandished the incendiary torch over the heads of our wives and children and to burn their homes, we were doing our utmost to sustain the honor of our country's flag, to perpetuate, if possible, those civil, social, and political liberties, they, who so malignantly hate us, have so fully enjoyed."

Only the arrival of infantry and artillery regiments fresh from the Gettysburg battlefield finally put an end to the outrage. About 119 people died and more than 300 suffered injuries as a result of the chaos, but the black community suffered the most. The destruction and loss

"New York—Hanging and Burning a Negro in Clarkson Street," from *Great Riots,* ca. 1880s.

proved so great that even New York's hardened leaders felt remorse. Wealthy city merchants—who depended upon African Americans for their domestic help—and Protestant clergy, with the city's cooperation, established a Committee of Merchants for the Relief of Colored People to compensate victims of the tragedy. A black clerical committee, headed by the Reverend Henry Highland Garnet, visited victims and approved levels of compensation. While regret over the incident helped create support for the organization of black New York army regiments, nothing could ever compensate the city's African American community for the murders, financial losses, and horror of the attacks.

THE 54TH MASSACHUSETTS VOLUNTEER INFANTRY REGIMENT

"The Gallant Charge of the Fifty Fourth Massachusetts (Colored) Regiment," Currier and Ives, 1863.

We have more to gain, if victorious, or more to lose, if defeated, than any other class of men." George E. Stephens, a Philadelphia cabinetmaker and sergeant in the 54th Massachusetts Volunteer Infantry Regiment, spoke for Northern blacks when, on April 11, 1863, he described the regiment's importance in the New York *Weekly Anglo-African*.

Since the Confederate attack on Fort Sumter in April 1861, African Americans had been offering their patriotism to help preserve the Union. But each time they volunteered their services, they heard the same refrain: "This is a white man's war." From the pulpit, the press, and the halls of Congress, a relentless barrage of insults insisted that blacks never could become effective soldiers. The very concept of white manhood would not permit black men to wear Union blue.

But two years of war brought the North no closer to victory, and the seemingly endless casualty lists convinced the Lincoln administration and many Northerners to experiment with black recruitment. Although some black troops had been in the field late in 1862 and the Congress had authorized the president to recruit black soldiers, President Lincoln did not do so until after he issued the Emancipation Proclamation on January 1, 1863. Boston's black leader Lewis Hayden then urged Massachusetts governor John A. Andrew to form a regiment of black troops, but as an abolitionist, Andrew needed little encouragement. On January 26 he received War Department approval to raise the 54th Massachusetts Infantry.

The governor enlisted Amos A. Lawrence, George Luther Stearns, William I. Bowditch, John Murray Forbes, Francis G. Shaw, and Morris L. Hallowell—wealthy elites—to serve on his advisory committee, carefully choose the unit's officers, and organize the regiment. Many local blacks rushed to the recruitment office to fight slavery and racism. But others hesitated, wondering if the government would keep its promise of equal pay, equipment, and benefits, and they were angered by the government's refusal to commission black officers. Then in March Frederick Douglass called out "Men of Color to Arms!" and the governor promised equal pay to the men (a promise the federal government would break). Black men from across the North traveled to Readville, Massachusetts, to join the regiment and prove the worth of black manhood.

The men felt the glare of white eyes and knew all too well that anything they did would reflect upon all African Americans. Nevertheless, as the black press explained, success of the 54th would represent the surest avenue to securing full civil rights for all African Americans. Failure was unthinkable. Under the command of twenty-five-year-old Robert Gould Shaw, the 54th left Boston, amid great celebration, on May 28 and arrived in the Department of the South (stretching from coastal South Carolina to northern Florida) on June 4.

The regiment immediately began to win support among local army commanders. In their first fight, the soldiers'

"54th Regiment!" recruitment poster, 1863.

quick and valiant rearguard action saved the Tenth Connecticut—a white unit—from capture or annihilation. The unit then volunteered to lead the attack on Fort Wagner (an earlier attempt had been a terrible failure) on July 18, 1863. At dusk, after the heaviest bombardment of the war, the regiment, with Colonel Shaw in front of his men, ran headlong at the sand-and-palmetto-log emplacement. The rebel defenders had hidden themselves in a bomb-proof shelter and emerged at full strength to meet the assault with a withering barrage of musket and cannon fire. Half of the regiment's attacking force (about six hundred) became casualties, and the regiment's young commander died on the fort's parapets; the fort would remain in Confederate hands until September.

Sergeant William H. Carney's heroics in rescuing the national flag later won him the Medal of Honor, and the unit's conduct provided convincing evidence that the "experiment" in black recruitment was a success. Although some Union commanders remained skeptical or, like General William T. Sherman, opposed to placing black men in uniform, the Union debate over black recruitment effectively ended after the 54th's heroics at Fort Wagner. Indeed, the unit's performance and the Christlike sacrifice of its handsome commander became celebrated in poetry and art, and a model of the fort even became a wildly popular attraction. Given the undeniable performance not only of the 54th but also of black units in South Carolina and Louisiana, the federal government organized the U.S. Colored Troops, leading to the recruitment of 178,000 black soldiers, about 10 percent of all Union troops. As even President Lincoln confessed, the North could not have triumphed without the aid of black troops.

FORT PILLOW

"The War in Tennessee—Confederate Massacre of Federal Troops after the Surrender at Fort Pillow, April 12, 1864," from *Scenes and Portraits of the Civil War: The Most Important Events of the Conflict Between the States Graphically Pictured* (New York: Mrs. Frank Leslie, 1894).

Black Civil War soldiers faced terrors that their white brethren hardly knew, should they fall into the hands of Confederate troops. The Confederacy, in December 1862, made clear its intentions regarding black soldiers. Captured white officers of black troops could be executed for instigating servile insurrections, and all black prisoners would be "returned to slavery." Although not official policy, Confederate forces routinely executed captured blacks, and the few who ended up in rebel prison camps, such as the infamous Andersonville, received the very worst treatment their captors could hand out. Others were shot or hanged from a tree with signs pinned to their corpses as a warning. In Union-held Louisiana in 1864, several soldiers of the 11th U.S. Colored Heavy Artillery were caught unaware by rebels and then butchered for effect. The unit's outraged white commander sent a note to his opposite number that in future cases an equal number of rebel soldiers would be put to the sword. The rebel commander replied that if Confederate soldiers or civilians were executed for "killing negroes under arms," an equal number of white Union soldiers would be executed. The standoff left the matter to be worked out on the battlefield, where the small number of black Union prisoners in rebel hands spoke to the result. In short, the South fought under the "black flag," and Confederate officers never hesitated after battles to inform their superiors that they took "no negro prisoners."[11]

A Confederate massacre of Union troops at Fort Pillow stands as a heinous act, rarely matched in the history of American warfare, but symptomatic of the fate African American soldiers faced on the battlefield. An earthen fortification overlooking the Mississippi River about forty miles above Memphis, the fort was manned by about 277 white soldiers of the 13th Tennessee Cavalry ("galvanized Yankees," or captured Confederate soldiers who had sworn allegiance to the Union) and some 270 blacks from the Sixth U.S. Colored

Heavy Artillery and the Second U.S. Colored Light Artillery. Confederate General Nathan Bedford Forrest, daring, relentless, and ruthless, wanted the fort's horses and supplies. At 4:30 a.m. on April 12, 1864, 1,500 of Forrest's men assaulted the fort and quickly seized the surrounding area, leaving the Mississippi River as the defenders' only possible escape route. That afternoon, under a flag of truce, Forrest demanded the garrison's surrender. The Union forces rejected the demand, and Forrest ordered his men to take the fort. As happens in combat, confusion reigned, and shooting apparently occurred even after the fort surrendered. Whatever happened, Confederate forces slaughtered the occupants, including civilians, turning a portion of the Mississippi River red with their blood. The extraordinary casualty rate tells the story: the fort's garrison suffered 231 killed, 100 wounded, and 226 captured. The black units suffered 64 percent killed, while the white units lost 33 percent. The attacking Confederates lost only 14 killed and 86 wounded.

Senator Benjamin F. Wade, an ardent abolitionist, oversaw the congressional investigation into the massacre (House Report, No. 65), and Congress printed forty thousand copies of its report, which became powerful wartime propaganda. The report contained testimony from survivors that was remarkably consistent and equally horrifying. Jacob Thompson, one of the many black civilians at the fort, explained that he had seen Confederates savagely murdering black troops; "they just called them out like dogs, and shot them down. I reckon they shot about fifty, white and black, right there. They nailed some black sergeants to the logs, and set the logs on fire . . . they nailed them to the logs; drove the nails right through their hands." Major Williams, a black private in the Sixth U.S. Heavy Artillery, "saw a white man burned up who was nailed up against the house. [Nailed] through his hands and feet right against the house." Ransom Anderson, also in the Sixth, testified that "all the men [who] were killed on our side were killed after the fight was over. They called them out and shot them down. Then they put some in the houses and shut them up, and burned the houses." As Woodford Cooksey of the Thirteenth Tennessee Cavalry testified,

I saw one of them shoot a black fellow in the head with three buckshot and a musket ball. The man held up his head, and then the fellow took his pistol and fired that at his head. The black man still moved, and then the fellow took his sabre and stuck it in the hole in the negro's head and jammed it way down, and said "Now, God damn you, die!" The negro did not say anything, but he moved, and the fellow took his carbine and beat his head soft with it. That was the next morning after the fight.[12]

EXTRAORDINARY HEROISM: NEW MARKET HEIGHTS

In late September 1864, Union General Benjamin F. Butler and his Army of the James were in Deep Bottom, southeast of Richmond, Virginia. In an attempt to penetrate Confederate lines south of the rebel capital and break the long siege, Butler moved his army north. Failing that goal, he would engage in a series of maneuvers to divert rebel attention from the Army of the Potomac, then at Petersburg. Union forces already had twice failed to seize rebel entrenchments at New Market Heights, outside Richmond, and General Butler believed that if black troops led the new attack and carried the day, it would once and

Christian A. Fleetwood (1840–1914). Born free in Baltimore, Fleetwood received private tutoring from a white businessman, who groomed him for work in the sugar-refining business. In 1863, he joined the Fourth Regiment, USCT, commanded by William Birney (son of the antislavery leader James G. Birney) and rose to the rank of sergeant major. His valor in saving the regiment's flag from capture won him the Medal of Honor. After the war, he worked for the Freedman's Bank and then in the War Department, becoming a leader of the thriving black community in Washington, D.C.

Milton M. Holland (1844–1910). A Texas-born slave, Holland was sent by his white father to Ohio in the 1850s to gain an education. At the outbreak of the war, he became a servant to a white officer in an Ohio regiment. In the summer of 1863, he joined the Fifth USCT. Holland also won his Medal of Honor at Fort Harrison, taking command of his company after all the officers had been killed or wounded. After the war he earned a law degree from Howard University, worked as an auditor, and in 1892 founded his own insurance company.

Powhatan Beaty (1839?-1916). Born a slave in Richmond, Beaty moved to Cincinnati in 1849, where he studied cabinetmaking and acting. In June 1863, he joined the Fifth Regiment, USCT. During the second attack at New Market, he assumed command of his company after all its officers were either killed or wounded and rescued the unit's flag, earning him the Medal of Honor. After the war he enjoyed a long career on the stage.

James D. Gardner (1839–1905). Born in Gloucester, Virginia, Gardner was probably a slave before joining the Second North Carolina Regiment in the fall of 1863. In January, the Second was redesignated the 36th USCT and guarded prisoners at Point Lookout, Maryland. In September, his unit attacked Fort Harrison, and Gardner was one of the first black soldiers to enter the rebel fortification. His heroism in the attack won him the Medal of Honor. After the war he farmed and worked on various railroads.

for all end lingering prejudice in the army against the use of black troops. As he later recalled in his memoir, Butler felt "determined to put them in position, to demonstrate the fact of the value of the negro as a soldier."

Soldiers from the First, Fourth, Fifth, Sixth, 22nd, 36th, 37th, and 38th U.S. Colored Troops engaged the enemy on September 29, 1864. The men had begun their preparations at three a.m.—after marching into position the same night—and at four a.m. General Butler visited them, proclaiming that the attack must succeed. A nearly impossible challenge faced the soldiers, he understood, and he fired their spirits by encouraging them to yell "Remember Fort Pillow" as they charged the entrenchments. At 5:30 a.m., as the sun was just breaking over the horizon and the battlefield was still shrouded in fog, the Fourth and Sixth USCT began the assault.

They had been ordered to use only the bayonet, which left them vulnerable to withering enemy fire, and they were stunned to find ravines, woods, swamps, roots, felled trees, and sharpened stakes blocking their approach. The few men who survived the obstacle course and reached the rebel lines were either captured or shot down. The rebels then summarily executed the wounded. The heroism of Christian A. Fleetwood, Alfred B. Hilton, and Charles Veal from the Fourth USCT and Thomas Hawkins and Alexander Kelly from the Sixth would earn them the Medal of Honor. Nevertheless, the initial assault failed.

At seven a.m. the Fifth, 36th, and 38th USCT renewed the attack over the very same ground, over the bodies of their comrades, and up into the enemy's trenches. So many officers (white) had been killed or wounded that black noncommissioned officers, such as Milton M. Holland, Robert Pinn, and Powhatan Beaty, took command of their companies; they would win the Medal of Honor for their courage and leadership. James Gardner of the 38th rushed the rebel lines and shot an enemy officer who was attempting to rally his men, then drove his bayonet up to the gun muzzle into the man's chest. Edward Ratcliff, a sergeant in the 38th from Yorktown, was the first enlisted man to enter the rebel trenches, leading Company C of the regiment, for which he also would win the Medal of Honor. In two days of fighting, Union forces lost 391 killed, 2,317 wounded, and 649 either missing or captured. In total, fourteen African American soldiers would win the Medal of Honor for their valor in the engagement.

As the main Union force chased after the retreating enemy, survivors of the Sixth USCT scoured the battlefield for their wounded comrades. One black sergeant, found lying on the field with two shattered legs, asked a lieutenant if the attack had succeeded. When told that the rebels had been driven from the heights, the sergeant cheered wildly. Fearing that the man would die instantly if he did not remain calm, the officer advised him that he probably would not survive his injuries. But the sergeant remained unconcerned and proudly declared that he had done his duty.

DEFENDING RIGHTS IN
THE MIDST OF WAR

The Civil War offered the possibility of ending slavery and gave African Americans the opportunity to assert their claim to full civil rights. While blacks in the North had claimed American citizenship since the eighteenth century, the war gave Southern blacks their first chance to do so.

New Orleans, captured by Union forces in April 1862, possessed a large, well-educated, and prosperous free black population, as well as many slaves. Expulsion of Confederate forces opened up unprecedented opportunities for the city's colored populations. One New Orleans free black who seized the moment was Louis Charles Roudanez. Born in St. James Parish in 1823 to a white French merchant and a free woman of color, Roudanez grew up as part of the city's black elite and in 1844 left for medical training in Paris, where he earned a medical degree in 1853. He returned to the United States, attended Dartmouth College, and earned a second medical degree in 1857.

The Union occupation moved Roudanez to join the struggle for full civil rights. He and other members of the city's black elite established the short-lived *Union*, a newspaper that gave voice to the local free black community. After its close, Roudanez and his brother Jean-Baptiste Roudanez established *The New Orleans Tribune*, the nation's first black daily newspaper, which represented the interests of free blacks and the former slaves. The paper took an uncompromising stand for black suffrage and full civil rights for all African Americans. It proved a sharp critic of the Lincoln administration's handling of the occupation and its earliest Reconstruction plans. Rather than give abandoned rebel lands to those who had been forced to labor on those fields, the

Louis Charles Roudanez (1823–90). Roudanez founded *The New Orleans Tribune*.

John S. Rock (1826–66). Born free in New Jersey, Rock was the first African American lawyer to win the right to practice before the U.S. Supreme Court. He was also a doctor and dentist, and one of Boston's most eloquent black abolitionists. During the war he helped recruit for the 54th Massachusetts Infantry and employed his legal skills to assist black troops in getting their bounties and pensions. From *Harper's Weekly,* February 25, 1865.

government leased the property, the paper reported on September 24, 1864, to "avaricious adventurers . . . whose sole endeavor and object was not to enlighten, improve and elevate, but to make as much money as possible out of the labor of these colored proletaries."

Until the paper closed in 1869, Roudanez's *Tribune* reported the activities of local Freedmen's Aid groups and provided a searing record of the increasing oppression of African Americans. "All over the state," the paper reported on July 18, 1865, "the Freedmen are threatened in their lives, robbed of their liberties and deprived of the fruits of their toils and labor. . . . In many parts of the state, a system of terror has been inaugurated, to keep down the Freedmen; several have already been murdered and many more will be if we do not resist." In response, the paper advised blacks to arm themselves. The former rebels, the paper advised, "must be taught to respect the lives of their fellow citizens." The *Tribune* also recommended that the government dispatch more federal troops to the city, especially "a few companies of colored troops into the worst parishes," which

the paper asserted "would do a great deal toward bringing the slaveholders to their senses. The black regiments carry with them the vivid and forcible image of the revolution, i.e. of the elevation of the downtrodden race to the level of citizens."

Northern blacks, who belonged to numerous Northern antislavery societies, also had formed their own fraternal, self-help, literary, and abolitionist organizations and had taken the lead in orchestrating Underground Railroad activities. Now, as blacks in liberated sections of the South had done, Northern black leaders took advantage of the war to advance the struggle for civil rights. In early October 1864 in Syracuse, they convened the National Convention of Colored Men, a national organization to advance black rights.

With delegates from eighteen states, it was the largest and most representative meeting of black leaders prior to Reconstruction. John S. Rock, a Boston black abolitionist leader who would be the first black lawyer to win the right to argue cases before the U.S. Supreme Court, addressed the convention on October 6. "I come from Massachusetts," he exclaimed, "where we are jealous of every right." He pointed to the heroism of the black soldiers at Milliken's Bend, Port Hudson, and Fort Wagner, and in the campaign to seize Richmond; their service in blood underpinned black claims to citizenship. Such patriotism, Rock explained, had typified the African American community since the American Revolution. He and members of the Syracuse convention recognized that a defining moment in the nation's history had arrived, and they were determined to place the nation back on the road to freedom and liberty. Black men, Rock exclaimed, wanted nothing special for their devotion. "We ask the same for the black man that is asked for the white man; nothing more and nothing less."[13]

The convention went on to form the National Equal Rights League (NERL). With extensive state and local auxiliaries, the NERL focused black protest and offered a platform to debate strategy and an independent organization to promote black interests and advance social change. While the national organization would be short-lived, failing to reach any consensus on strategy or tactics, several state auxiliaries would prove very effective and, at the close of the century, become models for further black efforts.

FRUIT OF A BITTER HARVEST: THE THIRTEENTH AMENDMENT

Fondly do we hope—fervently do we pray—that this mighty scourge of war may speedily pass away. Yet, if God wills that it continue, until all the wealth piled by the bondman's two hundred and fifty years of unrequited toil shall be sunk, and until every drop of blood drawn with the lash shall be paid by another drawn with the sword, as was said three thousand years ago, so still it must be said 'the judgments of the Lord are true and righteous altogether.'" Lincoln's enduring words from his Second Inaugural Address, coupled with the lawyerly Emancipation Proclamation, may leave the impression that a constitutional amendment to end slavery inevitably resulted from the war.

Such a consequence, however logical, was by no means inevitable. The North entered the war to preserve the Union and nothing more. The Emancipation Proclamation left the liberation of slaves to the army, which never encountered the overwhelming majority of enslaved people; the proclamation had no impact in the loyal border states or upon loyal slave owners. Moreover, a deeply divided Congress and a legally fastidious presi-

Resolution approving submission of the Thirteenth Amendment to the states for ratification, February 1, 1865.

142

dent largely groped their way toward solutions that would defeat the South. After two years of bitter war, the North finally—and reluctantly—concluded that no victory was possible without attacking the foundation of the war: slavery. The Republican Party did stand for such an amendment in the 1864 election, but it did not occupy much political debate, and public attention remained riveted on the war and the endless casualty lists. Despite his party's official stand on an amendment, Lincoln said nothing about the slow process of enabling legislation in the U.S. Senate, and especially in the House, until December 1864. Then the president, safely reelected, and with the city of Atlanta safely in General Sherman's pocket, informed party leaders in the House that he wished to have legislation passed before he gave his inaugural address in March.

The pressure on the Congress to act mounted as mammoth petitions from the Northern public rolled into the House insisting upon a final end to the institution of slavery everywhere. Both houses of Congress debated proposed resolutions for a constitutional amendment abolishing slavery. But when the final vote came on January 31, 1865, to victorious shouts, fifty-six congressmen still opposed it. The president insisted on signing the resolution, although as a congressional document it was entirely unnecessary. What, however, would the end of slavery mean? What rights did the former slaves now possess? Who determined the extent of their rights, and how would they be exercised? The Thirteenth Amendment to the Constitution only began that debate.

FIRST BLACK VOICE IN CONGRESS

No accident led Henry Highland Garnet to become the first African American to address Congress. Minister, editor, and intellectual, Garnet was one of the leading voices of black abolitionism in the 1850s. Born slaves in Maryland, as he was in 1815, his family escaped to Pennsylvania and in 1825 moved to New York City. There Garnet, his cousin Samuel Ringgold Ward (who also became a minister and an abolitionist), and the great pan-Africanist and minister Alexander Crummell attended the city's influential African Free School. Garnet went on to attend the Noyes Academy in Canaan, New Hampshire (where enraged whites closed the interracial school), and the Oneida Institute in Whitesboro, New York, which also enrolled Crummell.

Garnet's early experience with southern slavery and northern discrimination made him a resolute abolitionist, and he became a founding member of New York's American and Foreign Anti-Slavery Society. He wrote prolifically for the black press, particularly for *The Colored American, Voice of the Fugi-* *tive, The North Star,* and the New York *Weekly Anglo-African.* His best-known speech remains his 1843 "Address to the Slaves of the United States." Its call for slave insurrections was so radical that even John Brown sought to temper it and attendees at the Buffalo convention where Garnet delivered it refused to endorse it—an accurate version did not appear in print until March 1863, after the North had declared war on slavery.

Garnet became so influential that he served on the executive committee of the American Missionary Association, and he became the pastor of the Shiloh Baptist Church in New York City, a significant step up from his ministry in Troy, New York. Before the outbreak of the Civil War, Garnet founded the controversial African Civilization Society, which advocated that black Americans emigrate to Africa and evangelize it for Christianity. But once the war commenced, the society turned its attention to the relief of the freedpeople. In 1864, Garnet received the call to become pastor at Washington, D.C.'s Fifteenth Street Presbyterian Church. This was

Henry Highland Garnet (1815–82).

the pulpit of the Reverend John F. Cook, who had been part of the delegation that met with President Lincoln in August 1862, and it would later be occupied by the Reverend Francis J. Grimké, one of the founders of the NAACP. Garnet's church became the home for the Contraband Relief Association, founded by Elizabeth Keckley, Mrs. Lincoln's seamstress and a denizen of the White House.

At the outset of 1865, the chaplain of the U.S. House of Representatives, William H. Channing, a Boston-born abolitionist and Unitarian minister, invited Garnet to address the House and to urge the nation to ratify Congress's constitutional amendment to permanently end slavery in the United States; or in Garnet's words, to "speedily finish the work he [God] has given you to do." In his "Memorial Discourse" delivered on February 12, 1865, Garnet drew upon Matthew 23:4 to advise the Congress that a heavy responsibility now lay on it to act. For too long others have borne the "heavy and grievous burdens of duties

and obligation." The American church and all elected officials had always known the right course of action, but, Garnet said, like the biblical scribes and Pharisees, they refused to do right. Not one year earlier, Garnet reminded the Congress, New York City's Fernando Wood had proclaimed in the same halls that "the best possible condition of the negro is slavery." Although Americans spoke in hallowed terms of the Constitution's descent from the Magna Carta and believed that God had blessed the nation with religious liberty, that Con-

stitution nevertheless doomed others of the "same blood" to "life-long servitude and chains." Of this, Garnet could speak with authority: "The first sounds that startled my ear, and sent a shudder through my soul, were the cracking of the whip, and the clanking of chains." The Congress must act, Garnet exclaimed, and do so until "emancipation shall be followed by enfranchisement, and all men holding allegiance to the government shall enjoy every right of American citizenship."[14]

BUREAU OF REFUGEES, FREEDMEN, AND ABANDONED LANDS

The Civil War prompted the emancipation of almost four million slaves, but it also left the war-ravaged South in a state of physical, political, economic, and social ruin. On a human level, the war's end left most of the former slaves and displaced whites in desperation, facing a future of homelessness and near starvation. Clearly, a successful reconstruction of the Southern states would require large-scale relief efforts to assist their most vulnerable citizens. Accordingly, on March 3, 1865, the U.S. Congress adopted the Freedmen's Bureau bill, which established the Bureau of Refugees, Freedmen, and Abandoned Lands under the auspices of the War Department.

The "Freedmen's Bureau," as it became popularly known, was a comprehensive relief agency designed to facilitate the transition from slavery to freedom. Originally conceived as a temporary agency, the bureau's primary function was to address the immediate needs of freed slaves and war refugees by providing food, clothing, fuel, temporary living facilities, and medical treat-

"The Freedman's Bureau!" broadside, 1866. The Democratic Party, north and south, remained opposed to government intervention on behalf of the former slaves.

ment. But it rapidly developed a broader social service agenda that included the promotion of education, job placement, legal assistance, and settlement on abandoned or confiscated lands. Headed by Union general Oliver Otis Howard,

the bureau promised to expand the role of the federal government in overseeing the social welfare of its citizens. Although Congress did not appropriate any specific monies for this daring new federal agency, Howard drew from the

Glimpses at the Freedmen—the Freedmen's Union Industrial School, Richmond, Va., by James E. Taylor, wood engraving, 1866. Many of the first black schools established in the South received funding from the Freedmen's Bureau. Each school was required to submit detailed reports on the number of students instructed and the progress of their instruction. Women, black and white, and men—some former soldiers—went south to take up the cause of the freedpeople.

an unnecessary infringement on states' rights, Congress overrode the veto and enacted the bill.

Despite criticism by the president and its unpopularity among white Southerners, the Freedmen's Bureau continued its relief efforts and social welfare programs. The hundreds of reports by its many agents very often described the relentless exploitation and violence directed at former slaves, as well as their passion to acquire the education that slavery had denied them. Over time it became clear that one of the bureau's most essential and lasting contributions was the creation of freedmen's schools. Within a year of its founding, the bureau, assisted by Freedmen's Aid Societies and Northern missionary groups, had established 740 schools, serving nearly 100,000 students throughout the South. By 1870 the Freedmen's Bureau's educational network included more than 2,500 schools and 150,000 students, plus several colleges dedicated to training black teachers. Thanks to the bureau, and to the thousands of teachers who came South, often at considerable personal

War Department's budget and resources to fund a series of ambitious programs.

Howard hoped to lay the foundation for a biracial, free-labor society based on national citizenship. To a large extent, bureau employees often found themselves dealing with the immediate task of restoring order, especially in matters of land, law, and labor. In addition to leasing the lands under its control, the bureau established special tribunals in 1865 to adjudicate civil disputes between whites and blacks, and it assisted in formulating labor contracts between landowners and employees, usually to the detriment of the former slaves.

As its first year drew to a close, the bureau received additional support from Congress's Committee on Reconstruction. The committee, tasked with gathering information about the state of affairs in the South, recommended that Congress extend the term of the Freedmen's Bureau and increase its powers. Concerned about the emerging Black Codes, unfair labor practices, and increased Klan activity, Congress passed a new Freedmen's Bureau bill in February 1866. The bill provided for the indef-inite extension of the bureau's life and authorized increased power to supervise labor contracts. Although President Andrew Johnson vetoed the bill—as he would so many during his tenure—as

"Office of the Freedmen's Bureau, Memphis, Tennessee," from *Harper's Weekly,* 1866. Agents of the Freedmen's Bureau—many of them soldiers or former soldiers— acted as intermediaries between the ex-slaves and their former owners to establish just, free-labor work contracts and to protect the freedpeople from exploitation and abuse. The bureau, however, never had sufficient power to resist white domination.

risk and sacrifice, educational instruction for blacks on a mass scale—once unthinkable in the South—had become a reality.

Although Congress extended the bureau's tenure past its initial one-year term, public support for the bureau's activities waned as the decade of the 1860s drew to a close. Northerners were losing interest in the overall Reconstruction effort, and Ku Klux Klan violence and dogged political resistance weakened their resolve, leaving the Freedmen's Bureau politically vulnerable. In 1869, Congress voted to terminate all of the bureau's activities except for those involving education and veterans' affairs, and a year later it cut off the bureau's educational funding. With the elimination of its schools, the bureau lost most of its influence over Southern life. Two years later, in 1872, Congress closed the bureau altogether.

FREEDMAN'S BANK

When Congress established the Freedmen's Bureau on March 3, 1865, it also chartered the Freedman's Savings and Trust Company. The "Freedman's Bank," as it became known, was the brainchild of Congregational minister John W. Alvord, who saw that many black soldiers who had received back pay and bounty payments for their service in the Civil War had no safe place to deposit their money. In order to promote thrift, savings, and financial security, Alvord proposed the creation of an innovative financial institution designed to address the unique needs of African American veterans and the former slaves. Most Southern blacks, who had never received compensation for their work, were now encouraged to save their hard-earned wages and become a part of the economic mainstream. The Freedman's Bank, although a privately owned corporation, operated much like an arm of the government-run Freedmen's Bureau, and sought to help Southern blacks move from slavery to freedom. Advertisements for the bank commonly bore the images of President Lincoln and the U.S. flag. Freedmen's Bureau commissioner Oliver Otis Howard considered "the Freedman's Savings and Trust Company to be greatly needed by the colored people" and "welcomed it as an auxiliary to the Freedman's [sic] Bureau."[15]

Prompted by this ostensible federal backing, thousands of freedpeople opened individual savings accounts. Despite the depositors' meager resources (most of the accounts never had more than fifty dollars), the bank grew steadily over the years, and at its peak in the early 1870s its assets totaled nearly $3.7 million. With some thirty-four branch offices in seventeen states, the Freedman's Bank became an important symbol of self-sufficiency and economic promise.

Unfortunately, the success of the Freedman's Bank, like that of the broader Freedmen's Bureau, proved fleeting. In 1867, the bank moved its headquarters from New York City to Washington, D.C., and a new board of trustees soon adopted a riskier financial strategy. In 1870, the board persuaded Congress to amend the bank's charter and allow it to invest its assets in real estate mortgages.

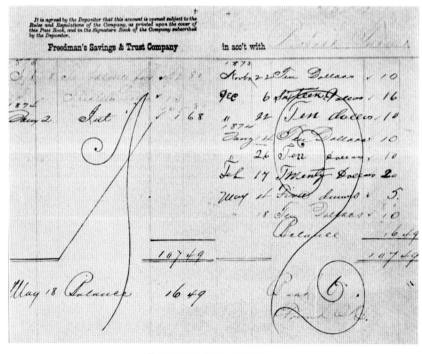

Freedman's Bank passbook.

Headquarters of the Freedman's Bank, at Pennsylvania and Madison Place, N.W., Washington, D.C., woodcut, ca. 1880.

Frederick Douglass (1818–95), lithograph, ca. 1870.

lass to take on the role of bank president. They hoped that his esteem among African Americans would inspire the faith of depositors and steady its reputation. Douglass, who seemed confident in the bank's standing, invested $10,000 of his own money to reassure the clientele.

After several months as president, however, Douglass realized that the bank was doomed, and in June 1874 the Freedman's Bank closed. Although Douglass had urged Congress to take steps to protect the investors, the bank had only $31,000 to cover its obligations when its doors closed; it left its more than 61,000 depositors with no financial protection. Despite the government's loose affiliation with the bank and its arguable moral obligation, Congress was not legally required to insure the depositors' lost funds. Ultimately, many freedmen received nothing from the bank, while others obtained just cents on the dollar. For several decades, depositors and their descendants unsuccessfully lob-

An economic panic in 1873, coupled with bad investments, unsecured loans, and runaway deflation, sent the bank spiraling toward its demise. In March 1874, in a last-ditch effort to rescue the failing bank, the board invited Frederick Doug-

bied the federal government to recompense those who had invested in the Freedman's Bank. In the end, however, having put their faith in an institution that had seemed so promising, African Americans across the country received only disappointment as their return.

THE LINCOLN ASSASSINATION

The fourteenth of April "will be a day forever memorable in history by an act of atrocity that has no parallel in the annals of men." On April 22, 1865, the New Orleans *Black Republican,* a newspaper founded on the day Lincoln died by the Reverend S. W. Rogers, a former slave, expressed its grief and shock at the news. "Who next?" the paper wondered. The cause, however, was no mystery: "These dreadful deeds are a fitting finale of this brutal and bloody rebellion. They are the natural results of it." African Americans understood all too well that the gun John Wilkes Booth had used to kill the president was also aimed at them. "The

greatest earthly friend of the colored race has fallen by the same spirit that has so long oppressed and destroyed us. In giving us our liberty," Rogers wrote, "he has lost his own life."

Booth had been in the audience to hear Lincoln's Second Inaugural Address—"a sacred effort," Frederick Douglass later told the president—and was present at his final public address, given from the second floor of the White House on April 11. Lincoln stated that in Louisiana, which in many ways served as a model for the general reconstruction of the Southern states, the "very intelligent" blacks and "those who serve our cause as soldiers" should be given

the right to vote. On the very day of Lincoln's address, the new chief justice of the U.S. Supreme Court, Salmon P. Chase, twice encouraged the president to support black suffrage, or at least as much as he felt was practical. Booth, on the other hand, after hearing Lincoln express support for black voting rights, decided that rather than kidnap the president, he would kill him. Devoted to the South and to white supremacy and viewing slavery as a divine blessing, Booth could not contain his rage at Lincoln's modest proposal.

The murder shocked a nation that believed it could no longer be shaken by death. For Union soldiers in the

"The Assassination of President Lincoln, at Ford's Theatre, Washington, D.C., April 14, 1865," Currier and Ives, 1865.

J. Sella Martin (1832–76). Born a slave in Charlotte, North Carolina, Martin taught himself to read and write and escaped to Chicago in 1856. Two years later he served as a minister in Buffalo, then moved to Boston. There he took over the Joy Street Church, also known as the First Independent Baptist Church, which was a focus of Underground Railroad activities and later a recruitment center for the 54th Massachusetts Infantry. An eloquent orator, Martin traveled to Britain in 1864 to raise funds for the freedpeople.

field—black and white—who thought the war had ended, sadness quickly turned to rage. Many wanted to reload their weapons and wipe out the Southern "race." Searching for some redeeming aspect of the killing, the editor of the New York *Weekly Anglo-African* opined on April 22 that Booth's murderous act at least might have put a stop to any quick reintegration of the South—"the wolves, serpents and savage barbarians who yet constitute the head and front of the Southern people"—into the Union. To a people weary of war and its terrible sacrifices, the paper warned that the Union had to remain alert to the dangers posed by those "whose hearts are now dancing the scalp dance over the remains of our murdered President."

But equally large dangers remained in the North, a fact that few African Americans would deny. When Lincoln's funeral train departed Washington for the long, slow journey to Springfield,

Illinois, black Americans gathered along the route to honor the martyred president. Officials in New York City—which had failed to support Lincoln in life—now wished to honor him in death with a huge funeral procession. On April 22, blacks learned from the city council that they could not participate in the march. Officials explained that the black request to participate came too late; more to the point, Irish and white Freemasons would refuse to participate if blacks were allowed into the procession. Swift reaction and cries of "Shame! Shame!" filled the papers. Even the Union League supported the New York blacks' request to march and pressured the council to reverse its ugly decision. The black minister and abolitionist J. Sella Martin denounced the city's move in a letter, which the *New York Evening Post* refused to print. Instead, *The Liberator* published it, allowing Martin to remind city officials that Lincoln's

last public words left no doubt that he would want those who helped save the Union to honor him with their presence. Only after the council received a telegram from the War Department did it reverse its decision and grant blacks permission to participate. But organizers placed all the black groups so far back in line that by the time they joined the procession, Lincoln's coffin already had left the city.

PART SEVEN

RECONSTRUCTING
A NATION

1866–1877

FORMATION OF THE KU KLUX KLAN

Shrouded in mystery, fear, and terror for more than a century, the Ku Klux Klan sparks images of violence, intimidation, and hatred. The organization's iconic hooded figures and burning crosses mark a shameful yet enduring chapter in American history.

The nation's most notorious terrorist organization traces its origins to the small town of Pulaski, Tennessee. Although the details are somewhat unclear, most pinpoint the founding of the KKK to the spring of 1866. Six ex-Confederate soldiers—Captain John C. Lester, Major James R. Crow, John B. Kennedy, Calvin Jones, Richard R. Reed, and Frank O. McCord—looking for amusement in the postwar tedium, established a fraternal organization. The group quickly took on a different mission, and Nathan Bedford Forrest, the Confederate general famed for the slaughter of black and white Union troops at Fort Pillow, became the KKK's first Grand Wizard. Ku Klux Klan, a combination of the Greek word for "circle," *kuklos,* and the alliterative spelling of *clan,* was modeled after the widespread college fraternity Kuklos Adelphon, or "old Kappa Alpha." The early Klan required absolute secrecy from its members; it maintained an elaborate hierarchy, and its members performed ritualistic initiation ceremonies. Klansmen dressed up in the now infamous conical hoods with holes for the eyes and nose, often in an attempt to frighten allegedly superstitious freedmen with ghostly images.

What began as a relatively harmless social club quickly became intricately involved in the bitter and violent struggles of the Reconstruction era. Within a year of its founding, the Klan had spread well beyond Tennessee into all the former Confederate states and Kentucky.

"The Union As It Was," by Thomas Nast, *Harper's Weekly,* October 24, 1874. Here the popular illustrator Nast warned about the dangers of the Klan.

The organization became a haven for white supremacist vigilantes, many of whom had served in the Confederate army, determined to maintain the social and political remnants of slavery. During a secret convention in Nashville in 1867, the Klan adopted its statement of "Organization and Principles." Ironically, the KKK's stated mission was "to protect the weak, the innocent, and the defenseless, from the indignities, wrongs, and outrages of the lawless, the violent, and the brutal" and "to protect and defend the Constitution of the United States, and all laws passed in conformity thereto."[1]

With its charter in hand, the self-righteous "institution of Chivalry, Humanity, Mercy, and Patriotism" embarked on a campaign of terror to thwart the Republican-controlled federal government's efforts to grant civil rights and political equality to the recently freed slaves. The Klan's principles rested on the basic premise that blacks were inferior members of society undeserving of citizenship or legal protection. Its main goals were to prevent blacks from voting and to disrupt Republican political activity. Targeting African Americans, white Republicans, and anyone who challenged the traditional racial hierarchy, the KKK committed countless acts of vandalism, intimidation, assault, and murder. Those who dared to stand up to the Klan risked injury or death, as local and state law enforcement officers, many of whom either belonged to the Klan or agreed tacitly or otherwise with its white supremacist ideals, turned a blind eye to the organization's brutality.

Klan violence spiraled out of control, and Congress responded by passing a series of federal acts to enforce the Fourteenth and Fifteenth amendments. The most important of the three enforcement acts was the Civil Rights Act of 1871, more commonly known as the Ku Klux Klan Act, which granted the federal rather than state governments the right to prosecute individuals who deprived or conspired to deprive citizens of their constitutionally guaranteed rights. The act also authorized military intervention and the suspension of habeas corpus to prevent lawlessness. The Klan Act yielded hundreds of indictments and arrests, effectively curtailing the KKK's power. By 1873 the organization had essentially disbanded. Unfortunately, this development brought little relief to the region, since the organization had already achieved its goal of neutralizing the effort to reconstruct the South. With the formal close of Reconstruction in 1877, the Klan's mystique as the primary force behind the white South's agenda for redemption was well established.

CIVIL RIGHTS ACT OF 1866

In 1865, the Thirteenth Amendment abolished slavery, but the full meaning of emancipation remained elusive. Vice President Andrew Johnson, although hailing from Tennessee, had been a staunch foe of secession and an enemy of the planter class. When he assumed the presidency after Lincoln's assassination, black abolitionists and their white allies believed they would have a sympathetic ear in the White House.

On February 7, 1866, representing the national convention of black leaders that was meeting in Washington to formulate goals for Reconstruction, Frederick Douglass, his son Lewis H. Douglass, George T. Downing (1819–1903), and several other blacks visited the White House to lobby the president. Downing, a wealthy Rhode Islander, addressed the president first. "We are Americans, native-born Americans; we are citizens," he asserted. "We see no recognition of color or race in the organic law of the land." During the Civil War the government justly reached "its strong arm into the States and demand[ed] from those who owe it allegiance, their assistance and support. May it not reach out a like arm to secure and protect its subjects upon whom it has a claim?" Douglass appealed to Johnson for black suffrage: "Your noble and humane predecessor placed in our hands the sword to assist in saving the nation, and we do hope that you, his able successor,

Frederick Douglass, ca. 1860.

will favorably regard the placing in our hands, the ballot with which to save ourselves."[2]

According to *The Christian Recorder*, which reported the meeting on February 17, 1866, the president astounded Douglass and his colleagues by advising the group to solve the nation's racial problems by colonizing themselves. Claiming to be "a friend of the colored man," Johnson rejected their pleas, declaring that "I do not want to adopt a policy that I believe will end in a contest between the races, which if persisted in will result in the extermination of one or the other." In response, the committee issued a public letter declaring that Johnson's views were "entirely unsound, and prejudicial to the highest interests of our race, as well as our country at large."[3]

The president, was, in fact, intent on reinstating white supremacy in the South. Radical Republicans in the Congress set out to thwart him. The Joint Committee on Reconstruction, established to investigate conditions in the South and to recommend legislation, proposed "an Act to protect all Persons in the United States in their Civil Rights, and furnish the Means of their Vindication." This Civil Rights Act of 1866 received near-unanimous support from Republicans and passed both houses of Congress. But on March 27, 1866, Johnson vetoed it, claiming that it unconstitutionally infringed upon states' rights. Undeterred, Congress voted on April 9 to override the veto, as it would do in so many other cases, making the Civil Rights Act of 1866 the law of the land.

Relying on the Thirteenth Amendment's enforcement clause ("Congress shall have power to enforce this article by appropriate legislation"), the 1866 law was the first federal statute designed to define and protect individual rights and liberties at the national level. Its first provision overruled the Supreme Court's decree in *Dred Scott v. Sandford* (1857) that blacks could never be citizens of the United States, asserting that "all persons born in the United States . . . are hereby declared to be citizens of the United States." Further, it ordered that "such citizens, of every race and color, without regard to any previous condition of slavery or involuntary servi-

Andrew Johnson (1808–75). The seventeenth U.S. president, Johnson began life as a tailor in North Carolina and resettled in Tennessee. Lincoln took on the War Democrat as his second vice president to shore up support in the border states. Johnson had been a vociferous opponent of secession and a critic of the planter class, thus winning support even among abolitionists. But after Lincoln's death, Johnson's repugnant racial views assumed center stage, and he opposed every effort by Congress to reconstruct the South and benefit African Americans.

"Andrew Johnson's Reconstruction, and How It Works," by Thomas Nast, *Harper's Weekly,* September 1, 1866.

tude . . . shall have the same right, in every State and Territory in the United States." All citizens thus could "make and enforce contracts, to sue, to inherit, purchase, lease, sell, hold, and convey real and personal property," and enjoy full access to "all laws and proceedings" designed to protect "the security of person and property."

Many congressional leaders, however, questioned whether the Thirteenth Amendment provided adequate authority for such sweeping legislation. Spurred by the lingering controversy, Congress passed the Fourteenth Amendment, which duplicated many of the provisions of the Civil Rights Act, and the Fifteenth Amendment, which prohibited denying a citizen the right to vote based on race. Operating under the enforcement provisions of these two constitutional amendments, Congress reenacted the Civil Rights Act in 1870, as well as other civil rights acts in 1871 and 1875.

But by the 1880s the Reconstruction-era civil rights legislation was having little practical effect. Kentucky's highest court, in *Bowling v. Commonwealth* (1867), explicitly declared the Civil Rights Act of 1866 unconstitutional, while other states simply ignored the law. The federal government made few attempts at enforcement, and the U.S. Supreme Court, in the 1883 Civil Rights Cases, effectively abrogated all civil rights legislation, declaring that Congress had no power to regulate private discrimination. The Civil Rights Act of 1866 (now codified as Section 1981 of the U.S. Code) languished as an unenforceable relic of Reconstruction, but during the 1960s NAACP attorneys persuaded the federal judiciary to restore its enforceability.

MURDER IN MEMPHIS, 1866

"Memphis, Tennessee," by Henry Lewis, hand-colored lithograph, 1854–57.

At the end of the Civil War, Memphis, Tennessee, was home to a growing number of freedpeople, as thousands of African Americans came to the city to seek the aid of the Freedmen's Bureau and to escape the plantations. Moreover, Fort Pickering, in south Memphis, was home to three regiments of black soldiers, the 59th and 61st U.S. Colored Infantry, and the Third U.S. Colored Heavy Artillery; along with them came networks of extended families that had traveled with them, and depended on the Union army for basic protection, food, money, and even clothing, in the form of discarded army uniforms.

White city leaders decried the presence of this population. The newest black residents were invariably vagrants, they claimed, and by refusing to work on the surrounding plantations they threatened to choke off the vital flow of raw materials into and out of the city. The presence of black troops, who regularly patrolled the streets around Fort Pickering, proved especially irritating to whites. The presence of former slaves, clothed in the uniform of the federal government and empowered to carry weapons and keep the peace as provost guards, starkly reminded them of the dramatic changes that the Union victory had brought to the South's social order.

On April 30, 1866, the last of the African American troops stationed at Fort Pickering were mustered out of service. Later that day, a group of Memphis policemen attempted to arrest a former soldier in the neighborhood outside the fort. Other former black soldiers in the area, still in uniform and still armed, intervened and exchanged shots with whites. Although contemporary accounts differ on which side fired first, at the end of the affair two whites were dead, both apparently killed accidentally by other whites. The ex-soldiers retreated to Fort Pickering, where the former cavalry officer General George Stoneman, commander of the post, disarmed them. For a time the incident appeared to have concluded.

Secretly, however, whites amassed additional support and proceeded to attack the south Memphis African American community beginning on May 1. For three days they ruthlessly attacked black men, women, and children; they especially targeted former black soldiers and anyone with ties to the fort. Five black women—four of whom were related to soldiers—were brutally raped during the violence. Two women were gang-raped by a group of seven men after photographs of Union officers were found in the women's home. Most of the forty-six blacks murdered in the riots were found dressed, at least partially, in Union blue. Additionally, the mob attacked other symbols of federal authority, including several schools and a hospital built by the Freedmen's Bureau. In addition to the dead, another eighty blacks were injured. Whites also burglarized more than one hundred homes and incinerated dozens of buildings in black neighborhoods. Finally General Stoneman declared martial law on May 3 and ordered federal troops to patrol the streets to keep the peace.

In the days after the riots, the Memphis press blamed African Americans, particularly the black soldiers from Fort Pickering, for the carnage. "It is only with the negro soldiers that trouble has ever existed," claimed the *Memphis Daily Avalanche* in mid-May 1866. "With their departure, will come order, confidence, and the good will of old days." Other voices blamed the city's poor Irish immigrants, who dominated the ranks of the police force and who, some claimed, felt the most threatened by the economic competition from the poor blacks. Scholars have since demonstrated, however, that native-born whites as well as Irishmen composed the mobs, which also included artisans and some city officials, poor white laborers, and even policemen. Contemporary reports recorded the presence of the mayor, attorney general, and other local officials among the bands of whites responsible for the violence.

As the story of the Memphis riot spread across the nation, Congress

"Scenes in Memphis, Tennessee, During the Riot," by Alfred R. Waud, *Harper's Weekly,* May 26, 1866.

launched an investigation to determine the cause. The congressional committee concluded, based on what happened in Memphis and elsewhere, that the lives of African Americans in the South depended upon federal protection. Their report helped build support within Congress for more thorough federal policies to govern the former Confederate states, ones that would soon come to be known as Radical Reconstruction. In the case of the Memphis incident, however, no one was ever arrested or punished for the crimes committed during the three days of violence in the spring of 1866.

FOURTEENTH AMENDMENT AND
BLACK CITIZENSHIP

In 1865, the adoption of the Thirteenth Amendment abolished slavery throughout the Union. But what did the newly won freedom mean for formerly enslaved African Americans? President Andrew Johnson rejected any notion of equal rights for blacks and unwaveringly opposed Republican attempts to institute a new social order in the South. After Congress passed the Civil Rights Act of 1866 over President Johnson's veto, Republicans proposed a second Reconstruction constitutional amendment designed to limit the power of the defeated Confederate states and to guarantee citizenship rights for former slaves. Led by Ohio congressman John Bingham, the Republicans secured passage of the Fourteenth Amendment— a constitutional revision that aimed at transforming the American legal system and securing the former slaves their rights as citizens. The amendment had passed both houses of Congress by June 13, 1866, but ratification by the states took more than two years to complete. The amendment did not become part of the federal Constitution until July 28, 1868.

Section 1 contains the bulk of the Fourteenth Amendment's weight. It provides a broad definition of citizenship, stating that "all persons born or naturalized in the United States, and subject to the jurisdiction thereof are citizens of the United States and of the State wherein they reside." Overruling the Supreme Court's controversial 1857 *Dred Scott* decision, this clause granted blacks full rights as citizens on both a state and federal level. Further, section 1 prevents states from enforcing laws that abridge "the privileges or immunities of citizens of the United States," and it prohibits the states from depriving "any

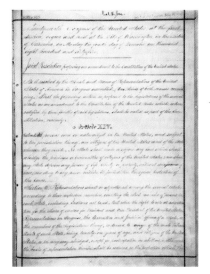

The Fourteenth Amendment, original text.

person of life, liberty, or property, without due process of law." This due process clause reiterated the words of the Fifth Amendment, instructing that both state and federal governments would abide by due process dictates. The final clause of section 1 requires the states to give all people "equal protection of the laws."

This equal protection clause ultimately became the linchpin of civil rights and equality movements.

Section 2 deals with congressional apportionment. Slaves previously had been counted as three-fifths of a person in determining population for representation and taxation purposes. Now

"We Accept the Situation," by Thomas Nast, *Harper's Weekly,* April 13, 1867.

newly emancipated freedmen and freedwomen were to be counted fully in apportioning seats in the House of Representatives. Section 3 prevented those who had "engaged in insurrection or rebellion" or who had "given aid or comfort to the enemies" of the Union from holding political office. Section 4 attempted to dispose of litigation over debt, stating that the national and state governments would not be obligated to pay for financial losses resulting from the Civil War and emancipation. Finally, section 5 explicitly granted Congress the power to make laws and enforce all provisions of the Fourteenth Amendment.

Considered by some a "mini Constitution" unto itself because of its diverse and influential subject matter, the Fourteenth Amendment would spawn more litigation than any other provision in U.S. history. In particular, section 1's due process and equal protection clauses have shaped protracted legal and public policy battles. Beginning in the 1920s judicial interpretation of the due process clause led to the incorporation of much of the Bill of Rights into state law, allowing for federal enforcement of these basic rights. But the Supreme Court initially took a narrow view of the equal protection clause, limiting

its scope in the Slaughterhouse Cases (1873), the Civil Rights Cases (1883), and *Plessy v. Ferguson* (1896), all of which granted states broad latitude in limiting the civil rights of citizens. However, in the post–World War II era the Court overturned some of its most controversial opinions by expanding its reading of the provision. The equal protection clause has become the foundation upon which several major civil rights and antidiscrimination cases have been built over the past half century, most notably employed in the landmark 1954 *Brown v. Board of Education* decision.

RECONSTRUCTION AND BLACK HIGHER EDUCATION

Emancipation, the Civil War, and the Thirteenth Amendment liberated nearly four million slaves from bondage, but the formerly enslaved population—many jobless and displaced—faced an uncertain future. By establishing the Freedmen's Bureau in March 1865, the federal government attempted to provide for the immediate needs of the freed slaves and war refugees by offering food, clothing, and shelter. But basic relief supplies were not enough to alleviate the effects of hundreds of years of slavery and oppression. Education was critical to freedom and for many would become the bedrock of Reconstruction policy.

As early as 1865, the Freedmen's Bureau, assisted by Freedmen's Aid Societies and Northern missionary groups, set out to establish schools specifically designed to meet the needs of freedpeople, adults as well as children. Additionally, within a few years, four of the most enduring institutions of African American higher education were

Senior Preparatory Class of Fisk University, Nashville, Tennessee, before 1906.

founded: Fisk University in 1865, Morehouse College and Howard University in 1867, and Hampton University in 1868. Although several black colleges had been founded in free states before the Civil War (Cheyney University in 1837, Lincoln University in 1854, and Wilberforce University in 1856), Fisk, Morehouse, Howard, and Hampton were among the first established in the South, and they all played a pivotal role in the history of black education, as dozens of historically black colleges and universities would seek to emulate them.

In October 1865, shortly after the Civil War ended, the Fisk Free Col-

Exterior view of Graves Hall, Morehouse College, Atlanta.

ored School was founded in Nashville by John Ogden, the superintendent of the Tennessee Freedmen's Bureau, and Erastus Milo Cravath and Edward P. Smith, both ministers and members of the American Missionary Association. The Fisk School was named for General Clinton Bowen Fisk of the Tennessee Freedmen's Bureau, who provided facilities for the new school in former Union army barracks. It held its first classes on January 9, 1866, beginning as an elementary school for all ages. Although largely serving the black population, Fisk was open to all, regardless of race. When the Tennessee legislature reopened the public schools in 1867 and required free elementary schooling for children of all races, Fisk began to focus on providing university-level liberal arts courses. On August 22, 1867, Fisk University was incorporated as a private, coeducational university for men and women, black and white.

Ministers in Augusta, Georgia, harbored similar ambitions to provide higher education to the black population. In February 1867 the Reverends William Jefferson White, Edmund Turney, and Richard C. Coulter, a former slave,

established the Augusta Institute (now Morehouse College) in the basement of the Springfield Baptist Church. The all-male school was primarily intended to prepare black men for careers in the ministry and teaching. The institute relocated to Atlanta's Friendship Baptist Church in 1879 and changed its name to the Atlanta Baptist Seminary. In 1897 the seminary moved to its current location in the west end of Atlanta and became Atlanta Baptist College. Finally in 1913 it was renamed Morehouse College, after Henry L. Morehouse, secretary

of the Northern Baptist Home Mission Society.

Howard University, located in Washington, D.C., originated when members of the District's First Congregational Society decided to create a seminary to train African American ministers. Plans quickly evolved to include a full-scale university, with college preparatory courses, undergraduate instruction, a normal school for teacher education, and graduate departments in law, medicine, theology, and agriculture. The society members proposed the idea to Congress, which chartered the school, and on March 2, 1867, President Andrew Johnson signed the congressional bill incorporating Howard University. Named for Oliver Otis Howard, the former Union army general who was now commissioner of the Freedmen's Bureau, Howard University received much of its early financial support from the bureau. The federally chartered and funded university was "for the education of youth in the liberal arts and sciences." Men and women, both black and white, were free to attend, and when the university opened its doors in May 1867, its first four students were white females, daughters of university trustees and faculty members. African American enrollment increased as Howard University grew, and when Howard's medical school opened on November 9, 1868, its first class of eight

Howard University, 1910 plans.

"Class in Cream Making at Hampton Institute," photograph
by Frances Benjamin Johnston, 1899–1900.

students consisted of seven blacks and one white.

In nearby Virginia, Samuel Chapman Armstrong, a former Union general and superintendent of the Freedmen's Bureau of Virginia's Ninth District, founded the Hampton Normal and Agricultural Institute. The Hampton Institute opened its doors on April 1, 1868, in Hampton, a locale on the Virginia Peninsula where thousands of African Americans had settled following emancipation. Armstrong obtained financial assistance from the American Missionary Association, the Freedmen's Bureau, and northern philanthropists for the school, which would emphasize practical experience in trade and industrial skills while fostering an academic environment. Armstrong's mission was "to train selected Negro youth who should go out and teach and lead their people first by example, by getting land and homes; to give them not a dollar that they could earn for themselves; to teach respect for labor, to replace stupid drudgery with skilled hands, and in this way to build up an industrial system for the sake not only of self-support and intelligent labor, but also for the sake of character."[4] During its first twenty years, enrollment averaged 350 students, both male and female, but it increased in the late nineteenth century. As American workforce needs changed in the twentieth century, Hampton's focus shifted from teaching vocational skills toward providing more college-level courses. Hampton Normal and Agricultural Institute was renamed the Hampton Institute in 1930, and it became Hampton University in 1984.

Since their founding in the 1860s, Fisk, Morehouse, Howard, and Hampton have had many distinguished graduates and faculty. Fisk graduates include the nation's most influential black scholar, W. E. B. Du Bois, the eminent historian John Hope Franklin, and the award-winning poet Nikki Giovanni. The poets Arna Bontemps, Sterling A. Brown, Robert Hayden, and James Weldon Johnson served on the Fisk faculty. Morehouse alumni include Martin Luther King, Jr., filmmaker Spike Lee, and activist Julian Bond. Howard University has graduated such famous figures as the U.S. Supreme Court justice Thurgood Marshall and the novelists Zora Neale Hurston and Nobel laureate Toni Morrison. No Hampton graduate achieved greater success in his time than Booker T. Washington. While controversial, no black leader of the late nineteenth century exerted more influence, wielded greater power, or attracted more followers than Washington. These institutions have been, for nearly 150 years, influential and vital academies of higher learning, their graduates affecting profoundly virtually every profession and the shape of race relations in American society.

FIFTEENTH AMENDMENT
TO THE CONSTITUTION

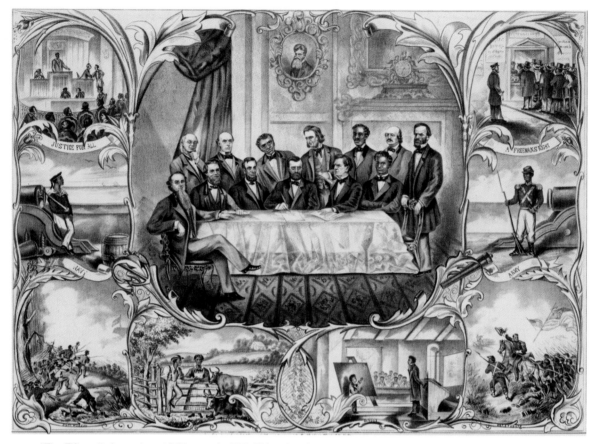

"The Fifteenth Amendment," lithograph, 1871. This print shows scenes of African Americans contributing to the nation's military history, to the legal system, to farming, and as educators and voters. They surround political leaders like Lincoln, President Grant, Salmon P. Chase, Benjamin F. Butler, and three African Americans: Frederick Douglass, Hiram Revels, and Robert Smalls. All are seated under a portrait of John Brown.

The last of the three Reconstruction amendments to the Constitution proclaimed: "The right of citizens of the United States to vote shall not be denied or abridged by the United States or by any State on account of race, color, or previous condition of servitude." Ratified five years after the Civil War, the amendment became the final piece in the Reconstruction plan to secure the freedom of the former slaves. Since 1865, the Republican-controlled Congress had achieved ratification of the Thirteenth Amendment to abolish slavery and the Fourteenth to grant blacks citizenship

rights, but a constitutional right to vote, for African American males, remained highly divisive.

Frederick Douglass, one of the greatest advocates of black male suffrage, asserted that the Civil War would not be over until African Americans gained the right to vote. Whites even in the North, however, remained deeply divided over the issue; many who had opposed slavery also ardently opposed black male suffrage. Even prominent female reformers like Elizabeth Cady Stanton, who had supported the antislavery movement, expressed

displeasure tinged with class prejudice, asserting that uneducated black males should not gain the vote before college-educated white women. Others argued that federally mandated voting qualifications interfered with states' rights, or that black men simply did not deserve the privilege of voting. Throughout his presidency, Andrew Johnson opposed black suffrage, preferring to give the vote back to those southern white men who had attempted to destroy the Union rather than extend it to the black men who fought to defend it. Even Radical Republicans dodged

The Fifteenth Amendment, original text.

the issue to prevent a political firestorm from their conservative constituents.

By the presidential election of 1868, however, Republicans realized that they needed the black vote to maintain their party majority. Republican candidate Ulysses S. Grant had won the presidency by a narrow margin (receiving only 52 percent of the vote), and Democrats had gained seats in both the House and the Senate. Thus, for Republicans, the fight for black suffrage became both an expression of principles and an exercise in self-interest.

Republicans initially disagreed over the scope of the amendment. Radicals, such as Massachusetts senator Charles Sumner, wanted to include a prohibition of literacy tests and poll taxes, which could be used to disenfranchise many of the potential new voters. More conservative congressmen felt satisfied with establishing black male suffrage but wished to relegate voter qualifications to the states. Congress proposed the moderate version of the Fifteenth Amendment on February 26, 1869, and sent it to the states for ratification. On March 1, 1869, Nevada became the first state to approve it, quickly followed by Republican-controlled legislatures in New England, New York, Pennsylvania, and the Midwest. States in the South had been forced to allow former slaves

"'One Vote Less.'—*Richmond Whig,*" by Thomas Nast, *Harper's Weekly,* October 19, 1872.

to vote since 1867, under mandates from Congress; all but Tennessee had agreed to its ratification. Congress required that Georgia, Mississippi, Texas, and Virginia ratify the amendment before they could be readmitted to the Union and send representatives to Congress. More than a year later, on March 30,

"The Fifteenth Amendment," lithograph, May 19, 1870. This print celebrates the new amendment by displaying the middle-class quality of black life, including educators, clergymen, Prince Hall Freemasons, and political and military leaders.

"The First Vote," by Alfred R. Waud, *Harper's Weekly,* November 16, 1867.

1870, three-fourths of the states had approved the amendment, thus certifying ratification.

Despite the victory, the amendment's aims would not be realized for nearly a century. As Sumner had feared, many states effectively disenfranchised African Americans through the use of poll taxes, literacy tests, and other voter qualifications. The Ku Klux Klan and other groups terrorized southern blacks to prevent them from voting. Although Congress passed enforcement acts in 1870 and 1871 to implement the Fifteenth Amendment and to protect black voters, the laws went largely unenforced. Courts interpreted the amendment narrowly, refusing to allow federal prosecution of individuals who prevented blacks from voting. In 1876, the Supreme Court crippled the effectiveness of the enforcement acts in *United States v. Reese,* holding that Congress had not provided adequate legislation to prosecute offenders. Black voters would have to wait until the Voting Rights Act of 1965 before the promises of the Fifteenth Amendment became reality.

AFRICAN AMERICAN DIPLOMATS

General U. S. Grant's election as president in 1868 gave African Americans renewed hope. Not only did he call openly for prompt ratification of the Fifteenth Amendment, but his election promised new opportunities in the federal patronage system. Certainly they could count on him to appoint an African American as minister to the Republic of Haiti—the first minister sent to the island republic since the Lincoln administration recognized Haitian independence, at long last, in 1862. (Haiti had become a republic in 1804.) Many black leaders aspired to the post, especially Frederick Douglass and George T. Downing, perhaps the nation's wealthiest African American. But upon taking office the next year, Grant chose the little-known Ebenezer Don Carlos Bassett—a man who would sail through the Senate confirmation process without debate.

Bassett, born in Litchfield, Connecticut, in 1833, had graduated with honors from the State Normal School in New Britain. While principal of a black high school in New Haven, Bassett attended Yale University. From 1857 until his appointment to the Haitian post, Bassett served as principal of Philadelphia's Institute for Colored Youth, the Quaker-founded school devoted to training black schoolteachers. Bassett earned great respect from Philadelphia's mayor, and when he was nominated to the Haitian post, twelve of his former teachers at Yale—where he studied French—wrote the State Department

Frederick Douglass, ca. 1880.

in support of his nomination. Bassett's appointment in 1869 made him the nation's first black diplomat.

His eight years in Haiti proved tumultuous. A series of Haitian presidents came and went. One was summarily shot; another spent several months hiding in Bassett's residence. Additionally, fears coursed through the island that the United States would either annex the Dominican Republic or force a naval coaling station upon Môle

Ebenezer Don Carlos Bassett (1833–1908), ca. 1855.

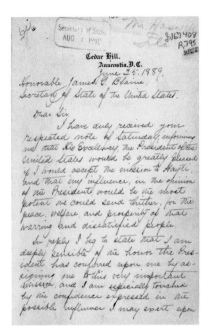

Frederick Douglass, letter to Secretary of State James G. Blaine, June 25, 1889, accepting the Haitian appointment.

Bassett's skills to Grant's secretary of state, Hamilton Fish. Bassett resigned at the end of Grant's term in 1877 and became the consul general for Haiti in New York. He remained there until 1889, when he accepted Frederick Douglass's offer to return to Haiti as his secretary and interpreter.

On June 25, 1889, Douglass informed Secretary of State James G. Blaine that he would accept President Harrison's offer of the Haitian diplomatic post. Although he greatly sympathized with the first black republic, and in the late 1850s had contemplated moving there, he spoke no French and knew little of the country's fierce and bloody politics or the overwhelming diplomatic pressures from the United States and Europe. He needed Bassett's help. In 1888 Haiti had been torn by revolution, and the United States remained divided over which of two Haitian generals to support. The U.S. Navy, the State Department, and New York merchant interests chose General Florvil Hyppolite, with the understanding that in return they

would receive the right to establish the coaling station at Môle St. Nicolas. While President Harrison remained decidedly cool over any U.S.-Haitian plans, the navy moved full steam ahead and attempted to compel Hyppolite's cooperation, desiring the port to support the projected canal across the Isthmus of Panama.

Additionally, Douglass served at a time when European powers and U.S. interests were attempting to wring debt payments out of the new government, casting him in the uncomfortable role of a mouthpiece for imperialists. When the Haitian government rejected the American insistence on a long-term lease of the port, many Democratic newspapers back home, especially in New York, blamed Frederick Douglass for the failure. Although President Harrison resisted calls for his minister's ouster—fearing loss of black Republican votes—Douglass nevertheless recognized his untenable situation and resigned on July 30, 1891.

St. Nicolas in Haiti. Despite extremely challenging circumstances, Bassett won the approval and respect of his diplomatic colleagues, both in the State Department and in the Haitian government. Even Frederick Douglass praised

---

HIRAM RHODES REVELS

On February 25, 1870, Hiram Rhodes Revels entered the U.S. Senate chamber to take the oath of office. The forty-two-year-old senator from Mississippi was greeted with both applause and jeers. Although many opposed his presence there, those assembled knew they were witnessing history as the first African American to serve in the U.S. Senate took his seat. Few occurrences better signified the dramatic transformation in American society that the Civil War had effected. Even a decade before, such an event had been unthinkable.

Revels was born free in 1827 in Fay-

etteville, North Carolina, to parents with mixed black and Indian ancestry. Little is known about his early life, but as a child he was educated at a private school for black children. As a teenager, he attended the Beech Grove Seminary near Liberty, Indiana, and in 1845 he entered the Darke County Seminary for Negroes in Ohio. During the 1840s he labored as an AME clergyman in the Indiana-Ohio region and traveled extensively, ministering to free blacks and slaves throughout the Midwest, Maryland, Kentucky, and Tennessee. He moved to St. Louis in 1853, but after a dispute with the local bishop, he aban-

Hiram Rhodes Revels (1827–1901).

doned the ministry to enroll at Knox College in Galesburg, Illinois. Upon finishing his studies, he relocated to Baltimore, where he became the first African American pastor of the Madison Street Presbyterian Church and the principal of a local African American high school.

At the beginning of the Civil War, Revels continued his clerical and educational pursuits, then served as a chaplain in the Union army, recruited African Americans for military service, and helped to establish schools for the freedpeople. In 1868, he moved to Mississippi and became the presiding elder at a church in Natchez. He made his first foray into public service when Adelbert Ames, the military governor of Mississippi, appointed him to the city board of aldermen. One of few highly educated African Americans in the area, Revels excelled in local politics and received the overwhelming support of the large black population, which had recently acquired the right to vote. In 1869, he ran for and handily won the Adams County seat in the Mississippi State Senate, one of thirty-six African Americans elected to the state's legislature that year.

As Mississippi prepared to reenter the Union in 1870, Revels's fellow state legislators called upon him to seek higher office. The state's U.S. Senate seats had been vacated when Mississippi seceded from the Union, and amid the Republican Party's postwar Reconstruction and reconciliation enthusiasm, many urged that a black American fill at least one of the vacancies. After much debate, on January 20 the state legislature voted that Hiram Revels would fill the unexpired U.S. Senate term of Jefferson Davis. Revels's appointment to the seat of the former president of the Confederacy was both ironic and highly symbolic. In late January the young black politician headed for Washington.

"Heroes of the Colored Race," chromolithograph, 1881. This print displays Revels alongside Douglass and Blanche K. Bruce, surrounded by images of African American patriotism, desire for education, and contributions to the American economy. John Brown is portrayed in these prints just as often as Lincoln.

Mississippi was not formally readmitted to the Union until February 23, at which point Revels presented his credentials. Predictably, several members of Congress attempted to prevent Revels's seating. After two days of fierce argument, Massachusetts senator Charles Sumner ended the debate with a passionate and stirring appeal to his colleagues: "The time has passed for argument. Nothing more need be said. . . . 'All men are created equal' says the great Declaration [of Independence]; and now a great act attests this verity. Today we make the Declaration a reality. For a long time a word only, it now becomes a deed. For a long time a promise only, it now becomes a consummated achievement."[5] The Senate voted 48–8 to seat Revels.

Revels served only one year, finishing out his term on March 3, 1871. He introduced three bills on the Senate floor, one of which—a petition for the removal of civil and political disabilities from an ex-Confederate—passed. Following his term, he returned to Mississippi to found Alcorn University in 1872. He served as its first president until 1873, when he was appointed Mississippi's secretary of state.

Although brief and uneventful, Hiram Revels's post in the U.S. Senate was a major milestone in American history. Only one other African American, Blanche Kelso Bruce (also of Mississippi), served in the Senate during the Reconstruction era. Unfortunately, the political triumphs of Reconstruction proved short-lived, and black citizens soon found themselves forcibly exiled from the democratic process. Not until the modern civil rights movement of the 1960s, nearly a century later, would another African American, Edward Brooke, a Republican from Massachusetts, take a seat in the U.S. Senate.

BLANCHE K. BRUCE, ROBERT SMALLS, AND AFRICAN AMERICANS IN CONGRESS

"The First Colored Senator and Representatives, in the 41st and 42nd Congress of the United States," by Currier and Ives, lithograph, 1872. Left to right: Hiram Revels of Mississippi, Benjamin Turner of Alabama, Robert DeLarge of South Carolina, Josiah Walls of Florida, Jefferson Long of Georgia, and Joseph Rainey and Robert B. Elliott of South Carolina.

Twenty-two African Americans served in the U.S. Congress between 1870 and 1901. Many of these men sat there even as whites toppled the Reconstruction governments in the South through campaigns of violence, intimidation, and fraud. Nevertheless, eight African American members served in the 44th Congress, which met between March 1875 and March 1877. One of the most prominent blacks to attain national office was Mississippi's Blanche K. Bruce, who became the first African American elected to serve a full six-year term in the U.S. Senate. (Hiram Revels had previously served from February 1870 to March 1871.)

Blanche Kelso Bruce, born a slave in Virginia in 1841, by his own account received relatively good treatment at the hands of his master—likely his own father. Whatever the nature of their relationship, Bruce benefited from the unusual opportunity to learn to read and write alongside his master's white children. Living in Missouri when the Civil War began, he took his first oppor-tunity to cross the border to the free state of Kansas. After the end of the war, he settled in Mississippi and quickly established himself both as a successful cotton planter and as a local politician. A popular Republican, Bruce was elected to the U.S. Senate by the Mississippi state legislature in 1874, just months before conservative Democrats reclaimed control of the state government.

A lame duck from the start, Bruce was unable to gather substantial support for any of his legislative initiatives in his single term, though he was widely respected by whites and blacks alike. He did oversee a careful and thorough review of the failed Freedman's Bank, and he endeavored to return as much money as possible to its depositors, who were largely poor African Americans. He also notably broke with his party in voting against the Chinese Exclusion Act and in speaking out for a more responsible federal policy toward American Indians. In 1880 Bruce was briefly put forward as a candidate for the vice presidential nomination at the Republican National Convention, as a show of respect for his abilities and service to the party. He received eight votes, more than four of the other candidates, before withdrawing his name from consideration.

Robert Smalls, the new representative from South Carolina's Fifth District, joined Bruce in the 44th Congress. As a slave, Smalls had enjoyed the freedom to work for wages, but he had had to relinquish most of his pay to his owner. In 1861, the talented Smalls became a deckhand on the *Planter,* a steamer that plied Charleston harbor. In short order he became the vessel's pilot. When Union forces began to capture the South Carolina Sea Islands and blockaded the harbor in 1862, Smalls and the black members of his crew gathered up their families and under cover of darkness sailed the craft out of the harbor and turned it over to the Union navy. Congress rewarded Smalls and his crew for liberating the *Planter,* an act that made headlines across the North and that abolitionists used to destroy stereotypes

Blanche K. Bruce
(1841–98).

Robert Smalls
(1839–1915).

of the contented slave and to push for emancipation. Smalls served the Union navy throughout the war, piloting the *Planter* as a troop transport; he even took the helm on a Union ironclad in an unsuccessful bid to run the gauntlet of Confederate forts surrounding the harbor and take Charleston.

After the war Smalls used his savings to purchase the house of his former master. He also became involved in South Carolina politics, serving in the state assembly from 1868 to 1874, when he was elected to the U.S. House of Representatives. As a state representative, he helped establish funding for the state's first public schools. With little formal education himself, he hired tutors to prepare him for the rigors of political life.

In his second term in Congress, Smalls was convicted of having accepted a bribe while serving in the South Carolina legislature. He appealed his conviction, but political opponents used the scandal to limit his effectiveness in Congress. In 1878, he lost his seat in an election when Red Shirts, armed bands of whites, prevented many African Americans from exercising their right to vote. He contested the election results and was eventually awarded his seat by the House Committee on Elections.

Despite these obstacles, Smalls served his constituents faithfully. He presented a bill to establish a naval station in his district and argued forcefully for a sustained military presence in the South to protect African Americans from white violence. When black disenfranchise-

ment ended their legislative careers in 1880 and 1886, respectively, Bruce and Smalls both remained active in Republican politics. For the rest of their careers, both enjoyed patronage appointments during Republican administrations and worked for the party while Democrats held power. Smalls regained office in 1898 and served until the arrival of the Woodrow Wilson administration in 1913, and its even more intolerant racial policies.

HARVARD AND YALE, 1870 AND 1876

Prior to the Civil War only a handful of African Americans graduated from institutions of higher education. A college education was only marginally more available to blacks in the North than in the South, which outlawed even the most basic elementary education of blacks. Although black colleges such as Cheyney, Lincoln, and Wilberforce had been founded in the pre–Civil War period, very few African Americans received bachelor's degrees, and even fewer attended the nation's historically white institutions. In 1870, Richard Theodore Greener became

the first African American graduate of Harvard University; four years later, Edward Alexander Bouchet became the first African American to receive a bachelor's degree from Yale University. Bouchet went on to complete his doctorate in physics, the first black to receive a Ph.D. from any American university.

Richard Theodore Greener was born on January 30, 1844, in Philadelphia to free parents Richard Wesley Greener and Mary Ann Le Brune. When his father disappeared during a gold-mining expedition in California, the nine-year-old Greener and his mother relocated to

Cambridge, Massachusetts, where he attended elementary school. At the age of twelve, however, financial hardship forced Greener to leave school and seek employment to help support his mother. His employer, Augustus E. Bachelder, offered him financial help and encouraged him to enroll in the two-year college preparatory program at Oberlin College.

He returned from Ohio to New England in 1864 and graduated from Phillips Academy in Andover, Massachusetts, in 1865. Although Greener had a rocky start at Harvard and had to repeat his first year, he ultimately excelled and

Richard Theodore Greener
(1844–1922), 1885.

Edward Alexander Bouchet
(1852–1918).

Washington, D.C., and became active in politics and the fight for racial equality. His activity with the Republican Party led to his appointment as U.S. consul in Vladivostok, Russia, where he served as commercial agent until 1905. Greener retired to Chicago, where he died in 1922.

Yale's first African American graduate, Edward Alexander Bouchet, was born in New Haven, Connecticut, on September 15, 1852. The youngest of four children of William Francis Bouchet and Susan Cooley, Bouchet attended the Artisan Street Colored School, a one-teacher, ungraded school—one of only three schools for black children in all of New Haven. In 1868, he entered Hopkins Grammar School, an institution that prepared young men for classical and scientific studies at Yale College. He graduated first in his class and became one of two black students accepted to Yale in 1870. Four years later Bouchet graduated sixth in his class—the first African American to receive a bachelor's degree from the school—and was the first black to be nominated to Phi Beta Kappa. He continued his studies at Yale the next fall, and in 1876 he completed his dissertation in geometrical optics. The first African American to earn a Ph.D. from an Amer-

during his sophomore year received the Boylston Prize for oratory; his senior dissertation won the inaugural Bowdoin Prize for research and writing. After receiving his bachelor's degree in 1870, Greener became principal of the Male Department at Philadelphia's Institute for Colored Youth (later Cheyney University). In 1873, he became professor of mental and moral philosophy at the University of South Carolina, where he taught Greek, mathematics, and constitutional law. He also served as the university's librarian, attended its law school, and earned an L.L.B. degree in 1876. He practiced law in both South Carolina and

ican university, he was only the sixth American of any race to earn a Ph.D. in physics. Like Greener, Bouchet began his career teaching in Philadelphia at the Institute for Colored Youth, where he remained until 1902. He thrived in the city's black community, becoming active in the black Episcopal church. After leaving Philadelphia, he held teaching positions at several schools, including Sumner High School in St. Louis; St. Paul's Normal and Industrial School in Lawrenceville, Virginia; and Lincoln High School in Gallipolis, Ohio. He returned to New Haven to retire and died there in 1918.

CIVIL RIGHTS ACT OF 1871— THE KU KLUX KLAN ACT

n March 23, 1871, President U. S. Grant advised Congress:

A condition of affairs now exists in some States of the Union rendering life and property insecure and the carrying of the mails and the collection of the revenue dangerous . . . Therefore, I urgently recommend such legislation as in the judgment of Congress shall

effectually secure life, liberty, and property, and the enforcement of law in all parts of the United States.[6]

Responding to a Senate investigative committee, Grant urged the Congress to adopt legislation that would give him the authority to halt the reign of terror—intimidation, assaults, cross burnings, and murder—that white

supremacist organizations, most notoriously the Knights of the Ku Klux Klan, were inflicting on blacks and their white allies in the former states of the Confederacy.

Established in 1866 in Tennessee, the Klan saw itself as defending southern culture and politics against blacks and the Republican-controlled governments that offered the newly freed slaves the equal protection of the laws. The

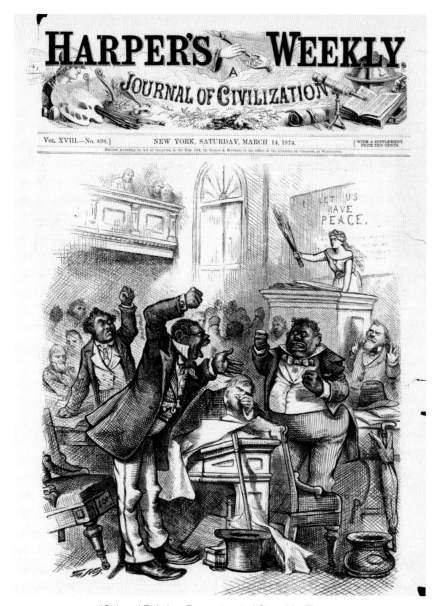

HARPER'S WEEKLY.

A JOURNAL OF CIVILIZATION

Vol. XVIII.—No. 898.] NEW YORK, SATURDAY, MARCH 14, 1874. [WITH A SUPPLEMENT PRICE TEN CENTS.

"Mississippi Ku-Klux in the Disguises in Which They Were Captured," *Harper's Weekly,* January 27, 1872.

"Colored Rule in a Reconstructed State," by Thomas Nast, *Harper's Weekly,* March 14, 1874.

Benjamin F. Butler (1818–93).

Thirteenth, Fourteenth, and Fifteenth amendments had been added to the Constitution in the wake of the Civil War, but their guarantees to African Americans remained unrealized.

Congress responded to the systemic violence and discrimination with a series of acts intended to enforce the new amendments. The Enforcement acts of 1870 and 1871 aimed to protect black citizens against infringements upon their civil rights; they forbade state officials to interfere with voting rights and authorized the appointment of election supervisors who could bring federal suits to prevent voter intimida-

tion and fraud. But the power of the Klan persisted.

In 1870, the radical Republican Benjamin Butler, a former Civil War general and a congressman from Massachusetts, had proposed a bill to break the back of white supremacist organizations, but he failed to find support. A year later a six-hundred-page Senate report detailed the activities of the Klan and the inability of state governments to cope with it. Congress could not ignore it. Representative David Perley Lowe of Kansas aptly argued, "While murder is stalking abroad in disguise, while whippings and lynchings and banishment have been

visited upon unoffending American citizens, the local administrations have been found inadequate or unwilling to apply the proper corrective." Lowe, Butler, and other like-minded congressmen introduced an "Act to Enforce the Provisions of the Fourteenth Amendment to the Constitution of the United States, and for other Purposes." President Grant gave his speech urging passage. The Civil Rights Act of 1871— sometimes referred to as the Third Enforcement Act, or more commonly the Ku Klux Klan Act—was approved on April 20, 1871. It gave federal officials the power to arrest anyone who sought to deprive citizens of their constitutionally guaranteed rights. It also authorized military invention and the suspension of habeas corpus (imposition of martial law) to suppress the violence and lawlessness that interfered with the rights of American citizens.

The Klan Act led to hundreds of indictments and the imprisonment of many Klansmen. In October 1871, President Grant found the lawlessness in South Carolina so vexing that he suspended the writ of habeas corpus and dispatched federal troops to occupy the region. Thousands of Klan members fled. Within a year the federal government's enforcement activities had effectively dislodged the Klan from its position of power and reduced the rampant violence.

As Reconstruction came to a close and southern Democrats regained national power, the federal government lost interest in enforcing the Civil Rights Act. Black citizens and their white allies—now without federal backing—lacked power to resist the Klan's renewed campaign of terror and the spreading legalization of Jim Crow segregation. Not until the landmark Supreme Court case of *Monroe v. Pape* (1961) did the Klan Act see a revival. Since then the act has been amended and codified as 42 U.S. Code 1983 and remains an important tool for civil rights litigation and enforcement.

THE DECLINE OF CIVIL RIGHTS, 1875–1883

As early as 1870 Senator Charles Sumner attempted to move the Congress to adopt a civil rights bill that would guarantee African Americans the right to serve on juries, to attend integrated schools, and to enjoy equal access to public accommodations. But Sumner was unable to overcome opposition from a reluctant Congress, and in March 1874 the great Massachusetts abolitionist senator died without achieving one of his most cherished ambitions. Prospects for passage of the bill without him appeared bleak. In the fall of 1874, white supremacist Democrats achieved landslide victories in elections across the South, where widespread violence and voter intimidation suppressed the black vote.

However, Republicans in the 43rd Congress again took up the civil rights bill. The seven African Americans serving in the Congress spoke passionately for it, many recalling personal injustices they had suffered on trains, in restaurants, and at inns. Robert B. Elliott, the English-born South Carolina editor and congressman, debated the bill with the former vice president of the Confederacy Alexander Stephens, and won. President U. S. Grant—having successfully put down a white insurrection in New Orleans in January 1875, sending federal troops into the Louisiana legislature to enforce order and prevent a Democratic coup—also wished to protect the rights of black voters. After a series of complicated political maneuvers to overcome conservative Republican and staunch Democratic opposition, the president signed the law on March 1, 1875. The clause mandating integrated schools

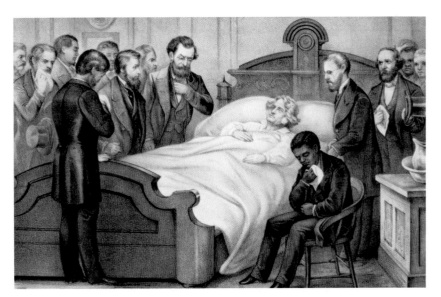
"The Death of Charles Sumner," Currier and Ives, lithograph, 1874.

had been dropped in a compromise to win congressional passage.

Section 1 of the Civil Rights Act required that "citizens of every race and color, regardless of any previous condition of servitude," must be "entitled to the full and equal enjoyment of the accommodations . . . and privileges of inns, public conveyances . . . theatres and other places of public amusement." In practice, however, whites across the South routinely ignored the statute.

"The Shackle Broken—By the Genius of Freedom," lithograph, 1874. This print celebrates Congressman Robert B. Elliott's House speech in support of the Civil Rights Act. The central image contains his famous words: "What you give to one class you must give to all. What you deny to one class, you deny to all."

African Americans attempted to use their political power to preserve their rights, and in 1881 the four black members of the Tennessee state legislature, along with their Republican backers, introduced a bill to ban discrimination on the state's railroads. Despite their vigorous efforts, the bill was narrowly defeated. Instead, a compromise measure became law, preventing railroad companies from charging black passengers for a first-class ticket and then requiring them to sit in the second-class or "smoker" car. The companies also had to provide separate first-class facilities for their black customers with "the same conveniences, and subject to the same rules governing other first class cars." Most historians have labeled this the South's first Jim Crow law, although it intended to improve conditions for African Americans. The law's enforcement provision allowed for individuals who had not been provided equal (although separate) privileges to sue any rail company for violation of the act, and be compensated.

Unfortunately, like the Civil Rights Act of 1875, even this modest law proved ineffective. Black Tennesseans, offended, turned to organized protests and the courts to defend their rights. For three straight days in the fall of 1881, blacks in Nashville attempted to take seats in white cars, in a deliberate attempt to establish a test case. In 1883, Ida B. Wells-Barnett (who would later play a leading role in the international movement to end lynching) sued a rail carrier in Tennessee when conductors forcibly

John Marshall Harlan (1833–1911). Born in Boyle County, Kentucky, Harlan trained as a lawyer and won election as a judge in Franklin County. He ran unsuccessfully for Congress in 1860, then, during the war, edited a Unionist newspaper and served in the Tenth Kentucky Volunteers. He opposed the Emancipation Proclamation and retained his slaves until adoption of the Thirteenth Amendment—which he also opposed. He won appointment to the Supreme Court in 1877 and, surprisingly, defended the newly won rights of African Americans.

"'Jim Crow' Cars," *Cleveland Gazette,* July 14, 1900.

A Jim Crow railcar in Fayetteville, North Carolina, 1929.

removed her from the white first-class (or ladies') car.

In 1883, however, the U.S. Supreme Court dealt a decisive blow to these efforts. In an 8–1 decision, in what became known as the Civil Rights Cases, the Court found the public accommodations section of the 1875 Civil Rights Act to be unconstitutional. The Fourteenth Amendment, the Court held, authorized Congress to pass laws necessary to prevent the states from infringing on the rights of individuals, but it did not prohibit individuals or corporations from engaging in discriminatory behavior. In the lone dissenting opinion, Justice John Marshall Harlan—a former slaveholder—challenged the majority opinion's twisted logic. Referring to the Reconstruction amendments, Harlan said:

With what rights, privileges, or immunities did this grant from the nation invest them? There is one, if there be no others— exemption from race discrimination in respect of any civil right belonging to citizens of the white race. . . . That, surely, is their constitutional privilege . . . unless the recent amendments be "splendid baubles," thrown out to delude those who deserved fair and generous treatment at the hands of the nation.[7]

African Americans reacted strongly against the court's decision. A Civil Rights Congress met in a packed Washington, D.C., hall to condemn the Court's action and to call on both political parties to guarantee equal rights through state legislation. Frederick Douglass publicly criticized the decision, and AME bishop Henry McNeal Turner declared, "Nothing has hurt us so much since the day we were emancipated as the decision of the Supreme Court."[8]

After the federal courts withdrew the formal protections of the Civil Rights Act of 1875, states began rejecting laws like Tennessee's that permitted segregation and adopting ones that required segregation. Mississippi enacted the first law mandating Jim Crow on its rails (1888), followed by Texas (1889), Louisiana (1890), Alabama, Kentucky, Arkansas, and Georgia (1891), South Carolina (1898), North Carolina (1899), Virginia (1900), Maryland (1904), and Oklahoma (1907).

FISK UNIVERSITY JUBILEE SINGERS

Founded in 1866, the Fisk Free Colored School was one of a string of American Missionary Association (AMA) schools established in the former Confederate states to offer education to the freedpeople. By 1871 the Nashville school had obtained a university charter but faced serious financial hardships. With university coffers dangerously close to empty, school treasurer and music professor George White, a white former Union army officer and Freedmen's Bureau worker, struck upon a novel idea. He selected nine of his students for a choral ensemble that would tour the nation to raise funds.

The AMA scoffed at the idea, noting that it ran counter to the school's religious goals and would subject the students to undue stress and torment. The association charged that the plan resulted more from White's ego than from any real desire to help the school. White persisted, however, and prepared his students for the tour.

Song selection proved critical. They prepared a set of popular and patriotic songs, but White also instructed them in African American spirituals. He then based their tour route on the path of the Underground Railroad. Taking most of what little money remained in the Fisk treasury (supplemented by his own funds) to provide for their expenses, White and his singers kicked off their tour in Cincinnati and then headed east and north. When the group set out on October 6, 1871, nobody knew quite what to expect.

Throughout Ohio they met hostility and prejudice and failed to attract any significant support. Rather than taking the stage in concert halls, they often had to sing on street corners. In both Ohio and upstate New York, they regularly

Fisk Jubilee Singers, by Allen & Rowell of Boston, ca. 1870s. The singers include George E. Barrett, Maggie L. Porter, Jennie Jackson, Ella Sheppard, F. J. Loudin, Mabel R. Lewis, R. A. Hall, and Patti Malone.

faced galling discrimination in lodging and food, at times having to rely on the goodwill of sympathetic church and missionary association members who took them into their homes. As winter neared, White struggled to raise money for adequate clothing for the group. After a disappointing night in Columbus, in an attempt to motivate the crew, White renamed them the Jubilee Singers, after the year of the Jubilee in the Bible.

In November they performed for the AMA members at the National Council of Congregational Churches, meeting at Oberlin College. Thereafter the tour began to succeed. In 1872 they performed at the World Peace Jubilee in Boston and, on March 5, for President Ulysses S. Grant at the White House. Shortly afterward they performed for the congregation of the famed New York minister Henry Ward Beecher. Beecher, who enjoyed a wide readership for his columns in *The Independent,* a popular Congregationalist newspaper,

wrote enthusiastically about the singers. The next day they performed to an adoring crowd at Steinway Hall in New York City. General Clinton B. Fisk, the AMA board member after whom Fisk University was named, sat in the audience. After the performance, he remarked that one of the singers, Thomas Rutling, once had been a runaway that his owner valued at $450. Now, Fisk joked, he was worth much more.

In May they made their London debut, which set the stage for a full-blown tour of Britain the following year. They drew thousands of people to their concerts and even performed for the Duke of Argyle and Queen Victoria. All told, the England tour raised more than $50,000. Successive tours brought the Jubilee Singers to Australia, India, and Japan. The money they raised would help to fund the education of generations of Fisk students, including the school's most notable alumnus, W. E. B. Du Bois.

Throughout the twentieth century

the Jubilee Singers (with ever-changing personnel) continued to perform, not only representing Fisk University, but becoming important guardians of black cultural traditions. Their music reemerged on the national stage during the civil rights movement of the 1950s and 1960s. In 1999, PBS aired an hour-long film documentary on the Jubilee Singers as part of its *American Experience* series. In 2000, the singers were inducted into the Gospel Music Association's Hall of Fame, and in 2008, the group received the National Medal of Arts, the nation's highest recognition for contributions to the arts. Not only did the Jubilee Singers rescue their school from financial failure, but they popularized and canonized some of the most original music created on the continent. As a result of their efforts, songs like "Steal Away" and "Swing Low, Sweet Chariot" were recorded for posterity. The singers themselves also became an institution, and in 1875 Fisk University built Jubilee Hall, a permanent building for the singers.

CHARLOTTE RAY

Just a few years after the Civil War and nearly fifty years before women were granted the right to vote, a young black woman from New York City blazed a path that few could have expected, but many have since followed. In February 1872, Charlotte E. Ray earned her law degree and became the first African American woman lawyer.

Born on January 13, 1850, to Charles Bennett Ray and his second wife, Charlotte Augusta Burroughs Ray, Charlotte was one of seven children. Unlike most African Americans of that era, she was born into relative affluence and raised in a home dedicated to social activism and education. Her father, pastor of the Bethesda Congregational Church in New York, gained national renown as an antislavery leader and editor of *The Colored American,* the most important black newspaper of the late 1830s. Charlotte Ray began her education at one of the few schools that accepted black female students: Myrtilla Miner's Institution for the Education of Colored Youth in Washington, D.C. (After the Civil War it would become the Miner Normal School.) After graduating in 1869, she became a teacher in Howard University's normal and preparatory department.

While teaching, Ray enrolled in the law department and attended classes in

Lutie A. Lytle (1875–1950?). Born in Murfreesboro, Tennessee, Lytle attended Central Tennessee College in Nashville and passed the state bar examination in 1897. She became the first black woman to practice law in the state and the third in the United States. But few clients would hire an African American lawyer, so she abandoned the practice and began teaching law at Central Tennessee, the first woman of any race to teach law at a chartered law school. After marrying, she moved to New York, where she became a supporter of Marcus Garvey.

the evenings, specializing in commercial law. Although Howard University had been established in 1866 to provide an education for freed slaves and their descendants, a woman's presence there was unprecedented. Upon receiving her degree in 1872, she was the first woman to graduate from its law department. Her pioneering efforts continued after she was admitted to the District of Columbia bar on April 23, 1872. With this rite of passage, she became the first female member of the District bar, and the first black female lawyer in the entire country. She soon opened her own law firm, but because of segregation and pervasive gender prejudice she could not attract enough clients to maintain her practice.

Ray returned to New York with her sister, the poet H. Cordelia Ray, to teach in the Brooklyn public school system. Little is known about her life in New York, and no image of her has ever been located, but she remained politically active, attending the National Woman Suffrage Association's annual convention in New York City in 1876 and becoming involved with the National Association of Colored Women. In 1897, she moved to Woodside in Queens, where she died at the age of sixty on January 4, 1911. Although her legal career was short-lived, Charlotte Ray's accomplishments proved an inspiration for black and white women. In her honor, the greater Washington area chapter of the Women Lawyers Division of the American Bar Association created the annual Charlotte E. Ray Award.

U.S. SUPREME COURT AND THE FOURTEENTH AMENDMENT: THE SLAUGHTERHOUSE CASES

Five years after the ratification of the Fourteenth Amendment, the Supreme Court received an opportunity to interpret its meaning, in the Slaughterhouse Cases.

In 1869, the Louisiana legislature had enacted a law "to protect the health of the city of New Orleans, to locate the stock-landings and slaughter-houses, and to incorporate the Crescent City Live-Stock Landing and Slaughter-House Company." It specified that all commercial livestock in the city must be slaughtered by the Crescent City Corporation or within its facilities. Several butchers brought suit, alleging that the law violated the Thirteenth and Fourteenth amendments: it imposed involuntary servitude upon them and deprived them of their privileges and immunities of citizenship, due process, and equal protection of the laws.

John Archibald Campbell, a former Supreme Court justice, argued on behalf of the butchers that the privileges and immunities clause of the Fourteenth Amendment granted federal safeguards for civil rights, which included the right to pursue one's occupation. The amendment's framers, he reasoned, intended to elevate the privileges and immunities of state citizenship to federal protection, just as the Constitution's framers had aimed to protect national citizenship in the similarly worded Article IV, Section 2. The state of Louisiana countered that the law was designed to isolate the noxious slaughterhouse activities and was valid pursuant to the state's police powers (powers to protect the safety, health, morals, and general welfare of the public).

Three related suits that challenged the law's constitutionality made it to the U.S. Supreme Court. In its 5–4 opinion, delivered April 14, 1873, and authored by Justice Samuel Taylor Miller, the Court upheld Louisiana's slaughterhouse law. The ruling had momentous

John Archibald Campbell (1811–89). Campbell served on the U.S. Supreme Court from 1853 until 1861, when he resigned to join the Confederacy. He had joined with the majority in the *Dred Scott* decision and had owned slaves, but he freed them upon joining the Supreme Court. Whatever his racial views, he firmly believed that the Fourteenth Amendment guaranteed all persons economic liberty that could not be restricted by the states.

consequences for the civil rights of all African Americans. The Court refused Campbell's invitation to diminish the states' responsibility and power over civil rights and increase the role of the federal government. Instead, it opted for a narrow reading of the Fourteenth Amendment, ruling that its privileges and immunities clause granted no new rights to citizens. The clause simply reiterated Article IV's instruction that states could not abridge citizens' rights of national citizenship (the right of mobility, the right to vote, the right to assemble peaceably, and the right to petition for redress of grievances). No provision of the Constitution, the Court declared, required a state to grant special privileges to its citizens beyond those explicitly protected by the Constitution. Thus, state legislatures were free to limit their citizens' rights, such as those relating to the performance of their occupation or, more specifically, the right to operate a slaughterhouse.

In rejecting Campbell's arguments, the Court examined the purpose of the Reconstruction amendments. It held that the amendments had been adopted for "unity of purpose," namely "the freedom of the slave race, the security and firm establishment of that freedom, and the protection of the newly made freeman and citizen from the oppressions of those who had formerly exercised unlimited dominion over him." In essence, the Court reasoned that the amendments were specifically designed and ratified to ban states from depriving blacks of their rights as U.S. citizens. But because states had long been granted authority over basic rights such as labor, the Fourteenth Amendment could not be used to abridge that authority.

Thus, the Slaughterhouse opinion pushed the privileges and immunities clause of the Fourteenth Amendment into obscurity, drawing a sharp divide between national and state citizenship: "It is quite clear, then, that there is a citizenship of the United States, and a citizenship of a State, which are distinct from each other, and which depend upon different characteristics or circumstances in the individual." By effectively nullifying this clause, the Supreme Court restricted the federal government's power to limit state infringement of civil liberties.

This narrow reading of privileges and immunities remains in force today, but more liberal jurists in the twentieth century turned to the Fourteenth Amendment's due process and equal protection clauses to give credence to civil rights claims and to strike down state laws that denied the full exercise of liberty.

THE CATHOLIC HEALYS

James Augustine and Patrick Francis Healy were two of ten children born to a wealthy Georgia planter named Michael Morris Healy and Mary Eliza, his slave. Settling in Georgia in 1818, the elder Healy quickly established himself as a land speculator and a cotton planter, accumulating a vast fortune and about fifty slaves. Unlike many slaveholders, Healy appears to have genuinely cared for Mary Eliza and their children. Although Georgia law prevented him from directly manumitting his children or their mother, Healy provided for Mary Eliza financially in his will and arranged for her to travel north, where she could live free, should he die before her. Healy also sent his nine surviving children to the North, where they could be educated and free. Healy, a Roman Catholic, enrolled four of his sons in the College of the Holy Cross, a newly founded Jesuit college in Worcester, Massachusetts.

In 1849, James Healy became the valedictorian of the school's first graduating class; Patrick graduated from Holy Cross one year later. The brothers' decision to join the Jesuits, born of their experiences at Holy Cross, was complicated by the fact that the order's novitiate was in Maryland, a slave state. While both brothers were light-skinned, James chose to attend seminary first in Montreal and then in France; Patrick appears to have passed as white while a novice at the Maryland school. In Paris, on June 10, 1854, James Healy took his vows in a ceremony at Notre Dame Cathedral, making him the first ordained African American Catholic priest.

Shortly after his ordination, James returned to the United States, taking a position as an aide to John Fitzpatrick, the Bishop of Boston. When Fitzpatrick became ill in 1857, Healy began to manage many of the bishop's daily responsibilities. In 1865, as the Civil War ground to a close, he played an important role in the founding of the Home for Destitute Catholic Children, many of whose charges had been left impoverished after the loss of their fathers in the war. After Bishop Fitzpatrick's death in 1866, Boston's new bishop named Healy as the pastor of St. James, the largest Catholic parish in the diocese. From this prominent post, Healy helped found the

Bishop James A. Healy (1830–1900).

House of the Good Shepherd, a home for homeless girls, and he lobbied successfully against anti-Catholic legislation at the statehouse in Boston.

Patrick Healy, meanwhile, taught at St. Joseph's College in Philadelphia and briefly at Holy Cross before going to Georgetown University in 1852 to further his own studies. Patrick's time in the slaveholding District of Columbia was short, likely because his race became known. Like his brother James, Patrick next traveled to Europe, where he was ordained as a priest in Belgium in September 1864. Patrick remained in Belgium, earning a Ph.D. in philosophy from the Catholic University of Louvain in 1865. One year later, he returned to Georgetown to teach philosophy. Healy's race does not appear to have been an issue at postbellum Georgetown, as he quickly rose to prominence

Patrick F. Healy (1834–1910).

within the university's administration. He served as university vice president in 1873 when John Early, the school's president, died suddenly. Healy was immediately named acting president, and in July 1874 church authorities in Rome confirmed him as Georgetown's twenty-ninth president, making him the first African American president of a predominantly white university.

In February 1875, less than a year after his brother Patrick became the head of Georgetown, Roman Catholic authorities named James Healy the second Bishop of Portland, a diocese that encompassed all of Maine and New Hampshire. While Healy's race was known throughout his career, it does not appear to have prevented him from successfully leading the majority-white diocese. Under his leadership, the Portland diocese experienced extraordinary growth: Healy presided over the founding of sixty new congregations, a new Catholic college, new schools, and new charitable organizations. As his prominence within the Catholic Church grew, James was invited several times to address the Congress of Colored Catholics. Yet up to his death in

Healy Hall, Georgetown University.

1900, he consistently refused to affiliate with groups organized by race.

Patrick Healy's influence as president of Georgetown paralleled his brother's impact as Bishop of Portland. Patrick Healy is often called Georgetown's "second founder" in recognition of his enormous contributions to the school. He updated the curriculum to include a greater emphasis on the sciences and modernized and expanded the library, the law school, and the school of medi-

cine. Healy's most lasting contribution to the physical campus remains the building that still bears his name. Healy Hall's Gothic architecture and two-hundred-foot tower evoke the style Healy knew from his studies in Belgium. His accomplishments as president of Georgetown University transformed a nineteenth-century-style college into an important twentieth-century research university. Fittingly, he died there in January 1910.

CONVICT LEASE

Before the Civil War southern prisons tended to be small and to hold almost exclusively white criminals. The slave system maintained its own unique form of discipline. On the plantation, slave owners—or specific whites assigned to manage the task—handed out punishments, either corporally or through the sale of the offending individual or their loved ones. In small towns and cities, local jails often served as centers to administer whippings or other immediate forms

of punishment rather than long-term confinement.

But in the aftermath of emancipation, the South's penal system was transformed so that it targeted freedpeople. In Mississippi, for instance, the new Black Codes made criminals of many African Americans for any number of petty transgressions, real or imagined. Black convicts soon overwhelmed the state's existing prison. Mississippi authorities sought inventive solutions both to ensure control over the black

population and to solve the overcrowding problem: they put the black population to work. Convict lease spread throughout the South during the late nineteenth and early twentieth centuries. Widespread use of convict labor not only allowed a select few southerners to expand their vast fortunes but also provided the crucial mechanism needed to rebuild the South's infrastructure, which had been devastated during the Civil War. Convicts worked the coal mines of Alabama, the forests of North

Southern chain gang, 1900–06.

Carolina, and the levees along both sides of the Mississippi; they built roads and railways and even worked plantations across the South.

On February 21, 1867, Mississippi governor Benjamin G. Humphreys signed the state's first convict lease law, allowing private parties to work convicts in exchange for a fee paid to the state. At first the act had relatively little impact. During Reconstruction federal authorities established a convict lease with Edmund Richardson, one of the South's leading planters and financiers. From 1868 to 1871 he used thousands of convicts, the large majority of whom were black, on public works, on his enormous cotton plantations, and on his railroads. He amassed a vast fortune, largely as a result of his use of convict labor. After the new state government formed in 1870, Richardson fell from favor and lost his exclusive rights to the lease in 1871, when it was transferred to Nathan Bedford Forrest, the former Confederate general intimately tied to the 1864 massacre of black soldiers at Fort Pillow and a founder of the Ku Klux Klan. Forrest leased convicts from Mississippi, Alabama, and Tennessee to work on a speculative railroad-construction project. After Forrest, the contract to lease Mississippi's convicts changed hands several times.

Prisoner punishment in Georgia, photograph by John L. Spivak, 1932.

Real growth in the convict population began after the end of Reconstruction and the enactment of the so-called Mississippi Plan of 1875, a violent and bloody strategy devised by whites to suppress the black vote and return Democrats to power. In 1876, the state allowed the leaseholder to sublease convicts to other parties. Former Confederate officer Jones S. Hamilton rarely worked convicts himself, but he subleased them for a profit. A large number of Mississippi's convicts found themselves, once again, compelled to work for the millionaire Edmund Richardson. The same year, the Mississippi legislature passed the infamous "pig law," which defined the theft of any livestock, such as a pig or a cow, as grand larceny. The years 1874 to 1877 saw a fourfold increase in the number of black men and boys convicted and sentenced to work in Mississippi's "justice" system.

For convicts under the lease system, life was brutish. The state offered almost no supervision, and leaseholders provided little in the way of food or proper shelter. Under these difficult conditions, many were literally worked to death. Mortality rates for convicts in Mississippi were ten to fifteen times higher than in many northern prisons during the same period. Some convicts described life under the convict lease as "worse than slavery." Slaves, after all, had represented a significant financial asset to their masters, who provided them with some basic necessities, if for no other reason than to protect their investment. Convicts, however, required no such protection. Moreover, the criminal "justice" system offered a seemingly endless supply of cheap labor; as one white southerner put it, "If one dies, get another."[9]

Public outcry at corruption in the convict lease system, more than concern for the treatment of prisoners, helped turn public opinion against the practice, at least in Mississippi. Leaseholders regularly failed to pay even the scant fees charged to them for the right to work the state's convicts without pay. Thus, the lease failed to benefit the state as Mississippians had been promised. The new state constitution of 1890 outlawed the convict lease system, replacing it with a system of state farms.

Remarkably, however, the practice of convict leasing continued under a system in which state farm lands, presupplied with convict labor, were leased to private planters. Not until 1906 did the state legislature end this practice. It was phased out in the first half of the twentieth century, but even then many south-

ern prisoners continued to be sentenced to hard labor, on public works, and on state and county-run prison plantations like Parchman Farm in Mississippi and Angola in Louisiana. To this day, prisoners at places like Angola work at tasks such as picking cotton by hand as part of the punishment for their crimes.

END OF RECONSTRUCTION AND
HO FOR KANSAS!

The presidential election of 1876 set the Democratic governor of New York Samuel Tilden against Republican Rutherford B. Hayes, then the third-term governor of Ohio. When the popular vote was counted, Tilden led by more than a quarter of a million votes and appeared to be the winner in the Electoral College as well. Republicans, however, contested returns from three southern states. In the complex and lengthy congressional negotiations that followed, southern Democrats agreed to break with northern members of their party and support Hayes's presidency in exchange for promises that included the withdrawal of federal troops from South Carolina and Louisiana, the last remaining Reconstruction governments. Historians have long cast "the Compromise of 1877," as these negotiations are known, as the de facto end of Reconstruction. In reality, however, the majority of southern states had already been returned to "home rule" by the time Hayes took office. In addition, both public and congressional support for federal intervention in defense of black rights had been waning for some time.

Nevertheless, Hayes was a more complicated figure. He required formal promises to protect black rights before he would relinquish federal control in South Carolina and Louisiana—none

"The 'Strong' Government 1869–1877," by James Albert Wales, *Puck,* May 22, 1880. In this sympathetic British view of the South under Reconstruction, President Grant plays the role of Napoleon.

of his predecessors had taken that step when reinstating southern state governments. He notably vetoed no less than seven congressional bills designed to weaken federal protection of voting

rights, although his actions did nothing to halt the rise of rigid segregation and the oppression of blacks. Finally, in an act of great symbolic importance, Hayes was the first president ever to host a for-

"Shall We Call Home Our Troops?" *Harper's Weekly,* January 9, 1875. A Union soldier stands between the former slave and his former masters, one of whom proclaims: "WE intend to beat the negro in the battle of life, and defeat means one thing—EXTERMINATION."

"Murder of Louisiana Sacrificed on the Altar of Radicalism," by A. Zenneck, wood engraving, 1871.

mal performance by an African American entertainer at the White House. In 1878, the renowned diva Marie Selika Williams performed an operatic concert for the president and his guests.

Despite the loss of federal protection, African Americans continued to defend their hard-won freedom with every means at their disposal. Many abandoned the South in search of a better life. While some focused on migration to Liberia, others turned west. As early as the mid-1870s Benjamin "Pap" Singleton, a carpenter and former slave, had begun to organize African Americans in

At the time this photograph of Nicodemus, Kansas, was taken in 1885, about seven hundred African Americans lived in the colony. The structure to the left of the general store was the First Baptist Church.

"Ho for Kansas," broadside,
March 18, 1878.

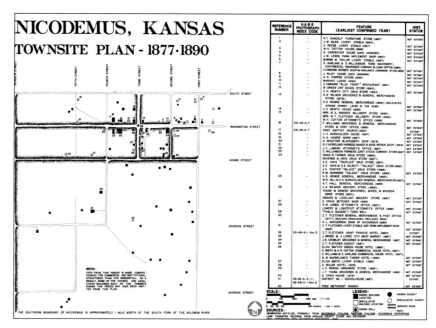

Nicodemus, Kansas, Townsite Plan, 1877–90. The Historic American
Buildings Survey reconstructed the Nicodemus town plan.

Henry O. Flipper
(1856–1940).

Tennessee to emigrate to Kansas, where cheap land was abundant, and where, he hoped, blacks would get a fair chance at developing economic independence. Singleton advertised his call throughout the South to build black colonies in Kansas. Driven by the growing violence and oppression in the South, many African Americans responded.

On July 30, 1877, African American settlers from Kentucky established the town of Nicodemus in western Kansas, the first of hundreds of predominantly black towns in the West. Early conditions in Nicodemus proved trying, and many of the settlers were extremely poor. Some groups arrived too late to plant crops for the first year. Residents often had to take jobs away from home or rely on charity to survive the first winter. Yet resolutely, waves of black settlers arrived to build up their homesteads and the town itself. Despite the hardships of establishing a new life under such difficult conditions, the promise of landownership and escape from southern oppression, especially lynch law, were appealing. Just two years after the founding of Nicodemus, as many as twenty thousand African Americans, known as Exodusters, flowed out of Louisiana, Mississippi, and Texas and into the new promised land: Kansas.

Joining the new residents of Nicodemus was Henry O. Flipper, the first African American graduate of the U.S. Military Academy at West Point. Though Flipper had been preceded at West Point by two other black cadets, he was the first to complete all four years required to graduate, enduring racism and rigorous training from his instructors as well as near total ostracism by his fellow cadets, who were intent on driving him out of the academy. After his graduation, Flipper was given the rank of second lieutenant and assigned to the all-black Tenth Cavalry Unit, stationed on the western frontier.

Henry Flipper spent five years in the army, distinguishing himself as a talented officer while engaging in engineering projects across the region. In the 1880 war with Apache chief Victorio, Flipper earned the respect of his superior officers and an assignment as acting assistant quartermaster, in recognition of his meritorious service. Just two years later, however, Flipper was court-martialed for allegedly embezzling thousands of dollars from the commissary fund he oversaw. Although Flipper was acquitted on the charges of financial mismanagement, he was found guilty of conduct unbecoming an officer and dishonorably discharged. He remained in the West for nearly fifty years, working in a variety of engineering, surveying, and mining activities. He also served terms as an agent of the U.S. Justice and Interior departments. Henry Flipper maintained, until his death in 1940, that he was innocent of the charges that had ended his military career and that his court-martial was the result of racial prejudice. In 1976, the U.S. Army posthumously granted him an honorable discharge.

PART EIGHT

"THERE IS NO NEGRO PROBLEM"

1877–1895

BLACK FRONTIERSPEOPLE AND COWBOYS

If we learned our history from Hollywood, we would think the Old West was populated almost exclusively by gunslinging males as white as the population of Frost, Minnesota—a city that as late as 2010 recorded no people of African descent. According to the 1870 U.S. Census, however, more than 250,000 African Americans lived in Texas; by 1880 that number had grown to 400,000. That same year the census recorded 43,000 black people living in Kansas; even the mountains and high plains of Montana were home to more than 300 African Americans. Settlement of the West clearly depended upon the contributions of black Americans—including black women.

"Stagecoach" Mary Fields, born a slave in Tennessee in 1832, left her home after the Civil War to work as a maid on the steamboat *Robert E. Lee*. She then moved to Toledo, Ohio, where she became a maid and "handyman" for the city's Ursuline Convent. The convent's mother superior, who may have been related to Fields's former owners, established an Indian mission in Montana and invited Fields to join her. Fields became the mission's jack-of-all-trades, learning tanning from the neighboring Indians. She made her own clothes, which included buckskin pants, a buffalo coat, and a black hat, which she accessorized with one of the new repeating rifles. She earned a reputation for toughness and may have beaten or shot to death a white man—an act that in most places would have led to her immediate lynching. The frontier offered her protection from the law. In the 1890s Fields began to work for Wells Fargo, driving a mail coach, where she earned her "Stagecoach" moniker. As a young boy, the actor Gary Cooper met Stage-

"Stagecoach" Mary Fields
(1832–1914).

coach Mary in Montana, and in 1959 he recalled that she "lived to become one of the freest souls ever to draw a breath or a .38."[1]

Gary Cooper's 1952 film *High Noon* helped to establish our popular image of the West: the solitary man struggling against evil amid an indifferent community. Clint Eastwood acted in many westerns, from the 1960s television series *Rawhide* to the 1992 film *Unforgiven*. In such films we find comely women, the occasional Mexican, and a few Indians—even a midget—but no one like Nat Love, commonly known as "Deadwood Dick."

Like Stagecoach Mary, Love was born a slave in Tennessee, in his case in 1854. He set out for the West in 1869. According to his entertaining 1907 autobiography, he herded cattle and shot his way through Kansas, Texas, Montana, Arizona, Mexico, and California; he recalled later that he was hardly the only black man punching cattle. His exploits on the range required mastery of the famed Colt .45, the repeating rifle, and the lasso; he excelled in the use of

Nat Love ("Deadwood Dick")
(1854–1921).

each. He was friends with Billy the Kid, Buffalo Bill Cody, Kit Carson, Bat Masterson, and the James brothers. Love claimed that he had been shot or stabbed fourteen times. He also claimed to have walked for days through a snowy desert carrying his prized saddle, which had to be pried from his frozen grip. Once, severely wounded, he was captured by an Indian tribe, he tells us, who nursed him back to health. When he regained his strength, the chief, according to Love, offered him his daughter in marriage. Rather than accept this fate, he escaped one night on a pony and rode bareback for more than one hundred miles in less than two weeks.

Love sought a wide readership for his autobiography and thus avoided uncomfortable subjects like racial prejudice on the frontier. But he firmly denounced the slavery he knew as a boy. Seven years old when the Civil War broke out, he could not contain his rage against the "peculiar institution." "Surely 'war is hell,'" he wrote, "—but slavery is worse." All his other exploits were generously spiked with self-deprecating humor. While living near Fort Dodge, Kansas, for instance, he recounted a whiskey binge that led him to lasso one of the fort's cannons and attempt to drag it out of the compound. Authorities looked unkindly on the move, he wrote, but a round of drinks offered by Bat Masterson resulted in dropped charges and good cheer.

The U.S. government officially declared the frontier closed in 1890; Love, foreseeing the end of the freewheeling life he had known, abandoned the range. For the next fifteen years he worked in California for various railroad lines as a Pullman porter, a dramatic contrast

Black cowboys.

to his cowboy days. Love spent his last days as a bank guard in, of all places, Los Angeles—where the American film industry blossomed by creating the most enduring of American myths, that of the taming of the West. But it ignored Love's story and the story of the black cowboys like him.

THE INVENTIVE LEWIS H. LATIMER

Lewis Howard Latimer was born in 1848, in Chelsea, Massachusetts. His parents, George Latimer and Rebecca Smith, had escaped slavery in Virginia in 1842 and settled in Boston, sparking the famed Latimer protests over the attempt to return the couple to slavery. Helped by mass protests, the Latimers successfully resisted attempts to reenslave them and remained in Massachusetts. The young Lewis worked in his father's barbershop and sold William Lloyd Garrison's abolitionist newspaper, *The Liberator*. In 1858, however, Lewis's father vanished mysteriously, leaving the family in a precarious financial position. Lewis's formal schooling quickly

ended, and to help provide for his family, he worked a variety of odd jobs, then took a low-level position in a Boston attorney's office. In 1864 Latimer joined the U.S. Navy and served until honorably discharged in July 1865.

Returning to Boston after the Civil War, Latimer took a post as an office boy in the Crosby and Gould patent law office and taught himself technical drafting. He quickly rose in the ranks, becoming the firm's chief draftsman by the mid-1870s. Some of his technical drawings survive, displaying enormous talent and artistry. While at the patent law office, he drafted the schematics for Alexander Graham Bell's patent

Lewis H. Latimer
(1848–1928).

application for the telephone, which was granted on February 14, 1876. Latimer's work on Bell's patent application gave him a small but noteworthy role in the development of a technology that would eventually transform the Western world.

In 1879, Latimer left Boston and resettled in Bridgeport, Connecticut, where he worked for the U.S. Electric Lighting Company. In the years to come, he would make a number of significant contributions to the nascent electrical lighting industry. In 1880, he assisted in the installation of New York City's first incandescent system in the Equitable Building. Later, he supervised the installation of many other lighting systems and helped develop the process of manufacturing new, more reliable carbon filaments for electric lamps. He patented new production techniques for these filaments and held other patents, including one for an electric lamp that he invented, known as the Latimer Lamp. In the early 1880s, he traveled to

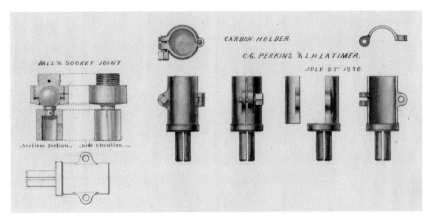

Arc light components, 1880. Latimer drew this component of an arc lamp, an early electric light, for the U.S. Electric Lighting Company.

London to oversee the development of an incandescent lamp factory there.

In 1883, Latimer joined the Edison Electric Light Company, working in the engineering division, and six years later joined the firm's legal department. His intimate knowledge of the development of electrical lighting technologies and his patent history made him essential to the legal department's work. In 1890, he published *Incandescent Electric Lighting, a Practical Description of the Edison System,* an

enormously popular volume that made the essential elements of the new technology accessible to the public. Latimer remained a member of the legal department when a merger in 1892 created the General Electric Company. He continued to work on patent issues until his retirement in 1924 and died four years later. In 1995, to recognize his "contributions to science and technology and American life," the Latimer house in Flushing became a New York City landmark.

KNIGHTS OF LABOR AND COLORED FARMERS' ALLIANCE

In 1879, a labor leader named Terence V. Powderly took over leadership of a small fraternal organization in Pennsylvania called the Noble and Holy Order of the Knights of Labor. Under Powderly's leadership, membership in the organization grew rapidly. In 1886, the Knights of Labor emerged as the first national labor movement in U.S. history, with more than 700,000 members in locals across the country. The Knights organized skilled and unskilled workers and reached out to black workers. During one tour of the South, Powderly reminded workers that whites and blacks "must sink their differences or

fall prey to the slave labor now being imported into this country."[2]

Initially distrustful of white labor organizations, many in the black press began to support the Knights as they gained strength in the South. By 1886 an estimated 75,000 African Americans had joined the order. To placate white southerners, Knights leaders adopted an unofficial practice of organizing black workers into separate locals, even though the organization formally called for equal treatment of all workers. Despite the segregated system, several black Knights rose to important leadership positions; others gained political

office on interracial labor-backed tickets in local elections.

Despite the Knights' compromise with the strengthening Jim Crow order, their efforts to organize black workers faced intense resistance. Strikes led by Knights seeking higher wages for cotton pickers in Arkansas and sugar workers in Louisiana, for instance, triggered violent reactions from local planters. Both strikes ended without success. In addition to courting violence, the practice of organizing poor black farmworkers also threatened the Knights' growing cooperation with an important new force in southern politics: the Farmers' Alliance.

George Washington Murray (1853–1926). Born in Sumter County, South Carolina, Murray attended the University of South Carolina at Columbia and taught school for fifteen years. He became inspector of customs, a coveted patronage position, at Charleston and was elected to Congress, serving from 1893 to 1897. He lectured for the Colored Farmers' Alliance for fifteen years.

First organized in Texas in 1877, the National Farmers' Alliance and Industrial Union (commonly known as the Southern Alliance) was, by 1886, well on its way to becoming the nation's largest agricultural organization. Alliance rhetoric called for political and economic policies to benefit America's producers—farmers and laborers—rather than capitalists. Unlike the Knights, however, the Southern Alliance maintained a policy of strict segregation. Moreover, many of its leaders were landed planters who regularly employed poor black farmworkers. The Knights' attempts to organize black agrarians demonstrated the limitations of the nascent producers' movement, divided by race and class. Weakened by these tensions, as well as by a failed strike against railroad giant Jay Gould, the Knights' power diminished rapidly from its peak in 1886—the same year that saw the formation of the American Federation of Labor (AFL). In the years to come, the AFL grew to fill the void left by the Knights. Unlike the Knights, however, the AFL concentrated only on organizing skilled laborers and excluded all black workers well into the twentieth century.

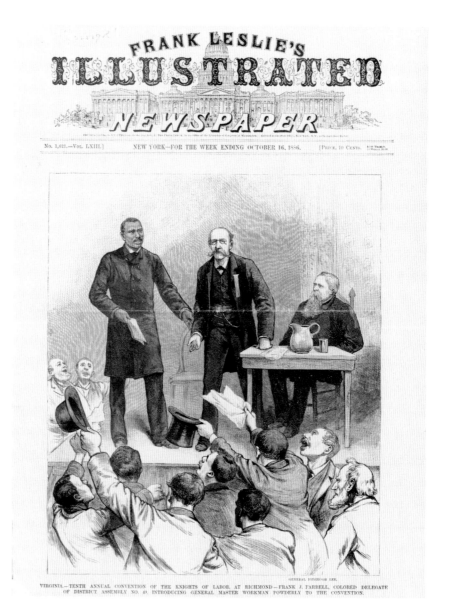

"Virginia—Tenth Annual Convention of the Knights of Labor, at Richmond—Frank J. Farrell, Colored Delegate of District Assembly No. 49, Introducing General Master Workman Powderly to the Convention—from a Sketch by Joseph Becker," *Frank Leslie's Illustrated Newspaper,* October 16, 1886.

Recognizing the power in the emergent Farmers' Alliance movement, a small group of black agrarians in Houston County, Texas, founded the Colored Farmers' National Alliance and Cooperative Union in 1886. A black farm owner named J. J. Shuffer became its first president, and African Americans filled most of its other leadership roles. A white man, however, named R. M. Humphrey became general superintendent of the Colored Alliance, tasked with the building of a coalition with the all-white Southern Alliance.

Over the next five years the Colored Alliance pushed its white counterpart for cooperation across racial lines. The two organizations did cooperate on some economic ventures and, at times, worked together to elect sympathetic figures to local and state office.

The Colored Alliance swept across the South. At one point it claimed more than one million members, ran its own national newspaper, and operated cooperative stores and exchanges. In politics, the Colored Alliance differed from its white counterpart by advocating a federal elections bill designed to protect black voting rights and by publicly

Cotton pickers, stereo view.

criticizing segregation. The Colored Alliance also joined with the Southern Alliance in calling for the development of a third political party based on Alliance ideals. From this coalition the Populist (or People's) Party was born.

In the fall of 1891, southern newspapers reported with great alarm that a national strike of cotton pickers, organized by the Colored Alliance, was imminent. Once again the economic and racial divides of the producers' move-

ment emerged. Although little is known about the origins of the strike plan, it clearly divided the Alliance movement in general and the Colored Alliance in particular. Landed black leaders in the Colored Alliance, ironically, joined with white planters in condemning the strike. Reports of sporadic strike activities appeared throughout the South, but a national movement never materialized. The failed strike badly damaged the Colored Alliance, although it remained an important part of the emerging Populist movement and individual black Alliance members continued to play prominent roles. George Washington Murray, for example, a former Colored Alliance lecturer from South Carolina, was elected to the U.S. Congress as a Republican in 1892.

EDUCATION AND PHILANTHROPY IN THE NINETEENTH CENTURY

When it first opened in a church basement on April 11, 1881, the Atlanta Baptist Female Seminary was one of hundreds of post-emancipation schools for African Americans. Founders Sophia Packard and Harriet Giles, both white women, began their school with fewer than a dozen students, but within a year more than two hundred women had registered. Beginning in 1882, John D. Rockefeller made the first of several donations, helping the school move to a new nine-acre campus in 1883. The following year the school was renamed Spelman Seminary (in 1924 it became Spelman College), in honor of Rockefeller's wife, Laura Spelman Rockefeller, and her abolitionist family. Initially the school offered high school diplomas and trained teachers, missionaries, and nurses. Spelman imple-

Students at Spelman Seminary, Atlanta, 1902.

mented a college curriculum in 1897 and awarded its first degrees in 1901, making it the first black women's college in the United States. Sophia B. Jones, a homeopathic doctor trained at the University of Michigan, was the first black female to join the school's faculty, in 1885. Not until 1953 would the college elect an African American—Alfred Manley—as its president; in 1987, Johnnetta Betsch

Tuskegee Normal and Industrial Institute, 1916.

Cole became the first black woman to lead Spelman. Among the school's prominent recent alumnae are Marian Wright Edelman, founder of the Children's Defense Fund, and Bernice Johnson Reagon, founder of the musical group Sweet Honey in the Rock.

Lingering pockets of black political power in the South in the last quarter of the nineteenth century helped establish Tuskegee Institute. Local blacks in Macon County, Alabama, agreed to support State Senator Wilbur Foster in his reelection campaign, in exchange for his promise to secure funding for a normal school to train black teachers. In February 1881, the legislature appropriated two thousand dollars for the establishment of the school. Initially, officials asked Virginia's Hampton Institute principal, Samuel Chapman Armstrong, to recommend a white candidate to lead the school. Armstrong, however, offered his strong endorsement of Hampton graduate Booker T. Washington.

Arriving in late June, Washington found that there were no buildings or even land for the school. Undaunted, he arranged for temporary housing for the initial crop of thirty-one students and selected a dilapidated building adjacent to the local AME church as the school's first building. On July 4, 1881, he formally opened the school. As Washington focused on raising funds for proper school buildings, the students, when not in class, were tasked with constructing the campus.

Tuskegee's early curriculum stressed the importance and dignity of manual, industrial, and craft labor. It taught the so-called higher subjects like literature, geography, and the sciences, however, as well. As the school's ambassador, Washington sought support from white philanthropists in the North and acceptance from local whites. To that end he publicly emphasized accommodationism, or submission to the prevailing segregationist culture, and avoided discussions of racial equality. As money flowed in from sources like Andrew Carnegie and John D. Rockefeller, Tuskegee's campus and prestige grew. By 1900 campus properties were valued at more than $300,000. The school's faculty developed as well. George Washington Carver, perhaps Tuskegee's most famous faculty member, arrived on campus in 1896. He helped revolutionize southern agriculture by ending its dependence on cotton and demonstrating the utility of diverse crops, including soybeans, sweet potatoes, and peanuts.

Alabama's early funding of the Tuskegee Institute notwithstanding, southern states in the early 1880s spent less and less on black education as black political power waned. Many northern whites began to fear that, without access to even a basic education, southern blacks would not be prepared to meet what they considered the moral and occupational demands of the working class. In April 1882, in an attempt to address this problem, a wealthy textile manu-

Black students studying corn and cotton at the Annie Davis School, near Tuskegee, photograph by Frances Benjamin Johnston, ca. 1902.

Slater Fund meeting report, *Cleveland Gazette*, May 21, 1887.

Booker T. Washington (1856?-1915). Born a slave in Virginia, Washington rose to become the most powerful and influential African American of his era. He is photographed here at his desk at the Tuskegee Institute. His insistence that African Americans drop their demands for full civil rights and focus on avocations that would bring economic stability to the race offended many black leaders, most notably W. E. B. Du Bois. But the "Wizard of Tuskegee" wielded enormous power, dispensing funds that only he could raise from sympathetic whites and patronage jobs from his contacts in a series of presidential administrations.

facturer named John Fox Slater donated more than $1 million in cash and bonds to establish a foundation to fund African American education in the former slave states. The purpose of the fund, Slater said in a letter to the Fund's Board of Trustees, was to confer a "Christian education" on black Americans, in order that they might become "good men and good citizens." Slater appointed former president Rutherford B. Hayes as the fund's leader.

Under Hayes and its general agent Atticus G. Haygood (who had been a chaplain in the Confederate army and president of Emory University), the Slater Fund led the movement to support industrial education for African Americans. In the first twenty years of its existence, it donated the modern equivalent of millions of dollars to colleges and universities that taught African Americans. Some of these schools taught the liberal arts, but all of them offered vocational training. In addition to institutional financial support, the fund also provided direct grants to some individuals. Most prominent of the scholars it aided was W. E. B. Du Bois, who pursued graduate research in sociology at the Friedrich Wilhelm University in Berlin in 1892 and 1893.

The Slater Fund soon abandoned support for blacks in higher education, however, and focused on the industrial arts. The decision forced Du Bois to abandon his studies in Germany and return to Harvard (where he earned his Ph.D. in 1895); as social policy, the change also helped sustain widespread prejudice that African Americans could not achieve intellectual distinction and were best suited to manual labor. At the turn of the century, the Slater Fund, the Peabody Education Fund (which began in 1867), and other smaller funds combined to form the General Education Board, which established a virtual monopoly over black educational philanthropy in the South.

MAJOR LEAGUE BASEBALL AND JIM CROW

Moses Fleetwood Walker (1857–1924). Moses is seated at the left. This image of the Oberlin College baseball team also includes his brother "Weldy" Walker, who is standing in the back row.

Modern baseball slowly took shape in the early 1880s. Team owners just had begun to pay their best players; four strikes equaled an out; players still fielded the ball without the aid of gloves; and walks were officially recorded as hits. Teams, even entire leagues, sprang up and then disappeared with regularity. Some teams, especially those in northern cities, included black players who could help make a team competitive. Black stars like Frank Grant, John W. "Bud" Fowler, and George Washington Stovey excelled in the minor leagues. At the close of the nineteenth century somewhere between thirty-five and seventy African Americans played with whites in organized baseball.

Among the earliest black players was Bud Fowler, who began in the Interna-

tional League (a minor league name often recycled) in 1878. Fowler experienced terrible treatment from fans and opposing players alike. As a second baseman, he endured countless runners who slid into second base with "spikes up." It happened so often that he wrapped the lower parts of his legs in wood.

The next year William Edward White, a Brown University student, played one game on June 21, 1879, for the Providence Grays, considered the first major league appearance by a black ballplayer. Frank Grant led his team—the Buffalo Bisons—in batting, but the other team members refused to be photographed with him, and opposing players sometimes chased him off the field. One player slammed into Grant so hard that he took three weeks to recover.

Among the first black professional ballplayers, Moses Fleetwood Walker— "Fleet," as he was known—had the longest career. He had been a star in 1881 on the first varsity team fielded by Oberlin College, famed for accepting African American and female students. Three years later Walker played for the Toledo, Ohio, Blue Stockings, part of the American Association, one of the three major leagues in organized baseball. In 1883, the team won the Northwestern League championship. A talented defensive catcher, Walker also earned a reputation as a speedy, if inconsistent, offensive threat.

A handful of other black players, including his younger brother, Welday "Weldy" Walker, joined Fleet in the big leagues, but they also experienced much racial prejudice. Particularly in southern cities, black players were subject to regular threats and insults. In Richmond, Fleet Walker received a letter indicating that a lynch mob would be waiting for him if he took the field against the local nine. He ignored the threat and, thankfully, no mob materialized.

In 1887, Fleet was playing in the minor league International Association; an exhibition with future Hall of Famer Adrian "Cap" Anson's major league club was scheduled. Anson, an Iowan with an uncontrollable disposition, successfully fought to bar Fleet and his black teammate from playing in the game.

Shortly thereafter, the International Association team owners agreed that all teams would stop signing black players. This so-called gentleman's agreement became an ugly precedent for all of organized baseball. Although black players continued to play in the International Association and other predominantly white leagues, they faced increasing hostility. Eventually they all either faded away from baseball or joined the emerging Negro Leagues.

Fleet Walker retired from baseball in 1889 and returned to Ohio, where he took up work as a railroad clerk. In 1891, he was involved in a bar fight with a group of white men who harassed and hurled racial epithets at him. In the brawl that ensued, Walker stabbed and killed one of the men. Tried for second-degree murder, Walker won acquittal based on the court's determination that he had acted in self-defense. Trouble, however, continued to hound Walker for the rest of his life. In 1898, he was convicted of mail fraud and sentenced to a year in jail. In the end, none of his business ventures equaled the success he had enjoyed on the diamond. In 1924, he died poor in Cleveland, Ohio.

MISSISSIPPI PLAN AND BLACK DISENFRANCHISEMENT

The state constitutions established in the late 1860s by Reconstruction governments, and the adoption of the Fifteenth Amendment in 1870, gave black men in the South the right to vote. But whites immediately undermined black civil rights through violence, intimidation, and fraud, especially in the former Confederate states. In 1889, the century's last significant Republican effort to protect black voting rights appeared in the form of Senator Henry Cabot Lodge's election bill. Called the "force bill" in the South, the legislation would have provided federal supervision of elections—a critical step in ensuring that black votes would be counted. Democratic politicians, however, vilified it as the worst form of northern interference in southern life. Although Lodge's bill passed through the House of Representatives easily, it met an unbreakable filibuster in the Senate.

Mississippians had already begun organizing a constitutional convention to limit the impact of Lodge's bill if it passed the Congress. While the Fifteenth Amendment mandated suffrage to all qualified male voters regardless of color, the power to determine what constituted a qualified voter still remained with the states. When Mississippi's constitutional convention met in August 1890, it sought one result: to eliminate the black vote. The Jackson *Clarion-Ledger,* on December 22, 1890, stated plainly that the convention was held "to restrict suffrage—negro suffrage, if you please."

Turnout for the election to nominate convention delegates was low, and in many races Republicans did not even field candidates. In Jasper County white supremacists assassinated one Republican who ran for a seat at the convention. As a result, the white, Democratic convention proposed a constitution aimed at limiting qualified voters. Voters would have to pay a new two-dollar poll tax and register at least four months in advance of an election. Anyone with a criminal conviction would be disqualified, and those seeking to register would have to demonstrate that they could

Isaiah T. Montgomery (1847–1924). A former slave, Montgomery had been a personal attendant to Joseph Davis, brother of Jefferson Davis, the president of the Confederacy. His support for black disenfranchisement in 1890 was meant to help ease racial tensions, but black leaders like Frederick Douglass expressed shock at his move. He remained active in local politics and the Republican Party for the rest of his life but dedicated himself to the economic development of the Mound Bayou community.

read a section of the state constitution and understand it. The "understanding" clause, at first, was designed to permit sympathetic registrars to admit poor, illiterate white voters, while still denying illiterate blacks the right to vote.

Isaiah Montgomery, founder of the black settlement Mound Bayou and the lone African American convention delegate, spoke in favor of the new suffrage clause. In a speech frequently hailed by white politicians and decried by the vast majority of black leaders, Montgomery acquiesced to what he called the convention's intention to "purify the ballot," in exchange for the promise of guarantees of basic legal protection for black Mississippians and an end to the violence inflicted on blacks. Montgomery thus offered to sacrifice the suffrage of what he calculated to be roughly two-thirds of African Americans and thereby secure an "unquestioned white supremacy." As reported in the New York *World* on September 28, 1890, he pleaded with the white delegates to accept the deal and bring peace and a measure of justice to black Mississippians: "Press the fated question home to your conscience and to your hearts—'What answer?'" he asked dramatically. "Is our sacrifice

"The Vampire that Hovers Over North Carolina," *News and Observer* (Raleigh), September 27, 1898.

accepted? Shall the great question be settled?"

Montgomery's strategy failed to produce either peace or basic legal rights for blacks in Mississippi. Even worse, the new constitution proved far more effective at disenfranchising blacks than Montgomery ever imagined. In 1868, roughly 87,000 blacks had registered to vote, representing almost 97 percent of the voting-age population in Mississippi. After the passage of the new constitution, fewer than 9,000 African Americans

registered for the election of 1892, less than 6 percent of the voting-age population. While the new constitution also significantly limited the number of poor whites who voted, the most significant impact fell upon blacks. The so-called Mississippi Plan established a blueprint for other southern states. South Carolina (1895), Louisiana (1898), North Carolina (1900), Alabama and Virginia (1901), Georgia (1908), and Oklahoma (1910) all used similar tactics to formally disenfranchise African American voters.

PROVIDENT HOSPITAL AND
DR. DANIEL HALE WILLIAMS

Born to prosperous parents in Philadelphia in 1856, Daniel Hale Williams's life was upended at eleven when his father died of tuberculosis. His mother struggled financially, and by age seventeen Williams and his sister Sally had moved to Janesville, Wisconsin. There he worked at Harry Anderson's Tonsorial Parlor and Bathing Rooms, where he approached Dr. Henry Palmer, a prominent physician

and his barbershop patron, concerning an apprenticeship. Palmer agreed. After two years, Palmer recommended that Williams receive formal medical school training, and with financial support from Anderson, he was able to. He graduated from the prestigious Chicago Medical College in 1883 and quickly established himself as a talented surgeon. He earned a position at the South Side Dispensary in Chicago

at a time when few black doctors had privileges in any American hospitals. In his private practice, Williams developed an interracial clientele, another rarity for black doctors of the day. As an instructor at Northwestern Medical School, he taught both white and black students, some of whom, like Charles Mayo (for whom the Mayo Clinic was later named), would go on to have very successful careers of their own. In 1889,

Daniel Hale Williams (1856–1931). From Booker T. Washington, Fannie Barrier Williams, and Norman Barton Wood, *A New Negro for a New Century, an Accurate and Up-to-Date Record of the Upward Struggles of the Negro Race* (Chicago: American Pub. House, 1900).

Provident Hospital, founded in 1891, located at 36th and Dearborn Streets in Chicago.

he was appointed to the Illinois State Board of Health.

Although he was personally successful, Williams was disturbed by the scarcity of options for African Americans needing medical treatment as well as for those who wanted to enter the health professions. To address these conditions, he opened Provident Hospital in 1891, the first black-operated hospital in the United States. At his insistence, the hospital maintained an integrated staff and accepted patients of all races. He also established the nation's first training program for black nurses—all other programs barred blacks from attending nursing schools. To increase professional development opportunities for African American doctors, Williams helped found the National Medical Association, an organization of black physicians excluded from membership in the all-white American Medical Association.

Though taxed with administrative responsibilities, Williams continued to hone his surgical skills. In July 1893, he completed one of the first successful open-heart surgeries. When a patient with a stab wound to the chest showed signs of steady decline, Williams faced a choice: wait and watch the man die, or operate and risk killing the man himself. Without the benefit of X-ray or any proven procedures, Williams opened the man's chest and carefully repaired a laceration of his pericardium (the fluid-filled sac around the heart). The patient recovered fully and lived for many years afterward. Williams would later perform one of the nation's first successful surgeries on a patient with a hemorrhaging spleen.

In 1913, he was included in the group of one hundred charter members of the American College of Surgeons, the only African American so recognized. With Provident as a model, Williams emerged as a leading national figure in the movement to develop black hospitals. In a 1900 speech, he made his case:

> In view of this cruel ostracism, affecting so vitally our race, our duty seems plain. Institute Hospitals and Training Schools. Let us no longer sit idly and inanely deploring existing conditions. Let us not waste time trying to effect changes or modifications in the institutions unfriendly to us, but rather let us seek to promote the doctrine of helping and stimulating our race.[3]

Following in his footsteps, African Americans built a dozen hospitals by 1900, just nine years after the founding of Provident. Fifty more emerged by 1912, and more than one hundred black hospitals existed by 1919.

IDA B. WELLS-BARNETT AND LYNCHING

Ida B. Wells-Barnett (1862–1931).

"Lynching of C. J. Miller, at Bardwell, Kentucky, July 7th, 1893." From Ida B. Wells, *A Red Record: Tabulated Statistics and Alleged Causes of Lynchings in the United States, 1892–1893–1894* (Chicago: Donohue & Henneberry, 1895).

We may never know the full extent of the lynching that took place in the United States from the late nineteenth to the early twentieth century. Scholars at the Tuskegee Institute attempted to track and publicize each murderous episode, seeking to raise national awareness about the frightening number of African Americans lynched by their white neighbors. Of the 230 incidents carefully catalogued in Tuskegee's files for 1892, perhaps none had a greater impact on the course of American history than those of Calvin McDowell, Thomas Moss, and William Stewart of Memphis, Tennessee. The murders of these men launched the antilynching crusade of Ida B. Wells (later Wells-Barnett), the cause's most eloquent and effective advocate. A former teacher, Wells began her career in journalism in the early 1880s and by 1892 had transformed her newspaper, the Memphis *Free Speech,* into an important voice for black rights.

One March evening that year, a fight broke out between blacks and whites in a predominantly black neighborhood called the Curve. Sensing an opportu-nity, W. H. Barrett, the white owner of a grocery store in the Curve, blamed the incident on leaders of the People's Grocery, a neighboring black-owned cooperative. In a naked attempt to eliminate his competitors, Barrett arranged for an arrest warrant to be issued for several blacks, including Thomas Moss, a close friend of Wells and the president of the joint stock company that owned the People's Grocery. A white posse organized to seize the men rushed the People's Grocery, only to be repelled by several armed blacks. Hysteria gripped much of white Memphis. Moss, Stewart, and McDowell were then quickly rounded up and taken to the city jail. A mob descended on the building and marched the men to a nearby field. When one of the three resisted, sadistic whites gouged out his eyes. Then the mob shot all three of the men.

Wells went on the attack. Since blacks could not live in safety in Memphis, she advised them to leave the city as soon as possible. Throughout the year, she denounced city authorities and all apologists for lynching. Then, on May 21, 1892, she published this editorial in her paper:

Eight negroes lynched since last issue of the Free Speech one at Little Rock, Ark., last Saturday morning where the citizens broke (?) into the penitentiary and got their man; three near Anniston, Ala., one near New Orleans; and three at Clarksville, Ga., the last three for killing a white man, and five on the same old racket—the new alarm about raping white women. The same programme of hanging, then shooting bullets into the lifeless bodies was carried out to the letter. Nobody in this section of the country believes the old threadbare lie that Negro men rape white women. If Southern white men are not careful, they will overreach themselves and public sentiment will have a reaction; a conclusion will then be reached which will be very damaging to the moral reputation of their women.

A seething white mob stormed the offices of the *Free Speech* and destroyed Wells's press. Out of town at the time, she received word of the attack. Friends advised her to stay away since whites had threatened to lynch her too. Under the pen name "Exiled," she published a series of editorials for T. Thomas Fortune's *New York Age,* an important reform newspaper, which became the basis for her many public lectures on lynching and her best-known work, *Southern Horrors.*

Southern Horrors was a landmark work and spawned a national campaign against lynching. Wells rejected the deadly and common but fanciful charge that black men represented a threat to white womanhood. Although few blacks had ever been officially charged with the crime of rape, defenders of lynch law asserted the propensity of black men to commit the crime. Clearly, Wells charged, whites had no interest in preventing rape, since no white man ever was punished for raping a black woman. She also presented cases where black men were lynched for having consensual sex with white women. Rape, then, she concluded, was not the cause of lynching. Lynching, rather, was an attempt on the part of whites to return African Americans to a level of subjugation not known since the days of slavery. Thus, she concluded, blacks should resist with any means at their disposal: emigration, boycotts, publicity through the press, and even the gun. "The lesson this teaches," she wrote, "which every Afro American should ponder well, is that a Winchester rifle should have a place of honor in every black home and it should be used for that protection which the law refuses to give."[4]

THE WORLD'S COLUMBIAN EXPOSITION AND THE BANJO LESSON BY HENRY OSSAWA TANNER

From August to October 1893, organizers of the World's Columbian Exposition focused international attention on Chicago and the progress of American "civilization" in the four hundred years since Columbus. For more than three years leading up to the fair, African American leaders fought to secure recognition of black achievement as part of the exposition. The fair's all-white organizing committee, however, consistently thwarted these efforts. When the fair opened to the public in

"Darkies' Day at the Fair. (A Tale of Poetic Retribution)," by Frederick Burr Opper, *Puck*, August 21, 1893.

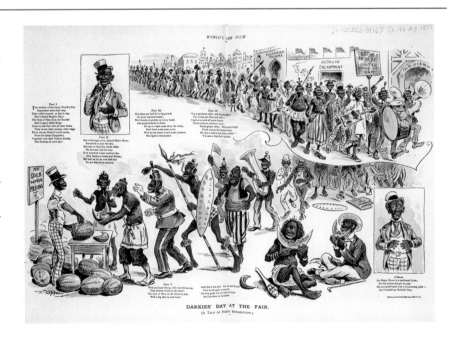

DARKIES' DAY AT THE FAIR.
(A TALE OF POETIC RETRIBUTION.)

Administration building at the World's Columbian Exposition, in Chicago, on opening day, May 1, 1893.

Henry Ossawa Tanner (1859–1937).

Banjo Player, by William Miller.

the summer of 1893, its fabled "White City" presented a narrative of American industrial, social, and artistic progress almost entirely devoid of the contributions of people of color.

In protest, activists led by Ida B. Wells (later Wells-Barnett) and Frederick Douglass published a pamphlet condemning the fair organizers' treatment of African Americans, comparing the damage done to the public image of blacks to the injuries caused by the evils of lynch mobs and the convict lease system. While Wells and Douglass collaborated on the pamphlet, *The Reason Why the Colored American Is Not in the World's Columbian Exposition,* they differed over the fair's planned "Jubilee Day." Fair organizers attempted to placate black leaders by granting African Americans free admission on a specially designated day. Wells feared the scheme would only provide further opportunity for the white press to disparage African Americans. Douglass believed it best to take advantage of any opportunity, however small, to show the world both the progress of African Americans and the growing threats to it.

On August 25, from his station within the fair as the honorary head of the Haitian delegation, Douglass held court, hosting black artists and leaders, hoping to make an impact on visitors. Paul Laurence Dunbar read a poem, the Fisk Jubilee Singers performed, and Douglass himself delivered an eloquent address calling for equality. "Men talk of the Negro problem," he said, "There is no Negro problem. The problem is whether or not the American people have honesty enough, loyalty enough, honor enough, patriotism enough to live up to their own constitution."[5] Regrettably, Wells's estimation of white reaction proved correct, as the day's festivities were lampooned by the reactionary white press ("Darkies' Day at the Fair"), reflecting the rising national tide of racism that accompanied the rise of Jim Crow segregation in the 1890s.

Among the black leaders present at the Columbian Exposition was the artist Henry Ossawa Tanner, who had temporarily returned to the States from Paris to recoup, both physically and financially, before returning to Europe, where he would spend most of his adult life. Born to deeply religious parents (his father, Henry Tanner, was a bishop in the AME Church, and his mother was involved in missionary work), Tan-

ner primarily painted works with biblical themes. Between 1893 and 1894, however, he focused on scenes of ordinary African American life. In October, shortly after his address at the Chicago World's Fair, Tanner exhibited *The Banjo Lesson,* his most famous work. The painting's two figures occupy the center of a large canvas: an older man, seated in a straight-backed chair, instructs a young boy. The roughhewn floorboards and sparse furniture and walls suggest a humble but honorable family.

In subject matter Tanner broke no

new ground. Nineteenth-century art commonly depicted poor blacks—and the banjo, specifically, was a common motif in both popular and artistic representations of African Americans. Minstrel shows, trade cards and postcards, sheet music, games and toys, and other aspects of popular culture frequently presented racist caricatures of blacks playing banjos. Many white artists indulged in black genre art, frequently portraying poor blacks playing the instrument, comically or mockingly. Even relatively sympathetic images, such as Thomas Hovenden's *I's So Happy* (1885), reinforced servile stereotypes of African Americans. While the original of Hovenden's work does not survive, the popular New York engraver William Miller, who had worked for one of Frank Leslie's magazines—an endless source of stereotypical images—produced a version of the painting.

These condescending elements in the Hovenden/Miller piece are entirely absent in *The Banjo Lesson*. Gone is the broken English of Hovenden's title—he created a similar painting of a black banjo player in 1882 titled *Dem Was Good Ole Times*. Gone too is the depiction of the happy-go-lucky black man. Instead, Tanner created an intimate portrait of hard work, intelligence, and the passage of knowledge from one generation to the next. Under his brush, the banjo was transformed from an instrument for white amusement into an educational tool to nurture a new African American generation. Tanner's characters were transformed as well, from stereotypes into fully realized individuals.

The Banjo Lesson, by Henry Ossawa Tanner, oil on canvas, 1893.

Even the art critic in the October 7, 1893, Philadelphia *Daily Evening Telegraph* who dubbed the painting's subjects "old Uncle Ned, bald and venerable," and "a bare-footed little darkey," felt compelled to acknowledge Tanner's great technical achievement: "the faces are informed with intelligence and expres-sion."[6] Though many whites still could not see past familiar stereotypes, Tanner's work signaled to the art world that a new generation of black artists would demand the right to represent black subjects as fully realized.

W. E. B. DU BOIS AND HARVARD UNIVERSITY

William Edward Burghardt Du Bois, the nation's preeminent African American scholar for more than six decades, was born in 1868 in rural Great Barrington, Massachusetts. The only son of Mary Silvia Burghardt, a domestic servant, and Alfred Du Bois, a barber and itinerant laborer of Haitian descent, Du Bois was the first black graduate of Great Barrington's racially integrated high school. Eager for academic distinction, he immediately went to work to earn money for college. In March 1885, however, his mother died, and since his father had previously abandoned the family, the chances for the young boy to attend college appeared dismal.

But Frank Hosmer, Du Bois's high school principal, and white members of the local Congregational church recognized his exceptional abilities and provided scholarship aid. As Du Bois explained in his book *Darkwater* (1920), "Harvard was the goal of my dreams . . . a mighty conjure-word in that hill town, and even the mill owners' sons had aimed lower."[7] The aid committee instead decided to send him to Fisk University, in Nashville, one of the best of the southern black colleges founded after the Civil War. Du Bois later wrote that the change in plans did not leave him disappointed. "I was going into the South; the South of slavery, rebellion and black folk; and above all, I was going to meet colored people of my own age and education, of my own ambitions."[8] He entered Fisk with sophomore standing, edited the school newspaper, *The Fisk Herald,* taught at a black school near Alexandria, Tennessee, and sang with Fisk's Mozart Society.

W. E. B. Du Bois (1868–1963), 1907.

After only three years the ambitious Du Bois received his B.A. and, receiving another scholarship, entered Harvard College. In 1870, Richard T. Greener (1844–1922) had been the first African American to graduate from Harvard College, and several other blacks had attended the university before Du Bois, but none had been admitted into the graduate program. "A determined effort was made in 1884 and later to make Harvard a more national institution," he recorded in his *Autobiography* (1968). "In my favor were my New England elementary education, and the fact that I was studying in the South and that I was colored."[9] At this time Harvard commonly enrolled students from less prestigious colleges as undergraduates before accepting them into the graduate program. In 1888, Du Bois enrolled as a junior (probably the sixth African American to do so) and, unable to live on campus, secured a room in the house of a black woman in Cambridge. The Glee Club rejected him, and he assumed that writing for the college newspaper would

be impossible because of his race. Thus, Du Bois later wrote, he was "in Harvard but not of it." Nevertheless, he excelled at his studies, attracting William James and George Santayana (philosophy), Frank Taussig (economics), and Albert Bushnell Hart (history) as his mentors. He won second prize in the Boylston oratorical competition, received his B.A. in philosophy cum laude (1890), and delivered a commencement oration on Jefferson Davis, which drew attention from the national press.

Du Bois preferred to concentrate in philosophy but concluded that no employment opportunities would exist for an African American professor in that field, so he studied history. He earned an M.A. in history in 1891 and won a grant from the Slater Fund to study at the Friedrich Wilhelm University in Berlin. He studied sociology with Max Weber and wrote a thesis on agricultural economics in the American South. Unable to continue his studies in Germany when the Slater Fund terminated his funding, he reluctantly returned to the United States. In 1894 he secured a position teaching classics at Wilberforce University in Ohio and a year later became the first person of African descent to receive a Ph.D. from Harvard. Within a year, Du Bois had published his doctoral dissertation, *The Suppression of the African Slave Trade to the United States of America, 1638–1870,* as volume one of the Harvard Historical Monograph Series. The university established an endowed chair in his honor in 1980, as well as the W. E. B. Du Bois Institute for African and African American Research, founded in 1975.

PART NINE

NEW NEGRO, OLD PROBLEM

1895–1900

BOOKER T. WASHINGTON AT THE ATLANTA COTTON STATES EXPOSITION

On September 18, 1895, Booker T. Washington took the podium at Atlanta's 1895 Cotton States and International Exposition. Exposition organizers had included Washington in the program to avoid the ugly controversy surrounding the exclusion of African Americans from Chicago's 1893 World's Columbian Exposition. Washington's speech that day not only defined the rest of his career but helped shape the very direction of African American history for decades to come.

After a brief introduction, Washington sketched out his vision for race relations in the next century in a speech that would become famously known as the "Atlanta Compromise." A people long denied liberty, he said, would understandably place great emphasis on politics and letters, rather than on more prosaic endeavors like agriculture and industrial training. This approach, he asserted, was ultimately foolhardy. "No race can prosper," he claimed, "till it learns that there is as much dignity in tilling a field as in writing a poem. It is at the bottom of life we must begin, not at the top." In response to those African Americans who advocated migration to escape lynching, disenfranchisement, and segregation, Washington offered a parable. America's black population, he suggested, was like a ship, adrift and without potable water. The distressed crew signaled again and again to another ship their need for drinking water, but they repeatedly received the response "Cast down your buckets where you are." Unknown to its crew, the ship had drifted into fresh waters. The South, Washington assured African Americans, now provided the ideal environment for black progress.[1]

In exchange for black loyalty to their

W. E. B. Du Bois, ca. 1907.

Booker T. Washington (1856–1915), by Harris and Ewing.

white neighbors, Washington asked white Americans for a reciprocal commitment. "To those of the white race," he said, "... I would repeat what I say to my own race, 'Cast down your bucket where you are.' Cast it down among the eight millions of Negroes whose habits you know, whose fidelity and love you have tested." If whites would offer African Americans a fair opportunity to develop an economic basis in agriculture and the trades, blacks would, in exchange, Washington assured his audience, eschew the political realm and abandon campaigns for social integration. "In all things that are purely social," he concluded, "we can be as separate as the fingers, yet one as the

Cotton States and International Exposition, Atlanta, 1895.

hand in all things essential to mutual progress."[2]

Whites reacted to Washington's speech with enormous, almost hysterical enthusiasm. From the podium Clark Howell, editor of the influential *Atlanta Constitution*, called the speech "the beginning of a moral revolution in America." The text was quickly reprinted in newspapers throughout the country. President Grover Cleveland met with Washington and said his ideas represented a "new hope" for African Americans. Initial reactions from African Americans were similarly positive. W. E. B. DuBois said of the speech, "Here might be the basis of a real settlement between whites and blacks in the South, if the South opened to the Negroes the doors of economic opportunity and the Negroes cooperated with the white South in political sympathy."[3]

Within a few years, however, Du Bois and many other black leaders reconsidered the impact of Washington's words. While southern whites were eager for blacks to acquiesce to new restrictions on their social and political freedoms, they ignored the second half of Washington's proposal, in which they were to give blacks a fair economic deal. Washington's compromise came under acid attack in Du Bois's *The Souls of Black Folk* (1903). The speech, dubbed the "Atlanta Compromise" by Du Bois himself, had made Washington the "most distinguished Southerner since Jefferson Davis, and the one with the largest personal following." But Washington's approach, Du Bois wrote, "tended to make the whites, North and South, shift the burden of the Negro problem to the Negro's shoulders and stand aside as critical and rather pessimistic spectators; when in fact the burden belongs to the nation." His philosophy, such as it was, Du Bois lamented, represented the "old attitude of adjustment and submission."[4] As the division over Washington's ideas grew, a Du Bois–led opposition organized itself to combat Washington's influence, starting with the Niagara Movement in 1905 and leading to the creation of the NAACP in 1909.

PLESSY V. FERGUSON

On June 7, 1892, in New Orleans Homer Adolph Plessy boarded an East Louisiana Railway train bound for Covington, Louisiana. He took a seat in the car designated for whites only. As the conductor came down the aisle collecting tickets, Plessy matter-of-factly informed him that under the laws of the state he was "colored." It didn't matter that Plessy was only one-eighth black and to any casual observer he appeared white. State law mandated that he sit in the "colored car." Plessy's polite refusal to vacate his seat set in motion a series of events that would shape the American social order for the next fifty years. He had known the risks of his action: he had been recruited by the New Orleans–based Citizens' Committee to Test the Constitutionality of the Separate Car Law (Comité des Citoyens), which set out to end Jim Crow by forcing the courts to recognize the basic rights promised to blacks by the Reconstruction amendments.

Homer Plessy was hauled off the train and jailed for violating Louisiana's 1890 law requiring that "all railway companies carrying passengers in their coaches in this state, shall provide equal but separate accommodations for the white, and colored races." He was then tried and convicted by Judge John H. Ferguson of the New Orleans Criminal Court. Four years later, the case reached the U.S. Supreme Court. Albion W. Tourgée, a liberal white Republican lawyer from Ohio, famed for his writings supporting Reconstruction, headed Plessy's legal team. He argued that the Separate Car Law violated the Fourteenth Amendment's equal protection clause. "A law assorting the citizens of a State in the enjoyment of a public franchise on the basis of race, is obnoxious to the spirit of republican institutions, because it is a legalization of caste," he asserted in his brief. Since the Fourteenth Amendment theoretically put all classes of citizens on an equal footing, to distinguish between citizens

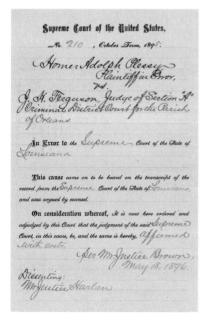

Plessy v. Ferguson decision, 1895.

"Negro Drinking at 'Colored' Water Cooler in Streetcar Terminal,
Oklahoma City, Oklahoma," by Russell Lee, July 1939. This image
symbolizes the long-term impact of the *Plessy* decision.

John Marshall Harlan, photograph by
Frances Benjamin Johnston, about the
time of the 1895 *Plessy* decision.

based on race was "to legalize caste and restore, in part at least, the inequality of right which was an essential incident of slavery."[5]

The Court rejected Tourgée's interpretation of the equal protection clause. In a 7–1 decision authored by Justice Henry Billings Brown, the Court conceded that the Fourteenth Amendment intended to establish absolute equality for the races. Justice Brown, however, was not convinced that forced segregation violated the spirit of the Constitution, noting that "it could not have been intended to abolish distinctions based upon color, or to enforce social, as distinguished from political, equality or a commingling of the two races unsatisfactory to either." Using as a precedent the 1850 Massachusetts decision by Judge Lemuel Shaw in *Roberts v. Boston,* Brown reasoned that segregation laws "do not necessarily imply the inferiority of either race to the other." In short, the Court authorized states to impose institutionalized segregation of the races on the premise that separate could be equal.

Justice John Marshall Harlan, the lone dissenter to the majority's opinion, warned: "The judgment this day rendered will, in time, prove to be quite as pernicious as the decision made by this tribunal in the Dred Scott Case."[6] *Dred Scott,* decided in 1857, had denied African Americans citizenship and attempted to relegate blacks to a permanent state of inferiority. Although the Reconstruction amendments had effectively overturned it, the Supreme Court's decision once again set the Constitution on the side of racism and injustice. *Plessy's* "separate but equal" doctrine left a shameful legacy, validating a system of de jure segregation that would pervade the Jim Crow South until 1954, when the Court finally overturned it in *Brown v. Board of Education.*

THE NATIONAL ASSOCIATION OF COLORED WOMEN AND THE AMERICAN NEGRO ACADEMY

In the last two decades of the nineteenth century, membership in black women's clubs mushroomed, sparking calls for the formation of a national organization. In 1893, African American women lobbied, unsuccessfully, for representation at the Chicago World's Columbian Exposition, and Ida B. Wells-Barnett inspired black women to join her in her campaign to end lynching. From these efforts two separate organizations emerged: the National Federation of Afro-American Women and the National League of Colored Women. The two organizations merged in July 1896 in Washington, adopting the name National Association of Colored Women (NACW). It elected Mary Church Terrell as its first president.

The daughter of the South's first black millionaire, Robert Reed Church, Terrell earned a B.A. from Oberlin College in 1884 and then traveled and studied in Europe for two years. Despite her father's objections that a lady of her standing should not work, Terrell began a career as a teacher, settling in Washington, D.C., where she met her future husband, Robert Terrell, principal of Dunbar High School. A dedicated reformer, Mary Terrell helped establish the Colored Women's League of Washington and thus was well positioned to take leadership of the new unified organization. Under her presidency the NACW adopted the motto "Lifting as We Climb" and declared its purpose:

> To secure and enforce civil and political rights for ourselves and our group. To obtain for our colored women the opportunity of reaching the highest standard in all fields of human endeavor. To

Mary Church Terrell (1863–1954). Born to the South's first black millionaire, Robert Reed Church, Terrell graduated from Oberlin College and taught at Wilberforce University and at the M Street Colored High School in Washington, D.C., before leading the National Association of Colored Women.

Alexander Crummell (1819–98), from William J. Simmons, *Men of Mark: Eminent, Progressive and Rising* (Cleveland: G. M. Rewell, 1887).

promote interracial understanding so that justice and good will may prevail among all people.

In the absence of government programs for poor African Americans, black women's clubs embarked on a remarkable program of service and reform. Emphasizing self-help, clubwomen organized care for the aged and indigent, encouraged education as a way for poorer African Americans to improve their lives, and protested segregation in public accommodations. In administering its vital social services, the NACW emphasized middle-class values like temperance, etiquette, and chastity, in the hope that if black women adopted these traits, it would help break down racial barriers. Regrettably, the assumption that racism could be defeated by rigorous adherence to a code of proper behavior was quickly and violently disproven. Nevertheless,

the NACW grew rapidly, and by the start of World War I, the group claimed more than one hundred thousand members. In the early twentieth century, it became increasingly political, focusing on issues ranging from women's suffrage to prohibition, and the passage of a federal antilynching statute.

One year after the founding of the NACW, a group of eighteen black intellectuals, led by the great clergyman, intellectual, and pan-Africanist Alexander Crummell, formally organized the American Negro Academy (ANA) in Washington, D.C. As blacks were barred from most white learned societies, Crummell and his colleagues created the academy to advance the race by promoting African American contributions to "Letters, Science, and Art." In its emphasis on higher learning, the ANA consciously critiqued Booker T. Washington's exclusive emphasis on practical education for African Americans, which

President Crummell disparaged as "this miserable fad of industrialism."[7]

Born in 1819, the son of a freeborn woman and an emancipated African man, Crummell was denied the opportunity to attend seminary because of his color, so he studied privately to be an Episcopal priest. An active member of the antislavery movement from a young age, he traveled to England in 1847 to attend Cambridge University and deliver a series of antislavery speeches. He then accepted a missionary position in Liberia, becoming a leading scholar and statesman in Monrovia. He joined the faculty of Liberia College at its founding and served in that role until 1865, when clashes with the college's leadership drove him back to missionary work. As would be the case throughout his career, Crummell's ambition, contentious personality, and uncompromising mind created rifts between himself and other black leaders. After a coup in 1871 ousted Crummell's political allies from the Liberian government, he returned to the United States and settled at St. Luke's Church, Washington's first independent African American Episcopal congregation. A prolific writer and speaker, Crummell, by the time the ANA was founded, had become a respected elder statesman among African American intellectuals.

Other founding members of the ANA included the great Harvard-trained scholar W. E. B. Du Bois; the Presbyterian minister Francis James Grimké; the classical scholar William Scarborough; the educator and AME bishop Levi J. Coppin; and John W. Cromwell, founder of *The People's Advocate,* a black newspaper published in the District. Later members included such notable scholars as John Hope, president of Morehouse College; historian Carter G. Woodson; Arthur A. Schomburg, the great collector and bibliophile; poet James Weldon Johnson; and John R. Clifford, publisher of the *West Virginia Pioneer Press,* the state's first black lawyer, and one of the founders of the Niagara Movement.

Despite its accomplished membership, the ANA never enjoyed the influence that Crummell and its founders had envisioned. In the thirty-one years of its existence, it published just twenty-two papers and thirty-one articles, because it lacked the funds to publish more regularly. Its publications did, however, enjoy a small but loyal readership among black and white intellectuals. The ANA reflected the restive nature of African American intellectuals who had begun to chafe under the dominance of Booker T. Washington. In its application of research and scholarly study to the problems of African Americans, the ANA—

John Wesley Cromwell (1846–1927). Born a slave in Portsmouth, Virginia, Cromwell was freed when his father bought his family and then moved them to Pennsylvania. He graduated from Philadelphia's Institute for Colored Youth in 1864. After the war he taught, became an agent for the American Missionary Association, and in 1874 graduated from the Howard University School of Law. He continued teaching and founded *The People's Advocate* in 1876, which he published until 1884, gaining considerable influence among the black elite. In addition to his work in the American Negro Academy, he practiced law and published *The Negro in American History* in 1914.

even with its limited influence in its time—offered a compelling model for other organizations seeking more widespread impact on African American life through contemplation and reflection.

WILMINGTON, NORTH CAROLINA, RACE RIOT OF 1898

The 1898 Wilmington race riot. White leaders of the riot proudly stand before their handiwork.

In the late 1890s Wilmington, North Carolina, was a thriving port city of roughly twenty thousand inhabitants. African Americans comprised a majority of them, boasting an affluent middle class of professionals and business owners. Wilmington blacks also enjoyed comparatively strong political representation: they held the deputy sheriff's post and half of the aldermanic positions. Wilmington's black political leaders, despite the South's growing repression and the disappearance of federal intervention, had managed to hold on to their power. Coalitions between Populists and black Republicans had managed to stave off Democratic challengers in many contests.

This state of affairs, however, increasingly disturbed Democrats, who sought to establish unchecked white supremacy over the city. As the November 1898 elections approached, white Democrats were prepared to claim power by any means necessary. They repeatedly threatened blacks with death if they ran for elected office and issued a racial tirade, the "Declaration of White Independence," announcing their intention to overthrow the city's black politicians. Armed groups like the Red Shirts routinely intimidated the city's black community.

Alex Manly, the editor of the African American daily *Wilmington Record,* published an article that incensed Wilmington's white community. Manly had attended the Hampton Institute but left for what he understood to be greater opportunities for blacks in Wilmington. In 1895, he launched the *Record,* as the willingness of white Populists to work with black leaders offered great hope. But that cooperation shattered when Rebecca Felton, the wife of a Populist leader, writing in the *Wilmington Morning Star* (a Democratic paper), demanded the use of lynching, "a thousand times a week if necessary," to protect white womanhood from black beasts. As Ida B. Wells-Barnett had done in Memphis, Manly went on the offensive and publicly attacked the South's favorite justification for lynching, the myth of the black-man-as-rapist. Consensual sex between a white woman and a black man was possible, he wrote, and such relationships did not constitute rape. The whites of Wilmington could not tolerate Manly's directness and honesty about this old taboo.

Alexander Manly (1866–1944).

On election day, Democratic intimidation produced sweeping but uneventful victories. Within two days, however, hundreds of armed whites raided Manly's newspaper office, destroyed his press, and sent its editor into exile. Later that night, groups of armed whites and blacks—refusing to tolerate the intimidation—clashed; one white man was shot. In response, whites swarmed into black neighborhoods, committing indiscriminate acts of violence and destroying homes and businesses.

At the same time leaders of the white mobs staged a coup; they forced the white Republican mayor and other city officials to resign and installed a Democratic city government. As many as thirty blacks were killed in the riot, while many other prominent African Americans were either jailed or driven from the city. In the wake of the riot, almost fifteen hundred black residents fled Wilmington; those who remained behind faced disenfranchisement and the systematic imposition of Jim Crow.

BUFFALO SOLDIERS

25th U.S. Infantry, at Fort Keogh, Montana, 1890. Some of the soldiers are wearing buffalo robes.

Although the 54th and 55th Massachusetts regiments and the nearly 178,000 men of the U.S. Colored Troops had contributed to Union victory in the Civil War, whites remained unconvinced that black men should serve in the peacetime army. Opposition to a permanent black presence in the army manifested itself in both houses of the Congress. But the opponents could not block Radical Republican efforts without the support of the yet-unreconstructed southern states. On July 28, 1866, President Andrew Johnson signed into law a military appropriation bill that provided for the establishment of the all-black Ninth and Tenth Cavalry as well as the 38th, 39th, 40th, and 41st Infantry, which in 1869 would be consolidated into the 24th and 25th Infantry regiments. Most of the recruits in the new regiments were young, often only eighteen or nineteen, but the units also contained many black Civil War veter-

Soldiers, probably from the Tenth U.S. Cavalry, by Frederic Remington. Remington did a series of images for U.S. magazines from 1889 to 1906.

ans, who enlisted to escape the South, to earn a regular wage, or perhaps chiefly to find adventure.

Sent west, the army's new black regiments eventually served along the entire span of the frontier, from the Dakotas to the Mexican border. They primarily served to keep the peace between white settlers and American Indians, especially to resist white encroachment on Indian lands guaranteed by treaty. At other times they protected Indians settled on reservations from raids by hostile Indian groups, or they protected residents of Indian Territory (now the state of Oklahoma) from threats by white settlers. But they also faced Native Americans in combat.

Throughout the last quarter of the nineteenth century, African American soldiers served in combat in the so-called Indian Wars, earning much recognition for their bravery and heroism. They earned the sobriquet Buffalo Soldiers, reportedly from the Native Americans they faced in combat. The Buffalo Soldiers served notably in clashes with Comanche Indians and in the Ghost Dance Campaign of 1889–90. In Mexico in 1916 they marched with the forces led by General John J. "Black Jack" Pershing to capture the Mexican revolutionary Pancho Villa. During the Spanish-American War, many Buffalo Soldiers faced Spanish forces in Cuba (under Theodore Roosevelt), Puerto Rico, and the Philippines. In all, twenty-three Buffalo Soldiers received the nation's highest military recognition, the Medal of Honor, for their heroic acts in combat on the western frontier and in the Caribbean.

From 1899 to 1904, African American regiments served in the summer months at the Sequoia and Yosemite national parks, becoming the nation's first "park rangers." They introduced the famed broad-brimmed hat that now is required of all park rangers.

The U.S. entry into World War I precipitated a permanent redeployment for the Buffalo Soldiers, fighting under French rather than American command in Europe. Some who remained stationed in the United States in August 1918 fought a skirmish against German and Mexican troops along the border. Although during World War II, the War Department disbanded the old units, many black troops continued to train in the West and were subsequently reorganized into the 92nd and 93rd Infantry Divisions, as well as support units.

WAR WITH SPAIN AND FOR AN EMPIRE

In the late 1890s international tensions were on the rise. The popular American press was filled with stories of Spanish cruelty in Cuba. Once the U.S. declared war on Spain in April 1898, expansionists like Theodore Roosevelt and Alfred T. Mahan viewed it as an opportunity to project American power across the globe and secure vital coaling stations and colonies, so the nation could compete in the race for colonial power. Moreover, Roosevelt trumpeted the war as an opportunity to affirm American manhood. Only small groups of influential Americans opposed the war, including the novelist Mark Twain.

Many African Americans offered their support. Some black leaders, Booker T. Washington most notably, hoped the war would provide African Americans with an opportunity to demonstrate their patriotism to skeptical whites, and that a lengthy conflict would provide jobs for African Americans and an improved market for southern-grown cotton. At first the war appeared to fulfill this promise. At the outset of hostilities, the U.S. Army contained a relatively meager twenty-five thousand soldiers, roughly one-tenth of whom were African Americans, the Buffalo Soldiers of the Ninth and Tenth Cavalry, as well as the 24th and 25th Infantry. President William McKinley authorized the raising of additional volunteer regiments, including, after intensive lobbying by the increasingly influential Booker T. Washington, several new African American units.

While a number of African Americans received temporary commissions to serve as officers with the new volunteer corps, only two of the more than fourteen hundred officers commissioned in the regular army between

"Some of our brave colored boys who helped to free Cuba," 1899.

December 1898 and July 1902 were black. African American soldiers fought valiantly during the conflict, and many received decorations for their acts of heroism. Four members of the Tenth Cavalry—Sergeant William Thompkins, Corporal George Wanton, Private Dennis Bell, and Private Fitz Lee—received the Medal of Honor for risking their lives to retrieve wounded comrades under heavy enemy fire on the beach at the tiny village of Tayabacoa in Cuba on June 30. One day later, at Santiago de Cuba, Sergeant Major Edward L. Baker, Jr., left cover and ran through a barrage of shelling and rifle fire to save a wounded man from drowning in a river, an act for which he too received the nation's highest military honor. As a result of the war, the United States acquired Puerto Rico, Cuba, Guam, and the Philippines, but black participation did not improve the economic or political conditions of most African Americans, even those who had risked their lives in battle. Indeed, seeing black men in uniform sometimes inflamed whites to riot and lynch.

Meeting of the Afro-American Council, Oakland, California, 1907.

Troubled by the increasingly violent racist backlash against African American political and economic power, T. Thomas Fortune, the brilliant editor of the *New York Age* and the leading black journalist of his era, and AME Zion bishop Alexander Walters established the Afro-American Council in a meeting at Rochester, New York, in September 1898.

The new organization sought to protest the suppression of black voters in the South; lynching; unequal funding of white and black schools; the southern penal system; and segregation on the rails and in public accommodations.

Fortune, the visionary behind the Afro-American Council, had previously formed the Afro-American League in 1890, intending it to be supported by state and local bodies. After the league's initial national convention, however, a strong national interest failed to materialize. The body collapsed amid financial pressures and divisions within its leadership.

The new Afro-American Council quickly became a critical theater in the war between the accommodationist philosophy of Booker T. Washington and supporters of more aggressive approaches to civil rights, especially those of W. E. B. Du Bois. Supporters of Du Bois generally saw Fortune as a close ally of the Tuskegee machine and Walters, the council's first president, as also too open to Washington's conciliatory approach. Ida B. Wells-Barnett, William Monroe Trotter, and W. E. B. Du Bois passionately resisted Washington's influence. At the council's second national convention, an entire session was consumed by debate over resolu-

T. Thomas Fortune (1856–1928). Born in Florida, Fortune attended Howard University and helped edit John Wesley Cromwell's *People's Advocate.* He moved to New York City in 1881 and became the city's most prominent black editor. His famed *New York Age* greatly benefited from Booker T. Washington's support. Fortune remained loyal to his benefactor but was always more militant on civil rights issues. From William J. Simmons, *Men of Mark: Eminent, Progressive and Rising* (Cleveland: G. M. Rewell, 1887).

Alexander Walters (1858–1917). Walters became bishop of the AME Zion Church at thirty-four, among the youngest ever to assume such a position in the church. For a time he tried to bridge the growing gap between followers of Booker T. Washington and those of W. E. B. Du Bois, but eventually he sided with Du Bois. Like Du Bois, he became interested in pan-Africanism, attended the 1900 London meeting, and in 1910 traveled to West Africa. President Wilson named him ambassador to Liberia, but Walters declined the honor. He joined with Du Bois in the Niagara Movement and in founding the NAACP. From James Walker Hood, *One Hundred Years of the African Methodist Episcopal Zion Church* (New York: A.M.E. Zion Book Concern, 1895).

tions condemning Washington. In 1900 Washington, fearing his influence over the council had weakened, sought to undermine it by establishing the National Negro Business League. In 1904 Fortune stepped down as council president, acknowledging that a lack of financial stability threatened its existence.

Despite its clear limitations, the Afro-American Council was an important early black national political association. In the wake of its demise, new organizations emerged, destined to have a much larger impact on African American history. Dissatisfied with the council's pro-Washingtonian slant, W. E. B. Du Bois broke with the group in 1905 to form the Niagara Movement to launch more direct attacks on white supremacy. In later years, organization members, including Bishop Walters, would defect to join the newly formed NAACP (1909) and the Urban League (1910).

W. E. B. DU BOIS: THE PARIS ALBUMS, 1900

To counter stereotypes of blacks as backward and culturally bankrupt, W. E. B. Du Bois compiled photographs of successful African Americans who thoroughly embodied American middle-class values into albums, called *Types of American Negroes* and *Negro Life, Georgia, USA*. Du Bois could find no better venue for his photographs than the 1900 Paris Exposition Universelle, an astounding world's fair that attracted millions of people from around the globe. He curated an exhibition, which included 363 photographs, with his old Fisk University classmate Thomas J. Calloway, a black lawyer and educator who, more than anyone, was responsible for the inclusion of African Americans in the exhibition. Congressman George Henry White, who would be the last black to serve in Congress until 1928, managed to wrangle $15,000 out of his white colleagues to fund Du Bois's "Negro Exhibit."

Mounting the albums, as the central part of the display, constituted a political act, a declaration of inherent nobility in the war over respectability and the nature of the Negro. The display ran in the Exposition des Negres d'Amérique from April 14 until November 10 in the Palace of Social Sciences. The remarkable images depicted dignified, well-dressed men and women living in comfortable and even lavish homes, whose furnishings reflected the occupants' sophisticated taste and refinement. One imagines that Du Bois selected this particular array of "types" for two reasons. First, they would be a counterdiscourse to "types" of Negroes summoned in the work of anthropologists such as Louis Agassiz a half century before.

And second, he wanted to create an archive of images that could refute the extremely popular images of black people as deracinated "sambos" and

Unidentified African American woman. Du Bois albums of photographs of African Americans in Georgia, exhibited at the Paris Exposition Universelle, 1900.

Piano lesson for young African American woman. Du Bois albums.

Daughter of Thomas E. Askew. Du Bois albums.

Officers of Tobacco Trade Union, Petersburg, Virginia. Du Bois albums.

lascivious "coons" that peppered trade cards, postcards, advertisements, sheet music, and virtually every other form of popular visual culture during the 1890s. As Jim Crow segregation was just then being legalized, culminating in the infamous *Plessy v. Ferguson* "separate but equal" Supreme Court decision (1896), Du Bois's exhibition assumed an enormous urgency. One can only imagine the surprise, the depth of disappointed expectations—and the frisson—generated in the white visitors who viewed the hundreds of images of black doctors, lawyers, and other professionals whose talents and aspirations matched or exceeded those of their white counterparts. Almost a century later the American media would be startled by the level of articulation of the parade of black upper-middle-class, well-educated witnesses in the Clarence Thomas–Anita Hill hearings; similar attitudes would be expressed in the reviews of Stephen Carter's novel about the black upper class on Martha's Vineyard (*The Emperor of Ocean Park,* published in 2002). Du Bois's hope was to use art, photography, as propaganda.

Today these images remind us of the historical struggle for control of the black image in American society, and of the political discourses into which all black art at the time was necessarily drawn. But they also make vivid the age-old class divisions in the African American community. Such class divisions were born in slavery and then were made more pronounced by the markedly different status of slaves and freedpeople over the course of slavery; they existed despite the *Dred Scott* decision and the Jim Crow "separate but equal" laws, which identified all black people, before the law, as members of one class, a class as defined by "All Negroes shall" or "All Negroes shan't." In 1860, the federal census recorded about 3.9 million slaves and 488,000 free Negroes; and some scholars speculate that the black middle class at the end of the nineteenth century—which Du Bois would name the "talented tenth"—was composed disproportionately of descendants of the free Negroes.

In 1900, black progressive politics had an enormous imperative to summon visual evidence of the "talented tenth," the middle-class, "college-bred" Negroes, as Du Bois would have put it, as prima facie evidence of the social and intellectual equality of the Negro in the battle against scientific racism, de jure and de facto segregation, and discriminatory legal statutes and social customs—in short, the prevalent antiblack racisms that pervaded American society in the era of Jim Crow. These photographs were the visual analogue of what Evelyn Brooks Higginbotham calls "the politics of respectability," proof that a "New Negro" existed.[8] And the images, paraded before the world at the Paris Expo, were to serve as proof that the Negro was "improvable"; that the gap between black and white,

Unidentified young man. Du Bois albums.

within the same class at least, was no gap at all.

Du Bois saw the people in these photographs as cultural warriors, as a vanguard, as missionaries of cultural and educational potential, promising massive social mobility for the entire race. Today, when class divisions within the black community are so starkly pronounced, these photographs seem to be evidence, in black and white, of the origins of that problem, which all of us must worry is becoming a permanent fixture of a complex and bifurcated African American social identity.

In addition to the beautiful photographs, the exhibit presented art and scholarship in a great variety of forms, including books, maps, and even patents.

Statistical charts illustrated the increase of black schools and the decrease in black illiteracy following emancipation. A display focused on black veterans drew particular attention to the loyalty and patriotism of African Americans. Additionally, the *Preliminary List of Books and Pamphlets by Negro Authors for Paris Exposition and Library of Congress* noted more than fourteen hundred books written by African Americans, a powerful statement of black accomplishment. For his work on the Exposition des Negres d'Amérique, Du Bois earned a gold medal from the judging committee.

The Alden Fruit Vinegar
trade card, ca. 1885.

"Is He Black All Over, Mammy?" by Fred Spurgin, 1922.

"Black Men Lynched. The Nigger Peril," 1908.

H. Cuthbertson & Son, Boots & Shoes trade card, 1883.

Seal of North Carolina Tobacco: Darktown Bowling Club posters, 1888.

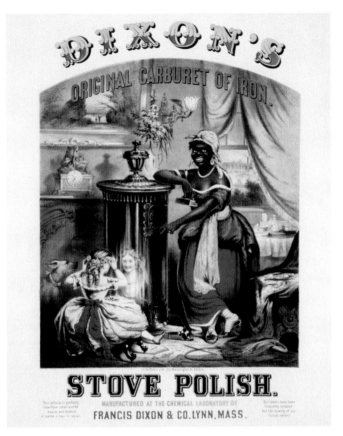

Advertisement for Dixon's Stove Polish Company,
Lynn, Massachusetts, ca. 1860.

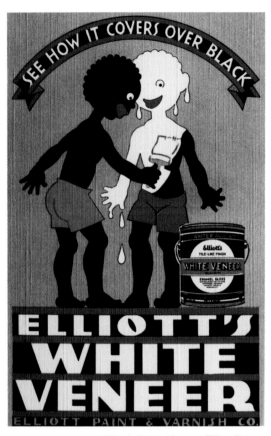

Advertisement for Elliott's White Veneer, Elliott Paint
& Varnish Company, Chicago, ca. 1935.

Gold Dust Washing Powder trade card, ca. 1890.

Sheet music for "Happy Darkies Barn Dance,"
by Arthur E. Godfrey, London, 1892.

Label for "Nigger Boy" brand Jamaican rum, ca. 1900.

Sheet music for "Ten Little Niggers," by G. W. Moore of the Original Christy Minstrels, ca. 1880.

Advertisement for Pears soap, 1893.

Tom Smith's Piccaninny Crackers, 1907.

H. D. Stone Wheat Meal Graham poster, by Van, 1892.

Sambo and Coal Black Rose, characters devised in the 1820s and usually found on popular sheet music, especially by George Washington Dixon, who gave birth to blackface minstrelsy.

Poster for one of the countless adaptations of Harriet Beecher Stowe's *Uncle Tom's Cabin,* ca. 1930.

"We Never Fade!!" advertisement for J & P Coats, thread manufacturer, ca. 1890.

PHOTO ESSAY: THE NEW NEGRO

The following images first appeared in a popular black journal of the early twentieth century, The Voice of the Negro. *John Henry Adams's "The New Negro Man," in the October 1904 issue, and "A Study of the Features of the New Negro Woman," in the August 1904 issue, like Du Bois's enormous collection of photographs of African Americans for the 1900 Paris Exhibition, sought to present images of black Americans not customarily seen in popular culture. While seeking to combat racial stereotypes, they also provided the magazine's readership with models to emulate. In the age of the "New Negro," magazines like* The Voice of the Negro *took on the important work of "uplifting the race" to eliminate racism by setting high standards or expectations for the new generation of black Americans. All captions are taken from the original images.*

PROF. JOHN HENRY ADAMS, Jr., of Morris Brown College. He is considered the rising negro Artist of the South. The Atlanta Constitution pronounces him "nothing short of a genius" and says that "he may some day startle the world with his paintings."

MR. WM. J. DECATUR, A. B.
In this characteristic pose can be seen one of the new forces of the race. For years a successful teacher. Mr. Decatur is now partner to Mr. J. B. Long, the successful builder and contractor. Decatur and Long represent the spirit and demand of the times—thoroughly competent mechanics.

Here one catches a glimpse of rare beauty. But it is not buried there alone, Eva.

We want more men who have the proper sense of appreciation of deserving women and who are deserving themselves. This is a death-knell to the dude and the well-dressed run-around. You ought to write a book on that, Eva.

You cannot avoid the motion of this dignified countenance. College training makes her look so.

An admirer of Fine Art, a performer on the violin and the piano, a sweet singer, a writer— mostly given to essays, a lover of good books, and home-making girl, is Gussie.

Dr. J. D. HAMILTON
Much has been added to the dental profession of Atlanta, in the person of Dr. Hamilton. He is rather socially inclined, but he knows the value of "sticking to business." His office shows the enterprise of the new Negro man.

CHAS. L. HARPER, A. B.
Mr. Harper is one of the strong young men in the government service of Atlanta. He is paving the way for himself for higher things in life.

In this admirable face rises a happy response to the lofty impulses of her poetic soul. In the language of art this is Lacolia.

In this face is an uncommon sweep
of kindness and affection, linked with
an industriousness of mind, which
have been the making of Lena.

This beautiful eyed girl is the result of
careful home training and steady schooling.
There is an unusual promise of intelligence
and character rising out of her strong
individuality. A model girl, a college
president's daughter, is Lorainetta.

THE "NEGRO" IN JOURNALISM
The above sketch shows Editor Jesse
Max Barber in his characteristic attitude
while engaged in study in what he calls
his "Sanctum Sanctorum." Mr. Barber
is a very close student of current,
economic and sociological questions,
as his narrations of current events in
"Our Monthly Review" will show.

MR. R. T. WEATHERBY, B. D.
This is the strong hand underneath
the successful Y.M.C.A. of Atlanta.
Mr. Weatherby has ability and
character, which elements have
raised him to the highest esteem
and confidence of the people. He is
a qualified Christian worker, and a
faithful secretary of the Association.

MR. GEO. WHITE, A. B.
Mr. White is a young man hardly 22
years old, but he has shown already
that he has a work to do in helping
to elevate the race. He is quiet and
modest and has a strong personality.

PART TEN

THE ORDEAL OF JIM CROW

1900–1917

GEORGE H. WHITE AND THE
ORDEAL OF BLACK POLITICS

By the turn of the twentieth century, southern states had deprived most African Americans of their rights as citizens. Disenfranchisement laws in particular decimated the political foundation that Congressman George H. White and other blacks had built in the years following the Civil War.

White, born into slavery in Rosindale, North Carolina, on December 18, 1852, worked for his father's farm and funeral home business after the war. After attending public schools in North Carolina, he went north and graduated from Howard University in 1877, then taught and worked as a principal in Raleigh and New Bern, North Carolina. In 1879, he passed the state bar. White found quick success in politics, winning a seat in the North Carolina House of Representatives in 1880. There he fought to gain funding for African American schools. In 1886, he became the solicitor and prosecutor for the state's Second Judicial District, a position he held for eight years.

In 1894, after serving two terms as prosecutor, White ran for Congress, where he faced off against his own brother-in-law, Henry Cheatham, in the Republican primary. White lost, but two years later he took the nomination. The election of 1896 threatened to effect great changes in southern politics, as the Populist Party's success in 1892 had led to fusion coalitions across the South. In North Carolina the fusion of Populists

George Henry White (1852–1918). Born of a mixed-race family in North Carolina, White graduated from Howard University in 1877 and settled in New Bern, where he taught and earned a law degree. Beginning in 1880, he served in the state legislature and in 1890 became the only black prosecutor in the country. In 1896, he won election to the U.S. Congress, where he served until 1901.

and Republicans gave White a majority victory in the November election.

Taking office in 1897, White confronted a transformed political landscape—indeed, he found himself the only African American left in Congress. Nevertheless, he continued to agitate for black rights, even as his demands went unheeded. He tried to convince his colleagues to allow more African Americans to fight in the Spanish-American War. He tried to move President McKinley to honor those black soldiers who did fight. He lobbied for a $1,000 appropriation for the family of a black South

Carolina postmaster who, along with his infant daughter, had fallen victim to a white mob. He sought federal funding for an African American exhibit at the 1900 Paris Exhibition Universelle. All were unsuccessful. He took care to enter into the official record the many stories of discrimination and violence in the Jim Crow South.

White barely won reelection in 1898—that year white supremacist political campaigns led to the triumph of the Democratic Party in the North Carolina state legislature. Nevertheless, he battled racial discrimination and lynching and attempted to fight disenfranchisement by asserting that the reduction of a state's voting population should bring an accompanying reduction in congressional representation. He also introduced a strong antilynching bill but garnered no support.

Seeing the impossibility of his own reelection, White declined to run in 1900, leaving office the next year. No African American would serve in Congress for the next twenty-eight years. The South and allied white supremacists in the Democratic Party had completed their destruction of black political influence. White admitted to one interviewer that he could no longer live in North Carolina "and be a man and be treated as a man."[1] He moved to Washington, D.C., and then to Philadelphia, where he practiced law and continued to fight for black civil rights until his death in 1918.

DINNER AT THE WHITE HOUSE

"Equality: Dinner given at the White House by President Roosevelt to Booker T. Washington, October 17 [*sic*], 1901," by C. H. Thomas.

On October 16, 1901, President Theodore Roosevelt invited Booker T. Washington to the White House. Roosevelt and Washington had met in 1898, and Roosevelt, like many American whites, appreciated Washington's message of black accommodation. When Roosevelt served as vice president, the "Wizard of Tuskegee" had promised to use his influence among blacks to gain him votes should he run for president. Roosevelt hoped that the support of the dwindling number of voting African Americans in the South—an area dominated by Democrats—would help him in what promised to be a tough primary in 1904. William McKinley's assassination on September 14, 1901, placed Roosevelt in the White House unexpectedly, and the new president soon asked Washington to visit him to discuss presidential appointments in the South. Washington had long avoided any public role in politics for fear of alienating southern whites, but he could not pass up the opportunity to work as an adviser to the president of the United States. Weeks later, Roosevelt invited Washington back; this time, however, the meeting would cause a national uproar.

When Washington arrived on October 16, he learned that the president had invited him to dinner, and that evening he ate with the Roosevelt family. The following day, *The Washington Post* reported the brief statement of the White House: "Booker T. Washington, of Tuskegee, Alabama, dined with the President last evening." For many Americans, white and black, the event carried much more significance than a single sentence could convey. A great number of African Americans celebrated the dinner as a sign that the president might hold more favorable racial views than his predecessors. (Roosevelt would soon disappoint them.) Many whites, on the other hand, reacted with horror. They could not understand why the president of the United States would have dinner with Washington (or any other African American), which symbolically, at least, seemed to threaten segregation. The New Orleans *Times-Democrat* asked, "White men of the South, how do you like it? White women of the South, how do you like it?" The *Richmond Times* asserted, "It means that the president is willing that Negroes shall mingle freely with whites in the social circle—that white women may receive attentions from negro men; it means that there is no racial reason in his opinion why whites and blacks may not marry and intermarry, why the Anglo-Saxon may not mix negro blood with his blood."[2] The leap from a business dinner to interracial sex revealed how much both men

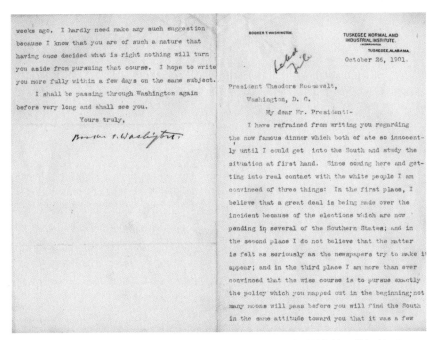

weeks ago. I hardly need make any such suggestion because I know that you are of such a nature that having once decided what is right nothing will turn you aside from pursuing that course. I hope to write you more fully within a few days on the same subject.

I shall be passing through Washington again before very long and shall see you.

Yours truly,

Booker T. Washington

BOOKER T. WASHINGTON.

TUSKEGEE NORMAL AND INDUSTRIAL INSTITUTE.
TUSKEGEE, ALABAMA.

October 26, 1901.

President Theodore Roosevelt,
Washington, D. C.

My dear Mr. President:-

I have refrained from writing you regarding the now famous dinner which both of ate so innocently until I could get into the South and study the situation at first hand. Since coming here and getting into real contact with the white people I am convinced of three things: In the first place, I believe that a great deal is being made over the incident because of the elections which are now pending in several of the Southern States; and in the second place I do not believe that the matter is felt as seriously as the newspapers try to make it appear; and in the third place I am more than ever convinced that the wise course is to pursue exactly the policy which you mapped out in the beginning; not many moons will pass before you will find the South in the same attitude toward you that it was a few

Booker T. Washington to Theodore Roosevelt, October 26, 1901. Here Washington diminishes the importance of the controversy over his appearance in the White House.

Theodore Roosevelt and Booker T. Washington at Tuskegee Institute, October 24, 1905. In his remarks, Roosevelt praised the school, its leadership, and the whites who supported it. Significantly, he condemned the lynching that plagued the entire United States. The "work of Tuskegee," he exclaimed, "is a matter of the highest practical importance to both the white man and the black man."

had underestimated the public response to their meeting.

It also placed Washington in a difficult position. For years he had courted the favor of whites by arguing that African Americans should avoid political concerns. Now, by his controversial meeting with the Republican president, he risked jeopardizing his position among southerners. He minimized the importance of the trip, and some white newspapers suggested that he had had no choice but to accept Roosevelt's invitation. But the event also spurred calls of hypocrisy from Washington's increasingly vocal black opponents who believed that his accommodationism actually meant capitulation to discrimination. For his part, Roosevelt did not host any other African Americans while in office. Although Washington remained an informal adviser, both par-ties kept the relationship discreet. But the import of the dinner—symbolic or otherwise—resonated with the American public well into the early twentieth century.

THE MUSIC OF JOHNSON, JOHNSON, AND COLE

No coons allowed / No coons allowed / This place is meant for white folks that is all / We don't want no kinky-head kind / So move on darky down the line / No coons allow'd in here at all." At first blush, Bob Cole's (1868–1911) "A Trip to Coon Town" (1897) would appear to be firmly rooted in the antebellum minstrel tradition. But through parody, signifying, irony, and the force of their considerable talents, Cole and other African Americans in the music and entertainment business at the turn of the century used "coon songs" to challenge the minstrel tradition and create important careers for African American performers and composers.

Cole, born Robert Allen Cole, Jr., in Athens, Georgia, in 1868, began his career in Asbury Park, New Jersey, then moved to Chicago, where he tried his hand at vaudeville. Unsuccessful, he moved to New York, where he published minstrel songs and starred in exotic shows. In 1891, he appeared in Sam T. Jack's *The Creole Show* (and later became its stage manager), where he created his popular character Willy Wayside. Willy the tramp conformed to what white audiences had come to expect from

"Lift Every Voice and Sing," 1900.

"I Ain't Gwine Ter Work No Mo," sheet music cover, 1900. The song was part of the score of *The Belle of Bridgeport* (1900), the first collaboration of Cole and the Johnson brothers.

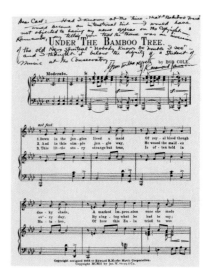

"Under the Bamboo Tree," sheet music.

black performers, or whites in blackface. In 1895 he joined the vaudeville group Black Patti Troubadours, performing similar roles, and wrote music for white performers like the vaudeville star and singer May Irwin, who won great popularity with her "Coon Shouting" and even appeared in popular cabinet cards (studio photographs for distribution) with black babies. But Cole also wrote respectable music for the Georgia Jubilee Singers (patterned after the Fisk Jubilee Singers) and even started the All-Star Stock Company in New York to train black performers.

The straitjacket of the racist expectations of white audiences proved wearisome, although profitable, and when the white producers of the 1896 minstrel show *At Jolly Coon-ey Island* rejected his request for higher pay and benefits, Cole bolted the production and the next year opened his own show, *A Trip to Coontown*. Running from 1897 to 1901, the musical, with songs like "Gimme De Leavin's" and "The Luckiest Coon in Town," was a smashing success, the first Broadway show written, produced, and managed by African Americans. The next year he issued the Colored Actor's Declaration of Independence, which, during the Harlem Renaissance almost three decades later, would find new expression in W. E. B. Du Bois's call for true black theater: "by us, for us, near us, and about us."

In 1902, Cole joined forces with composer and arranger John Rosamond Johnson (1873–1954) and his brother, the poet, writer, and civil rights activist James Weldon Johnson. The Johnson brothers (born in the early 1870s) grew up in a middle-class African American neighborhood in Jacksonville, Florida. James Weldon graduated from Atlanta University in 1894, then returned to Florida to work as a schoolteacher and

principal. At the same time, he began collaborating with his brother, known as J. Rosamond. In 1899, they sold their first tune, "Louisiana Lize." Their most enduring work was "Lift Every Voice and Sing," which began as a poem James Weldon wrote in 1900 to mark Abraham Lincoln's ninety-first birthday. Five years later, his brother set the words to music. The song drew upon the sufferings of African Americans to predict a brighter future: "Sing a song of the faith that the dark past has taught us, / Sing a song full of hope that the present has brought us . . . / Let us march on 'til vic-

James Weldon Johnson (seated), J. Rosamond Johnson (standing right), and Bob Cole.

James Weldon Johnson (1871–1938).

"Pliney Come Out in the Moonlight," sheet music cover, from the 1908 musical *The Red Moon*.

"Pliney Come Out in the Moonlight," sheet music.

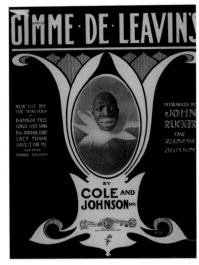

"Gimme De Leavin's," sheet music cover.

tory has won." The song soon became known as the "Negro National Anthem," and as recently as 2009, the Reverend Joseph Lowery recited its lines during the inauguration of President Barack Obama.

The Cole, Johnson, and Johnson collaboration proved an unprecedented Broadway success. Between 1902 and 1910 (James Weldon entered the U.S. diplomatic corps in 1906), they collaborated on about 150 songs, which Cole and J. Rosamond used in their own vaudeville acts and which white performers used for much of the twentieth century, as in Florenz Ziegfeld's *The Little Duchess* (1901). Sophie Tucker, the Russian immigrant and "last of the red hot mamas," grounded her popular career in Cole and Johnson tunes and in a variety of coon songs such as "I Wonder Where My Easy Rider's Gone?" and "Give Me Back My Husband, You've Had Him Long E'nuff."

In 1902, Cole and the Johnson brothers collaborated on "Under the Bamboo Tree," perhaps the highest-grossing song of the early twentieth century. Attesting to its popularity, it was sung forty-two years later by Judy Garland in *Meet Me in St. Louis*. The Johnson brothers had not realized the tune would become an international hit. They had based the song on the Negro spiritual "Nobody Knows De Trouble I See" and believed it was not dignified enough to meet the conservatory standards to which the formally trained J. Rosamond held himself. Thus they allowed Cole, well known for coon songs, to take sole credit. The song would be a staple of elementary school choruses throughout America in the 1950s and 1960s. Between 1906 and 1910 the Johnson brothers and Bob Cole also produced two all-black musicals: *The Shoo-Fly Regiment* and *The Red Moon*.

Once joining with the Johnsons, Cole's work moved away from minstrelsy, and he dropped his Willy Wayside character. Wherever they performed, they favored white tie and tails (attire that Fred Astaire would make famous during the 1920s) to dignify themselves and all African Americans. The quality and complexity of his music also increased because of J. Rosamond's influence—he had graduated from the New England Conservatory in 1899. But the success of their Broadway collaborations could not overcome Cole's declining health, and in fact perhaps contributed to it. After returning to vaudeville, an onstage physical collapse in 1910 was followed by a long stay in Bellevue. The following year Cole drowned. His presumed suicide in 1911 clearly deprived the nation of an immense talent.

James Weldon Johnson went on to publish a major novel, *The Autobiography of an Ex-Colored Man*, and a landmark book of poetry, *God's Trombones*; he also edited the first major anthology of canonical African American poetry, *The Book of American Negro Poetry* (1922, 1931) and two volumes of American Negro spirituals (1925, 1926). He served as the first black executive secretary of the NAACP.

J. Rosamond became director of the Hammerstein Grand Opera House in London, and after returning to the United States in 1914, founded the Music School Settlement for Colored People in New York. He established himself as the country's leading black stage manager and music arranger and was music director for the films *The Emperor Jones* (1933), starring Paul Robeson, and *Cabin in the Sky* (1935), starring Lena Horne.

CHARLES W. CHESNUTT AND JAMES WELDON JOHNSON

During the early years of the twentieth century, African American authors produced several influential literary works. In 1901, the poet and critic William Stanley Braithwaite, pointing to new works by Paul Laurence Dunbar, W. E. B. Du Bois, and Charles Chesnutt, called the period the beginning of a "Negro renaissance," which would realize itself as the New Negro Movement or Harlem Renaissance in the 1920s. While each of these writers played a seminal role in the black literary tradition, none was more important to the shaping of African American fiction by folklore than Charles W. Chesnutt.

Born in 1858, Chesnutt spent much of his youth in North Carolina, then relocated to his birthplace, Cleveland, Ohio, in 1884. He passed the bar exam and found financial success and security as a legal stenographer. But he yearned to write and spent much of his free time pursuing that dream, publishing sketches and stories in a variety of magazines and journals, including *Puck, The Outlook, Youth's Companion,* and *The Crisis.* His hard work paid off, and, in August 1887, he became the first African American to publish a short story, "The Goophered Grapevine," in *The Atlantic Monthly.* (Most of his readers could not have imagined that the author was a black man.)

After publishing other well-received short stories, he collected them as *The Conjure Woman,* published in March 1899 to wonderful reviews. Chesnutt's confidence grew: in the fall of that year, he published a second collection of short stories, *The Wife of His Youth.* A year later, he published his first novel, *The House Behind the Cedars,* followed by his most important novel, *The Marrow of Tradition,* in 1901. He published a biography

Charles W. Chesnutt (1858–1932).

of Frederick Douglass in 1899, in a series edited by Harvard University's Mark A. DeWolfe Howe. A final novel, *The Colonel's Dream,* was published in 1905, but to tepid reviews.

Chesnutt's writing did not turn a profit sufficient to enable him to live as a writer. He returned to legal stenography and stopped writing fiction. But for his pioneering role in the African American literary tradition, he was awarded the prestigious Spingarn Medal by the NAACP in 1928. He lived and worked in Cleveland until his death in 1932. His image was honored on a U.S. postage stamp on the occasion of his 150th birthday.

Most critics agree that *The Marrow of Tradition* is the most accomplished of his three novels. Set in Wilmington, North Carolina, in the aftermath of the brutal 1898 race riots, the novel focuses on the numerous—and often scandalous—intersections between the white Carteret family and the black Miller family. It served, implicitly, as a rebuttal of the numerous racist writings about miscegenation and rape published to justify Jim Crow segregation during the 1890s.

James Weldon Johnson (1871–1938). This pencil drawing was made by Winold Reiss for Alain Locke, ed., *The New Negro: An Interpretation* (New York: Atheneum, 1925).

Johnson's *The Autobiography of an Ex-Colored Man,* cover, 1912.

Few African Americans, and indeed few Americans, in the first third of the twentieth century had a career as interesting and successful as did James Weldon Johnson. He was a genius at reinventing himself, in entirely new directions, a true Renaissance man. After his prolific career in the music business, he served as consul to Venezuela and Nicaragua in the Theodore Roosevelt administration and in 1912 anonymously published *The Autobiography of an Ex-Colored Man*. The novel focused on the phenomenon of passing—that a black man with light skin could live as a white person. The unnamed narrator—a character based on Johnson's roommate at Atlanta University—travels to Atlanta, to Jacksonville, to New York, and even to Europe as he attempts to find his place in the world. He explores his own racial and class prejudice, is robbed by a black man, and eventually marries a white woman in New York City. A meditation on the meaning of race, *The Autobiography of an Ex-Colored Man* foreshadowed many of the themes that would come to prominence during the 1920s Harlem Renaissance. But the book did not catch on with audiences until Johnson reprinted it in 1927 under his own name.

Johnson went on to have an amazing career as a civil rights activist. He joined the NAACP in 1917 and became the organization's first black executive secretary in 1920. Under his leadership, the NAACP thrived. He returned to literature in the 1920s, when he published several major books and anthologies, including a masterful book of sacred vernacular poetry, *God's Trombones* (1927). The prefaces to his anthologies, *The Book of American Negro Poetry* (1922), and the first and second *Book of American Negro Spirituals* (1925, 1926) served as manifestos for the relation between traditional black vernacular forms and high literary art. He was the first black person to teach at New York University, and from there he went on to teach creative writing at Fisk. If there was one true Renaissance man during the Harlem Renaissance, it was Johnson.

PAUL LAURENCE DUNBAR
AND *IN DAHOMEY*

We wear the mask that grins and lies / It hides our cheeks and shades our eyes / This debt we pay to human guile / With torn and bleeding hearts we smile." If he had written nothing else, Paul Laurence Dunbar would hold a central place in the canon of the African American literary tradition for "We Wear the Mask." Composed in 1895, the poem perceptively embodies the cultural and psychological schizophrenia that was a by-product of slavery and Jim Crow segregation. Dunbar's mask metaphor for what W. E. B. Du Bois (elaborating on Dunbar's trope) would characterize as the American Negro's "double consciousness" and life "behind the veil" also captures the poet's own anguish as he struggled to assert his talent in a society defined by de jure segregation and disgraced by an epidemic of lynching.

Paul Laurence Dunbar, born in 1872, was the son of former slaves who had built a comfortable life in Dayton, Ohio. He began writing as a young boy; after graduating from high school, he edited the short-lived *Tattler,* a newspaper for African Americans published by Dunbar's former schoolmate Orville Wright (brother of Wilbur). He then supported himself through a series of miscellaneous jobs, particularly as an elevator operator, so that he could write poetry. He published his first collection, *Oak and Ivy,* in 1893 and visited the World's Columbian Exposition in Chicago. There he met Frederick Douglass, who gave him an opportunity to give a public reading of his poem "The Colored Soldiers."

The audience's enthusiastic response encouraged Dunbar to write more poetry, and he published his second book, *Majors and Minors,* two years later. William Dean Howells, the nation's leading literary critic, loved Dunbar's work and in a major review of *Majors*

Paul Laurence Dunbar (1872–1906).

and Minors praised him as the first "man of pure African blood and of American civilization to feel the negro life aesthetically and express it lyrically."[3] Sales of Dunbar's work soared, and his next book, *Lyrics of Lowly Life* (1896), sent him on a tour of Britain. He returned in 1897 and took up a position at the Library of Congress, which he quit the following

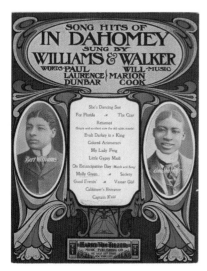

In Dahomey, sheet music
cover, ca. 1902.

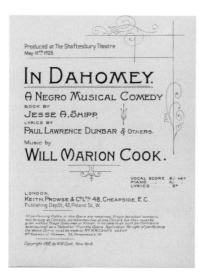

In Dahomey, theatrical program, 1902.

year to devote himself to writing his poetry. Dunbar was the first African American who managed to support himself through his writing. But declining health and addiction to alcohol proved ruinous and destroyed his brief marriage to the writer Alice Dunbar-Nelson. He died from tuberculosis in 1906.

During his most productive years, Dunbar also found great success composing lyrics for black musicals. He collaborated with the Broadway composer James Weldon Johnson and his brother J. Rosamond; and particularly with Will Marion Cook (1869–1944). Cook, who had studied music with Antonín Dvořák in New York City, dedicated his career to replacing "Old Negro" minstrelsy with "New Negro" music, part of the emerging New Negro Movement that critics such as William Stanley Braithwaite, John Henry Adams, and W. H. A. Moore welcomed between 1901 and 1903 with enthusiasm and hope. The first Dunbar-Cook collaboration was the 1899 musical *Clorindy: The Origin of the Cakewalk;* it was innovative beyond what whites had been accustomed to hear from African Americans, but it also remained firmly in the minstrel or "coon song" tradition. The musical proved a roaring success (however questionable it

would be to modern audiences) and, as Cook declared, put blacks on Broadway and kept them there. Dunbar struggled against the genre of dialect poetry that his own success forced him to adopt, so he determined to use dialect poems and lyrics in an attempt to transform white views of blacks. He had little commercial choice. As he remarked to James Weldon Johnson, "It is the only way I can get them to listen to me."[4]

Dunbar then swore off "plantation lyrics," but his next collaboration with Cook relied on them, although subversively; it proved even more successful than the first—indeed, it became a landmark in the history of African American performance. *In Dahomey* opened in New York City on February 18, 1903, the first full-length musical written and performed by African Americans to open on Broadway. One of its signal compositions, "Emancipation Day," proclaimed: "Coons dress'd up lak Masqueraders / Porters arm'd lak rude invaders," and "Brass ban' playin sev'ral tunes / Darkies eyes look jes lak moons." But it also asserted black authority and satirized whites: "On Emancipation Day / All you white folks clear de way . . . / When dey hear dem ragtime tunes / White folks try to pass fo' coons."[5] For

Cook, who composed all the music for *In Dahomey,* the musical represented the beginning of genuine black expression. *In Dahomey* ran for fifty-three performances, then went on tour to Britain. "My race," Cook told a reporter for the *London Daily News* on May 16, 1903, "has determined to make itself felt in painting, sculpture, and music." Starring Bert Williams (1874–1922) and George Walker (1873–1911), and with an all-black cast, *In Dahomey* opened in London on May 16, 1903; it played continuously for seven months, delighting audiences, judging by reviews and ticket sales. Williams, Walker, and their troupe even gave a performance for the royal family at Buckingham Palace. Word of the play spread quickly throughout Britain, and black Britons flocked to the performances—and afterward, frequented the pubs in central London. So many black people attended that pub owners began denying service to black clientele. Outraged at this extraordinary burst of discrimination, one man, whom the U.S. embassy described as "a gentleman of culture and refinement," successfully lodged a complaint against the pub owners at the local magistrate's court. The protester was Dr. W. E. B. Du Bois.[6]

THE BOSTON *GUARDIAN* AND THE *CHICAGO DEFENDER*

From his Atlanta Exposition speech in 1895 to his death in 1915, Booker T. Washington was the most visible and most powerful African American leader. But new and sometimes strident voices also emerged to critique the policies he advocated. William Monroe Trotter offered particularly sharp criticism of the "Wizard of Tuskegee."

Born to an elite black Boston family in 1872, Trotter graduated with highest honors from his majority-white high school (where he was class president) and in 1895 earned a bachelor's degree from Harvard University. Perhaps because his life demonstrated the importance of a college education to blacks, Trotter adamantly challenged Washington's emphasis upon vocational education and his apparent acceptance of segregation. Accommodation, he argued, would not convince whites that they could live beside African Americans as equals; rather, it reaffirmed black inferiority.

Beginning in 1901, Trotter publicized his dissenting opinions and founded the Boston Literary and Historical Association, which gave the growing anti-Washington contingent a conduit for expression. The same year he and George W. Forbes cofounded the Boston *Guardian,* one of the most important black papers of the early twentieth century. Within a year the *Guardian* boasted a circulation of 25,000. Trotter used its pages to skewer Washington as well as white politicians like Theodore Roosevelt. For his part, Washington did not appreciate the attacks and attempted to use his influence to cripple the paper. One of his supporters contacted Forbes's employer at the Boston Public Library. Library administrators, who also disdained the *Guardian*'s attacks, successfully pressured Forbes into resigning as the paper's coeditor. Trotter, however, would not be silenced. In 1903, he and his supporters attended a speech Washington delivered in Boston. They peppered him with hostile questions, until the tension in the room exploded into an all-out brawl. The so-called Boston Riot of 1903 led to a month-long prison term for Trotter, which only heightened his stature among anti-Washington blacks. He would remain at the forefront of civil rights activism in Boston until his death in 1934.

The early twentieth century also saw the birth of an important new newspaper in Chicago, one that would attract a national readership. Unlike Trotter, Robert S. Abbott, the son of former Georgia slaves, had long supported Washington; he even learned the printing trade at the Hampton Institute, Washington's alma mater. But Abbott, influenced by speeches he had heard by Frederick Douglass and Ida B. Wells-Barnett, also believed that blacks had a role in politics.

William Monroe Trotter (1872–1934). From Carter G. Woodson's *The Negro in Our History* (Washington, D.C.: Associated Publishers, 1922).

After earning a law degree at Chicago's Kent College of Law, Abbott started the *Chicago Defender* in 1905, with a start-up fund of twenty-five cents, and one employee—himself. Abbott's sensationalism and fearless politics immediately endeared the newspaper to the nation's

The *Guardian*'s office.

Chicago newsboy selling the *Defender,* photograph by Jack Delano, 1942.

Robert S. Abbott (1868–1940) with his wife, Helen Thornton Morrison.

black community. He offered a scathing critique of white supremacy, publicizing incidents of violence and lynching. At the same time, he emphasized black pride and published stories of the success that many African Americans had found in Chicago. While it was a northern paper, southern blacks relished reading what white society would never permit them to say aloud. While few southern blacks could afford the annual subscription charge, they shared copies of the paper throughout their communities, and many black-owned businesses, churches, and social clubs stocked it. For those who could not read, family members, friends, and neighbors read it aloud. Despite humble origins, the *Defender* would become the nation's most popular African American newspaper.

THE SOULS OF BLACK FOLK

"The problem of the twentieth century is the problem of the color line." These haunting words set the tone for W. E. B. Du Bois's 1903 masterpiece, *The Souls of Black Folk*. A collection of thirteen essays and a short story, written with poetic lyricism, *Souls* challenged African American readers to examine their own history and to confront white oppression. Du Bois combined his personal experiences with nuanced interpretations of African American history, sociology, and music, to examine the predicament that all blacks faced—"How does it feel to be a problem?"—and offered direction for change. The book was hailed as a classic as soon as it was published.

The Souls of Black Folk introduced a number of theoretical constructs and signal metaphors that would influence black thought, literature, and activism

throughout the twentieth century. Du Bois recalled when he had first determined that his blackness made him socially inferior to whites, "that I was shut out from their world by a vast veil." Such experiences contributed to Du Bois's argument that a "veil" separated him and other African Americans from white society. Yet while blacks lived behind the veil, whites' vision of black people, and of American culture and society, was obscured as well: they could not see African Americans as human beings, as social and political equals, as fellow citizens.

Perhaps "double consciousness" was the book's most enduring and influential idea. The color line, according to Du Bois, forced blacks to navigate difficult psychological terrain, particularly when it came to their own identities as simultaneously "an American [and] a

W. E. B. Du Bois (1868–1963).

Negro." For most blacks, white supremacy colored their view of their home country and of themselves. Although born in America, they could not fully embrace a nation whose most powerful people did not welcome or respect them. They could not—and to Du Bois's

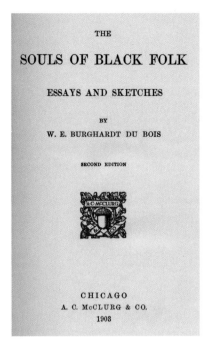

The Souls of Black Folk, title page, 1903. Du Bois's most influential work.

"Of Mr. Booker T. Washington and Others." Here he presented the "triple paradox" of Washington's accommodation philosophy. How, he asked, can black people fulfill Washington's dream of owning businesses and property if they lack the power to vote and defend their rights? How can they practice "thrift and self-respect" while experiencing daily instances of white supremacist degradation? And if all blacks eschewed higher education in favor of Washington's trade schools, who would do the teaching in the trade schools? This, Du Bois explained, was a prescription for perpetual subordination. He countered with a program insisting upon the vote, equality, and "the education of youth according to ability."[8]

He also argued quite eloquently against the increasingly popular view of Reconstruction, promulgated by Columbia University's William Dunning and others, as a tragic period of (black) political corruption. Dunning and his many followers blamed the failure of Reconstruction on the newly freed African Americans, who were inherently incapable of governance, and

their cynical abolitionist allies. But Du Bois, in his essay "Of the Dawn of Freedom," insisted that Jim Crow discrimination, peonage, and violence kept blacks in a state of pseudo-slavery and prohibited them from having a chance at genuine social, economic, and political equality. He refined this critique in his magnum opus, *Black Reconstruction,* published in 1935.

In another 1903 essay, Du Bois expressed his conviction that the "talented tenth"—the "college-bred Negro"—bore special responsibility to lead the race. *Souls* marked a turning point, as Du Bois articulated a new, activist agenda for turn-of-the-century blacks. The book would inspire millions of readers over several generations and would serve as a philosophical manifesto for the Niagara Movement, founded in 1905, and the NAACP four years later. Its metaphors of duality, double consciousness, and the veil would be repeated and revised by James Weldon Johnson, Jean Toomer, Zora Neale Hurston, Ralph Ellison, Ishmael Reed, Toni Morrison, Rita Dove, and Elizabeth Alexander, among many others.

mind, should not—disassociate themselves from black culture or the black past. These dual identities became "two warring ideals in one dark body, whose dogged strength alone keeps it from being torn asunder."[7]

Du Bois elaborated an especially searching critique of his archrival in

MARY MCLEOD BETHUNE AND AFRICAN AMERICAN EDUCATION

Despite criticisms by W. E. B. Du Bois and his followers, Booker T. Washington's ideology of racial uplift continued to find a ready audience. Mary McLeod Bethune, who received an extensive education at various southern mission schools and at Dwight L. Moody's evangelical Institute for Home and Foreign Missions in Chicago, believed in the transformative power

of schooling. When she reached adulthood, she set out to help other southern blacks, particularly women, follow her path. After teaching in South Carolina and unsuccessfully attempting to start a school in Palatka, Florida, Bethune moved to Daytona in 1904 to try again.

Daytona offered a number of advantages for an upstart school, including a location convenient to the railroad,

Mary McLeod Bethune (1875–1955). Gordon Parks photographed Bethune at Bethune-Cookman College, 1943.

Bethune standing with students outside White Hall
at Bethune-Cookman College, 1943.

Bethune's home at Bethune-
Cookman College, photograph
by Gordon Parks, 1943.

which promised easy transportation and a steady influx of new people. The city had an established African American community, and local blacks volunteered their time and money to support the school. Bethune's support for Washingtonian accommodationism and self-help attracted donations from local white women's groups, as well as from a number of wealthy tourists attracted to Daytona's beaches and resort atmosphere. She rented a house in an African American neighborhood and started the Daytona Literary and Industrial Training School for Negro Girls. Her first class consisted of five girls, ages six through twelve (joined by young Albert, Bethune's five-year-old son).

Bethune, in her 1906 *Record Book of the Bethune School,* remembered those precarious first years:

We burned logs and used charred splinters as pencils, and mashed elderberries for ink. I begged strangers for a broom, a lamp, a bit of cretonne to put around the packing case which served as my desk. I haunted the city dump and trash piles behind hotels, retrieving discarded linen and kitchenware, cracked dishes, broken chairs, pieces of old lumber. Everything was scoured and mended.

This dedication and inventiveness led to extraordinary success. In its first six years, the student body increased by 500 percent. The school expanded its curriculum beyond grammar, industry, and religious studies to include high school–level and liberal arts courses. Combining her belief in vocational training with her dedication to training black teachers, she renamed the school the Daytona Normal and Industrial Institute. Local volunteers helped build a four-story schoolhouse to hold the expanding enrollment, and Bethune held classes outside her facility for local workers and farmers, to integrate her mission into the black community. As with many African American schools, money always ran short. The school charged a modest tuition that did not come close to covering its actual operating costs; students who could not afford the payment sometimes donated food instead.

While Bethune played the key role in creating the curriculum, she also led crucial fund-raising efforts. In 1923, to help alleviate the chronic shortages, she merged the school with the nearby Cookman Institute, a coeducational school run by the Negro Education Board of the Methodist Episcopal Church. She remained president of the new school until 1942, guiding it to full accreditation in 1931. The institute eventually adopted the name Bethune-Cookman College, becoming a model for the education of young black women, and it established Bethune as one of the country's preeminent educators.

NIAGARA MOVEMENT

Founders of the Niagara Movement, pasted onto an image of Niagara Falls, 1905. Top row: H. A. Thompson, Alonzo F. Herndon, John Hope, possibly James R. L. Diggs. Second row: Frederick L. McGhee, Norris Bumstead Herndon, J. Max Barber, W. E. B. Du Bois, Robert Bonner. Third row: Henry L. Baily, Clement G. Morgan, W. H. H. Hart, B. S. Smith.

The 1903 publication of *The Souls of Black Folk* inflamed the long-standing feud between its author, W. E. B. Du Bois, and his political nemesis, Booker T. Washington. In January 1904, Washington invited Du Bois to a race conference in New York City. Du Bois attended, but, as he had feared, Washington ignored his suggestions and made no effort to include him in major decisions. He left New York disillusioned. Frustrated by personal dissension and political disagreements, Du Bois decided to hold his own conference, one without the influence—or indeed the presence—of Booker T. Washing-ton. He enlisted the help of other prominent African American intellectuals and activists, including fellow Harvard alumnus William Monroe Trotter.

On July 10, 1905, Du Bois hosted the first meeting of the Niagara Movement at the Erie Beach Hotel in Ontario, Canada. He had intended to hold the

The original twenty-nine founders of the Niagara Movement, collage, undated.

Niagara Movement delegates in Boston, 1907.

meeting in Buffalo, but hotel owners there refused to accommodate African Americans. The twenty-nine attendees agreed to a platform, and their manifesto, the *Declaration of Principles,* denounced segregation and disenfranchisement and the accommodationist policies of Booker T. Washington. The Niagara Movement demanded that African Americans receive the full benefits of citizenship, including desegregation, equal voting rights, fair treatment of black workers, and protection from white violence. It emphasized the right to a fair trial and insisted upon greater access to all forms of education, not just trade schools. Perhaps most important, it urged blacks to speak out when denied these rights: "Persistent manly agitation is the way to liberty."

The Niagara Movement would meet annually over the next five years. On August 15, 1906, the group—hosted by founding member John R. Clifford, West Virginia's first black lawyer and the editor of the *Pioneer Press* newspaper—met in Harpers Ferry, West Virginia, the site of John Brown's 1859 assault on slavery. Participants once more distanced themselves from Washington's conciliatory philosophy; the Massachusetts clergyman Reverdy Ransom memorably declared that blacks "should not submit to being humiliated, degraded, and remanded to an inferior place."[9] The organization's third meeting took place the following year at Boston's historic Faneuil Hall, where it challenged President Theodore Roosevelt's racial policies. The next conferences occurred at Oberlin College and in Sea Isle City, New Jersey. The Niagara Movement had thirty branch

Niagara Movement leaders at Harpers Ferry, 1906. Du Bois is seated next to J. R. Clifford in the center.

organizations around the country, but ultimately it could not overcome budget shortfalls, clashes with the followers of the "Wizard of Tuskegee," and internal dissension. It ended in 1911, but in its short life it represented a major turning point in black activism and articulated a new vision of how blacks should pursue social and political equality. When Du Bois disbanded the movement, he did so with the knowledge that by then another option existed for black activism: the National Association for the Advancement of Colored People.

THE ATLANTA RIOT, THE BROWNSVILLE RAID, AND THE REPUTATIONS OF THEODORE ROOSEVELT AND BOOKER T. WASHINGTON

When President Theodore Roosevelt hosted Booker T. Washington for dinner at the White House in 1901, the meeting underscored Washington's unparalleled place among his contemporaries; it signified that the American power structure had embraced the Atlanta Compromise as its preferred policy for the future of African Americans. Three years later, in the presidential election, blacks rewarded Roosevelt by voting for him in droves. But afterward Roosevelt's attention to the interests of blacks wavered. And perhaps more important, racial violence in Atlanta and in Brownsville, Texas, in 1906 threatened to destroy the notion that accommodation could mitigate racial tensions. Contrary to Washington's hopes, the fact that his famed speech had taken place in Georgia's capital did nothing to prevent this cruel and brutal venting of white violence on innocent black victims.

The summer of 1906 saw an outburst of incendiary racism in Georgia. White newspaper editors competed for readers by running fantastic and unfounded stories of black men attacking white women. In a similarly dangerous game of one-upmanship, gubernatorial candidates competed to assert their white supremacist credentials. Each candidate demeaned African Americans while accusing the other of catering to black interests. The powder keg exploded on

"Les 'Lynchages' aux États-Unis," *Le Petit Journal*, October 7, 1908. The Atlanta riot as depicted by a French daily newspaper.

September 22, 1906, when an armed mob of whites took to the streets in response to yet another hysterical newspaper story about black violence. Although the mayor and the police commissioner tried to halt the mob, it marched through the black business district and destroyed everything in sight, leaving ten blacks and one white dead during the five-day rampage.

African Americans nationwide exploded in anger. Washington expressed his forlorn hope that whites and blacks would unite after the riot, if only to protect Atlanta's reputation as a progressive New South city. But the savage violence led many blacks to question Washington's conciliatory approach. W. E. B. Du Bois led the chorus of opposition, mocking the fallacy of compromise in the *New York Independent*: "Behold this maimed black man. . . . They told him: Work and Rise!" Whites in the North blamed black criminals for instigating the riot, and in his State of the Union address that December, the president argued that blacks had brought it on themselves. "The greatest existing cause of lynching," he said, "is the perpetration, especially by black men, of the hideous crime of rape."[10]

The president's response to an incident of violence in Brownsville, Texas, further shocked African Americans. Stationed at Fort Brown on the Rio Grande, the African American First Battalion of the 25th Infantry Regiment had frequent altercations with local whites. A Texas senator even asked Secretary of War William Howard Taft to move the unit in order to prevent an outbreak of violence. Taft refused; the soldiers remained in their segregated barracks within the city and continued to face discrimination. Details of what exactly happened on the night of August 13, 1906, remain sketchy.

Late in the evening, gunshots rang out in bars and dance halls located near the fort. The shooting spree lasted

"Remember Brownsville," broadside, 1906.

approximately ten minutes. A white man died, and a police officer was seriously wounded. But nobody could definitively identify the shooters. Black soldiers assumed the violence came from a white mob, while local whites blamed unruly black soldiers. A number of whites came forward to say that they had witnessed infantrymen committing the crime, although an army investigation produced no conclusive evidence of the soldiers' participation in the fighting. The story seemed as though it would quietly fade away. It did not.

Roosevelt dismissed without a hearing three companies of the regiment (the black soldiers, not the white officers); the distinguished soldiers received dishonorable discharges and lost their pensions. But Roosevelt decided to wait until after the November midterm elections to announce the discharges, so as not to risk his party losing the votes of African Americans in key northern states. He did, however, inform Booker T. Washington of his plan a week in advance. Washington pleaded with the president to change his mind and stop "the great blunder." Roosevelt was unmoved. On November 7, the Republicans safely retained control of the House, and afterward Roosevelt made his decision public. Blacks criticized both the president and Washington. As T. Thomas Fortune wrote in the *Age*, "Neither Mr. Washington nor the colored people . . . can risk the hazard to be moved as mere pawns on the chess board of the President."[11]

The Brownsville Raid and Atlanta Riot signaled to a great number of African Americans that an alliance with the federal government—and accommodationism as a racial strategy—would fail to advance their interests. The events provided powerful ammunition to those like W. E. B. Du Bois who wanted to challenge Washington's leadership.

SPRINGFIELD RACE RIOT, THE FOUNDING OF THE NAACP, AND THE BEGINNING OF *THE CRISIS*

For African Americans, Springfield, Illinois, was not only the home of Abraham Lincoln—it held a special connection to the Union victory, to their own emergence from southern slavery, and to the achievement of black citizenship and the right to vote. At the turn of the century, Springfield's brickyards, coal mines, and railroads offered employment opportunities that attracted migrants, black and white, from the South. African Americans, comprising 5 percent of Springfield's population in 1908, had established successful businesses and provided a blueprint for upward mobility. Still, tensions ran high between white and black newcomers, especially in the Levee, the downtown saloon district.

Remnants of the home of an African American in Springfield, Illinois, 1908.

Junior Auxiliary of the Cleveland NAACP, 1929.

Fighting broke out in Springfield for several reasons: job competition between blacks and whites; white jealousy over the wealth that the black middle class had accrued; anxiety over lawlessness in the Levee; and fractious local politics. But the spark that ignited it occurred on August 14, 1908, when a white woman named Mabel Hallam accused local black worker George Richardson of raping her. Police took Richardson to jail, where he joined Joe James, an African American who had been accused of murdering a local white man a month earlier. A mob formed outside the prison. In hopes of staving off vigilante violence, the local sheriff put James and Richardson on a train to nearby Bloomington. Incensed that the police had deprived them of the opportunity to seek revenge, the mob revolted. "What the hell are you fellows afraid of?" one woman shouted to the angry men. "Women want protection. . . ."[12]

Whites responded with violence, destroying property and attacking citizens in black neighborhoods. "Lincoln freed you," shouted one member of the mob, "we'll show you where you belong."[13] About two thousand blacks fled the city; those who remained faced

assault and even death. One evening, in a particularly brutal incident, whites lynched an elderly black man named William Donnegan. By the time the National Guard stopped the riot the next day, six had died (including four whites), dozens had been injured, and property damage totaled more than $200,000. Even though the mass rioting had ended, small-scale attacks against Springfield blacks continued for the next month.

The Springfield violence made it clear that the South had no monopoly on lynching and terror. Journalist and labor reformer William English Walling traveled to the city to document the violence; on September 3, 1908, he published "Race War in the North" in the New York *Independent*. Walling appealed to the North's abolitionist past and warned that the racial violence so often blamed on the South would soon infect the entire nation. His essay concluded with a clarion call for the protection of African Americans: "Yet who realizes the seriousness of the situation, and what large and powerful body of citizens is ready to come to their aid?"

Walling's article drew immediate interest from a number of white reformers. Social worker Mary White Ovington, socialist muckraker Charles Edward Russell, and publisher Oswald Garrison Villard joined Walling in New York City to discuss possible responses to the increasingly ugly racism. Although at first they were in the minority, African Americans, including W. E. B. Du Bois, began aligning with the group, now called the National Negro Committee. Walling issued a call for a national conference. Originally it was scheduled on Lincoln's birthday for symbolic effect,

Du Bois in the office of *The Crisis*, 1920–21.

but delays pushed it ahead to May 31, 1909. Prominent black attendees of the first meeting of the National Negro Committee included Du Bois, Ida B. Wells-Barnett, and the Howard University sociologist Kelly Miller. While equality between whites and blacks was the meeting's overarching theme, African Americans shifted the discussion toward suffrage. The conference ended with the formation of the National Committee for the Advancement of the Negro.

By the beginning of 1910, the new organization had stalled. Donations failed to materialize, conflicts arose over who would lead it, and Booker T. Washington worked diligently to discredit it. But the second conference, held from May 12 to May 14, energized the members. It focused on voting rights, and the group adopted a new name, the National Association for the Advancement of Colored People. Members chose the word *colored* rather than *negro* to emphasize their international focus.

W. E. B. Du Bois resigned from Atlanta University to work full-time for the new organization, which issued its formal constitution the following year. The NAACP's leadership, white and black, understood the benefits of having Du Bois in a high-profile position: his Niagara Movement had attracted a great number of followers; his charisma would bring the NAACP attention and credibility; and perhaps above all else, the new organization needed his immense talent as a spokesperson and writer.

Setting up shop in Villard's *Evening Post* headquarters, Du Bois began work on a new monthly magazine, *The Crisis,* the "organ of the National Association for the Advancement of Colored People." Although some NAACP leaders doubted that the magazine could survive, the first issue, published in November 1910, sold out all 1,000 copies. Sales only multiplied thereafter: 6,000 by March 1911, and 25,000 by November 1912. The editorials and opinion pieces, written primarily by Du Bois, publicized issues confronting African Americans and helped to mold black public opinion across the country. The magazine created a community of shared interest and devotion. Marie Brown Frazier, wife of noted sociologist E. Franklin Frazier, remarked that during her youth, *The Crisis* was "just like the Bible to me."[14]

MADAM C. J. WALKER

Sarah Breedlove's childhood offered no indication that she would go on to become one of the wealthiest and most famous African Americans of her generation. Born in 1867 in Delta, Louisiana, Breedlove lost both parents when she was only seven years old. She married at age fourteen and lived in Mississippi, but her husband died six years later—of unknown causes—leaving her with a two-year-old daughter, A'Lelia. With little hope of advancement, she left Mississippi for St. Louis, where her three older brothers worked as barbers. She spent the next fifteen years struggling as a washerwoman to educate her daughter. Breedlove remarried in 1894, but the marriage disintegrated in 1903.

Fortunately, as a member of the St. Paul AME Church, she had met several middle-class clubwomen who assisted

Madam C. J. Walker driving with her niece Anjetta Breedlove, Alice Kelby, and Lucy Flint, forewoman and secretary at the Madam C.J. Walker Manufacturing Company, 1911.

"From a slave cabin to riches," advertisement (front and reverse) for Madam C. J. Walker's products.

her. She then became a sales agent for Annie Turnbo Pope Malone, owner of the Poro Company, a manufacturer of hair care products for black women. Perhaps Breedlove's own hair loss, caused by poor hair care, malnutrition, and stress, had attracted her to the hair care industry. With only $1.50 to her name, she moved to Denver, where a widowed sister-in-law and four nieces lived, and became a Poro salesperson. Then, in January 1906, she married Charles Joseph Walker, a St. Louis newspaper agent and promoter who had followed her to Denver.

Following a practice common to many businesswomen of the era, Walker adopted the marketable and dignified-sounding name Madam C. J. Walker. (The marriage lasted only six years, but the name change stuck.) She began to sell her own line of hair care products. She developed a hair restorer, a sulfur-based ointment, which she claimed came to her in a dream (assisted by Denver pharmacist E. L. Scholtz), and a new version of the hot comb. Used together, the Walker System could grow hair, remove kinks, and groom the hair

of African American women. When this method was later criticized as encouraging black women to conform to white standards of beauty, Walker denied that she sought to straighten black women's hair. But the practice blossomed nevertheless, and in the process Walker earned a fortune.

She traveled extensively, going door to door to sell her products. She moved to Pittsburgh in 1908 and opened the first of her many Lelia Colleges, where black women could learn the Walker System. In 1910, she moved her base of operations to Indianapolis, the largest manufacturing center in the Midwest. Her burgeoning business proved a boon to African American women, creating many jobs for black salespeople, agents, and beauticians. Additionally, Walker turned to philanthropic efforts, and her sales agents formed Walker Clubs, where they received cash prizes for charitable work. She distributed the prizes at the national conventions of the Madam C. J. Walker Hair Culturists Union of America.

She also joined civil rights organizations, including the National Associa-

tion of Colored Women and the NAACP. She donated money to the National Conference on Lynching, gave $1,000 to build a YMCA for blacks in Indianapolis, helped fund Bethune-Cookman College, and sponsored scholarships at the Tuskegee Institute.

But it was in the world of finance that Walker would receive the greatest attention. She moved to New York City in 1916, by which time her business was grossing more than a half million dollars per year, and she employed twenty thousand agents in the United States, Central America, and the Caribbean. She invested money in real estate and bought a $350,000 estate on the Hudson River. Estimates place her personal worth at between $500,000 and $1 million, the equivalent of about $20 million in modern currency, making her at the time the wealthiest African American business owner. When she passed away at her mansion on May 25, 1919, *The New York Times* noted her many accomplishments, giving her obituary the title "Wealthiest Negress Dead." Her remarkable success made her an inspiration for generations of black entrepreneurs.

MATTHEW HENSON

Admiral Robert E. Peary's team, Matthew Henson and Inuits Ooqueh, Ootah, Egingwah, and Seegloo, at the North Pole, April 7, 1909.

After leading the first successful expedition to the North Pole, U.S. Navy lieutenant Robert Peary earned a hero's welcome upon his return to the United States. In his many reports, Peary claimed he only received assistance from a few Eskimos. African American newspapers, however, told a different story. They revealed Matthew Henson's integral role in the famed polar exploration—and many others.

Henson was born to sharecroppers in Charles County, Maryland, on August 8, 1866. His parents died while he was young, and for a time he lived with an uncle and attended school in Washington, D.C. He left school at the age of twelve, moved to Baltimore, and took a job working as a cabin boy on the three-masted *Katie Hines*. By the time

he reached the age of twenty, he had established himself as an excellent merchant sailor. A chance connection led to the partnership with Peary. Between ocean journeys Henson worked a series of jobs, including at a hat store in the nation's capital. In 1886, as Lieutenant Peary was preparing a scouting trip for a prospective canal in Central America, Henson's boss recommended him to Peary. Peary later retained Henson's services when he explored Greenland in 1891. Through the rest of the decade, Henson accompanied Peary on a series of trips, working as a cook, blacksmith, sled builder, and sled driver, to name only a few of his many responsibilities. He also worked for Peary between expeditions at the League Island Navy Yard in Philadelphia.

Reaching the North Pole, however, remained Peary's primary ambition. During the 1890s and early 1900s, Henson, Peary, and his team made seven Arctic voyages, but the ferocious Arctic weather consistently blocked their path. One cannot overemphasize the importance of Henson to the various Peary expeditions. In their 1898 adventure, for instance, Peary suffered from frostbite— and Henson used his own body to keep him warm and even saved his life by transporting him to safety. On ice, the two worked as one, but back in America Peary reverted to common racial and class divisions.

In July 1908, Peary's team departed New York aboard a state-of-the-art ice-breaking ship, and seven months later, in February 1909, they arrived at Cape

Matthew Henson (1866–1955).

Henson (far right) and others seated on a sledge that went to the North Pole.

Sheridan, about five hundred miles from the North Pole. The weather again halted them, but they waited until the worst of the storm had passed before setting out across the polar ice cap. Victory came on April 6, when Peary, Henson, and four Eskimos finally reached the North Pole. According to Henson, Peary had asked him to remain behind, but he accidentally kept his pace and actually reached the North Pole before Peary. Henson's claim ruined their friendship.

Yet Henson's role in the expedition—at one point Peary conceded that he could have never made it without him—went largely unnoticed. African American newspapers and political leaders tried to bring attention to the accomplishment. Booker T. Washington and leaders at several black colleges such as Morgan State and Howard University granted him honorary degrees. The influential black Republican Charles Anderson of New York secured employment for him—he convinced President William Howard Taft in 1913 to appoint him as a messenger at the New York Customs House.

Henson retired in 1936, and the fol-lowing year national accolades finally began to arrive. Henson became the first black member of the Explorers' Club, in 1937, and after repeated attempts to honor him with a Medal of Honor, Congress issued all the members of the expedition such a medal in 1944. Even President Dwight D. Eisenhower welcomed Henson at the White House. In 1986, the U.S. Postal Service recognized him with a stamp, and in 1988 he and his wife were reburied in Arlington National Cemetery—near Peary's grave.

THE FOUNDING OF THE URBAN LEAGUE; THE HARLEM ATTACK AND THE DEATH OF BOOKER T. WASHINGTON

Even before World War I, black migrants had begun to flee to the North to escape the Jim Crow South and its plantation labor. Most, however, met only overcrowding and discriminatory practices in housing and employment. Those blacks who had already achieved a foothold in the industrial economy feared that the new-comers would increase racial tensions and place their own tenuous status in jeopardy. Newspapers like the *Chicago Defender* published advice for black new-comers, telling them to be polite, clean their homes, and keep their children in school. In New York City a number of organizations formed to confront both the issues that black migrants faced and conflicts with northern-born blacks. The National League for the Protection of Colored Women (NLPCW) and the Committee for Improving Industrial Conditions of Negroes in New York (CIICN) assisted southern migrants in making the difficult transition to life in the North. In 1910 the African American sociologist George Edmund Haynes and

National Urban League headquarters on South Wabash Avenue, Chicago.

the white reformer Ruth Standish Baldwin formed the Committee on Urban Conditions Among Negroes (CUCAN). Haynes believed that migrants needed help not only in finding jobs but also in assimilating into urban culture. To consolidate their strengths, the NLPCW, CIICN, and CUCAN came together in 1911 to form the National League on Urban Conditions among Negroes, which shortened its name to the National Urban League in 1916.

At first George Haynes set the group's agenda. Influenced by the larger trends of the Progressive Era, he and his fellow Urban League members utilized the tools of social science, such as interviews and fieldwork, to identify problems and formulate solutions. Statistics on crime in the cities, for instance, led them to argue for job-training opportunities and for additional educational programs. Indeed, one of the most important programs of the early years of the Urban League granted African Americans fellowships to study social work at universities. The Urban League also mediated between white employers and their black employees and eventually worked alongside labor unions as well. The Urban League held that by addressing social inequalities, it could also reform individual African Americans—a program that proved far more conservative than that offered by W. E. B. Du Bois and the NAACP. Its members strongly opposed direct action protest, believing that such activism emerged out of social maladjustment and would leave blacks vulnerable to the false promises of a few unrealistic radicals. In addition to its calls for jobs, the league demanded the creation of recreational spaces, arguing that it would lead to "the profitable

Lifting the Veil of Ignorance, bronze sculpture by Charles Keck, 1922. This statue of Booker T. Washington stands at the Tuskegee Institute.

Funeral of Booker T. Washington at Tuskegee, 1915.

George E. Haynes (1880–1960). Graduated from Fisk University in 1903, Haynes in 1910 became the first black graduate of Columbia University's School of Social Work, earning a Ph.D. in 1912. From 1921 until 1946 he worked for the National Council of Churches.

use of leisure." The league also advocated vocational training, asserting in the Washingtonian tradition that good jobs would promote good conduct and assimilation—coincidentally undercutting any support for "radicals" like Du Bois. No surprise, Booker T. Washington joined its board of directors in 1914.

The Urban League's early years coincided with the traumatic last years of the "Wizard of Tuskegee." On the evening of March 19, 1911, Washington traveled to uptown Manhattan to visit a friend. He arrived at the apartment building, and while searching the directory, a man screamed at him and accused him of trying to break into the building. The white man, a local kennel owner named Henry Alpert Ulrich, attacked Washington, first with his hands and then with a walker that he seized from a man on

the street. Although he spent time in the hospital, Washington refused to let the assault keep him from his work. He continued to travel at his typically frenetic pace. Four years later, his body could no longer handle the workload. He died on November 14, 1915, at the age of fifty-nine, likely from a combination of kidney failure, high blood pressure, and perhaps arteriosclerosis.

Washington's death left an enormous hole in African American leadership, which the NAACP and the Urban League sought to fill. The challenges would only grow more pronounced, however, as the league expanded in the northern cities, desperate to avert further violence between whites and the influx of black migrants. The events of the next decade justified those concerns.

EMANCIPATION ANNIVERSARY, CARTER G. WOODSON, ROSENWALD SCHOOLS

The year 1913 marked the fiftieth anniversary of the Emancipation Proclamation. Whites had dominated official remembrances of the Civil War with monuments to fallen generals, paeans to the Lost Cause, and stories of white heroism and supremacy. For their part, African Americans—particularly black veterans—took to the field in the growing battle over the meaning of the war in the public memory and sought to educate all Americans about black heroism in combat as well as the failed promise of Reconstruction. Joseph T. Wilson, Christian A. Fleetwood, Alexander H. Newton, Susie King Taylor, and others recounted their own actions in the war and those of their comrades in published histories, pamphlets, and memoirs. Veterans also met in Soldiers' and Sailors' National Conventions and

marched with other members of the Grand Army of the Republic to memorialize and affirm an antislavery interpretation of the war. Many blacks had long celebrated the anniversary of Emancipation Day and most notably the "Juneteenth" celebrations of June 19, the day Texas slaves received word of their freedom at the close of the Civil War.

The celebrations that occurred during the golden jubilee of 1913 stressed the achievements of African Americans in education, business, and the arts. Monroe N. Work of Tuskegee Institute published *The Negro Year Book* to catalogue black accomplishments. Chicago hosted an exposition where 130,000 people paid tribute to Lincoln and the progress of African Americans. In New York City, W. E. B. Du Bois organized the National Emancipation Exposition from

Carter G. Woodson (1875–1950). This image of Woodson, taken in Washington, D.C., was owned by W. E. B. Du Bois.

October 22 to October 31. The event culminated with *The Star of Ethiopia*—a pageant written by Du Bois, directed by Charles Burroughs, and with music

Julius Rosenwald (1862–1932). Shown here with one of his three daughters in 1926, Rosenwald was part owner of Chicago-based Sears, Roebuck, and Company. He established the Rosenwald Fund in 1917.

Cadentown Rosenwald School, Caden Lane, Lexington, Kentucky. Cadentown was one of twenty-five communities founded by blacks in Fayette County after the Civil War.

by J. Rosamond Johnson—that told the stories of Abraham Lincoln, Crispus Attucks, Nat Turner, Frederick Douglass, and David Walker. The fiftieth anniversary of the Emancipation Proclamation offered African Americans a novel way to educate the public.

African American historical scholarship found a new leader in Carter G. Woodson. Born to former slaves in Virginia in 1875, Woodson taught in the Philippines from 1903 to 1907. Upon his return to the United States, he earned bachelor's and master's degrees from

the University of Chicago and a Ph.D. from Harvard in 1912. In 1915, he organized the Association for the Study of Negro Life and History (chartered in Washington, D.C.), and the following year he published the first issue of the groundbreaking *Journal of Negro History*. Woodson hoped that the journal would promote black pride and mollify conflict between the races. It provided a scholarly rebuttal to the white supremacy that so thoroughly dominated academia. In the following decades, Woodson, who earned the nickname the "Father of Negro History," would publish many books and articles and guide the development of the association and its journal.

New elementary and secondary schools for African Americans also opened during the first decade of the twentieth century. Disenfranchisement had robbed southern blacks of their political voice, which made it nearly impossible for them to convince politicians to fund their schools. Instead, they depended on their own hard work and scarce resources, as well as the help of northern philanthropists. Perhaps none played a greater role in this process than

President Woodrow Wilson at the dedication of the Confederate Monument at Arlington National Cemetery, 1914.

Julius Rosenwald, the president of Sears, Roebuck. In 1917, he established the Rosenwald Fund, which supported five thousand Rosenwald Schools throughout the South over the next fourteen years. The schools, combined with the persistent activism of African Americans in their own communities, greatly improved the condition of black education. Aside from the new Rosenwald buildings, however, black schoolhouses were generally makeshift buildings that paled in comparison to their white counterparts, which benefited from state and local tax revenues. The battles over school segregation and inequality would continue throughout the twentieth century.

JACK JOHNSON AND WHITE AMERICA

Jack Johnson (1878–1946) with his first wife, Etta Terry Duryea, posing as Napoleon and Josephine at Vancouver, B.C., upon their arrival from Australia, 1909.

Hiss! A gloved left lines across the gap, a shoulder blocks the jab and launches a viperous answer into space as a cropped head shifts an inch, the short rights follow in, the lock snaps shut, again the tattoo drumming on the ribs." For the journalist Robert Alden Sanborn, writing in January 1917 in the journal *The Soil,* watching Jack Johnson in the boxing ring was like watching a battle between two "savage bulls." But when Johnson fought white men, thought Sanborn, there was more at stake than a mere boxing match; one saw "Greek and Barbarian, skill and Brute, light and dark, over and over—victory and defeat." As Sanborn wrote, "the Brute, he always wins"; and white America couldn't accept it.

Born in Galveston, Texas, in 1878, Jack Johnson became the first African American world heavyweight boxing champion. His first important match, against a white Jewish fighter, Joe Choynski, in 1901, landed both men in jail for violating a state law against prizefighting. After his release three weeks later, Johnson fought a series of black opponents and in 1903 secured the black heavyweight title. Strong, proud, and refusing to bow to white racial etiquette, he began challenging white fighters in 1905 and quickly gained renown for savagely

Johnson striking a pose, undated.

Jack Johnson, undated.

beating them. He hired a white manager, Sam Fitzpatrick, who booked fights in England and Australia; his international reputation grew. On December 28, 1908, Johnson went fourteen rounds in Australia with Tommy Burns, the reigning heavyweight champ, and knocked him out. Outraged that a black man could be so victorious, whites called for Jim Jeffries, the former heavyweight champion, to emerge from retirement and restore white pride. In Reno, Nevada, on July 4, 1910, the "fight of the century" saw Johnson pummel Jeffries in a fifteen-round ordeal. The black champion emerged with $110,000 and the title of world champion.

Johnson's victories swelled black pride, but they came at a time when Jim Crow segregation was growing and repression of southern blacks was reaching terrible depths. The boxer's challenge to white manhood provoked widespread anger, and his relationships with white females drove his enemies in the North and nearly every white politician in the South to distraction. After the suicide of his first wife, Etta Terry Duryea, in 1912, Johnson courted

a number of other white women, especially Lucille Cameron. The federal government charged him with abduction, attempting to secure the defeat of Johnson that whites could not obtain in the ring. The "trial" proved a farce—"witnesses" refused to appear—and enraged whites outside the courthouse called for his death. Yet Johnson was acquitted. Still, *The Chicago Daily News* on October 19, 1912, reported that the mob screamed, "Kill him, Lynch him."

On November 7, 1912, the government then charged him with violating the Mann Act—transporting women across state lines for immoral purposes. Johnson refused to buckle. His dalliances provoked reactions even from several black leaders, including Booker T. Washington, who believed that the boxer's taste for white women not only was an insult to his own race but dangerously inflamed racial tensions, at a time when lynchings took place with disturbing regularity throughout the country. In fact, whites lynched several blacks in direct response to Johnson's relationships with white women. Politicians throughout the South, especially in the boxer's native Texas, called for whites to administer a "dose of Southern hospitality" to him.[15] Others declared their intention to charter a train for Chicago and promptly lynch the intolerable insult to whiteness.

When Johnson and Cameron married, hue and cry coursed through most state legislatures and even in Congress. Legislatures in ten states introduced bills outlawing racial intermarriage, and representatives introduced twenty-one bills into Congress to end the practice everywhere. One of Georgia's U.S. representatives, Seaborn A. Roddenbery, introduced legislation for a constitutional amendment to end such marriages. Seething with desire for vengeance, Roddenbery exclaimed that

Johnson's offenses represented an act more brutal, infamous, and degrading than anything that had occurred in the history of slavery.

Whites obtained some measure of revenge when a jury convicted Johnson of violating the Mann Act in May 1913 and a judge sentenced him to one year in jail. Released on a bond, Johnson fled to Europe, where he resumed his boxing career. Four years later, after squandering his fortune, Johnson returned to the United States and spent a year in the federal prison at Fort Leavenworth. He divorced Cameron in 1921, married another white woman, Irene Pineau, and opened the Club Deluxe in Harlem. Johnson, however, could not successfully manage the club and sold it. In 1923, it reopened as the Cotton Club.

The greatest fighter in the history of boxing before Joe Louis, Jack Johnson became a hero to many African Americans and to all true fans of the sport; equally important, his persecution by the government exposed the depths of American racial anxiety about black male sexuality and economic competition at the height of the Jim Crow era.

WOODROW WILSON AND FEDERAL SEGREGATION

In the August 1912 edition of *The Crisis,* W. E. B. Du Bois made a stunning endorsement for the upcoming presidential election. The events of the previous years had alienated many blacks from the "Party of Lincoln." Theodore Roosevelt (running in 1912 on the Bull Moose ticket) had ordered the Brownsville dismissals, severely damaging his base support among blacks, and his successor, William Howard Taft, had done nothing to help African Americans. Given Roosevelt's and Taft's records, Du Bois argued that African Americans should vote for the Democratic candidate, Woodrow Wilson. Wilson, Du Bois wrote, "will not advance the cause of oligarchy in the South, he will not seek further means of 'Jim Crow' insult, he will not dismiss black men wholesale from office, and he will remember that the Negro in the United States has a right to be heard and considered."

Approximately one hundred thousand African Americans voted for Wilson. (With a two-million-vote margin of victory, however, he did not need black support.) Wilson's first months in office showed that Du Bois and other black leaders had completely misjudged their candidate. Wilson, a native Virginian, held white supremacist beliefs and filled his cabinet with southern whites whose views were more extreme. At a cabinet meeting on April 11, 1913, Postmaster General Albert Burleson and Treasury Secretary William G. McAdoo announced plans to segregate their departments. Wilson approved, thus formalizing the racial segregation of the federal government.

President Woodrow Wilson, seated at left, with his cabinet. Secretary of State William Jennings Bryan faces him on the right.

Over the following months, officials moved black workers to basement, windowless offices or literally screened them off from whites. Blacks ate in separate cafeterias and used separate restrooms, often located far from their offices. At the same time, the government hired fewer blacks. In 1914, it began requiring applicants for Civil Service Commission positions to submit photographs of themselves.

African Americans who had supported Wilson at first wondered if the president knew about the changes instituted by his chosen officials. But the president confirmed their worst fears in a letter to Oswald Garrison Villard. Wilson supported segregation, he wrote, "with the idea that the friction, or rather the discontent and uneasiness which had prevailed in many of the departments would thereby be removed."[16] He also speciously asserted that segregation would actually protect blacks from discrimination. Blacks protested; even Booker T. Washington, with nothing to lose with a Democrat in office, publicly disagreed. Du Bois skewered Wilson in *The Crisis.* The NAACP and the National Equal Rights League collected signatures on petitions that they delivered to the White House. The two organizations hosted mass protest rallies across the North. Religious groups from around the world wrote Wilson in protest. Black newspapers, so often divided by their loyalties to Du Bois or Washington, united in publicizing the unequal conditions and criticizing the president. The federal government, once seen as the protector of civil rights, had betrayed African Americans. An increasing number of blacks doubted the reasonableness of accommodation and began to believe that only protest would prevent the further erosion of their citizenship rights.

PART ELEVEN

RENAISSANCE

1917–1928

WORLD WAR I AND THE GREAT MIGRATION

The Migration of the Negro, panel 1, by Jacob Lawrence, tempura on hardboard, 1940–41.

orld War I afforded African Americans an opportunity to demonstrate their loyalty to the government, their full embrace of American ideals, and their sense of citizenship, in spite of the horrors of Jim Crow segregation, peonage, and second-class status. Eugene J. Bullard (1895–1961), a black Georgian whose parents had been slaves, left for Europe before the war and became the first African American to fight in the conflict. Bullard served in the French Army's Moroccan Division of the 170th Infantry Regiment, where he received the Croix de Guerre for heroism at the Battle of Verdun. Wounded twice and declared unfit for the infantry, he requested assignment to flight training, eventually flew twenty missions, and shot down at least one German aircraft.

When the United States officially entered the war on April 6, 1917, blacks enlisted in droves. W. E. B. Du Bois, in one of his most controversial editorials, entitled "Close Ranks," encouraged blacks to "forget our special grievances and close our ranks shoulder to shoulder with our white fellow citizens and the allied nations that are fighting for democracy."[1] A great many did just that. More than two million blacks registered for the draft, constituting 13 percent of all draftees. About 370,000 blacks served in the armed forces during the war, over half in France, and with great distinction. One hundred seventy members of the 369th Infantry Regiment earned the Croix de Guerre from the French government. Blacks also displayed their musical prowess: James "Tim" Flynn's 350th Field Artillery Regiment and

James Reese Europe's marching band brought African American music like ragtime to new and often wildly enthusiastic European audiences—audiences free of prejudices about the art produced by African Americans.

Despite their importance to the war effort and their long history of military service, African Americans suffered extreme racism in the American armed forces. As in the Civil War, the army relegated them to segregated units, but now under the command of more than one thousand black officers. The Army Air Corps, the Marines, and the Red Cross Nurses' Corps excluded blacks altogether. White officers sometimes harassed and sometimes beat black soldiers, forced them to work as menial laborers, or relegated them to quartermaster duty, and their accommoda-

255

African American soldiers, 1917–18.

Lieutenant J. Tim Brymn, 1917–18. Part of a collection of World War I images W. E. B. Du Bois collected for a study of black soldiers.

tions and equipment sometimes did not match those of white soldiers. Their training at camps in the South occasionally provoked protests and even rioting because of locals' fears about teaching African American men to bear arms.

But battlefield experiences told only half the story. On the home front, African Americans were on the move. Even before the nation entered the war, northern factories had increased pro-duction, but they faced a labor shortage as immigration slowed and as, eventually, native-born men joined the military. With more work to do and fewer laborers to do it, industry clamored for employees. African Americans in the South responded eagerly, fleeing their farms and plantations in hopes of finding a better life in the northern urban centers. During what became known as the Great Migration, as many as one million black southerners moved to cities in the North, West, and Midwest.

This mass movement continued after the war, and by 1930 the total black urban population in the North had more than doubled since 1910; it had nearly tripled in the mid-Atlantic states (New York, New Jersey, and Pennsylvania), and it had quadrupled in the East North Central states (Ohio, Indiana, Illinois, Michigan, and Wisconsin). The effect on New York City was quite dramatic: between 1910 and 1930, Central Harlem's black population went from 17,995 to 147,141, or from 9.89 percent to 70.18 percent of the city's population, and New York state's tripled, from 134,191 to 412,814. These dramatic figures were replicated throughout northern urban communities.

African Americans established communication networks to facilitate this migration. The *Chicago Defender* in particular published stories and editorials about the North as a financial promised land and served as a sounding board for blacks needing help moving north or finding a job. Labor recruiters went south, often using unscrupulous methods to convince blacks to come work in their factories. Southern whites were furious; while they believed in the inferiority of blacks, they also depended on their cheap labor. Across the South

Black officers of the 367th Infantry, 92nd Division, in France, ca. 1918.

blacks formed migration clubs and pooled their resources to make the trip.

But once they reached the northern cities, the realities of life often fell far short of the promise—they met discrimination and violence from whites who resented their growing presence and competition in the marketplace. Nevertheless, the opportunities proved irresistible to millions of black women and men. Urban black workers could make up to five dollars a day—many times more than what they could sweat out on a southern plantation. Larger cities also provided independence from the eyes of whites, and black neighborhoods grew. Few expressed any desire to return to their old southern homes, except to gather up additional friends and family members. The Great Migration was a historic demographic shift. Only in the last decades of the twentieth century would more black people in the North migrate to the South than vice versa, reversing the pattern.

THE BIRTH OF A NATION, NAACP PROTESTS, AND THE FOUNDING OF THE SECOND KKK

Viewers of the 1915 film *The Birth of a Nation* could not help but marvel at its cinematic sophistication. Director D. W. Griffith had created a technical masterpiece far beyond what anyone had achieved before. Most films to that point lasted about fifteen minutes—*The Birth of a Nation* stretched for three hours and used twelve reels. While most films ran at storefront nickelodeons, *The Birth of a Nation* traveled around the country as a roadshow. It was the first film to be screened at the White House, an event hosted by Woodrow Wilson, who sympathized with its racist message. The film cost an unprecedented $100,000 to make, but the filmmakers recouped their investment by charging an equally unprecedented two dollars per ticket. Millions of people in the United States and around the world watched the film. The original music, dramatic acting, and complex direction left most of them stunned.

The film's visceral impact, however, went beyond flash. Originally titled *The Clansman* and based on the novel by Thomas Dixon, *The Birth of a Nation* presents a version of American history that resonated with much of its white audience. The Civil War has ended in disorder, and Reconstruction has brought "Negro rule" to the South. Chaos reigns as corrupt African Americans conquer legislatures and black rapists run rough-

Scene from *The Birth of a Nation,* 1915.

shod across the countryside. In one notable scene, a black character (played, like all the major black characters, by a white man in blackface) chases a white woman. Faced with jumping off a cliff or submitting to an attack, the woman plunges to her death.

Woodrow Wilson proclaimed that the film was "like writing history with lightning" and that its content was "all so terribly true." African Americans, on the other hand, were outraged. Du Bois denounced Griffith for his representations of the black man "either as an ignorant fool, a vicious rapist, a venal or unscrupulous politician or a faithful but doddering idiot."[2] Fearing that the film would only increase the tensions caused by the Great Migration, the NAACP called for its censorship. It blocked showings in Pasadena, California, in Wilmington, Delaware, and in Chicago; in Boston it joined William Monroe Trotter to prevent a screening there. In New York City, the NAACP, the Urban League, and white and black reformers organized a march but failed to move the mayor to stop the film.

Stone Mountain, Georgia, site of the Klan revival in 1915 and neo-Confederate hallowed ground.

Movie poster for *The Birth of a Nation,* 1915.

Ku Klux Klan parade, Washington, D.C., September 13, 1926. Note that representatives of Connecticut and Rhode Island are in the lead.

The Birth of a Nation dramatically energized the NAACP, but it also galvanized white supremacists, who organized new racist political groups. In Georgia it inspired a white man named William Joseph Simmons to look to a myth-laden past. On Thanksgiving night 1915, he and friends convened at Stone Mountain with a flag, a Bible, and a wooden cross. They set the cross ablaze as they declared themselves the Knights of the Ku Klux Klan, giving new life to this old, largely defunct fraternity. With crucial help from the Southern Publicity Organization, the new Klan enlisted more than one hundred thousand members by 1921, the majority from the white middle classes.

The revived Klan maintained its commitment to white supremacy, preserving Christianity, and suppressing African Americans, just as the Reconstruction-era Klan had done. Members also continued the tradition of vigilante violence. But during the 1920s the new Klan expanded its targets, in an effort to capitalize on the increasing fears of white Americans. It targeted Catholics and Jews and argued for "pure Americanism" in response to the rise of communism overseas and the increasing number of immigrants. This broad-based politics of fear found a ready audience in the South and in many other parts of the nation. By the middle of the decade, Klan membership had reached five million, and in 1926 the organization proudly marched through the nation's capital in a massive show of force.

Throughout the 1920s the new Klan relied on *The Birth of a Nation* to recruit members. Klaverns hosted screenings in New York, Washington, and Chicago, as well as across the South. In some cases, they even organized parades to promote the film; hooded members would march through town on the day of a screening. The NAACP found some success in blocking *The Birth of a Nation* in the 1920s, but the second Klan diminished only with the onset of the Great Depression. Still, even in the civil rights period, the Klan continued to terrorize African Americans.

RIOTS IN EAST ST. LOUIS AND HOUSTON; THE RESPONSE OF THE NAACP, 1917

Silent protest parade against the East St. Louis riots, New York City, 1917.

American mobilization for World War I inadvertently provided opportunities for economic and social mobility for the nation's blacks, begetting the Great Migration. But opportunities to find jobs in urban centers and to serve in the military also led to violent racial strife. The year 1917 witnessed two race riots that recalled the chaos in Springfield a decade earlier.

Southern blacks had streamed into industrial East St. Louis, Illinois, in search of work in the factories of Armour, Swift, and Aluminum Ore. These companies had defeated workers' attempts to organize labor unions, and Aluminum Ore had taken to replacing white workers with lower-paid black newcomers.

Economic fear combined with xenophobia to foster antiblack animus in working-class whites; that situation was only exacerbated when African Americans voted Republican, as working-class whites, for the most part, voted Democrat. On July 1, whites staged drive-by shootings at two black homes. African Americans resolved to fight back: when they saw another car full of whites approach them, they fired. This car, however, was filled with plainclothes policemen. Two of the detectives died of gunshot wounds. When the morning paper publicized the incident, whites stormed black neighborhoods looking for revenge.

For the next four days, the rioting was intense. Whites burned black homes and shot African Americans at will. They threw their victims' bodies into the Mississippi River; floating, bloated corpses later surfaced as a grim reminder of the murders. In the tragic final toll, thirty-nine blacks and eight whites had died; rioters had destroyed $400,000 worth of property. Six thousand blacks left the city.

On behalf of the NAACP, W. E. B. Du Bois and Martha Gruening, a Jewish suffragist, visited the city to conduct an investigation. Their twenty-four-page report came out in the September issue of *The Crisis,* but Oswald Garrison Villard proposed that the NAACP make a more immediate and dramatic response. Du Bois and James Weldon Johnson, NAACP field secretary, agreed and organized a massive silent protest in New York City. On July 10, almost ten thousand African Americans marched down Fifth Avenue. A photograph of the event—men wearing black, women and children dressed in white—circulated

East St. Louis riot, 1917.

around the country, drawing attention to this and other race-fueled violence. It also reinforced the NAACP's growing reputation as the nation's preeminent civil rights organization.

That same year violence also broke out in Houston, Texas. Local white police repeatedly beat and arrested black soldiers of the 24th Infantry Regiment stationed there at Camp Logan. One well-meaning soldier attempted to intervene in the police beating of an arrested black woman. The overall abuse proved to be more than the soldiers could tolerate, and on August 23 more than one hundred black troops marched to Houston and attacked white officers and citizens, killing seventeen whites; two blacks died during the riot. After quick proceedings, the army executed nineteen men and issued life prison sentences to sixty-three others. It was the largest court-martial in American history. Martha Gruening investigated this case as well. The NAACP helped fund the soldiers' defense and presented Woodrow Wilson with a petition of twelve thousand signatures, convincing the president to commute five of the death sentences.

The riots in East St. Louis and in Houston were just two of the many episodes of the racial violence in American cities, north and south, during the war years. They made plain the widespread fears of black social mobility, and the deep social and economic fissures in the American working class.

PAN-AFRICAN CONGRESS

At the end of 1918 W. E. B. Du Bois traveled to France for a firsthand look at the aftermath of the Great War. Only a few months had passed since he asked African Americans to "close ranks" around the war effort; the war's devastating casualties, and the poor treatment that blacks received in service to the nation, dealt a considerable blow to his reputation as a resolute voice speaking truth to power. While ostensibly collecting data for a book on the black wartime experience, Du Bois hoped to give all people of African descent a voice as world powers determined peace terms at Versailles. "I went to Paris," he wrote in *The Crisis,* "because today the destinies of mankind for a hundred years to come" would be settled there.[3]

Du Bois also intended to organize a Pan-African Congress, modeled on a conference he had attended in London in 1900. He enlisted the help of Blaise Diagne, a Senegalese general who was the first African to hold a seat in the French parliament. Diagne convinced a reluctant French government to allow the conference to convene.

The Pan-African Congress began on February 19, 1919, at the Grand Hotel in Paris. Fifty-eight delegates attended, most of whom had never visited Africa.

W. E. B. Du Bois, photograph by Cornelius M. Battey, 1918.

Pan-African Congress in Brussels, photograph by Presto, 1921.

Sixteen people, including a number of whites, represented the United States. Most of the African American delegates, including John Hope and Addie Hunton, had already been in France—the State Department refused to grant new passports for prospective black attendees. For three days the delegates discussed European colonization and how to ensure the rights of colonized Africans around the world. They called for a law "for the international protection of the natives of Africa."[4] They demanded that the fledgling League of Nations supervise new colonies and that it abolish slavery and capital punishment in Europe's African colonies. The delegates argued for fairer treatment of African peoples, but they stopped short of calling for self-determination or decolonization.

After the congress, Du Bois mailed the resolutions to Woodrow Wilson, at his request. But neither the United States nor the European powers formally adopted any of its suggestions. The Pan-African Congress did, however, set the tone for future protests. The congress continued to meet through the 1920s and then again in 1945. More immediately, it energized Du Bois and

Representatives of the 1921 Pan-African Congress.

Panel discussion at the Pan-African Congress, 1921. Du Bois is seated at the far right.

other blacks who had become disillusioned following the war.

In May 1919, Du Bois wrote another *Crisis* editorial, "Returning Soldiers," which served as a rebuttal to his controversial "Close Ranks" essay. He eloquently and passionately expressed the protest mood: "By the God of Heaven, we are cowards and jackasses if now that the war is over, we do not marshal every ounce of our brain and brawn to fight a sterner, longer, more unbending battle against the forces of hell in our own land. We return. We return from fighting. We return fighting." These words would inspire blacks as they faced legal segregation in the 1920s.

THE RED SUMMER, THE TULSA RACE RIOT, AND MORE

In the summer of 1919, just two years after the bloody confrontations in East St. Louis and Houston, twenty-six race riots convulsed American cities, leading NAACP field secretary James Weldon Johnson to coin the phrase "Red Summer."

On May 10, in Charleston, South Carolina, a group of white sailors killed a local black man in a fight. The sailors resisted arrest and, armed, stormed the city's black neighborhoods. Charleston's mayor demanded they return to their base, but the defiant sailors instead unleashed a maelstrom of violence. Black residents fought back with shots of their own. During the riot, two blacks died and seventeen were wounded, while no whites died and only eight suffered injuries.

Although Charleston blacks found some support in the mayor, those elsewhere found none. In Longview, Texas, whites shot to death a black man known to have a white lover, but city officials refused to investigate the crime. An

Mounted police escorting a man during the July 1919 Chicago riots.

anonymous protest letter appeared in the *Chicago Defender,* which local whites attributed to Samuel L. Jones, a black schoolteacher. Militants attacked him on July 10; the following day a mob descended on Jones's house but met

gunfire from blacks waiting inside. The outraged rioters responded by riding through black neighborhoods setting homes ablaze. Police arrested twenty whites and twenty blacks. Longview remained under martial law until July 18.

Seizure of men from Tulsa's black community, 1921.

Two of the country's largest cities also experienced race riots. In July, *The Washington Post* ran a false story about a black man who targeted white women for assault and called for off-duty police to protect the city. The result was a terrifying mob. From July 19 to July 23, whites attacked black citizens and ransacked their homes, ending their rampage only after the army intervened. Later that month in Chicago, a white man at a local beach thought a black man was swimming too close to the designated white area. He threw a large stone at the swimmer and killed him. The following two weeks of fighting killed 23 blacks and injured 342 others; 15 whites perished as well.

More than twenty other riots racked the nation that year. In a horrific case in Omaha, Nebraska, on September 28, whites killed a black prisoner, set his body on fire, and then posed for photos with the smoldering corpse. The *Chicago Defender* ran one of the pictures on its front page. Police arrested fifty-nine whites in connection with the killing and the subsequent riot. Days later in Elaine, Arkansas, violence erupted when black sharecroppers and tenant farmers attempted to form a branch of the Progressive Farmers and Household Union of America. Whites seeking

to punish them for daring to organize killed at least twenty-five blacks.

One of the deadliest race riots in the nation's history occurred in Tulsa, Oklahoma, from May 31 to June 1, 1921. It began in an unlikely venue: an elevator. The bumpy elevator shook, causing nineteen-year-old African American Dick Rowland to accidentally step on the foot of the white elevator operator. She began to fall, but Rowland caught her. The woman, Sarah Page,

then accused Rowland of assault. When police took Rowland to jail, a mob stood waiting to lynch him. Hundreds of African American residents of the Greenwood neighborhood arrived at the jail too, finding the white mob growing in number. When a white man tried to wrench a gun from a black man, a firefight ensued, killing ten whites and two blacks. Rioting erupted, in which white assailants fired guns randomly into black homes. The mob burned

Results of the Tulsa riot, 1921.

263

Unidentified lynching of an
African American, 1925.

Destruction of Rosewood, Florida, 1923.

churches and destroyed middle-class homes and stores in forty-four blocks. Rather than bring order, police deputized members of the white mob, who rounded up thousands of blacks into makeshift internment centers. By the time the riot ended the following day, the mob had destroyed more than $1.5 million in property belonging to African Americans. Newspapers estimated that sixty-eight blacks and nine whites died in the fighting.

Postwar rioting in the rural South continued long past 1919. In the first week of 1923, furious violence came to the black community of Rosewood, Florida. White supremacists across the state had mobilized to destroy what they saw as African Americans pushing beyond their rightful place. Like many southern race riots, the Rosewood massacre resulted from whites responding to an alleged attack on a white woman. Fannie Taylor reported the attack on New Year's Day, but she could not identify any traits of the attacker, not even his race. Nevertheless, local whites assumed he was black and prepared for war. More than three hundred whites from Sumner and other surrounding communities traveled to Rosewood and systematically burned it to the ground, home by home. Six blacks and two whites died. The black residents of Rosewood had no choice but to flee.

White rioters most frequently justified their actions by claiming that they were seeking to punish an alleged black rapist, but the destruction of the most prosperous sections of these black communities revealed their economic motivation. Lynching, race riots, and indeed antiblack racism itself were the certain legacy of slavery and of the peonage system that replaced it.

MARCUS MOSIAH GARVEY

Perhaps no figure in post–World War I black America inspired more admiration and animus than Marcus Mosiah Garvey. A native of Jamaica, Garvey had formed the Universal Negro Improvement Association (UNIA) in Kingston in August 1914. Washington's autobiography *Up from Slavery* had profoundly influenced him, and he intended to use his new organization to promote industrial education. At the same time, he argued that all people of African descent should unite to overthrow white oppression around the globe.

In 1916, Garvey traveled to New York to bring his message of African solidarity to American blacks. In Harlem he founded the New York division of the UNIA. His fiery speeches protested the white injustices visited upon black people, and stridently and unapologetically called for black pride, for "Africa for the Africans," and for American Negro emigration to the motherland. His appeals found broad and enthusiastic audiences, both in black urban areas and throughout the South. "Up you mighty race," he instructed listeners desperate for relief from race riots, the spreading Klan, and Jim Crow segregation: "You may do as you will."[5] Garvey was primarily concerned with remaking American blacks' self-image in their own imaginations and shaping them into a coherent, united political force. His poems, such as "The Black Mother" and "The Black Woman," stressed the inherent nobility and beauty of African American women—black women held high positions in the UNIA. By 1920, when the UNIA held a national convention in Harlem, Garvey and his supporters claimed that two million blacks had joined the organization. Membership peaked three years later, reportedly

Marcus M. Garvey (1887–1940).

with six million members, all of whom Garvey attempted to link together with his lively and popular newspaper, *The Negro World*.

Despite his popularity, Garvey and the UNIA confronted a number of problems. For one, his "Back to Africa" message alienated many African American civil rights leaders. Garvey wanted to relocate blacks to Liberia, but the American leadership opposed that goal as another form of colonization. Making matters worse, in 1922 Garvey met with leaders of the Ku Klux Klan and voiced his opposition to desegregation and racial mixing. Prominent black activists responded with a "Garvey Must Go" campaign. Indeed, during these years, the only thing that black activists like Du Bois, A. Philip Randolph, Robert Abbott, and Cyril Briggs could fully agree upon was disdain for Marcus Garvey. The U.S. government shared this opinion; J. Edgar Hoover and the fledgling Bureau of Investigation monitored Garvey and the UNIA closely.

Financial ineptitude ruined the organization. In 1919, Garvey founded the Black Star Line, a steamship company designed to be the commercial link among black people in Africa, the Caribbean, and the United States. For five dollars, blacks could purchase stock in the company: Garvey intended to use

Universal Negro Improvement Association parade, 1924.

this start-up capital to buy more ships and increase the power of the line. Garvey had many noble qualities, but he was not a businessman. He overpaid for unseaworthy vessels, and when the ships failed mechanically, he lacked the money to fix them. He lied to potential investors, telling them that he owned more ships than he actually did. The stock became worthless, and investors accused Garvey of mail fraud. Seeing the opportunity to end Garvey's influence, the federal government convicted him of mail fraud in 1923. (He represented himself at the trial.) He went to prison in 1925. Two years later, the government deported him to Jamaica.

Garvey's influence has lived on through generations of African Americans. He created the largest mass movement of black people in American history. His calls for black pride and economic independence would fuel future black nationalist and African solidarity

Stock certificate in the Black Star Line, 1920.

movements. Without a doubt, he was the father of contemporary pan-Africanism. And his repression by the FBI was a fore-taste of more detailed and brutal repression of black political leaders during the civil rights and Black Power eras.

CLAUDE MCKAY AND "IF WE MUST DIE"

Claude McKay, author of some of the most sophisticated African American poetry in the Harlem Renaissance, was born in Sunny Ville, Jamaica, in 1890. His parents, fearing they could not provide him with an education, sent him to live with his schoolteacher brother. Under his tutelage, McKay began writing poetry and came to the attention of William Jekyll, a British-born benefactor who encouraged McKay's writing career. In 1912, McKay published two books of poetry: *Songs of Jamaica* and *Constab Ballads*. That same year, at age twenty-one, he left for the United States, where he attended Tuskegee Institute and then Kansas State College.

But in 1914 McKay abandoned school and moved to Harlem, where he worked low-paying jobs while continuing to write. He made friends with white and black radicals in Greenwich Village, and the socialist editor Max Eastman tapped him to coedit and eventually edit *The Liberator,* a radical monthly that Eastman established after the government closed down his radical journal *The Masses* during the First World War. MacKay never joined the Communist Party, but early in his career he expressed great sympathy with its ideals and even visited Moscow. His sympathies with socialism, and his embrace of an unflinching realism in his fiction, put him at odds with many other African American activists,

especially members of the NAACP. During the 1920s McKay emerged as one of

Claude McKay (1890–1948).

the most accomplished of the Harlem Renaissance writers. His book of poetry, *Harlem Shadows,* published in 1922, was very well received. He wrote a novel about the mores and manners of the black working class, *Home to Harlem,* in 1928, which critics as dissimilar as W. E. B. Du Bois and Marcus Garvey trashed for fulfilling white primitivist fantasies of the black lower-class other.

But it was an earlier work of his for which he will be remembered. In 1919, McKay was searching for a way to respond to the unprecedented anti-black violence of the Red Summer. His sublime sonnet, "If We Must Die," gave poignant voice to growing African American militancy and served as a call to arms. "If we must die," it begins, "let it not be like hogs / Hunted and penned in an inglorious spot." According to McKay, African Americans had to retaliate in order to preserve their dignity:

> If we must die, O let us nobly die
> So that our precious blood may
>   not be shed
> In vain; then even the monsters
>   we defy
> Shall be constrained to honor us
>   though dead!

He closed with this inspiring cry: "Like men we'll face the murderous, cowardly pack, / Pressed to the wall, dying but fighting back!"[6]

McKay's poem resonated with African Americans, and it is still one of the most anthologized poems from the Harlem Renaissance. It would serve as a call to arms to other oppressed peoples. Winston Churchill quoted the poem during his famous address to Congress during World War II, the poem was widely anthologized and read during the 1960s Black Power era, and it was recited by inmates during the Attica Prison Riot of 1971.

SADIE ALEXANDER, EVA DYKES, GEORGIANA SIMPSON, AND BESSIE COLEMAN

In the early 1920s, a number of extraordinary African American women reached unprecedented levels of success. In 1921 alone, three black women earned Ph.D. degrees. A Philadelphia native from a distinguished and accomplished family line, Sadie Tanner Mossell Alexander pursued graduate work in economics at the University of Pennsylvania. Eager to explain the economic implications of the Great Migration, she wrote *The Standard of Living among One Hundred Negro Migrant Families in Philadelphia* as her doctoral thesis, becoming the first African American woman to earn a Ph.D. in this country.

Although she earned her doctorate and later published her dissertation, the barriers of race and gender thwarted Alexander when she tried to find employment in economics. Undaunted, she enrolled in the University of Pennsylvania Law School and became its first black female graduate in 1927. She served on the board of the National Urban League and on the national advisory council of the American Civil Liberties Union. She also worked on official presidential committees, contributing to *To Secure These Rights* under Harry S Truman, serving on the Lawyers' Committee for Civil Rights under Law under John F. Kennedy, and becoming the chair of the White House Conference on Aging under Jimmy Carter.

Eva Beatrice Dykes earned a bachelor's degree in English from Howard University in 1914, whereupon an uncle convinced her to continue her studies at Radcliffe College. She excelled, getting her second B.A. in 1916, a master's degree in 1917, and finally her Ph.D. in English philology in 1921. Dykes pursued the life of an academic, teaching at Howard and later at Oakwood College in Huntsville, Alabama. In 1942, she published *The Negro in English Romantic Thought; or, A Study of Sympathy for the Oppressed,* which analyzed the portrayal of African Americans in English literature.

Georgiana R. Simpson took a more circuitous route to her Ph.D. Born in

Sadie Tanner Mossell Alexander (1898–1989).

Washington, D.C., around 1865, she began working as a teacher in the local public schools in 1885, spending time with German immigrants. Intrigued, she traveled to Germany and studied the language for more than a year. To further her knowledge of German culture and language, she enrolled at the University of Chicago, where she received

Eva Beatrice Dykes
(1893–1986), ca. 1917.

Georgiana Rose Simpson
(1865?–1944).

Bessie Coleman
(1892–1926).

her bachelor's degree in 1911 and her master's in 1920. The following year, her dissertation *Herder's Conception of "Das Volk"* earned her a Ph.D. in German literature. She taught at Dunbar High School in Washington, then received a professorship at Howard University, where she taught from 1931 to 1939.

Bessie Coleman won distinction as a graduate of a different sort. Coleman had grown up in Texas before moving to Chicago in 1912 at the age of twenty. After the First World War, her brother Johnny recounted stories of wartime

heroism and the fact that he had seen female pilots in France. Flying became her life's ambition, but no aviation school in the United States would accept her. On the advice of Robert Abbott, publisher of the *Chicago Defender*—and with his financial support—she traveled to France to attend an aviation school run by an aircraft-manufacturing company. She took lessons from a French pilot who reportedly had shot down thirty-one German planes. She earned her pilot's license from the French Fédération Aéronautique Internationale

in 1921, becoming the first licensed African American woman pilot. She returned to the United States and began a career as a stunt pilot, which unfortunately led to her death in 1926.

The accomplishments of Alexander, Dykes, Simpson, and Coleman demonstrated, in an era of rigid male chauvinism toward all women, that black women possessed the ability, talent, and fortitude to do anything that men—white or black—aspired to do.

HARRY PACE, TANNER AND FULLER AT THE NYPL, ROBESON IN *THE EMPEROR JONES,* HOWARD UNIVERSITY GALLERY OF ART

The Jazz Age and the Harlem Renaissance saw the flowering of the black arts, both inside Harlem and across the nation.

Atlanta University graduate Harry Pace had spent the first two decades of the twentieth century in exceptional jobs: collaborating with W. E. B. Du Bois on the *Moon Illustrated Weekly,* the nation's first black weekly maga-

zine, teaching school in Georgia and Missouri, and working for banks and insurance companies in Memphis and Atlanta. He moved to New York City in 1917, where he struck a partnership with the noted bluesman W. C. Handy; their business venture, called Pace and Handy Music, distributed sheet music. Four years later Pace left the collaboration and started a new record company,

Black Swan Records, the country's first black-owned label.

Making Black Swan—its name a tribute to the great nineteenth-century concert singer Elizabeth Greenfield—into a commercial success proved an uphill climb; whites controlled the recording business, including distribution and pressing plants, and they viewed Pace as an upstart, destined to fail. But in the

Bessie Smith (1894?–1937). The daughter of a Baptist preacher, Smith escaped grinding poverty to become one of the queens of blues during the 1920s and 1930s. Over the course of her career she sold between eight and ten million records. Tragically, she died in a car crash in Clarksdale, Mississippi. This photograph is dated 1936.

following two years the phenomenal popularity of one singer, Ethel Waters, had sales that carried the label. Pace believed, however, that the surprisingly popular radio industry would curtail the record business. That was his first mistake. His second was to fail to sign Bessie Smith to a contract. She would go on to become the nation's most famous black singer and would launch Colum-

bia Records. Meanwhile, white-owned labels responded to Black Swan's popularity and signed promising black artists. Outmaneuvered, Pace sold Black Swan to the Paramount Company in 1925 and returned to the insurance business. Despite its brief first incarnation, Black Swan Records would inspire many African Americans to pursue their dreams in music, both as artists and as producers.

Black artists in those years made other breakthroughs. In 1921, the 135th Street Branch of the New York Public Library hosted an exhibition, featuring the work of Henry Ossawa Tanner, and auguring the Harlem Renaissance. Tanner's *The Banjo Player* and other paintings proved extremely popular. The exhibition also featured the art of one of Tanner's students, Meta Vaux Warrick Fuller. Fuller had learned the art of sculpting at schools from Philadelphia to Paris, and she pioneered the use of African and African American themes in *The Spirit of Emancipation, The Awakening of Ethiopia,* and *A Silent Protest Against Mob Violence.*

In 1923, white real estate magnate and philanthropist William E. Harmon established the Harmon Foundation in New York City. The Harmon Foundation sponsored a wide array of activities geared toward helping African Americans, including issuing student loans, funding playgrounds, assisting the disabled, and noting black achievement. But it would become best known for promoting Africans and African Americans in the fine arts. In 1928, it organized its first exhibition solely of African American art; the show toured the country in 1931. William H. Johnson, a South Carolinian who studied art in Paris, returned to the United States in 1929 and entered six of his pieces in the Harmon Foundation competition and won the gold medal. He would work for the WPA during the Depression.

The year after the Harmon Foundation was created, Eugene O'Neill's widely heralded play *The Emperor Jones*

The 135th Street branch of the New York Public Library, photograph by Wurts Brothers.

made its debut in London with the African American actor Paul Robeson in the title role. Robeson's performance brought him worldwide acclaim, and he went on to find enormous success as a singer and actor. He would use his success as a weapon to fight for civil rights and, more controversially during the McCarthy era, against American imperialism.

As the decade came to a close, How-

Logo of Black Swan Records.

Paul Robeson (1898–1976). Athlete, actor, and singer, Robeson was also a leader of the struggle for African American civil rights. His many acting roles, especially as Othello, won him international acclaim. His acting career began in 1924 in Eugene O'Neill's *The Emperor Jones,* and the next year he sang at Carnegie Hall. Photograph ca. 1930s.

James V. Herring (1887–1969). Herring, a landscape and seascape artist, founded Howard University's art department in 1922 and in 1930 organized the university art gallery. He opened the Barnett-Aden Gallery in Washington, D.C., in 1943, the earliest institution to collect, preserve, and exhibit African American art. Unfortunately, it closed after Herring's death. Portrait by James A. Porter, oil on canvas, 1923.

ard University stepped forward to further document black artistic accomplishments. In 1928, the Howard University Gallery of Art became the nation's first art gallery owned and operated by African Americans. James V. Herring, who had founded Howard's department of art in 1921, took over as the first director, and one of his first acquisitions was one of Henry Ossawa Tanner's last creations, *Return from the Crucifixion*. The gallery would showcase the best in African American art throughout the twentieth century.

Street Musicians, by William H. Johnson, silkscreen, ca. 1940. Johnson (1901–70) left his native South Carolina in 1918 for New York City to become an artist. He worked at many menial jobs until discovered by the National Academy of Design in 1921. In 1929, he entered six pieces of his artwork into the Harmon Foundation competition and won a gold medal. He traveled extensively in Europe and during the Depression worked for the WPA.

SCHOMBURG COLLECTION AND *OPPORTUNITY*

For members of the National Urban League, the Red Summer of 1919 and later race riots reinforced the fact that urban blacks needed help immediately. From his professorship at Atlanta University two decades before, W. E. B. Du Bois had argued that expanding the social science research agenda could help solve black social problems. In 1921, with an $8,000 grant from the Carnegie Corporation, the Urban League established a department of research, led by Charles S. Johnson of Chicago. The department streamlined the league's surveys and fieldwork and used the findings to assist blacks in need and to target areas for new Urban League branches.

As the Urban League amassed data, the leadership considered how to make the findings accessible to the public. In 1926, it brokered a $10,000 grant from the Carnegie Corporation to the New York Public Library to buy Arthur Schomburg's collection of books and artifacts on African American life. Schomburg himself served as curator for the collection from 1932 until his death in 1938. Two years later, the NYPL named the division in his honor. The Schomburg collection gave New York residents and scholars around the world access to an unparalleled archive of information about the black world.

In 1921, the Urban League's Department of Research began publishing the bimonthly *Urban League Bulletin,* edited by Johnson. It soon expanded into a monthly magazine, and, on January 1, 1923, the first issue of *Opportunity: Journal of Negro Life* became available at bookstores and newsstands. Within four years, the magazine's circulation would peak at about eleven thousand. *Opportunity* served a number of goals for the Urban League: it publicized League announcements and news; published recommendations and information about programs based on the results of the organization's research; and examined the social, economic, and health problems that plagued blacks in America's cities. Reflecting the organization's founding values, the articles in *Opportunity* stressed that blacks would find success through hard work, self-help, humility, and proper dress and behavior. The magazine hoped to convince both blacks and whites of the value of social cooperation across the color line.

Equally important, *Opportunity* also provided African American writers and artists a venue for expression. Here, the magazine's influence transcended its circulation statistics, serving as the launching pad for a number of great writers who would be pivotal figures in the Harlem Renaissance. Langston Hughes, Countee Cullen, Claude McKay, and Alain Locke all published early work in its pages. From 1924 to 1926, the

Charles S. Johnson (1893–1956). After graduating from Virginia Union College, Johnson attended the University of Chicago to study sociology. In 1920, he moved to New York and thereafter assumed the editorship of *Opportunity*. He published many books on African American society and established a race relations institute at Fisk University.

magazine held literary contests, just as Du Bois's *Crisis* did. The dinners at which the winners were announced were major cultural events in the black

The Schomburg collection.

and liberal white elite artistic communities. Johnson organized awards and banquets as ways for black writers to connect with white publishers and thus disseminate their work to larger audiences. Hughes later wrote in his memoir *The Big Sea* that Charles S. Johnson "did more to encourage and develop Negro writers during the 1920s than anyone else in America."[7] Even though Johnson left the magazine in 1928, *Opportunity* continued until 1949 to illuminate the challenges to and the accomplishments of urban blacks.

A. PHILIP RANDOLPH, *THE MESSENGER*, BROTHERHOOD OF SLEEPING CAR PORTERS

Asa Philip Randolph was born in Crescent City, Florida, on April 15, 1889. Beginning in 1903, he attended the Cookman Institute, where his studies convinced him to search beyond the menial jobs open to him in the South. So he moved to New York City in 1911. Working during the day and attending City College at night, he fell into the city's network of radical socialists. He formed an immediate bond with Chandler Owen, a law student at Columbia University, who shared his conviction that black workers lacked a public voice. In November 1917, they began publishing *The Messenger*, self-described as "the only magazine of scientific radicalism in the world published by Negroes."[8]

America's first black socialist magazine stridently called for economic equality and unionization across racial lines. As Randolph wrote in the editorial "Our Reason for Being," published in 1919, "First, as workers, black and white, we all have one common interest, viz., the getting of more wages, shorter hours, and better working conditions." Randolph and Owen also endorsed pacifism, a controversial opinion during World War I and one that put the editors at odds with W. E. B. Du Bois. Their opinions earned them jail time after they published an antiwar article titled "Pro-Germanism Among Negroes." In a report on radical black publications, the Department of Justice called the magazine "by long odds the most able and the most danger-

Chandler Owen (1889–1967). Owen graduated from the Virginia Union University and attended New York's Columbia University and the New York School of Philanthropy. During the Red Scare of 1919, his was a major voice in opposing the repression. He and Randolph rejected the accommodationism of Booker T. Washington and found even W. E. B. Du Bois insufficiently militant. Owen took Marcus Garvey as a primary target of criticism, seeing his interest in Africa as an impediment to the achievement of full civil rights for African Americans.

Asa Philip Randolph (1889–1979). Editor, labor leader, and civil rights activist, Randolph graduated from the Cookman Institute and moved to New York in 1911. In 1916, he joined the Socialist Party, where he met Chandler Owen. His career in organizing black labor took a major step with the founding of *The Messenger* in 1917. He soon took over as head of the Brotherhood of Sleeping Car Porters and gained affiliation with the American Federation of Labor, a major accomplishment. Perhaps his most important accomplishments after World War II were helping to organize the 1963 March on Washington and exposing the racism in the modern American labor movement. Photograph ca. 1911 or 1912.

ous of all the Negro publications."[9] In an attempt to silence it, the federal government even suspended *The Messenger's* mailing privileges.

In the face of government persecution, Randolph continued to fight for black rights, particularly for black workers. Previously, he had attempted to organize African American laborers into unions, but in 1925 he began to organize the porters at the Pullman Company, perhaps his most important career deci-

"Why Negroes Should Be Socialists," from *The Messenger,* November 1919.

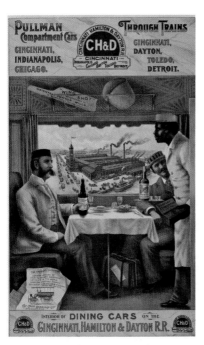

Pullman Compartment Cars, advertisement. The illustration shows the cars' luxurious appointments, and a Pullman porter.

sion. Working as a Pullman porter was one of the most prestigious jobs available to an African American working-class male. While the pay of black porters was lower than that of most of their white counterparts, they easily made enough money to support their families comfortably, and they benefited from travel across the country. Still, they hoped for better pay and better treatment, and they wanted the benefits that white porters enjoyed, such as money for food and lodging while on the rails.

Since African Americans made up the majority of Pullman porters, Randolph saw them as a good target for unionization. He organized the Brotherhood of Sleeping Car Porters (BSCP) on August 25, 1925, and *The Messenger* became its official magazine. More than half of the porters joined the union, and the wives and female relatives of union members organized "ladies' auxiliaries" to lead fund-raising efforts. For years, however, the Pullman Company ignored the union and its demands. Believing it a lost cause, a number of members quit the BSCP, and *The Messenger* ceased publication.

But the election of Franklin Delano Roosevelt in 1932 and his New Deal policies, designed to combat the worst of the Great Depression, brought renewed interest in the union. Workers scored a victory in 1933 with the passage of the National Industrial Relations Act, section 7A of which legalized collective bargaining. As a result, the American Federation of Labor recognized the BSCP in 1935. Two years later, on August 25, 1937, the Pullman Company signed a contract with the union, which had begun publishing a new magazine, *The Black Worker.* These successes made Randolph one of the nation's foremost civil rights activists.

ALAIN LOCKE AND *THE NEW NEGRO*

The son of a lawyer and a schoolteacher, Alain Leroy Locke (1885–1954) understood the value of an education and the promise of economic mobility. Born in Philadelphia on September 13, 1885, he attended Central High School and the Philadelphia School of Pedagogy. He attended Harvard University, where he earned his bachelor's degree in 1907. That year Locke became the first African American Rhodes Scholar and moved to England to study at Hertford College at the University of Oxford. He joined the faculty of Howard University in 1912. With W. E. B. Du Bois's encouragement, he returned to Harvard, where he earned his Ph.D. in philosophy in 1918.

Locke's earliest writings engage the intersected issues of race and class. The same year he earned his doctorate, he wrote "The Role of the Talented Tenth," an essay in support of Du Bois's central idea concerning the responsibilities of the college-educated Negro toward the larger community. Locke especially believed that nurturing black literature and the arts would help lift all African Americans. His public profile grew in the early 1920s, when he began writing for Charles S. Johnson's *Opportunity* magazine. In March 1924, Locke served as master of ceremonies at a

THE NEW NEGRO
AN INTERPRETATION

EDITED BY ALAIN LOCKE

BOOK
DECORATION
AND
PORTRAITS
BY
WINOLD
REISS

ALBERT AND CHARLES BONI
NEW YORK   1925

The New Negro: An Interpretation, cover.

Alain Leroy Locke, oil on canvas by
Betsy Graves Reyneau, ca. 1943–44.

literary banquet that Johnson organized at the Civic Club in Manhattan. Paul Kellogg, the editor of the magazine *Survey Graphic,* found Locke so impressive that he asked him to edit a special issue of the magazine on the transformations occurring in Harlem as a result of the Great Migration and the Jazz Age. Locke embraced the opportunity to showcase the artistic works of African Americans, to encourage even more black artistic achievement, and to counter racist stereotypes. The Harlem issue of *Survey Graphic* was published in March 1925, signaling the birth of the Harlem Renaissance.

To bring the work of black artists to an even larger audience, Locke expanded the issue of *Survey Graphic* and published it that same year as the seminal anthology *The New Negro: An Interpreta-*

tion. "The pulse of the Negro world," he wrote in the preface, "has begun to beat in Harlem." Harlem, Locke emphasized, had become the national center for black artistic and intellectual achievement. It was more than a neighborhood in Manhattan; it was a metaphor and a conduit for the creation of black literature and art in a movement that could counter racial prejudice by demonstrating black intellectual parity with white Americans. "Harlem has the same role to play for the New Negro as Dublin has had for the New Ireland or Prague for the New Czechoslovakia," Locke asserted.[10]

Through its essays, fiction, poetry, and drama, its stunning visual images (some in color) and its germinal cultural criticism, the anthology served as a manifesto for the burgeoning Harlem Renaissance, also known as the New Negro Movement. Locke was a brilliant anthologist and propagandist. He published short stories by Zora Neale Hurston, a selection from Jean Toomer's pathbreaking novel *Cane,* and poems by Langston Hughes, James Weldon Johnson, Georgia Johnson, and Arna Bontemps. Essays by Hughes, Locke, and J. A. Rodgers explicated the sublimity of African American music, while Arthur Schomburg, Locke, and others trumpeted the achievements of black history and folklore. James Weldon Johnson and W. A. Domingo offered social commentary about the role of Harlem in the American imagination, and Paul Kellogg analyzed "The Negro Pioneers." Kelly Miller discussed the role and accomplishments of Howard University, the "capstone of Negro education."[11]

Not to be outdone, Robert R. Morton related the histories of Hampton and Tuskegee. Melville Herskovits and Walter White examined the consequences of being black in a white-dominated country. Elise Johnson McDougald pondered "The Task of Negro Womanhood." W. E. B. Du Bois, fittingly, had the last word with the essay "The Negro Mind Reaches Out."

One cannot overestimate the impact of *The New Negro,* or of Locke's role as the veritable dean of the Harlem Renaissance in shaping African American literary history from the 1920s through the Black Arts Movement of the 1960s. *The New Negro* remains an enduring, resonant portrait of the flowering of African American intellect and art during the Jazz Age. Until his death in 1954, Locke continued to publish criticism of art and literature, philosophical essays, and analyses of African American culture and education.

LOUIS ARMSTRONG AND DUKE ELLINGTON

Among its many other ramifications, the Great Migration transformed the cultural complexion of northern urban America. It brought to New York, Chicago, and other cities men and women (such as Mamie and Bessie Smith) who would invent or master the entirely new musical genres of classic blues and jazz. Of these several artists, none was more original or innovative than Louis Armstrong.

Louis "Satchmo" Armstrong was born into a poor New Orleans family on August 4, 1901. His interest in music seems to have begun when his misadventures landed him in the New Orleans Colored Waifs' Home for Boys between 1913 and 1914, where he received music lessons. By 1918 he had begun playing trumpet and cornet professionally, winning the friendship of noted musician Joe "King" Oliver. Four years later, Armstrong joined Oliver's Creole Jazz Band in Chicago, where they played the Lincoln Gardens Café. Armstrong's visibility rose dramatically in 1924, when he moved to New York City to join the Fletcher Henderson Orchestra, the country's most famous African American band. During his performances at the Roseland Ballroom, he electrified audiences with his unique timbre, rhythm, and style. He also cut jazz records with the accomplished saxophonist Sidney Bechet.

In 1925, Armstrong returned to Chicago, where he formed a new band with his second wife, Lillian Hardin. The Hot Five (later the Hot Seven, when they added a bassist and a drummer) recorded a number of classic songs, including "Heebie Jeebies," "Skid-Dat-De-Dat," and "Hotter Than That." In 1929, he moved back to New York and then took his act on the road. He turned to big band music

and rapidly became one of America's most popular musicians. His fame soon stretched beyond music: he became an icon in the film industry, appearing in nearly fifty motion pictures over the next four decades.

Armstrong did receive criticism for playing stereotypical, diminutive roles in films like *Rhapsody in Black and Blue* (1932) and *Pennies from Heaven* (1936), and for using black vernacular humor (sometimes attacked as a form of minstrelsy) in his performances. But Armstrong was a staunch supporter of the civil rights movement and quite publicly and forcefully voiced his hatred of Jim Crow restrictions. While his later career lacked the stunning innovation of his early years—an exception being the poignant and wildly popular vocal "What a Wonderful World," recorded near his death—the genius of his originality cannot be gainsaid. He was one of the two pivotal figures in the early history of jazz.

Just as Louis Armstrong parlayed

Louis Armstrong (1901–71), photograph taken in New York by William P. Gottlieb in the summer of 1946.

his big band success into a film career, Edward Kennedy "Duke" Ellington rode his to superstardom. Duke Elling-

Louis Armstrong and his Hot Five band.

Edward Kennedy Ellington
(1899–1974).

Duke Ellington.

ton was born to a middle-class family in Washington, D.C. As a teenager, he developed an interest in music and at seventeen began playing piano professionally. In 1923 he moved to New York City and made his name playing "jungle" music, characterized by the growling trumpet sounds and twisting rhythms of black primitivist modernism. In 1927 he began a residency at the Cotton Club, performing for its all-white audience.

But Ellington's music traveled well beyond Harlem and New York City through the new medium of radio. Beginning in 1927, the city's radio station, WHN, broadcast his performances. When CBS radio began playing them weekly, the entire country could listen to "Black and Tan Fantasy," "Mood Indigo," and "Creole Love Call," classic compositions that introduced the broad swath of the American public to Ellington as a major American artist. Ellington's performance of the jazz symphony *Black, Brown, and Beige* at Carnegie Hall in 1943 was a landmark in African American history. Ellington's career in music continued for more than fifty years as he and his band toured the world many times over and wrote and performed hit records at an astounding pace. Though awarded a Pulitzer Prize for Music only posthumously, during his lifetime Ellington received the Presi-

dential Medal of Freedom in 1969 and the French Legion of Honor in 1973. He was an icon of all that was elegant in the history of jazz.

Together Duke Ellington and Louis Armstrong perhaps did more than any other Harlem Renaissance artists to fundamentally transform American popular culture. Ken Burns, in his monumental film documentary *Jazz*, would compare Armstrong and Ellington's role in the history of jazz to that of Beethoven and Bach in the history of Western classical music. Their music constitutes the double helix structure of jazz's DNA.

PAUL ROBESON

Like James Weldon Johnson, Paul Robeson was truly a Renaissance man, a man of enormous talents, gifted in a wide variety of professions. Born in Princeton, New Jersey, on April 9, 1898, Robeson excelled in his studies and in 1914 earned a scholarship to Rutgers College, only the third African American to attend the school. At Rutgers he found academic and athletic success, graduating as valedictorian in 1919 and named a national All-American in football in 1917 and 1918.

After completing his degree, Robeson enrolled at Columbia University Law School and earned money to pay his tuition by playing football for the Akron Pros and the Milwaukee Badgers. At the urging of his wife, he also pursued his passion for acting. He joined a Greenwich Village theater group called the Provincetown Players, where he fortuitously met the playwright Eugene O'Neill. In 1924, O'Neill's masterpiece *The Emperor Jones* premiered in London with Robeson playing the title role. His performance brought him worldwide acclaim, and he continued acting in plays like *All God's Chillun Got Wings* (1924) and *Othello* (1943). He also starred in *Show Boat* (Broadway 1932, film 1936) and toured the country performing concerts, astonishing audiences with his sonorous and resonant baritone voice. His records sold phenomenally well.

Robeson defined himself as a committed political activist as well as an artist, and his politics shaped his performances. He sang primarily African American spirituals and folk songs, even when asked to perform classical numbers, and accepted only acting roles that he felt dignified African Americans. His politics would shape—and haunt—the remainder of his life.

Paul Robeson (1898–1976). Photograph by Carl Van Vechten, June 1, 1944.

He discovered socialism through George Bernard Shaw in 1928. Distressed by the racism he experienced at Rutgers, in law school, and in the entertainment world, he left America for Europe and developed particular admiration for pan-Africanism and for the Soviet Union; even when he returned to the United States during World War II, he would maintain his support of the Soviet Union. In the 1930s he led efforts to promote international equality and to undermine fascism. In 1937, he helped found the International Council on African Affairs, which morphed into the Council on African Affairs five years later. He chaired the organization, which counted among its ranks W. E. B. Du Bois, Ralph Bunche, and Mary McLeod Bethune. The CAA protested colonialism, promoted pan-African consciousness, and called for greater economic assistance to Africa.

After World War II Robeson's politics became a severe liability in the eyes of the U.S. government. While the nation had allied with the Soviet Union during the war, the postwar years ushered in extreme tensions and the Cold War between the two superpowers. An unprecedented Red Scare, led by Senator Joseph McCarthy of Wisconsin, swept the nation. Anti-communists equated international civil rights organizations with communism, and government officials targeted Robeson.

In 1946, Robeson appeared before a legislative committee in California to answer questions under oath about his relationship to communism. He denied joining the Communist Party, but he refused on principle, citing the Fifth Amendment, to explain further his political allegiances. Even after the leadership of the Soviet Union denounced Stalinism in 1956, he refused to renounce the Soviet Union or, more stubbornly, the repression and anti-Semitism of Stalinism. Instead, he argued that the Soviets cared more about racial equality than did the supposedly democratic United States.

These statements angered whites and blacks across the country. Rutgers alumni attempted to wipe Robeson from the school's records. Newspapers decried his perceived disloyalty. And the FBI in 1950 revoked his passport. For an international performer, the effects were devastating. He could not take advantage of lucrative offers overseas, and American venues would not book him. In 1947, Robeson had earned $100,000; five years later, he earned $6,000. Severely battered and depressed, neither Robeson nor his career ever fully recovered.

In 1958, the Supreme Court ruled that Congress could not withhold passports due to citizens' "beliefs and associations." That year Robeson toured Europe, where a number of countries hosted parties to celebrate his sixtieth

Paul Robeson meeting W. E. B. Du Bois at the 1949
World Peace Conference in Paris.

birthday. But his career never returned to its former heights. While he eventually gained recognition as a civil rights pioneer and emerged a hero to a great number of African Americans (the U.S. Postal Service placed his image on a stamp in 2003), his harassment and persecution by the government are indicative of the terrible consequences that an African American who dared to question the nation's commitment to its own principles would be allowed to suffer during the McCarthy era. One can only imagine the trajectory of Robeson's career in music and acting in the 1950s and 1960s had he been allowed to thrive.

PART TWELVE

GROWING AUTHORITY

1928–1939

OSCAR DE PRIEST AND ADAM CLAYTON POWELL, JR.

During the first half of the twentieth century, while disenfranchisement laws eliminated black voting in the South, African Americans in the North made great political strides. The increasing black population in specified neighborhoods in industrial cities opened the possibility that black candidates could win significant elective offices.

Oscar De Priest moved to Chicago at the age of seventeen. Finding financial success as a contractor, he turned to politics and joined the Republican Party. He proved skilled at rallying blacks to the polls, winning election as Cook County commissioner in 1904. In 1915, he was elected to the city council, thanks to the Great Migration influx of black voters and to the votes of women, who had gained municipal suffrage two years earlier. In 1928, De Priest supported a former rival, Nelson Madden, in his bid for reelection to represent the First District of Chicago in Congress. When Madden died shortly after winning the primary, De Priest ran in his place. He won the election, becoming the first African American congressman since George H. White left office in 1900 and the first black from a northern state ever to serve in the House of Representatives.

While in office, De Priest found himself at the center of controversy when First Lady Lou Hoover invited his wife, Jessie Williams De Priest, to the White House for tea. For outraged white supremacists, it recalled Theodore Roosevelt dining with Booker T. Washington in 1901; for African Americans, it offered hope for a softening of racial barriers. De Priest lost a reelection bid in 1934, but to another African American, the Democrat Arthur W. Mitchell. De Priest opened the door for a black seat in Con-

Oscar De Priest (1871–1951).

gress from the South Side of Chicago for years to come.

Blacks in other sectors of the North could not elect a representative until New York's Adam Clayton Powell, Jr., won a seat in Congress in 1944. The son of the minister of Harlem's large and powerful Abyssinian Baptist Church, Powell earned a bachelor's degree at Colgate University in 1930 and a master's from Columbia University in 1932. Upon returning to Harlem, Powell agitated for the rights of African Americans. He organized soup kitchens and community services, as well as picket lines and marches against discrimination in hiring. He took over his father's pulpit and began a newspaper, the *People's Voice,* which increased his visibility. In 1941 he won a seat on the New York City Council.

Three years later, redistricting created a new congressional district in Harlem, and Powell won election to the House of Representatives. As the con-

Adam Clayton Powell, Jr.
(1908–72).

gressman from Harlem, Powell became the nation's most influential black politician. He fought for fair employment, voting rights, and social services for poor blacks. After the 1954 *Brown* decision, he promoted the "Powell Amendment," a rider that would withhold federal funds from southern schools that refused to comply with the Court's desegregation order. Powell attached the amendment to a host of bills until he achieved victory with Title VI of the Civil Rights Act of 1964.

While Powell gained unprecedented popularity and influence during the 1950s and 1960s, he spent the second half of the latter decade battling controversy. He was accused of corruption, and a sixty-six-year-old woman whom Powell had called a "bag lady" filed a lawsuit. When he refused to pay the woman a settlement, the court found him in contempt, and the House refused to seat him. The following years saw a sad and debilitating back-and-forth battle between Powell and the House. Powell eventually won in 1969, but at the cost of his seniority. He lost his seat in 1970 to a young challenger named Charles Ran-gel. Suffering from cancer, Powell died two years later.

Adam Clayton Powell left Congress with an unprecedented legacy of courageous, unflinching agitation for the rights of African Americans, providing a model for a new generation of black politicians to utilize the legislative process to combat de jure segregation and other remnants of America's racist past.

SCOTTSBORO AND WALTER WHITE

Throughout the Great Depression, men and women boarded boxcars on rail lines seeking a free ride, food, work, shelter, or a sense of excitement amid the chaos and despair of everyday life. On March 25, 1931, some young hoboes on a train traveling west from Chattanooga to Memphis got into a fight, which changed the course of American history.

In the fight a group of young blacks squared off against several young whites and threw the whites off the train. The victors, who ranged in age from twelve to twenty-one, were surprised when the train slowed to a stop in Paint Rock, Alabama. When they slid open a train door, they discovered angry, armed white men approaching. The white boys had gone to the Scottsboro police and claimed the African Americans had attacked them. The police—with the all-too-willing help of white civilians—seized the nine blacks, tied them together with plow line, and took them to jail.

The assault charge came as no surprise. The rape charge, on the other hand, shocked them. When the cops boarded the train, they found two white prostitutes in the same car. The women likely

Walter White (1893–1955). Born in Atlanta to parents who had been slaves, White graduated from Atlanta University and became a successful businessman. His organizational work for the Atlanta branch of the NAACP brought him to the attention of field secretary James Weldon Johnson. He joined the New York branch of the association in 1918.

made the rape accusation to avoid facing arrest. The nine African Americans sat in jail, assuming that, like many other black men accused of rape, they would never make it out alive. The trial, held twelve days later, went as expected. The white women offered contradictory testimony. The court learned that disease had left one of the young men incapable of sexual intercourse. Nevertheless, a jury found all nine defendants guilty and sentenced all but the youngest to death.

Word of the injustice traveled across the nation, and numerous people and organizations volunteered their help. The most persistent protest came from the International Labor Defense (ILD), a legal group sponsored by the American Communist Party. Believing that the Great Depression signaled the beginning of the end of capitalism, the party had increased its efforts to appeal to African Americans, whose participation it thought pivotal. While its assistance often had as much or more to do with strengthening the party than it did with helping black people, many African Americans appreciated the effort. The Communist Party called the Scottsboro verdict a "legal lynching," and it mobilized support for the young men by encouraging Americans to send gifts and letters. More important, ILD lawyers visited them in jail. The prisoners and their parents at first found it difficult to trust the whites from the Communist Party, but they agreed to allow the ILD to handle the case, even as their inept former attorney, the prison offi-

Attorney Samuel Leibowitz accompanies four of the newly freed Scottsboro defendants as they arrive to cheering crowds in New York on July 26, 1937. Three others remained in an Alabama prison.

"Save the Scottsboro Boys." Donation pin created by the Communist Party–affiliated International Labor Defense, the organization that represented the Scottsboro defendants.

cials, and indeed every other white person they met warned them to stay away from the communists.

The NAACP also opposed communist involvement. The association, long at the forefront of struggles to secure legal rights for African Americans, responded slowly to the Scottsboro case. The blame fell squarely on Walter White, who only weeks before the arrests had succeeded James Weldon Johnson as executive secretary. White had joined the national staff in 1918 with an impressive track record of investigating lynchings, which he could do surreptitiously because he could pass for white. Still, he had prejudices of his own and avoided the Scottsboro case, afraid to associate the NAACP with teenage delinquents. More to the point, he speculated that the youths might actually have committed the crime and worried that their conviction and execution would adversely affect the association. Moreover, he had

no desire to work with the Communist Party in any capacity, which would have been anathema to his financial backers.

The black press and high-ranking NAACP officials, however, pressured White to act. About a month after the verdicts, amid a rising chorus of complaints, he decided to stall, using the time-honored method of collecting facts, seeking to gain assistance from white liberals, and advocating trust in the courts. In January 1932, the NAACP officially withdrew what little involvement it had offered, much to the delight of the ILD. Although White would later guide the NAACP to legal successes, the Scottsboro case brought his leadership skills into question.

The ILD represented the Scottsboro Nine as their cases proceeded through the courts. At first the Alabama Supreme Court upheld their convictions. On appeal, the U.S. Supreme Court ordered a new trial since the lower court had

denied the defendants due process. For the next round of proceedings, the ILD enlisted prominent lawyer Samuel Leibowitz, who did not belong to the Communist Party. The guilty verdicts in the lower courts remained the same. The Supreme Court reversed the decision in 1935. By the time the third set of trials began in 1937, the nine had spent six miserable years in Alabama jails. Fortunately, in the next few years, most of the prisoners gained parole. In 1948, Haywood Patterson, the last "Scottsboro Boy" still jailed (though others had returned for parole violations), took matters into his own hands and escaped. Although the FBI captured him in Michigan, the governor refused to extradite him to Alabama. The prisoners all eventually returned to freedom, but the Scottsboro case became an iconic instance of American racial injustice.

TUSKEGEE SYPHILIS STUDY

In 1929, the U.S. Public Health Service (PHS), in conjunction with the Rosenwald Fund, began an investigation into the prevalence and treatment of syphilis among African Americans in six rural counties in six southern states, including Macon County, Alabama. The program found rates of the disease at many stages, from a low of less than 10 percent to a high of nearly 40 percent, in those men and women contacted. While treatment was started, the onset of the Great Depression made it impossible financially to continue the project.

In 1932, the PHS returned to Macon County, home of the Tuskegee Institute, expecting to do a short study on latent syphilis in men who were thought to be no longer infectious. The study began with treatment, but it too ran out of funds. Then the idea for the study shifted. Rather than instituting mass treatment, officials wondered what would happen if they left the syphilis untreated and monitored its ravages. There was a medical debate at the time about whether the preferred treatment for those who were asymptomatic did more harm than good. With the participation of the Tuskegee Institute, the PHS in 1932 began the "Tuskegee Study of Untreated Syphilis in the Negro Male."

Scientists enrolled more than four hundred African American men with the latent form of the disease and almost two hundred others to serve as a control group. The doctors falsely told subjects that they would receive treatment for their "bad blood." Instead they received aspirin, iron tonics, and diagnostic spinal taps that were called "special treatment," as well as hot meals, medical exams, and, ironically, burial insurance.

President Bill Clinton and Vice President Al Gore acknowledge Herman Shaw, age ninety-four, one of the last surviving participants of the infamous Tuskegee syphilis study, May 16, 1997.

In the minds of the PHS researchers, the study would yield valuable scientific dividends at minimal human cost. After all, they reasoned, most of those involved in the study could never have afforded treatment anyway. What began as a six-month study continued for decades.

Remarkably, the study was not kept secret and, when it began, was not particularly controversial. Its first published findings appeared in the journal *Venereal Disease Information* in 1936; thirteen more papers would follow between then and 1973. The study proceeded even after PHS doctors began using penicillin to treat latent syphilis cases in other parts of the country in the late 1940s. Criticism of the study surfaced in the 1950s, but the study continued. The Centers for Disease Control, which took over monitoring the program from the PHS, called a meeting in 1969 and decided to continue it. Not until a former syphilis investigator named Peter Buxtun brought the study to the attention of an AP reporter did a public uproar bring the study to an end.

On July 25, 1972, the Associated Press sent the story to newspapers around the nation. Six months later, in response, the Department of Health, Education, and Welfare stopped the study and began providing treatment to surviving participants. Civil rights attorney Fred Gray, one of the lawyers of the Montgomery bus boycott, filed a $1.8 billion class-action lawsuit against the participating federal and state institutions. They settled out of court for $10 million; the money went to the seventy-four surviving subjects and the heirs of those who had died. The study also led in part to the formation of institutional review boards to monitor scientific experiments.

In 1997, after lobbying by politicians, survivors, and academics, President Bill Clinton issued an official apology to the men in the study, six of whom were still alive, and to their families. Nonetheless, the study has become a metaphor for irresponsibility and racism in the use of human subjects in scientific research.

ETTA MOTEN, OLIVER LAW, AND WILLIAM HASTIE

Etta Moten grew up the daughter of a Methodist minister in Weimar, Texas, a small town less than one hundred miles west of Houston. Known through the town for her amazing voice, she sang in the church choir. She divorced her husband after seven years of marriage to earn a college degree in voice and drama from the University of Kansas. Her successful senior recital in 1931 led to a performance with the Eva Jessye Choir in New York. (She stopped in Chicago en route and met her second husband, Claude Barnett, the founder of the American Negro Press.) Moten won roles in the Broadway plays *Fast and Furious* (1931) and *Sugar Hill* (1931), then relocated to Los Angeles to pursue voiceover work. In California she sang parts for Barbara Stanwyck and Ginger Rogers, and in *Gold Diggers of 1933* she performed the song "Remember My Forgotten Man." Her Hollywood work brought her to the attention of the new first lady, Eleanor Roosevelt, who invited her to perform for her husband's

William H. Hastie (1904–76). In the spring of 1942, Hastie was a civilian aide to Secretary of War Cordell Hull. Here he is shown speaking with Undersecretary of War Robert P. Patterson.

Oliver Law (1900–37). Born in West Texas, Law served in the U.S. Army from 1919 to 1925. As head of the Abraham Lincoln Brigade, he was the first African American to lead an integrated military force.

birthday on January 31, 1934, making her the first African American to perform at the White House since the Fisk Jubilee Singers did so in 1881. Moten went on to star in other productions—most notably *Porgy and Bess* (1942)—and would work for a number of social and political organizations, including the National Council of Negro Women. She died in 2004 at the age of 102.

Just two years after Moten's performance at the White House, an African American named Oliver Law made military history. Law had served the United States in World War I and, after the war, moved to Chicago, where he worked a series of odd jobs. The Great Depression awakened his political consciousness, and he joined the Communist Party. He took particular interest in international affairs, especially the Italian

fascist Benito Mussolini's invasion of Ethiopia. To fight fascism, he traveled to Spain in 1937, where he joined the International Brigade defending the republican government during the Spanish Civil War. Law served with sixty to eighty other African Americans in the integrated Abraham Lincoln Brigade. He so impressed his superiors that they named him battalion commander, making Law the first African American to command an integrated military force. He died in combat on July 9, 1937.

William Hastie attended Dunbar High School in Washington, D.C., and graduated as valedictorian from Amherst College in 1925. He graduated from Harvard Law School in 1930 (he would earn a second degree in 1933) and returned to practice law in the nation's capital. In Washington he participated in civil rights protests, including "Don't Buy Where You Can't Work" campaigns. During the 1940s, Hastie also worked with Thurgood Marshall and the NAACP on key civil rights cases, including *Smith v. Allwright* (1944) and *Morgan v. Virginia* (1946).

While practicing law, Hastie made inroads into politics as a member of Franklin Roosevelt's informal "Black Cabinet." Roosevelt rewarded his service on March 26, 1937, by appointing him district judge in the Virgin Islands, making him the first black federal court judge in American history. From 1946 to 1949, he served as governor of the Virgin Islands and on the U.S. Court of Appeals, Third Circuit. He remained active in the law and in civil rights work until his death in 1976.

THE APOLLO THEATER

In 1914, Hurtig and Seamon's New (Burlesque) Theater opened in Harlem at 253 West 125th Street between Seventh and Eighth avenues, across the street from Blumstein's department store. For more than a decade, Hurtig and Seamon's hosted vaudeville and burlesque shows exclusively for white audiences. By the end of the 1920s, however, the popularity of burlesque had declined, and the demographics of the neighborhood had dramatically changed. Black migrants from the South had been streaming into Harlem, and the neighborhood was now the national center of black culture and intellectual life.

During the Great Depression, businessman Sidney Cohen purchased the theater, renamed it the Apollo Theater, and began pitching to an African American audience. It opened on January 26, 1934, with the show *Jazz à la Carte*. For the first time African Americans could enter the building, fill its two balconies, and enjoy the show.

As the first theater on 125th Street to welcome blacks, the Apollo consistently drew large crowds, even in the depths of the Great Depression. Within its first few years, the stage hosted many of the nation's most popular black entertainers, including Lionel Hampton, Louis Jordan, Duke Ellington, Bessie Smith, Billie Holliday, and Lena Horne. The Apollo's Amateur Night—held each

Arnett Cobb and Walter Buchanan perform at the Apollo Theater, August 1947.

Wednesday—garnered particular attention. In 1934 the disk jockey Ralph Cooper began hosting his *Harlem Amateur Hour Radio Show* from the Apollo. Ambitious black artists hoped to break into professional show business with a successful performance on the program.

On one Amateur Night, November 21, 1934, a very nervous Ella Fitzgerald, having passed her audition, prepared to sing live in front of the world-famous Benny Carter Orchestra. She performed "Judy" and "The Object of My Affec-

tion." Initially she struggled, sparking fierce booing from the tough crowd. But she quickly rebounded, and her performance that night launched her spectacular career. Sarah Vaughan and Pearl Bailey were among the other entertainers whose paths to stardom began at the Apollo's Amateur Night.

The Apollo became the most important venue in the United States for black singers, many of whom released live albums from their performances, such as James Brown's legendary *Live at the*

Apollo in 1963. The theater maintained its popularity by adapting to the popular musical climate. In the 1940s, the prominence of swing music brought Count Basie to the Apollo; Sammy Davis, Jr., and Nat "King" Cole also performed there. During the 1950s, the Apollo opened its stage to rhythm and blues, gospel, and rock and roll artists. It also consistently welcomed comedians like Redd Foxx, Moms Mabley, and Pigmeat Markham. In the 1960s, Smokey Robinson, the Jackson Five, Dionne Warwick, and Stevie Wonder excited Apollo crowds. More recently James Brown held his seventieth birthday concert there, playing to an audience filled with the contemporary version of Du Bois's "talented tenth."

In a sad irony, however, the success of the Apollo and its performers contributed to its decline. Many of the gifted black artists who began there became so successful that they could play larger rooms and command larger fees. Nationwide, promoters engaged in bidding wars for black artists, a competition that the small Apollo could not win. The theater declared bankruptcy in 1977. It opened and closed numerous times during the 1980s but could not regain its footing as a profit-making entity. In 1991, the Apollo Theater Foundation, a nonprofit led by Harlem congressman Charles Rangel, gave the Apollo the resources to return to prominence. In the last two decades, the theater has once again hosted performances from the world's most famous artists.

NATIONAL NEGRO CONGRESS

In May 1935, Howard University hosted a conference called "The Position of the Negro in Our National Economic Crisis." A remarkable example of Popular Front activism, the participants—communists and non-communists, blacks and whites, middle class and working class—offered a radical, class-based critique of American society. Ralph Bunche, the lawyer John P. Davis, and Robert C. Weaver led the conference. A. Philip Randolph and W. E. B. Du Bois skewered Jim Crow unions and segregationist whites. James Ford gave a talk called "The Communist's Way Out for the Negro." Excited by the possibilities, the group planned a formal national conference for the following year.

The National Negro Congress (NNC) met on the South Side of Chicago on February 14, 1936. Eight hundred seventeen delegates, representing more than 550 black organizations from across the country, attended. Again, non-communists like Randolph, Bunche, and Langston Hughes worked side by side with communists like Ben Davis and Angelo Herndon. Over three days they covered topics as varied as the rights of black sharecroppers, women in the workforce, the shortcomings of the Social Security Act, and the Italian occupation of Ethiopia. Above all, the NNC articulated a vision of freedom defined by access to jobs and working-class unity across the color line. The NNC named veteran labor leader A. Philip Randolph president.

An unprecedented mix of enthusiastic African Americans from different class and political backgrounds, the NNC seemed poised for success in the turbulent social and political climate of the late 1930s. The Wagner Act protected and legitimized unionism. The Congress of Industrial Organizations instituted "Operation Dixie" to organize blacks in the South. Thousands of African Americans joined labor unions for the first time. Over the next three years the NNC organized black laborers in the steel and textile industries; many other unions, such as autoworkers and tobacco workers, were much more resistant to incorporating African Americans. It also expanded its platform to organize protests against lynching and in support

A. Philip Randolph (1889–1979), the first president of the National Negro Congress, is shown here standing with an unidentified man at a Washington, D.C., meeting of the NNC in 1940, the year he resigned from the organization over the increasing influence of its communist members.

of fair housing for blacks. And it continued to protest European fascism. At its peak the NNC had seventy local chapters across the nation.

The NNC's coalition might have collapsed eventually, but world events

for full employment after the war
REGISTER ⚙ VOTE
CIO POLITICAL ACTION COMMITTEE

"For full employment after the war, register, vote," poster by Ben Shahn, 1944.

in 1939 accelerated the process. On August 23, Nazi Germany and the communist Soviet Union, once mortal enemies, signed a nonaggression pact and united against the democratic nations of Europe. After years of equating white supremacy with fascism, American communists of both races suddenly faced the conundrum of how to follow the party line and recognize fascist Germany as an ally. When Hitler and Stalin carved up Poland between themselves, party members and fellow travelers lost a great deal of credibility in the eyes of non-communists. How could communists oppose fascism in America, many former supporters asked, if their party supported it in Europe? Nationwide, the rising tide of anti-communism began to stifle any leftist critique of American society. The Popular Front could not exist under such constraints.

These issues came to a head at the April 1940 meeting of the NNC. A. Philip Randolph did not hide his distaste for what the Soviet Union had done. In his address he accused both Nazi Germany and communist Russia of using censorship and violence to subvert democracy. Most of the white delegates stormed out of the room in anger. When the communists who remained passed a resolution that condemned any American intervention in the new European conflict, Randolph resigned as president.

The NNC would continue to exist on a much smaller scale throughout World War II, but the fissure over communist influence—both real and unfounded—would only increase as Americans of both races felt the chill of the Cold War. Still, the National Negro Congress represented an inspiring, if fleeting, moment of united protest framed around unionism and international politics, subjects far too rarely associated with the struggle for civil rights.

JESSE OWENS AND JOE LOUIS

During the Great Depression, Americans searched not only for jobs, food, and shelter but also, amid the misery of day-to-day survival, for hope. African Americans found inspiration in the sports world, with the rise to prominence of track star Jesse Owens and heavyweight boxing champion Joe Louis.

Jesse Owens had first demonstrated his athletic prowess at an early age. Born in Alabama in 1913, he moved to Detroit with his family seven years later, during the Great Migration. In high school he shattered track and field records and nearly made the Olympic team. He attended Ohio State University, where he found similar success, setting world records in the sprint, hurdles, and long jump. As an African American, he often endured the jeers of white crowds, which mentally prepared him for his greatest challenge. He made the U.S. track team for the 1936 Berlin Olympic Games, held in the capital of Nazi Germany. A black man challenging Hitler's Aryan athletes carried heavy symbolism, which delighted African Americans. As Hitler watched in the stands, assuming the German squad would easily carry the day, Owens raced to four gold medals in the 100-meter sprint, the 200-meter sprint, the four-by-100-meter relay, and the long jump. His stunning performance undermined the fallacy of white physical supremacy. Hitler took little note of Owens's success, but Leni Riefenstahl's documentary of the games, *Olympia,* released in 1938, prominently featured Owens.

Jesse Owens (1913–80) at
the 1936 Olympics.

Joe Louis (1914–1981) knocking out Max Schmeling, June 22, 1938.

Perhaps the only black athlete more popular than Owens during these years was another Alabama native, Joe Louis. Born Joe Louis Barrow (he inadvertently dropped his last name while completing paperwork for his amateur boxing card), Louis and his family moved to Detroit, where he took up boxing. After a successful amateur career, he went to Chicago in 1934, where he turned professional. Louis soon demonstrated the same dominance he had shown as an amateur. By the end of 1935 he had won more than twenty consecutive fights, including a knockout of former champion Primo Carnera at New York's Yankee Stadium. The following year he squared off against Max Schmeling, a German fighter who, like the German Olympians, symbolized to black Americans Hitler's ideology of white supremacy. On June 18 in New York, Schmeling knocked Louis out in the twelfth round. The defeat stunned African Americans; Langston Hughes reported seeing grown men in tears afterward.

But Louis quickly returned to the ring, and if he doubted his skills after the dramatic defeat, he did not show it. Former champion Jack Sharkey fell to his knockout power, and on June 22, 1937, Louis defeated Jim Braddock, to capture the heavyweight championship. African Americans celebrated, and Louis and his fans anticipated the day he would have a rematch with Schmeling. Louis got his wish one year to the day after winning the heavyweight crown, on June 22, 1938.

Promoters and journalists hyped the fight as the conflict of two races and two cultures, with Louis representing the democratic United States and the promise of the race, and Schmeling representing Nazi Germany and white supremacy. (Schmeling himself did not endorse white supremacy, and the two men later became friends.) The New York rematch could not have gone more differently from the first. Three years earlier, Schmeling had defeated Louis only after a long, grueling match. This time, Louis knocked the German out in the first round. African Americans

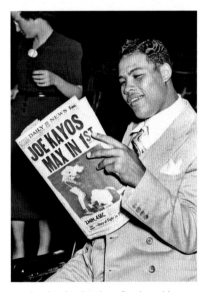

Joe Louis, the day after knocking
out Max Schmeling.

rejoiced; their hero had disposed of a hated symbol of white supremacy.

The achievements of Owens and Louis played significant roles in the growing movement for civil rights for African Americans.

ZORA NEALE HURSTON, ARNA BONTEMPS, RICHARD WRIGHT

The literary flowering of the Harlem Renaissance continued with far less fanfare and self-consciousness through the Great Depression and World War II.

Zora Neale Hurston grew up in Eatonville, Florida, and by the middle of the 1920s had published in *Opportunity,* earning a reputation as a skilled writer of short stories. She studied with Alain Locke at Howard University and then earned her B.A. from Barnard College in 1928, where she studied under the influential anthropologist Franz Boas. As a graduate student in anthropology at Columbia, Hurston spent several years conducting field research and collecting folklore across the South. She received two Guggenheim fellowships and published two scholarly essays based on her studies. In 1930, she collaborated with Langston Hughes to write the play *Mule Bone.* She published her first novel, *Jonah's Gourd Vine,* in 1934, and a collection of black folklore entitled *Mules and Men* in 1935.

But Hurston cemented her literary legacy with her 1937 masterpiece, *Their Eyes Were Watching God.* At the time, black male critics—especially her nemesis, Richard Wright—treated the book harshly, accusing it of using minstrel-like methods to pander to white racist tastes, rather than serving as a testament against white racism. The novel is an exploration of a young, poor black woman's successive victimization by black men, focusing on the protagonist, Janie Crawford, and a series of mentally and physically abusive relationships. Janie liberates herself from her second husband's oppression by standing up for her right to speak, defending herself verbally, and finding her voice. Eventually, following this husband's death, she finds

Zora Neale Hurston (1891–1960), photograph by Carl Van Vechten, April 3, 1938.

Arna W. Bontemps (1902–73), photograph by Carl Van Vechten, August 15, 1939.

a fulfilling relationship with Tea Cake (Vergible) Woods, but she ultimately is forced to shoot him to save herself from his rabid attack. Hurston died penniless in 1960, but a generation of feminist critics and readers, fueled by Alice Walker's interest in her work, would resurrect Hurston's reputation and install her in the canon.

Arna Bontemps also published his most recognized work during the Great Depression. Bontemps grew up in Los Angeles and in 1923 graduated from Northern California's Pacific Union College, a Seventh-Day Adventist institution. Like many aspiring black writers, he moved to Harlem and, just as Hurston had done, published in *Opportunity.* In 1931, he moved to Huntsville, Alabama, to work for Oakwood College. While in Huntsville he wrote both serious novels like *God Sends Sunday* (1931) and children's fiction like *You Can't Pet a Possum* (1934). In 1936, he published his most influential work, *Black Thunder,* an exploration of Gabriel Prosser's failed slave revolt in 1800. The book established Bontemps as one of the

country's most important black novelists. In 1939, he completed *Drums at Dusk,* a novel about the Haitian Revolution. Uncertain about the future, he earned a library science degree from the University of Chicago in 1943 and became the long-serving librarian at Fisk University.

Hurston's *Their Eyes Were Watching God,* cover, 1937.

He continued to write adult fiction and poetry. He edited a number of poetry collections and a variety of other collections of black writings, most notably *The Harlem Renaissance Remembered,* as a visiting professor at Yale University in 1969.

Richard Wright, one of the twentieth century's most important black writers, also came to prominence during these years. Frustrated with menial jobs and the climate of repression in the South, Wright moved to Chicago in 1927. There he worked for the Federal Writers' Project and discovered the Communist Party, one of the few political parties that sought black membership and fully supported the civil rights movement. He moved to Harlem in 1937, where he served as an editor for the communist *Daily Worker* newspaper, and in 1938 he published a collection of short stories, *Uncle Tom's Children,* all of which deal in some way with racial oppression. Two years later, Wright published his most acclaimed work, *Native Son.* It is the masterwork of African American naturalism. The novel's success made him the most famous black writer in the world.

Its plot centers on Bigger Thomas, a black man who accidentally kills the young white daughter of his wealthy employer and, in an attempt to hide the evidence, dismembers and burns her corpse in the family's furnace. Fleeing a citywide police dragnet, Bigger murders his girlfriend, Bessie. Wright intended the book's themes of race, violence, and sex to show how racist culture could twist the lives of its victims, but some African Americans criticized it for focusing on a brutish black murderer. Nevertheless, the novel proved an astonishing success, making Wright the first black author to produce a Book-of-the-Month Club selection.

Wright's next book was also a Book-of-the-Month Club selection. *Black Boy* explored his own life in the South. Before its publication in 1945, Wright had left the Communist Party, as detailed

Richard Wright (1908–60).

in his essay "I Tried to Be a Communist." In 1947, he left the United States for France, where a number of black expatriate writers and artists went to live, including James Baldwin, Wright's disciple. Wright closely associated with French intellectuals such as Jean-Paul Sartre and Simone de Beauvoir, as well as other expatriate writers such as Gertrude Stein. In addition, he had frequent interactions with African and Caribbean intellectuals associated with the Negritude Movement, such as Leopold Senghor and Aimé Césaire. Wright published several books in Paris, but none had the traction or force of *Native Son*

and *Black Boy.* He remained in Paris until his death in 1960. While he played little direct role in the civil rights movement, his writings were held up as the model of the committed author in the Black Arts Movement of the 1960s.

Wright's first novel is such a dominant force in the African American literary tradition that some scholars have termed the period between its publication in 1940 and the end of the Black Arts Movement as "The Age of Richard Wright." But very few black writers of the contemporary generation utilize his naturalistic style of writing.

MARY MCLEOD BETHUNE AND THE NATIONAL COUNCIL OF NEGRO WOMEN, THE NATIONAL YOUTH ADMINISTRATION, AND THE BLACK CABINET

Mary McLeod Bethune (standing at front, center), with Mary Church Terrell to her right, White House Conference Group of the National Women's Council, 1938.

Mary McLeod Bethune's life as an activist went beyond her pathbreaking work in the field of education. While her efforts at her Daytona school reflected the early influence of Booker T. Washington, Bethune also agitated for change in more direct ways. During the 1930s, she seized both private and public opportunities to fight for gender and racial equality. On the private side, Bethune participated in the burgeoning black women's club movement. Since white clubs excluded them, African American women formed their own organizations for social betterment, including temperance agencies, religious groups, and political clubs. Particularly through her membership in and presidency of the National Association of Colored Women, Bethune addressed the dual discrimination of race and gender that she and all black women faced. But she found the NACW lacking, contending that many members held a bias against poor women. Addressing the structural dimension of inequality rather than individual behavior, Bethune argued, would go further to promote equality. Additionally, on an organizational level, Bethune felt that the NACW's lack of a unified national program and infrastructure was a problem. To this end, she called for a new organization, the National Council of Negro Women.

On December 7, 1935, Bethune hosted a meeting of thirty women representing women's groups from around the country. Notable attendees included Charlotte Hawkins Brown, Mary Church Terrell, and Daisy Lampkin, all prominent black women activists themselves. Bethune hoped that black women would use the NCNW to develop a unified platform that could translate into political influence. The NCNW called for voter registration efforts, political education for black women, and pressure on government officials to address social problems. Bethune reminded the women of the accomplishments of previous leaders "who dared to stand for right." The group expanded over the following years and eventually offered

Young men and women received
training for defense jobs during
World War II under the direction of
the National Youth Administration,
Daytona Beach, Florida, 1943.

Mary McLeod Bethune as chief of the "Negro Section" of
the National Youth Administration, ca. 1938.

assistance to African Americans in the
military.

Bethune had reason to believe the
NCNW could wield political power, as
she herself had reached the higher ech-
elons of the federal government. As her
stature as an educator grew during the
1920s, Bethune had worked with government agencies concerned with African
American children. In 1936, President
Franklin Delano Roosevelt chose her
to head the Office of Minority Affairs
of the National Youth Administration,
which aided young Americans during
the Great Depression. She helped guarantee that African Americans would
benefit from the program, ensuring
that support went to black secondary
schools and colleges, that black youth
received defense industry jobs and training, and that black college students participated in the Civilian Pilot Program
and learned to fly.

Bethune also organized African
American New Deal administrators into
an informal group called the Federal
Council on Negro Affairs, better known
as the unofficial "Black Cabinet." The
sole woman member and the leader of

Mary McLeod Bethune meeting with Eleanor Roosevelt and
Aubrey Williams, the executive director of the NYA.

the group, Bethune hosted the meetings
of the Black Cabinet in her apartment
or her office. While the Black Cabinet
had little say on official policy, its members did keep the interests of African
Americans on the table. Bethune not
only showed that blacks could advance

in politics, but she used the knowledge
she had gained to help younger African
Americans negotiate the political process. A monumental figure in the history
of black education and politics, Mary
McLeod Bethune continued to speak out
for equal rights until her death in 1955.

PART THIRTEEN

THE ERA OF WORLD WAR II

1939–1950

MARIAN ANDERSON PERFORMS
AT THE LINCOLN MEMORIAL

Marian Anderson (1897–1993), performing alongside the pianist Kosti Vehanen, Lincoln Memorial, April 9, 1939.

The world-famous contralto Marian Anderson enjoyed performing in Washington, D.C., but she rarely had the opportunity to sing for everyone who wanted to hear her. The city had few integrated venues, forcing her to hold recitals in black churches or small theaters. In 1933, Howard University professor Charles Cohen began the Lyceum Concert Course to feature African American artists. Anderson would be the series' highlight, if only he could find a concert hall to hold her ever-growing number of fans. She performed at the Armstrong High School auditorium in 1936; the following day Eleanor Roosevelt invited her to sing at the White House. She sang at Armstrong again in 1937 and moved up to the two-thousand-seat Rialto Theater in 1938. Each time, event organizers turned away hundreds at the door.

In 1939, Cohen wanted her for an Easter Sunday Lyceum concert that he planned to hold at Constitution Hall, the city's largest auditorium. But the hall, owned by the Daughters of the American Revolution (DAR) and just a few steps from the White House, fiercely maintained the color line. Cohen attempted to schedule Anderson anyway, but as expected, the DAR turned him down. So he contacted the NAACP's Walter White, who hatched a plan to bring national attention to the incident. He arranged for Eleanor Roosevelt to present Anderson the prized Spingarn Medal at the NAACP annual convention; she then publicly resigned from the DAR. Despite the bad publicity, the DAR refused to budge. White then proposed an outdoor venue, one that would not only make the concert accessible to thousands of people but would also call upon history to judge the DAR's gross act of discrimination. White enlisted a number of powerful politicians, including three Supreme Court justices, to sponsor the event. With lobbying from Anderson's manager, the legendary impresario Sol Hurok, secretary of the interior Harold Ickes permitted them to use the Lincoln Memorial—just one week before the April 9 Easter Sunday concert.

The predicted bad weather failed to materialize, and seventy thousand

Marian Anderson at the Lincoln
Memorial, April 9, 1939.

people, whites and blacks, attended the concert. Anderson opened with a stirring rendition of "America," where she subtly changed the lyrics: "My country 'tis of thee, sweet land of liberty, of thee we sing." About thirty minutes later she closed the recital with "Nobody Knows the Trouble I've Seen." The crowd roared its applause and rushed the stage as Anderson delivered a heartfelt thank-you. While the concert had no immediate effect on segregation and discrimination, in 1943 the DAR changed its policy and invited Anderson to perform in the hall. More important,

the Lincoln Memorial concert changed the lives of many who witnessed it and became an iconic event in American history. As Mary McLeod Bethune wrote to Charles Hamilton Houston on April 10, 1939, the day after the event, "Through the Marian Anderson protest concert we made our triumphant entry into the democratic spirit of American life."[1] The concert also transformed the Lincoln Memorial into a site of protest, one that African Americans would use to the fullest extent during the 1960s civil rights movement.

THE MARCH ON WASHINGTON MOVEMENT AND EXECUTIVE ORDER 8802

Asa Philip Randolph knew firsthand the domestic turmoil that accompanied world war. As the United States began to mobilize for World War II, he remembered that, for African Americans, the Great War had "neither won democracy abroad or at home."[2] Even more galling, the same issues blacks faced during World War I resurfaced in the 1940s. In the military, they encountered the same unequal and segregated treatment, and in war-related industries white officials and managers conspired to keep them out altogether. Many skilled unions refused to admit any black workers.

Despite the influence of Mary McLeod Bethune and the "Black Cabinet" on the administration, President Roosevelt had done very little explicitly about racial discrimination. In 1940, Randolph, Walter White, and T. Arnold Hill of the Urban League met with the president to urge him to desegregate the military and defense jobs. Roosevelt made no promises and then issued a statement that made the civil rights lead-

ers appear to agree with the necessity of segregation. When Roosevelt delivered his famous Four Freedoms speech on January 6, 1941, Randolph resolved to hold the president to his words. On January 15, he called for ten thousand African Americans to march on Washington to demand the desegregation of the armed services and defense industries. "We loyal Negro-American citizens," he said, "demand the right to work and fight for our country."[3] The idea swiftly gained support, and the new March on Washington Movement established thirty-six branches across the country.

Randolph decided to permit only African Americans to participate in the march, which caused concern among his supporters. But he argued that it would build racial solidarity and, just as important, would counter accusations of communist influence. The previous year Randolph had resigned as president of the National Negro Congress, an organization formed in 1936 to address problems faced by black workers. A remarkable example of Popular

EXECUTIVE ORDER

REAFFIRMING POLICY OF FULL PARTICIPATION IN
THE DEFENSE PROGRAM BY ALL PERSONS, REGARDLESS
OF RACE, CREED, COLOR, OR NATIONAL ORIGIN, AND
DIRECTING CERTAIN ACTION IN FURTHERANCE OF
SAID POLICY.

WHEREAS it is the policy of the United States to encourage
full participation in the national defense program by all
citizens of the United States, regardless of race, creed, color,
or national origin, in the firm belief that the democratic way
of life within the Nation can be defended successfully only with
the help and support of all groups within its borders; and

WHEREAS there is evidence that available and needed workers
have been barred from employment in industries engaged in defense
production solely because of considerations of race, creed, color,
or national origin, to the detriment of workers' morale and of
national unity:

NOW, THEREFORE, by virtue of the authority vested in me by
the Constitution and the statutes, and as a prerequisite to the
successful conduct of our national defense production effort, I
do hereby reaffirm the policy of the United States that there shall
be no discrimination in the employment of workers in defense
industries because of race, creed, color, or national origin, and
I do hereby declare that it is the duty of employers and of labor
organizations, in furtherance of said policy and of this order, to
provide for the full and equitable participation of all workers
in defense industries, without discrimination because of race, creed
color, or national origin;

And it is hereby ordered as follows:

1. All departments and agencies of the Government of the
United States concerned with vocational and training programs for
defense production shall take special measures appropriate to assure
that such programs are administered without discrimination because
of race, creed, color, or national origin;

Executive Order 8802,
June 25, 1941.

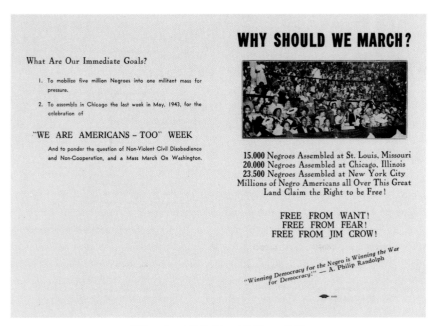

"Why Should We March?" flyer, 1941.

Front activism, the NNC welcomed both communists and non-communists into its ranks, but the rising tide of anti-communism threatened to destroy any movement or organization with perceived communist influence. Randolph's argument proved convincing, and the NAACP and Urban League supported the march.

The idea of tens of thousands of blacks flooding the nation's capital in protest rattled administration members. Even Eleanor Roosevelt, a friend of African American civil rights, asked Randolph to call off the march. Her husband asked Randolph, Walter White, and the black labor leader Layle Lane to attend a meeting at the White House on June 18. There he promised them that he would contact defense plants to ensure that they hired more blacks. Randolph insisted that nothing short of an executive order would do, and they would support it only if Randolph could review the order before the president issued it. With the crucial mediation of New York mayor Fiorello La Guardia and National Youth Administration head Aubrey Williams, the activists forced the president to act. On June 25, Roosevelt issued Executive Order 8802 that ended "discrimination in the employment of workers in defense industries or government because of race, creed, color, or national origin." Additionally, it created a temporary Fair Employment Practices Committee (FEPC) to enforce the order and review all complaints of racial discrimination. In return for issuing the order, Randolph called off the march—only six days before the crowds were to gather on the National Mall.

The limitations of Roosevelt's order left Randolph open to criticism for "caving in" to the president. The FEPC lacked effective enforcement powers and suffered from chronic underfunding—it began with a six-person staff and a budget of $80,000. Despite the FEPC's impotence, the number of African Americans in war industries increased from 3 to 8 percent. To be sure, employers still consigned blacks to the lowest-paying jobs, and whites often reacted with anger and violence to their presence and resisted working alongside them. But Executive Order 8802 marked a turning point in the struggle for black equality, won by black leaders and the threat of a major protest march. Randolph's dream of a March on Washington would be fulfilled in August 1963, when the Reverend Dr. Martin Luther King, Jr., delivered his famous "I Have a Dream" speech on the steps of the Lincoln Memorial.

A. Philip Randolph delivers an address at a rally for the Fair Employment Practices Committee at Madison Square Garden, New York, February 28, 1946.

MOVING TOWARD THE DOUBLE V

The African American community knew World War II primarily for the "Double V" campaign: victory over fascism abroad and victory over racism at home. But during the war, black people, incredibly, made great gains in the arts and sciences.

Jacob Lawrence's family had left the South during the Great Migration. After his parents separated, he moved with his mother, first to Philadelphia and then to Harlem in 1930. In New York, the young Lawrence found plenty of trouble, so his mother enrolled him in an after-school program to keep him off the streets. There Jacob met Charles Henry Alston, who encouraged him to pursue his passion for art. Even after dropping out of high school to earn money for his family, Lawrence continued painting. He moved into a shared space at Alston's studio, where he met luminaries like Langston Hughes, Ralph Ellison, and Alain Locke.

Lawrence realized that he too was a "race man" and began to employ African and African American themes in his art. In 1936, he held his first solo exhibition at the Harlem Artists Guild. His profile grew so quickly that only two years later the Harlem YMCA invited him for a solo exhibition. Lawrence soon finished a series of forty-one paintings on the Haitian revolutionary Toussaint L'Ouverture. Later he would complete series on Harriet Tubman and Frederick Douglass. He also created series on historical moments, including the Great Migration (which launched his career in 1940), the civil rights movement, the American bicentennial, and the 1972 Olympic Games. He produced murals for Harvard University and the Times Square subway station. He remained actively creative until his death.

Hattie McDaniel rose to national acclaim through her singing and acting talents. Born in 1895, McDaniel grew up in Denver, where she sang at school and in local groups. In 1931 she moved with her sisters to California to try to make it in Hollywood. She had minor roles in the films *Judge Priest* (1934), *Alice Adams* (1935), and *The Mad Miss Manton* (1938). Her experiences playing a maid contributed to her earning the part of Mammy in the 1939 film adaptation of Margaret Mitchell's *Gone With the Wind*. McDaniel won an Oscar for her performance, making her the first African American to win an Academy Award. Although she would never reach that level of success again, McDaniel performed in film and radio until her death from breast cancer in 1952.

Charles R. Drew made his mark in medicine. Success both in the classroom and on the football field at Dunbar High

Jacob Lawrence (1917–2000), photograph by Carl Van Vechten, 1941.

School in Washington, D.C., earned him a scholarship to Amherst College in 1922. He continued to play well at Amherst, but a leg injury led him to consider a career in medicine. Drew graduated in 1926 and worked for two years as

Hattie McDaniel (1895–1952) with Clark Gable in *Gone With the Wind,* 1939.

The Migration of the Negro, panel 3, by Jacob Lawrence, tempera on hardboard, 1940–41.

Charles R. Drew
(1904–50).

Frederick Douglass Patterson
(1901–88), photograph portrait, 1962.

University. There in 1940 Drew finished his doctoral thesis, *Banked Blood: A Study in Blood Preservation,* which concluded that plasma could replace whole-blood transfusions. Largely because of his work, blood plasma came to be mass-produced, which saved countless lives during the war. He remained committed to his studies, and in 1944 he won the Spingarn Medal from the NAACP for his criticism of the Red Cross's baseless policy of segregating white and black blood.

Frederick Douglass Patterson worked to ensure that more African Americans could get an education like the one Drew received. Raised in Texas by his older sister, Patterson earned a number of degrees: a doctorate of veterinary medicine (1923), a master of science (1927) from Iowa State College, and a second doctorate from Cornell University in 1932. He taught for four years at Virginia State College, then went to the Tuskegee Institute in 1928. From 1935 to 1953 he served as Tuskegee's president. A stellar leader, he aimed to help other black schools find the same success. In 1943, he called on black colleges to work together

an athletic director at Morgan College in Baltimore; he then enrolled in medical school at McGill University in Montreal. He graduated in 1933, completed an internship and residency in Montreal, and then began teaching pathology at the Howard University Medical School. The dean of the medical school, Numa P. G. Adams, nominated him for a fellowship to study medicine at Columbia

to raise money for their collective advancement. The next year, Patterson and other notable African Americans, including Mary McLeod Bethune, officially formed the United Negro College Fund. The UNCF declared that "a mind is a terrible thing to waste" and continues to this day to fund African American schools and students.

AFRICAN AMERICANS IN THE MILITARY DURING WORLD WAR II

During World War II African Americans increased their calls for social and political equality. Since the American Revolution, they argued, they had served their country in the military and therefore deserved the full rights of citizenship. They organized the "Double V" campaign, signifying victory against the Axis abroad and against racism at home. Begun by *The Pittsburgh Courier* in 1942, black newspapers around the country printed images of the Double V with an eagle and the words "Democracy" and "At Home—Abroad." Even sheet music covers carried the insignia.

Before the United States entered the war, however, blacks had begun breaking racial barriers in the military. On October 25, 1940, after forty-two years of service, Benjamin O. Davis, Sr., became the first African American general in the army. His leadership during the war earned him the Bronze Star and the Distinguished Service Cross, the nation's second-highest military honor. In 1945, Colonel Benjamin O. Davis, Jr., commander of the Tuskegee Airmen, followed in his father's footsteps and became the first African American to command a military base when he took over Goodman Field in Kentucky.

In 1942, the U.S. Marine Corps, long known as a bastion of white manhood, accepted its first African American soldiers. Blacks demonstrated their valor during combat and proved that they deserved high-ranking appointments. When the Japanese attacked Pearl Harbor on the morning of December 7, 1941, an African American messman named Doris "Dorie" Miller not only helped save his injured comrades but also manned a machine gun and shot down four Japanese aircraft. For his efforts he earned the prestigious Navy Cross.

Even though Miller and most other blacks remained confined to the lowest ranks, often given menial noncombat positions, African Americans continued to distinguish themselves on the battlefield. In 1943 the black pilots of the 99th Pursuit Squadron, later the 332nd Air Expeditionary Wing—known as the Tuskegee Airmen—flew in the North African Campaign and over Italy. The little-known 51st Defense Battalion of marines fought in the Pacific theater, and at least five hundred African American soldiers participated in the D-Day invasion of Normandy. (Countless popular films have depicted the momentous

Benjamin O. Davis, Sr. (1880–1970). Davis began his military career in the Spanish-American War. In 1901 he became one of three black officers in the entire U.S. Army. He later served in the Philippines and after World War I attained the rank of lieutenant colonel. He made full colonel in 1930, the only black officer in the army at the time, and was promoted to general in 1940.

Admiral Chester W. Nimitz gives the Navy Cross to Doris Miller, May 27, 1942. Miller (1919–43) had joined the U.S. Navy in 1939. After basic training, he was assigned to the USS *West Virginia*. Miller, who shot down several Japanese planes during the attack on Pearl Harbor, received his well-deserved award only because *The Pittsburgh Courier*, an influential black newspaper, waged a campaign to compel the navy to recognize his heroism. The navy balked, and President Roosevelt personally ordered that Miller receive the medal.

invasion, but all have ignored black participation.) In 1944, African Americans in the 333rd, 578th, and 969th Field Artillery battalions fought in the Battle of the Bulge. Eleven members of the 333rd paid the ultimate price when German soldiers captured and executed them.

Despite their valor, blacks continued to face discrimination in the military. The overwhelming majority of black soldiers worked at low-level tasks: digging ditches, cooking, cleaning, and laboring in the motor pools. African

Black marine gun crew of the 51st Defense Battalion at a Pacific military base, 1945. These marines named their cannon "Lena Horne."

Lieutenant General George S. Patton, commander of the Third Army, pins the Silver Star on Private Ernest A. Jenkins for gallantry during the liberation of Chateaudun, France, October 13, 1944.

Americans comprised less than 2 percent of all officers and often received assignments deemed unfit for their white counterparts. Others, however, worked in engineering units and built important supply roads in all theaters of the conflict. Many black soldiers—and their civilian brethren—could only bear it in silence when German soldiers imprisoned in the South enjoyed privileges denied to African American citizens.

Conflicts over the color line occurred

Platoon of black troops just off Omaha Beach, near Vierville-sur-Mer, June 10, 1944.

Agana, Guam.

on American bases overseas as well. In Agana, Guam, racial tension built throughout 1944. Numerous times white servicemen assaulted and even fired on their black comrades. On Christmas Eve a full-scale riot erupted and continued through Christmas Day. White soldiers fired on blacks in their barracks, who returned the volley. Military police arrested forty-four blacks but no whites. Despite the intervention of Walter White and the NAACP, the accused soldiers received jail sentences of up to four years. In 1946, the NAACP successfully appealed to the War Department to reverse the sentences, but the case demonstrated the depth of discrimination that black soldiers faced.

THE TUSKEGEE AIRMEN

Thanks in part to the persistence of Mary McLeod Bethune, the Civilian Pilot Training Program solicited the participation of African American colleges and universities, including the Tuskegee Institute. When World War II began, the federal government made Tuskegee the most important hub of civilian pilot training in the country. The first class of black pilots began preparation on July 19, 1941. The students completed rigorous programs of navigation and meteorology, then moved to actual flight training at the new (and segregated) Tuskegee Army Base. The first five African American pilots earned their "silver wings" and graduated as fighter pilots on March 7, 1942. During the war Tuskegee trained 962 black pilots, 450 of whom flew in combat.

While the existence of black pilots was a notable story by itself, African Americans also distinguished themselves in combat in nine different squad-

Edward C. Gleed of Lawrence, Kansas, leans on a wing tank of a P51-D fighter at the airbase of the 332nd Fighter Group at Ramitelli, Italy, March 1945.

Members of the 332nd Fighter Group at a briefing in Ramitelli, Italy, March 1945. From left to right are Robert W. Williams, William H. Holloman, Ronald W. Reeves, Christopher W. Newman, and Walter M. Downs.

rons: the 332nd Fighter Group, the 99th, 100th, 301st, 302nd Fighter Squadrons, and the 616th, 617th, 618th, and 619th Bombardment Squadrons, which flew medium (two-engine) bombers. Called "Red Tails" because they painted their planes' tail sections red to distinguish them, the 99th Squadron began on March 10, 1941, and remained active until July 1, 1949.

The squadrons of the 332nd Fighter Group, led by Colonel Benjamin O. Davis, Jr., battled in North Africa and in the Mediterranean. The 332nd flew 179 bomber escort missions, and its members shot down 111 Axis aircraft. They also destroyed ground fighters, as well as enemy trucks and railroads. On March 24, 1945, the 332nd participated in the longest bomber escort mission of the war and in the process shot down three of the revolutionary German ME-262 jet fighters and damaged five others without losing any of their own bombers or planes.

Together the 99th and 332nd flew more than fifteen hundred missions during the war, earning the respect of many Army Air Corps bomber pilots for their fighter protection and for losing very few bombers to enemy air attacks. In recognition of their professionalism, the airmen earned Silver Stars, Distinguished Flying Crosses, and Purple Hearts. Sixty-six Tuskegee Airmen died during the war, and the 332nd received a Distinguished Unit Citation for "outstanding performance and extraordinary heroism."

Colonel Davis understood that the

mission of the Tuskegee Airmen went beyond victories on the battlefield. By demonstrating their courage and valor, these black pilots destroyed the racist myth that African Americans lacked the intelligence and discipline and courage to successfully fly a plane in combat (far more insidious than the myth that black men couldn't play quarterback). When black activists pressed President Harry Truman to eliminate segregation in the military, they could point to the Tuskegee Airmen to show that they deserved equal treatment.

WORLD WAR II–ERA RACE RIOTS

Mobilization for World War II brought hundreds of thousands of new migrants into American cities. Competition for defense industry jobs, housing, and other scarce resources created many of the same problems that had plagued urban areas during the Great Migration. Tensions between blacks and whites over jobs often exploded into violence: in 1943 alone, incredibly, race riots erupted in forty-seven cities.

The deadliest World War II–era race riot occurred in Detroit, where more than sixty thousand African Americans streamed looking for work in the defense industries. For years Detroit had suffered housing and food shortages; this new influx of migrants angered the working-class whites. During the summer of 1943, racial conflict intensified into the bloodiest American race riot since the 1921 Tulsa insurrection.

On June 20, thousands of Detroiters—whites and blacks—went to Belle Isle Park to escape the summer heat. The cauldron of humidity and close proximity resulted in dozens of racially

Mob surrounds a streetcar in Detroit, June 22, 1943.

motivated fights involving more than two hundred people. As day turned to night, wild, irresponsible rumors spread through both white and black neighborhoods: blacks had raped and murdered a white woman on a bridge; whites had killed a black woman and thrown her

baby into the water. In a frenzy, whites, often with the assistance of police, went into black neighborhoods and attacked African Americans at random. By the time the chaos ended two days later, twenty-five blacks and nine whites had died.

White rioters attacking a car owned by African Americans in Detroit, June 20–22, 1943.

A month later, New York's Harlem erupted in violence for a much different reason. A white police officer had injured an African American during an arrest; rumors then transformed the incident such that the officer allegedly committed murder. Since that happened with shocking regularity, most residents never questioned the story. Seeking revenge, black residents began looting and destroying white-owned businesses, resulting in the death of six residents.

Wartime urban strife occurred in the South as well, especially in the increasingly crowded coastal shipping boomtowns. The workforce at the Alabama Dry Dock and Shipbuilding Company in Mobile had grown from 1,000 to 30,000, including 7,000 blacks. The FEPC demanded that the company desegregate its workforce; after months of resistance, it finally acquiesced. On May 24, 1943, it promoted twelve African Americans to skilled welding positions. Whites, feeling that their jobs and racial privilege had been assaulted, attacked black workers and ejected them from the plant. Army troops stationed at

nearby Brookley Field had to quell the fighting.

On June 15, rioting exploded in Beaumont, Texas, when a white woman accused a black man of raping her. A mob rushed nearby black neighborhoods, destroying stores, restaurants, and more than one hundred homes. The mayor placed the city under martial law and called in the Texas National Guard.

The rioting peaked in 1943 but did not end with the war. In Columbia, Tennessee, on February 25–26, 1946, a black veteran and a white clerk at a radio repair shop began fighting. The city moved toward mayhem, and police swept into the black business district, but rather than keep the peace, these officers, with the assistance of state troopers, shot into black homes and businesses, looted stores, stole weapons, and arrested more than one hundred African Americans.

Ugly racial eruptions also occurred when African Americans, including veterans, attempted to purchase homes in the booming postwar suburbs. Many of these communities, such as the one at Levittown, New York, refused to sell houses to blacks. Buttressing this galling discrimination, banks refused to extend loans to prospective black buyers, and the federal government failed to distribute postwar benefits fairly to black servicemen and their families. In 1951, when a black family moved into a formerly all-white apartment building in the Chicago suburb of Cicero, thousands of whites responded with violence. The family and their real estate agent then were indicted on charges of conspiring to lower property values. In Cicero and elsewhere in suburbia, racial hatred and persistent discrimination belied the nation's wartime aims of ending oppression and preserving democracy.

The same year brought tragedy to Florida. Harry T. Moore had founded the Brevard County branch of the NAACP in 1934, then organized the statewide branch seven years later. After the Supreme Court outlawed the whites-only primary in its 1946 *Smith*

Mobile's Alabama Dry Dock and Shipbuilding Company, founded in 1917, was one of the largest shipbuilding firms in the country. Out of a workforce that eventually reached 30,000, approximately 7,000 were African Americans.

v. Allwright decision, Moore organized the Progressive Voters League and helped more than one hundred thousand blacks register. His persistent critique of segregation, inequality, and lynching made him a convenient target for white supremacists, who retaliated: in 1946, both Moore and his wife lost their teaching jobs. But the Moores would not relent. Harry Moore led the charge to investigate a rape and murder case that had occurred in Groveland, Florida, and Moore called for the resignation of the local sheriff. Six weeks later, on Christmas Day 1951, a bomb exploded in Moore's bedroom, killing both him and his wife. The crime remains unsolved.

Orkin's clothing store on 125th Street, one of about thirty shops damaged during the Harlem riot, August 2, 1943.

JOHN H. JOHNSON, *EBONY*, AND *JET*

John H. Johnson rose from poverty to become the nation's most famous black publisher. Born in 1918 in Arkansas City, Arkansas, he attended grade school to the eighth grade, but his hometown had no black high school. So Johnson's mother scraped together enough money for them to move north to Chicago in 1933. There Johnson attended the segregated Du Sable High School, known for its rigorous academic standards, with classmates Nat "King" Cole and Redd Foxx, and graduated with distinction in 1936.

During the Depression, the family struggled but obtained assistance from the WPA and the National Youth Administration, which offered full- and part-time job opportunities and training to high school– and college-age young men and women. Johnson earned a scholarship to attend the University of Chicago but did not complete his studies. Because of an impressive speech

John H. Johnson (1918–2005), in his office, February 1974.

Johnson delivered at a meeting of the National Urban League, Harry Pace of the Supreme Liberty Life Insurance Company offered the aspiring young man a job. While at the company, Johnson conceived of a *Reader's Digest*–style magazine for African Americans and in

1942 began publishing the *Negro Digest*. Within six months circulation reached 50,000; eventually, it would rise to 100,000. The Johnson media empire had been born.

Johnson had financed that magazine with a loan from his mother. Once that venture proved successful, in November 1945, he founded another imprint, which he named *Ebony*. With initial sales of 25,000 copies, *Ebony* was an immediate success and has remained the largest circulating black publication since the first issue hit newsstands. Patterned in appearance after *Life,* the magazine addressed issues of race and black culture that the mainstream press largely ignored. It reported on racism, segregation, civil rights legislation, and freedom rides and marches, and especially important, it highlighted black economic and social success.

In 1951, Johnson began still another publication, a weekly newsmagazine that he named *Jet*. (Named for the color jet black, it was often referred to as "The Jet" in the black vernacular.) It too covered the civil rights movement, but in a smaller and abridged format, and it subsequently focused on fashion, beauty, personal advice, and news of black celebrities, like the later *People* magazine. Building on his success, Johnson published *African American Stars* and *Ebony Jr.,* a children's magazine. Although successful, none of the new ventures could compete with *Ebony*, which in its fortieth year of publication reached a circulation of 2.3 million, making Johnson one of the most successful publishers in the history of American journalism, and one of the wealthiest individuals in the United States.

After founding *Jet,* Johnson expanded his empire into book publishing, radio stations, and television production. In 1958, Ebony Fashion Fair, run by his wife, Eunice Walker Johnson, became the world's largest traveling fashion show. Since its inception, the fair has raised more than $51 million for the United Negro College Fund and other scholarship programs. In 1957, Johnson accompanied Vice President Richard M. Nixon on a goodwill tour of nine African countries, and in 1961, President John F. Kennedy appointed him special U.S. ambassador to the independence ceremonies of the Ivory Coast. In 1973, Johnson launched Fashion Fair Cosmetics to serve African American women,

whose skin-care needs had traditionally been ignored by mainstream cosmetic companies. Johnson was the first African American to appear on *Forbes* magazine's list of the four hundred wealthiest Americans. In 1966, he received the Spingarn Medal, the highest honor of the NAACP, for his contributions to African American culture. In 1972, he was named publisher of the year by the major U.S. magazine publishers. In 1988, the Martin Luther King Jr. Center for Nonviolent Social Change recognized his philanthropic and humanitarian work. And in 1995, President Bill Clinton awarded him the Presidential Medal of Freedom, the nation's highest civilian honor.

THE CONGRESS OF RACIAL EQUALITY AND THE JOURNEY OF RECONCILIATION

On April 9, 1947, an interracial group of nine activists, trailed by two reporters from black newspapers, boarded a bus in the nation's capital and set out to test the enforcement of the *Morgan v. Virginia* decision (1946). The Supreme Court had ruled segregation in interstate transit unconstitutional, but southerners remained recalcitrant—bus companies continued to segregate passengers, arguing that, as private companies, they could do as they pleased. Members of a relatively new civil rights organization, the Congress of Racial Equality (CORE), organized the test.

Originating in Chicago in 1942, CORE was a political offshoot of the pacifist Fellowship of Reconciliation (FOR). Inspired by Gandhian protest in India, CORE's founders—James Farmer, George Houser, and Bernice Fisher—hoped to use nonviolent resistance to advance the cause of black civil rights. Houser and fellow CORE activist

James Farmer (1920–99). The son of a Texas Methodist minister who had earned a Ph.D. in religion from Boston University, Farmer attended Howard University and began his career opposing segregation by working with the Fellowship of Reconciliation, a Quaker organization. Inspired by the teachings of Gandhi, he went on to help found CORE. Manhattan, June 20, 1964.

Journey of Reconciliation members Worth Randle, Wally Nelson, Ernest Bromley, Jim Peck, Igal Rodenko, Bayard Rustin, Joe Felmet, George H. Houser, and Andy Johnson outside the office of Attorney S. W. Robinson in Richmond, Virginia, 1947.

Bayard Rustin saw protesting bus segregation as an ideal way to advance civil rights and expand their fledgling organization into the South. They decided to focus only on the Upper South, however, fearing that further penetration would result in needless violence and possible death. Much to the chagrin of activists like Pauli Murray and Ella Baker, CORE leadership decided that the ride should be all male. Rustin and Houser called the project the "Journey of Reconciliation."

In January, Rustin and Houser traveled through Virginia, North Carolina, Tennessee, and Kentucky to scout the planned route. They sought out local activists and laid the foundation for support for the ride. In early April, they organized a meeting of sixteen volunteers in Washington to prepare for the trip. Over two days they conducted seminars that attempted to brace the young

men for what they would encounter south of the Mason-Dixon Line. They acted out the roles of antagonistic bus drivers, violent police, and militant segregationists, and they formulated a list of rules about where to sit on the bus and what to do when arrested.

When the nine riders left Washington on April 9, they believed they would change society. They divided into two groups: one boarded a Trailways bus, the other a Greyhound. The first leg of the trip, which finished in Richmond, went exceedingly well. The riders met no serious resistance, and in a few cases they even garnered the support of bus drivers and their fellow passengers. The second leg, en route to Petersburg, Virginia, went equally well, although one black passenger warned the riders, "Some bus drivers are crazy, and the further South you go, the crazier they get."[4]

Indeed, the road got rougher almost

immediately. As the Greyhound group prepared to leave Petersburg, they met harassment not only from whites but also from African Americans who appeared threatened by the agitation. When the Trailways group reached Durham, North Carolina, police arrested Rustin, Johnson, and James Peck for refusing to abide by segregation rules. The riders enjoyed a brief sanctuary in the relatively liberal college town of Chapel Hill, where a number of progressive whites supported them. But when they tried to leave for Greensboro, more riders were arrested, and local whites assaulted James Peck on the street. They had to travel to Greensboro by car to resume the ride while one of their white supporters in Chapel Hill, the Reverend Charles M. Jones, faced death threats for cooperating with the protest.

The remainder of the journey produced similarly mixed results in North Carolina, Tennessee, and Kentucky. Although the group found some success in desegregating individual buses—and even a train car—they continued to face resistance and arrest. James Peck and the African American musician Charles Banks were sentenced to thirty days of hard labor for sitting next to each other on a bus in Asheville, North Carolina. Out on bail, Banks was again arrested in Culpeper, Virginia. By the time the riders returned to Washington on April 23, CORE recorded twenty-six desegregated buses. Twelve protesters, however, had been arrested. The rides received little attention from the white press, and the efforts resulted in little change on interstate transit. But they had demonstrated that nonviolent direct action could have an impact, even in the South. More important, they provided a blueprint that, fourteen years later, a new group of CORE activists would carry out to great success.

JOHN HOPE FRANKLIN

Few academic publications have had the lasting impact of John Hope Franklin's *From Slavery to Freedom: A History of African Americans*. First published in 1947, Franklin's book made it possible to teach a survey course in African American history using one textbook. This would have, over the crucial next two decades especially, an enormous impact on the institutionalization of African American history in college and high school curricula.

Franklin was not the first professional historian to write about African Americans. The autodidact George Washington Williams, about whom Franklin would write a major biography, wrote perhaps the first comprehensive history. And several major black historians—W. E. B. Du Bois, Carter G. Woodson, Rayford W. Logan, and Charles Wesley among them—earned their Ph.D.s at Harvard in the field and published works on various aspects of the African American experience. But major white scholars paid scant attention to "Negro history," and not even the academically trained black historians had completed a comprehensive narrative that could be utilized in the classroom for a one- or two-semester survey course.

A young Harvard history Ph.D. teaching at the North Carolina College for Negroes (now North Carolina Central University), Franklin stepped in to fill the void. He recast "Negro history," framing it not simply as a discrete subset of American history but as a saga inextricably intertwined with American history as a whole. *From Slavery to Freedom* traces the story of African Americans from their origins in Africa to the rise of slavery, from the evolution of a distinct culture among the enslaved and freed blacks to emancipation and the

John Hope Franklin (1915–2009).

ongoing struggle for freedom in the United States, the Caribbean, and Latin America.

In his 2005 autobiography, *Mirror to America,* Franklin described what moved him to write the text:

In the planning and writing of my work, I had witnessed more than five hundred years of human history pass before my eyes. I had seen one slave ship after another from Portugal, Spain, France, Holland, England, and the United States pile black human cargo into its bowels as it would coal or even gold had either been more available and profitable at the time. I had seen them dump my ancestors at New World ports as they would a load of cattle and wait smugly for their pay for capture and transport. I had seen them beat black men until they themselves became weary and rape black women until their ecstasy was spent leaving their brutish savagery exposed. I had heard them shout, "Give us

liberty or give us death," and not mean one word of it. I had seen them measure out medication or education for a sick or ignorant white child and ignore a black child similarly situated. I had seen them lynch black men and distribute their ears, fingers, and other parts as souvenirs to the ghoulish witnesses. I had seen it all, and in the seeing I had become bewildered and yet in the process lost my own innocence.[5]

Originally published in 1947, Franklin's impassioned work was not immediately recognized as a masterpiece; nor did it sell. In his autobiography, he recalls a stinging review in *The New York Times* and disappointing first-year sales. But as the civil rights movement gained strength in the 1950s, the academic community began to appreciate what the African American scholar of American literature William Harrison called in his *Boston Chronicle* review "the impressive grandeur of the total achievement."[6] By the time Franklin published a second edition in 1956, *From Slavery to Freedom* was widely recognized as essential to a full understanding of American history. The ninth edition, rewritten by Evelyn Brooks Higginbotham, was published in 2010. Since its initial publication, *From Slavery to Freedom* has sold nearly four million copies and has been translated into several languages.

Franklin's death in March 2009, at the age of ninety-four, marked the end of a long career of scholarship and public service. His contributions to academia went well beyond his most famous work. He published a dozen notable books, as well as more than one hundred scholarly articles, and he taught and inspired countless students at a variety of institutions, including Fisk University, St. Augustine's College, North Carolina Central University, Howard University, Brooklyn College, the University of Chicago, and Duke University. A consummate public intellectual, he became well known for his work on pressing social issues. In the early 1950s, he assisted Thurgood Marshall and the NAACP Legal Defense team with preparations for *Brown v. Board of Education,* and in the 1990s, President Clinton appointed him chair of a national commission on race. By then an iconic figure, Franklin was awarded the Presidential Medal of Freedom, the nation's highest civilian honor, in 1995.

JACKIE ROBINSON AND BLACK BASEBALL

Rube Foster's team, the American Giants, at Schorling Field in Chicago, panoramic view. The former home of the White Sox, the field had been known as South Side Park, but Foster named the field after his business partner John C. Schorling, a South Side saloon keeper and the son-in-law of the owner of the White Sox.

While baseball's major leagues began excluding African Americans in 1887, blacks found alternative ways to play the game. The first attempt to form an all-black league failed, but black independent teams continued to play around the country. The Homestead Grays, the Philadelphia Giants, and the New York Lincoln Giants regularly competed on the East Coast. The Midwest featured the Indianapolis ABCs, the St. Louis Giants, and a number of teams based in Chicago. In the South clubs formed in Atlanta, Birmingham, and Jacksonville. All these teams often played informal championship games but lacked a formal league structure. That changed in 1920 when Rube Foster founded the Negro National League (NNL).

Foster had had a distinguished career in his own right as a star pitcher for the Cuban X Giants and the Philadelphia Giants and was a successful manager for the Chicago American Giants. For the next eleven years, the NNL fielded teams across the Midwest and Deep South, including the Detroit Stars, the Kansas City Monarchs, and the Birmingham Black Barons. Although the league folded in 1931 as a casualty of the Great Depression, it set the blueprint for future Negro Leagues, including a new Negro National League in 1933 and the Negro American League in 1937. All the while teams kept playing barnstorming games outside the league schedule. Great players like Satchel Paige and Josh Gibson showed that African Americans could compete equally with even the most outstanding professional white players.

Ironically, the death of the Negro Leagues in the 1940s and 1950s resulted from something a great number of black ballplayers wanted: the desegregation of major league baseball. On April 9, 1947, the Brooklyn Dodgers announced the signing of Jack Roosevelt Robinson. Jackie Robinson grew up in Pasadena, California, where he proved himself to be one of the state's most gifted ballplayers. After serving in the military in the early 1940s, Robinson joined the Kansas City Monarchs and hit for a .387 average in forty-seven games in 1945. Meanwhile, Branch Rickey, the owner of the Brooklyn Dodgers, saw the potential for bringing an African American player onto his team. Not only did Rickey personally dislike the exclusion of black players, but he also believed that signing skilled African Americans would make his team more competitive and more

Jackie Robinson (1919–72) at Ebbets Field, New York, legendary home of the Brooklyn Dodgers, April 11, 1947.

Rube Foster (1879–1930). Born Andrew Foster in Calvert, Texas, Rube seemed born to play baseball and even organized a team while in grade school. By the age of eighteen, he had become a star pitcher. A strong player and a determined businessman, Foster ended his days in a state mental asylum. Nevertheless, his fame endured, and upon his death his body lay in state for several days to accommodate the crowds who wished to pay their respects.

profitable. He chose Robinson because he felt that his education and youth in majority-white Pasadena prepared him for the firestorm he would enter.

During his first season with the Dodgers in 1947, Robinson endured abuse from all corners. On the field, pitchers threw at his head, and opposing players deliberately slid into him with their spikes up. Fans booed and heckled. He even received numerous death threats. Despite the harassment and jeers of whites across the country, Robinson not only broke the color line but demonstrated his great talent and skills, earning the Rookie of the Year Award and going on to win the Most Valuable Player Award in 1949. All the while, the

Dodgers set attendance records. In one of the most famous plays in baseball history, Robinson stole home against the New York Yankees during the 1955 World Series, which the Dodgers would go on to win. In 1962 Robinson was the first African American player elected to the Baseball Hall of Fame.

In some ways Robinson's success was bittersweet. In the next decade, many of the best players of the Negro Leagues—including Roy Campanella, Willie Mays, and Ernie Banks—found success in the majors. Without its top talent, the Negro Leagues could not continue. The second Negro National League collapsed in 1948, and the Negro American League ceased operations in

1960. Still, the desegregation of major league baseball held great importance for the game and for the nation. Desegregating baseball, it turned out, was a dry run for desegregating other parts of American society.

Perhaps no player better symbolized the importance of blacks to the national pastime than Henry "Hank" Aaron. Aaron played with the Indianapolis Clowns of the Negro American League before making his major league debut with the Milwaukee Braves in 1954. Nearly every year, a model of consistency, Aaron hit thirty or forty home runs and drove in more than one hundred runs. Soon Aaron's talents brought him within striking distance of baseball's greatest record: Babe Ruth's 714 career home runs. As Aaron drew closer, he bore the wrath of many angry white fans, several of whom threatened to kill him. As he ended the

1973 season with 713 home runs, he had reason to believe he might not make it to the next season. But at the beginning of the 1974 season, he tied Ruth's record in Cincinnati. And on April 8, 1974, in front of his home crowd in Atlanta, Aaron hit home run number 714, making him baseball's home run king. Like Jackie Robinson's debut in the majors, Jack Johnson's heavyweight championship, Joe Louis's stunning defeat of Max Schmeling, and Jesse Owens's four gold medals in the 1936 Olympics, Aaron's achievement had a much larger, symbolic significance in the history of American race relations. Sports in America was a metaphorical battleground for larger and more sweeping social change.

EXECUTIVE ORDERS AND TO SECURE THESE RIGHTS

President Harry Truman knew he faced an uphill climb toward reelection. The nation's economy had faltered after the war, and political opponents accused him of weakness in dealing with the Soviet Union. The Republicans took control of Congress during the midterm elections of 1946, and Thomas Dewey promised a strong challenge for the presidential election of 1948. Within his own party, Truman had to contend with challenges from the left (the progressive Henry Wallace) and the right (the South Carolina Dixiecrat senator Strom Thurmond).

African Americans took advantage of Truman's uncertain future to push him for change. In the summer of 1946, the White House faced a barrage of pickets and marches from black activists. African Americans knew they had something the president coveted: votes. Truman responded with a series of executive orders aimed at dismantling racial discrimination. On December 5, 1946, he issued Executive Order 9808, which created the President's Committee on Civil Rights. Truman charged the interracial committee with compiling a report on how "current law-enforcement measures and the authority and means possessed by federal, state, and local governments may be strengthened and improved to safeguard the civil rights of the people." The committee's report, *To Secure These Rights,* detailed the forms

Portrait of Committee of Southern Governors, March 13, 1948, Washington, D.C. The committee attempted to rally white southerners to resist President Truman's civil rights program and those who proposed it. Left to right, seated: J. Strom Thurmond, South Carolina; James E. Folsom, Alabama; William Preston Lane, Jr., Maryland, chairman; Fielding L. Wright, Mississippi; standing—Ben T. Laney, Arkansas; M. E. Thompson, Georgia; and Beauford H. Jester, Texas.

of discrimination that black people suffered, and called for antilynching legislation and an immediate end to segregation and the poll tax. It asserted that discrimination was morally wrong, that it hurt the nation's economy by eliminating blacks as producers and consumers, and (in Cold War language) embarrassed the United States in the eyes of the world.

On February 2, 1948, Truman made an unprecedented civil rights address to Congress, calling for the implementation of the Civil Rights Committee's findings. The conservative southern wing of the party responded later that

313

ESTABLISHING THE PRESIDENT'S COMMITTEE ON
EQUALITY OF TREATMENT AND OPPORTUNITY IN
THE ARMED SERVICES

WHEREAS it is essential that there be maintained in the
armed services of the United States the highest standards of
democracy, with equality of treatment and opportunity for all
those who serve in our country's defense:

NOW, THEREFORE, by virtue of the authority vested in
me as President of the United States, by the Constitution and the
statutes of the United States, and as Commander in Chief of the
armed services, it is hereby ordered as follows:

1. It is hereby declared to be the policy of the President
that there shall be equality of treatment and opportunity for all
persons in the armed services without regard to race, color,
religion or national origin. This policy shall be put into effect
as rapidly as possible, having due regard to the time required
to effectuate any necessary changes without impairing efficiency
or morale.

2. There shall be created in the National Military Establishment an advisory committee to be known as the President's
Committee on Equality of Treatment and Opportunity in the Armed
Services, which shall be composed of seven members to be designated by the President.

3. The Committee is authorized on behalf of the President
to examine into the rules, procedures and practices of the armed
services in order to determine in what respect such rules, procedures and practices may be altered or improved with a view
to carrying out the policy of this order. The Committee shall
confer and advise with the Secretary of Defense, the Secretary

Executive Order 9981, July 26, 1948.

year by walking out of the Democratic National Convention. Convinced that black voters could make the difference in the election, Truman issued two more executive orders on July 26, 1948. Number 9980 called for fair employment in the federal government and established a Fair Employment Board and fair employment officers, to respond to complaints of discrimination in the workplace. Executive Order 9981 ordered an end to unequal treatment and eventually to segregation in the armed forces. Truman intended this latter order to end the embarrassment of a Jim Crow military overseas, where the Soviet Union and its allies could easily and convincingly point to American hypocrisy.

Truman won reelection, famously displaying an issue of the *Chicago Tribune* that had erroneously proclaimed "Dewey Defeats Truman." Blacks had voted for him in unprecedented numbers, but the president failed to live up to his civil rights agenda. Conservative congressmen blocked his attempts at reform, and military desegregation did not occur until the Korean War two years later. Congress also voted down legislation that would have made the FEPC permanent. Still, Truman's executive orders had formalized the importance of equality and ensured that Democratic politicians, to win elections, would have to account for the interests and concerns of African American voters.

THE ARTISTRY OF GORDON PARKS

Gordon Parks, Sr., born in 1912 in Fort Scott, Kansas, one of fifteen children, was the first black mainstream representative of the art of American photography. His early years, however, had predicted a different outcome. After his mother's death in 1928, his father sent him to live with a sister in Minneapolis–St. Paul, but conflict with his brother-in-law sent young Parks into the streets. He rode railcars at night and stayed in pool halls during the day. He attended school only episodically, and in high school one teacher advised all the black students to forget college since they would never amount to anything but porters and maids. He wandered, played piano in a brothel, and then moved to Harlem in search of work. In 1933, Parks joined the New Deal's Civilian Conservation Corps and the next year found employment with two railroad companies.

Gordon Parks (1912–2006).

In 1937, Parks picked up a discarded magazine and peered at images taken by Farm Security Administration photographers Walker Evans, Dorothea Lange, Ben Shahn, and Arthur Rothstein. This chance discovery proved transforming.

Parks bought a camera and began publishing his own photographs in hometown Minnesota newspapers; then he moved to Chicago where he found success as a fashion photographer. In 1941 he won a Julius Rosenwald Fellowship, the first ever awarded for photography, and an apprenticeship in the Farm Security Administration (which had initially sparked his interest in photography). As these images show, he possessed a keen eye for finding the extraordinary in the ordinary. He extensively photographed black life in Washington, D.C., and his image of Ella Watson with mop and broom, often referred to as "American Gothic, Washington D.C."—after the Grant Wood painting—was one of the most important images ever created by an American photographer.

In 1943, Parks went to work for the Office of War Information and photographed many of the Tuskegee Air-

Ella Watson, August 1942. One of Gordon Parks's best-known images.

Black women workers, New Britain, Connecticut, 1943.

men. The accomplished photographer Edward Steichen recognized his great talent and helped him get assignments at *Glamour* and *Vogue* magazines. Two books of Parks's photographs, *Flash Photography* (1947) and *Camera Portraits* (1948), enhanced his reputation. In 1948, *Life* magazine hired him as its first African American photographer, establishing a relationship that endured for twenty years. The result was some of the best photojournalism the magazine ever published. Over the course of his career, Parks photographed virtually everyone of significance, from dictators and gangsters to artists, writers, and presidents.

In addition to publishing three autobiographies, Parks also wrote poetry and three novels and ventured into filmmaking. Among his films are *The Learning Tree* (1969, based on his autobiographical novel), which the Library of Congress placed on its National Film Registry; the iconic *Shaft* (1971); and *Solomon Northup's Odyssey* (1984). Shortly before he died, Parks was honored by the Anisfield-Wolf Book Award, for lifetime achievement, for "being a national treasure."

Watson grandchildren, Washington, D.C., August 1942.

PART FOURTEEN

FOUNDATIONS OF THE NEW CIVIL RIGHTS MOVEMENT

1950–1963

BREAKING A BARRIER: BILLY ECKSTINE

Billy Eckstine (1914–93), *Life,* April 24, 1950.

In the 1940s and 1950s, Billy Eckstine was a major national recording star. His remarkably resonant and lyrical baritone and bebop trumpet catapulted him to stardom; in 1942, his rendition of "Skylark" outsold Bing Crosby's. By 1948, Eckstine had gained such an enormous following that he could reject Jim Crow venues and write into his contracts that he would be treated as a guest in whatever hotel he sang and that no racial restrictions would be placed on his audiences. While white marketers refused to capitalize on his sex appeal, his female audience thought otherwise. This image of Eckstine being adored by white female fans appeared in *Life* magazine on April 24, 1950, four years before the *Brown v. Board of Education* Supreme Court decision. In the history of black performers in America, it was unprecedented for a mainstream magazine to depict a black male with white females, except in an avuncular relationship, such as Uncle Tom or Stepin Fetchit. Singer Harry Belafonte recalled the enormous political impact that this photograph had within the black community as an explicit image of interracial sexual attraction. When we remember that interracial marriage was not legalized nationally until 1967, we can begin to understand how revolutionary this photograph was. And *Life,* part of Henry Luce's media empire, was not exactly a liberal publication. As Belafonte put it, "When that photo hit, in this national publication, it was as if a barrier had been broken."[1]

POSTWAR ACCOMPLISHMENTS: ALICE COACHMAN, WESLEY BROWN, GWENDOLYN BROOKS, AND RALPH BUNCHE

The years immediately following World War II saw African Americans achieve notable firsts in a number of fields.

Alice Coachman had dominated American track and field, the high jump in particular, since her youth in Georgia and Alabama. In the early 1940s, she attended high school and college at the Tuskegee Institute, where she won Amateur Athletic Union national championships in the high jump, the 50- and 100-meter dashes, and the 200-meter relay. In 1947, she transferred to Albany State College, where she became known as the "Tuskegee Flash." Olympic triumph seemed certain, but because of the war her Olympic dreams were postponed until 1948, when she became the first African American woman to take a gold medal. That year, nine of the twelve women on the women's Olympic team were black. She won the high jump competition with a record leap of 5 feet 6.5 inches. Although she retired after the games, Coachman remained active in athletic and charitable pursuits, and in 1996 she was named one of the hundred greatest Olympic athletes in history.

Wesley A. Brown had worked a number of odd jobs while growing up in Baltimore and Washington, D.C., from sorting clothes at a dry cleaner to delivering newspapers. At the age of fifteen, while attending Dunbar High School, he took a job in the mailroom at the Navy Department, working full-time and participating in the Cadet Corps two days a week. He also joined Carter G. Woodson's Association for the Study of Negro Life and History and attended Howard University. He

graduated in 1944 and, through family connections, came to the attention of Harlem congressman Adam Clayton Powell, Jr., who sponsored his enrollment in the Naval Academy. A previous black recruit had been unable to stand the constant bullying and punishment and had dropped out. Brown too faced discrimination, including severe paddling from higher-ranking cadets, vandalism of his property, and verbal abuse.

Still, he remained in the academy, won over many of his white peers through his determination, and in 1949 was its first African American graduate. He went on to a distinguished career in the Civil Engineer Corps, earning the rank of lieutenant commander.

Gwendolyn Brooks developed a love for writing while growing up in Chicago during the 1920s. Her stories and poems gained her the attention and

Alice Coachman (b. 1923), at the 1948 Olympics.

Wesley A. Brown (b. 1927), midshipman, at U.S. Naval Academy, 1949.

Ralph Bunche (1904–71), photograph by Carl Van Vechten, May 16, 1951.

and her womanhood. In 1950, *Annie Allen* made Brooks the first African American to win a Pulitzer Prize, and in 1968, the state of Illinois made her its poet laureate, succeeding Carl Sandburg. In 1976, she was the first black woman to be elected to the National Institute of Arts and Letters. She would build an accomplished career as a writer, with notable books including *Maud Martha* (1953), *The Bean Eaters* (1960), and *Riot* (1969). During the 1960s and 1970s, as the last title indicates, she participated in civil rights, the Black Arts Movement, and Black Power protests.

Like Brooks, Ralph Bunche's accomplishments make for a lengthy résumé. He earned a bachelor's degree in 1927 from the University of California at Los Angeles, where he graduated summa cum laude as class valedictorian. He continued his education with a master's and eventually a Ph.D. from Harvard University in 1934. He earned a reputation as an activist and scholar, helping to found the short-lived National Negro Congress and providing research for Gunnar Myrdal's influential 1944 *An American Dilemma.*

During the 1940s, Bunche pursued government work, becoming an analyst with the OSS (Office of Strategic Services), the forerunner of the CIA, and in 1946 attended the first session of the United Nations General Assembly. The same year he became director of the UN's trusteeship program and remained there for the remainder of his career. He played the key role in negotiating the armistice between the new state of Israel and the surrounding Arab states. For this achievement he won a Nobel Peace Prize in 1950, the first African American to receive that prestigious award. Shortly afterward, he was offered a tenured professorship at Harvard, the first black professor to be extended that privilege.

friendship of Langston Hughes. In 1945, she published her first book, *A Street in Bronzeville,* followed four years later by *Annie Allen.* The three-part book examines a girl's growing up and coming to terms with her race, her environment,

Bunche consistently condemned American racism and declined a position in the State Department because of the intense discrimination in the nation's capital. He participated in the 1965 march from Selma to Montgomery with Martin Luther King, Jr., and continued to work for the United Nations. President Kennedy honored him with the Medal of Freedom in 1963.

Gwendolyn Brooks (1917–2000) with Langston Hughes celebrating the publication of an award-winning anthology, *The Poetry of the Negro,* 1949.

BROWN V. BOARD OF EDUCATION AND SCHOOL DESEGREGATION

African American students of the famous *Brown v. Board of Education* case and their parents, Topeka, Kansas, 1953. Left to right, front row: Vicki Henderson, Donald Henderson, Linda Brown, James Emanuel, Nancy Todd, and Katherine Carper; back row: Zelma Henderson, Oliver Brown, Sadie Emanuel, Lucinda Todd, and Lena Carper.

During the 1930s, the NAACP adopted a novel strategy to dismantle de jure segregation: it would use the court system to concentrate on education. This was a bold strategy, and a risky one. Lawyers in the NAACP's Legal Defense Fund, organized in 1939 under the direction of Charles Hamilton Houston, hoped that showing the persistent inequality would force the courts to overturn *Plessy v. Ferguson,* the 1896 landmark decision that had ensconced the "separate but equal" doctrine in constitutional law.

Houston, trained at Harvard Law School and the dean of the law school at Howard, adopted a clever strategy that focused on the "equal" half of the "separate but equal" doctrine. In the 1930s, the NAACP convinced the Court to declare

unconstitutional the common practice in Missouri of forcing black law students to attend schools in neighboring states and paying their tuition. After the end of the Second World War, the NAACP grew in membership, and the victories of the previous decade encouraged the organization's new chief counsel, Thurgood Marshall, to challenge segregation head-on. In two cases decided the same day, June 5, 1950, the Supreme Court modified—but did not overturn—*Plessy.*

Heman Sweatt had sued because the University of Texas, rather than allow him to attend law school on campus in Austin, created an inferior school for blacks 150 miles away in Houston. In its *Sweatt v. Painter* decision, the Court agreed with Sweatt, saying that the university had violated his Fourteenth

Amendment rights and denied him the intangibles of studying at the prestigious Austin school. George McLaurin was a black schoolteacher who was nearly seventy years old in 1948 when he applied to attend the University of Oklahoma's School of Education. The school admitted McLaurin, but it separated him from his classmates by forcing him to sit in his own row and often in his own room. The Court ruled in *McLaurin v. Oklahoma* that segregation denied McLaurin the intangibles of studying and discussions that would train him as a leader of society.

In the early 1950s, a new chief justice unexpectedly made the Supreme Court more likely to abolish segregation. President Dwight D. Eisenhower would later call the appointment of

Attorneys George E. C. Hayes, Thurgood Marshall, and James M. Nabrit celebrate their victory in *Brown v. Board of Education,* 1954.

The Court conceded that *Brown* addressed nominally equal schools; therefore it addressed a different question than *Sweatt* or *McLaurin*. Segregation, it argued, existed only as a result of racism. "In the field of public education," the decision read, the "doctrine of separate-but-equal has no place. Separate educational facilities are inherently unequal." The Court overturned *Plessy* and with it the legal foundation of segregation.

The *Brown* decision did not read like a typical Supreme Court verdict. It cited few legal precedents; it was comparatively short; and it rested on sociological evidence, including two important books, Gunnar Myrdal's *An American Dilemma* (1944) and E. Franklin Frazier's *The Negro in the United States* (1939). Warren skillfully navigated a unanimous decision to remove any doubt about the strength of the Court's opinion. To unify the Court—and to court public opinion—Warren postponed a decision on enforcement until the following year.

Earl Warren the "biggest damn fool mistake I ever made."[2] Warren's résumé did not indicate any liberal leanings. He had built a career as a ruthless, anti-communist district attorney in Alameda County, California. He supported Japanese internment camps during World War II, and while he later apologized for the roundup of Japanese citizens, he maintained that the government could suppress personal liberties during wartime. He grew more moderate in the 1950s but gave no indication whatsoever that he would seek to transform American race relations as a Supreme Court justice. But he did just that.

In the fall of 1950, the NAACP sued on behalf of third-grader Linda Brown of Topeka, Kansas. Brown's parents wanted her to attend the local white school, since it was much closer to their home than the segregated school that the city forced Linda to attend. Marshall argued that segregation stigmatized children, stamping them with the badge of inferiority that the Court had ostensibly forbidden in the *Plessy* decision. On appeal, the Supreme Court heard the suit in combination with others from Virginia, Delaware, South Carolina, and Washington, D.C. (The case was named after Brown because her name came first alphabetically.) On May 17, 1954, a unanimous Supreme Court ruled in favor of the black students.

George W. McLaurin sits apart from other students in a classroom, 1948. McLaurin (1887–1968) applied to the all-white University of Oklahoma for an advanced degree in education. Because Oklahoma statutes outlawed integrated classrooms, his application was rejected. He filed a complaint against the university on the state court level and won. This photograph shows how the school accommodated his presence. In 1950, McLaurin again sued and won, helping to pave the way for the *Brown v. Board of Education* case.

In the *Brown II* decision in 1955, the Court ruled that school desegregation must occur with "all deliberate speed." Recalcitrant white southerners interpreted the vague phrase "all deliberate speed" to mean "slow" or "never." Local and state officials went out of their way to minimize *Brown*'s import and keep schools segregated. White supremacists and opportunistic politicians targeted those schools that attempted to integrate peacefully. Additionally, southern states halted most or all financial assistance previously allocated to local black colleges and universities, severely hampering the effectiveness of these institutions, which had educated the overwhelming percentage of black students since the Civil War. It would take more than a decade for meaningful desegregation to begin in many parts of the South. But the *Brown* decision had overturned *Plessy* and set the stage for dramatic advances in civil rights.

INVISIBLE MAN

Perhaps the most insidious and least understood form of segregation is that of the word," Ralph Ellison declared in "Twentieth-Century Fiction and the Black Mask of Humanity," an essay he wrote shortly after World War II.[3] Segregation of the word, Ellison argued, manifested itself in the racist stereotypes used in American literature to circumscribe the lives of African Americans; it was the literary equivalent of Jim Crow. Just as legalized racial segregation limited how African Americans could live, so did literary stereotypes of African Americans as deracinated clowns, lascivious criminals, and meek, childlike Aunt Janes and Uncle Toms. Little did Ellison know, at the time he wrote this essay, that his novel, *Invisible Man* (1952), would perhaps more effectively challenge the literary color line than any other book before it.

A first-person narrative of a nameless black protagonist, the novel incorporates surrealism, African American vernacular forms (such as the blues, jazz, black humor, and folklore), and brilliantly subtle echoes of an astonishing range of canonical American and European literature to depict the challenges and ultimate ironic triumph of a young man in search of his identity. In this sense, the novel is a classic bildungsroman. Tracing the protagonist's migra-

Ralph Waldo Ellison (1913–94), photograph by Gordon Parks, ca. 1950.

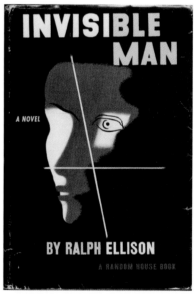

Invisible Man, cover, 1952.

tion from the South to Harlem, Ellison's novel explores the mystery and diversity of the black American experience. By moving away from the protest tradition's emphasis on victimization caused by an all-oppressive antiblack racism, as in Richard Wright's *Native Son* (1940), Ellison crafted a novel that probed America's racial dilemma without sacrificing the complexity of his leading character. His protagonist, Ellison famously said, is invisible only because of his own refusal to run the gamut of his personality, not because white people refuse to see him. This was a radical claim for an African American writer to make, especially in the wake of the crushing of Bigger Thomas's character by the naturalistic forces of capitalism and racism depicted in *Native Son*.

Born in Oklahoma City on March 1, 1913, Ralph Waldo Ellison was the second of three sons of Lewis Ellison, a coal and ice salesman, and his wife, Ida Millsap Ellison, a domestic worker. Named after the great American essayist and philosopher Ralph Waldo Emerson, Ellison grew up conscious of the high expectations that his name carried. His first love was music, and in

1933 he won a music scholarship to the Tuskegee Institute to study classical music and dreamed of becoming a composer.

His discovery of T. S. Eliot's *The Waste Land* (1922), however, inspired him to pursue writing. He recognized in Eliot's work a connection between poetry and jazz: "somehow its rhythms were often closer to those of jazz than were those of the Negro poets . . . its range of allusion was as mixed and as varied as that of Louis Armstrong."[4] African American musical forms, such as jazz, blues, and spirituals, would become the aesthetic foundation of his work. Instead of allowing segregation to define their lives, African Americans had created their own social institutions and cultural traditions, universal forms that transcended simple protest: art, in other words, not propaganda. And truly universal, timeless art must speak across racial, social, temporal, and national boundaries, he held. Because the protagonist was a man rather than primarily the representative of a particular black experience, *Invisible Man* was able to speak to the human condition, using the experience of African Americans as a metaphor for postmodernity and the challenges of multiple identities. The novel's concluding sentence aptly captures Ellison's aesthetic mission: "who knows but that, on the lower frequencies, I speak for you?"[5]

Invisible Man gained the attention of the literary establishment shortly after its publication in 1952. It won the National Book Award for fiction the following year, making Ellison the first African American writer to win that coveted prize. In 1965, a group of critics judged his novel to be the most significant work of fiction published since World War II. Though Ellison died before completing his second novel, two books of criticism further cemented his place as a major creative writer and critic of American literature and culture, and the African American's role in both.

THE WHITE CITIZENS' COUNCIL

The Supreme Court's decision in *Brown v. Board of Education* elated African Americans and liberals but enraged white supremacists. While anti-black violence had never ceased completely anywhere in the United States since the end of the Civil War, the years immediately before *Brown* had been relatively calm. The Tuskegee Institute even reported that no lynchings had occurred anywhere in the United States during 1952. Almost overnight, however, the *Brown* decision destroyed this fragile peace.

State legislatures passed laws designed to circumvent—or outright avoid—the ruling (a task made possible by the Court's own evasion of an enforcement order). Hundreds of thou-

Robert Patterson,
1956.

White Citizens' Council meeting in Sturgis, Kentucky,
photograph by Myron Davis, *Life,* September 1956.

sands of whites across the South registered their anger by joining new private organizations aimed at preserving white supremacy. The most influential was formed on July 11, 1954, in Indianola, Mississippi. Robert Patterson, a Mississippi State College alumnus and local plantation manager, called a meeting to determine how to forestall school desegregation. The fourteen participants included bankers, lawyers, and even the mayor; a subsequent rally at the local town hall drew seventy-five whites. The attendees called their new organization the White Citizens' Council (WCC) and pledged to stop desegregation through any legal means necessary. New branches of the WCC spread rapidly through the state, and by October more than 25,000 Mississippians had signed up—most adherents were in counties with black majorities. Soon the movement crossed the Magnolia State's borders, and in 1956, Alabama state senator Sam Englehardt boasted that more than eighty thousand Alabamians had joined the WCC. The council drew most of its strength from whites in Black Belt states, but branches also took hold in Arkansas, Tennessee, and the Carolinas.

The Citizens' Council publicly sought to distance itself from the Ku Klux Klan, and rather than parade in hoods under the cloak of night, it maintained a high public profile. It even criticized the Klan's unrestrained violence and claimed to favor legal tactics, such as economic coercion, to carry out its plans. Whites used their control of businesses to prevent African Americans from obtaining essential services

Montgomery, Alabama, teenagers, allied with the Klan and White Citizens' Councils, protesting desegregation. Photograph by Flip Schulke, September 1963.

such as insurance and credit. They petitioned school boards to stop desegregation, bankrolled the establishment of whites-only private "academies," and ostracized whites who resisted their efforts. WCC members were able to avoid the bad press that attended murderous Klan activities yet achieve the same ends. In a culture of white supremacy, where whites made and enforced the laws, acts of lawlessness aimed at suppressing blacks were deemed archaic, brutal, and unnecessary.

For all their rhetoric about working within the law, however, Citizens' Council members often resorted to vigilante tactics. They wrote threatening letters and made menacing phone calls to NAACP members. While they did not espouse violence directly, they rarely made any serious efforts to find and punish perpetrators. The WCC and Klan strategies worked together. In

1956, WCC member and Montgomery, Alabama, mayor W. A. "Tacky" Gayle offered a reward for the identification of the person who had bombed Martin Luther King, Jr.'s, home. Police never identified a culprit.

Other WCC members ignored the party line altogether and committed acts of deadly violence. In perhaps the most notable example, WCC member Byron de la Beckwith murdered NAACP field secretary Medgar Evers in his driveway in Jackson, Mississippi, on July 12, 1963. While the WCC may not have directly precipitated brutality, its goals encouraged such violence. White Citizens' Councils declined in number and influence after 1964, when the federal government stepped up its involvement in civil rights issues. But for a decade they presented a serious obstacle to African Americans fighting for change in the South.

EMMETT TILL

In August 1955, fourteen-year-old Emmett Louis Till took the train from Chicago to Money, Mississippi, to visit his great-uncle, Mose Wright. The gregarious youngster, weeks away from beginning the eighth grade, spent his first few days in Mississippi relaxing and enjoying the company of his cousins and new friends. Till amused his southern companions by bragging about having a white girlfriend back home. Doubting Till's claims—and unconvinced by his bravado—his friends dared him to talk to Carolyn Bryant, a white woman who worked the counter at her husband's convenience store. Till took the bet and went inside.

We will never know for sure what happened next on that hot afternoon of August 24. Carolyn Bryant said that Till grabbed her hand, called her "baby," and asked her on a date. Other reports accused Till of whistling at Bryant. Till's mother, Mamie Bradley (later known as Mamie Till Mobley), assumed that he simply had trouble speaking to Bryant

Defendants Roy Bryant and J. W. Milam, with their attorney, September 1955. The two men were charged with murdering Emmett Till.

because of his stuttering problem. He tried to ask for bubble gum, Bradley reasoned, but Bryant mistook the stutters for whistles. Whatever the specifics of Till's encounter with Bryant, white vengeance came swiftly. Three nights later,

Roy Bryant—Carolyn's husband—and his half-brother J. W. Milam appeared at Mose Wright's house. Armed, they demanded that the sixty-four-year-old Wright surrender the boy. If Wright refused or told anyone what had happened, Bryant and Milam told him, "you'll never live to be sixty-five." They put Till in the back of Milam's 1955 Chevrolet pickup and sped off into the Delta night. The two white men pistol-whipped Till for his perceived transgression. Then they shot him in the head, tied a seventy-five-pound weight around his neck, and threw him in the Tallahatchie River. A white boy found the body while fishing three days later. It had so badly decomposed that only an initialed ring could identify it as the fourteen-year-old from Chicago.

The murder and kidnapping trial proceeded as so many others had during those years in the South. The jury, after deliberating for just over an hour, acquitted Bryant and Milam, even as a

Emmett Till with his mother, Mamie Bradley, ca. 1950.

grieving Mose Wright risked his life to identify the murderers from the witness stand. The verdict drew applause from the whites in the courtroom. A juror joked that they would have reached the verdict sooner had they not taken a soda break. Bryant and Milam promptly sold their story—and their confession—to *Look* magazine for $4,000.

Unlike many other southern lynchings, however, the murder of Emmett Till made national headlines. Refusing to allow her son to become another faceless victim, Mamie Bradley spoke candidly and frequently to the American people through the press. She insisted on an open-casket funeral in Chicago, displaying for all to see what Bryant and Milam had done to her son. She allowed *Jet* magazine to run shocking photos of Till's mutilated body on its cover. While the murderers escaped unscathed, Till's tragic death and his mother's defiance brought the violence of the South into the lives of all Americans. Abstract racial violence now wore the face of an innocent fourteen-year-old boy. Bradley's courageous decision to publicize her son's brutal murder and her own grief gave great emotional and moral momentum to the growing civil rights movement.

ROSA PARKS AND BOYCOTTING THE BUSES

Pools of Defiance by Colin Bootman, oil on canvas, 2001.

Less than four months after Emmett Till's murder, an event three hundred miles to the east of Money, Mississippi, again forced Americans to confront the painful realities of Jim Crow. For African Americans across the South, the everyday act of riding the bus to work meant sometimes risking harassment but always accepting the code of racial segregation. City laws separated white and black riders and in many cases granted white passengers the power to take seats already claimed by blacks. In Montgomery, Alabama, blacks could never sit in the first ten rows of the bus. If the black section was filled to capacity, African Americans had to stand, even if the white section remained empty. When whites boarded to find the first ten rows full, they forced blacks to move. Bus drivers carried guns, and they often verbally and physically tormented black passengers.

Whatever their social or political or religious differences, Montgomery blacks shared the experience of riding what they called the "yellow monsters."

Deputy Sheriff D. H. Lackey fingerprints Rosa Parks
after her arrest in Montgomery, 1956.

Rouge blacks had boycotted the buses for eight days until the city agreed to enforce its own, less onerous segregation code. The brevity of the protest, its goal of a more equitable segregation, and its occurrence before the *Brown* decision kept the Baton Rouge bus boycott from making national news.

The Montgomery story would end differently. The weekend following the arrest, Nixon, Parks, local college professor Jo Ann Robinson, and hundreds of others tirelessly publicized the boycott. That Monday, December 5, nearly every African American stayed off the buses. The streets flooded with thousands of residents walking to work, who delightedly watched empty buses traverse their neighborhoods. At a mass meeting that evening, locals voted to continue the boycott indefinitely. They formed the Montgomery Improvement Association (MIA) to coordinate the protest, and they chose a newcomer to town, the Reverend Martin Luther King, Jr., to head the organization. Local leaders feared that King had not lived there long enough to overcome the internecine conflicts that had long hampered effective activism within the black community. Neverthe-

It left some feeling a quiet sense of rage, while others exploded in anger. During 1955 three black women were arrested for refusing to give up their seats to whites. The third arrest occurred on December 1, after a white passenger attempted to take the seat occupied by Rosa Parks. Parks, who was sitting in the black section of the bus, refused to move. The bus driver called the police, who took her to the city jail. Although she projected a docile image, Rosa Parks had a lengthy record of activism and served as secretary of the local branch of the NAACP. Her refusal to submit to Jim Crow regulations was a deliberate act of protest. News of her arrest sent shock waves through the city's black neighborhoods.

The local NAACP president, E. D. Nixon, a Pullman porter, bailed Parks out of jail. Together they hatched a plan to stage a one-day boycott that they hoped would force the city to modify segregated seating on city buses; they never expected the system to be dismantled entirely. Black Montgomerians were not the first southerners to take such a dramatic step. At the turn of the twen-

tieth century, blacks in Mobile and even Montgomery itself had staged streetcar protests. And as recently as 1953, blacks in Baton Rouge had organized a bus boycott. Angry over fare increases and violent treatment by whites, the Baton

Martin Luther King, Jr., addresses a mass rally at the Holt
Street Baptist Church in Montgomery, 1956.

less, the MIA created a carpool system to facilitate transportation, and protesters prepared for a protracted boycott.

Although the boycott developed slowly, it captured the attention of the country, and the increasingly confident protesters expanded their goals. Discussions with the city produced no results, so the MIA decided in January 1956 to challenge segregation head-on. The association filed a class-action lawsuit that would compel the federal courts to rule on the constitutionality of bus segregation. Four women, all of whom had faced the wrath of bus drivers or police when they refused to vacate their seats, agreed to initiate legal proceedings: Aurelia Browder, Claudette Colvin, Mary Louise Smith, and Susie MacDonald.

As the lawsuit made its way through the courts, the city and its black citizens engaged in a series of challenges. On February 22, 1956, eighty-nine blacks faced indictment for breaking the city's antiboycott laws. They peacefully turned themselves in—wearing their nicest clothes—presenting an image of civility and dignity to the world. The boycott ran through the summer. In November, the city appeared to strike a crippling blow, winning an injunction to stop the MIA's carpool system. But it soon became clear that the carpool case did not matter. On December 13, the Supreme Court in *Browder v. Gayle* decided in favor of the protesters, declaring segregation on intrastate travel unconstitutional. Blacks continued the boycott until the final desegregation order came on December 20.

After 381 days of walking, carpooling, and waiting, Montgomery blacks won the right to sit wherever they chose. They had carried out the longest mass-action protest in American history, and they had provided an inspiration and a blueprint for others who sought to dismantle de jure or de facto segregation. But the protests in the former "Cradle of the Confederacy" had only just begun.

LITTLE ROCK AND THE CIVIL RIGHTS ACT OF 1957

On September 4, 1957, a federal court order provided nine black students with the opportunity to enroll in Central High School in Little Rock, Arkansas. In response, Arkansas's governor Orval Faubus declared a state of emergency, maintaining that the students' enrollment constituted an "imminent danger of tumult, riot and breach of peace," and deployed the Arkansas National Guard.[6] One cannot imagine the bravery that fifteen-year-old Elizabeth Eckford summoned as more than two hundred whites harassed her with racial taunts along her way to school and state authorities twice blocked her from entering the building. As she made her way to a bus stop to return home, she pleaded with the Arkansas National Guard for assistance, but under Faubus's order, they ignored her, closed ranks, and even blocked her access to the sidewalk, forcing her to endure thirty-five minutes of intense verbal harassment by scores of whites. Her frightening ordeal and her courageous stance splashed across newspaper front pages, from the London *Times* to *The Times of India* to the *South China Morning Post*. Moreover, television cameras captured the events, and Little Rock became a local, state, national, and international media spectacle, an embarrassment to liberal whites and a window onto the perniciousness of race relations in the South.

President Dwight D. Eisenhower, although not an integrationist, could not tolerate the state of Arkansas's defiance of the U.S. Constitution. For the first time since Reconstruction, a president of the United States dispatched federal troops to the South to protect the rights of black citizens. Eisenhower first federalized the Arkansas National Guard and then sent in regular army troops to guarantee enforcement of the federal court order to desegregate Central High School and to protect the lives of the nine African American students. On September 25, 1957, after three weeks of waiting to enroll in Central High, the nine black students ("The Little Rock Nine") entered the school.

The legendary 101st Airborne Division escorted them up the front steps to keep order while mobs of jeering whites shouted racial epithets. Once again the nation and the world witnessed shocking images of American racism, including three white protesters driven from the school at bayonet point. The media's juxtaposition of images of resolute, well-dressed and well-mannered African American students versus unruly, ill-mannered, viciously racist white people dramatically strengthened the moral authority of the civil rights movement at home and abroad. The victimization of innocent black teenagers by racist adults also threatened to weaken President Eisenhower's Cold War policies promoting democracy overseas. The Soviet Union especially exploited America's hypocritical claims to democracy and equality of opportunity in the face of the reality played out on the world

Whites scream at Elizabeth Eckford as she attempts to enter Central High School in Little Rock, Arkansas, 1957. National Guardsmen can be seen in the background of this iconic image.

first law since Reconstruction to protect the rights of African Americans: the Civil Rights Act of 1957. The act established the Commission on Civil Rights, a body of six presidential appointees with the power to hear complaints from African Americans denied their right to vote and to investigate instances of discrimination. The act also created a new assistant attorney general, who would preside over the new civil rights division in the Justice Department. But the Civil Rights Act of 1957 had met staunch opposition from southern Democratic senators. Most famously, J. Strom Thurmond responded with the longest filibuster in congressional history: twenty-four hours and eighteen minutes. Thurmond read from the Constitution and Declaration of Independence before killing time with inanities about his grandmother's recipes. While the bill eventually passed, southern Democrats succeeded in negotiating out most of its strong enforcement provisions. Lyndon Johnson in particular preserved the fragile unity of his party by orchestrating a compromise about key provisions of the law. While the Civil Rights Act had little immediate impact, it did set the stage for greater federal involvement in the civil rights struggle in later years.

stage at Central High School. The 101st Airborne Division withdrew from Little Rock in November 1957, while the Arkansas National Guard under federal orders gradually withdrew, with some troops remaining at the school until the end of the school year. Forty years after the crisis at Little Rock, the white woman in the center of the Eckford image asked for forgiveness.

The Little Rock crisis actually overshadowed the September 9 passage of the

---

SOUTHERN CHRISTIAN LEADERSHIP CONFERENCE AND THE STABBING OF MARTIN LUTHER KING, JR.

The success of the Montgomery bus boycott made the Reverend Dr. Martin Luther King, Jr., the national face and voice of civil rights activism. King embraced his newfound stature and hoped to form a new national organization for African American rights. Shortly after the *Browder v. Gayle* decision in December 1956, King invited southern preachers to the Negro Leaders Conference at his father's Ebenezer Baptist Church in Atlanta. Sixty of the most active progressives in the South attended, including King's confidant Ralph Abernathy, Fred Shuttlesworth of Birmingham, and C. K. Steele of Tennessee. Bayard Rustin, a Quaker and an expert in nonviolent political action, also volunteered to help King organize the group.

The conference was scheduled to begin on January 10, but early that morning bad news arrived from Montgomery. White supremacists had bombed Abernathy's home, as well as four black churches and the home of Robert Graetz, a white Montgomery Improve-

Martin Luther King, Jr.; his wife, Coretta Scott King; Ralph Abernathy; and other leaders of the SCLC march to the Georgia State Capitol, Atlanta, 1966.

ment Association member and pastor of the African American Trinity Lutheran Church. King and Abernathy returned to the Alabama capital, while Coretta Scott King, Shuttlesworth, and Rustin remained in Atlanta to organize the conference. The Southern Negro Leaders Conference on Transportation and Nonviolent Integration would focus on bus protests, but it also included broader plans for voting rights and nonviolent direct action protests. The participants outlined their goals in "A Statement to the South and the Nation," which they sent to President Eisenhower, Vice President Richard Nixon, and Attorney General Herbert Brownell. Predictably, federal officials ignored the document, though King did meet with Nixon that summer. The preachers continued to refine the organization over the following months.

In February 1957, ninety-seven preachers met in New Orleans to elect officers, naming King president. In August, they convened at Montgomery and adopted the name the Southern Christian Leadership Conference (SCLC). In a significant move later that year, Bayard Rustin recruited the prolific activist Ella Baker to join the organization. She moved to Atlanta and became executive secretary of SCLC in 1958. SCLC would emerge as one of the nation's preeminent civil rights organizations.

Ella J. Baker (1903–86). A graduate of Shaw University, Baker began work with the NAACP in 1938 and for more than two years in the late 1950s served as executive director of the SCLC. Few matched her determination or organizational skills.

Martin Luther King, at Harlem Hospital, recovers from the stabbing, 1958.

King, however, paid a steep price for his fame. In mid-September, he traveled to New York to appear on the *Today* show and promote his book on the Montgomery bus boycott, *Stride Toward Freedom*. On September 20, he attended a book signing at Harlem's Blumstein's department store. A woman in a blue raincoat asked the man signing books if he was Martin Luther King. When King answered in the affirmative, the woman, a forty-two-year-old black maid from Georgia named Izola Ware Curry, pulled a knife and stabbed him in the chest. As police took Curry away, an ambulance rushed King to Harlem Hospital, the blade still stuck between his heart and his lung. After a complicated surgery, doctors successfully removed the knife; a movement as simple as a sneeze could have jostled it enough to puncture King's heart. Curry, diagnosed as a paranoid schizophrenic, was committed to a mental institution, and King returned to Montgomery to recuperate. King would recover quickly, but the Harlem stabbing indicated that he would remain a target for attackers, even, as in this case, an African American without political motivation.

A RAISIN IN THE SUN

At the end of the turbulent 1950s, Lorraine Hansberry's *A Raisin in the Sun* became the first play produced on Broadway by an African American woman. Set on Chicago's South Side during the 1950s and inspired by an experience of Hansberry's family, the play compellingly dramatizes the tension between racism as an external social force and the moral choices individual black people must make within that context. The play takes its title from Langston Hughes's well-known poem "Harlem," which opens with: "What happens to a dream deferred? / Does it dry up / like a raisin in the sun? / Or fester like a sore— / And then run?"[7] Its main characters, Walter Lee Younger, Jr., his wife, Ruth, his mother, Lena, and his sister, Beneatha, define themselves through their dreams and aspirations

Lorraine V. Hansberry (1930–65). The Chicago-born Hansberry experienced intense white rage after her father moved the family into a white neighborhood. She studied drama at the University of Wisconsin, then moved to New York and worked for Paul Robeson's newspaper, *Freedom*. She quit her job to focus on writing *A Raisin in the Sun*. After its success she continued to write and assist in the civil rights movement until her untimely death from cancer.

Ruby Dee, Claudia McNeil, and Sidney Poitier in the film version of Hansberry's *A Raisin in the Sun,* 1961.

and in the process help define race and economics in an America on the cusp of vast social and economic changes. It was an astonishingly prescient work of literature, and it echoes and reworks themes and tropes from Richard Wright's novel *Native Son*.

The play's conflict revolves around what Lena should do with a $10,000 life insurance check, her husband Walter Lee, Sr.'s legacy to his family. Both Ruth and Beneatha see this windfall as belonging to their mother. Walter Lee, Jr., however, feels he has some claim at least to part of the money, as head of the family and as his father's son. He wants to leave his dead-end job as a chauffeur (Bigger Thomas's occupation in Wright's novel) and start a business, a liquor store. His mother, wisely, wants

to buy a house and finds her dream home in an all-white neighborhood. Divided by age, education, gender, and social philosophy, the Younger family seems destined for self-destruction.

Lena buys her new home. They are then visited by Karl Lindner, a white man and chairman of the neighborhood's "improvement" association who wishes to buy them out solely because they are black. As the play progresses, the audience witnesses the transformation of thirty-five-year-old Walter Lee Younger, Jr., from an immature and insecure man who blames his family and society for his limited choices in life, to a man who stands up to white authority and oppression and claims his rightful place as head of the family.

In 1961, Columbia Pictures and Hans-

berry adapted the play into a popular and well-reviewed film directed by Daniel Petrie and starring Sidney Poitier. Poitier earned a Golden Globe nomination for his performance and would become the most successful black actor of his generation. The film represented what was perhaps Hollywood's first attempt to portray realistically a black lower-middle-class family's struggle to achieve the American dream, and the ugly forces restricting it. Hansberry died tragically young of cancer. Her autobiography, *Young, Gifted, and Black,* was published posthumously. Her work inspired a new generation of black women and lesbian writers in the black women's literary movement, beginning in 1970.

STUDENT NONVIOLENT COORDINATING COMMITTEE AND SIT-INS

On February 1, 1960, four black students from North Carolina A&T College—Ezell Blair, Joseph McNeil, Franklin McCain, and David Richmond—sat down at the whites-only lunch counter at Woolworth's department store in Greensboro, North Carolina. The four students knew the staff would not serve them; they sat at the counter as a deliberate, premeditated protest designed to bring attention to the fact that the largest department store in the city would allow them to shop for clothing but would not allow them to eat lunch with whites. The students purchased small items in the store, kept the receipts, and asked for coffee at the counter. After the staff refused service, the students returned to campus and told their peers what had happened.

The following day twenty more students joined the original four. As the pro-

Ronald Martin, Robert Patterson, and Mark Martin, freshmen from the North Carolina Agricultural and Technical College, request service at an F. W. Woolworth lunch counter in Greensboro, North Carolina, February 1, 1960.

Picketing at the F. W. Woolworth store in Harlem in support of lunch-counter protests in Greensboro, Charlotte, and Durham, North Carolina, February 13, 1960.

test continued and grew throughout the week, whites retaliated, throwing food, cursing, and spitting at the students. The sit-ins spread throughout the South, with the most active protests occurring in Nashville and Atlanta. In Nashville, James Lawson, John Lewis, Marion Barry, Diane Nash, and other students at Fisk University and Vanderbilt Divinity School already had staged sit-ins the previous year. The attention given to the Greensboro protest inspired them to hold more. In Atlanta, Julian Bond and Lonnie King, then Morehouse students, led a number of coordinated sit-ins, protesting in ten restaurants at once. Many of the students of Atlanta University spent time in jail. Blacks also organized sit-ins in Hampton, Virginia; Rock Hill, South Carolina; Montgomery, Alabama; and Little Rock, Arkansas. A movement had begun.

From a tactical standpoint, the sit-ins failed. Very few establishments desegregated, and a great number of protesters did jail time and felt the violent wrath of white supremacists. But their sacrifices established a new form of nonviolent direct action protest and initiated a younger group of activists into the civil rights movement. College students, rather than middle-class minis-

ters, began staging protests in towns and cities across the South. For these young activists, the question turned to organization. Should they align with an established group, like the SCLC, CORE, or the NAACP? Or should they instead form their own organization? The students felt a generation gap between themselves and their elders, yet they

also wanted their support and their organizational and financial muscle.

The answer came from Ella Baker, who had grown increasingly alienated from what she saw as the timidity of the SCLC leadership. Baker believed that the power of protest came from grassroots community organizations, not from charismatic leaders like King. She issued a call for student activists to meet at Shaw University in Raleigh, North Carolina, "to help chart future goals for effective activism."[8] One hundred fifty students (including a dozen whites) poured into Raleigh on April 16, 1960, where they discussed what they should do. Most found the NAACP too conservative. They respected Martin Luther King's and CORE's emphasis on nonviolence, but Ella Baker encouraged them to set their own course. They voted to form their own group, the Student Nonviolent Coordinating Committee (SNCC). The following month they named Marion Barry as their first chairman. In another year, they would align with the NAACP, CORE, and the SCLC to challenge segregation in interstate transit.

Stokely Carmichael (in glasses) at an SNCC rally in Montgomery, Alabama, June 14, 1967.

BILOXI WADE-IN, ATLANTA KNEEL-IN, JACKSONVILLE VIOLENCE, UNIVERSITY OF GEORGIA RIOT

The 1960 sit-ins inspired a variety of novel protests across the South. In Mississippi, coastal cities for years had prohibited African Americans from enjoying public beaches. On May 15, 1959, physician Gilbert Mason took a group of children swimming in the Gulf of Mexico off the coast of Biloxi. When police officers ordered them out of the water and off the beach, Mason complained to the local police chief. The authorities, however, believed that Mason wanted nothing more than to inspire civil rights protests. Mason and other local blacks responded with a series of letters and meetings with local government officials. When desegregation failed to materialize, they organized a protest.

On April 24, 1960, 125 African Americans staged a nonviolent "wade-in" on the beach. A mob of whites attacked them with baseball bats, pipes, clubs, and even billiard cues. Police knew the wade-in would occur, but they stood by idly during the violence. By that evening four blacks and one white had been shot. The following day, white vigilantes bombed Mason's home. A federal Justice Department lawsuit filed in the wake of the incident finally forced the desegregation of Mississippi beaches in 1968.

Atlanta had seen its share of sit-ins in 1960, but that summer local activists designed a new idea for mass-action protest. In an appeal to the religious consciousness of the city and the nation, they organized "kneel-in" demonstrations at local white Protestant churches. On Sunday, August 7, twenty-five black students converged on six local churches. Only two allowed them into the service; the other four required that the group remain in the lobby. The following Sunday even more protesters attempted to desegregate ten church services. Only five congregations welcomed them. While the kneel-ins effected little change, they demonstrated the inge-

Hamilton Holmes and Charlayne Hunter remain confident after a court order struck down their suspension from the University of Georgia, 1961. Both Holmes (1941–95) and Hunter (b. 1942) had applied many times for admission to the university, in vain. The state's NAACP branch and the legal team of Constance Baker Motley, Donald Hollowell, Vernon Jordan, and Horace T. Ward fought on their behalf, and finally a 1961 court ruling ordered the university to admit the two. After white students objected, a dean suspended the two blacks "for their own safety." In 1963 Holmes would enter Emory University's School of Medicine and, after earning his medical degree, become chief of orthopedics at the Veterans Administration hospital in Atlanta. He would also open a private practice, become medical director of Grady Memorial Hospital, and serve as associate dean at Emory. Hunter, later Hunter-Gault, would become a successful journalist in print, television, and radio.

Dr. Gilbert Mason, Sr., a founder of the Biloxi branch of the NAACP, led the effort to desegregate Biloxi's public schools and its public beaches.

The University of Georgia newspaper covers Holmes and Hunter's attempt to integrate the university, January 9, 1961.

nuity of civil rights protesters and the hypocrisy of southern Christians. In this case, direct action protest did not lead to retaliatory violence.

A different story unfolded later that month in Jacksonville, Florida. After a failed spring campaign, the local NAACP youth council led sit-in protests at the Woolworth lunch counter on August 13 and throughout the following week. On August 27, the Ku Klux Klan mobilized the downtown area and threatened both black activists and white business owners who might give in to the NAACP's demands. After twenty-five students staged a sit-in that morning, more than one hundred Klansmen, wielding baseball bats and ax handles, attacked them. When three thousand blacks gathered downtown in nonviolent protest, they faced a Klan attack as well. But when the Klan entered black neighborhoods, African Americans fought back with violence of their own. More than fifty people suffered injuries in the fighting. The police did nothing to stop the bloodshed.

The fall of 1960 saw racial turmoil beyond mass-action protest. Two African American students, Charlayne Hunter and Hamilton Holmes, announced their intention to enroll in the all-white University of Georgia. Although six years had passed since the *Brown* decision, the school fought to keep black students out. After a series of losses in the federal courts, their legal team—under the direction of the NAACP Legal Defense Fund lawyer, Constance Baker Motley, and a young Vernon E. Jordan—prevailed. The university was forced to admit Hunter and Holmes on January 10, 1961. The following day, a large group of white students—made angrier by the school's loss in a basketball game that evening—massed outside Hunter's dormitory. They threw rocks and firecrackers at her window, all the while shrieking derogatory names and racial slurs. State troopers refused to help at first but eventually joined local police in breaking up the mob. The university dean conveniently suspended Hunter and Holmes and removed them from the campus, but the faculty passed a resolution condemning the riot and calling for the reinstatement of the suspended students. Hunter and Holmes returned on January 16, and while they still faced insults and ostracism, they graduated from the school in 1963, bravely setting a precedent for desegregation of the South's colleges and universities.

FREEDOM RIDES

Fourteen years after the Journey of Reconciliation, James Farmer, back with CORE after a stint working for the NAACP, resolved to try again. In the spring of 1961, he organized the Freedom Rides, interracial bus trips designed to convince the federal government to enforce desegregation in interstate transit. Farmer's plan gained the support of SCLC, the NAACP, and SNCC. On May 4, 1961, thirteen riders—seven black and six white—boarded two buses and left Washington, D.C. Much like the riders on the Journey of Reconciliation, the Freedom Riders met trouble when they arrived in the Lower South. When John Lewis tried to enter the white restroom at the Greyhound terminal in Rock Hill, South Carolina, a group of white hoodlums beat him to a pulp. Recognizing the violence as a harbinger of things to come, the riders prepared for danger as they passed through Atlanta and crossed the border into Alabama.

On May 14, the first bus passed through Anniston, Alabama, en route to Birmingham. Angry whites had lined the streets in anticipation. When the bus arrived, the mob slashed its tires and threw stones through the windows. The flat tires stopped the bus, and the whites rushed the riders. The governor of Alabama had placed an undercover officer on the bus, less to protect the riders themselves than to thwart the negative publicity their mission would bring. The officer halted the mob, but soon everyone left the bus, and it burst into flames from a Molotov cocktail. The second bus met a similar mob in Anniston but made it to Birmingham. At the Greyhound terminal there, whites

Freedom Riders escape the arson attack on their bus in Anniston, Alabama, 1961.

attacked the riders with no policemen in sight. Police Chief Bull Connor said that his men had the day off for Mother's Day, even though everyone knew that violence and bloodshed would occur.

With the support of reinforcements organized by Diane Nash in Nashville, the Freedom Riders regrouped and headed south to Montgomery. Upon arrival, John Lewis noted an eerie silence. The calm did not last; only minutes after the bus stopped, whites ran from nearby streets and buildings and attacked. One hit Lewis with a milk crate; since white ambulances would not pick him up, he lay in the street unconscious. Whites also assaulted federal official John Seigenthaler as well as many reporters on the scene. That night Martin Luther King, Jr., held a rally at First Baptist Church. Outside, a mob threatened to burn the church to the ground, which would have killed the twelve hundred people inside.

Dr. King eventually convinced a reluctant President Kennedy and his brother, Attorney General Robert Ken-

nedy, to send federal marshals to dispel the mob. As the riders prepared to go to Mississippi, the Kennedys made a deal with Senator James Eastland. Eastland pledged that police would protect the

riders, but only if the federal government did not prevent their arrest for traveling "for the avowed purpose of inflaming public opinion."[9] Arrested in Jackson, the Freedom Riders were sent

May 24, 1961, map showing a planned Freedom Ride aimed at the heart of the segregated South.

to Mississippi's jails and brutal prison farms, where they faced violence and beatings. They slept on soiled blankets spread on concrete floors. Many of them worked outside in the oppressive heat of the summer sun. Guards beat them at will, saving the most violent beatings for those who sang freedom songs. James Farmer received so little food that he lost thirty pounds.

Even with the assistance of the NAACP, the riders' legal fees drove CORE deep into debt. Unlike the Journey of Reconciliation, however, the Freedom Riders accomplished their immediate goal. The Interstate Commerce Commission finally enforced laws against bus segregation, and fearing the intervention of the Kennedys, local and state governments began to comply.

The majority of bus terminals eliminated their separate black restrooms, and over the next year bus segregation ended. President Kennedy's commitment to civil rights, however, remained in doubt, because he depended for support in Congress on southern Democrats known as Dixiecrats.

BILL RUSSELL AND THE BOSTON CELTICS

Coach Red Auerbach and Bill Russell are carried by jubilant fans on April 27, 1964, after the team's sixth consecutive world championship.

No American athlete has won more professional sports championships than basketball star Bill Russell. Born February 12, 1934, in Monroe, Louisiana, Russell moved with his family to Oakland, California, where he attended the University of San Francisco on a basketball scholarship. He led his team to NCAA championships in 1955 and 1956. His 20.7 points and 20.3 rebounds per game caught the attention of Boston Celtics coach and general manager Red Auerbach, who traded up in the draft in order to pick the six-foot-nine center. After winning another title—this time a gold medal in the 1956 Summer Olympics—Russell joined the NBA the following December.

Initially, the Russell trade looked bad for the Celtics. The star they had traded, Ed Macauley, led his new team, the St. Louis Hawks, to the 1958 NBA championship. But Auerbach knew that the addition of a defensive force like Russell

Bill Russell and Wilt Chamberlain of the Philadelphia 76ers.

would propel the Celtics' high-powered offense to a different level. The plan worked almost immediately. During Russell's rookie campaign, the Celtics marched through the regular season and captured the NBA championship in a thrilling double-overtime, game-seven victory at home in Boston over the St. Louis Hawks. The Celtics lost to the Hawks in the NBA finals the following season, due in large part to a knee injury Russell suffered in the third game. Nevertheless, Russell won the MVP award that year. During the 1958–59 season, the Celtics triumphed over the Minneapolis Lakers to begin an unprecedented streak of eight consecutive NBA championships.

At the same time, Russell's friendly antagonist and rival, Philadelphia 76ers center Wilt Chamberlain, made headlines by revolutionizing the offensive game. He scored 100 points in one historic game on March 2, 1962, and edged out Russell in rebounding in several seasons. In the 1961–62 season Chamberlain averaged an astonishing 50.4 points per game, compared to Russell's 18.9. But the Celtics center still won the league

MVP award that year in recognition of his pivotal leadership and central importance to the overall success of a championship team. It would take Chamberlain (just as it would the early Michael Jordan) several seasons to emerge as a team player as effective as he was as an individual player.

Russell did not shy away from a commitment to civil rights. (He preferred the phrase *human rights*.) He publicly aligned with the civil rights movement, staged integrated basketball camps in the South after the assassination of Medgar Evers, and openly supported Muhammad Ali's refusal to be drafted. He also accused basketball team owners of insisting upon a certain number of white superstars on each team. As a result, he faced racial slurs, threats, and vandalism, even from his hometown fans in Boston. The Celtics had been the first basketball team to recruit a black player, Chuck Cooper, in 1950, and under Red Auerbach the Celtics became the first team to abandon the infamous "three-fifths" rule, mandating that a majority of team players on the court be white. Auerbach's Celtics were the first professional basketball team to start four black players, and then five.

Despite his role in creating the Celtics' unprecedented dominance of the NBA, Russell did not escape racial discrimination. In 1961, after playing an

Bill Russell plays center for the Boston Celtics, 1960s.

Coach Red Auerbach and the Celtics celebrate their defeat of the Los Angeles Lakers
with Governor John Volpe of Massachusetts on April 18, 1962.

Russell won eleven NBA
championships with the Celtics.

NBA exhibition game in Marion, Indiana, he and several other black players went out for hamburgers. Outraged at the restaurant's refusal to serve them, Russell went to Mayor Jack Edwards's house, woke him in bed, and returned the keys to the city that the mayor had given him just a few hours earlier. Defying racism meant more to Bill Russell than any championship title.

Russell also broke new ground in the NBA in 1966–67, when, following Auerbach's retirement, he became the league's first African American head coach, while remaining a starting player on the team. Although the Philadelphia 76ers defeated the Celtics in the finals that year, he led the team to two more championships before retiring in 1969. His accumulated individual statistics were staggering. He won five MVP awards and made twelve All-Star appearances. He made 21,620 rebounds (second all-time only to Wilt Chamberlain) and scored an average of 22.5 points per game. During his thirteen seasons with the Celtics, the team won eleven titles. The Associated Press named him the outstanding professional basketball player of the 1960s, and the NBA placed him on its 25th Anniversary All-Time Team in 1970, as well as its 35th anniversary team in 1980. In 1974, he was elected to the Naismith Memorial Basketball Hall of Fame.

JAMES BALDWIN'S *GO TELL IT ON THE MOUNTAIN*

If Martin Luther King was the spoken voice of the civil rights movement, James Arthur Baldwin was its written voice, the movement in essays. Born in New York City in 1924, James Baldwin wrote more than twenty works of fiction and nonfiction, including *Go Tell It on the Mountain, Another Country, Notes of a Native Son,* and *The Fire Next Time. Go Tell It on the Mountain* (1953), his first major work, was an autobiographical novel based on his experiences as a teenage Pentecostal minister in Harlem. Although he once repudiated the protest novel, in a scathing critique of the fiction of both Harriet Beecher Stowe and Richard Wright, as crippling to the craft of the writer, Baldwin's fiction never achieved its promise formally and never was as accomplished as the best of his essays, which are routinely taught in college expository writing classes as masterpieces of prose.

Known as both a homosexual and an atheist, Baldwin spent much of his career in Europe (in Paris, in Istanbul, in Switzerland, and especially in St. Paul de Vence, in the South of France) and chose to bear witness as an outsider to the political, social, and cultural changes occurring at home. His writing was not always well received by critics, especially because of the forcefulness with which he treated violence and hatred. His second novel, *Giovanni's Room* (1956), received a harsh response because of its sympathetic treatment of homosexuality, a subject rarely given such open and approving consideration in the American literature of his era, let alone in African American literature.

James Baldwin (1924–87) in New York City, 1963.

On May 17, 1963, Baldwin appeared on the cover of *Time* magazine under the headline "Birmingham and Beyond: The Negro's Push for Equality." After a decade of publications, he had, with some irony, established himself as the civil rights movement's first literary celebrity. *The Fire Next Time,* released in May 1963 in the centennial year of the Emancipation Proclamation, galvanized the movement. When the book appeared, the popular public intellectual Max Lerner described Baldwin as "an avenging angel." Right from the title page, Baldwin challenged white America: "God gave Noah the rainbow sign, No more water, the fire next time!" It was written in two parts: "My Dungeon Shook: A Letter to My Nephew on the One Hundredth Anniversary of Eman-

cipation" and "Down at the Cross: Letter from a Region in My Mind." With its unforgiving and unrelenting social commentary on American race relations, it rocked the literary world and the body politic. Characterized as both a plea and a warning to the nation, *The Fire Next Time* propelled Baldwin from author and activist to icon. He wrote with courage and determination, his voice mingling with Martin Luther King, Jr.'s, as the public voice of the the struggle for black freedom and liberation.

Baldwin became an international phenomenon, a consummate and complete man of letters. From *Go Tell It on the Mountain* in 1953 to *The Price of the Ticket: Collected Nonfiction, 1984–1985* in 1985, he wrote a total of six novels, six books of essays, three plays, and a screenplay, as well as a book of poems and a collection of short stories with a depth and a breadth about social, racial, and gendered relationships unparalleled by any other author at the time. In 1986, he became a Commander of the Legion of Honor in France, an award established by Napoleon Bonaparte in 1802. While he traveled frequently to the United States, he spent most of his last two decades in the South of France. He taught briefly at Hampshire College in Amherst, Massachusetts. He died in St. Paul de Vence in 1987. His funeral at the Cathedral of St. John the Divine was a major tribute to the greatest essayist in the history of African American literature, and to his uncompromising voice in black America's struggle for freedom and dignity.

PART FIFTEEN

THE MOVEMENT AT HIGH TIDE

1963–1968

MARTIN LUTHER KING, JR.'S "LETTER FROM BIRMINGHAM JAIL"

A police officer arrests Martin Luther King, Jr., after an antisegregation
march in Birmingham, Alabama, 1963.

By the time he arrived in Birmingham, Alabama, in 1963, Martin Luther King had begun to doubt his role in the civil rights movement. The previous year, his Southern Christian Leadership Conference had organized protests in Albany, Georgia, aimed at desegregating the city and getting the attention of the White House. Albany police chief Laurie Pritchett shrewdly ordered his men to refrain from beating protesters, and he made sure he had access to enough jails to contain the arrested. Without violence, nonviolent provocation garnered little attention, and the Albany program failed. At the behest of Fred Shuttlesworth, however, King traveled to Birmingham to assist (and to bring attention to) an ongoing desegregation campaign. Birmingham had a

reputation as the most violent city in the South; a series of bombings had earned it the nickname "Bombingham." King knew that Sheriff Bull Connor would never show Pritchett's level of restraint. He intended to get as many arrests as possible in order to fill up the jails. The police obliged.

While incarcerated for more than a week in Birmingham, Martin Luther King, Jr., wrote "Letter from Birmingham Jail," one of the most important documents of the civil rights movement, on the margins of newspapers, on scraps of paper, and on a memo pad. In January 1963, eight prominent, "liberal" Alabama clergymen had published an open letter to King, calling upon him to halt his nonviolent demonstrations in the South. Rather than direct action, they

argued, he should employ the local and federal courts to fight segregation.

In responding to the clergymen's criticism, King marshaled history and his mastery of biblical text and black church rhetoric to justify the movement's tactics. By focusing on nonviolent civil disobedience, King's "Letter from Birmingham Jail" placed Christian discipleship at the heart of the African American struggle for equality. Although it had little effect on the events in Birmingham at the time, King's statement quickly gained national and international recognition. The Quaker American Friends Service Committee reprinted it, and more than a million copies were distributed to churches across the country. Newspapers and magazines, including the *New York Post, Ebony, The Liberation,* and *The Christian Century,* reprinted excerpts. Representative William Fitts Ryan of New York even read a portion of it into the *Congressional Record.*

King began his "Letter" noting that other clergymen had labeled his tactics as "unwise and untimely," and likely to produce violence. They urged blacks to wait, wait, wait—a tiresome call ever since the movement began. He rejected such criticism, asserting that the times cried out for nonviolent direct action and, more important, that Christians had an obligation to conduct such protest. "I am in Birmingham because injustice is here," King explained. "I cannot sit idly by in Atlanta and not be concerned about what happens in Birmingham. Injustice anywhere is a threat to justice everywhere." Based on his reading of Saint Augustine, he could advocate breaking some laws—while obeying most—by distinguishing between just and unjust laws: "'an unjust law is no law at all.'" His impatience with white moderates proved shrewd and timely: "Shallow understanding from people of good will is more frustrating than absolute misunderstanding from people of ill will. Lukewarm acceptance is much more bewildering than outright rejection."[1]

King's rhetorical strategy also engaged on a practical level, exposing the clergymen's ill-considered approval of the conduct of the Birmingham police force:

King in the Birmingham jail, 1963.

I doubt that you would have so warmly commended the police force if you had seen its dogs sinking their teeth into unarmed, nonviolent Negroes. I doubt that you would so quickly commend the policemen if you were to observe their ugly and inhumane treatment of Negroes here in the city jail; if you were to watch them push and curse old Negro women and young Negro girls; if you were to see them slap and kick old Negro men and young boys; if you were to observe them, as they did on two occasions, refuse to give us food because we wanted to sing our grace together. I cannot join you in your praise of the Birmingham police department.[2]

The "Letter from Birmingham Jail" is critical to understanding King's belief in nonviolent direct action as the movement's primary weapon against segregation. The next year it appeared in *Why We Can't Wait,* King's account of the Birmingham campaign. The piece resonated with American readers in the 1960s and went on to become a manifesto for other movements for freedom and liberation, including the anti-apartheid movement in South Africa.

MARCH ON WASHINGTON AND THE SIXTEENTH STREET BAPTIST CHURCH BOMBING

Upon his release from the Birmingham jail, Martin Luther King, Jr., and the SCLC decided upon a controversial plan to continue the protest: they would fill Birmingham's jails with children. On May 2 children and teenagers gathered in Kelly Ingram Park and at the Sixteenth Street Baptist Church to march through the city. Police cared little about the age of the protesters, rounding them up for arrest in school buses after they ran out of vans. By the end of the day, more than nine hundred children sat in jail. The next day, Sheriff Bull Connor and his men turned fire hoses and attack dogs on the protesters, adults and children alike.

Images of children being arrested and African Americans facing fire hoses strong enough to break bones shocked the nation. The demonstrations—and the national and international outrage over the actions of the police—accomplished their intended goal. President Kennedy mobilized federal troops and threatened to use them if Birmingham whites did not halt the violence. The city's white business community, feeling the effects of the negative publicity, agreed to integrate lunch counters. But negotiations between King and the city did not go smoothly. Without Fred Shuttlesworth to assist him, King agreed to a watered-down agreement that put no deadline on the city for integration. Still, desegregation of public accommodations did eventually occur in Birmingham.

On the national level, the chaos in Birmingham finally convinced President Kennedy to take a firm stand on civil rights. On June 11, the president made a civil rights address to Congress (only hours before the murder of Medgar

A fire hose pummels protesters during a demonstration in Birmingham, May 5–9, 1963.

Evers), and on June 19 he sent a comprehensive civil rights bill to Congress. To keep the pressure on Kennedy and Congress, A. Philip Randolph and Bayard Rustin organized the March on Washington for Jobs and Freedom. Randolph had organized a march on Washington in 1941, but a last-minute compromise with President Franklin Roosevelt had convinced him to call it off. Not this time. This march would be Randolph's greatest political achievement, a brilliant strategic move in a complex battle for moral suasion over an American public deeply and profoundly ambivalent over Negro rights.

Randolph, King, James Farmer of CORE, Roy Wilkins of the NAACP, John Lewis of SNCC, Whitney Young of the Urban League, and other prominent activists cast aside their differences and united for the event. On August 28 more than two hundred thousand people converged on the Lincoln Memorial in the

The March on Washington, photograph by Warren K. Leffler, August 28, 1963.

Martin Luther King, Jr., delivering his "I Have a Dream" speech.

nation's capital to demand civil rights. The historic event culminated with Martin Luther King, Jr.'s stirring "I Have a Dream" speech, in which he outlined his vision of a racially egalitarian America. Afterward Kennedy—who privately opposed the protest—invited the organizers to the White House for coffee, a sign of his commitment to civil rights.

While the March on Washington ended on a sublime note, an event in Birmingham on September 15 reminded the nation that seething opposition to racial equality remained virulent in the South. A bomb exploded in the basement of the Sixteenth Street Baptist Church, killing four black girls: Addie Mae Collins, Denise McNair, Carole Robertson, and Cynthia Wesley. As for the culprits, one man, Robert Chambliss, was arrested and convicted, but not until 1977. In 2000, the FBI announced that three other Klansmen had helped perpetrate the murders. One, Herman Cash, had already died; the others, Thomas Blanton and Bobby Frank Cherry, were tried and convicted. But in 1963 one could hardly overstate the sense of visceral shock that coursed through the rest of the country, and around the world, over the bombing. On November 22, 1963, another act of violence took place, this time in Texas: President Kennedy was assassinated in Dallas. The fate of the civil rights bill fell to the new president, Lyndon Baines Johnson.

Bomb damage at the Sixteenth Street Baptist Church in Birmingham, September 15, 1963.

LIVE AT THE APOLLO

James Brown already had exceeded expectations when he took the stage at the Apollo Theater on Wednesday evening, October 24, 1962, for what would become perhaps the most legendary performance in the history of that proving ground of African American culture. Brown was born in 1933 into abject poverty in Barnwell, South Carolina. When he reached the age of four, his parents separated, leaving his great-aunt in Augusta, Georgia, as his foster mother. He spent his childhood earning money by tap-dancing in the street and shining shoes rather than attending school. At eight he taught himself to play the organ; at eleven he won a singing contest. At fifteen, in 1948, he was arrested for stealing a car and received a lengthy sentence in the Georgia Juvenile Training Institute, where he earned the nickname "Music Box" and formed a gospel group.

Released on parole in 1952, Brown

James Brown (1933–2006) and the Famous Flames at the Apollo Theater, October 24, 1962.

joined the Avons, a rhythm and blues group that soon changed its name to the Flames with Brown as the lead vocalist. Word of the group's intense performances spread throughout the South and came to the attention of Little Richard's manager, Clint Bradley. The Flames' 1955 single "Please, Please,

Please" was released by King Records in Cincinnati. King had balked at first, but the song soon reached number six on *Billboard*'s rhythm and blues chart, and Brown and the Flames were on their way. Subsequent singles sold poorly until the 1958 ballad "Try Me" climbed to number one on the R&B charts. Brown and the band scored another hit with the song "Think" in 1960.

Increasingly, Brown and his band became known for their epic live performances. In concert, they stretched each song to the breaking point, engaging in complex polyrhythms and mesmerizing the audience with crescendo after crescendo. For his part, Brown was an amazing front man, and his signature style—falling on his knees and pretending to faint, then rising slowly, marching quickly in place, and fainting all over again—and the band's signature multiple encores, made Brown the performer among performers. His growing fame gave Brown the novel idea of recording a concert and releasing it as an album—something that had never been done for an African American artist. King Records refused to finance it, thinking that a live record would not make money. If Brown wanted to make the recording, he would have to finance it himself. Brown put up the money, and King agreed to release the result.

Brown, billed as "The Hardest Working Man in Show Business," chose the October 1962 date at the Apollo to make

the album. Brown and the Famous Flames marched through an astonishingly compelling set; the recording captured both the energy of the performers and the call-and-response of the exceptionally receptive crowd. From the moment Fats Gonder introduced "Mr. Dynamite, The Amazing Mr. Please, Please Himself," electricity filled the theater. The band opened with "I'll Go Crazy" and continued with the hits "Try Me," "Think," and "I Don't Mind." Then Brown half-narrated and half-crooned the ballad, "Lost Someone," extending it to ten full minutes, and introducing a form of "rapping" that would inform Isaac Hayes's version of "By the Time I Get to Phoenix" in 1969, and that would be imitated widely in rap and hip-hop. Brown and the Flames continued with a medley of favorites, including "I Want You So Bad," "Strange Things Happen," and "Bewildered," bookended by two helpings of "Please, Please, Please." They closed out the set with a vibrant performance of their latest single, "Night Train."

The album *Live at the Apollo* hit record stores in January 1963, and it shot to number two on the charts. *Live at the Apollo* is to this day regarded as one of the greatest albums of all time, live or studio (*Rolling Stone* magazine placed it at number twenty-four in 2003), and the Library of Congress enshrined the album in its National Recording Registry. Brown would reprise performances

Brown performs at the fortieth anniversary of his album *Live at the Apollo,* September 18, 2003.

of some of the songs he made classics that night in 1962 at his seventieth birthday celebration at the Apollo in 2003, attended by many prominent members of the group W. E. B. Du Bois would have likely called the twenty-first century's "talented tenth," including Citigroup chairman Richard Parsons, American Express CEO Kenneth Chenault, HBO Video president Henry McGee, and Random House vice president and executive editor Erroll McDonald.

LEROI JONES'S *BLUES PEOPLE* AND KING'S NOBEL PEACE PRIZE

While the Freedom Riders were beginning to capture the attention of the country, their generational contemporaries in the arts, as we might expect, were using their cultural expressions to further the movement, both directly and indirectly. Among the new generation of writers, none would be more important to the politics of black culture over the next two decades than the poet and playwright Amiri Baraka.

Amiri Baraka was born LeRoi Jones in Newark, New Jersey, in 1934. He moved to the Lower East Side of Manhattan in 1957 after receiving a bachelor's degree from Howard University and serving a three-year stint in the U.S. Air Force. In New York's Greenwich Village, he began a stunning career as a writer, editor, and activist by integrating the Beat Movement and copublishing with his wife, Hettie Cohen, *Yugen,* a short-lived literary magazine, and founding the Totem Press publishing house. At the same time Jones launched his phenomenal writing career with three brilliant and well-reviewed publications: his first book of poetry, *Preface to a Twenty Volume Suicide Note* (1961), and two plays, *The Slave* (1962) and *The Toilet* (1962). The following year he published the landmark book *Blues People: Negro Music in White America,* perhaps his most important contribution to the field that would be known as black studies, which would emerge in the academy at the end of the decade.

Blues People was perhaps the first critical and sociological analysis of the full sweep of the history of African American music—the work songs, hollers, and spirituals, but especially the blues and jazz—from the time of slavery through John Coltrane and Ornette Coleman. As the book's subtitle indicates, Jones had become increasingly interested in how

Amiri Baraka (b. 1934), photograph by Leroy McLucas, 1965.

African Americans expressed their experiences of race (and racism) in cultural forms. No other scholar before him had tackled the subject of black cultural history and the consciousness of the race in quite this way. The result was an astonishing analysis, a book with many

deeper implications for our understanding of the history of African Americans, exceeding even his important insights into how black musical forms emerged and then melded into new forms over time. His book was almost a history of the self-consciousness of a people, and it informed subsequent narrative accounts of the broader history of African Americans.

Jones used the history of music to interpret the ways blacks had adapted to white society and culture and, in turn, had merged black forms born of slavery into something new, something American and black. Blues, he argued, "could not exist if the African captives had not become American captives."[3] Jones's focus on black responses to American racism, combined with the influence of the civil rights movement unfolding around him, would lead him toward increasingly radical politics. Soon he would move to Harlem (and then back

Martin Luther King, Jr., accepts the Nobel Peace Prize in Oslo, Norway, and receives congratulations from Crown Prince Harald and King Olav, December 10, 1964.

to Newark), change his name to Amiri Baraka, and become one of the founders (with the poet Larry Neal) of the Black Arts Movement and one of the leaders (with Maulana Karenga) of the black nationalist group US. He became an active force in Newark politics and culture, especially through his organization Spirit House. In 1973, he would abandon his black nationalist politics and embrace a Marxist critique of American capitalism and racism.

In 1964, a thirty-year-old LeRoi Jones had won the prestigious Obie Award from *The Village Voice* for his play *Dutchman*. That same year, the thirty-five-year-old Martin Luther King, Jr., became the youngest person to win the Nobel Peace Prize. King, suffering from exhaustion, was lying in a hospital bed at St. Joseph Infirmary in Atlanta on October 14 when his wife, Coretta, called to give him the news. He promptly announced that he would donate "every penny" of the $54,000 prize to civil rights issues. Congratulations poured in from around the world. (Not surprisingly, segregationists such as Sheriff Bull Connor condemned the decision.) "I accept the Nobel Prize for Peace," King said in Norway at his December 10 acceptance speech, "at a moment when twenty-two million Negroes of the United States of America are engaged in a creative battle to end the long night of racial injustice. I accept this award on behalf of a civil rights movement which is moving with determination and a majestic scorn for risk and danger to establish a reign of freedom and a rule of justice." He used the international stage to recognize the unknown leaders and foot soldiers of the movement, and he made it clear that much work remained left to accomplish in the civil rights struggle.

CHANEY, GOODMAN, AND SCHWERNER, AND FREEDOM SUMMER

The Civil Rights Act of 1964 addressed de jure segregation, but African Americans demanded stronger voting rights provisions. Black protesters and their white allies thought voting rights offered perhaps the most direct route to political change. In 1961, under the leadership of Bob Moses, SNCC began organizing a voter-registration campaign in rural Mississippi. The following year, SNCC united with the SCLC and CORE to form a new organization, the Council of Federated Organizations (COFO). Although these groups often clashed over tactics and personalities, they united in the hope that COFO and its Voter Registration Project would help African Americans exercise their right to vote.

The project succeeded in registering blacks in many urban areas of the South, but Mississippi proved much more difficult. Despite the constant threat of violence, activists from the North, whites and blacks, traveled to the Magnolia State to help the cause. Although some local blacks worried that white newcom-

Burned automobile of civil rights workers James Chaney, Michael Schwerner, and Andrew Goodman, June 1964.

ers might be seeking to gain publicity for themselves, Moses believed that if nothing else, the presence of sympathetic whites would bring greater attention to southern violence. In 1964, Moses instituted Freedom Summer, a broad-based voter-registration drive aimed at ushering blacks into a new political party, the Freedom Party. Tensions remained high between local blacks and white college students and among feuding civil rights organizations, and all lived with the threat of violence.

Threats turned to tragedy on June 21, 1964. James Chaney, a twenty-one-year-old African American from Meridian, Mississippi, and two New Yorkers, Andrew Goodman, age twenty, and Michael Schwerner, twenty-four, traveled to Philadelphia, Mississippi, for COFO to investigate a church burning. Before leaving, Schwerner told a friend

Martin Luther King, Jr., holding a photograph of the slain
civil rights workers, December 4, 1964.

Fannie Lou Hamer (1917–77). One of twenty siblings, Hamer grew up in Mississippi picking cotton and had left school by age twelve. In 1962, she encountered James Forman of SNCC and James Bevel of the SCLC and tried to register to vote. She spent the rest of her career fighting segregation and politically organizing the poor blacks of Mississippi.

to call all the local hospitals and jails if they did not return by four o'clock. Not only did they not return that evening, they disappeared for weeks. Even President Lyndon Johnson intervened to help find the missing men and ordered an unwilling FBI to join in the search. White supremacists had murdered the three activists, buried their bodies in an earthen dam, and burned the automobile they had been driving. In October, the FBI arrested eighteen whites, but state prosecutors, claiming a lack of evidence, refused to try the case. In 1967, seven men were convicted on federal conspiracy charges and given sentences of three to ten years, but none served more than six, and no one was tried on the charge of murder until 2005.

Concerted white resistance did not stop Moses and COFO. They held elections to choose delegates for the Mississippi Freedom Democratic Party (MFDP), an alternative to the all-white Democratic Party. Sixty-eight MFDP delegates—including four whites—traveled to the Atlantic City Democratic National Convention, where they would attempt to unseat the official state Democratic Party. Lyndon Johnson, the party's presidential nominee, saw the convention as a celebration of his success and feared the attention that the MFDP

movement would attract. Without question, conceding to the challengers would have catapulted white southerners from the Democratic Party into the arms of the conservative Republican candidate, Barry Goldwater, who vocally opposed all civil rights legislation. Many southern delegations had in fact threatened to walk out if the convention seated the dissidents.

Mississippi sharecropper and civil rights activist Fannie Lou Hamer did not care about inconveniencing the president and his party. She presented the MFDP's case before the Democratic National Committee's credentials committee—and in front of live television cameras. In harrowing detail, Hamer testified about the violence she and others had endured and the threats they had faced for trying to register blacks to vote. Turning to the television cameras, Hamer declared, "If the Freedom Democratic Party is not seated now, I question America. Is this America? The land of the free and the home of the brave? Where we have to sleep with our telephones off the hook, because our lives be threatened daily?"[4]

Horrified, Johnson called his own press conference to divert attention from Hamer. It did not work. The Democrats offered a compromise, allowing

two MFDP members to have at-large seats at the convention but without voting privileges. The MFDP refused the compromise. At the same time, all but three of the official Mississippi delegates walked out of the convention. MFDP delegates borrowed passes from sympathetic delegates from other states and took the seats vacated by the Mississippi contingent. Representatives of the Democratic Party escorted them out. When the MFDP returned the next day, they found that convention organizers had removed the empty seats, so they stood and sang freedom songs.

The MFDP did not succeed in gaining official recognition, but its members brought national attention to the cause of black voting rights. The following year a protest in Selma would force the federal government, at long last, to act to ensure that black people could exercise the right to vote.

WAR ON POVERTY, ECONOMIC OPPORTUNITY ACT, MOYNIHAN REPORT, ROBERT WEAVER, CONSTANCE BAKER MOTLEY, THURGOOD MARSHALL

Lyndon Johnson's domestic agenda stretched beyond a narrow definition of civil rights. On January 8, 1964, the president declared an "unconditional war on poverty." He believed that the inequalities of American society, including racial discrimination, resulted from an unequal distribution of wealth. Taking a calculated risk by raising the issue during an election year, Johnson hoped to pass legislation that would help all poor Americans, white and black. On August 20, he signed the Economic Opportunity Act, a broad antipoverty bill designed "to eliminate the paradox of poverty in the midst of plenty in this Nation by opening to everyone the opportunity for education and training, the opportunity to work, and the opportunity to live in decency and dignity."

The act created the Office of Economic Opportunity to implement and manage an astonishing array of new services. The Volunteers in Service to America (VISTA) resembled a domestic Peace Corps, establishing jobs that allowed Americans to help the poor; the Job Corps provided educational training and experience to the nation's youth; Work Study programs helped students to earn money through working part-time jobs; Upward Bound aimed to help lower-income high school students attend college; Community Action Programs encouraged urban and rural communities to fight poverty themselves; and Head Start programs provided preschool education for young children. While historians have debated the effectiveness of these programs, at the very least they signaled Johnson's willingness to build on the example of the New Deal and use federal power to help the poor. But the rise of conservatism (in part a reaction to the victories of the civil rights movement) and the costly war in Vietnam would eventually undermine Johnson's ambitious domestic agenda.

Daniel Patrick Moynihan (1927–2003). Although born in Tulsa, Oklahoma, Moynihan is forever identified with New York and selfless government service. One of the brightest politicians to hold public office, he held cabinet or subcabinet positions under presidents John Kennedy, Lyndon Johnson, Richard Nixon, and Gerald Ford; was ambassador to India; was U.S. ambassador to the United Nations; and served in the U.S. Senate from 1977 to 2001.

Robert C. Weaver (1907–97), the nation's first African American cabinet secretary, is shown here after taking the oath of office as secretary of housing and urban development at a White House ceremony. President Lyndon B. Johnson congratulates Weaver, who is holding his commission of office.

Constance Baker Motley
(1921–2005), 1965.

Thurgood Marshall (1908–93). Marshall won renown as the lead attorney in *Brown v. Board of Education.* In 1961 he won appointment to the U.S Court of Appeals for the Second Circuit in New York, and in 1965 President Johnson appointed him U.S. solicitor general. Two years later the president named him to the U.S. Supreme Court.

While President Johnson presided over two of the most important civil rights bills in American history, his administration had a complicated relationship with race. Specifically, the March 1965 publication of *The Negro Family: The Case for National Action* drew outrage from a number of black scholars and activists. Dubbed the Moynihan Report, after its author, assistant secretary of labor Daniel Patrick Moynihan, the report supported the increasingly popular notion that African Americans lived in a "culture of poverty." It argued that the legacy of slavery had undermined the roles of black men in the family, and the preponderance of single-parent households in black communities contributed to a cycle of destitution. At the same time, Moynihan and others called on the federal government to do more to help poor blacks, calls that conservatives characterized as unfair, preferential treatment. Still, some African Americans wondered if they could trust a government that blamed poverty on their own life choices.

While the politics of race loomed large in his administration, Johnson did go further than any other president had in appointing African Americans to prominent federal offices. In 1966, he named Robert Weaver secretary of housing and urban development, making him the first black cabinet member in the history of the United States. He chose a black woman, Constance Baker Motley, for a federal judgeship in New York City. And in 1967, he named Thurgood Marshall to the U.S. Supreme Court. The man who had masterminded the NAACP's case in *Brown v. Board of Education* now sat on the highest court in the land. While the Vietnam War would damage his legacy, Lyndon Johnson took dramatic steps toward advancing the cause of African Americans, including ensuring the passage of the Civil Rights Act of 1964 and the Voting Rights Act of 1965.

CIVIL RIGHTS ACT OF 1964 AND VOTING RIGHTS ACT OF 1965

The direct action protests of the 1960s paid dividends. In 1964 and 1965, the Johnson administration orchestrated the passing of the two most significant civil rights bills since Reconstruction. The Birmingham protests and the March on Washington had convinced President Kennedy to forge ahead with a civil rights bill in 1963. But his assassination on November 22, 1963, left the passage of the bill in question. President Johnson, who to that point had an unfavorable record concerning civil rights, had come to believe in the importance of federal protection for African Americans and deftly tied the civil rights bill to the memory of Kennedy.

Perhaps the most skilled parliamentarian of his generation, Johnson pledged to circumvent a filibuster from southern conservatives and usher the bill through Congress. In the House, Howard Smith of Virginia even tacked on a women's rights provision in hopes of sabotaging the bill. Still, it cleared the House by a vote of 290–130. While the Senate proved even more reluctant, enough senators supported the bill to guide it through cloture and then to pass it. Johnson signed the act on July 2, 1964. The Civil Rights Act of 1964 outlawed discrimination in public accommodations engaged in interstate commerce, including hotels, restaurants, and theaters. It forbade state and local governments from restricting access to public facilities on the grounds of "race, color, religion, or national origin." It empow-

President Johnson shakes hands with Martin Luther King, Jr., after signing the civil rights bill into law, July 2, 1964.

Civil Rights Act of 1964.

Voting Rights Act of 1965.

ered the Justice Department to initiate lawsuits to desegregate schools. Ten years after the *Brown* decision, real (though often short-lived) school desegregation had begun to occur in the South, but resistance persisted. The new Civil Rights Act threatened to withdraw federal funding from any agency or organization that discriminated against African Americans. Title VII of the act, ironically, formalized Representative Smith's amendment to prevent discrimination based on gender.

Despite passage of this far-reaching bill, African Americans still faced barriers to their right to vote. While the Civil Rights Act of 1964 addressed voting rights, it did not eliminate many of the tactics recalcitrant southerners used to keep blacks from the polls, such as violence, economic intimidation, and literacy tests. But the Freedom Summer protests in Mississippi and the Selma-to-Montgomery march the following year led to the passage of the Voting Rights Act of 1965. Johnson had already begun work on a bill before the Selma march, and he again urged Congress to pass it. On March 15, 1965,

he addressed both houses of Congress. With words that brought tears of joy to many African Americans watching this historic speech on television, the president repeated the mantra of the civil rights movement:

There is no Negro problem.
There is no Southern problem.
There is no Northern problem.
There is only an American problem . . . What happened in Selma is part of a far larger movement which reaches into every section and state of America. It is the effort of American Negroes to secure for themselves the full blessings of American life. Their cause must be our cause too. Because it's not just Negroes, but really it's all of us, who must overcome the crippling legacy of bigotry and injustice. And we shall overcome.[5]

Debates over the new bill exposed the conservatives' intransigence. Republican William Moore McCulloch of Ohio proposed an alternate bill autho-

rizing action by the federal government once it had received twenty-five "meritorious complaints" of voter discrimination. When Democratic congressman William Tuck of Virginia declared his preference for McCulloch's idea because it was "milder," he demonstrated that conservatives sought the weakest law possible and helped turn the tide of public opinion toward Johnson's bill.

On August 3, the bill passed the House by a vote of 328–74; the following day, it passed the Senate, 79–18. Johnson, flanked by civil rights activists including Martin Luther King, Rosa Parks, and Vivian Malone, signed it into law on August 6. "Today," the president said at the signing, "is a triumph for freedom as huge as any victory that has ever been won on any battlefield."[6]

The Voting Rights Act of 1965 prohibited states from using measures "to deny or abridge the right of any citizen of the United States to vote on account of race or color." It abolished literacy tests and extended the federal shield over states where fewer than 50 percent of eligible voters had cast ballots in 1964. Those states had to obtain clearance from the Justice Department before implementing voting or districting changes. It also authorized the replacement of reluctant local registrars with federal government workers to prevent voter fraud and intimidation. These measures increased black voter registration quickly and

President Johnson and Roy Wilkins (1901–81), executive director of the NAACP, discuss the Voting Rights Act of 1965 in the White House.

dramatically. Mississippi had had only 6 percent of eligible African Americans registered in 1965; by 1968 that number had increased to 44 percent. While insidious discrimination continued, the two new measures represented the most significant legislative triumphs in the twentieth-century struggle for racial equality before the law.

MANCHILD IN THE PROMISED LAND AND THE AUTOBIOGRAPHY OF MALCOLM X

The publication of two books in 1965, the same year in which the Voting Rights Act was signed, gave Americans new insights into the lives of urban, working-class black people. In his autobiography, *Manchild in the Promised Land,* Claude Brown offered a compelling vision of his childhood in the dilapidated tenements and crowded streets of postwar Harlem. He illuminated the economic and social forces that challenged this first generation from the South to grow up in northern ghettos—the ironically titled "Promised Land."

To find his voice, Brown looked to recent black writers, especially Richard Wright, whose *Black Boy* Brown analyzed carefully while writing *Manchild*. On the other hand, *Manchild in the Promised Land* broke new ground with its blistering candor about the crime, prostitution, drugs, and violence that dominated postwar Harlem. Brown had committed petty theft and sold marijuana, leading to as much time in juvenile detention centers as out of them. He briefly experimented with heroin and witnessed his neighborhood capitulate to the drug. Misogyny defined his relationships with women, and the violence he endured from his father subsided only when he proved too drunk to beat him.

Yet Brown's book contained a redemptive quality. Thanks to a counselor at one of the reform schools he attended, Brown cleaned up his life. He worked odd jobs, attended night school, and left the life of crime. As the story of a man who overcame such tragedy, *Manchild in the Promised Land* earned both strong critical praise and a large readership. Critics realized that Brown had introduced a new voice, a new rhetoric, into the corpus of African American autobiography. Just after its publication in 1965, the novelist Tom Wolfe wrote in *The New York Herald Tribune* that "Claude Brown makes James Baldwin

Claude Brown (1937–2002). The Harlem-born author memorably captured his troubled early years in his novel *Manchild in the Promised Land*. Although he tried to earn a law degree, his growing fame kept him on a lucrative lecture circuit. In 1976, he followed up his influential novel with a second, *The Children of Ham*.

and all that old Rock of Ages rhetoric sound like some kind of Moral Rearmament tourist from Toronto come to visit the poor." And Norman Mailer echoed the reaction of many white Americans when he wrote that *Manchild* was "the first thing I ever read which gave me an idea of what it would be like day to day if I'd grown up in Harlem."[7]

In October 1965, shortly after the Watts Riot and nine months after Malcolm's assassination, the novelist Alex Haley published *The Autobiography of Malcolm X*. Compiled from interviews Haley had conducted over the previous two years, the *Autobiography* humanized Malcolm X to a public that had felt threatened by his rhetoric and by the hate-filled image of him and his fellow members of the Nation of Islam depicted in journalist Mike Wallace's 1959 CBS television program, *The Hate That Hate Produced*. Not unlike *Manchild in the Promised Land,* the *Autobiography* told the story of a young black man who eventually escaped a downward spiral of crime and drugs. The book chronicled his childhood alienation from whites; his

years as a drug dealer and pimp; his discovery of the Nation of Islam in prison; his role as a public figure and leader of the increasingly militant Black Muslims; his conflicts with Elijah Muhammad and ultimate break with the Nation of Islam; and his embrace of a progressive humanism in the final year of his life, following his departure from the Nation of Islam and his pilgrimage to Mecca.

A tremendous critical and commercial success, the book solidified Malcolm X's role as a great leader and as a martyr, and reviewers responded to the book extremely positively. *The New York Times* praised it as "a brilliant, painful, important book." *Manchild in the Promised Land* and the *Autobiography* offered mainstream America its first autobiographical accounts of the lives of the black urban poor, written by truly gifted authors who had had those firsthand experiences. But the realization that the "racial problem" in American society had a fundamental economic foundation was only beginning to dawn as the civil rights movement neared its culmination.

MALCOLM X AND THE NATION OF ISLAM

Born in Omaha, Nebraska, on May 19, 1925, Malcolm Little's painful experiences with antiblack racism began at an early age. His politically active father, Earl, died after falling under a streetcar (perhaps thrown under the car by whites) when Malcolm was only six years old. His mother, Louise, ended up in a psychiatric hospital seven years later, unable to accept her husband's death. At first Malcolm excelled in school, but when a white teacher told him he could not be a lawyer because of his race, he lost the motivation to

continue. The young Malcolm Little was shuttled between foster families in Michigan before moving to Boston to stay with his sister, Ella.

In Boston Malcolm combined work as a busboy with a life of crime, selling drugs, running numbers, and pimping. In January 1946, police arrested him on weapons charges, larceny, and breaking and entering. He spent the next six years in jail, where he took English, German, and Latin courses and, through letters from his brother, discovered the Nation of Islam. He corresponded with Elijah

Muhammad, leader of the Nation, and adopted the surname *X* to symbolize his lost African heritage and name. After his release from prison in 1952, Malcolm X quickly rose to the top of Elijah Muhammad's organization and two years later became minister of the Nation of Islam's Harlem Temple No. 7.

Unlike other prominent civil rights activists, Malcolm X did not call for integration. "You cannot find one black man," he argued, "I don't care who he is, who has not been personally damaged in some way by the devilish acts of the

Malcolm X (1925–65),
iconic image, 1963.

Malcolm X steps out of his car in front of his firebombed house
in East Elmhurst, New York, February 14, 1965.

collective white man."[8] He criticized calls for integration as giving concessions to the oppressor. When Martin Luther King, Jr., won the Nobel Peace Prize in 1964, Malcolm X said, "If I'm following a general, and he's leading me into battle, and the enemy tends to give him rewards, or awards, I get suspicious of him. Especially if he gets a peace award before the war is over."[9] Malcolm X's radical critique of white society appealed to a great number of

African Americans and instilled fear in many whites. Estimates pegged Nation of Islam membership in the early 1960s at between five thousand and fifteen thousand, with a great deal more unofficial believers and sympathizers. His message resonated in particular in the urban ghettos of the North and the West Coast, but it angered others who believed that he offered no plan for reshaping society. As James Farmer recorded in his 1985 memoir *Lay Bare the*

Heart: An Autobiography of the Civil Rights Movement, he once asked him: "Brother Malcolm, don't tell us any more about the disease . . . tell us, physician, what is thy cure?"[10]

By 1963 Malcolm X had begun to lose faith in the Nation of Islam. He grew impatient with its insular character and sought more active protest to answer his critics and provide solutions to the social problems he and the Nation had so earnestly identified. But he especially lost faith in Elijah Muhammad who, Malcolm X discovered, had fathered six children with former secretaries, none of whom were his wife. He also recognized that Muhammad envied his popularity and had begun to reduce his role, especially after Malcolm X's ill-advised comment after the assassination of President Kennedy that the "chickens [were] coming home to roost."[11]

In 1964, Malcolm X left the Nation of Islam and began a search for a new ideology and, perhaps, a new identity. During the spring of 1964, he made a life-altering pilgrimage to Mecca, where he softened his hardline separatist beliefs and changed his name to el-Hajj Malik el-Shabazz. Upon his return, he announced the formation of the Organization of Afro-American Unity (OAAU). While he continued to advocate black

Bullet holes in back of the stage where Malcolm X was shot, 1965.

nationalism, he hoped to align with sympathetic whites in the name of civil rights. Malcolm X also understood that he had become a target for assassination and told his friend Gordon Parks, "It's a time for martyrs now. And if I'm to be one, it will be in the cause of brotherhood."[12]

In the early morning hours of February 14, 1965, vigilantes firebombed his East Elmhurst, New York, home. At first, he blamed the Nation of Islam, but he later speculated that the police or government agents had been responsible. On February 21, minutes after he began his address to an OAAU meeting at the Audubon Ballroom in Harlem, three Nation of Islam members pulled out revolvers and sawed-off shotguns and shot him to death. The next day Elijah Muhammad denied in a public statement that either he or the Nation had had anything to do with the assassination. Today Malcolm's autobiography is a staple of the African American literary canon.

JAMES MEREDITH AND MEDGAR EVERS

James Meredith (b. 1933), surrounded by John Doar of the Department of Justice and U.S. marshals, arrives on the University of Mississippi campus. Photograph by Marion S. Trikosko, October 1, 1962.

In the early 1960s the nation watched a civil rights drama unfold in Mississippi. In 1962, a twenty-eight-year-old air force veteran named James Meredith decided to transfer from the all-black Jackson State College to the all-white University of Mississippi. Although eight years had passed since the Supreme Court's *Brown* decision, school desegregation had not occurred in most areas of the state. Ole Miss had no intention of letting Meredith disturb that trend, and the university summarily rejected his application. A federal court, however, decided that the school could not deny Meredith admission on account of his race and ordered Ole Miss to permit him to register.

Mississippi governor Ross Barnett ignored the court's order and pledged to block Meredith's enrollment. On September 20, 1962, the day Meredith intended to select classes, Barnett traveled to the Oxford campus and stood in the path of the admissions office. To circumvent Barnett, Meredith appealed to the federal Justice Department. Attorney General Robert Kennedy called Barnett and instructed the governor to allow Meredith to enter the school. Barnett defiantly refused, leading Kennedy to send five hundred federal marshals to the state. On September 30,

Memorial march for Medgar Evers,
Jackson, Mississippi, June 1963.

Meredith finally moved in to his new dorm room.

But the chaos had only begun. A mob formed outside Meredith's dorm and soon outnumbered the federal marshals. With courage in numbers, the angry whites pelted the marshals with rocks, who returned fire with tear gas. When word of the escalating confrontation spread, more whites joined the mob and threw bricks and even acid on the marshals. Without using their guns, the

marshals fended off the mob, albeit suffering 160 injuries. The following day Kennedy sent in reinforcements: five thousand army troops. The soldiers squelched the mob, and university faculty restored order on campus. While Meredith faced constant harassment in the classroom and in his dormitory, he graduated in August 1963.

But only two months before Meredith's graduation, tragedy struck Mississippi. Since 1954, Medgar Evers had

worked as field secretary for the Mississippi branch of the NAACP. Evers and other Mississippi members pressed for change in more direct and radical ways than was the official policy of the national NAACP. Beginning in 1960, Evers led a series of protests in Jackson aimed at desegregation and gaining voting rights. He showed great skill in organizing grassroots protests, although he understood that civil rights activism in Mississippi came with the constant threat of white violence. His wife Myrlie Evers's worst nightmare was that her husband's activism would get him killed, leaving her a widow and their son without a father.

After midnight on June 12, 1963, Medgar Evers returned home from a long night of political activity. He pulled into his driveway, and as he got out of his car, a shotgun blast hit him in the back. His murderer, Byron de la Beckwith, evaded responsibility for the crime and was not convicted until thirty-one years later, in 1994. The Evers murder sent shock waves through Mississippi and the nation. But the following summer would only bring more violence to the state, as blacks sought to gain the right to vote.

CIVIL RIGHTS PROTESTS AND URBAN RIOTING IN THE NORTH

During the 1960s, while the nation's attention focused on events in the Deep South, African Americans in the North also mounted civil rights protests, especially concerning segregation and inequality in public schools. In New York City parents and NAACP members formed the Parents' Workshop for Equality in New York City Schools. When lobbying local and state officials failed to produce change, they asked Bayard Rustin to help organize

a school boycott. On February 3, 1964, more than 450,000 students stayed home from school and instead attended one of the many protest rallies. Blacks also staged boycotts and protests aimed at destroying school segregation in Cleveland, Cincinnati, Chicago, and Boston. While these protests had little effect on the racial composition of local schools, they did reveal that the North was not free of the racism being confronted so dramatically throughout the South.

Resistance to racial prejudice also took the form of urban violence and rioting. Perhaps nothing incited more violence than police brutality. When a white police officer shot a black teenager in Harlem on July 18, 1964, the NAACP and CORE responded with nonviolent marches, but far more blacks took to the streets. Over the following six days, the rioting and looting grew, eventually spreading into the Bedford-Stuyvesant neighborhood in Brooklyn. The vio-

Buildings burn after rioting on
Avalon Boulevard in Watts, Los
Angeles, August 13, 1965.

National Guard troops patrol the streets during the Watts riot.

lence claimed one life and led to 100 injuries and 450 arrests.

In Rochester, New York, tensions between local blacks and police had long simmered. When police arrested a young black man at a block party on July 24, local African Americans believed that the police brutalized him. Three days of rioting followed, stopping only when Governor Nelson Rockefeller called in the National Guard. In August, black people in Philadelphia rioted in response to what they believed was an incident of police brutality against a local black woman. Odessa Bradford refused to move her car after it had broken down. When police tried to remove her, a black man intervened. After police arrested both Bradford and the Good Samaritan, rumors spread through black neighborhoods that police had beaten a pregnant black woman. The ensuing two-day riot injured nearly 350 people. Similar riots engulfed Chicago, as well as Jersey City, Paterson, and Keansburg, New Jersey.

The most deadly riot occurred the following year in the Watts neighborhood of Los Angeles. Profoundly impoverished, Watts had a male unemployment rate of 34 percent; a full two-thirds of its residents received welfare assistance. The community's 250,000 people com-prised a population density four times greater than any other neighborhood in the city. This widespread poverty and despair, unmitigated by any signs of relief, combined with long-standing tensions with the overwhelmingly white police force, created all the elements for a violent incident. And predictably it occurred, but on a scale that shocked the nation and the world.

On August 11, 1965, the police pulled over a drunk driver, an African American man named Marquette Frye. But Frye's fear of going to jail led him to lash out against the police. When Frye's brother Ronald joined the fray, onlook-

State troopers seizing violators of the citywide curfew,
Rochester, New York, July 25, 1964.

Harlem riot, January 1964.

ers sensed that another incident of police brutality might occur. Rumors spread through the neighborhood, and it took little evidence to convince Watts residents that the police had once again mistreated one of their neighbors. They responded with six days of riots and looting. L.A. police needed the help of fourteen thousand National Guard troops to put down the insurrection. Thirty-four people died; nine hundred blacks suffered injuries; and thousands were arrested. Just days after the passage of the Voting Rights Act, the Watts riot, along with others in Chicago and Philadelphia that year, forced the country to confront the potential ramifications of persistent economic inequality.

SELMA, 1965

In 1963, the SNCC began a voting rights campaign in Selma, Alabama, a small city located about fifty miles west of Montgomery. As in many southern cities, white registrars in Selma had concocted a number of ways to keep African Americans off the rolls, disqualifying applications for menial omissions such as punctuation and spelling errors, and for failing to answer complicated questions about constitutional law. As a result, African Americans, a majority of Selma's population, made up only 1 percent of registered voters.

On the streets, Sheriff Jim Clark ruled with an iron fist. He and his posse stood ready to thwart any protest, and voter-registration efforts stalled. In response, local ministers invited Martin Luther King, Jr., to Selma, much to the chagrin of SNCC activists, who believed that King would monopolize resources and publicity. But John Lewis pledged support, and SNCC did not

State troopers attack SNCC leader John Lewis during the
Selma-to-Montgomery march, held on March 7, 1965.

break with King. Almost immediately after King arrived in January 1965, a white supremacist assaulted him outside his hotel. The incident suggested the extreme danger of the situation. The protest ebbed and flowed over the following month. Blacks staged marches

and Clark arrested them, King and the Reverend Ralph Abernathy included.

At the beginning of March, King prepared to launch his largest protest: a march to the state capitol in Montgomery. He hoped the march would keep pressure on President Lyndon

Aerial view of marchers crossing the Edmund Pettus Bridge from Selma to Montgomery.

Viola Liuzzo's car after her assassination by Klansmen, March 26, 1965.

Johnson, who had pledged that a voting rights bill was imminent. But when six hundred demonstrators met at Brown Chapel Church on March 7 to begin the protest, King did not attend. He had been warned of an assassination plot and preferred to delay the march until it received the approval of the federal court. The protesters left the church anyway and made it to the Edmund Pettus Bridge on the edge of town.

There they met armed state troopers whom Governor George Wallace had mobilized to stop them. When the demonstrators refused to retreat, the police attacked with clubs and tear gas. Television networks cut in to regularly scheduled programming to broadcast the incident, which became known as "Bloody Sunday." Two days after Bloody Sunday, King led a second march. He had already made a deal with a federal mediator that the marchers would retreat at Edmund Pettus Bridge, but he had not informed the demonstra-

tors themselves. The police, well aware of the compromise, cleared the road to allow the march to continue. King, true to his word, led a prayer and then turned around, which angered many of the young activists. A generational split over strategy in the movement was about to erupt.

The third and final Selma-to-Montgomery march began on March 21. Federal Judge Frank Johnson granted permission to the protesters, and President Johnson convinced George Wallace to allow it to happen. (Wallace summarized Johnson's persuasive skills: "If I hadn't left when I did, he'd have had me coming out for civil rights.")[13] As many as 25,000 people, white and black, made the trek, which culminated in Montgomery on March 25. In a stirring speech King told the crowd, "Mine eyes have seen the glory of the coming of the Lord; He is trampling out the vintage where the grapes of wrath are stored; He has loosed the fateful lightning of

his terrible swift sword; His truth is marching on. . . . Glory hallelujah! Glory hallelujah!"[14]

The march ended on that triumphant note, but the celebration did not last long. That evening, a white civil rights activist from Detroit named Viola Liuzzo was driving along the parade route when a group of Klansmen (including an undercover FBI agent) shot her. In part because of the shocking national impact of Liuzzo's brutal murder and other related forms of racist brutality, the marchers pressed the federal government to act and succeeded in moving Congress to adopt the Voting Rights Act of 1965. Signed into law on August 6, the legislation outlawed literacy tests and bolstered federal enforcement of black suffrage. The act paid dividends almost immediately, and the number of black voters skyrocketed, as would the number of black elected officials.

SAMMY YOUNGE, VERNON DAHMER, AND THE MARCH AGAINST FEAR

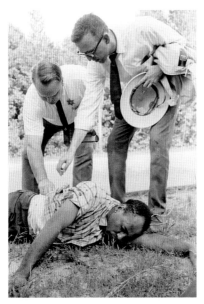

Police inspect James Meredith after a Klansman unloaded his shotgun on the civil rights worker during his one-man March Against Fear, Mississippi, June 6, 1966.

Martin Luther King, Jr. (center, with a hand on his sunglasses), joins other civil rights leaders, such as Stokely Carmichael (third from right, in short-sleeved white shirt), to continue the March Against Fear in James Meredith's honor, June 9, 1966.

Passage of the Voting Rights Act in 1965 did little, at first, to advance the struggle for civil rights and incited elements in the white South to increase the reign of terror on African Americans and their white allies. In January 1966, two murders galvanized protest and suggested how far blacks still had to travel before achieving equality. On January 3, SNCC member and navy veteran Samuel "Sammy" Younge stopped at a gas station in Tuskegee, Alabama. Younge had a reputation for local activism, and just that morning he had led forty blacks to attempt to register to vote at the Macon County Courthouse. When the white attendant, Marvin Segrest, saw the twenty-two-year-old Younge heading for the whites-only restroom—a distinction ostensibly rendered illegal by the Civil Rights Act of 1964—he pulled out a gun and shot him. An all-white jury found Segrest not guilty.

Just days later in Mississippi, white rage found the businessman, Sunday school teacher, and farmer Vernon Dahmer. In Forrest County, where he lived, Dahmer led the local NAACP branch and had organized voter-registration drives throughout the 1960s. Like Younge, Dahmer's activity earned him the undesirable attention of white supremacists. On the evening of January 10, 1966, they firebombed Dahmer's home while he and his family were inside. During the ensuing chaos, his family escaped, but Dahmer remained inside and shot back at the attacking whites. He never made it out alive. Four men were convicted of the attack, and a fifth pleaded guilty. Yet the mastermind of the attack, Klansman Sam Bowers, managed to escape conviction four times. Not until 1998 did he receive a guilty verdict and a sentence of life in prison.

The most publicized incident of violence in Mississippi that year involved someone from the state's recent civil rights past. James Meredith, in 1966 a law student at Columbia University, left Memphis on June 5 with a plan to march alone through rural Mississippi. He hoped to show that blacks could stand up to white supremacy and assert their right to vote. But as soon as he crossed the state line into Mississippi the following morning, a Klansman shot him. Meredith survived, and from his hospital bed he renounced nonviolence. Civil rights leaders vowed to continue the march in Meredith's honor.

With Meredith's approval, Martin Luther King, Jr., of the SCLC, Stokely Carmichael of SNCC, and Floyd McKissick of CORE planned the March Against Fear. Roy Wilkins of the NAACP and Whitney Young of the Urban League attended as well. While marchers in Selma had been able to overcome the

Protest in front of the White House, January 11, 1966, over the killing of Samuel Younge, Jr. (1944–66).

Remains of Vernon Dahmer's firebombed home, January 11, 1966.

deep cleavages among these organizations, reaching common ground proved much more difficult in Mississippi. King found himself caught between the more militant faction led by Carmichael and McKissick and the conservative faction led by Young and Wilkins. Eventually deciding that the march would turn into a Black Power display or a personal attack against President Johnson, Young and Wilkins left the state.

King, McKissick, and Carmichael remained, and they began the march on June 9. Although local blacks responded en masse to support the March Against Fear, the marchers increasingly argued among themselves. Their dis-

agreements would become public over the course of the 220-mile trek. Dr. King continued his emphasis on nonviolence, even as he grew more critical of the Vietnam War. After his arrest in Greenwood, Mississippi, on June 16, Carmichael gave his first Black Power speech. The effect was electrifying. He and SNCC's Willie Ricks increasingly used the term *Black Power* to explain their goals and to criticize white society. They also championed abandoning the term *Negro* for the race and replacing it with *black*.

When they all reached the state capital of Jackson on June 26, rival factions chanted either "Black Power" or "Freedom Now." King, who still maintained

close ties to the Democratic Party, and his assistants handed out American flags; this angered SNCC workers, who were beginning to formulate a black nationalist critique of the relation between racism and economic disparities in the United States and colonialism in Africa and the Third World. Civil rights organizations had always disagreed to some extent over strategy, and of course they had found themselves competing for scarce funds and publicity for their efforts, but the Mississippi march brought these tensions to the forefront of the movement and to the attention of the nation.

"FLOAT LIKE A BUTTERFLY, STING LIKE A BEE"

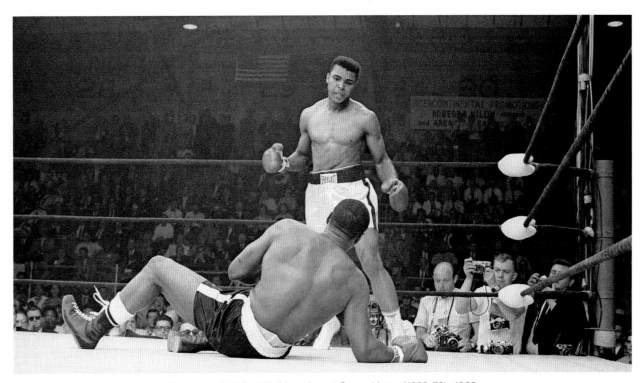

Muhammad Ali (b. 1942) knocks out Sonny Liston (1932–70), 1965.

Muhammad Ali was born Cassius Marcellus Clay, Jr., in 1942, named after a pugnacious and mercurial Kentucky antislavery journalist. He began boxing lessons at age twelve and soon decided to become a professional fighter. After graduating high school, his considerable talents began to emerge, and he quickly won six state championships. In 1960, he won a gold medal in the Rome Olympics.

His unconventional style, his unmatched speed and strength, his handsome appearance, his charisma, his penchant for rhymed couplets, and his witty commentary on the world unfolding around him earned him considerable media attention from the start. He bragged about his abilities and good looks, demeaned his opponents with sarcasm and a wink, and, prior to the 1974 "Rumble in the Jungle" with George Fore-

man, memorably declared that he could "float like a butterfly [and] sting like a bee." His brief appearance in Rod Serling's 1962 film *Requiem for a Heavyweight* only heightened his growing fame. In 1963, he proclaimed, "I am the greatest," and even released an album of that title through Columbia Records. In Miami on February 25, 1964, Clay met Sonny Liston, a boxer who had gained renown for defeating Floyd Patterson, an Olympic athlete who had been the youngest heavyweight world champion in history. The boxing world considered Clay overmatched and bet heavily on a victory by the much bulkier Liston. Clay, with astonishing style and unprecedented bravado, engaged in antics to draw attention to the fight and to unnerve his opponent. The tactic apparently worked: a seemingly astonished, delirious Clay defeated Liston in seven rounds. The two met

again on May 25, 1965; this time he sent Liston to the mat in the first round.

After Clay's first defeat of Liston, he shocked the world by declaring that he had not only joined the Nation of Islam but had changed his name to Muhammad Ali. Stunned Americans, who considered the Nation an antiwhite, angry, radical assertion of Black Power, felt betrayed by Ali's conversion and fearful of its meaning. No African American since Jack Johnson generated more controversy and hatred. When the army changed Ali's draft status to 1-A, making him eligible for service, he refused to join. Part of the growing national criticism of the Vietnam War, Ali responded to a reporter's question about the draft and the war with "I ain't got no quarrel with them Vietcong."[15] The government was outraged. He applied for conscientious-objector status, claiming to be a minister, but was rejected and ordered to appear for induction. In 1966, the federal government brought him to trial for draft evasion, convicted him, stripped him of his boxing title, and barred him from the ring. Ali's popularity within the African American community and throughout Europe, the Middle East, Africa, and Asia only grew. Nevertheless, for several years he was censured for his stand by public figures and the American public. But in 1970, especially after the National Guard murdered several students during an antiwar rally at Kent State University, public opinion turned against the war, criticism relented, and Ali was allowed back in the ring. In 1971 the U.S. Supreme Court unanimously overturned his conviction.

In 1971 too he lost an important bout to Joe Frazier and in 1973 suffered another defeat to Ken Norton. Seeking to reassert his authority, Ali challenged George Foreman to a title fight in Kinshasa, Zaire. Ali's victory at

Ali points to a newspaper headline on the Vietnam War, showing that he is not alone in opposing the war, March 1966. Sitting next to him is Rozaa Rio, a recording artist from Chicago.

what he dubbed the "Rumble in the Jungle" on October 30, 1974, placed the thirty-two-year-old fighter at the pinnacle of the sport and reinforced his status as an international celebrity. Muhammad Ali transformed the sport of box-

ing and the role of the black athlete in American politics and became during his prime the dominant American cultural icon throughout the world, sometimes said to be the most photographed man in history.

BLACK PANTHERS, US, KWANZAA

While the nation watched the civil rights movement unfold on national television, the mid-1960s also saw a flowering of organizations dedicated to Black Power and black nationalism. None, however, attracted more attention than the Black Panther Party for Self Defense. Formed in October 1966 in Oakland by Huey P. Newton and Bobby Seale, the Panthers began as an organized patrol to monitor Oakland's police, a force well known

for abusing black citizens. As the party evolved, leaders—using the work of various theorists of revolution, especially Frantz Fanon—connected the struggles of African Americans with the struggles of oppressed peoples around the world.

Unlike every other black political organization, the Black Panthers embraced a socialist program for revolutionary social change. Their "Ten Point Program" manifesto called for equal housing and education, an end to police

Ron Karenga (b. 1941; later Maulana Karenga) was not only the leader of US but a highly respected teacher offering classes in Swahili and African history to children at a Westminster Neighborhood Association facility in Watts, California.

Black Panther Party founders Bobby Seale (b. 1936)
and Huey P. Newton (1942–1989).

Eldridge Cleaver (1935–89), minister
of information for the Black Panther
Party. Photograph by Marion S.
Trikosko, October 18, 1968.

brutality, and black self-determination. Their "free breakfast" program was enormously popular within the black community. While they demanded a number of structural changes in American society, they earned the most attention for their willingness to carry guns openly. The group and its high-profile members, including Newton, Seale, Eldridge Cleaver, and Angela Davis, became the face of post–Malcolm X radical activism.

SNCC and CORE turned to radical black nationalism during these years, purging their organizations of white members. And in 1967 Stokely Carmichael brokered a short-lived merger of SNCC and the Panthers. But national civil rights organizations, Black Power organizations, and others disagreed as often as they agreed on effective means to improve the lives of African Americans. The alliance between SNCC and the Panthers failed. But the Panthers—who embraced socialism—

found their fiercest conflict with the cultural nationalist organization US, founded by Maulana Ron Karenga in 1965 in the aftermath of the Watts riot. Soon Karenga would be joined by Amiri Baraka, and the two would share leadership of the movement.

Karenga demanded that African Americans recapture their African roots. US members adopted Swahili names, spoke Swahili, and wore traditional African clothing. Karenga adopted the name Maulana, Swahili for "master teacher," renounced the blues and Christianity, and argued that African Americans could never be truly free until they "decolonized their minds," embracing African aesthetic and ethical principles. To Newton and the Black Panthers, however, Karenga offered little of practical value to the black masses; they accused him of mystification, of substituting one religion for another. US, for its part, declared that the Panthers were puppets of left-wing white groups and that their

socialist ideology was ineffective in the world's leading capitalist country. The two organizations engaged in a bitter feud, a conflict made worse by the interference of the FBI, which culminated in gunfire and murder on the UCLA campus in January 1969. The FBI's COINTELPRO (counterintelligence program) fabricated inflammatory correspondence to heighten tensions between the groups, resulting in a series of gunfights. The combination of personal and political antagonisms and the interference of the FBI exacerbated significant ideological differences among the various Black Power organizations.

While US faded from the headlines after Baraka abandoned the movement and the FBI systematically destroyed the Panthers, Karenga did not. Karenga would become a highly respected professor of African American studies at California State University in Long Beach. In 1966, he founded the holiday Kwanzaa, a seven-day celebration of African culture. Karenga framed the holiday around a philosophy he named Kawaida, which he defined as the seven cardinal principles of people of African descent: Umoja (unity), Kujichagulia (self-determination), Ujima (collective work and responsibility), Ujamaa (cooperative economics), Nia (purpose), Kuumba (creativity), and Imani (faith). While he initially conceived of the holiday as an alternative to Christmas, he softened his oppositional tone as millions of African Americans adopted some form of Kwanzaa celebration as a supplement to Christmas, and the celebration entered the cultural mainstream, from Hallmark greeting cards to U.S. postage stamps. Karenga is a prolific author and is active in teaching and administration at his university.

EDWARD BROOKE AND JULIAN BOND

For African Americans in politics, 1966 proved both memorable and contentious. Edward W. Brooke grew up in Washington, D.C., and graduated from Howard University. At the outset of World War II, he joined the all-black 366th Regiment—which took the name Buffalo Soldiers as its moniker—and saw combat in Italy. Upon his return after the war, he attended law school at Boston University, graduating in 1948. Brooke mixed his interest in the law with an interest in politics; he ran as a Republican for the Massachusetts state legislature in 1950 and 1952. Although he lost both elections, his ambitions remained. He lost a third election for secretary of state in 1960, but in the year of the Kennedy ascendancy, the Republican Brooke lost by only 112,000 votes.

After working as the chair of the Boston Finance Committee for two years, Brooke was elected state attorney general in 1962. He won reelection in 1964 despite the Democratic landslide in nearly every other contest in the state. Over the following two years he cultivated his political base, appealing to Republicans and Democrats, to African Americans and whites. His efforts yielded results when, on November 8, 1966, he was elected to the U.S. Senate, besting his Democratic opponent by 438,712 votes.

With his victory, Brooke became the first black senator since Blanche K. Bruce in the previous century, and the first black senator ever from any northern state. Because the Seventeenth Amendment, adopted in 1913, mandated the direct election of senators, Brooke also became the first African American popularly elected to the Senate. During his twelve years in office, he demonstrated a willingness to break with his party, most notably with President Richard Nixon. He voted against two of Nixon's Supreme Court nominees, and he was the first Republican to ask the president to resign following the Watergate scandal. Brooke received the Presidential Medal of Freedom from President George W. Bush in 2004.

Julian Bond (b. 1940) served in the Georgia General Assembly for twenty years before becoming the chairman of the NAACP.

For Julian Bond, however, 1966 was somewhat less triumphant. Bond is the son of Dr. Horace Mann Bond, the first black president of Lincoln University, where he had been a student. A graduate of Morehouse, Bond was one of the founders of SNCC. In 1968, his name was entered into nomination for the vice presidency of the United States, at a time when the election of a black person to the White House was unthinkable. Only twenty-eight at the time and not interested in the position, Bond declined the nomination. But it was a testament

Senator Edward Brooke
(b. 1919) of Massachusetts.

to his enormous popularity and the high regard in which he was held.

The longtime civil rights activist had won election to the Georgia House of Representatives the previous fall. But Bond had become an outspoken opponent of the Vietnam War, and, although he won a fair election, his new colleagues had no intention of welcoming him into the legislature. He faced opposition not only from white conservatives but also from white liberals, who believed that Bond had harmed the Democratic Party with his "radicalism." On January 10, 1966, the Georgia state assembly barred Bond from taking his new seat. Martin Luther King, Jr., defended Bond, referencing his own turn away from the war. The Supreme Court agreed with Bond, ruling in December 1966 that the legislature had to swear him into office. Bond finally took his seat on January 9, 1967.

He served in the Georgia House for seven years, and then in the state senate until 1987, when he lost to fellow civil rights activist John Lewis in a bid for the U.S. Senate. Bond also served as the first president of the Southern Poverty Law Center from 1971 to 1979. Although his political career ended in 1987, his career as an activist did not. He served brilliantly as chairman of the board of the NAACP from 1998 to 2010, revitalizing that organization during his tenure.

LOVING V. VIRGINIA, 1967

In June 1958, Mildred Jeter married Richard Loving. The young couple's story would not have been particularly noteworthy had it not been for the color of their skin. Virginia state law made their union illegal, so Jeter, a black woman, and Loving, a white man, crossed the border to the District of Columbia for their marriage ceremony. Shortly afterward, the newlyweds returned to their home in Caroline County, Virginia. There a grand jury issued an indictment charging the Lovings with violating Virginia's ban on interracial marriage. Tried, convicted of a felony, and sentenced to one year in jail, the Lovings received a suspended sentence after they agreed to leave the state and not return together for twenty-five years. They took up residence in D.C. to avoid jail, but their story did not end until the Supreme Court's landmark decision, *Loving v. Virginia*.

Section 20-59 of Virginia's 1924 Racial Integrity Act proclaimed, "If any white person intermarry with a colored person, or any colored person intermarry with a white person, he shall be guilty of a felony and shall be punished by confinement in the penitentiary for not less than one nor more than five years." This law had been on the books in some form

Mildred Jeter Loving (b. 1939) and Richard Loving (1935–75). Their marriage led the Supreme Court to overturn Virginia's antimiscegenation law. Richard Loving's life was cut short by a drunk driver in 1975. His wife lost her right eye in the same incident.

since the 1600s, and in 1967 sixteen other states still similarly prohibited interracial marriage. In 1963, in the midst of the civil rights movement, the Lovings turned to the American Civil Liberties Union for help. Lawyers Bernard S. Cohen and Philip J. Hirschkop took the case, filing appeals before Virginia trial court and the Virginia Supreme Court of Appeals. When their efforts to set aside the Lovings' conviction proved unsuccessful, they turned to the U.S. Supreme Court.

Presenting their case on April 10, 1967, Cohen and Hirschkop argued that Virginia's antimiscegenation statute directly violated the Fourteenth Amendment's equal protection and due process clauses. Virginia's assistant attorney general, citing the Tenth Amendment, countered that the regulation of marriage should be left exclusively to the states and that, because the miscegenation statute punished equally both the white and black participants in interracial marriage, they did not violate the equal protection clause's prohibition of invidious discrimination based upon race. The Court, however, agreed with Cohen and Hirschkop. Its unanimous decision, handed down on June 12, 1967, struck down Virginia's antimiscegenation law. Chief Justice Earl Warren's clearly worded opinion announced that such statutes "cannot stand consistently with the Fourteenth Amendment." The opinion explained that state-imposed regulations on marriage must not infringe upon federally protected rights, and thus it declared all race-based legal restrictions on marriage unconstitutional.

The two-part decision examined both the equal protection and due process arguments made by the Lovings' attorneys. Warren explained, "At the very least, the Equal Protection Clause demands that racial classifications, especially suspect in criminal statutes, be subjected to the 'most rigid scrutiny' . . . There can be no doubt that restricting the freedom to marry solely because of racial classifications violates the central meaning of the Equal Protection Clause." The opinion explicitly overturned the Court's 1883 decision in *Pace v. Alabama* that had upheld a conviction under an Alabama statute forbidding adultery or fornication between whites and blacks. The *Loving* decision also struck down antimiscegenation laws on due process grounds. Chief Justice Warren asserted that to deny the Lovings the fundamental freedom to marry "on so unsupportable a basis as the racial classifications embodied in these statutes, classifications so directly subversive of the principle of equality at the heart of the Fourteenth Amendment, is surely to deprive all the State's citizens of liberty without due process of law."

The Lovings' 1967 victory dealt a blow to one of the last pillars of the Jim Crow system. But many states adopted the Court's edict slowly, as societal approval lagged behind judicial authorization. Public acceptance of the Court's decree proved uneven and often grudging, and vestiges of the old laws remained until 2000, when Alabama became the last state to repeal its constitutional ban on mixed-race marriage.

RIOTS, NEWARK, ELECTION OF BLACK MAYORS

In 1967, riots again ignited across America. Conflict with police led to strife in Tampa, Florida; Winston-Salem, North Carolina; and at Fisk University in Nashville. San Francisco, Cleveland, Buffalo, Minneapolis, East St. Louis, New Haven, and Milwaukee also saw violence that year. Rioting convulsed smaller towns as well. On July 24, SNCC leader H. Rap Brown delivered a typically militant speech in Cambridge, Maryland, a town of 13,000 people located about ninety miles east of Washington. There he warned whites that "if America don't come around, we going to burn it down, brother. We're going to burn it down, brother, if we don't get our share of it."[16]

This sort of language was typical of Brown's rhetoric in his stump speeches to black audiences. However, his words had never before been taken literally. Immediately following the speech, incredibly, African Americans took to the streets and burned twenty buildings across two city blocks. The National Guard arrived, and amid the chaos, gunshots grazed Brown's head.

The Cambridge riot had lasting repercussions. For one, it led to the national rise of Maryland governor Spiro Agnew. Previously known as a moderate, Agnew capitalized on white anger and eventually became Richard Nixon's vice president thanks to the "law and order" credentials he won during his response to the violence. The Cambridge riot also fed into the media's portrayal of the leaders of the Black Power movement as violent rabble-rousing agitators like Brown and Stokely Carmichael.

Violence struck Detroit on July 23,

Black Power leaders Stokely Carmichael and H. Rap Brown at Columbia University, April 26, 1968.

National Guard march along Springfield Avenue in Newark, July 14, 1967.

when local police raided an illegal club, a "blind pig," in one of that city's African American neighborhoods. Officers arrested more than seventy people, and Detroit's inner city erupted into an insurrection. As soon as the police pulled away from the club, members of the crowd that had gathered around the scene began breaking windows in a nearby store. Over the next five days, rioting engulfed the city; homes and businesses burned along Woodward Street and Grand River. Police refused to patrol the scene, deciding that stopping the violence and protecting the city was not worth the risk to their lives. After observing the chaos from a helicopter, Governor George Romney asked President Johnson for help. Johnson sent National Guard troops and tanks from the 82nd Airborne Division. The five-day riot claimed forty-three lives and led to nearly twelve hundred injuries and more than seven thousand arrests.

Violence also rocked Newark, New Jersey (and nearby Plainfield), shortly after the announcement that the city would host a Black Power conference. Police arrested African American cab driver John Smith for a minor traffic violation, and officers beat him severely on their way to the station. A crowd gathered at the jail heard rumors that Smith had died. (Police actually had taken him to a hospital at the request of local black leaders.) Blacks began throwing rocks at the jail and, after police intervention, vented their anger on nearby homes and businesses. The arrival of the National Guard, however, made matters worse, as they randomly shot into buildings, supposedly rooting out snipers and looters. The riot lasted six days; twenty-three people died, including six women, two children, and a seventy-three-year-old man.

The aftermath of the riots hung over Newark's Black Power conference of July 20. The eleven hundred blacks who attended debated ways to simultane-

Time magazine featured Carl Stokes's victory in Cleveland, November 17, 1967.

Richard Hatcher (b. 1933) shakes hands with workers outside a U.S. Steel plant during his campaign for mayor of Gary, Indiana.

ously resist white racism and improve the living conditions of African Americans. They considered boycotting the Olympics, protesting the Vietnam War, establishing black-owned banks and local institutions, and teaching armed self-defense. The conference drew well-known activists like H. Rap Brown, Ron Karenga, Dick Gregory, and Newark native Amiri Baraka. The meeting also welcomed businessmen, NAACP and Urban League members, Black Muslims, and members of the clergy. (Indeed, the chair of the conference was Episcopal minister Nathan Wright, Jr.)

The same year that rioting dominated the newspaper headlines and the meeting in Newark, African Americans gained formal political power for the first time in two American cities. On November 13 in Cleveland, Carl Stokes, a former army solider and state repre-sentative, captured the mayor's office. That same day, Richard Hatcher became mayor of Gary, Indiana, a position he would hold for the next twenty years. The rise to prominence of two black mayors in increasingly black northern cities foreshadowed the turn toward electoral politics that many Black Power advocates would pursue in the 1970s.

MARTIN LUTHER KING: CHICAGO, VIETNAM, AND ASSASSINATION

The events of the early 1960s had made Martin Luther King, Jr., internationally famous and led to the passage of the Civil Rights and Voting Rights acts. But inequality and racial discrimination persisted in the South and remained pervasive in the North as well. According to law, blacks enjoyed equality, but housing inequality, school segregation, hiring discrimination, underemployment, and incidents of police brutality told a different story. In 1966, after witnessing the violence in Watts and gaining a better understanding of the problems blacks faced in northern and western cities, King and the SCLC planned the Campaign to End Slums in Chicago.

King believed that what had brought success in the South would also work in the North: nonviolent direct action and the support of liberal whites and the federal government. Much to his surprise, however, he found that a large number of blacks believed that nonviolent direct action had run its course. Like Laurie Pritchett in Albany, Georgia, four years earlier, Mayor Richard J. Daley knew that the best opposition to nonviolence was nonviolence: he succeeded in keeping the police from beating pro-

Dr. King is hit by a rock during a housing discrimination protest, Chicago, August 5, 1966. Despite his pacifism, he faced frequent assaults.

testers. But residents of white neighborhoods pelted King and his marchers with stones and fireworks. Soon allies rescinded their support for the campaign. King then arranged an agreement with local real estate agents to end housing discrimination—a pact they promptly ignored. The Chicago campaign proved a dismal failure. The experience came as a shock to the civil rights leader.

Nevertheless, King pressed on. He had grown increasingly disillusioned with President Johnson, specifically with how he continued to subjugate his domestic reform agenda to support the escalating war in Vietnam. In 1967, King began criticizing the war and the president. On April 4 in New York City, he delivered the speech titled "Beyond Vietnam," in which he called on the

Dr. King marches arm in arm with (from left) Dr. Benjamin Spock, Monsignor Charles Rice, and Cleveland Robinson of the Negro American Labor Council during an anti–Vietnam War demonstration, New York, April 17, 1967.

nation to end a war that compromised its morals and principles. "We still have a choice today," he told the crowd, "nonviolent coexistence or violent coannihilation." The speech infuriated the Johnson administration, and King lost whatever influence he still had with the federal government. Undeterred, King announced that the SCLC would organize the Poor People's Campaign: three thousand people would build a shantytown in the middle of the nation's capital to dramatize the problem of poverty. He also offered his support to striking garbage workers in Memphis, Tennessee, again demonstrating how his ideas of reform now contained an explicitly economic focus. But Memphis brought problems as well, as nonviolent marches turned violent, and President Johnson offered to send in the National Guard to squelch the protests. King even considered a hunger strike in a desperate attempt to end the infighting among blacks.

On April 3, 1968, shortly after the president announced that he would not run for reelection, King returned to Memphis. In a frightening premonition,

Aftermath of the riot, Washington, D.C.
Photograph by Warren K. Leffler, April 16, 1968.

he told a crowd, "I've seen the Promised Land. I may not get there with you. But I want you to know tonight that we as a people will get to the Promised Land. . . . I'm not fearing any man." Early the next evening an assassin's bullet killed King on the balcony of the Lorraine Motel. Over the following week, 125 cities in twenty-nine states and Washington, D.C., experienced riots that claimed the

lives of forty-six people and led to 35,000 injuries. Hundreds of thousands of Americans—white and black—grieved in more peaceful, personal ways. Civil rights activism had lost its most prominent leader. For all intents and purposes, the civil rights movement, as Dr. King had spearheaded it since 1955, had come to a violent, tragic end.

CIVIL RIGHTS ACT OF 1968

President Lyndon Johnson signs the Civil Rights Act of 1968.

In the 1960s, 73 percent of African Americans resided in urban ghettos, while whites who could afford to do so had fled to the suburbs. Although African Americans had won the right "to inherit, purchase, lease, sell, hold, and convey real and personal property" with the Civil Rights Act of 1866, neither the states nor the federal government devoted much effort toward enforcing it, allowing for segregated housing policies to grow over the next century. In the North, pervasive legal restrictions, discrimination in mortgage lending, and countless pernicious practices largely confined blacks to ghettos.

Until 1948, when the Supreme Court struck them down in *Shelley v. Kraemer,* racially based restrictive covenants were common. Such covenants had prohibited landowners from ever selling property to African Americans, Jews, or other "undesirable" individuals. After 1948, landlords, real estate agents, and mortgage brokers employed

unwritten methods, such as racial steering and "redlining," to maintain the racial homogeneity of neighborhoods. In racial steering, brokers and agents directed a particular race to certain neighborhoods and away from others. They would steer a black family to available homes in black neighborhoods, and the family would never know of houses on the market where whites lived. Financial services companies des-

Equal Housing Lender symbol.

ignated areas on maps dominated by affluent middle- and upper-middle-class whites in green, while they outlined predominantly black areas in red. This practice came to be known as redlining. Companies either would not invest in these neighborhoods or would increase the cost of services, leading to the "ghettoization" of African American neighborhoods—characterized by abandoned buildings, deteriorating school buildings, lowered property values, and a dearth of businesses.

The civil rights movement of the 1960s achieved historic successes in breaking down racial barriers. The Civil Rights and Voting Rights acts had granted fundamental rights to the black community. However, residential segregation remained a key impediment to full realization of equal opportunity. Prior attempts to end racist housing policies had failed. For example, a 1962 executive order had directed all departments of the executive branch to prevent

An African American couple consider a prospective purchase in suburbia. Photograph by Roland L. Freeman, December 16, 1969.

discrimination in all federally administered housing programs, while Title VI of the Civil Rights Act prohibited housing discrimination by programs receiving federal financial assistance. But these enactments were rarely enforced and covered only a minute percentage of housing units.

In order to fill the gaps in previous legislation, Congress passed the Civil Rights Act of 1968, and President Lyndon Johnson signed it into law on April 11, 1968. It contained Title VIII, commonly referred to as the Fair Housing Act, which prohibited discrimination based on "race, color, religion, or national origin" in the sale, rental, and mortgaging of housing. Amendments in 1974 and 1988 extended the protections of the Fair Housing Act to include gender, disability, and family status. Title VIII made housing discrimination a federal crime, subject to enforcement by the U.S. attorney general and the Department of Housing and Urban Development (HUD).

By passing the Civil Rights Act of 1968, the government finally gained the power to enforce laws prohibiting segregation in housing. Although illegal discriminatory practices still occur, the Fair Housing Act remains a critical victory in the campaign to achieve full equality for African Americans.

THE ORANGEBURG MASSACRE AND THE KERNER REPORT

On February 6, 1968, a group of black students from South Carolina State College in Orangeburg staged a protest against a bowling alley that refused to admit black patrons. The protest ended in chaos. Police beat one of the female students; nine students and one police officer went to the hospital with injuries. The conflict simmered over the following two days; then, on February 8, students lit a bonfire on the campus in protest. School officials called the fire department, and state troopers moved in to monitor the scene. A banister rail struck a trooper in the head, and seventy local police officers arrived on the campus to provide reinforcements. One officer, concerned about the growing number of students, fired warning shots; other officers began shooting, hitting a number of students in the back as they fled the scene. Three students died, and twenty-seven others suffered injuries. The event would be dubbed the Orangeburg Massacre. The follow-ing year a jury acquitted the nine state troopers who fired the shots but convicted Cleveland Sellers of SNCC for starting the riot. Sellers, who had suffered an injury in the riot, served seven months in jail and did not receive a pardon until 1993.

The alarming number of urban disturbances—the Detroit riot of 1967 in particular—pressured President John-

The National Guard at Orangeburg, South Carolina, 1968.

Kerner Commission chairman Otto Kerner (left) with New York mayor and commission vice chairman John Lindsay, 1967.

son into action. On July 27, 1967, he convened the National Advisory Commission on Civil Disorders and appointed Governor Otto Kerner of Illinois as its chair. The Kerner Commission investigated the causes of urban rioting and sought to formulate a government strategy to prevent future outbreaks. It issued its report on February 29, 1968, shortly after the Orangeburg Massacre. It argued in memorable words that "our nation is moving toward two societies, one black, one white—separate and unequal."[17] While many white Americans thought that the report should have blamed African Americans for instigating the violence, Kerner and his fellow commissioners found that discrimination and economic exploitation bore the primary responsibility for the growing social chaos afflicting American cities.

Although many social commentators responded thoughtfully to the commission's findings, Republican presidential candidate Richard Nixon pointed to the report as evidence that Democrats did not sufficiently punish (black) criminals. He successfully campaigned as a crusader for "law and order," tapping into the resentment of white Americans who believed that blacks had gained equal rights but had not accepted equal responsibility for their own behavior and for their own fates.

Johnson, preoccupied by the failing war in Vietnam, made insufficient use of the report's findings. On March 31, he announced he would not seek reelection, leaving him to serve the rest of his term as a lame duck.

POOR PEOPLE'S CAMPAIGN AND RESURRECTION CITY

The Civil Rights and Voting Rights acts had eliminated the formal vestiges of Jim Crow society, but they could not resolve structural problems of inequality of opportunity, racial discrimination, and poverty. In 1967 Martin Luther King, Jr., planned to unify the poor of all races into a broad-based coalition to fight poverty. King boldly imagined a Poor People's Campaign, a series of protests in Washington, D.C., that would include picketing federal buildings and building shantytowns on the grounds of the Capitol. King hoped these tactics would gain national attention, as had the protests in Selma and Birmingham, and force the federal government into action.

But times had changed. After the failure of the Chicago protest and the increasing likelihood of a Republican taking the White House in 1968, the idea

Protest outside the U.S. Department of Agriculture, May 1968.

of a Poor People's Campaign lay dormant. After King's assassination, however, his longtime confidant and new SCLC president, the Reverend Ralph David Abernathy, took up the mantle of protest. The Montgomery native had worked with King since his arrival in the Alabama

capital in 1954. He hoped that the Poor People's Campaign would provide a tribute to his fallen friend and establish him as a civil rights leader in his own right.

Abernathy, Jesse Jackson, and other SCLC leaders announced plans for "Resurrection City," a city within a city built on the National Mall. Beginning on May 12, protesters and small crews began constructing the A-frame shanties where protesters would live. Thousands of demonstrators began arriving on mule trains from around the country. But Resurrection City faced dire problems. The buildings of plastic and plywood did not shield their new residents from the cold. On May 23 a torrential rain transformed the campsite into a mud pit and undermined the morale of the three hundred–plus people living there. The most substantial problem, however, was that the SCLC leader-

Ralph Abernathy (center, in short sleeves) at Resurrection City, ca. May 1968.

Campaign stood little chance of succeeding. In the first month of the campaign, SCLC organized forty picket lines in front of government buildings. The protests accomplished nothing. Fifty thousand people attended a mass rally called Solidarity Day on June 19, but compared to the March on Washington in the same location five years earlier, it seemed a disappointment. In spite of calls to solidarity, conflicts erupted among African American, Latino, and Native American residents and organizers. Moreover, the SCLC failed to elaborate sufficiently on what exactly the campaign hoped to achieve. Less than a week after Solidarity Day, Resurrection City came to an end. On June 24, local police ordered residents to leave. After using tear gas, they arrested the 170 people who still remained and mowed down the shanties. Uncertainty clouded the future of the civil rights movement.

ship could not figure out how to garner the attention of, much less concessions from, those in power. Most Americans believed that civil rights legislation had eliminated systemic inequality and that the remaining problems resulted from individual shortcomings that government intervention could not solve. Since Washington, D.C., had seen rioting in the wake of King's assassination, government officials looked unsympathetically upon the presence of Resurrection City.

In this climate, the Poor People's

TOMMIE SMITH AND JOHN CARLOS AT THE 1968 OLYMPICS

By the end of the 1960s, the Black Power movement pervaded many aspects of African American culture, not least the world of sports. Earlier in the decade heavyweight boxing champion Cassius Clay had shocked the nation when he converted to Islam, joined the Nation of Islam, and changed his name to Muhammad Ali; his refusal to serve in the Vietnam War catapulted him to a level of renown perhaps unprecedented for any athlete and underscored how extensively repercussive the politics of sports could be. Ali was stripped of his boxing title in 1966 for five years, at the height of his form and prowess, robbing him of the chance to establish a record of unmatched dominance as the titleholder. While he became a pariah to the ever-shrinking numbers of Americans who supported the war, Ali became a hero to the radical left, to the swelling numbers of Americans who opposed the war, and to an astonishing number of citizens throughout the world. Through this action and as a result of his charismatic personality, Muhammad Ali would become the most famous person in the world.

With Ali as a most compelling exam-

American sprinters Tommie Smith (center) and John Carlos (right) raise their gloved fists in a Black Power salute during the medal ceremony at the 1968 Summer Olympics.

In dark berets, American runners (left to right) Lee Evans, Larry James, and Ronnie Freeman hold their hands up in a Black Power salute after the medal ceremony at the 1968 Summer Olympics.

ple of the power of sports figures to focus international attention on injustice, inequality, and discrimination, other black athletes looked for ways to use their fame for positive social ends. As student uprisings unfolded around the country and throughout the world in the pivotal year of 1968, San Jose State College sociology professor Harry Edwards hit upon an idea: African Americans should boycott the Summer Olympic Games in Mexico City and join the Olympic Project for Human Rights (OPHR), which Edwards had formed. While no formal boycott occurred, Lew Alcindor (later Kareem Abdul-Jabbar) refused to play basketball on the U.S. Olympic team, and the OPHR earned the support of a great number of African Americans.

For two black American athletes, however, the 1968 Olympics would offer an extraordinary platform from which to address a worldwide audience with a dramatic gesture. On October 17, in the 200-meter sprint competition, Tommie Smith took the gold medal with a world record time of 19.83 seconds, and John Carlos captured bronze by completing the race in 20.1 seconds. Peter Norman, a white runner from Australia, finished between the two in 20.06 seconds, for the silver. When the medals ceremony began, Smith and Carlos emerged wearing black socks and no shoes to symbolize the plight of the black poor. Smith donned a black scarf, and Carlos wore a beaded necklace to represent decades of lynching victims. The sympathetic Norman also displayed an OPHR badge

on his jacket. As "The Star Spangled Banner" played and the American flag hung high, Smith and Carlos bowed their heads in silence and raised their fists in the Black Power salute. A smattering of boos came from the confused crowd. "If I win I am an American, not a black American," Smith explained afterward at the press conference. "But if I did something bad then they would say 'a Negro.' We are black and we are proud of being black. Black America will understand what we did tonight."[18]

The backlash came quickly. The angry International Olympic Committee called the protest "a deliberate and violent breach of the fundamental principles of the Olympic spirit."[19] The U.S. Olympic Committee, concerned that the IOC would make good on its threat to ban all American sprinters from further competition, expelled Smith and Carlos from the Olympic Village. The event made front-page news (*The New York Times* ran the headline "2 Black Power Advocates Ousted from Olympics"), and much of the American press criticized Smith and Carlos for their actions. *Chicago American* columnist Brent Musburger went so far as to dub them "black-skinned stormtroopers" shortly after the incident. But Smith's statement at the press conference proved correct: African Americans did understand and supported the symbolism of the runners courageous gesture, and they abhorred the outrageous reaction of the IOC and the press. Overnight Smith and Carlos became heroes within the black community, symbols of the courage of conviction. Their censuring by the press, and the subsequent discrimination that they experienced in their careers, made them martyrs in the African American community, their martyrdom of a piece with the persecution of other black political militants in the second half of that decade. The photograph of the medal ceremony continues to resonate as one of the most poignant images of individual courage from the Black Power era.

PART SIXTEEN

CULTURAL INTEGRATION

1969–1979

QUINCY JONES: AMERICAN NATIONAL TREASURE

Quincy Jones (b. 1933) in a recording studio,
October 1974.

Jones at the Grammy Awards, 1991.

The music that accompanied the first manned space flight to the moon in 1969 was Quincy Jones's arrangement of "Fly Me to the Moon," recorded by Frank Sinatra. Born in 1933, on the South Side of Chicago, Jones overcame poverty and family disruptions to become one of the greatest forces in the music and entertainment industries. As a youngster he lived with his father in Seattle, and he formed his first band as a teenager with a young pianist named Ray Charles. Poor and without family support, Jones was nearly swept into a life of crime; then, during the 1940s, the many jazz musicians who came through Seattle inspired him to change course. In junior high school, he took trumpet lessons and later convinced a member of Count Basie's orchestra to offer him tutelage as well. Jones showed enormous promise and won a scholarship to Boston's Berklee School of Music. He studied there for a year before with-

drawing to play in Lionel Hampton's band. In 1951, he moved to New York City and began an extraordinary career as a music arranger for some of the most popular names in the music business, such as Count Basie and Dinah Washington, which catapulted him to the top of the industry. He toured the Middle East and South America with Dizzy Gillespie, and then moved to Paris to study with Nadia Boulanger and to write and perform.

In 1961, Jones returned to New York and worked for Mercury Records, becoming the company's vice president three years later, the highest position an African American had ever achieved in the music industry. He was soon arranging music for Frank Sinatra, Sarah Vaughan, and Peggy Lee. Just as important, in 1964 Jones began to write musical scores for Hollywood films, starting with Sidney Lumet's memorable *The Pawn Broker*. Subsequently, he wrote the

scores for *In Cold Blood* (1967); *In the Heat of the Night* (1967); *Cactus Flower* (1969); and *Bob & Carol & Ted & Alice* (1969). He also scored music for television, including *The Bill Cosby Show* (1969); *Ironside* (1967–75); *Sanford and Son* (1972–77); and the landmark series *Roots* (1977), which won Jones the first of myriad Emmys. At the same time, he composed and played his own jazz music. In the 1980s he moved to Warner Bros. and in 1983 produced Michael Jackson's two greatest albums, *Off the Wall* and *Thriller,* the latter of which sold more than 50 million copies.

In 1985, Jones coproduced Steven Spielberg's adaptation of Alice Walker's novel *The Color Purple.* In 1990 he established Quincy Jones Entertainment and created the television series *Fresh Prince of Bel-Air* (1990–96), the riveting documentary *The History of Rock and Roll* (1995), and *Tupac Shakur: Thug Angel* (2002). With seemingly endless

Michael Jackson and Quincy Jones at the 1984 Grammys. Jones produced Jackson's best-selling album *Thriller*.

energy and drive, Jones founded his own music publishing business and the magazine *Vibe*, devoted to black popular music. Testifying to his ubiquitous influence and creativity, Jones has received seventy-seven Grammy nominations and won twenty-six, and has been nominated six times for an Oscar. In 2000, Harvard University created the Quincy Jones Professorship of African American Music; the next year he was made a Commander of the Legion of Honor. In addition to his versatility as a musician and a composer, Quincy Jones will be remembered as one of the first black musicians who owned and produced his own music and films.

ARTHUR ASHE: A STUDY IN BRAVERY

The story of Arthur Ashe is one of grace, dignity, compassion, and quiet strength. Primarily known as a tennis star, Ashe was the first African American male to win a Grand Slam title. (Before Ashe, Althea Gibson had been the first black person to win a Grand Slam title, in 1956. And she won Wimbledon in 1957 and 1958.) Ashe shattered the white-dominated world of tennis at the height of the civil rights movement, and his accomplishments on the court paved the way for future African American athletes.

Arthur Robert Ashe, Jr., born on July 10, 1943, in Richmond, Virginia, took up playing at an early age on the segregated tennis courts at Brook Field Park. His natural talent attracted the attention of physician and tennis coach R. Walter Johnson of Lynchburg. Johnson had also been the coach of Althea Gibson and saw enormous potential in the young Ashe. Under Johnson's instruction, Ashe cultivated his talents

Arthur Ashe (1943–93) in action at Forest Hills, New York, 1964.

Ashe celebrates his Wimbledon victory over Jimmy Connors, 1975.

and became the first African American junior player to be ranked by the U.S. Lawn Tennis Association (USLTA). But in segregated Richmond, Ashe could play only black opponents, on segregated outdoor tennis courts.

In order to expand his playing options, he moved to St. Louis in 1960 to continue his training with Richard Hudlin. Ashe accepted a tennis scholarship to the University of California, Los Angeles, one of the country's best college tennis programs. He became an All-American, and in 1963 he was selected for the Davis Cup competition, making him the first African American to play for the U.S. team. By the time he graduated in 1966, Ashe had gained recognition among tennis enthusiasts as a rising star. He joined the U.S. Army and continued to play in the Davis Cup and other tournaments. While still an amateur and a lieutenant stationed at West Point in 1968, Ashe entered the inaugural U.S. Open. On September 9, he defeated Tom Okker of the Netherlands in the championship match. With this win, Ashe became the first African American male to win a Grand Slam tournament, and he remains to this day the only African American man to hold

Althea Gibson (1927–2003). Born in South Carolina, Gibson grew up in Harlem and attended Florida A&M University. After national tennis champion Alice Marble condemned the segregation that kept Gibson from playing tournaments, her career took off. In 1951, she was the first African American to play at Wimbledon. Here she reaches for a shot against Christine Truman of Britain in the Wimbledon ladies' singles semifinal match, 1957.

the U.S. Open title. He turned professional the next year, and his successes on the international tennis stage continued. In 1970, he won his second Grand Slam title at the Australian Open, and five years later, he defeated Jimmy Connors to win the coveted Wimbledon singles title. He was the first, and remains the only, black man to win the prestigious tournament.

Throughout the late 1960s and early 1970s, Ashe grew into one of the most famous tennis players in the world. Brilliant, articulate, and skilled, he embodied a mannerly style, discipline, and grace—characteristics that gained him acceptance in the white-dominated tennis world and that made him a national

icon in the midst of the often brutal and ugly struggle for racial equality. He channeled his celebrity to garner attention to issues he was passionate about, and he gained a reputation for his social and political consciousness. His early activism led him to help found the Association of Tennis Professionals (ATP) in 1972, which enabled tennis players to earn a living as professional athletes. After he was denied a visa in 1969 to compete in the South African Open, he began a campaign calling for South Africa's expulsion from the International Lawn Tennis Federation and Davis Cup play because of its strict apartheid policy of racial segregation that excluded blacks from competition.

His crusade gained considerable international support, drawing early attention to the injustices of South African apartheid. Ashe received a visa in 1973 and became the first black person to play in the South African Open.

Ashe suffered a heart attack in 1979 and underwent quadruple-bypass surgery, ending his tennis career. After a second heart attack and bypass surgery in 1983, he received a blood transfusion that he later discovered had been contaminated with HIV. Nevertheless, he remained active both in the world of tennis and in public life. He served as the nonplaying captain of the U.S. Davis Cup team until 1985, continued to speak out against apartheid, established tennis programs for inner-city youths, and wrote his three-volume *A Hard Road to Glory: A History of the African-American Athlete* (1988). In 1992, Ashe announced that he had developed AIDS. He used his personal tragedy to shine a spotlight on the worldwide HIV/AIDS crisis and established the Arthur Ashe Foundation for the Defeat of AIDS to raise money for AIDS research and treatment, as well as the Arthur Ashe Institute for Urban Health to assist public health programs for urban minority populations. Less than a year after he announced his disease, Ashe died on February 6, 1993, of AIDS-related pneumonia, at the age of forty-nine.

CHICAGO EIGHT, FRED HAMPTON, ANGELA DAVIS

Controversy followed the Black Panther Party and its members through the end of the decade. The 1968 Democratic National Convention in Chicago saw one of the largest protests in American history, as young people arrived by the thousands to speak out against the escalation of the Vietnam War. Bobby Seale attended the protests, although he did not play a major role, and found himself one of eight people (dubbed the Chicago Eight) indicted and brought to trial on charges of conspiracy to incite a riot.

In the courtroom, the protesters immediately transformed the trial into a spectacle of the absurd. Seale sat alongside Abbie Hoffman, Jerry Rubin, and other members of the Youth International Party who put their feet up and pretended to sleep, wore outrageous costumes like judicial robes, and ate candy during the proceedings. Seale, the lone African American on trial, developed a bitterly adversarial relationship with Judge Julius Hoffman. Seale wanted to represent himself, but Judge Hoffman refused to allow it. He responded by constantly berating Hoffman, calling him a pig and a racist, until, in an

Bobby Seale is restrained and gagged during the Chicago Eight trial, 1969. Drawing by Howard Brodie.

astounding act, Hoffman ordered Seale bound and gagged so that he could not interrupt the trial. In November 1969, Judge Hoffman sentenced Seale to four years in prison for contempt of court and ruled that his case would proceed separately from the rest, leaving them the Chicago Seven.

While Seale was serving his sentence, he briefly visited New Haven, Connecticut, where even bigger legal difficulties soon began: authorities accused him of ordering the murder of Panther Alex Rackley, a police informer. In the spring of 1970 the trial of Seale and several other Panthers began, bringing chaos, protests, bombings, and the National Guard to New Haven. In mid-April, as an expression of outrage, Yale students went on strike to protest the government's persecution of the Panthers. Eventually students at most colleges and universities followed suit, especially after the illegal bombings of Cambodia ordered by President Richard M. Nixon. On May 1, one hundred thousand students and supporters descended on New Haven for the "May Day" rally to support the Panthers and protest the Vietnam War. State leaders and Yale University officials cooperated to guard against violence and accommodate them. Legal authorities and elected officials alike expected that the Panthers and their supporters would attempt to burn down the city. Yale University's president Kingman Brewster sought to avoid violence by offering the protesters food and accommodations. Famously, he publically expressed doubt that Seale or any Black Panther could receive a fair trial in America. Perhaps because of the

Angela Davis (b. 1944). Panther advocate, social critic, and academic, Davis earned a Ph.D. in philosophy from the University of Frankfurt. She is shown here with her trademark Afro. Photograph by Bernard Gotfryd, 1974.

Chicago police remove the body of Black Panther leader Fred Hampton after he was shot on Chicago's West Side, December 4, 1969.

protests, or because the government had little evidence to convict Seale, he was acquitted in 1971.

The government, however, maintained its campaign to destroy the Panthers. Back in Chicago, tension between the Panthers and local police had long run high. On December 4, 1969, violence—from the police—exploded again. In the early morning hours, fourteen police officers—armed with intelligence from the FBI—attacked local Panther headquarters in a surprise raid, killing Fred Hampton and Mark Clark. The police claimed they fired in self-defense, but evidence later showed that officers had shot Hampton in the head, point-blank. The shootings gained the attention of prominent civil rights leaders and actually helped the Panthers' image in the eyes of the public.

The following year, the Panthers precipitated an act of violence. On August 7, 1970, seventeen-year-old Jonathan Jackson engineered an attempt to free his brother, Panther George Jackson, from Northern California's Soledad prison. An armed Jonathan Jackson entered the Marin County Courthouse and, with the help of three men on trial, kidnapped the judge, prosecutor, and three jurors. Once outside, Jonathan Jackson, two convicts, and the judge were killed in a shootout with guards. The FBI traced Jackson's guns to Angela Davis, a communist, Panther, and UCLA faculty member. A nationwide hunt culminated in the arrest of Davis in New York City on October 13. Despite an enormous amount of protest and publicity from all sides in the controversy, Davis did not come to trial until June 4, 1972, when she was acquitted. Her case had made her a cause célèbre among African American and left-wing groups. Davis remained one of the most visible and influential black activists, a genuine icon of the black revolutionary movement.

1972 EQUAL EMPLOYMENT OPPORTUNITY ACT

Title VII of the Civil Rights Act of 1964 prohibited employment discrimination based on race, sex, color, religion, or national origin. Intended to rectify centuries of disparate treatment of historically disadvantaged sectors of society, Title VII outlawed discrimination in recruitment, hiring, wages, assignment, promotions, benefits, discipline, discharge, layoffs, and almost every aspect of employment. It also created the Equal Employment Opportunity Commission (EEOC), a bipartisan agency charged with eliminating unlawful employment practices. But within a few years of its enactment, lawmakers acknowledged that the 1964 act did not go far enough to eradicate persistent discrimination.

A Senate report declared that "employment discrimination is even more pervasive and tenacious" than the Congress had assumed in 1964. Little progress had been made for minorities in any occupational field; they remained in lower-paid jobs, and significant pay disparities remained linked to discrimination. The resulting Equal Employment Opportunity Act of 1972 contained key amendments to Title VII, expanding its scope and increasing its muscle. The report accompanying the bill stated, "The time has come for Congress to correct the defects in its own legislation. The promises of equal job opportunity made in 1964 must be made realities."[1] To accomplish this task, the 1972 act expanded coverage of

Equal Employment Opportunity Commission seal.

Title VII to include all employers hiring fifteen or more employees (decreased from twenty-five). It also extended the provisions to cover employees of federal, state, and local government, as well as elementary, secondary, and higher educational institutions. Significantly, the act also increased the enforcement power of the EEOC by granting it the power to sue offending companies.

Since its enactment, the Equal Employment Opportunity Act has become a staple of American life, guiding fair hiring practices across the country and building up affirmative action programs. Its decisions, policy guidelines, and amicus briefs have helped shaped employment discrimination law, including how to prove discrimination and what remedies are available under the law. In the 1970s, the EEOC brokered many high-profile settlements involving systemic discrimi-

nation, including a $31 million settlement in 1974 from the steel industry and a $29.4 million settlement in 1978 from General Electric. Throughout its more than forty-year history, the EEOC has investigated countless discrimination claims, initiated thousands of lawsuits, and negotiated settlement agreements on behalf of thousands of mistreated employees.

The act was bolstered by passage of the 1973 Rehabilitation Act, which prohibited the federal government as an employer from discriminating against qualified individuals with disabilities; the 1978 Pregnancy Discrimination Act, banning discrimination against pregnant women; the 1990 Americans with Disabilities Act, often described as the Emancipation Proclamation for the physically impaired; the 1990 Older Workers Benefit Protection Act; the Civil Rights Act of 1991, which strengthened the Age Discrimination in Employment Act and the Americans with Disabilities Act by permitting injured parties to request jury trials and allowing plaintiffs to recover compensatory and punitive damages when intentional employment discrimination is proven. Finally, the Genetic Information Nondiscrimination Act of 2008 outlawed discrimination against employees or applicants because of genetic information, including an individual's (and family) genetic tests, as well as information about any disease, disorder, or condition of an individual's family medical history.

GROWTH OF BLACK POLITICAL POWER

Shirley Chisholm (1924–2005) announcing her presidential candidacy, 1972.

Charles C. Diggs (1922–98), World War II veteran, represented Detroit in Congress from 1955 to 1980.

The Voting Rights Act of 1965 led to an explosion in the number of registered black voters and, as a result, the number of black officeholders. Shirley Chisholm sought to take advantage of the possibilities opened by the new law. Born and raised in Brooklyn, Chisholm established herself as an educator, completing a master's degree in teaching at Columbia University in 1952 and becoming a consultant for the New York City Division of Day Care in 1959. Five years later, she began her political career and won a spot in the state legislature. In 1968, redistricting in Brooklyn created a new seat in the U.S. House, and Chisholm, with the campaign slogan "Unbought and unbossed," defeated three other black candidates in the primary. Her subsequent victory in the general election made her the first African American woman to serve in Congress.

By 1971 thirteen African Americans had won congressional seats. Sensing their own potential as a lobbying bloc, they formed the Congressional Black Caucus (CBC) on January 12 of that year. Representative Charles C. Diggs of Michigan served as the first chairman. The CBC aimed to keep issues of importance to African Americans at the forefront of the congressional agenda, and its members did not hesitate to use dramatic action to draw attention to their priorities. After President Richard Nixon repeatedly refused to meet with them, CBC members boycotted his State of the Union address. The protest worked, and Nixon finally agreed to a meeting.

But CBC members soon learned that attempting to balance black politics with personal interests and constituent demands often led to dissension. A notable rift occurred in 1972, when Shirley Chisholm ran for the Democratic presidential nomination. CBC members believed that she had placed her own political ambitions and her desire for new alliances—such as with white women and Hispanics—above the goals of the CBC. Only two CBC members publicly endorsed her campaign, although she did receive a respectable 10 percent of primary votes. While the CBC often disagreed on particular issues, it remains to this day perhaps the most important legislative mechanism for the rights and interests of African Americans.

African Americans also hoped to express their political power outside traditional political venues. Seeking to unite African Americans across political parties, Gary, Indiana, mayor Richard Hatcher, Charles C. Diggs, and Amiri Baraka hosted the National Black Political Convention in Hatcher's home city from March 10 to March 12, 1972. More than 2,700 delegates—along with thousands more alternates—discussed African American political participation, the

Founding members of the Congressional Black Caucus, left to right: (front row) Robert Nix, Sr., Charles Diggs, Jr., Shirley Chisholm, Augustus Hawkins; (second row) Parren Mitchell, Charles Rangel, William Clay, Sr., Ronald Dellums, George Collins, Louis Stokes, Ralph Metcalfe, John Conyers, Jr., Walter Fauntroy.

persistence of discrimination and poverty, and international affairs. But the convention suffered from intense factionalism, particularly over the divisive issues of school busing and American support of Israel. The National Black Political Convention also failed to endorse Chisholm's presidential campaign.

Despite the infighting at the convention, African Americans made significant gains during the midterm elections of 1972: Barbara Jordan and Andrew Young became the first African Americans from the South elected to Congress since 1898. Jordan, the first black woman to represent a southern state, grew up in Houston, where she practiced law after earning a degree in 1960 from Boston University. Her interest in politics blossomed after working for the Kennedy campaign that year. After two failed bids for the Texas House of Representatives, she won election to the state senate in

Andrew J. Young (b. 1932). Graduating from Howard University in 1951, Young earned a theological degree from the Hartford Theological Seminary. He joined the civil rights movement in 1955, worked directly for Dr. King, and in 1970 ran for Congress in Georgia, winning on his second try in 1972. In 1977 he became the U.S. ambassador to the United Nations.

Representative Barbara Jordan (1936–96). With her electrifying voice, Jordan delivered the keynote address at the 1976 Democratic National Convention. In 1972 the Texas-born lawyer was the first black woman from the South elected to Congress. She served until 1978.

Tom Bradley (1917–98). Born in a log cabin on a cotton plantation in Robertson County, Texas, Bradley worked for twenty years on the Los Angeles police force before becoming mayor in 1973. This photograph shows him campaigning in 1973.

Maynard Jackson (1938–2003). Atlanta's first black mayor took the oath of office on January 7, 1974.

Coleman Young (1918–97). Born in Tuscaloosa, Alabama, Young grew up in Detroit, served in World War II, and became a union organizer. He won election to the state senate before becoming Detroit's mayor in 1973.

1966. When redistricting increased the strength of Houston's African American voters, Jordan captured a seat in Congress. In Washington she proved a compelling champion of civil rights and a strong opponent of corruption. Indeed, she gained national recognition for her dramatic speech at the beginning of Richard Nixon's impeachment trial.

For Andrew Young, election to Congress seemed a victory both for himself and for his organization, the Southern Christian Leadership Conference. Young had joined the SCLC in 1961 and became one of Martin Luther King's most trusted advisers. During his congressional campaign, he forged what he called the "New South Coalition" of African Americans, white liberals, and white workers. Young's election began a political career that would include serving as UN ambassador under President Jimmy Carter and, later, two terms as mayor of Atlanta. For a generation, Young symbolized the future of the civil rights movement.

African Americans made gains at the local level as well. In May 1973, Tom Bradley captured the mayor's office in Los Angeles, the first African American to do so in the modern era. In Atlanta, the New South Coalition also elected Maynard Jackson as the city's first black mayor in 1973. He would serve until Andrew Young's election in 1980. In Detroit, Coleman Young became that city's first black mayor on November 6. The office of mayor was coming to be thought of, in many cities, as the province of black politicians.

SOUL TRAIN

Dancers on *Soul Train*.

on Cornelius badly wanted his own radio show, and he took dramatic steps to realize his dream. In 1966, the Chicago native left his steady job at Golden State Mutual Life and took a position (and an accompanying pay cut) at WVON radio as a fill-in disk jockey, a role that held little hope for future advancement. Fearing that radio would be a dead end, Cornelius accepted a job in 1968 as a sports broadcaster on the local television show *A Black's View of the News,* at WCIU-TV. This job inspired Cornelius to combine what he loved about radio and television into a new program that would target an African American audience starved for programming. With his own money, Cornelius shot a pilot for a dance show, a black version of *American Bandstand*. He shopped the pilot to sponsors; most expressed no interest. But a manager at the Chicago-based Sears, Roebuck department store chain proved

an exception, as he saw the show as an opportunity to boost record sales. With Sears's sponsorship, WCIU allowed Cornelius to broadcast his show on the network. Cornelius memorably named his invention *Soul Train.*

The first episode broadcast to the Chicago market on August 17, 1970, and aired weekday afternoons. The show found quick success, and Cornelius became famous in his home city. The next year he attracted a new sponsor in Johnson Products Company, the African American beauty company famous for its line of successful hair products such as Afro-Sheen. Johnson's sponsorship helped Cornelius place the show into other markets. It grew exponentially. Within a year *Soul Train* gained twenty-five new markets; in two years it was in fifty-two markets. By the middle of the decade, it had entered nearly one hundred markets. The program went into syndication in 1971 and

continued until 2006, becoming the longest-running syndicated television program in history. *Soul Train* was a harbinger of, and conduit for, the crossover market, cultural artifacts that appealed equally to white and black consumers.

Soul Train's format changed very little from its first episode, although Cornelius ended his role as permanent host in 1993. For twenty-two seasons, Cornelius, with his baritone voice, was the embodiment of cool in his sharp suits and wide ties. The former substitute deejay became an arbiter of taste in popular culture. He chose all the music for the show, selecting the hottest songs on the soul, rhythm and blues, and, later, rap charts. The show also hosted major African American performers as guests; Curtis Mayfield, Ike and Tina Turner, Michael Jackson, Aretha Franklin, Stevie Wonder, and Marvin Gaye all graced *Soul Train's* stage, generally lip-synching

Soul Train founder Don Cornelius (b. 1936).

their performances, as artists did on *American Bandstand*. The biggest stars of the show, however, were unquestionably the dancers. Young black men and women, decked out in the colorful, often flamboyant styles of the day, performed the most popular dances, serving effectively as dance instructors for thousands of black, Hispanic, and white viewers, nationalizing black culture to an extent not possible before.

Just as black people dominated the show in front of the camera, they also held the major production roles behind it. The program thrived for more than three decades, weathering a number of fads along the way. In 1985 Cornelius created the Soul Train Awards to recognize the achievements of black artists, so often ignored by the white-dominated Academy Awards and Grammys. Until it ceased production in 2006, *Soul Train* shaped the tastes of popular American culture in a way that no single program has done before or since. Its place in the history of black popular culture and black business is sui generis.

BUSING IN BOSTON

In 1954, the Supreme Court's landmark *Brown v. Board of Education* decision declared void the "separate but equal" doctrine that had allowed for legal segregation in the public school system. Southern states notoriously battled over school integration, with international news erupting out of Little Rock, Arkansas, and elsewhere. Although northern school systems, which lacked Jim Crow's de jure system of segregation, largely avoided widespread conflict over civil rights in the 1950s and 1960s, throughout the postwar period black leaders struggled to obtain better schools and hire black teachers. But by the mid-1970s the civil rights movement took center stage in the North when Boston found itself embroiled in a protracted school-desegregation scandal that shocked the nation and forced many to confront the depth of prejudice that existed even in one of the country's most historically liberal cities.

The Massachusetts state legislature had passed the Racial Imbalance Act of 1965, which aimed to eliminate student body compositions of more than 50 per-

Soiling of Old Glory, photograph by Stanley Forman, April 5, 1976. A busing opponent attempts to spear Ted Landsmark (b. 1946), who was innocently on his way to city hall when he was attacked and beaten to the ground. Forman won the 1977 Pulitzer Prize for spot photography for this image.

cent minority students. Despite passage of the law, Boston schools remained racially imbalanced. During the 1971–72 school year, 84 percent of Boston's white students attended schools that were more than 80 percent white and 62 percent of black students attended schools with more than 70 percent black students.

Assisted by the NAACP, a group of parents filed suit, alleging that the Boston School Committee intentionally violated the Fourteenth Amendment with its conscious policy of racially seg-

Louise Day Hicks (1916–2003), lawyer and former congresswoman, shown at the lower right, leads the opposition to the integration of Boston public schools, May 2, 1973.

regated schools. The parents claimed that the committee deliberately adopted policies, school-districting lines, and transportation practices that promoted the schools' racial homogeneity. Insisting it had done all it could to eliminate racial imbalances, the committee asserted that the racial makeup of Boston schools resulted not from deliberate policy but from residential segregation, which they could not control.

On June 21, 1974, U.S. District Court Judge W. Arthur Garrity, Jr., handed down his opinion in *Morgan v. Hennigan*. He found a recurring pattern of racial discrimination and intent by the Boston School Committee. Moreover, he concluded, the committee had established a system that deliberately separated black and white students and underfunded black schools. The U.S. Supreme Court, in *Swann v. Charlotte-Mecklenburg* (1971) and *Keyes v. School District No. 1, Denver* (1973), had granted judges wide latitude to remedy deliberate segregation in schools. To correct Boston's racial

imbalance, Garrity set out a "comprehensive plan," which among other things required white students to be bused to predominantly black schools and vice versa.

The plan, involving nearly eighteen thousand students, was to take effect in the fall of 1974. The abruptness of the change led to panic, but the most provocative element of Garrity's plan involved busing students from the insular Irish Catholic neighborhood of South Boston to the economically depressed black ghetto of Roxbury. The judge's decision sparked a firestorm, and many parents refused to abide by the court mandate. Led by South Boston mother and former Boston School Committee chairperson Louise Day Hicks, the antibusing movement spawned organizations such as Restore Our Alienated Rights (ROAR). They saw forced busing as an infringement of parents' authority, and outrage ignited across the city. Just before the fall semester began on September 12, thousands of parents gathered on the

Boston Common to protest the busing plan. Some protesters hurled insults and even rotten vegetables at Senator Edward Kennedy, who had come to the Common to try to calm parents' fears.

Although the first days of the desegregation plan went smoothly in most areas, violence dominated South Boston, Hyde Park, and Charlestown. South Boston High School became the center of the antibusing movement, when, on the first day of school, graffiti containing racial epithets was discovered scrawled on school walls. Angry mobs gathered outside and pelted schoolbuses carrying black children with rocks. Despite a surge of police presence in the most affected areas, cross-racial violence continued. Both whites and blacks retaliated against those they saw as a threat. Amid the volatile and often dangerous situation, many students feared going to school, and many parents prohibited their children from attending.

ROAR, Hicks's organization, called for a boycott, and school attendance fell by nearly 50 percent during the first year. For three years the battle over busing in Boston raged amid dwindling school attendance and seething racial tensions. Undaunted, Judge Garrity continued to oversee the busing plan for eleven years, issuing some four hundred orders to achieve compliance.

Ultimately the violence subsided, largely because many of the most militant white parents sent their children to private schools or turned to home schooling and private tutors. White attendance at Boston public schools dropped significantly in the mid- to late 1970s and never fully recovered. To many observers, Garrity's desegregation plan achieved a pyrrhic victory: while it fostered a measure of racial integration in the schools, it heightened racial tensions and sparked white flight from the inner city.

BLACKS IN THE MILITARY: SAMUEL GRAVELY, JANIE MINES, DANIEL JAMES

African Americans continued to rise in the military during the 1970s. Samuel L. Gravely's long, pioneering career in the U.S. Navy began when he enlisted in the naval reserve in 1942 at age twenty. But even after becoming the first African American to graduate from the Columbia University Midshipmen's School, he confronted the same segregation in the navy that he experienced every day in his hometown of Richmond, Virginia. Still, he persisted, serving during World War II, working as a recruiter for the navy after it desegregated in 1948, and seeing combat in the Korean War. His valor allowed him to set a number of precedents for African Americans over the following years.

In 1962, he took command of the *Falgout,* as the first black skipper of a modern American warship. In 1963, he was one of the first two African Americans to complete study at the Naval War College. Eight years later, he again made history by earning the rank of rear admiral, and his command of the *Jouett* during the Vietnam War made him the first African American to achieve flag rank. Gravely won the Legion of Merit and Bronze Star, as well as the Meritorious Service and Navy Commendation medals before he retired in 1980.

Women broke new ground in the navy as well. In 1976, the Naval Academy admitted women for the first time. One African American woman joined the inaugural class, Janie L. Mines of South Carolina. Four years later she was the first black woman to graduate from the academy; she served in the supply corps, the navy annex in the Pentagon, and aboard the USS *Emory S. Land.* After the navy, Mines earned an M.B.A. from the Sloan School of Business Manage-

Samuel L. Gravely, Jr. (1922–2004). A World War II veteran, Gravely was the first African American to earn a naval reserve officer's commission. He endured galling discrimination from white comrades and was even jailed in Miami for impersonating an officer. He joined the regular navy during the Korean War and took command of his first vessel at the outset of the Vietnam War. From 1976 to 1978 he commanded the U.S. Third Fleet.

General Daniel "Chappie" James (1920–78). Born in Pensacola, Florida, James graduated from Tuskegee Institute in 1942, trained to be a pilot, and earned a commission in 1943 but spent the war in the United States. He flew more than one hundred combat missions in Korea and seventy-eight more during the Vietnam War.

ment at MIT and started a nonprofit organization, Boyz to Men Club, to help poor children. She also established her own consulting firm, and while a senior vice president at Strategic Sourcing, she held responsibility for a procurement program of more than $2 billion.

African Americans also made gains in other branches of the military. Daniel "Chappie" James began his military career at the Tuskegee Institute. While working toward his bachelor's degree in physical education, he participated in the Civilian Pilot Training Program. Although he did not see combat in World War II, he remained in the air force and trained as a fighter pilot. After

serving for six years on bases in the United States, he arrived in the Philippines in 1949 and the next year flew 101 combat missions in the Korean War. He spent the next decade training officers in the United States, Britain, and Thailand, before flying 78 combat missions in Vietnam in 1967. The winner of dozens of civilian and military awards, James achieved the ultimate military goal on September 1, 1975, when he took over command of Peterson Air Force Base in Colorado and became the first African American four-star general in the nation's history. The F-4 Phantom he flew in Vietnam remains enshrined on the Tuskegee campus.

ALEX HALEY AND *ROOTS*

Alex Haley followed a most unusual path to becoming one of the most famous writers of his generation. Born in 1921, Haley grew up in Alabama and Tennessee. After attending Elizabeth City State Teachers College in North Carolina, in 1939 he joined the U.S. Coast Guard, where he worked primarily as a cook and spent his free time writing pulp romance fiction. When he shifted his focus to writing about the history of the coast guard, the branch named him chief journalist. When he retired from the coast guard in 1950, Haley moved to Greenwich Village to pursue writing full-time. He published articles in *Reader's Digest* and *The Saturday Evening Post*. His break came when *Playboy* commissioned him to interview some of the country's most famous Afri-

can Americans, including Miles Davis, Cassius Clay, and Malcolm X, as well as the head of the American Nazi Party, George Lincoln Rockwell. Haley's interview with Malcolm X would form the basis of his classic *Autobiography of Malcolm X,* published in 1965.

In 1976, Haley published his second book, a novel, *Roots: The Saga of an American Family. Roots* sprang from Haley's long-standing interest in his own family tree. Indeed, for the previous fifteen years Haley had traveled the United States and Africa to trace his lineage. The book begins in 1750 with the story of Kunta Kinte in a village in Gambia. Kunta Kinte is captured, sent as a slave to Annapolis, Maryland, and sold to a plantation owner from Virginia. The slave owner tries to strip Kunta Kinte of his name (by renaming him Toby) and his Muslim religion, but Kunta resists. The slave owner shows no mercy, inflicting the harshest punishment and even selling Kunta's daughter, Kizzy, to a North Carolina slave owner named Tom Lea. Lea rapes and impregnates Kizzy almost immediately after purchasing her. He eventually sells their son, George, to a man in Britain as payment for a gambling debt. The story continues through the Civil War and Reconstruction and ends with the death of Alex Haley's own father.

Roots scored with critics and the public alike, becoming a best seller and winning a Pulitzer Prize. But its influence would soon dramatically transcend the written word. From January 23 until January 30, 1977, ABC television aired an eight-part adaptation of the book. The miniseries focused on the pre–Civil War years and starred Louis Gossett, Jr., John Amos, Maya Angelou, and LeVar Burton. Many analysts predicted that

LeVar Burton in *Roots,* 1977.

a miniseries about the horrors of slavery would never find a mainstream audience. But Americans watched in record numbers—Nielsen Media Research recorded that the episodes averaged from 28.8 million to 36.3 million households. The concluding episode scored a 51.1 rating with a 71 share and stood for six years as the most-watched program in television history. *Roots* also captured nine Emmy Awards. Its popularity led to a sequel, *Roots: The Next Generation,* two years later. The wildly successful sequel, which covered the Reconstruction years, was viewed by 22.5 million households.

Despite its success, *Roots* incurred its share of controversy. Critics accused Haley of blurring the line between historical fact and fiction, but they forgot that the book was a novel, not a work of history. More seriously, authors brought charges of plagiarism, and

Alex Haley (1921–92), April 1, 1977, in London, England.

after a five-week trial Haley settled for $650,000 with novelist Harold Courlander, who rightly claimed that Haley had plagiarized from his 1967 book, *The Slave*. Margaret Walker made a similar claim. Nevertheless, *Roots* has had a last-ing impact and helped clear the way for serious discussions of slavery, violence, and history on television and in film. Equally important, the book and mini-series inspired a generation of Americans, black and white, to study their genealogy and family history, as seen in the popularity of Henry Louis Gates, Jr.'s *African American Lives* and *Faces of America* PBS documentary series.

BLACK WOMEN ACTIVISTS OF THE 1970S

During the 1970s black women continued to agitate for change. While racism remained a target, many black women began to call greater attention to the sexism they encountered in their own communities. In May 1973, thirty African American women, organized by Margaret Sloan-Hunter of *Ms.* magazine, came together in the New York City offices of the National Organization for Women (NOW). They discussed the meaning of black feminism, moving beyond the movement's national focus on white, middle-class women. They analyzed the racism of the women's movement and the sexism of the civil rights movement and sought to provide a voice for the average black women who daily confronted these issues.

Civil rights lawyer and future congresswoman Eleanor Holmes Norton drafted a statement of purpose, and three months later, the women officially formed the National Black Feminist Organization (NBFO). More than five hundred black women from across the country attended the inaugural conference that November. The NBFO addressed a wide variety of issues, including rape and domestic violence; homophobia and the "triple discrimination" that black lesbians faced; the poverty of working women; and the need for women to engage in formal politics. At its peak, the NBFO counted more than two thousand members, and

Eleanor Holmes Norton (b. 1937). In 1977, President Jimmy Carter appointed Norton to serve as the first woman chair of the U.S. Equal Employment Opportunity Commission. She is now is in her tenth term as the nonvoting congresswoman for the District of Columbia. She is also the chair of the House Subcommittee on Economic Development, Public Buildings, and Emergency Management and a tenured professor of law at Georgetown University.

it inspired the formation of other feminist groups, including the Boston-based Combahee River Collective. Though it lasted only four years, it established a foundation for African American feminists to organize in the future.

Marian Wright Edelman has dedicated her life to civil rights causes, in particular to the right of all children to receive a good education. A native of South Carolina, Edelman earned a bachelor's degree from Spelman College and studied abroad in Paris, Geneva, and Moscow. Upon returning to the United States, she became involved in the civil rights movement, which inspired her to study law in order to fight discrimination through the courts. She graduated from Yale Law School in 1963. The following year she moved to Mississippi, where she became the first African American woman admitted to the state bar and the director of the NAACP Legal Defense and Education Fund. She continued her activism throughout the 1960s, working for the Poor People's Campaign in Washington, D.C., in 1968.

After directing the Center for Law and Education at Harvard, Edelman in 1973 began the Children's Defense Fund (CDF), a research and lobbying organization aimed at obtaining aid for children. The CDF found immediate legislative success, convincing the federal government to increase attention to handicapped children in 1975, to pass a $150 million increase in Head Start funding in 1977, and to pass the Adoption Assistance and Child Welfare Act in 1980. Today Edelman and the CDF remain diligent in their pursuit of equal rights for children.

Patricia Roberts Harris sought change through the federal government. After earning her law degree from George Washington University in 1960, she worked for the Justice Department and as a law professor at her undergraduate alma mater, Howard University.

Marian Wright Edelman (b. 1939). A graduate of Spelman College and Yale Law School, Edelman was the first black woman admitted to the Mississippi bar. She directed the NAACP Legal Defense and Educational Fund office in Jackson, Mississippi, and in 1968 moved to Washington, D.C., to become counsel for the Poor People's Campaign. She founded the Washington Research Project, a public interest law firm and the parent body for the Children's Defense Fund. She remains president of the CDF and an advocate for disadvantaged Americans.

Patricia R. Harris (1924–85). Born in Mattoon, Illinois, Harris graduated from Howard University in 1945 and then worked for the Chicago Young Women's Christian Association. In 1949, she became assistant director for the American Council for Human Rights. After earning a law degree in 1960, she worked for the criminal division of the U.S. Department of Justice and taught at the Howard University Law School. In 1965, President Lyndon Johnson appointed her ambassador to Luxembourg. Her extensive experience brought her to the attention of President Jimmy Carter in 1977. This image shows Harris on the television news program *Meet the Press*.

In 1965, she accepted President Lyndon Johnson's appointment as ambassador to Luxembourg, making her the first black woman to hold an ambassadorship. She briefly returned to Howard in 1967, but by the turn of the decade she had dedicated herself to private practice and helping the poor. By 1977 her work with the National Urban League and the American Council of Human Rights caught the attention of the recently elected president, Jimmy Carter. Carter made Harris the first African American woman to hold a cabinet post when he named her head of the Department of Housing and Urban Development. In 1979, she became the secretary of health, education, and welfare (later the Department of Health and Human Services). She returned to private life after Ronald Reagan took office in 1981. Although she failed in a bid to become mayor of Washington, D.C., Harris symbolized the strides black women had made in official government positions. She died of cancer in 1985.

THE MOREHOUSE SCHOOL OF MEDICINE AND LOUIS SULLIVAN

In the early 1970s, the century-old Morehouse College began planning a two-year medical school to train African American doctors to help poor people in the rural South and in the country's inner cities. Morehouse enlisted accomplished physician Louis Sullivan to lead the school as its first dean.

The son of an undertaker and a schoolteacher, Sullivan grew up in Atlanta. His parents emphasized education and also believed in the civil rights struggle, founding the Blakely, Georgia, branch of the NAACP. Sullivan carried these examples with him and combined his professional aspirations with social justice goals. He graduated from Morehouse in 1954 and, four years later, from the Boston University Medical School. He went on to hold a number of prestigious internships and fellowships at institutions including Harvard University, Seton Hall University, the New Jersey College of Medicine, and Massachusetts General Hospital. He returned to Massachusetts in 1966 to found the Boston University Hematology Service at Boston City Hospital. Although he had risen to full professor at Boston University, Sullivan welcomed the chal-

Morehouse School of Medicine, Atlanta.

lenge of building Morehouse's new medical school.

The school opened in 1975, welcoming about two dozen students to its single building on the Morehouse campus. But growth came quickly. Six years later, the medical school split from the college, and the Morehouse School of Medicine became an independently chartered four-year institution. In 1983, the school earned the support of Barbara Bush, the wife of then–vice president George H. W. Bush, who served on its board of trustees. Morehouse School of Medicine gained full accreditation and began granting M.D. degrees in 1985, and by the turn of the twenty-first century, it offered accredited M.D., Ph.D., and M.P.H. degrees. Hundreds of doctors have graduated from the school, and it continues to train physicians to confront the health problems faced by African Americans and the poor of all races.

Sullivan remained president of the School of Medicine until 1989, when his friend George Bush became president of the United States. He appointed Sullivan the secretary of the U.S. Department of Health and Human Services—the only African American in Bush's cabinet. During his time in Washington, Sullivan made difficult choices and alienated many supporters

Louis Sullivan (b. 1933) with
President George H. W. Bush.

with political concessions. He waffled on his opinion regarding abortion after the administration chafed at his support of the *Roe v. Wade* decision. Sullivan eventually claimed to oppose the ruling and abortion so that his nomination would pass muster with conservatives. He also backtracked on his earlier support for needle-exchange programs for intravenous drug users. Indeed, critics charged him with abandoning his focus on stemming the AIDS crisis once he joined the Republican cabinet.

Nevertheless, Sullivan used his position to fight for causes important to African Americans. He led a campaign against the tobacco industry for targeting advertising to blacks; worked to institute new disease-prevention and public health campaigns; and played a key role in forcing food companies to more accurately label their products. After Bush left office in 1993, Sullivan returned to the Morehouse School of Medicine, where he remained president until his retirement in 2002. He continues to advocate for minority health issues.

BIRTH OF HIP-HOP

Grandmaster Flash, DJ Kool Herc, Afrika Bambaataa, and Chuck D attend Columbia University's Rap Summit, New York City, November 1993.

A failed war, forgotten promises, and economic blight set an unlikely stage for the rise of hip-hop culture. By the mid-1970s, the nation had been torn apart and depleted by the war in Vietnam. All major civil rights legislation had become federal law, but racism and economic inequality remained, and no one seemed to know precisely why.

Moreover, the civil rights movement never recovered from the deaths of Martin Luther King, Jr., and Bobby Kennedy, and the FBI's war on the Black Panthers. The promised "peace dividend" from the end of the war never materialized, at least for African Americans. As a result, nearly all major cities suffered crushing economic declines and white flight to the suburbs, turning urban residential regions into volatile landscapes that bore a striking resemblance to a war's aftermath.

In New York's Bronx community, the decline had set in with construction of the Cross-Bronx Expressway, begun in 1948 and finally completed in 1972; it obliterated a wide swath of housing and choked off the black neighborhood to the south. By the advent of the 1970s, six hundred thousand manufacturing jobs had disappeared, and average family income had plummeted. Gangs staked out territory throughout the borough, fueled by youth unemployment that averaged 60 percent, with some portions of the region reaching more than 80 percent. The South Bronx lost 43,000 housing units, and in one four-year period in the 1970s, 30,000 fires had been set in the borough.

At the same time, the Bronx became a tantalizing stew of African American, Caribbean, and Hispanic cultures. At the close of the summer of 1973, the eco-

nomic realities and the cross-cultural mixture produced a pivotal event at 1520 Sedgwick Avenue in the West Bronx. Clive Campbell, a Jamaican, soon to become known as DJ Kool Herc, modified a powerful sound system to merge two turntables with the ability to broadcast his own voice—and someone to flicker the lights in his building's recreation room—and commenced what would become a worldwide cultural revolution. Two years later, Herc (short for Hercules) opened his own club, the Twilight Zone, with an even more powerful sound system and became the biggest draw in the Bronx, where pop sounds mixed with Jamaican rhythms and break dancing. His unique disk jockey style propelled him to renown and, sensing a new avenue to wealth and fame, sparked other deejays who sometimes mixed their party work

Grandmaster Flash (b. 1958), ca. 1980.

South Bronx, 1975.

with music production and recording through sampling—combining portions of other recordings into a driven, aural montage.

The 1977 power failure and accompanying riots in New York boosted the authority of the new performers who took to the streets, illegally tapping into streetlights for power, to perform. The anger and frustration in the borough sparked the social and musical events with an explosion of break dancing and graffiti art. It also inspired a number of competing deejays who rose to prominence, especially Joseph Saddler, the son of Barbados immigrants, who became known as Grandmaster Flash and perfected the sampling genre. His release of *Superrappin* in 1979 as Grandmaster Flash and the Furious Five made him a mogul of hip-hop in the Bronx. At the same time, Kevin Donovan, born in the South Bronx, gained

a following as Afrika Bambaataa. He established the Zulu Nation, a loosely affiliated group of politically conscious rappers, break dancers, and graffiti artists to combat the prevalence of gangs in the Bronx communities. A group that at one point included Queen Latifah among its members rechristened itself the Universal Zulu Nation to sponsor community action and development projects in New York and around the world. By 1976, "deejaying" became a fine art, and Afrika Bambaataa set the standard for the practice. In 1980 his band the Soul Sonic Force debuted *Zulu Nation Throwdown,* followed by *Jazzy Sensation* and *Planet Rock,* immensely popular records that picked up loyal mainstream listeners.

In 1979, Carlton Douglas Ridenhour—Chuck D—from Queens came to the attention of Rick Rubin of Def Jam Records. With performers Terminator X,

Flavor Flav, Professor Griff, and the Bomb Squad, they formed Public Enemy. Their song "Fight the Power" was composed as the theme song of Spike Lee's 1989 film, *Do the Right Thing.* The song and the album that followed the next year, *Fear of a Black Planet,* sparked worldwide interest in rap and hip-hop, especially because it linked political consciousness with hip-hop culture. Moreover, the album's prediction that riots would afflict Los Angeles as a result of widespread racism, especially among the police, proved prescient in 1992 with the acquittal of the police in the infamous Rodney King incident. Thereafter, hip-hop became a cultural phenomenon, and today it has manifestations on every continent and in virtually every country in the world. With the exception of the Internet, hip-hop is arguably the most far-reaching cultural phenomenon in the world over the past thirty years.

THE *BAKKE* CASE AND AFFIRMATIVE ACTION

The mere mention of "affirmative action" usually sparks heated debate. The policy emerged in the late 1960s to increase opportunities for historically disadvantaged groups—particularly African Americans and women—in hiring, college admissions, and the awarding of government contracts. The groundbreaking Title VII of the Civil Rights Act of 1964 specifically banned discrimination in employment and effectively laid the groundwork for the development of affirmative action policies by mandating that a workforce match its applicant pool. In 1969, responding to the continuing racial inequities in the workforce, the Nixon administration instituted the Philadelphia Plan, the first formal enactment of affirmative action. This Republican plan required federally assisted contractors to set specific goals for hiring minorities.

Resistance mushroomed almost immediately. Critics insisted that a policy favoring certain groups violates the principles of equal protection and offers unfair advantages to minorities. In 1971, the first test of affirmative action reached the Supreme Court in *Griggs v. Duke Power Co.* The Duke Power Company required a high school diploma or a minimum IQ score for positions outside its labor department. African American applicants, less likely to hold a high school diploma and with lower average IQ test scores than white applicants, were effectively rendered ineligible for promotion.

The Supreme Court held that standardized tests, such as those used by Duke Power, had a disproportionate impact on minority groups and were not "reasonably related" to the job for which the tests were required. Further-

Allan Bakke on his first day as a student at the medical school of the University of California, Davis, September 25, 1978.

more, the Court explained, Title VII banned "not only overt discrimination but also practices that are fair in form but discriminatory in operation." The *Griggs* decision motivated many employers to adopt policies designed to increase minority hiring and promotion. One year later, the Equal Opportunity Act of 1972 expanded Title VII protections to educational institutions, leading to affirmative action policies at colleges and universities. In the many years since *Griggs,* the Supreme Court has maintained the constitutionality of affirmative action in the face of many "reverse discrimination" challenges and intense political pressure. The Court has, however, restricted the scope of affirmative action in several high-profile and controversial cases.

In 1973 and 1974, Allan Bakke, a white male, was rejected from the University of California, Davis, School of Medicine.

He filed suit to compel his admission, alleging that the university's admissions program violated the equal protection clause of the Fourteenth Amendment by excluding him on the basis of his race, while favoring minority applicants with lower academic scores. In *Regents of the University of California v. Bakke,* handed down on June 28, 1978, the Supreme Court ruled in Bakke's favor, declaring that universities could not establish rigid quota systems requiring admission of a set number of minorities. But it also found that creation of a racially and ethnically diverse student body was a "compelling interest" and that schools could consider race, ethnicity, gender, and even economic status as factors when evaluating applicants.

Subsequently, the Supreme Court has upheld some affirmative action policies as appropriate to remedy past discrimination, while striking down others. In

A protest of the *Bakke* decision in Oakland, October 8, 1977.

United Steelworkers v. Weber (1979) the Court held that a voluntary training program giving preference to minorities was constitutional; *Fullilove v. Klutznick* (1980) upheld a 10 percent "set-aside" for hiring minority contractors on federally funded public works projects; and *Metro Broadcasting v. Federal Communications Commission* (1990) affirmed federal laws designed to increase the number of minority-owned radio and television stations. But in *Wygant v. Jackson Board of Education* (1986) the Court struck down a plan to protect minority teachers from layoffs at the expense of white teachers with greater seniority, and in *Richmond v. J. A. Croson Co.* (1989) it invalidated a nonfederal set-aside program for minority contractors.

In 1995, the regents of the University of California voted to end all affirmative action in hiring and admissions, and the next year California voters approved Proposition 209, an initiative that ended affirmative action throughout the state. Other states soon followed California's lead. The Supreme Court remained largely silent until 2003, when it granted certiorari on two cases challenging affirmative action at the University of Michigan. In *Grutter v. Bollinger*, issued on June 23, 2003, a 5–4 majority of the Court upheld the ruling in *Bakke* that a diverse student body was indeed "a compelling state interest that can justify the use of race in university admissions." The Court, however, insisted that affirmative action policies must be narrowly tailored to achieve diversity goals and must be temporary. In a companion case, the Court declared strict quotas and point systems for minority applicants to be unconstitutional. While schools may consider race in setting diversity goals, the current Court clearly has directed affirmative action onto a narrowing road that many fear will eventually disappear.

PART SEVENTEEN

ACHIEVEMENT

1980-2008

AFRICAN AMERICANS IN ENTERTAINMENT AND THE ARTS DURING THE 1980S

Throughout the 1980s African Americans continued to gain visibility in the entertainment industry and the arts. Most notably, a number of television shows focused on black life, especially the nation's most successful prime-time program, *The Cosby Show.* Its examination of an upper-middle-class African American family marked a virtual revolution in television programming, which previously had either ignored black life or presented little more than racial stereotypes.

Just as black characters became more prominent on the screen, African Americans played greater roles behind the scenes as well. In 1980, Robert L. Johnson founded the first cable network dedicated to African American programming, Black Entertainment Television (BET). Over the following decade BET grew in popularity, and in 1991 it became the first black-controlled company traded publicly on the New York Stock Exchange. In 2003, Johnson sold the company to Viacom for $3 billion, making him the nation's first black billionaire.

But a black woman would soon usurp Johnson's title as the richest African American. Oprah Gail Winfrey, born into poverty in rural Tennessee on January 29, 1954, overcame a number of hardships, including sexual abuse, to graduate from Tennessee State University in 1971. After beginning her television career on news broadcasts in Nashville and Baltimore, Winfrey moved to Chicago in 1983 to host the *AM Chicago* morning program. Within two years the show, now named *The Oprah Winfrey Show,* was syndicated around the country; until she ended its run in 2011, it remained consistently one of the highest-rated programs on

Robert L. Johnson (b. 1946). Born in Hickory, Mississippi, Johnson grew up in Illinois and graduated from the University of Illinois with a degree in history. He earned a master's degree in public administration from Princeton and began his career with the Corporation for Public Broadcasting and the Urban League. With a $15,000 bank loan, he fulfilled his dream and created a cable network aimed at African Americans.

television. She began her own production company, Harpo, and in 1997 won three Emmy Awards. She has now founded her own network, the Oprah Winfrey Network (OWN). She remains one of the most influential, popular, and wealthy women in the world.

African Americans made notable accomplishments in the arts as well. In 1983, Alice Walker won the Pulitzer Prize and the National Book Award for her novel *The Color Purple.* Walker had long fought for civil rights causes and organized voter-registration drives in Georgia, attended the Youth World Peace Festival in Finland, and worked for a Head Start program in Jackson, Mississippi. Her novels focus on many of the problems she sought to rectify as an activist, including racial violence and extreme poverty. Written in 1982, *The Color Purple* traced the life of Celie, an African American woman who endures sexual abuse and poverty in Jim Crow Georgia. Yet she finds strength through other women, and her sexual relationship with her husband's mistress allows her to find self-worth. The novel's tremendous success led to a 1985 film adaptation directed by Steven Spielberg and costarring Oprah Winfrey.

Walker was not alone in winning the Pulitzer Prize during the 1980s. Rita Dove grew up in Akron, Ohio, and graduated summa cum laude from Miami University in Oxford, Ohio, in 1973. From there she continued her academic success, studying for a year on a Fulbright scholarship in Germany before earning an M.F.A. from the University of Iowa in 1977. In 1987, her third poetry collection, *Thomas and Beulah,* earned her the Pulitzer Prize in poetry, making her the first black woman to take the award since Gwendolyn Brooks thirty-seven years earlier. Dove would remain one of the nation's most famous and respected poets, and in 1993 she became the first African American to serve as poet laureate of the United States and consultant of poetry at the Library of Congress.

The African American playwright August Wilson won two Pulitzer Prizes for drama. His ten-play cycle tracing black life in the twentieth century was based mostly in the Hill District of Pittsburgh, a black neighborhood where he grew up. He focused on African Americans often ignored by the rest of society: domestic workers, criminals, menial laborers. He won his first Pulitzer Prize in 1985 for *Fences,* a play about a black garbage collector and his family. *Fences* also won a Tony, and the Broadway production set a record by grossing $11 million in one year. Despite the play's popularity, Wilson refused to allow a Hollywood production of the film unless an African American directed it. As a result, the film has never been made. Wilson won the Pulitzer again five years later for *The Piano Lesson*. In this play a brother and a sister argue over whether to sell the family piano, which Wilson uses as a device to analyze the history of the family and the black community for which it is a metaphor. Notable actors including Charles S. Dutton, Whoopi Goldberg, Phylicia Rashad, and Angela Bassett earned their first national attention in Wilson's plays, which have been performed on Broadway almost eighteen hundred times.

Oprah Winfrey (b. 1954).

Rita F. Dove (b. 1952).

Alice M. Walker (b. 1944). Born in Eatonton, Georgia, into a sharecropping family, Walker attended Sarah Lawrence College. She invested her personal struggles into her writing, found encouragement from Langston Hughes, and participated in the civil rights struggle. She not only emerged as one of the country's greatest writers, but she resurrected the career of Zora Neale Hurston in 1979.

August Wilson (1945–2005). Born in Pittsburgh, Wilson quit school in the ninth grade after a black teacher accused him of plagiarizing, refusing to believe that the young boy possessed such powerful writing skills. He ensconced himself in the public library and taught himself. At age twenty he became part of the emerging Black Arts Movement and soon became the nation's greatest black playwright. August Wilson (standing) with director Lloyd Richards on stage for *The Piano Lesson,* 1987. Photograph by Gerry Goodstein.

MARTIN LUTHER KING DAY

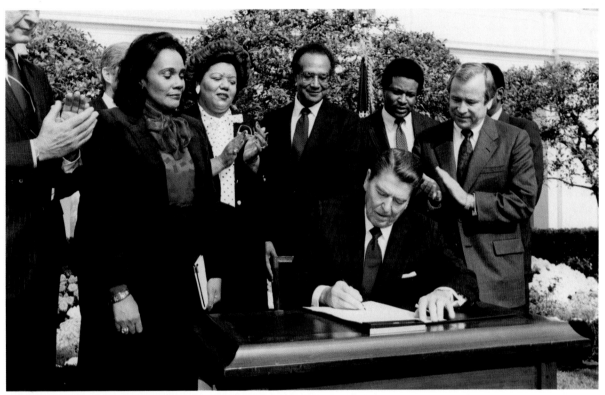

President Ronald Reagan signs the legislation creating the federal holiday for
Dr. King, as Coretta Scott King looks on, November 2, 1983.

The assassination of Dr. Martin Luther King, Jr., in 1968 led to immediate calls for official recognition of his life and work. Representative John Conyers of Michigan, who had a direct connection to the Montgomery story, led the charge. In 1965, he had hired Rosa Parks as a member of his staff—where she remained until 1988. Only four days after King's death, Conyers introduced legislation that would declare Martin Luther King, Jr., Day a federal holiday. But support for the move grew slowly, and like most civil rights issues, it sparked resistance and a sluggish governmental response.

On June 26, 1968, Coretta Scott King founded the Martin Luther King, Jr. Center for Nonviolent Social Change in Atlanta. Establishment of a holiday to honor her husband and his work ranked near the top of its agenda. On King's birthday the following January, the center hosted a celebration and called on Americans to remember the slain leader through a national holiday and, equally important, to continue to work for civil rights. The center asserted, "On this day we commemorate Dr. King's great dream of a vibrant, multiracial nation united in justice, peace and reconciliation. . . . We are called on this holiday, not merely to honor, but to celebrate the values of equality, tolerance and interracial sister- and brotherhood he so compellingly expressed in his great dream for America."[1]

Despite the vocal support of many, the movement for a King holiday proceeded fitfully during the 1970s. The Southern Christian Leadership Conference sent a petition with three million signatures to Congress, which had no immediate effect. Dozens of bills, mostly initiated by Conyers in the House and by Edward Brooke of Massachusetts in the Senate, went nowhere. While the federal government stood pat, a number of state governments began to recognize the holiday: Illinois in 1973; Massachusetts and Connecticut in 1974; and New Jersey in 1975.

The gains of the 1970s persuaded Coretta Scott King to campaign even harder in 1979—the year her fallen husband would have turned fifty. On February 19 she testified before the Senate Judiciary Committee, and on March 27 she testified before a joint hearing of Congress. Throughout the year she continued to use the King Center to mobilize public support, staging rallies and gathering signatures. Her efforts even earned the support of President Jimmy Carter. But when the measure came up again that November, it failed by five votes. Republicans in particular opposed the bill, arguing that a federal holiday would cost too much money (employees would still get paid) and that no precedent existed for an official holiday recognizing a public citizen.

Despite the setback in Congress, Mrs. King's campaign continued. She encouraged states and municipalities to recognize King's birthday. She again testified before Congress in support of the holiday and for a King national historic site, and in 1982 the King Center hosted a conference of one hundred organizations to recognize the March on Washington. Later that year, along with Stevie Wonder, King presented Speaker of the House Tip O'Neill with a petition bearing more than six million signatures. Finally, in 1983, the tide turned. In August, Conyers's years of persistence paid off, as the House passed the King holiday bill by a vote of 338–90. Martin Luther King Day would be observed on the third Monday every January. Despite the vocal protests of Senator Jesse Helms, who led a sixteen-day filibuster against the bill, the Senate passed it 78–22, and President Ronald Reagan signed it into law on November 2, 1983. The first holiday was celebrated on January 20, 1986, although it took time for all states to recognize the date. Arizona did not celebrate the holiday until 1993, and New Hampshire held out until 1999.

THRILLER AND PURPLE RAIN

Born in 1958, Michael Jackson achieved astonishing success from a very young age. But the release of his *Thriller* album and music video took his career to an unprecedented level of fame. He had sold millions of records and had become a household name as the young frontman of the Jackson Five, the group he formed with his brothers Jermaine, Tito, Jackie, and Marlon. Their hits—including "I Want You Back," "ABC," and "I'll Be There"— dominated the airwaves and the charts throughout the 1970s. When Michael Jackson released his solo album *Off the Wall* in 1978, four of its songs cracked the top ten—a record. It would reach platinum status eight times over in the United States, with millions of additional sales worldwide.

Still, Jackson wanted more. He teamed up with *Off the Wall* producer and collaborator Quincy Jones on his next solo album, *Thriller.* Released December 1, 1982, the recording became an instant international phenomenon. Every song was a hit: the uptempo opener "Wanna Be Startin' Something"; the Paul McCartney collaboration "The Girl Is Mine"; the hard-rocking "Beat It"; the haunting "Billie Jean"; the dance-floor smash "P.Y.T. (Pretty Young Thing)"; and the ballad "Human Nature." The album topped the Billboard 200 charts for thirty-seven consecutive weeks. Today it reigns as the all-time best-selling album, having sold upward of 100 million copies.

Despite all the hit singles, the video of the album's title track left the most

The Jackson Five, 1971. In addition to Michael, the group included Jackie, Tito, Jermaine, and Marlon.

indelible mark. Jackson teamed with John Landis, the director of the films *Blues Brothers* and *Animal House,* to create a fourteen-minute tour de force of dancing zombies and horror suspense. Before the video's release in 1983, the burgeoning MTV network had played white artists almost exclusively. Jackson

Thriller album cover, 1982,

Michael Jackson (1958–2009) performing his trademark moonwalk step, 1996.

Prince (b. 1958).

Prince.

Prince at the height of his fame in the 1980s.

became its first black star, creating commercial opportunities for other African American artists to combine music and video in creative and profitable ways.

The year after the *Thriller* video debuted, another black artist combined music and film to successful ends. Prince Rogers Nelson, born in Minneapolis on June 7, 1958, had begun playing in bands in junior high school. He released his first album as "Prince," *For You,* on Warner Bros. Records at the age of twenty. His mix of rock, funk, and soul found a ready audience, which grew with each successive album, *Prince* (1979), *Dirty Mind* (1980), *Controversy* (1981), and the megahit *1999* (1983). Prince was already on his way to becoming one of the nation's most notable artists—black or white—of the 1980s, but his 1984 project *Purple Rain* took him to even further heights. Released as a feature-length film, *Purple Rain* portrayed the story of a Minneapolis musician overcoming a violent home life and battling rivals to form a band, The Revolution. The film grossed more than $80 million, but it was the soundtrack, credited to Prince and the Revolution, that took the nation by storm. The record offered a potent mix of pop, R&B, funk, and even elements of psychedelia and heavy metal. The rocking lead track, "Let's Go Crazy," became a hit, as did the fiery guitar ballad "Purple Rain." The album's biggest hit, "When Doves Cry," offered an abstract meditation on romance and with striking innovation did not even feature a bass guitar line. It earned the performer two Grammy Awards as well as an Oscar for the best original film score, and sold twenty million copies worldwide.

JESSE JACKSON AND RONALD BROWN

In 1984, a number of candidates vied for the Democratic nomination to challenge Ronald Reagan in the November election. None proved more notable—or more controversial—than Jesse Louis Jackson. Jackson grew up in Greenville, South Carolina, the son of an unwed teenage mother. He graduated from North Carolina A&T College, but after a brief stint at the Chicago Theological Seminary, he shelved further studies in divinity school in order to work more closely with Martin Luther King, Jr., and the Southern Christian Leadership Conference. (He did, however, become an ordained minister in 1968.)

Jackson participated in the Selma-to-Montgomery march and played key roles in campaigns in Chicago and Memphis; he was with Dr. King when he fell to an assassin's bullet. In 1971, after a falling-out with Ralph Abernathy, he formed Operation PUSH (People United to Save Humanity). Based in Chicago, Operation PUSH worked to remedy inequality in employment and housing and staged boycotts of prominent companies, including Coca-Cola. By the 1980s, as blacks nationwide were winning more political offices than ever before, Jackson hoped to channel his civil rights experience into political success. He formed what he called a Rainbow Coalition of people of all colors and backgrounds to support him in a bold new mission: campaigning for the Democratic presidential nomination. He appealed to people who felt left out of Reagan's America—the poor, African Americans, working mothers—and those who supported greater attention to social programs such as welfare and affirmative action. The economic recession of 1982 seemed to bolster his criti-

cisms. Jackson and his allies focused on voter registration, and the campaign gained support from prominent Americans, including the popular feminist Gloria Steinem, U.S. representative John Conyers, and Gary, Indiana, mayor Richard Hatcher.

Jackson did well in the early primaries and even won Virginia, South Carolina, and Louisiana; he took half of Mississippi's delegates. He also performed well in televised debates. But many of his choices alienated him from voters. He aligned with the controversial leader of the Nation of Islam, Louis Farrakhan, which alarmed not only whites but also many African Americans; the NAACP and the National Urban League resisted supporting his campaign. When reporters recorded Jackson referring to Jews as "Hymies" and calling New York City "Hymietown," his campaign derailed. Although he apologized, anti-Semitism would haunt the rest of his political career. Still, the 1984 campaign estab-

Jesse L. Jackson, Sr. (b. 1941), 1983.

lished Jackson as a legitimate candidate and forced the Democratic Party to consider placing African Americans in high-ranking positions.

Encouraged by his success in the

Jackson with Michael Dukakis, the eventual Democratic Party presidential candidate, in San Francisco, May 25, 1988.

southern primaries, Jackson decided to run again in 1988. He confronted another crowded field of contenders who hoped to defeat Reagan's vice president, George H. W. Bush. Again, Jackson proved an able debater and campaigner. He took 55 percent of the vote in Michigan and won a total of five caucuses and seven primaries. But the controversies of 1984 still haunted him, and his 6.8 million votes fell short of Michael Dukakis's 9.7 million. Jackson had nevertheless established African Americans once and for all as viable candidates for national office, and the Democratic Party responded. On February 7, 1988, the Democratic National Committee elected Ronald H. Brown, a former deputy campaign manager for Senator Edward Kennedy, as chair, making him the first African American chair of a major American political party.

FRED GORDEN AND BARBARA HARRIS

In 1877, Henry Ossian Flipper was the first African American to graduate from the U.S. Military Academy at West Point. It would take more than a century for an African American to reach the post of commandant of cadets. Born in 1940 in Anniston, Alabama, Fred A. Gorden was raised by his aunt in Atlanta. When Gorden reached the age of ten, the family left the segregated South and moved to Battle Creek, Michigan. There Gorden excelled in school, played basketball, and worked part-time jobs. After one year at a local community college, he enrolled at West Point in 1958 and graduated in 1962—the only African American in his class. Gorden recalls experiencing no discrimination at West Point. The *Washington Post* writer S. I. Waxman wrote about the first year, "Misery knew no favorites." Gorden's freshman roommate recalled that all plebes " 'were . . . treated rotten!' "[2]

Gorden's military career continued with a commission in field artillery. He also found time to earn a master's degree in Spanish at Middlebury College. Five years later he served in Vietnam as captain of a field artillery unit of the 101st Airborne Division and earned a Bronze Star. After his tour in Vietnam, he taught Spanish at West Point; held military posts in Schofield Barracks, Hawaii, and Fort Ord, California; and directed the office of the assistant secretary of defense for international security in Washington, D.C. On October 28, 1987, the army chose Gorden as the 61st Commandant of Cadets, placing him in charge of the discipline and training of the Corps of Cadets. Another racial barrier had fallen in the American military.

Two years later, an African American woman broke through another kind of barrier. Barbara Clementine Harris was born on June 12, 1930, to a steelworker father and a church-organist mother in Philadelphia. She followed her parents into the Episcopal Church, organizing clubs and playing piano during services. After high school, she graduated from the Charles Morris Price School of Advertising and Journalism and

Barbara C. Harris (b. 1930).

Fred A. Gorden (b. 1940) with the family of former president Richard Nixon, April 26, 1994.

went into the public relations field. She worked for Joseph V. Baker Associates in Philadelphia before joining the Sun Oil Company in 1968. At the same time, she participated in the civil rights movement in Mississippi and Alabama.

In 1976, the Episcopal Church began ordaining women. Harris immediately began taking courses at Villanova University and informally at the Episcopal Divinity School in Cambridge, Massachusetts. She moved quickly up the ranks,

becoming a deacon in 1970 and a priest the following year. She worked out of Norristown, Pennsylvania, counseling prisoners in Philadelphia and directing the Episcopal Church Publishing Company. In her latter role, she provoked controversy by criticizing church doctrine and arguing that the church played an insufficient role in combating social injustice.

Still, when the church announced in 1986 that it would begin to ordain

women bishops, Harris knew her next goal. In the fall of 1988, she won election to become bishop of the Massachusetts diocese, and on January 29, 1989, the church ratified her election. On February 11, more than seven thousand people attended her ordination in Boston as the first woman bishop of the Episcopal Church. She served the diocese until her retirement on November 1, 2002.

SPIKE LEE

Few filmmakers of the last three decades—black or white—can match the success and social impact of Spike Lee. Born in Atlanta on March 20, 1957, Shelton Jackson Lee moved with his family to the Fort Greene neighborhood of Brooklyn at the age of two. His jazz musician father and art teacher mother ensured that Lee and his siblings would experience education and culture from an early age; the family often attended plays, concerts, and films. Lee graduated from Morehouse College in 1979, and began an M.F.A. program in film production three years later at New York University's Tisch School of the Arts. His final project at NYU, the film *Joe's Bed-Stuy Barbershop: We Cut Heads,* earned the 1983 Student Academy Award for best director.

After completing his M.F.A. degree— and finding little outside funding for his films—Lee began his own film production company: 40 Acres and a Mule Filmworks. He shot his first feature, *She's Gotta Have It* (1986), on a tight

budget and an even tighter schedule: twelve days. The story of Nola Darling and her relationships with different men

Spike Lee was born Shelton Jackson Lee in Atlanta in 1957.

(including Mars Blackmon, played by Lee himself) opened at the San Francisco Film Festival in 1986 and went on to win the Prix de Jeunesse at the Cannes Film Festival for the best new film by a young talent. Lee's second feature

film, *School Daze* (1988), was a bold examination of black intraracial relations, particularly the conflicts between dark-skinned and light-skinned blacks on a college campus. It grossed $15 million.

The following year, Lee released *Do the Right Thing,* his most provocative film to that point. *Do the Right Thing* explored conflicts between blacks and Italian Americans in Brooklyn's Bedford-Stuyvesant neighborhood. It received the Los Angeles Film Critics Best Picture Award, as well as four Golden Globe and two Academy Award nominations. The film elevated Lee to national prominence, and he began directing commercials, starring alongside Michael Jordan in commercials for Nike's Air Jordan sneakers. He then made two popular feature films, including *Mo' Better Blues,* starring Denzel Washington, in 1990 and *Jungle Fever,* starring Wesley Snipes, in 1991. His epic biopic *Malcolm X* grossed $48 million following its 1992 release. The film cemented Lee as the

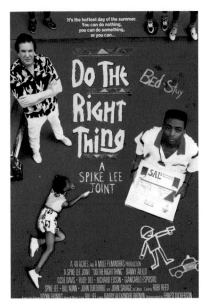

Do the Right Thing,
poster for Lee's 1989 film.

Malcolm X, poster for Lee's 1992
biographical film. Featuring a riveting
performance by Denzel Washington, the
film stuck very close to the life outlined in
Malcolm X's published autobiography.

foremost African American filmmaker in history.

After the success of *Do the Right Thing,* Lee traveled a number of different paths. Extraordinarily prolific, he directed sev-eral more films, including *Crooklyn* (1994), *Clockers* (1995), *Girl 6* (1996), *He Got Game* (1998), *Summer of Sam* (1999), *Inside Man* (2006), and *Miracle at St. Anna* (2008). He also directed more commercials and television programs and expanded into the world of music videos, perhaps most notably directing Public Enemy's "Fight the Power." Lee continued to probe racial issues with the 1996 drama *Get on the Bus,* featuring Ossie Davis and chronicling participants in the Million Man March. His documentaries found even more suc-cess. In *4 Little Girls* (1997), Lee told the powerful story of the 1963 bombing of Birmingham's Sixteenth Street Baptist Church, earning him an Academy Award nomination for best feature documen-tary. In 2006, he released the four-part HBO miniseries *When the Levees Broke: A Requiem in Four Acts,* a poignant docu-mentary that so very effectively captured the pain and the chaos surrounding Hurricane Katrina, while serving as a stinging indictment of the Bush admin-istration. *When the Levees Broke* won the NAACP Image Award, the Peabody Award, and two Emmys. Spike Lee will be remembered as the first successful black filmmaker in American history.

GROWING POLITICAL POWER, 1989–1991

African Americans continued to gain some of the most promi-nent political offices in the nation. On November 7, 1989, David Dinkins won election as mayor of New York City, and Norm Rice took the mayor's office in Seattle. That same day, an African Amer-ican triumphed in a gubernatorial elec-tion for the first time. L. Douglas Wilder had grown up in segregated Richmond, Virginia, and graduated from Virginia Union College in 1951. After serving in the Korean War, Wilder attended How-ard University Law School, earning his degree in 1959. He worked in private practice for ten years before beginning a pathbreaking career in politics. In 1969, he was the first African American elected to the Virginia state senate since Recon-struction. In 1985, he was elected lieuten-ant governor and four years later won the state's highest office, the first African American governor in the nation's his-tory. After his swearing-in the following January, the NAACP awarded Wilder the Spingarn Medal for his accomplish-ment. Although he returned to private life in 1994, his political career had not ended, and in 2004 Wilder became mayor of his hometown of Richmond.

Another Howard University Law School graduate also reached a mile-stone for African Americans in 1990. After finishing her law degree in 1968, Washington, D.C., native Sharon Pratt Dixon worked in her father's practice and taught law before taking a posi-tion as associate counsel of the Potomac Electric Power Company (PEPCO) in 1976. Pratt also entered politics, and in 1979 she became a member of the Demo-cratic National Committee. In 1989, she announced that she would challenge the incumbent Marion Barry in the 1990 election for mayor of the nation's

L. Douglas Wilder (b. 1931) at his historic inauguration, January 13, 1990. Photograph by Clement Britt.

Sharon Pratt Kelly (b. 1944).

Carol Moseley Braun (b. 1947).

capital. Shortly after her announcement, reports flooded the country regarding videotape evidence of Barry smoking crack cocaine. He withdrew from the race, and Sharon Pratt Dixon, who would soon remarry and change her name to Sharon Pratt Kelly, became the first African American woman mayor of a major American city.

Two years later an African American woman would reach an unprecedented national office. Carol Moseley grew up in Chicago and graduated from the University of Illinois in 1969. She returned to her hometown to complete a law degree at the University of Chicago in 1972 and there met her husband, Michael Braun. (Although they later divorced, she continued to use both names.) Through the 1970s and 1980s, Moseley Braun marched steadily up the ranks of local and state politics. She served as a prosecutor in the U.S. attorney's office (1973–77), in the state house of representatives (1978–88), and as the Cook County recorder of deeds in 1988. In 1992, she ran for the Senate, winning an upset victory in the Illinois Democratic primary. That November she defeated her Republican opponent and became the first black woman elected to the U.S. Senate.

During her term in office, she served on powerful committees, worked to pass laws geared toward helping African Americans and women, and faced off against Senator Jesse Helms of North Carolina over the meaning of the Confederate flag. Questions raised about her campaign financing cast a pall over her term in office, and she lost her reelection bid, but she spent the next two years as U.S. ambassador to New Zealand. She mounted brief presidential campaigns in 2000 and 2004. Although her career

David N. Dinkins (b. 1927). Born in Trenton, New Jersey, Dinkins was one of the first African Americans to serve in the U.S. Marine Corps. After World War II, he graduated from Howard University and earned a law degree from the Brooklyn Law School in 1956. He served in a variety of New York City offices, including Manhattan borough president, before winning election as mayor in 1989.

Norman B. Rice (b. 1943). At Seattle's University of Washington, Rice earned both a degree in communications and a master's degree in public administration. He worked as a reporter and also as assistant director of Seattle's Urban League before serving eleven years in the city council. He first ran for mayor in 1985 and won in 1989, emerging from a crowded field of candidates. He won reelection in 1993.

in national politics proved brief, she returned to the local stage when she ran for mayor of Chicago in 2011. She lost the bid to Rahm Emanuel, the former chief of staff for President Obama. Moseley Braun, like L. Douglas Wilder and Sharon Pratt Kelly before her, demonstrated the real progress African Americans had made in the nation's political life.

RIOTS IN HOWARD BEACH, BENSONHURST, VIRGINIA BEACH, AND LOS ANGELES

Crowds march to protest the murder of Yusuf K. Hawkins, August 23, 1989.

Virginia Beach riot, Labor Day 1989.

While African Americans continued to make social and political strides during the 1980s, the ugly specter of racial violence always loomed. Racial tension remained particularly high in the nation's cities, especially in the North. On December 20, 1986, Michael Griffith, Cedric Sandiford, Timothy Grimes, and Curtis Sylvester drove to the borough of Queens in New York City to pick up a paycheck. But their car broke down in the predominantly white Howard Beach neighborhood just after midnight. Leaving Sylvester in the car, the three others left to get assistance.

After grabbing a quick meal at the nearby New Park Pizzeria, the men were attacked by a gang of about a dozen whites. Grimes escaped and made it home, but the two others continued to fight off the assailants. Sandiford suffered a severe beating. Griffith, beaten as well, attempted to escape by crossing the busy Shore Parkway. A car hit and killed him. City officials and African Americans responded to the violence with outrage; Mayor Ed Koch told *The New York Times* that the beating was like "the kind of lynching party that took place in the Deep South."[3] The Reverend Al Sharpton organized a series of protests against the violence. Three of the attackers went to jail on manslaughter charges, while three others faced minor rioting convictions.

Three years later, on August 23, sixteen-year-old Yusuf Hawkins and three of his friends traveled to the Bensonhurst neighborhood in Brooklyn to inquire about an advertisement for a used 1982 Pontiac. When they got off the N train around nine p.m., they encountered an armed white mob. Keith Mondello, an eighteen-year-old white Bensonhurst resident, had organized the mob to gain revenge for a perceived racial transgression. The woman he hoped to date had turned him down, as he understood it, because she preferred to date black and Latino men. Hawkins and his friends had nothing to do with the situation, but they paid the price for Mondello's anger. Witnesses heard four shots, and Hawkins lay in the street fighting for his life with two bullets lodged in his chest. He died

Rodney King (right) stands with his attorney Edi M. O. Faal, August 16, 1995. His arrest and beating in 1991, and the acquittal of the accused police officers the next year, sparked some of the worst riots in California history. Photograph by Reed Saxon.

before the ambulance could get him to the hospital.

New York blacks expressed outrage over the senseless racist killing. On August 27, the Reverend Al Sharpton and local civil rights lawyer Alton Maddox organized a march of three hundred African Americans through Bensonhurst. Fights broke out all along the march route. Whites shouted racial epithets and even held up watermelons to chastise the marchers. "You couldn't get any uglier scene than this in Mississippi," Sharpton told *The New York Times*.[4] Protest marches continued over the next two years, as the perpetrators of the violence were either acquitted or given light sentences. Sharpton nearly lost his life during a January 12, 1991, march, when a drunk, twenty-seven-year-old white man named Michael Riccardi emerged from a crowd of onlookers and stabbed him in the chest. While Sharpton made a full recovery, the incident demonstrated the dangers that racial hatred still posed, even in New York.

On Labor Day 1989, race riots occurred in the vacation town of Virginia Beach during its annual "Greekfest," a predominantly black fraternity and sorority celebration. City officials feared an overflow of students, and placed the National Guard on alert. They also announced the cancellation of concerts and the closing of public facilities. Black students saw these actions as examples of government officials trying to exclude them. Once the party began, conflict among black students, local youth looking for trouble, and police snowballed into looting and rioting. Police in riot gear cleared the streets and beaches a number of times, often using brutal force. Partygoers, a great number of whom had little do to with the college students, responded with looting, vandalism, and violence of their own. The riot caused $1.4 million in damages and, like Bensonhurst, made national headlines as a symbol of the nation's persistent racism.

The incident that led to the deadliest riot since the 1960s occurred two years later and three thousand miles away in Los Angeles. Just after midnight on March 3, 1991, local police pulled over an African American driver named Rodney King. King had led the officers on a high-speed chase, and they sought revenge. After pulling King from his car, four officers beat him for fifteen minutes, leaving him with a broken leg, fractured cheekbones, and a fractured skull. Eleven other policemen stood by and watched.

Unknown to the police, a witness recorded the beating and sent it to a local television station. The nation watched the incident in horror. Yet when the officers came to trial in 1992, the jury—one Latino, one Asian, and ten whites—acquitted them. The predominantly African American neighborhood of South Central Los Angeles exploded in furious violence. Entire blocks burned. Young blacks pulled white truck driver Reginald Denny from his truck, beat him, and smashed a cement block against his skull. Gangs looted businesses and targeted Korean-owned stores. Television networks broadcast the chaos around the world. King himself pleaded, "Can we all get along?" But the violence continued. The five days of rioting killed more than fifty people, destroyed four thousand businesses, and caused $1 billion in property damage. More than a quarter century had passed since the Watts riot, yet the underlying cauldron of racial tension was as explosive as ever.

CLARENCE THOMAS

Nominations to the U.S. Supreme Court have in recent years become contentious and politically divisive. Few nominees, however, have sparked as much controversy as Clarence Thomas did in 1991. Thomas's confirmation hearing, marked by deep concerns within the African American community over his conservative interpretation of the law (especially on issues of race, such as affirmative action), and a sexual harassment allegation, captivated the nation. The tumultuous events surrounding his confirmation made him a household name—maligned by some, championed by others.

Thomas's improbable journey to the nation's highest court began in the small community of Pin Point near Savannah, Georgia. Born in 1948 to M. C. Thomas and Leola Anderson, Thomas spent his early years in the Gullah region of coastal Georgia and grew up speaking the Gullah language, a mix of English and West African languages. After moving to Savannah at the age of seven, Thomas attended Roman Catholic schools and eventually enrolled in the Conception Seminary in Missouri. He received his B.A. degree, cum laude, from the College of the Holy Cross in 1971, followed by a J.D. from Yale Law School in 1974.

Thomas took his first job with Missouri's Republican attorney general, John Danforth. During the Reagan administration, Thomas served as assistant secretary for civil rights with the U.S. Department of Education (1981–82) and as chairman of the U.S. Equal Employment Opportunity Commission (1982–90). In 1989, President George H. W. Bush nominated him for the U.S. Circuit Court of Appeals for the District of Columbia; he was confirmed on March 6, 1990.

Clarence Thomas (b. 1948).

Just one year after joining the D.C. judiciary, Thomas received the call of a lifetime. Liberal stalwart Justice Thurgood Marshall resigned his seat on the Supreme Court on June 27, 1991, and President Bush was determined to find a conservative jurist to replace him. As legal scholar Jeffrey Toobin explains, "The dilemma facing Bush and the Republicans was clear. If Marshall left, they could not leave the Supreme Court an all-white institution; at the same time, they had to choose a nominee who would stay true to the conservative cause."[5] Clarence Thomas fit the bill, and on July 1, 1991, Bush announced him as his nominee.

Many immediately opposed the choice. The NAACP Legal Defense Fund and the National Organization for Women spoke out against the nomination because of Thomas's prior statements against affirmative action and fear that he would vote to overturn *Roe v. Wade* and end legal access to abortion. Despite this disapproval, Thomas's confirmation process began rather

uneventfully. He described his humble beginnings and how hard work had taken him through law school to a successful career. Although his conservative ideals were evident from his prior activities, Thomas refused to answer questions about his judicial philosophy. The Senate was set to vote on Thomas's nomination when Professor Anita Hill emerged at the hearings, profoundly altering the course of the confirmation process for the would-be justice.

Hill, a former colleague of Thomas's at the Equal Employment Opportunity Commission, alleged that Thomas had sexually harassed her. Her allegations and the hearings that followed launched a media frenzy. Thomas denied Hill's accusations and lashed out against the Senate's questioning, responding:

> This is a circus. It's a national disgrace. And from my standpoint, as a black American, it is a high-tech lynching for uppity blacks who in any way deign to think for themselves, to do for

Anita Hill (b. 1956) is sworn in before the Senate committee investigating Thomas's suitability for the Supreme Court. Hill endured vicious attacks for her testimony but never retracted her story.

themselves, to have different ideas, and it is a message that unless you kowtow to an old order, this is what will happen to you. You will be lynched, destroyed, caricatured by a committee of the U.S. Senate rather than hung from a tree.[6]

In spite of the heated battle, the Democratic-controlled Senate ultimately confirmed Thomas by a vote of 52–48, one of the closest margins ever recorded for a Supreme Court nominee.

On October 23, 1991, Clarence Thomas took his seat as associate justice and became the second African American to serve on the Court. Although not as outspoken as Justice Anto-

nin Scalia, Thomas has been described as the most ideologically conservative member of the Supreme Court. Unswayed by public opinion or the idea of historically specific interpretive paradigms, Thomas maintains a hard-line originalist approach to the Constitution, believing that justices must adhere to the "true" intent of the framers. He supports a limited role for the federal government and the judiciary, desires to overturn federal protections for abortion, embraces religious participation in public life, and seeks an end to affirmative action. Despite the increasingly conservative bent of the Court, he is known for his silence on the bench, where he rarely participates in oral arguments but does, on occasion, read the majority opinion.[7]

AIR JORDAN

Born in Brooklyn, New York, on February 17, 1963, Michael Jordan grew up in Wilmington, North Carolina, harboring dreams of playing professional basketball. Cut from his high school basketball team as a sophomore, his hopes appeared to be dashed. But one year and one growth spurt later, he made the team and went on to become a high school All-American. He attended college at the University of North Carolina, where as a freshman he scored the winning basket in the 1981–82 national championship game. He earned NCAA College Player of the Year honors in 1983 and 1984, as well as winning an Olympic gold medal in 1984 as a member of the U.S. men's basketball team. That same year the Chicago Bulls chose Jordan as the third overall pick in the NBA draft. Almost immediately ticket sales jumped by 90 percent. It was the beginning of an era, both in

Chicago and in the history of professional basketball.

Jordan started strong with the Bulls, winning the Rookie of the Year Award in 1985. He continued to improve his second year, when, despite sitting out sixty-four games because of a broken foot, he made the All-Star Team and scored 63 points in a playoff loss to the Boston Celtics. The Celtics would again keep Jordan's Bulls from advancing in the playoffs in the 1985–86 season, when the Larry Bird–led squad swept Chicago in the first round of the playoffs. But Jordan averaged 43.7 points in the playoffs, scoring 63 points in the second game alone. (He had scored more than 50 points in eight games during the 1986–87 season.) Although the Celtics had beaten the Bulls convincingly, Larry Bird remarked that in the playoffs he had faced "God disguised as Michael Jordan."

The following year the Bulls would

Michael Jordan (b. 1963) in classic form, June 10, 1998.

meet a new foe, the Detroit Pistons, a team that would send them home for three consecutive seasons. Jordan, however, ended all doubts about his leader-

Statue of Michael Jordan outside the Chicago Bulls' United Center. Photograph by David Walberg.

ing to the creation and trademarking of the word *three-peat*. Jordan also led the "Dream Team," the U.S. All-Star Team that romped to a gold medal in the 1992 Olympics. But in 1994 he unexpectedly retired, ostensibly to pursue a dream of playing major league baseball. He played only one year for the double-A Birmingham Barons in the Chicago White Sox system before returning to the court. He emerged as though he had never left. The Bulls won the championship in 1995 and 1996—with an astounding 72–10 record. Jordan accomplished another three-peat the following season, when he hit a game-winning shot over Byron Russell of the Utah Jazz with only 6.6 seconds remaining.

Jordan again retired after the second three-peat, although he did return to play two seasons with the Washington Wizards in 2001–03. During his unprecedented career he won six championships, six NBA Finals MVP Awards, five league MVP awards, and ten scoring titles. He

was also elected to the NBA All-Star Team fourteen times, the NBA First Team ten times, and the NBA All-Defensive Team nine times. His 30.1 points-per-game average remains an NBA record, and he joined the National Basketball Hall of Fame in 2009.

Jordan also achieved a cultural status that no basketball player has ever known. His trademark gravity-defying dunks and shaved head, as well as his supremely self-confident and wry off-court persona, made him a marketer's dream. Nike created the "Air Jordan" sneaker, which, with the help of Spike Lee–directed commercials, became the most popular shoe of all time. Gatorade crafted the "Be Like Mike" campaign around him, and he even starred in the film *Space Jam*. Almost a decade after his retirement from professional basketball, the greatest offensive player in basketball history (the Celtics' Bill Russell is the greatest defensive player and team leader) remains an icon in American life and culture.

ship when he finally led Chicago to the NBA championship in 1990, winning the Finals MVP Award and losing only two games in the entire postseason. The victory would mark the first of three consecutive championships, lead-

PHOTO ESSAY: MODERN OLYMPIANS

Left: Jackie Joyner-Kersee (b. 1962) and her sister-in-law Florence Griffith-Joyner (1959–98) after the 1988 Summer Olympics in Seoul. Above: Jackie Joyner-Kersee.

Florence Griffith-Joyner.

Carl Lewis (b. 1961) at the 1984 Summer Olympics in
Los Angeles. He won four gold medals.

Edwin C. Moses (b. 1955) at the 1988
Summer Olympics in Seoul.

Shani Davis (b. 1982). Born in Chicago, Davis was the first black athlete from any
nation to win a gold medal in an individual Winter Games sport. At age twenty-two,
he won his third consecutive U.S. All-Around Championship and became the first
American skater to make all three world teams in the same season: World Sprint,
World All-Around, and World Short Track. At the 2006 Olympics in Torino, Italy, he
won gold and silver medals. Here he skates at the 1,000-meter World Cup race in
Heerenveen, Netherlands, March 14, 2010. Photograph by Vincent Jannink.

Michael D. Johnson (b. 1967) won a total of four Olympic gold medals in the 1990s.
He is the only athlete to win both the 200-meter and the 400-meter events at the
same Olympics, which he accomplished at the 1996 Summer Games in Atlanta.

Venus (b. 1980) and Serena Williams (b. 1981) have dominated American and world women's tennis since the late 1990s and won gold medals in doubles in the 2000 Summer Olympics in Sydney.

Justin Gatlin (b. 1982) won a gold medal in the 100-meter and silver and bronze medals at the 2004 Summer Olympics in Athens. His time in the 100-meter race is the third fastest in Olympic history. In Helsinki in 2005, Gatlin beat his competitors by the widest margin ever at a men's World Championship 100-meter race, thus capturing the Olympic–World Championship double.

ADVANCEMENT IN THE SCIENCES

In the 1970s African Americans expanded their roles in the sciences and conducted cutting-edge research both on earth and in outer space. Frederick Drew Gregory left Amherst College after one year to pursue a career in the air force and graduated from the academy in 1964. Two years later he served in the Vietnam War but remained with the military and accepted a position as a test pilot at NASA's Langley Research Center in Hampton, Virginia. In 1978 NASA selected him as an astronaut, and he made his first space voyage in 1985. Four years later he became the first African American to command a space shuttle when he led the *Discovery*. All told, Gregory took three trips into space, where he spent a total of 455 hours.

Four years after the *Discovery* mission, Mae Carol Jemison made history of her own. A graduate of Stanford, where she majored in chemical engineering and African and African American studies, Jemison earned her M.D. degree at Cornell Medical School. Before joining

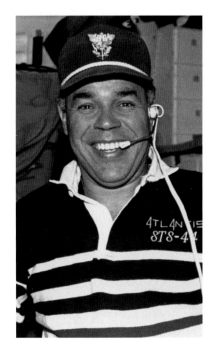

Frederick D. Gregory (b. 1941) graduated from the U.S. Air Force Academy and earned a master's degree from George Washington University. He flew 550 combat missions during the Vietnam War and subsequently flew as a test pilot. The air force assigned him to the NASA Langley Research Center, and he entered the astronaut program in January 1978. During his time with NASA, he logged three shuttle missions and more than 455 hours in space.

Mae Carol Jemison (b. 1956) was born in Decatur, Alabama, but grew up in Chicago. In 1977, she graduated from Stanford and in 1981 earned her medical degree from Cornell. On September 12–20, 1992, she served as the science mission specialist for Spacelab. During the eight-day mission, she did 127 orbits of the Earth and managed 44 Japanese and American science experiments. Kennedy Space Center.

M. Joycelyn Elders (b. 1933). Born a tenant farmer's daughter in rural Arkansas, Elders labored in the cotton fields and attended segregated schools. After working as a nurse's aide in a Veterans Administration hospital in Milwaukee, in 1953 she joined the U.S. Army, where she trained as a physical therapist. In 1956, she enrolled at the still-segregated University of Arkansas Medical School and completed her medical degree in 1960. Seven years later, she earned a master's degree in biochemistry. In 1993, President Bill Clinton appointed her surgeon general.

Helene Doris Gayle (b. 1955). Born and raised in Buffalo, New York, Gayle earned a B.A. in psychology at Barnard College, an M.D. from the University of Pennsylvania, and an M.P.H. from Johns Hopkins University. She is one of the country's leading authorities on the epidemiology of HIV/AIDS in children and teenagers.

NASA in 1987, Jemison's varied career included posts as a general practitioner in Los Angeles and as the area Peace Corps medical officer in Sierra Leone and Liberia. On September 12, 1992, she became the first African American woman in space. Aboard the *Endeavor*, Jemison and other scientists orbited the earth 127 times over the course of eight days, conducting bone cell research.

While Dr. Jemison made history circling the planet researching life science, other African American women reached unprecedented distinction in the field of medicine. Born in 1933, M. Joycelyn Elders grew up in a poor farming community in Arkansas. She attended Philander Smith College in Little Rock, where a presentation by a black doctor inspired her career choice. Elders spent time in the army, and in 1956 she used the G.I. Bill to attend the University of Arkansas Medical School. After graduating, she became chief resident at the school—an African American woman in charge of white doctors at the formerly segregated institution. Over the following decades she researched public health issues, with a particular focus on diabetes and sex education. Her research led Arkansas governor Bill Clinton to name her the head of the Arkansas Department of Health in 1987. When

Clinton became president six years later, he turned to Elders to fill a critically important post. Although conservatives opposed her progressive views on sex education, Clinton appointed her the first African American (and only the second woman) surgeon general in 1993.

Two years after Joycelyn Elders began her term as surgeon general, Helene Doris Gayle became the first African American and the first woman to direct the National Center for HIV, STD, and TB Prevention for the Centers for Disease Control and Prevention (CDC). Gayle earned her M.D. from the University of Pennsylvania and her M.P.H. from Johns Hopkins University in 1981. Three years later, she joined the CDC, where she researched malnutrition among poor children in the United States and Africa. She joined the CDC's AIDS program in 1987 and established herself as an expert on the worldwide devastation of HIV and AIDS in young people. This research made her the ideal choice to lead the national center. She remained there for six years before continuing her research in the private sector, first as director of the Bill & Melinda Gates Foundation's HIV, TB, and Reproductive Health Program and then as the president and CEO of the humanitarian antipoverty organization CARE in 2006.

GIANT STEPS

The Republican Party largely overlooked African Americans during the administrations of Ronald Reagan, George H. W. Bush, and George W. Bush. Nevertheless, two African Americans gained unprecedented power and recognition that carried enormous symbolic freight.

Born in Harlem in 1937 to Jamaican immigrants, Colin Powell began his military career when he joined the ROTC as a student at the City College of New York. When he graduated in 1958, he transitioned into the army as a second lieutenant. In 1962 and again in 1968, he served in Vietnam, where he received a Bronze Star, two Purple Hearts, and a legion of other military decorations for his valor in combat.

In 1972, he began working in government, rising to the rank of assistant to the deputy secretary of defense under President Jimmy Carter. In 1987, President Ronald Reagan named him national security advisor, making him the first African American to hold that post. Two years later, President George H. W. Bush named him the first African American chairman of the Joint Chiefs of Staff. As the highest-ranking member of the Department of Defense, Powell oversaw operations in the first Gulf War of 1991. He earned a reputation for steady leadership among a great number of Americans—white and black, Republican and Democrat, hawk and dove.

In 2001, President George W. Bush named Powell secretary of state, the highest government position ever held by an African American. The Senate confirmed the nomination unanimously. But Powell would face considerable controversy and embarrassment when President Bush sent him to the United Nations to justify the administration's

Colin Powell (b. 1937).

plans to invade Iraq to capture "weapons of mass destruction" following the September 11, 2001, attacks on New York City and Washington, D.C. While Powell feared that Bush's plan had flaws—in particular that the president intended to invade without a strong international coalition—he publicly pledged support.

In a self-consciously symbolic reprise of Adlai Stevenson's testimony before the Security Council during the Cuban Missile Crisis, Powell testified persuasively at the United Nations that the U.S. government possessed evidence that Iraq had stockpiled weapons of mass destruction in preparation for war. But no such weapons have ever been found. In 2004, Powell acknowledged that he had been wrong about Iraq and resigned as secretary of state. Many observers felt that he could have become the first African American president had he chosen to run following Clinton's second term. Despite the setback in his career over his UN testimony, General Powell has remained a popular and influential political figure, as evidenced by his key endorsement of Senator Barack Obama during the 2008 presidential campaign.

Upon taking office, George W. Bush also named the first African American woman as national security advisor. An expert in Russian history and diplomacy, Condoleezza Rice was born in Birmingham, Alabama, during the year of the *Brown* decision, 1954. Diligent and scholarly, Rice earned a bachelor's degree from the University of Denver (where her father was a dean) at the age of nineteen, under the mentorship of Madeleine Albright's father, Josef Korbel, who would direct her Ph.D. dissertation. By the age of twenty-six, she had earned a master's degree from Notre Dame and a Ph.D. at the University of Denver. Over the following two decades, she published a number of important studies on foreign affairs and international history, including a book, *The Soviet Union and the Czechoslovakian Army, 1948–1983: Uncertain Allegiance.*

Rice worked under George H. W. Bush as an adviser on Soviet affairs, then took a position as provost at Stanford University in 1993. After serving for four years as national security advisor, Rice became the first black woman to serve as secretary of state when President Bush chose her in 2005 to replace Colin Powell. In 2004, *Forbes* magazine named her the most powerful woman in the world. Rice steadfastly and expertly directed the administration's course through wars in Iraq and Afghanistan. She returned to Stanford as a fellow at the Hoover Institution and has published her autobiography, *Extraordinary, Ordinary People: A Memoir of Family.*

Condoleezza Rice (b. 1954) stands with President George W. Bush.

THE ACHIEVEMENTS OF CARL LEWIS AND TIGER WOODS

When ten-year-old Carl Lewis posed for a photo with Jesse Owens, nobody could have predicted that the smiling young man would someday match the accomplishments of his hero. Born on July 1, 1961, Frederick Carlton Lewis grew up in Willingboro, New Jersey, a middle-class community about twenty miles north of Philadelphia. Lewis excelled at track and field in high school and at the University of Houston. As a freshman he won the NCAA long jump championship. He qualified for the 1980 Olympics but he could not compete because of the U.S. boycott of the Moscow games. His athletic prowess so impressed the Dallas Cowboys that the team drafted him in 1984, even though he did not play football in college. Lewis did not pursue football, nor did he join the Chicago Bulls of the NBA when that organization drafted him.

Lewis continued to dominate competition in track and field, leading to his historic triumph at the 1984 Olympics in Los Angeles, where he won gold in the 100 meters, achieving an astonishing time of 9.9 seconds. He then set an Olympic record by winning the 200 meters in 19.8 seconds, and he anchored the gold medal–winning relay team. Lewis also captured gold in his signature event, the long jump: with the wind blowing in his face, he jumped more than 28 feet.

Lewis's four gold medals matched Jesse Owens's in 1936, but his accomplishments did not end there. Four years later in Seoul, he became the first athlete to repeat as the long jump champion. He also became the first to win gold in consecutive 100-meter races after the initial winner, Ben Johnson of Canada, had his medal stripped after testing positive for steroid use. All told,

Carl Lewis (b. 1961) at the 1984 Summer Olympics in Los Angeles.

Carl Lewis in the long jump at the 1988 Seoul Summer Olympics,
where he set yet another world record in the 100-meter race.

Eldrick "Tiger" Woods (b. 1975).

Lewis went a full decade without losing a long jump competition. He added two more Olympic gold medals in 1992 and an improbable fourth consecutive long jump gold medal at the age of thirty-five at the 1996 games in Atlanta. At the close of his Olympic career, Lewis had won nine gold medals and one silver and had set ten world records.

The same year Lewis won his last gold medal, a young African American golf phenomenon turned pro. Eldrick Tont "Tiger" Woods was born in Cypress, California, on December 30, 1975, to an African American father and a mother of Thai descent. Tiger's father, Earl, began training him almost as soon as he could walk. He first demonstrated his golfing

skills on national television at age two and six years later appeared with his father on the ABC television program *Good Morning America.* Woods attended Stanford University, where he racked up amateur win after win, leading him to turn pro in 1996. The following year he captured the Master's Championship, making him the first African American and, at twenty-one, the youngest person ever to win the tournament. And he had done it by an astounding 12 shots, shooting 18 under par.

Woods quickly became an international phenomenon, winning on the course and capturing a number of lucrative endorsements that constantly kept him in the public eye. He began an incredible run of major championships, winning the Master's three more times, taking four PGA Championships, and winning the U.S. Open and the British Open Championship three times apiece. In 2000, he became the youngest golfer to win the career grand slam by earning a victory in each of these four events. The following year, he held all four championships simultaneously—the first golfer ever to accomplish that feat. Not only did he rise to become one of the most successful golfers in the history of the sport, but he did so at an astonishingly young age. In another unprecedented achievement, in 2009 Woods became the first athlete to earn more than $1 billion.

Tiger Woods wins a playoff round against Rocco Mediate
at Torrey Pines, San Diego, June 16, 2008.

PULITZER PRIZE STORIES: TONI MORRISON AND GEORGE WALKER

Toni Morrison (b. 1931) at a press conference at the Louvre in Paris, November 8, 2006.

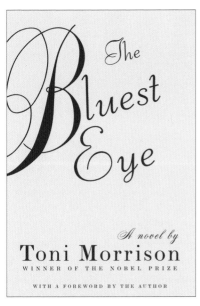

Morrison's first novel, *The Bluest Eye,* cover, 1970.

Toni Morrison, born Chloe Anthony Wofford in Lorain, Ohio, on February 18, 1931, graduated from Howard University with a major in English in 1953. She earned her master's degree from Cornell two years later and then taught at Texas Southern and at Howard. After a divorce, she began working as an editor at Random House and continued her own writing. She published her first novel, *The Bluest Eye,* in 1970. A renaissance in black women's writing would unfold over the next three decades; some scholars date its beginning to the publication of this book.

Set in Depression-era Lorain, the novel focuses on a young African American woman named Pecola who faces the perils of poverty and sexual assault. Idolizing Shirley Temple, Pecola naïvely believes that having blue eyes would make her beautiful to herself and to the rest of the world. Three years later, Morrison published *Sula,* which earned a National Book Award nomination. In *Sula* Morrison explores the meaning of good and evil through the story of two friends turned enemies, Sula and Nel, and their different paths in and out of the Bottom, a black community in Ohio. In 1977, she published *Song of Solomon,* the story of Macon "Milkman" Dead III, who begins a quest to discover a lost treasure but instead travels the South in an attempt to understand his roots. *Song of Solomon* became a selection of the Book-of-the-Month Club, which had not chosen a novel by an African American author since *Native Son* in 1949. Morrison followed with *Tar Baby* in 1981.

In 1987, Morrison published her masterpiece, *Beloved,* a devastating story about the lengths to which one woman would go to protect her children from slavery. Grounded in the real story of the fugitive slave Margaret Garner, Sethe, a slave and mother of four, escaped the violence of her southern plantation and fled to Cincinnati. For a month she lived in peace with her family, but her master soon found them. Believing death a better alternative than slavery, Sethe attempts to kill her children. She succeeds in killing the youngest and has the word *beloved* carved into the infant's headstone. The book found unprecedented success, winning the Pulitzer Prize in 1988, and it was made into a film starring Oprah Winfrey. *The New York Times* in 2006 called *Beloved* the greatest novel of the past twenty-five years. In 1993, Morrison became the first African American to win the Nobel Prize in literature. She has published four more novels since 1987, including *Jazz,* which some critics think rivals *Beloved* in quality.

Three years later, another African American broke a barrier. When seventy-six-year-old George Walker found out he had won the 1996 Pulitzer Prize for music, he briefly kept the news to himself for fear that it was not true. Walker was born in Washington, D.C., in 1922.

George Walker (b. 1922).

Both his parents played the piano, and he took his first lesson at the age of five. He went on to earn a series of diplomas and degrees from the Oberlin Conservatory of Music, the Curtis Institute, and the American Academy in Fontainebleau; in 1957 he received his doctorate at the Eastman School of Music. He has enjoyed a most prolific career as a writer, performer, and teacher and has published more than seventy compositions. The New York Philharmonic and the Kennedy Center for the Performing Arts are just two of the prestigious organizations that have commissioned works from him. He has toured the world performing. He taught at Dillard, the New School, Smith College, and elsewhere before going to Rutgers University, where he would retire. He won the Pulitzer for *Lilacs,* a song cycle commissioned by the Boston Symphony Orchestra and based on Walt Whitman's poem on the assassination of President Abraham Lincoln, "When Lilacs Last in the Dooryard Bloom'd."

TOM JOYNER

Born in Tuskegee, Alabama, in 1949, Tom Joyner graduated from Tuskegee Institute in 1970. Immediately afterward he began his career in broadcasting and worked at several radio stations in the South, then moved to WJPC-TV in Chicago. He briefly hosted a television show before taking over a morning radio program at KKDA in Dallas and an afternoon show at WGCI in Chicago. Earning the sobriquets "The Hardest Working Man in Radio" and "The Traveling DJ," Joyner would open his Dallas program in the morning and then fly to Chicago to host his afternoon program. Remarkably, he maintained this grueling pace from 1986 to 1993.

Joyner's black urban format became so successful that in 1994 the ABC Radio Network put the *Tom Joyner Morning Show* into syndication, making him the first African American male to host a national radio program. By 2006 Joyner's audience had grown to eight million listeners. Through his programming, he pushed advertisers to address the black markets they traditionally had ignored; he highlighted discriminatory practices and launched voter-registration drives to increase African American power. As a philanthropist, he established the Tom Joyner Foundation to provide financial assistance to students at historically black colleges and universities. By 2006 he had raised about $30 million. After Hurricane Katrina, he raised several million dollars to repair the damage done to Dillard, Xavier, and Southern universities, and he provided $1,000 each to students who had been enrolled at the three schools at the time of the flooding.

While Tom Joyner is very much a man of the present, he recently learned about a tragic family history. During the filming of *African American Lives, Part 2,* Joyner discovered that in 1913 two of his granduncles, Tom and Meeks Griffin, had been unjustly executed by the state of South Carolina. They had been convicted of murdering an elderly Confederate veteran. The real killer—also an African American—had probably fingered the Griffin brothers to throw off investigators, and also perhaps out of jealousy: the two Griffins were relatively wealthy black landowners. Because of

Tom Joyner (b. 1949).

his false testimony, the two men were executed in the electric chair. The tragic tale moved Joyner to clear his family name, and in 2009 a legal team headed by South Carolina attorney Stephen K. Benjamin won a posthumous pardon for the Griffin brothers. Although we cannot change the past, Joyner proved that we can change how we remember it.

LOUIS FARRAKHAN AND THE
MILLION MAN MARCH

The Million Man March at the National Mall, Washington, D.C., October 16, 1995.

Louis Abdul Farrakhan, born Louis Eugene Walcott on May 11, 1933, in the Bronx, grew up in the Roxbury neighborhood of Boston. He then headed south to attend Winston-Salem Teachers College in 1951, but the teaching profession could not compete with his true love: music. A talented singer and violinist, Walcott returned to Boston in 1953 to pursue a career as a musician. He also became politically active during the 1950s and in 1955 during a visit to Chicago joined the Nation of Islam. Just as Malcolm Little had done, he replaced his last name with an X in order to renounce his "slave name." Elijah Muhammad then gave him the Muslim surname Farrakhan.

Farrakhan worked under Malcolm X at Temple No. 7 in Harlem, and when Malcolm broke with the Nation of Islam in 1964, Farrakhan succeeded him as head minister. Second in command in the Nation hierarchy, he expected to succeed Elijah Muhammad as the group's national leader. But when Muhammad died in 1975, one of his sons, Wallace Muhammad (later Warith Deen Muhammad), took control, adopted tenets of traditional Islam, and moved away from black nationalism. Three years later Farrakhan broke from the group and formed a new organization, also called the Nation of Islam, geared toward recapturing the ideologies promoted by Elijah Muhammad. Throughout the 1970s and 1980s, Farrakhan invited controversy with inflammatory statements about whites, Jews, and homosexuals, yet his calls for black pride and black autonomy drew tens of thousands of admirers.

Farrakhan sought to make a national statement through a mass-action demonstration at the site of the 1963 March on Washington. In 1995, he and the Nation of Islam organized what they called the Million Man March. Farrakhan, along with co-organizer Benjamin Chavis, hoped to bring more than one million black men to the nation's capital to focus on African American unity, promote family values, and encourage the rebuilding of urban neighborhoods. Speakers included Marion Barry, Rosa Parks, James Bevel, Cornel West, Betty Shabazz, Jesse Jackson, Maya Angelou, and of course Farrakhan. Subject matter ranged from recommitting to God and ending black-on-black crime to exterminating the drug trade in black neighborhoods. Many speakers and attendees stressed the importance of voting and maintaining a black voice in formal politics. The march remained peaceful, and attendees hoped to lend support to embattled black males and encourage racial healing across the nation.

While many commentators saw great merit in bringing attention to the severe problems faced by black men, others criticized the gathering because of Farrakhan's participation; many black women, notably Angela Davis, resented their exclusion. Even the number of participants at the National Mall proved controversial. The National Park Service, long the official record-keeper, pegged it at 400,000 to 500,000. Boston University researchers estimated it at 870,000 (with a 25 percent

Louis Farrakhan (b. 1933), at far right, with Malcolm X, in Chicago.

margin of error). Farrakhan as well as some city officials argued that it easily topped one million. Whatever the final number, attendance far exceeded that of the 1963 March on Washington. More

important, the event offered Farrakhan and the Nation of Islam a role in public debates and drew national attention to an all-too-often neglected aspect of race in American life.

PROPOSITION 209 AND THE TEXACO DISCRIMINATION SUIT

National coverage of the 1996 election focused on incumbent president Bill Clinton successfully fending off Republican challenger Bob Dole, just two years after the Contract with America had led to a Republican triumph in Congress. But in California a statewide measure also made headlines, inspiring protest both within the state and beyond. Ward Connerly, an African American businessman from Sacramento, cofounded the American Civil Rights Institute (ACRI) in 1996. Despite

its name, the ACRI actually sought to eliminate affirmative action programs. Indeed, the group's other cofounder was the conservative *National Review* editor Thomas L. "Dusty" Rhodes.

Arguing that the civil rights movement had solved the problem of formal inequality in California, and that affirmative action equaled "reverse discrimination" against whites, Connerly and his primarily Republican supporters pushed for a law that would end race and sex criteria in state-level government pro-

Ward Connerly (b. 1939). The Louisiana-born businessman and political activist grew up in California, campaigned against housing discrimination, established a successful land-use consulting firm, and drifted into Republican politics. Believing that racial preferences caused more harm than good, he waged a nationwide campaign to end affirmative action programs.

Kweisi Mfume (b. 1948) was elected to the Baltimore city council in 1979 and served there for seven years. In 1984, he completed an M.A. from Johns Hopkins University and two years later won election to the U.S. Congress. There he represented Maryland's Seventh Congressional District for ten years. In 1996 he became head of the NAACP.

while opponents charged that it ignored persistent racial discrimination. Presidential candidates initially avoided the issue, but Dole soon offered praise while Clinton cautioned that the "right kind" of affirmative action still made sense.

Election Day, November 5, brought a dramatic victory to ACRI and to opponents of affirmative action. Of more than nine million votes cast, 54.6 percent supported Proposition 209. Opponents immediately initiated court proceedings and achieved a victory in federal district court, but a conservative federal appeals court upheld the constitutionality of the law. The largest public protests occurred at California colleges and universities. Students from the University of California's Berkeley and Santa Cruz campuses and from San Francisco State University organized walkouts and town hall meetings. But the law stood, and it dealt a deadly blow to many attempts to remedy the lingering structural inequality in California society. Enrollment of African American and Hispanic students at public universities plummeted.

The same month Proposition 209 passed, the Texaco Oil Company announced a historic settlement in a discrimination lawsuit brought by its African American employees. The suit had begun two years earlier when six black workers sued the company for blocking African Americans from promotions and for encouraging a racially hostile workplace. The break in the case came when *The New York Times* revealed the existence of audio recordings of Texaco executives using racial slurs and threatening to destroy evidence related to the case. A national uproar followed; Jesse Jackson called for a boycott of Texaco. The tidal wave of bad publicity pushed the previously reluctant Texaco leadership to the bargaining table.

Kweisi Mfume, the head of the NAACP, negotiated the terms of the settlement with Texaco, and the company promised to pay $115 million into a benefit pool for its fifteen hundred black employees. It also promised to provide salary increases. The total settlement would exceed $140 million, making it the largest settlement ever for a racial discrimination lawsuit. Texaco also pledged to overhaul its affirmative action plan and to work to create a more welcome and equitable corporate environment. To avoid a federal government lawsuit, the company agreed to allow the Equal Employment Opportunity Commission to supervise its hiring and promotion. While Proposition 209 appeared to signal the death knell of affirmative action, the Texaco case demonstrated the need for such programs.

grams and institutions, including public schools and colleges. The law, Proposition 209—formally called the California Civil Rights Initiative—would come up for popular vote that November. Such a charged issue led to intense arguments on both sides: proponents claimed the bill would fulfill Martin Luther King, Jr.'s dream of a fully color-blind society,

THOMAS JEFFERSON, SALLY HEMINGS, AND DNA

In 1802, halfway through Thomas Jefferson's first term in office, a Virginia newspaper reporter made a startling accusation about the president. James T. Callender of the *Richmond Recorder* gave life to a rumor that had circulated for some time: that Jefferson had fathered a child with his own slave, Sally Hemings. If true, the story painted Jefferson as a base hypocrite, someone who had argued the innate inferiority of black people while sleeping with a woman he owned. The allegations threatened his reputation and his legacy; indeed, the controversy would rage for two centuries. Not surprisingly, his family and many supporters denied the story. Jefferson himself, however, remained mum on the topic, and his silence only heightened the speculation. Even in private correspondence, he never directly addressed the accusation.

Did Jefferson father a child—or even multiple children—with Hemings? Circumstantial evidence seemed to support the theory. Jefferson inherited Hemings—along with her five broth-

Monticello, Thomas Jefferson's hilltop home.

ers and sisters—when his father-in-law, John Wayles, died in 1774. Evidence indicates that Hemings was Wayles's daughter and thus a half-sister of Jefferson's wife (who died in 1782). Hemings spent two years in France with Jefferson between 1787 and 1789; they allegedly began their relationship then. Hemings gave birth to her first child, Tom Woodson, not long after they returned to Virginia. She received her freedom upon Jefferson's death.

Records place Jefferson at Monticello during the periods when Hemings would have conceived each of her six children. The children had such light skin that three of them lived as whites once they grew up; contemporary reports claimed that Hemings's children even looked like Jefferson. Jefferson family members answered the charges by claiming that the president's nephews, Peter and Samuel Carr, had fathered the children. For their part, Hemings's descendants always believed their bloodline began with Jefferson. And Jefferson appeared to acknowledge some sort of special connection, as he freed Hemings's children, something he did not do for any of his other slaves.

Although this circumstantial evidence swayed few of Jefferson's defenders, belief in the story increased as the American social climate changed toward the end of the twentieth century. Many Americans, particularly academics, criticized Jefferson's racial beliefs and argued the likelihood that Jefferson, like a great many southern slaveholders, had had a sexual relationship with his slave. But not until the 1990s could anyone provide a scientific answer. In 1998, a team of scientists from the United States and Europe, led by Eugene Foster, used DNA testing to determine whether Jefferson fathered Hemings's youngest

child, Eston, who was born in 1808 and later in life adopted the last name Jefferson. They analyzed the DNA from male-line relatives of Thomas Jefferson, Eston Hemings Jefferson, Thomas Woodson, and Samuel and Peter Carr. The scientists compared Y chromosomes, which pass from father to son without changing.

The team released its results on October 31, 1998; *Nature* published the report on November 5. The team found no match with Woodson, whose family members had long maintained their relationship to Jefferson. They also found no match between Eston Hemings Jefferson and Samuel and Peter Carr, eliminating that theory. The results for Thomas Jefferson, however, told a different story. The researchers used DNA from five male-line descendants of two sons of Field Jefferson, Thomas Jefferson's paternal uncle. (Jefferson had no surviving sons.) The DNA results matched those of Eston Hemings, meaning that Jefferson was very likely the father. The possibility of coincidence was less than 1 percent. Critics pointed out that the same result could have been obtained if Jefferson's brother Randolph or nephew Isham had fathered the child. But no record places these relatives at Monticello, and the fact that their names surfaced only after the DNA test suggests the dubious nature of the claim. The DNA test confirmed what many African Americans had long believed, as well as the hypocrisy of America's most famous slave owner, the man who famously wrote that "all men are created equal."

ABNER LOUIMA AND AMADOU DIALLO

On August 6, 1997, Abner Louima talked his ill brother Jonas Louisma (who spelled his last name differently) into coming out to the East Brooklyn sewage plant where he worked second shift as a security guard. Louima had moved to New York City from Port-au-Prince, Haiti, nearly seven years earlier. He had a wife and a one-year-old son. When his shift ended at eleven that evening, Abner convinced Jonas to shake off his illness and join him in visiting a popular nightclub, Club Rendez-Vous, to see a Haitian band called Phantom. The band wrapped up, and the club closed at four a.m. When Abner and Jonas walked outside, they noticed a group of women fighting. Abner went to take a closer look and may have tried to stop the fight. Witnesses reported that a police officer grabbed Louima and began exchanging punches with him. Officers arrested Louima on charges of disorderly conduct and resisting arrest. Little did Louima know that when the police shoved him into the

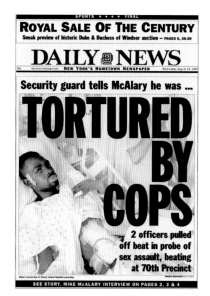

"Tortured by Cops." The Abner Louima headlines reverberated from New York across the country, in August 1997.

squad car, it would mark the beginning of an unspeakable horror.

On the way to the police station, the officers repeatedly spewed racial slurs at Louima and twice stopped the car so that they could beat him. When

they arrived at the 70th Precinct station house, two officers dragged Louima into a bathroom, removed his pants, and sodomized him with the broken wooden handle of a plunger. Louima suffered a torn rectum and punctured bladder, and the profuse bleeding and risk of infection put his life in danger. Still, the police, before calling an ambulance to transfer him to Coney Island Hospital for emergency surgery, left him in a holding cell.

News of the attack outraged the city. Mayor Rudolph Giuliani immediately criticized the police, saying, "These charges, if substantiated, should result in the severest penalties, including substantial terms of imprisonment and dismissal from the force."[8] One of the attackers, Justin Volpe, received a thirty-year prison sentence. Another officer, Charles Schwarz, received fifteen years. Although he was released on the grounds that he had not received a fair trial, Schwarz returned to jail on perjury charges. Louima sued the city, ultimately settling the case for $8.75 million.

Amadou Diallo.

Diallo's coffin, February 1999.

Two years later, police brutality in New York again captured the attention of a repulsed nation. Amadou Diallo had emigrated from Guinea in hopes of rescuing himself and his family from poverty. He shared with two other men a small apartment in the Soundview neighborhood of the Bronx. Each day he left home at noon and traveled to Manhattan, where he worked as a peddler on Fourteenth Street. He usually returned home around midnight. Shortly before one a.m.

on February 4, 1999, four plainclothes police officers approached Diallo in the doorway of his building, ostensibly to question him about his possible involvement in an open rape case. (He was not involved.) When Diallo reached into his jacket for his wallet to show his identification, the officers, believing Diallo was going for a gun, unleashed a barrage of gunfire. Forty-one shots were fired; nineteen bullets struck Diallo, and he died.

As in the Louima case, the community

responded with outrage. Three days after the murder, one thousand people staged a rally in front of Diallo's apartment. Protesters shouted "Forty-one bullets," "Four officers," and "One man dead." In this case, however, a jury acquitted all four policemen of murder charges. These two cases of extreme violence against people of color revealed the shocking persistence of deep-seated racism among some members of New York's police force.

STELLAR ACHIEVEMENTS

During the first decade of the new century, African Americans earned highest honors in the entertainment field. In 2002 two black actors took home Academy Awards. Halle Berry starred in the film *Monster's Ball* as Leticia Musgrove, a widow who becomes the lover of a white man who helped execute her husband, a convicted murderer. Her gripping performance made Berry the first African American woman to win the award for best actress. Denzel Washington had tasted Oscar success before: he won the best supporting actor award for his role in *Glory,* the drama based on the history of the Civil War's 54th Massachusetts Volunteer Infantry Regiment, and he had earned best actor nominations for *Malcolm X* and *The Hurricane.* In 2002, he finally won the Academy Award for best actor for his role in *Training Day,* where he played a corrupt cop who shows his young white apprentice how to survive on the streets—by any means necessary. He was the first black actor to win the prize since Sidney Poitier in 1963. Subsequently, Jamie Foxx won the award for *Ray* in 2004 and Forest Whitaker for *The Last King of Scotland* in 2006.

African American accomplishments also extended into other media worlds. Born in Gulfport, Mississippi, Tavis Smiley grew up in the mostly white community of Kokomo, Indiana. He developed an interest in politics at an early age, and after graduating from Indiana University, moved to Los Angeles to work for Mayor Tom Bradley. He came up short in a bid for a seat on the city council, but then discovered an alternative way to press for change in society: talk radio. He produced *The Smiley Report,* a series of short social and political commentaries syndicated around the nation. In 1994, *Time* magazine named the thirty-year-old Smiley one of fifty future American leaders. His popularity, his youth, and his compelling presence and thoughtfulness made him extremely attractive to radio programmers targeting the elusive younger audience.

Smiley's profile only grew in the following decade. He offered commentaries on the popular *Tom Joyner Morning Show* and hosted the television show *BET Tonight.* He published the books *Hard Left* (1996) and *On Air* (1998). He left BET in 2001 and worked as a commentator for the PBS, ABC, and CNN

Halle Berry and Denzel Washington at the 2002 Academy Awards ceremony.

television networks. Three years later, he became the first African American to host his own show on National Public Radio. He left NPR the same year, however, claiming that the network did not do enough to target minority listeners. Still, by 2005 his voice had returned to many NPR stations with the inception of a new show produced by Public Radio International. And by 2006 Smiley stood as one of the most noted African American journalists in the country.

Smiley wisely used his popularity to publish a new book, *The Covenant with Black America,* based upon the State of the Black Union symposia that he hosted following various presidential State of the Union addresses. The book, according to Smiley, sought "to create a national plan of action to address the primary concerns of African Americans today." It possessed a deliberate political component: "*The Covenant* is required reading for any person, party, or powerbroker who seeks to be supported politically, socially, or economically by the masses of black people in the coming years. So start reading."[9] To analyze problems confronting the black community and offer potential solutions, Smiley assembled an impressive list of scholars and commentators: Cornel West, former surgeon general David Satcher, National Urban League president Marc Morial, Columbia professor Edmund Gordon, activist Angela Glover Blackwell, and longtime children's advocate Marian Wright Edelman. The book found unprecedented success. The paperback version was the first book published by an African American company—Third World Press—to reach number one on the *New York Times* nonfiction best-seller list. The book spawned subsequent volumes on related themes and a Web site, evolving into a movement for social change.

Tavis Smiley (b. 1964).

BARACK OBAMA IN THE U.S. SENATE

In many ways, the story of Barack Obama embodies the fulfillment of the civil rights movement and the American Dream. Born on August 4, 1961, in Honolulu, to a white woman from Kansas and a black man from Kenya, Obama attended school in Hawaii, Indonesia, and Los Angeles before earning his bachelor's degree from Columbia University in 1983. The following year he relocated to Chicago to work as a community organizer on the city's predominantly black South Side. In 1988, he entered Harvard Law School, where he became the first black editor of the *Harvard Law Review.* He finished his degree in 1991 and returned to Chicago, where he worked with the law firm Miner, Barnhill & Galland and taught courses on constitutional law at the University of Chicago Law School.

Having worked as an organizer on the South Side, Obama understood the cutthroat world of Chicago politics. His political career began in earnest in 1996,

Barack Obama (b. 1961) entered Harvard University Law School in 1988, became editor of the *Law Review,* and graduated magna cum laude in 1991.

when he won election to the Illinois state senate. He proved an adept legislator and worked to pass bills aimed at reforming campaign finance laws and helping children and the poor. Though he lost badly in a 2001 attempt to unseat U.S. representative Bobby Rush (a former Black Panther) during the Democratic primary, he returned to the state senate and continued laying the foundation for a run for national office. Three years later, he mounted a campaign for the U.S. Senate, after the incumbent Republican decided against running for reelection. Unlike most Democrats at the time, Obama campaigned against the Iraq War. In the six-person race he captured the majority, taking 53 percent of the vote. After a general-election race against the black conservative Alan Keyes, Obama became the fifth popularly elected African American senator in U.S. history, and the second from Illinois. The summer before the general election, he gave a stirring keynote address at the Democratic National Convention in Boston, making a strong first impression before a national audience. The speech launched his national career.

While in the Senate, Obama worked on a number of important issues, including reform of federal lobbying laws, transparency in government activities, immigration reform, and nuclear arms control. He served on the Senate Committees on Foreign Relations; Health, Education, Labor, and Pensions; Homeland Security; Veterans' Affairs; and Environment and Public Works. He also joined the Congressional Black

In 2004, Obama won a landslide victory for the U.S. Senate from Illinois, becoming only the fifth African American to serve in that body. The most recent was Carol Moseley Braun, also from Illinois.

Caucus. In 2007, the *National Journal* declared him the most liberal U.S. senator. His work in Congress, however, was overshadowed by the constant talk that he would run for president. By 2006 Senator Obama was the author of two best-selling books, *Dreams from My Father* and *The Audacity of Hope,* and thanks to the DNC speech, he was one of the most

popular and visible Democrats in the country. On February 10, 2007, Obama called a press conference in front of the Illinois statehouse and announced his candidacy for president. "So let us begin," he told one of the last small audiences he would ever see. "Let us begin this hard work together. Let us transform the nation."

HURRICANE KATRINA

On August 24, 2005, the Category 1 hurricane Katrina slammed into the state of Florida. Eighteen people died, and the storm caused upward of $600 million in property damage. While over land the hurricane lost steam, the warm waters of the Gulf of Mexico made Katrina even stronger. Over the following two days, as the storm moved across the gulf, the National Weather Service tracked it, anticipating its next landfall would occur on the coasts of Mississippi and Louisiana. Government

officials prepared for disaster, and private organizations, including the Red Cross and Wal-Mart, readied relief efforts. By Saturday, the now Category 3 storm appeared to be headed for New Orleans. A direct hit on the historic city would be catastrophic, as the city sat below sea level. Many experts doubted that the levees that protected the city could stand the force of such a storm.

On Saturday, August 27, New Orleans mayor Ray Nagin called for evacuations and readied the Superdome, the home

of the New Orleans Saints football team, as a shelter for residents who could not or chose not to evacuate. The following day he ordered the first mandatory evacuation of an American city since the Civil War. At the same time, meteorologists notified President Bush and government officials that the levees might not withstand the storm. Hurricane Katrina, now Category 5, hit New Orleans just after six o'clock on Monday morning, August 29.

Even before the storm struck, levees

Remains of a barbershop in the Ninth Ward, New Orleans, 2005.

broke and flooding began. Many of the levees that had withstood the initial onslaught proved too low to keep the water from flooding the city. By 8:30 a.m. a twenty-foot tidal wave had obliterated the canal levees. While the National Weather Service, Louisiana state officials, and the Army Corps of Engineers reported the breaches of the levees, the federal government stood immobilized.

Michael Brown, the head of the Federal Emergency Management Agency (FEMA), even went on CNN television and denied that any levee breaches had occurred. The statements of Brown and other federal officials during the early hours of the storm foreshadowed the government's devastatingly inadequate response to the catastrophe.

Twenty-four hours after Katrina

struck New Orleans, 80 percent of the city was underwater; chaos reigned in the streets and in the halls of government. When most local police officers fled to save their own lives, the National Guard arrived to protect the city and rescue residents surrounded by deep water. President Bush, on vacation in Texas, did not immediately travel to New Orleans. Mayor Nagin, Governor Kathleen Blanco, and FEMA officials bickered over who should fund and implement the relief efforts.

All the while, more than twelve thousand people sat in the Superdome, where conditions had fallen to intolerable levels. Toilets overflowed, rain poured in through holes in the roof, and people lacked adequate food and clothing. As a global audience watched and read about the unfolding horror, the issue of race loomed large. New Orleans was overwhelmingly black and poor; about 30 percent of its black population lived below the poverty line. While evacuation made sense in theory, a full quarter of New Orleans blacks did not have access to a car. While wealthier residents had fled the city, many others

Only the steps of this house remain, Mississippi coast, 2005.

Hurricane Katrina.

had had little choice but to wait out the storm and hope it would change course or weaken at the last minute.

When African Americans did leave the city, before, during, and after the storm, they often faced resentment and outright hostility. In one dramatic example, the town of Gretna, just across the Mississippi River, refused to allow African American refugees to enter. Armed police stood on the bridge and turned people back.

On every level, Hurricane Katrina was the costliest natural disaster in U.S. history. It ravaged not only New Orleans but also coastal towns to the east in Mississippi, killing more than twelve hundred people. Property damage topped $80 billion, and hundreds of thousands of people lost their homes. The federal government's inept response undermined the president's reputation and drew attention to the interconnection of racial and class discrimination in the United States.

THE 2006 ELECTIONS

John Conyers, Jr. (b. 1929), a Korean War veteran, became a lawyer in 1958. He won election to the Congress in 1964 and is now the longest-serving African American in the House of Representatives. In his distinguished career in Congress, including helping to create the Black Caucus, he became chair of the House Judiciary Committee in 2006.

Charles Rangel (b. 1930) also served in the Korean War, and after returning to Harlem, earned a law degree. He quickly became involved in Harlem politics, served in the state general assembly, and in 1970 defeated the politically damaged Adam Clayton Powell, Jr., to represent Harlem in Congress. Enormously influential and powerful, few other congressmen can match his list of accomplishments.

Bennie G. Thompson (b. 1948) became mayor of Bolton, Mississippi, in 1973. His many accomplishments as mayor brought him to Congress in 1993. He became a voice for the rural poor and has worked tirelessly to compensate black farmers for decades of discrimination. In recognition of his growing importance, in 2006 he became chair of the House Homeland Security Committee.

Americans viewed the midterm elections of 2006 as a referendum on the Bush administration's war in Iraq. With public confidence in the war at an all-time low, the Democrats seized the advantage and took control of the House of Representatives and the Senate. The return of the Democratic Party to prominence meant that a number of ranking African American members of Congress would reach new political heights. Indeed, for the first time four members of the Congressional Black Caucus chaired full committees.

Representative John Conyers of Michigan had first been elected to the House in 1965. A cofounder of the CBC, he had served on the Judiciary Committee during the Watergate investigation in 1974 and had led efforts to create a holiday honoring Martin Luther King, Jr. In 2006, he became chairman of the House Committee on the Judiciary, which monitors the federal courts and the Department of Justice.

Another original member of the CBC, Charles Rangel, had succeeded the leg-

Juanita Millender-McDonald (1938–2007).

Governor Deval Patrick (b. 1956) with President Obama.

endary Adam Clayton Powell, Jr., as representative from Harlem in 1971. Rangel dedicated his work to helping the urban poor, combating drug addiction, fighting for gun control, and advocating other issues of concern to urban blacks. He had led the charge in 1987 to punish companies that invested in apartheid South Africa. In 2006 he became the first African American chairman of the House Ways and Means Committee (although he abandoned the post in 2010 amid ethics violations).

The former mayor of Bolton, Mississippi, Bennie Thompson won election to the House of Representatives in 1993. Bolton worked to create the National Center for Minority Health and Health Care Disparities, and he kept public health at the top of his agenda, particularly after the disaster of Hurricane Katrina. In 2006, he became the second chair of the Committee on Homeland Security.

Juanita Millender-McDonald made her name in California politics, most visibly as a delegate to the Democratic National conventions in 1984, 1988, and 1992. After serving on the Carson, California, city council and the California state assembly, she won election to the U.S. House of Representatives in 1996. She served on a number of committees—Small Business and Transportation and Infrastructure among them—and paid particular attention to women's issues. In 1999 she even organized a sit-in at the offices of Senator Jesse Helms when he threatened to block the appointment of Carol Moseley Braun as ambassador to New Zealand. After the 2006 election, she became chair of the House Administration Committee but sadly passed away from cancer the following year.

The 2006 election also saw an African American make history at the state level. Born in a poor neighborhood of Chicago, Deval Patrick moved to Milton, Massachusetts, in 1970 at the age of fourteen. He attended the prestigious Milton Academy, then earned a bachelor's and law degree from Harvard University. He worked for the NAACP Legal Defense Fund and remained in private practice until 1994, when President Bill Clinton named him assistant attorney general for civil rights. When Clinton left office, Patrick returned to private practice and worked as a corporate lawyer. He also chaired Texaco's Equality and Fairness Task Force, which aimed to implement changes at the company following its $176 million discrimination lawsuit.

Patrick became Texaco's executive vice president and general counsel in 1999, and he served in the same position at Coca-Cola beginning in 2001. But he still hoped to make a change in the public sector and decided to run for governor of Massachusetts in 2006. Adopting the campaign slogan "Yes we can," Patrick capitalized on citizens' dissatisfaction with the Republican Party, the base of the outgoing governor, Mitt Romney. He handily defeated Lieutenant Governor Kerry Healey to become the second African American popularly elected to a governorship (after L. Douglas Wilder in Virginia).

BARACK OBAMA'S PRESIDENTIAL CAMPAIGN

As a presidential candidate, Barack Obama's mantra was change—eight years of the Bush administration had destroyed the economy, and contrary to administration claims, the president had not made the country safer. Millions of young Americans responded to this message, and Obama's chief strategist, David Axelrod, built an unprecedented grassroots campaign and fund-raising machine. Latching on to new technology—particularly Internet sites like Facebook and YouTube—Obama believed that he could compete in all fifty states, regardless of their traditions as "red" or "blue." But he faced an uphill climb, squaring off against the favored Democrat Hillary Rodham Clinton, as well as former vice presidential candidate John Edwards.

In the primaries, Obama and his advisers utilized the same strategy that had led them to success in Illinois: forge a coalition of white liberals, African Americans, and young people. Many African American politicians, however, supported Hillary Clinton out of loyalty to her husband's administration. Additionally, both Obama and Clinton could lay claim to breaking through a political glass ceiling. Edwards faded early, but the two remaining candidates fought a protracted campaign up to the last primaries. Clinton argued that Obama lacked experience; Obama focused on Clinton's support for the Iraq War and other consistencies with current policies that seemed to have failed the country. Gradually Obama gained the support of African American

leaders, especially after his stunning victory in Iowa, and he steadily built a delegate lead during the long, hard-fought primary season.

Obama also deftly handled the issue

Barack Obama, presidential portrait.

of race, especially after the broadcast of inflammatory remarks made by his former pastor, the Reverend Jeremiah Wright. Wright, an AME minister at Chicago's Trinity United Church of Christ, had made caustic comments concerning the treatment African Americans endured from their fellow Americans. The sermon, in which the pastor shouted "God damn America," found its way to the Internet. Politicians, media members, and American citizens all asked Obama to respond.

On March 18, 2008, in Philadelphia, Obama did so in a lengthy, eloquent, and deeply personal speech on racial discrimination in America. Obama strongly denounced what Wright had said, but he refused to renounce his pastor and sought to contextualize the admittedly incendiary remarks. He acknowledged the historical persistence of racism but encouraged whites, blacks, and Latinos to work together to form a new social order. Appealing to the constitutional idea of a "more perfect union," Obama explained, "It requires all Americans to realize that your dreams do not have to come at the expense of my dreams; that investing in the health, welfare, and education of black and brown and white children will ultimately help all of America prosper." The speech earned Obama rave reviews and defused an incident that could have exploded his campaign.

Obama won the nomination and chose Senator Joe Biden of Delaware as his running mate. The campaign pitted Obama against the Republican senator John McCain of Arizona, a longtime politician with a reputation for military valor and relatively moderate leadership. He campaigned as a "maverick," someone who would neither toe the party line nor play by the traditional rules of Washington politics. In an attempt to deflate the novelty and inspiration of the Democratic National Convention, McCain named Governor Sarah Palin of Alaska as his running mate, a move that made headlines but gradually backfired as vot-

Inauguration of President Obama, January 20, 2009.

Historic inauguration of Barack H. Obama, shown here with his family.

ers increasingly questioned her credentials, judgment, and experience.

Obama's campaign raised money at a record pace, giving him a substantial financial advantage over the Republicans—a rare instance for recent campaigns. While McCain refused to engage the issue of Obama's race or the Jeremiah Wright controversy, his supporters possessed little reservation. The militant tone at many McCain campaign rallies prompted Representative John Lewis to remark that they reminded him of George Wallace's segregationist campaign rallies during the 1960s. All signs pointed to Obama winning the election, but many Americans wondered if voters would really elect an African American as president.

They did. Obama won the Electoral College 365–173, and the popular vote 53 percent to 46 percent. The celebration at Grant Park in Chicago on the night of his victory brought thousands, including former presidential candidate Jesse Jackson, to joyful tears, hardly believing what they had just witnessed. Many states that had gone to the Republicans in recent elections—Virginia, Indiana, Ohio, Colorado, New Mexico, and Nevada—went to Obama. His broad base of support came in large part from first-time voters who found inspiration in his message of change.

Obama's election would once have been unfathomable. While he downplayed race during the campaign—with the notable exception of the Philadelphia speech—he and his supporters understood the enormous significance of his achievement. On January 20, 2009, Obama took the oath of office as the forty-fourth president of the United States and, for so many Americans, validated centuries of struggle by African Americans.

NOTES

PART ONE
ORIGINS: 1513–1760

1. Henry Louis Gates, Jr., "Ending the Slavery Blame-Game," *New York Times,* op-ed, April 22, 2010. The fullest account of the Angolan origins of the slave trade occur in Linda M. Heywood and John K. Thornton, *Central Africans, Atlantic Creoles, and the Foundation of the Americas, 1585–1660* (Cambridge: Cambridge University Press, 2007), and John Thornton, *Africa and Africans in the Making of the Atlantic World, 1400–1800,* 2nd ed. (Cambridge: Cambridge University Press, 1998).

2. The estimates regarding the slave trade in this section can be found at the authoritative www.slavevoyages.org. David Eltis, the leading expert on the slave trade, in a communication to me on January 29, 2011, estimated that the total number of slaves sent to Peru and Mexico *combined* was approximately 700,000.

3. Excellent discussions of the black presence in the colonial Americas and in Europe are found in Thomas C. Holt, *Children of Fire: A History of African Americans* (New York: Hill and Wang, 2010); John Hope Franklin and Evelyn Brooks Higginbotham, *From Slavery to Freedom: A History of African Americans,* 9th ed. (New York: McGraw Hill, 2011); George Reid Andrews, *Afro-Latin America, 1800–2000* (New York: Oxford University Press, 2004); and Frank Moya Pons, *The Dominican Republic: A National History* (Princeton, N.J.: Markus Wiener Publishers, 1998).

4. Hugh Thomas, *The Slave Trade: The Story of the Atlantic Slave Trade, 1440–1870* (New York: Simon & Schuster, 1997), pp. 95–96.

5. Franklin and Higginbotham, *From Slavery to Freedom,* p. 23.

6. Quoted in Herman L. Bennett, *Africans in Colonial Mexico: Absolutism, Christianity, and Afro-Creole Consciousness, 1570–1640* (Bloomington: Indiana University Press, 2003), p. 16.

7. Quoted in Dedra S. McDonald, "To Be Black and Female in the Spanish Southwest: Toward a History of African Women of New Spain's Far Northern Frontier," in Quintard Taylor and Shirley Ann Wilson Moore, eds., *African American Women Confront the West, 1600–2000* (Norman: University of Oklahoma Press, 2003), p. 32.

8. Jane Landers, *Black Society in Spanish Florida* (Urbana: University of Illinois Press, 1999), pp. 8–9.

9. Kai Wright, ed., *The African American Experience: Black History and Culture Through Speeches, Letters, Editorials, Poems, Songs, and Stories* (New York: Black Dog & Leventhal, 2009), p. 25.

10. Ira Berlin, *Many Thousands Gone: The First Two Centuries of Slavery in North America* (Cambridge, Mass.: Belknap Press of Harvard University Press, 1998), p. 39; Heywood and Thornton, *Central Africans, Atlantic Creoles,* pp. 49–108.

11. Quoted in Graham Russell Hodges, *Root and Branch: African Americans in New York and East Jersey, 1613–1863* (Chapel Hill: University of North Carolina Press, 1999), p. 9.

12. Heywood and Thornton, *Central Africans, Atlantic Creoles,* pp. 312ff.

13. *Proceedings of the Massachusetts Historical Society* 45 (February 1912): 422.

14. Worthington C. Ford, ed., "Diary of Cotton Mather, 1681–1708," *Collections of the Massachusetts Historical Society,* ser. 7, vol. 7 (1911): 579.

15. Quoted in Landers, *Black Society in Spanish Florida,* p. 38.

PART TWO
FORGING FREEDOM: 1760–1804

1. Quoted in Dickson D. Bruce, Jr., *The Origins of African American Literature, 1680–1865* (Charlottesville: University of Virginia Press, 2001), p. 44.

2. Ibid., p. 45.

3. Quoted in Herbert Aptheker, ed., *A Documentary History of the Negro People in the United States, from Colonial Times Through the Civil War* (New York: Citadel Press, 1951), p. 7.

4. "Proclamation of Earl of Dunmore," *Africans in America,* Part 2, PBS (http://www.pbs.org/wgbh/aia/part2/2h42t.html).

5. Quoted in Julian P. Boyd, ed., *The Papers of Thomas Jefferson,* 36 vols. (Princeton, N.J.: Princeton University Press, 1950), 1:243–47.

6. Samuel Johnson, "Taxation No Tyranny: An Answer to the Resolutions and Address of the American Congress," in *The Works of Samuel Johnson,* 16 vols. (Troy, N.Y.: Pafraets & Company, 1903), 14:93–144.

7. "To the Honorable Counsel & House of [Representa]tives for the State of Massachusetts Bay in General Court assembled, Jan. 13, 1777," quoted in Herbert Aptheker, *The American Revolution, 1763–1783* (New York: International Publishers, 1960), p. 215.

8. Philip S. Foner, "A Plea Against Reenslavement," *Pennsylvania History* 39, no. 2 (April 1972): 240–41.

9. Quoted in David Brion Davis, "Impact of the French and Haitian Revolutions," in David P. Geggus, ed., *The Impact of the Haitian Revolution in the Atlantic World* (Columbia: University of South Carolina Press, 2001), p. 3.

PART THREE

"IT SHALL EVER BE OUR DUTY TO
VINDICATE OUR BRETHREN": 1800–1834

1. Thomas Clarkson, *Essay on the Slavery and Commerce of the Human Species* (London: J. Phillips, 1788), p. 86.
2. "Hard Scrabble, or Miss Philises Bobalition," broadside, Boston, 1824.
3. *David Walker's Appeal: To the Coloured Citizens of the World, but in particular, and very expressly, to those of the United States of America,* introd. by James Turner (Baltimore: Black Classic Press, 1993), p. 46.
4. Samuel Joseph May, *Some Recollections of Our Antislavery Conflict* (Boston: Fields, Osgood, & Co., 1869), pp. 36–37.
5. Thomas R. Gray, *The Confessions of Nat Turner, the Leader of the Late Insurrection in South Hampton, VA* (Baltimore: Lucas & Deaver, 1831), p. 12.
6. Quoted in Dorothy Sterling, *We Are Your Sisters: Black Women in the Nineteenth Century* (New York: W. W. Norton, 1984), p. 113.
7. Jarena Lee, *Religious Experience and Journal of Mrs. Jarena Lee, Giving an Account of Her Call to Preach the Gospel* (Philadelphia: n.p., 1849), p. 77.
8. William Wilberforce, *An Appeal to the Religion, Justice, and Humanity of the Inhabitants of the British Empire, in Behalf of the Negro Slaves in the West Indies* (London: J. Hatchard and Son, 1823), p. 32.
9. Elizabeth Heyrick, *Immediate, Not Gradual Abolition: or, An Inquiry into the Shortest, Safest, and Most Effectual Means of Getting Rid of West Indian Slavery* (Boston: Isaac Knapp, 1838), p. 7.
10. Steven Tomkins, *William Wilberforce: A Biography* (Oxford: Lion Hudson, 2007), p. 218.

PART FOUR

RACE AND RESISTANCE: 1834–1850

1. Richard Newman, Patrick Rael, and Phillip Lapsansky, eds., *Pamphlets of Protest: An Anthology of Early African-American Protest Literature, 1790–1860* (New York: Routledge, 2001), p. 138.

2. Frederick Douglass, *Narrative of the Life of Frederick Douglass,* ed. Gerald Fulkerson, John W. Blassingame, John R. McKivigan, and Peter P. Hinks (New Haven, Conn.: Yale University Press, 2001), p. 13.
3. Ibid., p. 3.
4. Charles Edwards Lester, *Life and Public Services of Charles Sumner* (New York: United States Publishing Company, 1874), pp. 75–79.
5. Derrick Bell, *Silent Covenants:* Brown v. Board of Education *and the Unfulfilled Hopes for Racial Reform* (New York: Oxford University Press, 2004), p. 89.

PART FIVE

EMERGENCE: 1850–1860

1. Fanny Jackson-Coppin, *Reminiscences of School Life, and Hints on Teaching* (Philadelphia: A.M.E. Book Concern, 1913), p. 24.
2. Wendell Phillips, "Introduction to Pamphlet Edition," in William Cooper Nell, *The Colored Patriots of the American Revolution,* with an introduction by Harriet Beecher Stowe (Boston: Robert F. Wallcut, 1855), p. 8.
3. Albert J. von Frank, "Anthony Burns," in *African American National Biography,* ed. Henry Louis Gates, Jr., and Evelyn Brooks Higginbotham, 8 vols. (New York: Oxford University Press, 2008), 2:68–69.
4. *Dred Scott v. Sandford,* 60 U.S. 393 (1857).
5. Harriet E. Wilson, *Our Nig: or, Sketches from the Life of a Free Black,* ed. and introd. by Henry Louis Gates, Jr. (New York: Vintage, 2002), p. 3.
6. Ibid., pp. 34–35.
7. Ibid., p. 129.
8. Ibid.

PART SIX

WAR AND ITS MEANING: 1859–1865

1. Quoted in David S. Reynolds, *John Brown, Abolitionist: The Man Who Killed Slavery, Sparked the Civil War, and Seeded Civil Rights* (New York: Vintage, 2005), p. 366.

2. Milton Meltzer, *The Black Americans: A History in Their Own Words, 1619–1983* (New York: HarperCollins, 1984), p. 70.
3. Quoted in Forrest G. Wood, *Black Scare: The Racist Response to Emancipation and Reconstruction* (Berkeley: University of California Press, 1970), p. 43.
4. Abraham Lincoln, *The Collected Works of Abraham Lincoln,* ed. Roy P. Basler, 11 vols. (New Brunswick, N.J.: Rutgers University Press, 1953–90), 5:169, 192.
5. Carla L. Peterson, *"Doers of the Word": African-American Women Speakers and Writers in the North, 1830–1880* (New York: Oxford University Press, 1995), pp. 116–17.
6. Dudley Taylor Cornish, *The Sable Arm: Negro Troops in the Union Army, 1861–1865* (New York: W. W. Norton, 1996), p. 44.
7. Henry Louis Gates, Jr., and Donald Yacovone, eds., *Lincoln on Race and Slavery* (Princeton, N.J.: Princeton University Press, 2009), p. xxxvi.
8. Lincoln, *Collected Works,* 5:420.
9. John Stauffer, *Giants: The Parallel Lives of Frederick Douglass and Abraham Lincoln* (New York: Twelve, 2008), p. 245.
10. Edna Greene Medford, "Imagined Promises, Bitter Realities: African Americans and the Meaning of the Emancipation Proclamation," in Harold Holzer, Edna Greene Medford, and Frank J. Williams, *Emancipation Proclamation: Three Views,* with a foreword by John Hope Franklin (Baton Rouge: Louisiana State Press, 2006), p. 20.
11. General Robert E. Lee appeared to oppose the killing of black prisoners. See Lynda Lasswell Crist, Barbara J. Rozek, and Kenneth Williams, eds., *Papers of Jefferson Davis,* 12 vols. to date (Baton Rouge: Louisiana State University Press, 1971–), 11:98.
12. Frank Moore, *The Rebellion Record: A Diary of American Events* (New York: D. Van Nostrand, Publisher, 1865), pp. 17–23 passim.
13. Christian G. Samito, ed., *Changes in Law and Society During the Civil War and Reconstruction* (Carbondale:

Southern Illinois University Press, 2009), p. 171.

14. Henry Highland Garnet, *Memorial Discourse,* ed. James McCune Smith (Philadelphia: Joseph M. Wilson, 1865).

15. Quoted in George H. White, "Defense of the Negro Race— Charges Answered" (Washington, D.C.: U.S. Government Printing Office, 1901), p. 13.

PART SEVEN

RECONSTRUCTING A NATION: 1866–1877

1. J. C. Lester and D. L. Wilson, "Organization and Principles of the Ku Klux Klan," ed. W. L. Fleming (1868).

2. Quoted in *Christian Recorder,* February 17, 1866.

3. Quoted in Booker T. Washington, *Frederick Douglass* (Philadelphia: George W. Jacobs & Company, 1906), p. 261.

4. "The Hampton Normal School," http://www.hamptonu.edu/about/history.cfm.

5. Charles Sumner, *The Works of Charles Sumner,* 15 vols. (Boston: Lee and Shepard, 1870–83), 13:337.

6. Wyn Craig Wade, *The Fiery Cross: The Ku Klux Klan in America* (New York: Oxford University Press, 1998), p. 89.

7. Milton R. Konvitz, *Fundamental Rights: History of a Constitutional Doctrine* (New Brunswick, N.J.: Transaction Publishers, 2007), p. 31.

8. Stephen Ward Angell, *Bishop Henry McNeal Turner and African American Religion in the South* (Knoxville: University of Tennessee Press, 1992), p. 168.

9. Matthew J. Mancini, *One Dies, Get Another: Convict Leasing in the American South, 1866–1928* (Columbia: University of South Carolina Press, 1996), p. 3 and passim.

PART EIGHT

"THERE IS NO NEGRO PROBLEM": 1877–1895

1. Gary Cooper as told to Marc Crawford, "Stagecoach Mary," *Ebony,* October 1959.

2. Terence Vincent Powderly, *Thirty Years of Labor, 1859–1889* (Columbus, Ohio: Excelsior Publishing House, 1889), p. 657.

3. Vanessa Northington Gamble, "Roots of the Black Hospital Reform Movement," in *Sickness and Health in America: Readings in the History of Medicine and Public Health,* ed. Judith Walzer Leavitt and Ronald L. Numbers, 3rd ed. (Madison: University of Wisconsin Press, 1997), p. 369.

4. Paula J. Giddings, *Ida: A Sword Among Lions: Ida B. Wells and the Campaign Against Lynching* (New York: Harper-Collins, 2009), p. 228.

5. Quoted ibid., p. 277.

6. Albert Boime, "Henry Ossawa Tanner's Subversion of Genre Source," *The Art Bulletin* 75, no. 3 (1993): 423. The art critic in question may have been Riter Fitzgerald, a friend of the American realist painter Thomas Eakins.

7. W. E. B. Du Bois, *Darkwater* (New York: Harcourt, Brace and Company, 1920), p. 8.

8. W. E. B. Du Bois, *Dusk of Dawn* (New York: Harcourt, Brace and Company, 1940), p. 22.

9. W. E. B. Du Bois, *The Autobiography of W. E. B. Du Bois: A Soliloquy on Viewing My Life from the Last Decade of Its First Century* (New York: International Publishers, 1979), p. 125.

PART NINE

NEW NEGRO, OLD PROBLEM: 1895–1900

1. "Atlanta Compromise" speech, September 18, 1895, Oxford African American Studies Center, http://www.oxfordaasc.com/article/primary/ps0007?hi=0&highlight=1&from=quick&pos=4.

2. Ibid.

3. Quoted in Louis R. Harlan, *Booker T. Washington: Volume I: The Making of a Black Leader, 1865–1901* (New York: Oxford University Press, 1972), p. 225.

4. W. E. B. Du Bois, *The Souls of Black Folk: Essays and Sketches* (Chicago: A. C. McClurg & Co., 1903), pp. 43, 58, 50.

5. Mark Whitman, Brown v. Board of Education: *A Documentary History* (Princeton, N.J.: Markus Wiener Publishers, 2004), p. xv.

6. Ibid., p. 16.

7. Quoted in Leon F. Litwack and August Meier, eds., *Black Leaders of the Nineteenth Century* (Urbana: University of Illinois Press, 1988), p. 249.

8. Evelyn Brooks Higginbotham, *Righteous Discontent: The Women's Movement in the Black Baptist Church* (Cambridge, Mass.: Harvard University Press, 1993), p. 185.

PART TEN

THE ORDEAL OF JIM CROW: 1900–1917

1. "The Negroes' Temporary Farewell: Jim Crow and the Exclusion of African Americans from Congress, 1887–1929," *Office of History and Preservation, Office of the Clerk, Black Americans in Congress, 1870–2007* (Washington, D.C.: U.S. Government Printing Office, 2008).

2. Quincy Howe, *A World History of Our Own Times from the Turn of the Century to the 1918 Armistice,* vol. 1 (New York: Simon & Schuster, 1949; rpt. Mahomedan Press, 2007), pp. 200–201.

3. Henry Louis Gates, Jr., and Gene Andrew Jarrett, eds., *The New Negro: Readings on Race, Representation, and African American Culture, 1892–1938* (Princeton, N.J.: Princeton University Press, 2007), p. 418.

4. James Weldon Johnson, Preface to *The Book of American Negro Poetry, Chosen and Edited with an Essay on the Negro's Creative Genius,* ed. Johnson (New York: Harcourt, Brace and Company, 1922), p. xxxiv.

5. Will Marion Cook, Paul Laurence Dunbar, and Jeese A. Ship, "Emancipation Day," in *In Dahomey,* 1903.

6. Jeffrey P. Green, " 'In Dahomey' in London in 1903," *The Black Perspective in Music* 11, no. 1 (Spring 1983): 38.

7. W. E. B. Du Bois, *The Souls of Black Folk: Essays and Sketches* (Chicago: A. C. McClurg & Co., 1903), p. 3.

8. Ibid., pp. 52–53.

9. Quoted in David Levering Lewis, *W. E. B. Du Bois: Biography of a Race, 1868–1919* (New York: Henry Holt, 1993), p. 329.

10. Quoted in Louis R. Harlan, *Booker T. Washington: The Wizard of Tuskegee, 1901–1915* (New York: Oxford University Press, 1983), p. 319.

11. Lewis, *Biography of a Race,* pp. 332–33.

12. James L. Crouthamel, "The Springfield Race Riot of 1908," *Journal of Negro History* 45, no. 3 (July 1960): 170–71.

13. Merrill D. Peterson, *Lincoln in American Memory* (New York: Oxford University Press, 1995), p. 167.

14. Quoted in Lewis, *Biography of a Race,* p. 433.

15. Philip Dray, *At the Hands of Persons Unknown: The Lynching of Black America* (New York: Modern Library, 2003), p. 194.

16. Kenneth O'Reilly, "The Jim Crow Policies of Woodrow Wilson," *Journal of Blacks in Higher Education* 17 (August 1997): 118.

Part Eleven
Renaissance: 1917–1928

1. David Levering Lewis, *W. E. B. Du Bois: Biography of a Race, 1868–1919* (New York: Henry Holt, 1993), p. 556.

2. Ibid., p. 507.

3. Ibid., p. 575.

4. Ibid., p. 577.

5. Marcus Garvey, "Look Up, You Mighty Race," *Black Man* 2 (Sept.–Oct. 1936):3–4

6. Claude McKay, *Harlem Shadows: The Poems of Claude McKay,* introd. by Max Eastman (New York: Harcourt, Brace and Co., 1922), p. 53.

7. Langston Hughes, *The Big Sea: An Autobiography,* introd. by Arnold Rampersad (New York: Hill and Wang, 1993), p. 218.

8. Jervis Anderson, *A. Philip Randolph: A Biographical Portrait* (Berkeley: University of California Press, 1986), p. 139.

9. Ibid., p. 82.

10. Henry Louis Gates, Jr., and Gene Andrew Jarrett, eds., *The New Negro: Readings on Race, Representation, and African American Culture, 1892–1938* (Princeton, N.J.: Princeton University Press, 2007), pp. 95, 92.

11. Kelly Miller, "The Past, Present, and Future of the Negro College," *Journal of Negro Education* 2, no. 3 [A Survey of Negro Higher Education] (July 1933): 422.

Part Thirteen
The Era of World War II: 1939–1950

1. The letter is held in the Marian Anderson/DAR Controversy Collection at the Moorland-Spingarn Research Center, Howard University Library. Noted in Scott A. Sandage, "A Marble House Divided: The Lincoln Memorial, the Civil Rights Movement, and the Politics of Memory, 1939–1963," *Journal of American History* 80, no. 1 (June 1993): 136.

2. Glenda Elizabeth Gilmore, *Defying Dixie: The Radical Roots of Civil Rights, 1919–1950* (New York: W. W. Norton, 2008), p. 356.

3. Jervis Anderson, *A. Philip Randolph: A Biographical Portrait* (Berkeley: University of California Press, 1986), p. 249.

4. John D'Emilio, *Lost Prophet: The Life and Times of Bayard Rustin* (New York: Free Press, 2003), p. 136.

5. John Hope Franklin, *Mirror to America: The Autobiography of John Hope Franklin* (New York: Farrar, Straus and Giroux, 2005), pp. 127–28.

6. Ibid., p. 135.

Part Fourteen
Foundations of the New Civil Rights Movement: 1950–1963

1. Quoted in Henry Louis Gates, Jr., *Thirteen Ways of Looking at a Black Man* (New York: Vintage Books, 1997), p. 163.

2. Quoted in *Time,* July 22, 1974.

3. Ralph Ellison, "Twentieth-Century Fiction and the Black Mask of Humanity," in *Shadow and Act* (New York: New American Library, 1966), p. 42.

4. Arnold Rampersad, *Ralph Ellison: A Biography* (New York: Alfred A. Knopf, 2007), p. 75.

5. Ralph Ellison, *Invisible Man* (New York: Vintage Books, 1995), p. 581.

6. Mary L. Dudziak, *Cold War Civil Rights: Race and the Image of American Democracy* (Princeton, N.J.: Princeton University Press, 2000), p. 115.

7. Langston Hughes, "Harlem [2]," in *The Collected Poems of Langston Hughes,* ed. Arnold Rampersad (New York: Vintage Books, 1994), p. 426.

8. Clayborne Carson, *In Struggle: SNCC and the Black Awakening of the 1960s* (Cambridge, Mass.: Harvard University Press, 1995), p. 20.

9. Kwame Anthony Appiah and Henry Louis Gates, Jr., eds., *Africana: Civil Rights: An A–Z Reference of the Movement That Changed America* (Philadelphia: Running Press, 2004), p. 119.

Part Fifteen
The Movement at High Tide: 1963–1968

1. Martin Luther King, Jr., "Letter from Birmingham Jail," in *Why We Can't Wait,* afterword by Reverend Jesse L. Jackson, Sr. (New York: Signet Classic, 2000), pp. 64, 65, 70, 73.

2. *The Crisis* 89 (Nov. 1982): 33.

3. Imamu Amiri Baraka, "African Slaves/American Slaves: Their Music," from *Blues People,* in *The LeRoi Jones/Amiri Baraka Reader,* ed. William J. Harris (New York: Thunder's Mouth Press, 1991), p. 21.

4. Chana Kai Lee, *For Freedom's Sake: The Life of Fannie Lou Hamer* (Urbana: University of Illinois Press, 1999), p. 89.

5. President Lyndon Baines Johnson, Speech Before Congress on Voting Rights, March 15, 1965; transcript from Miller Center of Public Affairs, University of Virginia.

6. President Lyndon Baines Johnson, Remarks on the Signing of the Voting Rights Act, August 6, 1965; tran-

script from Miller Center of Public Affairs, University of Virginia.

7. Quoted in *New York Times,* February 6, 2002. The Mailer quote is from the book's cover.

8. *The Autobiography of Malcolm X as Told to Alex Haley* (New York: Ballantine Books, 1999), p. 272.

9. Interview with Claude Lewis, December 1964.

10. James Farmer, *Lay Bare the Heart: An Autobiography of the Civil Rights Movement* (Fort Worth: Texas Christian University Press, 1998), p. 225.

11. Taylor Branch, *Pillar of Fire: America in the King Years, 1963–65* (New York: Simon & Schuster, 1998), p. 184.

12. Quoted ibid., p. 596.

13. Taylor Branch, *At Canaan's Edge: America in the King Years, 1965–68* (New York: Simon & Schuster, 2006), p. 170.

14. Quoted in David L. Lewis, *King: A Biography* (Urbana: University of Illinois Press, 1978), p. 283.

15. Quoted in David Remnick, *King of the World: Muhammad Ali and the Rise of an American Hero* (New York: Vintage Books, 1999), p. 287. Ali is often quoted as adding, "No Vietcong ever called me nigger," though that statement has never been verified.

16. Clayborne Carson, *In Struggle: SNCC and the Black Awakening of the 1960s* (Cambridge, Mass.: Harvard University Press, 1981), p. 261.

17. Branch, *At Canaan's Edge,* p. 706.

18. "1968: Black athletes make silent protest," BBC, October 17, 1968.

19. Ibid.

PART SIXTEEN

CULTURAL INTEGRATION: 1969–1979

1. "The 1970s: The 'Toothless Tiger' Gets Its Teeth—A New Era of Enforcement," U.S. Equal Employment Opportunity Commission 35th Anniversary Report, http://www .eeoc.gov/eeoc/history/35th/1970s/ index.html.

PART SEVENTEEN

ACHIEVEMENT: 1980–2008

1. Coretta Scott King, "The Meaning of the Martin Luther King, Jr. Holiday," The King Center, http://www.the kingcenter.org/Default.aspx.

2. S. I. Waxman, "At West Point, A Commanding Example: Gen. Fred Gorden, at Ease as the Cadets' First Black Commandant," *Washington Post,* September 27, 1987.

3. Joseph P. Fried, "Night of Hatred by Whites Is Depicted at Racial Trial," *New York Times,* December 10, 1987.

4. Nick Ravo, "Marchers and Brooklyn Youths Trade Racial Jeers," *New York Times,* August 27, 1989.

5. Jeffrey Toobin, *The Nine: Inside the Secret World of the Supreme Court* (New York: Anchor Books, 2008), p. 30.

6. Clarence Thomas Second Hearing, Day 1, Part 4, Senate Judiciary Committee, C-SPAN Video Library, http://www .c-spanarchives.org/program/ ID/152447&start=1023&end=1123.

7. Adam Liptak, "No Argument: Thomas Keeps 5-Year Silence," *New York Times,* February 12, 2011.

8. David Kocieniewski, "Injured Man Says Brooklyn Officers Tortured Him in Custody," *New York Times,* August 13, 1997.

9. Tavis Smiley, ed., *Covenant with Black America* (Chicago: Third World Press, 2006), p. xi and passim.

BIBLIOGRAPHY

Anderson, James D. *The Education of Blacks in the South, 1860–1935.* Chapel Hill: University of North Carolina Press, 1988.

Anderson, Jervis *A. Philip Randolph: A Biographical Portrait.* Berkeley: University of California Press, 1986.

Andrews, George Reid. *Afro-Latin America, 1800–2000.* New York: Oxford University Press, 2004.

Andrews, William L. *To Tell a Free Story: The First Century of Afro-American Autobiography, 1760–1865.* Urbana: University of Illinois Press, 1986.

Angell, Stephen Ward. *Bishop Henry McNeal Turner and African American Religion in the South.* Knoxville: University of Tennessee Press, 1992.

Appiah, Kwame Anthony, and Henry Louis Gates, Jr., eds. *Africana: Civil Rights: An A–Z Reference of the Movement That Changed America.* Philadelphia: Running Press, 2004.

Aptheker, Herbert. *The American Revolution, 1763–1783.* New York: International Publishers, 1960.

Aptheker, Herbert, ed. *A Documentary History of the Negro People in the United States, from Colonial Times Through the Civil War.* New York: Citadel Press, 1951.

Arsenault, Raymond O. *Freedom Riders: 1961 and the Struggle for Racial Justice.* New York: Oxford University Press, 2006.

The Autobiography of Malcolm X as Told to Alex Haley. New York: Ballantine Books, 1999.

Baker, Houston A. *Modernism and the Harlem Renaissance.* Chicago: University of Chicago Press, 1987.

Baldwin, James. *Collected Essays.* Ed. Toni Morrison. New York: Library of America, 1998.

Bell, Derrick. *Silent Covenants:* Brown v. Board of Education *and the Unfulfilled Hopes for Racial Reform.* New York: Oxford University Press, 2004.

Bennett, Herman L. *Africans in Colonial Mexico: Absolutism, Christianity, and Afro-Creole Consciousness, 1570–1640.* Bloomington: University of Indiana Press, 2003.

Berlin, Ira. *Many Thousands Gone: The First Two Centuries of Slavery in North America.* Cambridge, Mass.: Belknap Press of Harvard University Press, 1998.

———. *Slaves Without Masters: The Free Negro in the Antebellum South.* New York: Oxford University Press, 1975, 1992.

Berlin, Ira, and Leslie M. Harris, eds. *Slavery in New York.* New York: The New Press, 2005.

Blatt, Martin H., Thomas J. Brown, and Donald Yacovone, eds. *Hope and Glory: Essays on the Legacy of the 54th Massachusetts Regiment.* Amherst: University of Massachusetts Press, 2001, 2009.

Boime, Albert. "Henry Ossawa Turner's Subversion of Genre Source." *Art Bulletin* 75, no. 3 (1993): 415–42.

Branch, Taylor. *At Canaan's Edge: America in the King Years, 1965–68.* New York: Simon & Schuster, 2006.

———. *Parting the Waters: America in the King Years, 1954–63.* New York: Simon & Schuster, 1988.

———. *Pillar of Fire: America in the King Years, 1963–65.* New York: Simon & Schuster, 1998.

Brooks, George E. *Landlords and Strangers: Ecology, Society and Trade in Western Africa, 1000–1630.* Boulder, Colo.: Westview Press, 1993.

Brown, Scot. *Fighting for US: Maulana Karenga, the US Organization, and Black Cultural Nationalism.* New York: New York University Press, 2003.

Bruce, Dickson D., Jr., *The Origins of African American Literature, 1680–1865.* Charlottesville: University of Virginia Press, 2001.

Brundage, William Fitzhugh. *Lynching in the New South: Georgia and Virginia, 1880–1930.* Urbana: University of Illinois Press, 1993.

Bundles, A'Lelia. *On Her Own Ground: The Life and Times of Madam C. J. Walker.* New York: Scribner, 2002.

Carson, Clayborne. *In Struggle: SNCC and the Black Awakening of the 1960s.* Cambridge, Mass.: Harvard University Press, 1981.

Cecelski, David S. *The Waterman's Song: Slavery and Freedom in Maritime North Carolina.* Chapel Hill: University of North Carolina Press, 2001.

Cecelski, David S., and Timothy B. Tyson, eds. *Democracy Betrayed: The Wilmington Race Riot of 1898 and Its Legacy.* Chapel Hill: University of North Carolina Press, 1998.

Chang, Jeff. *Can't Stop Won't Stop: A History of the Hip-Hop Generation.* New York: St. Martin's Press, 2005.

Chisholm, Shirley. *The Good Fight.* New York: Harper & Row, 1973.

———. *Unbought and Unbossed.* Boston: Houghton Mifflin, 1970.

Clegg, Claude A., III. *The Price of Liberty: African Americans and the Making of Liberia.* Chapel Hill: University of North Carolina Press, 2004.

Cooper, Wayne F. *Claude McKay: Rebel Sojourner in the Harlem Renaissance. A Biography.* Baton Rouge: Louisiana State University Press, 1987.

Cornish, Dudley Taylor. *The Sable Arm: Negro Troops in the Union Army, 1861–1865.* New York: W. W. Norton, 1996.

Coughtry, Jay. *The Notorious Triangle: Rhode Island and the African Slave Trade, 1700–1807.* Philadelphia: Temple University Press, 1981.

Crawford, Vicki L., Jacqueline Anne Rouse, and Barbara Woods, eds. *Women in the Civil Rights Movement: Trailblazers and Torchbearers, 1941–1965.* Bloomington: Indiana University Press, 1993.

Crouthamel, James L. "The Springfield Race Riot of 1908." *The Journal of Negro History* 45, no. 3 (July 1960): 164–81.

Curry, Leonard. *The Free Black in Urban America, 1800–1850: The Shadow of the Dream.* Chicago: University of Chicago Press, 1981.

Curtin, Philip D. *The Rise and Fall of the Plantation Complex: Essays in Atlantic History.* New York: Cambridge University Press, 1998.

Curtin, Philip D., et al. *African History: From Earliest Times to Independence.* 2nd ed. London: Longman, 1995.

Daniel, Pete. *The Shadow of Slavery: Peonage in the South, 1901–1969.* Urbana: University of Illinois Press, 1972, 1990.

Davis, David Brion. *Inhuman Bondage: The Rise and Fall of Slavery in the New World.* New York: Oxford University Press, 2006.

———. *The Problem of Slavery in Western Culture.* Ithaca, N.Y.: Cornell University Press, 1966.

D'Emilio, John. *Lost Prophet: The Life and Times of Bayard Rustin.* New York: Free Press, 2003.

Dittmer, John. *Local People: The Struggle for Civil Rights in Mississippi.* Urbana: University of Illinois Press, 1994.

Douglass, Frederick. *Narrative of the Life of Frederick Douglass.* Ed. Gerald Fulkerson, John W. Blassingame, John R. McKivigan, and Peter P. Hinks. New Haven, Conn.: Yale University Press, 2001.

Dray, Philip. *At the Hands of Persons Unknown: The Lynching of Black America.* New York: Modern Library, 2003.

Duberman, Martin B. *Paul Robeson.* New York: Alfred A. Knopf, 1988.

Du Bois, W. E. B. *The Autobiography of W. E. B. Du Bois: A Soliloquy on Viewing My Life from the Last Decade of Its First Century.* New York: International Publishers, 1979.

———. *Darkwater.* New York: Harcourt, Brace and Company, 1920.

———. *Dusk of Dawn.* New York: Harcourt, Brace and Company, 1940.

———. *The Souls of Black Folk: Essays and Sketches.* Chicago: A. C. McClurg & Co., 1903.

Dudziak, Mary L. *Cold War Civil Rights: Race and the Image of American Democracy.* Princeton, N.J.: Princeton University Press, 2000.

Dunn, Richard S. *Sugar and Slaves: The Rise of the Planter Class in the English West Indies, 1624–1713.* Chapel Hill: University of North Carolina Press, 1972, 2000.

Dyson, Michael Eric. *Come Hell or High Water: Hurricane Katrina and the Color of Disaster.* New York: Basic Civitas, 2006.

Egerton, Douglas R. *He Shall Go Out Free: The Lives of Denmark Vesey.* Rev. ed. Lanham, Md.: Rowman & Littlefield, 2004.

Ellison, Ralph. *Invisible Man.* New York: Vintage Books, 1995.

———. *Shadow and Act.* New York: New American Library, 1966.

Eltis, David, and Lawrence C. Jennings. "Trade Between Western Africa and the Atlantic World in the Pre-Colonial Era." *American Historical Review* 93 (1988): 936–59.

Engs, Robert Francis. *Educating the Disenfranchised and Disinherited: Samuel Chapman Armstrong and the Hampton Institute, 1839–1893.* Knoxville: University of Tennessee Press, 1999.

Fairclough, Adam. *A Class of Their Own: Black Teachers in the Segregated South.* Cambridge, Mass.: Belknap Press of Harvard University Press, 2007.

Farmer, James. *Lay Bare the Heart: An Autobiography of the Civil Rights Movement.* Fort Worth: Texas Christian University Press, 1998.

Foner, Eric. *Reconstruction: America's Unfinished Revolution, 1863–1877.* New York: Harper & Row, 1988.

Foner, Philip S. "A Plea Against Reenslavement." *Pennsylvania History* 39, no. 2 (April 1972): 239–41.

Franklin, John Hope. *The Free Negro in North Carolina, 1790–1860.* Chapel Hill: University of North Carolina Press, 1943.

———. *Mirror to America: The Autobiography of John Hope Franklin.* New York: Farrar, Straus and Giroux, 2005.

Franklin, John Hope, and Evelyn Brooks Higginbotham. *From Slavery to Freedom: A History of African Americans.* 9th ed. New York: McGraw-Hill, 2011.

Franklin, John Hope, and Loren Schweninger. *Runaway Slaves: Rebels on the Plantation.* New York: Oxford University Press, 1999.

Fry, Sylvia R. *Water from the Rock: Black Resistance in a Revolutionary Age.* Princeton, N.J.: Princeton University Press, 1991.

Garrow, David J. *Bearing the Cross: Martin Luther King, Jr., and the Southern Christian Leadership Conference.* New York: Vintage Books, 1988.

Gates, Henry Louis, Jr. *The Trials of Phillis Wheatley: America's First Poet and Her Encounters with the Founding Fathers.* New York: Basic Civitas, 2003.

Gates, Henry Louis, Jr., and William L. Andrews, eds. *Pioneers of the Black Atlantic: Five Slave Narratives from the Enlightenment, 1772–1815.* New York: Basic Civitas, 1998.

Gates, Henry Louis, Jr., and Evelyn Brooks Higginbotham, eds. *African American National Biography.* 8 vols. New York: Oxford University Press, 2008.

Gates, Henry Louis, Jr., and Gene Andrew Jarrett, eds. *The New Negro: Readings on Race, Representation, and African American Culture, 1892–1938.* Princeton, N.J.: Princeton University Press, 2007.

Gates, Henry Louis, Jr., and Donald Yacovone, eds. *Lincoln on Race and Slavery.* Princeton, N.J.: Princeton University Press, 2009.

Geggus, David P., ed. *The Impact of the Haitian Revolution in the Atlantic World.* Columbia: University of South Carolina Press, 2001.

Giddings, Paula. *Ida: A Sword Among Lions: Ida B. Wells and the Campaign Against Lynching.* New York: HarperCollins, 2009.

Gilmore, Glenda Elizabeth. *Defying Dixie: The Radical Roots of Civil Rights, 1919–1950.* New York: W. W. Norton, 2008.

Glatthaar, Joseph T. *Forged in Battle: The Civil War Alliance of Black Soldiers and White Officers.* New York: Free Press, 1990.

Goodman, James E. *Stories of Scottsboro.* New York: Vintage Books, 1995.

Goodwin, Robert. *Crossing the Continent, 1527–1540: The Story of the First African-American Explorer of the American South.* New York: HarperCollins, 2008.

Gordon-Reed, Annette. *The Hemingses of Monticello: An American Family.* New York: W. W. Norton, 2008.

Graham, Lawrence. *The Senator and the Socialite: The True Story of America's First Black Dynasty.* New York: HarperCollins, 2006.

Gray, Thomas R. *The Confessions of Nat Turner, the Leader of the Late Insurrection in South Hampton, Va.* Baltimore: Lucas & Deaver, 1831.

Green, Jeffrey P. "'In Dahomey' in London in 1903." *The Black Perspective in Music* 11, no. 1 (Spring 1983): 22–40.

Gregory, James N. *The Southern Diaspora: How the Great Migrations of Black and White Southerners Transformed America.* Chapel Hill: University of North Carolina Press, 2005.

Grossman, James R. *Land of Hope: Chicago, Black Southerners and the Great Migration.* Chicago: University of Chicago Press, 1989.

Guelzo, Allen C. *Lincoln's Emancipation Proclamation: The End of Slavery in America.* New York: Simon & Schuster, 2004.

Gutman, Herbert G. *The Black Family in Slavery and Freedom, 1750–1925.* New York: Vintage Books, 1977.

Hahn, Steven. *A Nation Under Our Feet: Black Political Struggles in the Rural South from Slavery to the Great Migration.* Cambridge, Mass.: Harvard University Press, 2003.

Hahn, Steven, et al. *Freedom: A Documentary History of Emancipation, Land, and Labor, 1865.* Chapel Hill: University of North Carolina Press, 2008.

Hamilton, Kenneth. "The Origins and Early Promotion of Nicodemus: A Pre-Exodus, All-Black Town." *Kansas History* 5 (1982): 220–42.

Hardwick, Kevin R. "'Your Old Father Abe Lincoln Is Dead and Damned': Black Soldiers and the Memphis Race Riots of 1866." *Journal of Social History* 27, no. 1 (1993): 109–28.

Harlan, Louis R. *Booker T. Washington.* 2 vols. New York: Oxford University Press, 1972, 1983.

Harold, Claudrena N. *The Rise and Fall of the Garvey Movement in the Urban South, 1918–42.* New York: Routledge, 2007.

Harris, William J., ed. *The LeRoi Jones/Amiri Baraka Reader.* New York: Thunder's Mouth Press, 1991.

Harris, William M. *Keeping the Faith: A. Philip Randolph, Milton P. Webster, and the Brotherhood of Sleeping Car Porters, 1925–37.* Urbana: University of Illinois Press, 1991.

Haygood, Wil. *King of the Cats: The Life and Times of Adam Clayton Powell, Jr.* Boston: Houghton Mifflin, 1993.

Henri, Florette. *Black Migration: Movement North, 1900–1920.* Garden City, N.Y.: Anchor Press, 1975.

Henri, Florette, and Arthur E. Barbeau. *The Unknown Soldiers: African-American Troops in World War I.* New York: Da Capo Press, 1974, 1996.

Heyrick, Elizabeth. *Immediate, Not Gradual Abolition: or, An Inquiry into the Shortest, Safest, and Most Effectual Means of Getting Rid of West Indian Slavery.* London: Hatchard, 1824.

Heywood, Linda M., and John K. Thornton. *Central Africans, Atlantic Creoles, and the Foundation of the Americas, 1585–1660.* New York: Cambridge University Press, 2007.

Higginbotham, Evelyn Brooks. *Religious Discontent: The Women's Movement in the Black Baptist Church, 1880–1920.* Cambridge, Mass.: Harvard University Press, 1993.

Hilliard, David. *This Side of Glory: The Autobiography of David Hilliard and the Story of the Black Panther Party.* Boston: Little, Brown, 1993.

Hine, Darlene Clark. "Black Migration to the Urban Midwest: The Gender Dimension, 1915–45." In Joe William Trotter, Jr., ed., *The Great Migration in Historical Perspective*, pp. 127–46. Bloomington: Indiana University Press, 1991.

Hinks, Peter P. *To Awaken My Afflicted Brethren: David Walker and the Problem of Antebellum Slave Resistance.* University Park: Pennsylvania State University Press, 1997.

Hodges, Graham Russell. *Root and Branch: African Americans in New York and East Jersey, 1613–1863.* Chapel Hill: University of North Carolina Press, 1999.

Holt, Thomas C. *Children of Fire: A History of African Americans.* New York: Hill and Wang, 2010.

Holzer, Harold, Edna Greene Medford, and Frank J. Williams. *Emancipation Proclamation: Three Views.* Foreword by John Hope Franklin. Baton Rouge: Louisiana State Press, 2006.

Horton, James O., and Lois E. Horton. *In Hope of Liberty: Culture, Community, and Protest Among Northern Free Blacks, 1700–1860.* New York: Oxford University Press, 1996.

Howe, Quincy. *A World History of Our Own Times from the Turn of the Century to the 1918 Armistice.* Vol. 1. New York: Simon & Schuster, 1949; rpt., Mahomedan Press, 2007.

Huggins, Nathan I. *Harlem Renaissance.* New York: Oxford University Press, 1978, 2007.

Hughes, Langston. *The Big Sea: An Autobiography.* Introd. Arnold Rampersad. New York: Hill and Wang, 1993.

———. *The Collected Poems of Langston Hughes.* Ed. Arnold Rampersad. New York: Vintage Books, 1994.

Hwang, Hyesung. "World War I and the New Negro." *Journal of North American Studies* 1 (1995): 43–68.

Jackson, Kenneth T. *The Ku Klux Klan in the City, 1915–1930.* New York: Oxford University Press, 1967.

Jackson-Coppin, Fanny. *Reminiscences of School Life, and Hints on Teaching.* Philadelphia: A.M.E. Book Concern, 1913.

Jeffries, Judson L. *Black Power in the Belly of the Beast.* Urbana: University of Illinois Press, 2006.

Jennings, Lawrence C. *French Anti-Slavery: The Movement for the Abolition of Slavery in France, 1802–1848.* Cambridge: Cambridge University Press, 2000.

Johnson, James Weldon, ed. *The Book of American Negro Poetry, Chosen and Edited with an Essay on the Negro's Creative Genius.* New York: Harcourt, Brace and Company, 1922.

Johnson, Michael, and James L. Roark. *Black Masters: A Free Family of Color in the Old South.* New York: Oxford University Press, 1984.

Johnson, Samuel. "Taxation No Tyranny: An Answer to the Resolutions and Address of the American Congress." In *The Works of Samuel Johnson*, vol. 14, pp. 93–144. Troy, N.Y.: Pafraets & Company, 1913.

Johnson, Walter. *Soul by Soul: Life Inside the Antebellum Slave Market.* Cambridge, Mass.: Harvard University Press, 1999.

Jonas, Gilbert. *Freedom's Sword: The NAACP and the Struggle Against Racism in America, 1909–1969*. New York: Routledge, 2005.

Jones, Beverly Washington. *Quest for Equality: The Life and Writings of Mary Eliza Church Terrell, 1863–1954*. Brooklyn, N.Y.: Carlson, 1990.

Jones, Norrece. *Born a Child of Freedom, Yet a Slave: Mechanisms of Control and Strategies of Resistance in Antebellum South Carolina*. Middletown, Conn.: Wesleyan University Press, 1989.

Joyner, Charles. *Down by the Riverside: A South Carolina Slave Community*. Urbana: University of Illinois Press, 1984.

Kelley, Robin D. G. *Race Rebels: Culture, Politics, and the Black Working Class*. New York: Free Press, 1996.

———. *Yo Mama's Disfunktional! Fighting the Culture Wars in Urban America*. Boston: Beacon Press, 1997.

Kerby, Jack Temple. "The Southern Exodus, 1910–1960: A Primer for Historians." *Journal of Southern History* 49 (1983): 585–600.

King, Martin Luther, Jr. *Why We Can't Wait*. Afterword by Reverend Jesse L. Jackson, Sr. New York: Signet Classic, 2000.

Klein, Herbert S. "African Women in the Atlantic Slave Trade." In Claire C. Robertson and Martin A. Klein, eds., *Women and Slavery in Africa*, pp. 29–33. Portsmouth, N.H.: Heinemann, 1983, 1997.

Konvitz, Milton R. *Fundamental Rights: History of a Constitutional Doctrine*. New Brunswick, N.J.: Transaction Publishers, 2007.

Kulikoff, Allan. *Tobacco and Slaves: The Development of Southern Cultures in the Chesapeake, 1680–1800*. Chapel Hill: University of North Carolina, 1986.

Landers, Jane. *Black Society in Spanish Florida*. Urbana: University of Illinois Press, 1999.

Lapp, Rudolph M. *Blacks in Gold Rush California*. New Haven, Conn.: Yale University Press, 1977.

Law, Robin. *The Slave Coast of West Africa, 1550–1750: The Impact of the Slave Trade on an African Society*. New York: Oxford University Press, 1991.

———. "Slave-Raiders and Middlemen, Monopolists and Free-Traders: The Supply of Slaves for the Atlantic Trade in Dahomey, c. 1715–1850." *Journal of African History* 30 (1989): 45–68.

Leavitt, Judith Walzer, and Ronald L. Numbers, eds. *Sickness and Health in America: Readings in the History of Medicine and Public Health*. 3rd ed. Madison: University of Wisconsin Press, 1997.

Lee, Chana Kai. *For Freedom's Sake: The Life of Fannie Lou Hamer*. Urbana: University of Illinois Press, 1999.

Lee, Jarena. *Religious Experience and Journal of Mrs. Jarena Lee, Giving an Account of Her Call to Preach the Gospel*. Philadelphia: n.p., 1849.

Lepore, Jill. *New York Burning: Liberty, Slavery, and Conspiracy in Eighteenth-Century Manhattan*. New York: Alfred A. Knopf, 2005.

Lester, Charles Edwards. *Life and Public Services of Charles Sumner*. New York: United States Publishing Company, 1874.

Lewis, David L. *King: A Biography*. Urbana: University of Illinois Press, 1978.

———. *W. E. B. Du Bois: Biography of a Race, 1868–1919*. New York: Henry Holt, 1993.

———. *W. E. B. Du Bois: The Fight for Equality and the American Century, 1919–1963*. New York: Henry Holt, 2000.

———. *When Harlem Was in Vogue*. New York: Penguin, 1981, 1997.

Lichtenstein, Alex. *Twice the Work of Free Labor: The Political Economy of Convict Labor in the New South*. New York: Verso, 1996.

Littlefield, Daniel F., Jr. *The Chickasaw Freedmen: A People Without a Country*. Westport, Conn.: Greenwood Press, 1980.

Litwack, Leon F. *Been in the Storm So Long: The Aftermath of Slavery*. New York: Alfred A. Knopf, 1979.

———. *Trouble in Mind: Black Southerners in the Age of Jim Crow*. New York: Alfred A. Knopf, 1998.

Litwack, Leon F., and August Meier, eds. *Black Leaders of the Nineteenth Century*. Urbana: University of Illinois Press, 1988.

Logan, Rayford W. *The Betrayal of the Negro: From Rutherford Hayes to Woodrow Wilson*. New York: Da Capo Press, 1965, 1997.

Love, Nat. *The Life and Adventures of Nat Love, Better Known in the Cattle Country as "Deadwood Dick," by Himself*. Los Angeles: Privately published, 1907.

Lovejoy, Paul E. *Transformations in Slavery: A History of Slavery in Africa*. New York: Cambridge University Press, 2000.

Mancini, Matthew J. *One Dies, Get Another: Convict Leasing in the American South, 1866–1928*. Columbia: University of South Carolina Press, 1996.

Marks, Carole. *Farewell, We're Good and Gone: The Great Black Migration*. Bloomington: Indiana University Press, 1989.

May, Samuel Joseph. *Some Recollections of Our Antislavery Conflict*. Boston: Fields, Osgood, & Co., 1869.

McFeely, William S. *Frederick Douglass*. New York: W. W. Norton, 1991.

McKay, Claude. *Harlem Shadows: The Poems of Claude McKay*. Introd. Max Eastman. New York: Harcourt, Brace and Co., 1922.

McMurray, Linda O. *To Keep the Waters Troubled: The Life of Ida B. Wells*. New York: Oxford University Press, 1998.

McNeil, Genna Rae. *Groundwork: Charles Hamilton Houston and the Struggle for Civil Rights*. Philadelphia: University of Pennsylvania Press, 1983.

McPherson, James. *The Abolitionist Legacy: From Reconstruction to the NAACP*. Princeton, N.J.: Princeton University Press, 1975, 1995.

Meier, August. *Negro Thought in America, 1880–1915: Racial Ideologies in the Age of Booker T. Washington*. Ann Arbor: University of Michigan Press, 1963.

Meier, August, and John H. Bracey. "The NAACP as a Reform Movement, 1909–1965: To Reach the Conscience of America." *Journal of Southern History* 59 (1993): 3–30.

Melish, Joanne Pope. *Disowning Slavery: Gradual Emancipation and "Race" in New England, 1780–1860*. Ithaca, N.Y.: Cornell University Press, 1998.

Meltzer, Milton. *The Black Americans: A History in Their Own Words, 1619–1983*. New York: HarperCollins, 1984.

Miller, Edward A. *Gullah Statesmen: Robert Smalls from Slavery to Congress, 1839–1915*. Columbia: University of South Carolina Press, 1994.

Miller, Floyd J. *The Search for a Black Nationality: Black Emigration and Colonization, 1787–1863.* Urbana: University of Illinois Press, 1975.

Miller, Joseph C. *Slavery and Slaving in World History: A Bibliography.* Armonk, N.Y.: M. E. Sharpe, 1999.

———. *Way of Death: Merchant Capitalism and the Angolan Slave Trade, 1730–1830.* Madison: University of Wisconsin Press, 1988.

Miller, Kelly. "The Past, Present, and Future of the Negro College." *The Journal of Negro Education* 2, no. 3 [A Survey of Negro Higher Education] (July 1933): 411–22.

Mohr, Clarence L. *On the Threshold of Freedom: Masters and Slaves in Civil War Georgia.* Baton Rouge: Louisiana State University Press, 1986, 2001.

Moore, Frank. *The Rebellion Record: A Diary of American Events.* New York: D. Van Nostrand, Publisher, 1865.

Morgan, Edmund S. *American Slavery, American Freedom: The Ordeal of Colonial Virginia.* New York: W. W. Norton, 1975, 2003.

Morgan, Marcyliena. *The Real Hiphop: Battling for Knowledge, Power, and Respect in the LA Underground.* Durham, N.C.: Duke University Press, 2009.

Morgan, Philip D. *Slave Counterpoint: Black Culture in the Eighteenth-Century Chesapeake and Lowcountry.* Chapel Hill: University of North Carolina Press, 1998.

Moses, Wilson J. *The Golden Age of Black Nationalism, 1850–1925.* New York: Oxford University Press, 1978, 1988.

Nash, Gary B. *The Forgotten Fifth: African Americans in the Age of the Revolution.* Cambridge, Mass.: Harvard University Press, 2006.

Nell, William Cooper. *The Colored Patriots of the American Revolution.* Introd. Harriet Beecher Stowe. Boston: Robert F. Wallcut, 1855.

Nelson, Peter. *A More Unbending Battle: The Harlem Hellfighters' Struggle for Freedom in World War I and Equality at Home.* New York: Basic Civitas, 2009.

Newman, Richard S. *Freedom's Prophet: Bishop Richard Allen, the AME Church, and the Black Founding Fathers.* New York: New York University Press, 2008.

Newman, Richard, Patrick Rael, and Phillip Lapsansky, eds. *Pamphlets of Protest: An Anthology of Early African-American Protest Literature, 1790–1860.* New York: Routledge, 2001.

Norell, Robert. *Up from History: The Life of Booker T. Washington.* Cambridge, Mass.: Belknap Press of Harvard University Press, 2009.

O'Reilly, Kenneth. "The Jim Crow Policies of Woodrow Wilson." *The Journal of Blacks in Higher Education* 17 (August 1997): 17–19.

Oshinsky, David. *"Worse Than Slavery": Parchment Farm and the Ordeal of Jim Crow Justice.* New York: Free Press, 1996.

Ovington, Mary White. *Black and White Sat Down Together: The Reminiscences of an NAACP Founder.* New York: Feminist Press at the City University of New York, 1995.

Pearson, Hugh. *The Shadow of the Panther: Huey Newton and the Price of Black Power in America.* Reading, Mass.: Addison-Wesley, 1994.

Perdue, Theda. *Slavery and the Evolution of Cherokee Society, 1540–1866.* Knoxville: University of Tennessee Press, 1979.

Perman, Michael. *Struggle for Mastery: Disfranchisement in the South, 1880–1908.* Chapel Hill: University of North Carolina Press, 2001.

Perry, Bruce. *Malcolm: The Life of a Man Who Changed Black America.* Barrytown, N.Y.: Station Hill Press, 1991.

Peterson, Carla L. *"Doers of the Word": African-American Women Speakers and Writers in the North, 1830–1880.* New York: Oxford University Press, 1995.

Pleck, Elizabeth. "Kwanzaa: The Making of a Black Nationalist Tradition, 1966–1990." *Journal of American Ethnic History* 20 (2001): 3–28.

Pons, Frank Moya. *The Dominican Republic: A National History.* Princeton, N.J.: Markus Wiener Publishers, 1998.

Powderly, Terence Vincent. *Thirty Years of Labor, 1859–1889.* Columbus, Ohio: Excelsior Publishing House, 1889.

Quarles, Benjamin. *The Negro in the American Revolution.* Chapel Hill: University of North Carolina Press, 1961, 1996.

Rabinowitz, Howard N. *Race Relations in the Urban South.* Athens: University of Georgia Press, 1978, 1996.

Raboteau, Albert. *Canaan Land: A Religious History of African Americans.* New York: Oxford University Press, 2001.

Raines, Howell. *My Soul Is Rested: Movement Days in the South Remembered.* New York: Putnam, 1977.

Rainwater, Lee, and William L. Yancey. *The Moynihan Report and the Politics of Controversy.* Cambridge, Mass.: MIT Press, 1967.

Rampersad, Arnold. *The Life of Langston Hughes.* New York: Oxford University Press, 2002.

———. *Ralph Ellison: A Biography.* New York: Alfred A. Knopf, 2007.

Reed, Christopher Robert. *"All the world is here!": The Black Presence at White City.* Bloomington: Indiana University Press, 2000.

Reidy, Joseph. *From Slavery to Agrarian Capitalism in the Cotton Plantation South: Central Georgia, 1800–1880.* Chapel Hill: University of North Carolina Press, 1992.

Remnick, David. *King of the World: Muhammad Ali and the Rise of an American Hero.* New York: Vintage Books, 1999.

Reverby, Susan. *Examining Tuskegee: The Infamous Syphilis Study and Its Legacy.* Chapel Hill: University of North Carolina, 2009.

Reynolds, David S. *John Brown, Abolitionist: The Man Who Killed Slavery, Sparked Civil War, and Seeded Civil Rights.* New York: Alfred A. Knopf, 2005.

Ripley, C. Peter, et al. *The Black Abolitionist Papers.* 5 vols. Chapel Hill: University of North Carolina Press, 1985–92.

Rolinson, Mary. *Grassroots Garveyism: The Univeral Negro Improvement Association in the Rural South, 1920–1927.* Chapel Hill: University of North Carolina Press, 2007.

Rose, Willie Lee. *Rehearsal for Reconstruction: The Port Royal Experiment.* Athens: University of Georgia Press, 1999.

Samito, Christian G., ed. *Changes in Law and Society During the Civil War and Reconstruction.* Carbondale: Southern Illinois University Press, 2009.

Sandage, Scott A. "A Marble House Divided: The Lincoln Memorial, the Civil Rights Movement, and the Politics of Memory, 1939–1963," *Journal of American History* 80, no. 1 (June 1993): 135–67.

Schama, Simon. *Rough Crossings: Britain, the Slaves and the American Revolution.* New York: HarperCollins, 2006.

Schneider, Mark. *Boston Confronts Jim Crow, 1890–1920.* Boston: Northeastern University Press, 1997.

———. *"We Return Fighting": The Civil Rights Movement in the Jazz Age.* Boston: Northeastern University Press, 2002.

Schweninger, Loren. "Black-Owned Businesses in the South, 1790–1880." *Business History Review* 63 (1989): 22–60.

———. "Property-Owning Free African-American Women in the South, 1800–1870." *Journal of Women's History* 1 (1990): 13–44.

———. "A Vanishing Breed: Black Farm Owners in the South, 1651–1982." *Agricultural History* 63 (1989): 41–60.

Seraile, William. *Fire in His Heart: Bishop Benjamin Tucker Tanner and the AME Church.* Knoxville: University of Tennessee Press, 1998.

Sernett, Milton C. *Bound for the Promised Land: African Amerian Religion and the Great Migration.* Durham, N.C.: Duke University Press, 1997.

Sitkoff, Howard. *A New Deal for Blacks: The Emergence of Civil Rights as a National Issue, The Depression Decade.* New York: Oxford University Press, 1978, 2009.

Skocpol, Theda, Ariane Liazos, and Marshall Ganz, eds. *What a Mighty Power We Can Be: African American Fraternal Groups and the Struggle for Racial Equality.* Princeton, N.J.: Princeton University Press, 2006.

Smiley, Tavis, ed. *Covenant with Black America.* Chicago: Third World Press, 2006.

Sobel, Mechal. *The World They Made Together: Black and White Values in Eighteenth-Century Virginia.* Princeton, N.J.: Princeton University Press, 1987.

Soderlund, Jean R. *Quakers and Slavery: A Divided Spirit.* Princeton, N.J.: Princeton University Press, 1985.

Spivey, Donald. *Schooling for the New Slavery: Black Industrial Education, 1868–1915.* Westport, Conn.: Greenwood Press, 1978.

Stauffer, John. *Giants: The Parallel Lives of Frederick Douglass and Abraham Lincoln.* New York: Twelve, 2008.

Sterling, Dorothy. *We Are Your Sisters: Black Women in the Nineteenth Century.* New York: W. W. Norton, 1984.

Sugrue, Thomas J. *Sweet Land of Liberty: The Forgotten Struggle for Civil Rights in the North.* New York: Random House, 2008.

Sullivan, Patricia. *Days of Hope: Race and Democracy in the New Deal Era.* Chapel Hill: University of North Carolina Press, 1996.

———. *Lift Every Voice: The NAACP and the Making of the Civil Rights Movement.* New York: The New Press, 2009.

Sumner, Charles. *The Works of Charles Sumner.* Vol. 13. Boston: Lee and Shepard, 1880.

Taylor, Quintard, and Shirley Ann Wilson Moore, eds. *African American Women Confront the West, 1600–2000.* Norman: University of Oklahoma Press, 2003.

Thomas, Hugh. *The Slave Trade: The Story of the Atlantic Slave Trade, 1440–1870.* New York: Simon & Schuster, 1997.

Thomas, Lamont D. *Rise to Be a People: A Biography of Paul Cuffe.* Urbana: University of Illinois Press, 1986.

Thornbrough, Emma Lou. *T. Thomas Fortune: Militant Journalist.* Chicago: University of Chicago Press, 1972.

Thornton, John K. *Africa and Africans in the Making of the Atlantic World, 1400–1800.* New York: Cambridge University Press, 1998.

———. "The African Experience of the '20 and Odd Negroes' Arriving in Virginia in 1619." *William and Mary Quarterly* 55 (1998): 421–34.

Tomkins, Steven. *William Wilberforce: A Biography.* Oxford: Lion Hudson, 2007.

Toobin, Jeffrey. *The Nine: Inside the Secret World of the Supreme Court.* New York: Anchor Books, 2008.

Trelease, Allen W. *White Terror: The Ku Klux Klan Conspiracy and Southern Reconstruction.* Westport, Conn.: Greenwood Press, 1971, 1979.

Tushnet, Mark V. *The NAACP's Legal Strategy Against Segregated Education, 1925–1950.* Chapel Hill: University of North Carolina, 1987, 2004.

Tuttle, William M. *Race Riot: Chicago in the Red Summer of 1919.* Urbana: University of Illinois Press, 1970, 1996.

Tygiel, Jules. *Baseball's Great Experiment: Jackie Robinson and His Legacy.* New York: Vintage Books, 1983.

Van Deburg, William. *New Day in Babylon: The Black Power Movement and American Culture, 1965–1975.* Chicago: University of Chicago Press, 1992.

Vaughn, William. *Schools for All: The Blacks and Public Education in the South, 1865–1877.* Lexington: University of Kentucky Press, 1974.

Vorenberg, Michael. *Final Freedom: The Civil War, Abolition of Slavery, and the Thirteenth Amendment.* New York: Cambridge University Press, 2001.

Wade, Wyn Craig. *The Fiery Cross: The Ku Klux Klan in America.* New York: Oxford University Press, 1998.

Walker, David. *David Walker's Appeal: to the Coloured Citizens of the World, but in particular, and very expressly, to those of the United States of America.* Introd. James Turner. Baltimore: Black Classic Press, 1993.

Warren, Naguelyalti. "Pan-African Cultural Movements: From Baraka to Karenga." *Journal of Negro History* 75 (1990): 16–28.

Washington, Booker T. *Frederick Douglass.* Philadelphia: George W. Jacobs & Company, 1906.

Whitman, Mark. *Brown v. Board of Education: A Documentary History.* Princeton, N.J.: Markus Wiener Publishers, 2004.

Wilberforce, William. *An Appeal to the Religion, Justice, and Humanity of the Inhabitants of the British Empire, in Behalf of the Negro Slaves in the West Indies.* London: J. Hatchard and Son, 1823.

Wilkinson, J. Harvie, III. *From Brown to Bakke: The Supreme Court and School Integration, 1954–1978.* New York: Oxford University Press, 1979.

Wilson, Harriet E. *Our Nig: or, Sketches from the Life of a Free Black.* Ed. and introd. Henry Louis Gates, Jr. New York: Vintage Books, 2002.

Wilson, William Julius. *More Than Just Race: Being Black and Poor in the Inner City.* New York: W. W. Norton, 2009.

Winch, Julie. *A Gentleman of Color: The Life of James Forten.* New York: Oxford University Press, 2002.

Wintz, Cary D. *African American Political Thoughts, 1890–1930: Washington, Du Bois, Garvey, and Randolph.* Armonk, N.Y.: M. E. Sharpe, 1996.

———. *Black Culture and the Harlem Renaissance.* Houston: Rice University Press, 1988.

Wood, Forrest G. *Black Scare: The Racist Response to Emancipation and Reconstruction.* Berkeley: University of California Press, 1970.

Wood, Peter H. *Black Majority: Negroes in Colonial South Carolina from 1670 through the Stono Rebellion.* New York: W. W. Norton, 1975.

———. *Strange New Land: Africans in Colonial America.* New York: Oxford University Press, 2003.

Woodson, Carter G. *Free Negro Owners of Slaves in the United States in 1830.* Washington, D.C.: Assocation for the Study of Negro Life and History, 1924.

Wright, Kai, ed. *The African American Experience: Black History and Culture Through Speeches, Letters, Editorials, Poems, Songs, and Stories.* New York: Black Dog & Leventhal, 2009.

Yacovone, Donald, ed. *A Voice of Thunder: The Civil War Letters of George E. Stephens.* Urbana: University of Illinois Press, 1997.

Zangrando, Robert L. *The NAACP Crusade Against Lynching, 1909–1950.* Philadelphia: Temple University Press, 1980.

INDEX

Page numbers in *italics* refer to illustrations.

465

ILLUSTRATION CREDITS

The Abbott Sengstacke Family Papers/Robert Abbott Sengstacke/Getty Images: 234 *(top center)*

AFP/Getty Images: 364 *(top left)*, 422 *(top right)*

Agence France Presse/Getty Images: 380

akg-images: 3, 31

Alabama Drydock and Shipbuilding Company Collection, University of South Alabama Archives, Mobile, Ala.: 306 *(bottom)*

Alamy: 15 *(bottom)*

Alfred Eisenstaedt/Time & Life Pictures/Getty Images 301 *(bottom left)*

American Antiquarian Society: 19 *(top right)*, 114

American Antiquarian Society/Bridgeman Art Library: 29, 124 *(top)*

Andover Historical Society: 76

Andy Lyons/Getty Images: 427 *(top right)*

Anne S. K. Brown Military Collection, Brown University Library: 32 *(top left)*

AP/MBR/Virginian Pilot/Press Association Images: 417 *(right)*

AP Photo/JL/Press Association Images: 353 *(top left)*

AP Photo/Mamie Till Mobley Family/Press Association Images: 327 *(bottom)*

AP Photo/Press Association Images: 385 *(right)*

Archives du 7e Art/DR/Photo12.com: 415 *(right)*

Archives of the Academia das Cienas, Lisbon: 11 *(bottom)*

Art Archive: 88 *(right)*

Associated Press/Bay State Banner: 379 *(top)*

Associated Press/Press Association Images: 263 *(bottom)*, 289 *(top right)*, 332 *(bottom right)*, 336 *(left)*, 349 *(top)*, 358, 372, 373 *(bottom left)*, 385 *(left)*, 387 *(left)*, 387 *(right)*, 391 *(top left)*, 408 *(top left)*

Atwater Kent Museum of Philadelphia/ Courtesy of Historical Society of Pennsylvania Collection/Bridgeman Art Library: 56 *(bottom)*

Bachrach/Getty Images: 355 *(top right)*

Courtesy of the Bancroft Library, University of California, Berkeley: 89, 210 *(top)*

Bay State Banner: 233 *(bottom left)*

Bebeto Matthews/Associated Press/Press Association Images: 434 *(bottom right)*

Beinecke Rare Book and Manuscript Library, Yale University: 228 *(bottom left)*, 228 *(top left)*, 228 *(top center)*, 321 *(bottom)*, 324 *(right)*, 408 *(bottom right)*

Courtesy of Berea College Archives: 111

Bernard Gottfryd/Hulton Archive/Getty Images: 324 *(left)*

Bettmann/Corbis UK Ltd: 28 *(top)*, 42 *(bottom)*, 53 *(top right)*, 98 *(top right)*, 101 *(top right)*, 102 *(top)*, 120 *(bottom right)*, 126 *(bottom right)*, 172, 245, 262 *(bottom)*, 263 *(top)*, 264 *(top right)*, 265 *(bottom)*, 267, 276 *(left)*, 276 *(right)*, 281 *(bottom)*, 282, 283 *(left)*, 291, 293 *(bottom)*, 299 *(bottom)*, 301 *(bottom right)*, 302 *(right)*, 303 *(bottom)*, 305, 306 *(top)*, 307 *(top)*, 307 *(bottom)*, 308, 313, 314 *(top)*, 320, 323 *(top)*, 323 *(bottom)*, 327 *(top)*, 331, 332 *(top)*, 333 *(left)*, 334, 335 *(top)*, 336 *(right)*, 338 *(top)*, 338 *(bottom)*, 339, 340 *(top)*, 340 *(bottom)*, 341 *(top)*, 341 *(bottom)*, 345, 346, 351 *(bottom)*, 352, 353 *(right)*, 354 *(left)*, 354 *(right)*, 355 *(left)*, 356 *(top left)*, 359 *(top right)*, 362 *(top left)*, 362 *(bottom)*, 363 *(top)*, 364 *(right)*, 365 *(left)*, 366 *(left)*, 366 *(right)*, 367, 368 *(top)*, 368 *(bottom)*, 371, 374, 375 *(bottom)*, 377 *(bottom)*, 391 *(top right)*, 394, 395 *(right)*, 396 *(bottom)*, 403, 408 *(bottom left)*, 409

Bibliothèque Nationale, Paris, France/ Bridgeman Art Library: 4 *(top)*

Bill Wilson/Kenan Research Center at the Atlantic History Center: 370 *(right)*

Bob Adelman/Corbis UK Ltd: 342

Bob Daugherty/Associated Press/Press Association Images: 378 *(top)*

Boston Athenaeum/Bridgeman Art Library: 100 *(bottom left)*

Brady-Handy Collection/Library of Congress: 166 *(left)*

British Library/akg-images: 53 *(bottom)*

British Library, London, UK/© British Library Board/Bridgeman Art Library: 43 *(top)*

Brown University Library: 229 *(top right)*, 232 *(top left)*

Brown/Special Collections and University Archives, University of Massachusetts Amherst: 248 *(bottom)*

Buyenlarge/Getty Images: 130 *(bottom)*, 258 *(bottom)*, 363 *(top)*

Courtesy of the California History Room, California State Library, Sacramento: 90 *(top)*

Carl Iwasaki/Time & Life Pictures/Getty Images: 322

Carl Van Vechten/Library of Congress: 300 *(top)*, 321 *(top right)*

CBW/Alamy: 410 *(left)*

Charles Moore/Black Star/Alamy: 347 *(top)*

Charles Smith/Corbis UK Ltd: 176

The Charleston Library Society: 51 *(bottom)*

Chicago History Museum/Getty Images: 28 *(bottom)*, 312 *(right)*

Children's Defense Fund: 398 *(left)*

Chris Carlson/Associated Press/Press Association Images: 427 *(bottom)*

Cole/Special Collections and University Archives, University of Massachusetts Amherst: 242 *(top)*

Collection of Henry Louis Gates, Jr.: 115, 220 *(left)*, 220 *(center)*. 220 *(right)*, 221 *(top left)*, 221 *(top center)*, 221 *(top right)*, 221 *(bottom left)*, 221 *(bottom center)*, 221 *(bottom right)*, 222 *(top left)*, 222 *(top center)*, 222 *(top right)*, 222 *(bottom left)*, 222 *(bottom right)*, 244

Collection of the Maryland State Archives: 12 *(bottom)*

© Collection of the New-York Historical Society/Bridgeman Art Library: 18 *(right)*, 19 *(left)*, 20, 57 *(left)*, 57 *(center)*, 63 *(bottom)*, 78 *(bottom)*

Courtesy of the College of the Holy Cross Photo Archives: 175 *(right)*

The Colonial Williamsburg Foundation: 10 *(top)*

Congressional Black Caucus Foundation/ CBC Archives, Moorland-Springarn Research Center, Howard University: 390 *(top)*

J. R. Eyerman/Time & Life Pictures/Getty Images: 86 (left)

Kansas State Historical Society: 121 (center), 121 (right), 173

Kean Collection/Getty Images: 168 (bottom right), 208 (left)

Keith Srakocic/Press Association Images: 74 (bottom right)

Ken James/Corbis UK Ltd: 431 (bottom)

Kevin Lamarque/Reuters/Corbis UK Ltd: 440 (right)

Kevin Mazur/WireImages/Getty Images: 400

KEYSTONE Pressedienst/Photo12.com: 359 (top left)

Lake County Museum/Corbis UK Ltd: 217 (top right)

The Library Company of Philadelphia: 8, 41 (top right), 81 (bottom)

Library of Congress: 9, 15 (top right), 22 (bottom), 27 (bottom left), 30 (top), 35 (top), 39 (top left), 39 (bottom), 51 (top left), 59 (top left), 59 (bottom), 67, 77, 78 (top), 79 (top), 83 (top left), 83 (top right), 85, 86 (right), 88 (left), 90 (bottom), 93 (center), 93 (right), 97, 98 (top left), 102 (bottom), 103 (top), 108, 112 (left), 113, 119, 120 (top left), 122, 123 (left), 123 (right), 124 (bottom), 125 (top), 125 (bottom), 126 (bottom left), 126 (top right), 127, 128, 129, 132 (bottom), 133, 134 (top), 139, 140 (center), 140 (right), 140 (left), 141 (right), 144, 147 (left), 148 (top), 151, 152, 153 (right), 155, 156 (bottom), 157, 158 (top), 158 (bottom), 159, 160, 162 (top), 162 (bottom right), 163 (bottom), 164, 165, 168 (top left), 168 (top right), 169, 170 (top), 170 (bottom), 174, 177 (left), 178, 179 (top left), 179 (top right), 180 (top right), 186 (right), 187 (top), 188 (top), 188 (bottom), 189 (left), 195, 196 (top left), 201 (top right), 201 (bottom), 203 (left), 203 (right), 204 (left), 207 (bottom), 209, 211 (bottom), 212 (top left), 212 (top right), 212 (bottom), 213, 227 (left), 229 (left), 229 (center), 233 (bottom right), 234 (bottom), 235 (bottom), 241 (top), 246 (left), 246 (right), 247 (bottom right), 249 (top left), 249 (top right), 249 (bottom), 250, 251 (left), 251 (right), 258 (top right), 260 (bottom), 264 (left), 265 (top), 269 (top left), 269 (bottom right), 272 (left), 275 (top), 281 (top), 285 (top), 289 (top left), 290 (top left), 290 (top right), 293 (top right), 299 (top), 304 (bottom left), 304 (bottom right), 309, 315 (top left), 347 (bottom), 359 (bottom), 360, 369 (right), 375 (top), 376 (top), 377 (top), 389 (left), 390 (bottom left), 390 (bottom right), 412 (top), 433, 438 (top), 438 (bottom)

Lynn Pelham/Time & Life Pictures/Getty Images: 365 (right)

M&N/Alamy: 218 (top left)

Manuel Balce Ceneta/Associated Press/Press Association Images: 437

Manuscript Division, Library of Congress: 35 (bottom)

Manuscripts and Archives, Yale University Library: 167 (right)

Manuscripts, Archives and Rare Books Division, Schomburg Center for Research in Black Culture, The New York Public Library, Astor, Lenox and Tilden Foundations: 10 (bottom right), 41 (bottom), 50 (top), 59 (top right), 68 (left), 98 (bottom), 101 (left), 105 (top right), 110, 186 (left), 194 (right), 205, 211 (top), 274 (left)

Mary Evans Picture Library: 6, 214 (right), 215 (top), 218 (top right), 218 (bottom left), 218 (bottom right), 240

Mary Evans Picture Library/EDWIN: 217 (bottom right), 219 (top right)

Courtesy of Massachusetts Archives: 37 (left)

Courtesy of Massachusetts Historical Society: 17 (left), 84 (top right), 109 (top left)

Courtesy of Massachusetts Historical Society, Boston, Mass./Bridgeman Art Library: 17 (top right), 37 (right), 64, 100 (top left), 106, 107 (bottom left), 137, 148 (bottom)

Maurice Savage/Alamy: 92 (top)

Mel Finkelstein/NY Daily News Archive/Getty Images: 373 (top)

© Michael Graham-Stewart/Bridgeman Art Library: 45 (left), 49, 70 (left)

Michael Ochs Archives/Corbis UK Ltd: 410 (right), 411 (bottom right)

Michael Ochs Archives/Getty Images: 349 (bottom), 392 (top)

Mike Nelson/AFP/Getty Images: 435

Mike Powell/Allsport/Getty Images: 421 (bottom right)

Monica Almeida/NY Daily News Archive/Getty Images: 417 (left)

Moorland-Springarn Research Center: 268 (center)

Morehouse School of Medicine: 399 (top)

MPI/Getty Images: 21, 36, 75, 208 (right)

Musée de la Ville de Paris, Musée Carnavalet, Paris, France/Archives Charmet/Bridgeman Art Library: 32 (bottom left)

© Museum of London: 52 (right)

The Museum of Modern Art, New York/Photo Scala, Florence: 255, 288

Myron Davis/Time & Life Pictures/Getty Images: 325 (right)

Mystic Seaport, G. W. Blunt White Library: 266 (top)

NASA: 424 (top left)

National Archives—Digital Vers/Science Faction/Corbis UK Ltd: 39 (top right)

The National Archives/Heritage Images/Image State: 14

National Archives and Records Administration (NARA): 32 (bottom right), 33, 38 (top), 142, 156 (top), 161 (top left), 163 (top), 202, 298 (bottom), 303 (top left), 356 (top right), 356 (bottom)

National Gallery of Canada: 42 (right)

National Gallery of Denmark, Copenhagen/© SMK Photo: 11 (left)

© National Maritime Museum, Greenwich, London: 50 (bottom)

National Museum of American Art, Smithsonian Institution: 196 (top right)

National Park Service: 5 (top)

National Photo Company Collection/Library of Congress: 252

National Portrait Gallery, Smithsonian Institution/Art Resource/Scala, Florence: 230 (top right)

Courtesy of Naval History and Heritage Command: 321 (top left), 395 (left)

Neal Preston/Corbis UK Ltd: 411 (bottom left)

Nelson Ching/Bloomberg/Getty Images: 423 (top left)

New York Public Library: 161 (bottom)

The New York Public Library Archives, The New York Public Library, Astor, Lenox and Tilden Foundations: 271 (bottom)

Niday Picture Library/Alamy: 69

NOAA/Corbis UK Ltd: 439 (top)

Nova Scotia Archives and Records Management: 34 (bottom)

NY Daily News Archive/Getty Images: 289 (bottom), 434 (top)

Oberlin College Archives: 73, 74 (top), 74 (bottom left), 121 (left), 190, 429 (top)

Office of the Clerk, U.S. House of Representatives: 439 *(bottom left)*, 439 *(bottom right)*

Ohio Historical Society: 171 *(left)*, 189 *(right)*

Pablo Martinez Monsivais/Associated Press/Press Association Images: 440 *(left)*

Patricio Sauzzi/Foto Gioberti srl: 11 *(top left)*

Pennsylvania State Archives: 37 *(center)*

Peter Newark American Pictures/Bridgeman Art Library: 66 *(bottom)*, 132 *(top)*, 193 *(left)*

Peter Pelham/Library of Congress: 22 *(top)*

Peter Read Miller/Sports Illustrated/Getty Images: 421 *(bottom left)*

Peter Southwick/Associated Press/Press Association Images: 413 *(top)*

Phil Dent/Redferns/Getty Images: 411 *(top left)*

© The Phillips Collection: 301 *(top)*

Photo12.com: 87

Photographs and Prints Division, Schomburg Center for Research in Black Culture, The New York Public Library, Astor, Lenox and Tilden Foundations: 53 *(top left)*, 54 *(left)*, 62 *(bottom)*, 83 *(bottom)*, 126 *(top left)*

Photography Collection, Harry Ransom Humanities Research Center, University of Texas at Austin: 177 *(right)*

PhotoQuest/Getty Images: 348

Photo Scala, Florence: 274 *(right)*

Picture Collection, The New York Public Library, Astor, Lenox and Tilden Foundations: 55, 99, 105 *(bottom)*, 134 *(bottom)*, 135 *(top)*, 138, 145 *(bottom)*, 161 *(top right)*

Pierpont Morgan Library/Art Resource/Photo Scala, Florence: 4 *(bottom)*

Courtesy of the P. K. Yonge Library of Florida History/George Smathers Libraries, University of Florida: 230 *(bottom)*

Press Association Images: 329 *(top)*, 370 *(left)*, 383 *(left)*, 384 *(top)*, 419, 422 *(bottom right)*

Presto, Brussels, Belgium/Special Collections and University Archives, University of Massachusetts, Amherst: 261 *(top)*, 262 *(top)*

Print Collection, Miriam and Ira D. Wallach Division of Art, Prints and Photographs, The New York Public Library, Astor, Lenox and Tilden Foundations: 143

Private Collection/Bridgeman Art Library: 52 *(left)*, 328

Private Collection/© Michael Graham-Stewart/Bridgeman Art Library: 15 *(top left)*

Private Collection/Peter Newark American Pictures/Bridgeman Art Library: 180 *(top left)*, 180 *(bottom)*, 183 *(right)*, 184 *(top)*

Private Collection/The Stapleton Collection/Bridgeman Art Library: 5 *(bottom)*

Private Collection/Courtesy of Swann Auction Galleries/Bridgeman Art Library: 43 *(bottom)*

Quaker Collection, Haverford College Library: 16

Courtesy of the Queens Borough Public Library, Long Island Division, Lewis H. Latimer Collection: 84 *(left)*, 184 *(bottom)*

Reed Saxon/Associated Press/Press Association Images: 418

Reuters/Jason Reed/Corbis UK Ltd: 416 *(top right)*

Rex Features: 350, 421 *(top)*

Rex Hardy, Jr./Time & Life Pictures/Getty Images: 272 *(right)*

Richard Harbus/Getty Images: 434 *(bottom left)*

Rick Diamond/WireImage/Getty Images: 429 *(bottom)*

Robert Abbott Sengstacke/Getty Images: 351 *(top)*

Robert L. Haggins/Time & Life Pictures/Getty Images: 431 *(top)*

Robert W. Kelley/Time & Life Pictures/Getty Images: 325 *(left)*

Roland Grant Archive: 396 *(right)*

Rolls Press/Popperfoto/Getty Images: 379 *(bottom)*

Ross Marino/Sygma/Corbis UK Ltd: 411 *(top right)*

San Francisco Examiner/Associated Press/Press Association Images: 369 *(left)*

S&G and Barratts Sport/Press Association Images: 384 *(bottom)*

Sangamon Valley Collection, Lincoln Library: 241 *(bottom)*

Saul Loeb/AFP/Getty Images: 426 *(top)*

The Schlesinger Library, Radcliffe Institute, Harvard University: 268 *(left)*

Science, Industry & Business Library, The New York Public Library, Astor, Lenox and Tilden Foundations: 40 *(left)*

Scott Applewhite/Associated Press/Press Association Images: 399 *(bottom)*

Scurlock Studio Records, Archives Center, National Museum of American History, Smithsonian Institution: 292

Seattle Municipal Archives: 416 *(bottom right)*

Seth Cole, Jr./Corbis UK Ltd.: 100 *(bottom right)*

Society for the Preservation of Long Island Antiquities: 27 *(top)*

Smithsonian American Art Museum/Art Resource/Scala, Florence: 270 *(right)*

Special Collections and University Archives, University of Massachusetts Amherst: 198, 201 *(top left)*, 237, 238, 239, 256 *(top left)*, 256 *(top right)*, 260 *(top)*, 261, 278

A SPIKE LEE JOINT/Ronald Grant Archive: 415 *(left)*

Stephen Crowley/New York Times Co./Getty Images: 416 *(top center)*

Steve Jennings/WireImage/Getty Images: 424 *(top right)*

Steve Nelson Photographs Collection, Abraham Lincoln Brigade Archives/Tamiment Library, New York University: 285 *(bottom)*

Stock Montage/Getty Images: 27 *(bottom right)*, 61 *(bottom right)*

Swim Ink 2, LLC/Corbis UK Ltd: 214 *(left)*, 215 *(bottom)*, 216, 217 *(bottom left)*, 219 *(top left)*, 219 *(bottom left)*, 219 *(bottom right)*

Terry Ashe/Time & Life Pictures/Getty Images: 432

Thomas D. McAvoy/Time & Life Pictures/Getty Images: 297, 298 *(top)*

Time & Life Pictures/DMI/Getty Images: 383 *(right)*

Time & Life Pictures/NASA/Getty Images: 423 *(bottom)*

Tim Wright/Corbis UK Ltd: 408 *(top right)*, 416 *(top left)*

Tony Duffy/Allsport/Getty Images: 422 *(top left)*

TopFoto: 57 *(right)*, 93 *(left)*, 335 *(bottom)*

Courtesy of the Trustees of the Boston Public Library/Rare Books: 61 *(bottom left)*, 68 *(right)*

Underwood & Underwood/Corbis UK Ltd: 333 *(right)*

University Archives, Central Connecticut State University: 162 *(bottom left)*

University of North Carolina at Chapel Hill, *News and Observer;* North Carolina Collection: 192, 207 *(top)*

U.S. Department of Housing and Urban Development: 376 *(bottom)*

A NOTE ABOUT THE AUTHOR

Henry Louis Gates, Jr., is the Alphonse Fletcher University Professor and the Director of the W. E. B. Du Bois Institute for African and African American Research at Harvard University. An influential scholar in the field of African American studies, he is the author of fourteen books and has hosted and produced ten documentaries for PBS and the BBC. He is the recipient of fifty-one honorary degrees and numerous awards, including the MacArthur "genius grant" and the National Humanities Medal, conferred on him by President Bill Clinton in 1998.

A NOTE ON THE TYPE

This book was set in Dante, a typeface designed by Giovanni Mardersteig (1892–1977). Conceived as a private type for the Officina Bodoni in Verona, Italy, Dante was originally cut only for hand composition by Charles Malin, the famous Parisian punch cutter, between 1946 and 1952. Its first use was in an edition of Boccaccio's *Trattatello in laude di Dante* that appeared in 1954.

Composed by North Market Street Graphics,
Lancaster, Pennsylvania

Printed and bound by RR Donnelley,
Willard, Ohio

Designed by Michael Collica